Research Anthology on Human Resource Practices for the Modern Workforce

Information Resources Management Association
USA

Volume I

Published in the United States of America by
    IGI Global
    Business Science Reference (an imprint of IGI Global)
    701 E. Chocolate Avenue
    Hershey PA, USA 17033
    Tel: 717-533-8845
    Fax: 717-533-8661
    E-mail: cust@igi-global.com
    Web site: http://www.igi-global.com

Library of Congress Cataloging-in-Publication Data

Names: Information Resources Management Association, editor.
Title: Research anthology on human resource practices for the modern
  workforce / Information Resources Management Association, editor.
Description: Hershey, PA : Business Science Reference, 2021. | Includes
  bibliographical references and index. | Summary: "This book presents a
  dynamic and diverse collection of global practices for human resource
  departments, discussing the emerging practices as well as modern
  technologies and initiatives (machine learning, organizational culture,
  and social entrepreneurship) that affect the way human resources can be
  conducted"-- Provided by publisher.
Identifiers: LCCN 2021042081 (print) | LCCN 2021042082 (ebook) | ISBN
  9781668438732 (hardcover) | ISBN 9781668438749 (ebook)
Subjects: LCSH: Personnel management. | Management--Environmental aspects.
  | Organizational change.
Classification: LCC HF5549 .R4598 2021 (print) | LCC HF5549 (ebook) | DDC
  658.3--dc23
LC record available at https://lccn.loc.gov/2021042081
LC ebook record available at https://lccn.loc.gov/2021042082

British Cataloguing in Publication Data
A Cataloguing in Publication record for this book is available from the British Library.

The views expressed in this book are those of the authors, but not necessarily of the publisher.

For electronic access to this publication, please contact: eresources@igi-global.com.

List of Contributors

Abe, Ethel N. / *University of KwaZulu-Natal, South Africa* 1177

Abe, Isaac Idowu / *University of KwaZulu-Natal, South Africa* 1177

Adeola, Oladele Stephen / *Department of Computer Science, Federal University of Technology, Akure, Nigeria* 814

Afedzie, Richard / *Pentecost University, Ghana* 2103

Ahmad, Rizal / *Bandung Institute of Technology, Indonesia* 1743

Akgül, Yakup / *Alanya Alaaddin Keykubat University, Turkey* 1094

Al-Ajlouni, Mahmoud Mohammad / *Northern Border University, Saudi Arabia* 695

Albors-Garrigos, Jose / *Universitat Politècnica de València, Valencia, Spain* 735, 1990, 2022

Al-Dmour, Rand H. / *The Univeristy of Jordan, Jordan* 1468

Alharahsheh, Husam Helmi / *University of Wales Trinity Saint David, UK* 35, 1823

Altunoz, Ozlem / *Ankara Haci Bayram Veli University, Turkey* 1390

Ambrosius, Judith / *University of Erlangen-Nuernberg, Germany* 892

Anjum, A. / *Glorious Sun School of Business and Management, Donghua University Shanghai, China* 1021

Aquino, Jr., Perfecto G. / *Duy Tan University, Vietnam* 233

Arora, Amit Kumar / *KIET Group of Institutions, Delhi-NCR, Ghaziabad, India* 2053

Arora, Shilpa / *Manav Rachna International Institute of Research and Studies, India* 73

Asare, Enoch / *Texas A&M University, Texarkana, USA* 2179

Attah-Panin, James / *Pentecost University, Ghana* 2103

Ayandibu, Ayansola Olatunji / *University of Zululand, South Africa* 2202

Ayodeji-Ogundiran, Amina I. / *The Chicago School of Professional Psychology, USA* 1040

Bajaj, Badri / *Jaypee Institute of Information Technology, Noida, India* 93, 491

Bakhru, Kanupriya Misra / *Jaypee Institute of Information Technology, India* 471

Baniski, Gislaine Martinelli / *Ponta Grossa State University, Brazil* 564

Baporikar, Neeta / *Namibia University of Science and Technology, Namibia & University of Pune, India* 1666

Barberi, Larissa Cristina / *FESL, Brazil* 1944

Barbieri da Rosa, Luciana Aparecida / *Universidade Federal de Santa Maria, Brazil & International University of La Rioja, Spain & Federal Institute of Education, Science, and Technology of Rondônia, Brazil* 1944

Basharat, Taimoor / *University of Management and Technology, Lahore, Pakistan* 803

Baykal, Elif / *İstanbul Medipol University, Turkey* 200, 1908

Bayram, Gul Erkol / *Sinop University, Turkey* 1390

Berber, Nemanja / *Faculty of Economics in Subotica, University of Novi Sad, Serbia* 939

Berning, Sue Claire / *University of Erlangen-Nuernberg, Germany* 892

Bhusal, Roshee Lamichhane / *Kathmandu University, Nepal* 1132

Boaventura, Helena / *Polytechnic Institute of Cávado and Ave, Portugal* 636

Borg, Naomi / *RMIT University, Australia* 1884

Bornay-Barrachina, Mar / *Pablo de Olavide University, Spain* 141

Brace, Richard / *Pentecost University, Ghana* 2103

Brightenburg, Mark E. / *University of Dallas, USA* 2179

Buabeng-Andoh, Charles / *Pentecost University College, Ghana* 448

Burrell, Darrell Norman / *The Florida Institute of Technology, USA* 17, 1040

Čambál, Miloš / *Slovak University of Technology in Bratislava, Slovakia* 1762

Cazarez, Jorge Alberto Delgado / *Universidad de Guadalajara, Mexico* 251

Cézanne, Cécile / *Université Côte d'Azur, France* 2068

Charidimou, Dimos Savvas / *Department of Informatics, School of Sciences, Aristotle University of Thessaloniki, Greece* 1491

Choi, Youngkeun / *Sangmyung University, Seoul, South Korea* 1727

Chowdhury, Mohammad Ashraful Ferdous / *Shahjalal University of Science and Technology, Bangladesh* 340

Conceição, Oscarina / *Polytechnic Institute of Cávado and Ave, Portugal & DINÂMIA'CET-IUL, ISCTE, Instituto Universitário de Lisboa, Portugal & UNIAG, Portugal* 636

Cristofaro, Concetta Lucia / *University Magna Graecia di Catanzaro, Italy* 1193

Crowne, Kerri Anne / *Widener University, Chester, USA* 1001

Cruz, Ana Campos / *University of Aveiro, Portugal* 659

Čulková, Katarína / *Technical University of Košice, Slovakia* 1800

Das, Richa / *IMS Unison University, India* 129

Davarpanah, Ashkan / *Universiti Teknologi Malaysia, Malaysia* 1314

Dede, Nurten Polat / *Istanbul Medipol University, Turkey* 180, 1230

Deogaonkar, Anant / *Shri Ramdeobaba College of Engineering and Management, India* 911

Dev, Santosh / *Jaypee Institute of Information Technology, Noida, India* 93, 491

Dieguez, Teresa / *Polytechnic Institute of Cávado and Ave, Portugal* 636, 1623

Dinçer, Füsun Istanbullu / *Istanbul University, Turkey* 1390

Doğru, Çağlar / *Ufuk University, Turkey* 358

Dohroo, Mitali / *Amity Business School, Amity University, Noida, India* 291

Duarte, Isabel / *Universidade Lusófona de Humanidades e Tecnologias, Portugal* 1375

Duggal, Taranjeet / *Amity Business School, Amity University, Noida, India* 291

Duncan, Terrence / *Liberty University, USA* 17

Elayan, Malek B. / *Institute of Public Administration, Saudi Arabia* 711

Fapohunda, Tinuke / *Lagos State University, Nigeria* 403

Fernando, A. G. N. K. / *Uva Wellassa University of Sri Lanka, Sri Lanka* 2138

Flamini, Giulia / *University of Rome Tor Vergata, Italy* 303

Franco, Edgar Cossio / *Universidad Enrique Díaz de León, Mexico* 251

French, Roderick / *George Mason University, USA* 1040

Gaba, Loveleen / *Rukmini Devi Institute of Advanced Studies, India* 791

Galli, Brian J. / *Assistant Professor and Graduate Program Director, Master of Science in Engineering Management Industrial Engineering, Hofstra University, USA* 114, 526

Ganiyu, Adesina Rafiu / *Ladoke Akintola University of Technology, Ogbomoso, Nigeria* 814

Ganiyu, Idris Olayiwola / *University of KwaZulu-Natal, South Africa* 2121

García-Alcaráz, Jorge Luis / *Autonomous University of Ciudad Juarez, Mexico* 760
Genty, Kabiru Ishola / *Lagos State University, Nigeria* 1278
Gera, Rajat / *Manav Rachna International Institute of Research and Studies, India* 73
Gnan, Luca / *University of Rome Tor Vergata, Italy* 303
Godoy, Tais Pentiado / *Universidade Federal de Santa Maria, Brazil* 1944
Goeke, Richard J. / *Widener University, Chester, USA* 1001
Göktaş, Pınar / *Süleyman Demirel University, Turkey* 1094
Gouloudis, Stylianos Euaggeos / *Independent Researcher, Greece* 1491
Gregar, Ales / *Tomas Bata University in Zlín, Czech Republic* 1601
Güler, Burcu Kümbül / *Dokuz Eylul University, Turkey* 1524
Gupta, Minisha / *Quality Cognition Private Limited, India* 1122
Gupta, Sakshi / *Rukmini Devi Institute of Advanced Studies, India* 791
Hamid, Zainab / *University of Kashmir, India* 1
Hasan, Ikramul / *Independent University, Bangladesh* 340
Hashim, Nurul Afza / *Universiti Tun Abdul Razak, Malaysia* 1743
Hobbs, Harry L. / *The Florida Institute of Technology, USA* 1040
Hurd, Brian / *Washington University, USA* 17
Islam, MD. Nazmul / *University of Malaya, Malaysia* 340
Iwashita, Hitoshi / *Faculty of Economics and Management, Vietnamese German University, Vietnam* 1868
Jain, Geetika / *FMS, Amity University, Noida, India* 911
Jain, Ruchi / *Amity University, India* 1436
Jalagat Jr., Revenio C. / *Al-Zahra College for Women, Oman* 233
Jalaludin, Farah Waheeda / *Universiti Tunku Abdul Rahman, Malaysia* 1743
Janošková, Mária / *Department of Management in Poprad, Catholic University of Ružomberok, Poprad, Slovakia* 1800
Jaoua, Fakher Moncef / *College of Economics and Administrative Sciences, Riyadh, Al Imam Mohammad ibn Saud Islamic University, Riyadh, Saudi Arabia & University of Sfax, Sfax, Tunisia* 1707
Jiménez-Macías, Emilio / *University of La Rioja, Spain* 760
Justin, Mercia Selvia Malar / *Xavier Institute of Management and Entrepreneurship, India* 233
Kalambi, Mihir Dilip / *S.K. Somaiya College of Arts Science and Commerce, Mumbai, India* 1344
Kaseeram, Irrshad / *University of Zululand, South Africa* 2202
Kesti, Marko / *University of Lapland, Lapland, Finland* 1783
Khandelwal, Ruchi / *Amity University, India* 1436
Khashman, Aysar Mohammad / *The World Islamic Sciences and Education University, Amman, Jordan* 1352
Kim, Minkyoung / *University of West Florida, USA* 545
Koç Aytekin, Güner / *Ufuk University, Turkey* 962
Kumah, Peace / *Ghana Education Service, Accra, Ghana* 448, 1251
Kumar, Sanjeev / *Lovely Professional University, Punjab, India* 219
Laker, Dennis R. / *Widener University, Chester, USA* 1001
Lakhera, Anupama / *Delhi School of Professional Studies and Research, India* 1337
Lawal, Ibrahim Olanrewaju / *Kwara State University, Malete, Nigeria* 987
Lim, Doo Hun / *University of Oklahoma, USA* 545
Lindsay, Preston Vernard Leicester / *The University of Maryland, College Park, USA* 1040

Loufrani-Fedida, Sabrina / *Université Côte d'Azur, France* 921
Maldonado-Macías, Aide Aracely / *Autonomous University of Ciudad Juarez, Mexico* 760
Malik, Sahil / *Manav Rachna International Institute of Research and Studies, India* 73
Manna, Rosalba / *National Institute for Documentation, Innovation, and Educational Research, Italy* 1412
Marchisio, Emiliano / *"Giustino Fortunato" University of Benevento, Italy* 1578
Marin, Maria Rosario Perello / *Universitat Politècnica de València, Valencia, Spain* 1990, 2022
Marnoto, Sandra / *Instituto Universitário da Maia, Portugal & Universidade do Porto, Portugal* 1965
Martins-Rodrigues, Maria Carolina / *CinTurs, University of Algarve, Portugal* 1944
Melina, Anna Maria / *University Magna Graecia di Catanzaro, Italy* 1193
Mendy, John / *University of Lincoln, UK* 162
Meskelis, Simone / *University of Dallas, USA* 2179
Mikulášková, Justína / *Slovak University of Technology in Bratislava, Slovakia* 1762
Min, Gihong / *Department of Game Engineering, Paichai University, Daejeon, South Korea* 513
Ming, X. / *Glorious Sun School of Business and Management, Donghua University Shanghai, China* 1021
Mohamed, Norshidah / *Prince Sultan University, Saudi Arabia.* 1314
Müceldili, Büşra / *Yıldız Technical University, Turkey* 1928
Muzamil, Muhammad / *University of Kashmir, India* 1
Naderpajouh, Nader / *RMIT University, Australia* 1884
Nanoty, Sampada / *M. S. University Vadodara, India* 911
Narayana, Alamuri Surya / *Osmania University, India* 1132
Oladejo, Olufemi Michael / *University of KwaZulu-Natal, South Africa* 2121
Olawoyin, Femi Stephen / *Kwara State University, Malete, Nigeria* 987
Olgun, Bülent Özgür / *Başkent University, Turkey* 962
Ovalle-Mora, Omar Orlando / *EAN University, Colombia* 1644
Özcan, Ahmet / *Adana Science and Technology University, Turkey* 619
Padhi, Sushree Lekha / *Xavier University, India* 867
Palumbo, Rocco / *University of Rome "Tor Vergata", Italy* 1412
Panchal, Ankit / *KIET Group of Institutions, Delhi-NCR, Ghaziabad, India* 2053
Park, Sunyoung / *Louisiana State University, USA* 545
Pellegrini, Massimiliano / *University of Rome "Tor Vergata", Italy* 1412
Perello-Marin, M. Rosario / *Universitat Politècnica de València, Valencia, Spain* 735
Perez-Uribe, Rafael Ignacio / *EAN University, Colombia* 1644
Pérez-Uribe, Rafael Ignacio / *EAN University, Colombia* 1052
Pius, Abraham / *Arden University, UK* 35, 1823
Polakovič, Ľuboš / *Lotes Centrum s.r.o., Slovakia* 1762
Puig, Lilian Consuelo Mustelier / *Glorious Sun School of Business and Management, Donghua University Shanghai, China* 1021
Pupo, Fabricio Palermo / *Positivo University, Brazil* 564
Puri, Roma / *International Management Institute Kolkata, India* 847
Quansah, Fidelis / *University of Professional Studies, Accra, Ghana* 2103
Radant, Olaf / *Ginkgo Management Consulting, Germany* 374
Rahim, Emad / *Bellevue University, USA* 17
Ramírez-Garzón, María Teresa / *La Salle University, Colombia* 1052

Ramirez-Salazar, Maria Del Pilar / *EAN University, Colombia* 1644
Realyvásquez-Vargas, Arturo / *Instituto Tecnológico de Tijuana, Mexico* 760
Reina, Rocco / *University Magna Graecia di Catanzaro, Italy* 1193
Reis, Rosana Silveira / *Institut Supérieur de Gestion, Paris, France* 564
Rezwan, Roksana Binte / *Hiroshima University, Japan* 1549
Rocha Fernandes, Bruno Henrique / *Pontifical Catholic University of Parana, Brazil* 564
Rožman, Maja / *University of Maribor, Slovenia* 1843
Sachdeva, Geeta / *National Institute of Technology Kurukshetra, India* 55
Saglietto, Laurence / *Université Côte d'Azur, France* 2068
Saha, Nibedita / *Tomas Bata University in Zlín, Czech Republic* 1601
Sáha, Petr / *Tomas Bata University in Zlin, Czech Republic* 1601
Salcedo-Perez, Carlos / *EAN University, Colombia* 1644
Salih, Ahmad Ali / *Middle East University, Jordan* 1074
Sanyang, Saikou / *Arden University, UK* 35, 1823
Schoeneberg, Klaus Peter / *Beuth University of Applied Sciences Berlin, Berlin, Germany* 735
Schoeneberg, Klaus-Peter / *Beuth University of Applied Sciences, Berlin, Germany* 1990, 2022
Schultz, Martin / *HAW Hamburg, Hamburg, Germany* 735
Scott-Young, Christina M. / *RMIT University, Australia* 1884
Sengupta, Pooja / *International Management Institute Kolkata, India* 847
Sfeir, Elizabeth Kassab / *Université Antonine, Lebanon* 422, 1297
Shah, Shawkat Ahmad / *University of Kashmir, India* 1
Sharma, Alka / *Jaypee Institute of Information Technology, India* 471
Sharma, Pooja / *Institute of Information Technology and Management, Delhi, India* 1337
Shenoy, Nagaraj / *Dayananda Sagar Junior Business School, India* 680
Shetty, Susheela / *Brindavan College, Bangalore, India* 606
Shrivastava, Archana / *Jaypee Business School, Jaypee Institute of Information Technology,
    India* 911
Singh, Amrik / *Lovely Professional University, Punjab, India* 219
Slavić, Agneš / *Faculty of Economics in Subotica, University of Novi Sad, Serbia* 939
Soonthodu, Sachin / *Garden City University, India* 606
Sosa, Liliana Avelar / *Autonomous University of Ciudad Juarez, Mexico* 760
Sousa, Célio A.A. / *Instituto Universitário da Maia, Portugal* 1965
Sousa, Maria José / *ISCTE, Instituto Universitário de Lisboa, Portugal* 1944
Springs, Delores / *Regent University, USA* 2092
Srivastava, Sonalee / *Jaypee Institute of Information Technology, Noida, India* 93, 491
Stantchev, Vladimir / *SRH Hochschule-Berlin, Germany* 374
Statti, Aubrey / *The Chicago School of Professional Psychology, USA* 588
Stefanova, Marina / *UNGC Network Bulgaria, Bulgaria* 1158
Sutha, Jayaranjani / *Uva Wellassa University of Sri Lanka, Sri Lanka* 2138
Tari, Inci / *Arel University, Turkey* 2155
Tatar, Berivan / *Gebze Technical University, Turkey* 1928
Tomar, Jitendra Singh / *Amity University, India* 1436
Torres, Kelly M. / *The Chicago School of Professional Psychology, USA* 588
Treven, Sonja / *University of Maribor, Slovenia* 1843
Ubrežiová, Iveta / *Department of Management in Poprad, Catholic University of Ružomberok,
    Poprad, Slovakia* 1800

Uçar, Pınar / *Antalya AKEV University, Turkey* 1688

Urbanovičová, Petra / *Slovak University of Technology in Bratislava, Slovakia* 1762

Vakkala, Hanna / *University of Lapland, Lapland, Finland* 1783

Van der Heijden, Beatrice I.J.M. / *Radboud University Nijmegen, The Netherlands & Open University of the Netherlands, The Netherlands & Kingston University, UK* 1601

Vasanthapriyan, Shanmuganathan / *Sabaragamuwa University of Sri Lanka, Sri Lanka* 1211

Ventura, Marzia / *University Magna Graecia di Catanzaro, Italy* 1193

Wang, Bo / *Department of Electrical Engineering, Shanxi Institute of Technology, Xi'an, China* 513

Whittington, J. Lee / *University of Dallas, USA* 2179

Xu, Jing / *Department of Economics Management, Shanxi Institute of Technology, Xi'an, China* 513

Yadav, Neha / *Rukmini Devi Institute of Advanced Studies, India* 791

Yaokumah, Winfred / *Department of Information Technology, Pentecost University College, Accra, Ghana* 448

Yap, Ching Seng / *Curtin University, Malaysia* 1743

Ylitalo, Aino-Inkeri / *University of Lapland, Lapland, Finland* 1783

Zezzatti, Carlos Alberto Ochoa Ortiz / *Universidad Autónoma de Ciudad Juárez, Mexico* 251

Ziebell, Robert-Christian / *Universitat Politècnica de València, Valencia, Spain* 735, 1990, 2022

Zingoni, Matthew / *University of New Orleans, USA* 276

Table of Contents

Preface xxv

Volume I

Section 1
Fundamental Concepts and Theories

Chapter 1
Strategic Human Resource Management 1
Zainab Hamid, University of Kashmir, India
Muhammad Muzamil, University of Kashmir, India
Shawkat Ahmad Shah, University of Kashmir, India

Chapter 2
Understanding Green Human Resources in Healthcare 17
Terrence Duncan, Liberty University, USA
Emad Rahim, Bellevue University, USA
Darrell Norman Burrell, The Florida Institute of Technology, USA
Brian Hurd, Washington University, USA

Chapter 3
Trends and Issues in Strategic Human Resources Management 35
Abraham Pius, Arden University, UK
Husam Helmi Alharahsheh, University of Wales Trinity Saint David, UK
Saikou Sanyang, Arden University, UK

Chapter 4
Impact of Psychological Contract on Employees' Performance: A Review 55
Geeta Sachdeva, National Institute of Technology Kurukshetra, India

Chapter 5
Emotional Labor in the Tourism Industry: Strategies, Antecedents, and Outcomes 73
Rajat Gera, Manav Rachna International Institute of Research and Studies, India
Shilpa Arora, Manav Rachna International Institute of Research and Studies, India
Sahil Malik, Manav Rachna International Institute of Research and Studies, India

Chapter 6
Human Resource Information System Adoption and Implementation Factors: A Theoretical
Analysis.. 93
    Sonalee Srivastava, Jaypee Institute of Information Technology, Noida, India
    Badri Bajaj, Jaypee Institute of Information Technology, Noida, India
    Santosh Dev, Jaypee Institute of Information Technology, Noida, India

Chapter 7
How Can Human Resource Management Help the Theory of Constraints 114
    Brian J. Galli, Assistant Professor and Graduate Program Director, Master of Science in
        Engineering Management Industrial Engineering, Hofstra University, USA

Chapter 8
Human Resource Management in Indian Microfinance Institutions 129
    Richa Das, IMS Unison University, India

Chapter 9
International Human Resource Management: How Should Employees Be Managed in an
International Context?... 141
    Mar Bornay-Barrachina, Pablo de Olavide University, Spain

Chapter 10
Key HRM Challenges and Benefits: The Contributions of the HR Scaffolding............... 162
    John Mendy, University of Lincoln, UK

Chapter 11
The Role of E-HRM Practices on Digital Era 180
    Nurten Polat Dede, Istanbul Medipol University, Turkey

Chapter 12
Digitalization of Human Resources: e-HR 200
    Elif Baykal, İstanbul Medipol University, Turkey

Chapter 13
Identifying Innovations in Human Resources: Academia and Industry Perspectives 219
    Amrik Singh, Lovely Professional University, Punjab, India
    Sanjeev Kumar, Lovely Professional University, Punjab, India

Section 2
Development and Design Methodologies

Chapter 14
Legal Framework on the Implementation of the Human Resource Management Reforms in the
Philippines After the Marcos Era Up to the Duterte Administration.................................. 233
    Perfecto G. Aquino, Jr., Duy Tan University, Vietnam
    Revenio C. Jalagat Jr., Al-Zahra College for Women, Oman
    Mercia Selvia Malar Justin, Xavier Institute of Management and Entrepreneurship, India

Chapter 15
Implementation of an Intelligent Model Based on Machine Learning in the Application of Macro-
Ergonomic Methods in a Human Resources Process Based on ISO 12207 251
    Edgar Cossio Franco, Universidad Enrique Díaz de León, Mexico
    Jorge Alberto Delgado Cazarez, Universidad de Guadalajara, Mexico
    Carlos Alberto Ochoa Ortiz Zezzatti, Universidad Autónoma de Ciudad Juárez, Mexico

Chapter 16
Human Resource Management in Agile Scrum Processes 276
    Matthew Zingoni, University of New Orleans, USA

Chapter 17
Sustainable and Green Human Resource Practices... 291
    Mitali Dohroo, Amity Business School, Amity University, Noida, India
    Taranjeet Duggal, Amity Business School, Amity University, Noida, India

Chapter 18
The Role of Awareness in Designing Human Resources Management Practices in Family Firms:
A Configurational Model 303
    Giulia Flamini, University of Rome Tor Vergata, Italy
    Luca Gnan, University of Rome Tor Vergata, Italy

Chapter 19
Transformational Human Resource Management: Crafting Organizational Efficiency 340
    Ikramul Hasan, Independent University, Bangladesh
    MD. Nazmul Islam, University of Malaya, Malaysia
    Mohammad Ashraful Ferdous Chowdhury, Shahjalal University of Science and Technology,
        Bangladesh

Chapter 20
An Integration of Human Resources and Supply Chain Management for a Sustainable
Competitive Advantage: A Resource-Based View 358
    Çağlar Doğru, Ufuk University, Turkey

Chapter 21
A Critical Assessment and Enhancement of Metrics for the Management of Scarce Human
Resources 374
    Olaf Radant, Ginkgo Management Consulting, Germany
    Vladimir Stantchev, SRH Hochschule-Berlin, Germany

Chapter 22
Greening the Compensation Design and Management of the Human Resource Function................ 403
    Tinuke Fapohunda, Lagos State University, Nigeria

Chapter 23
The Wasta Model: Impact on Human Resource Practices and HRM Within Lebanese
Universities 422
    Elizabeth Kassab Sfeir, Université Antonine, Lebanon

Chapter 24
Identifying HRM Practices for Improving Information Security Performance: An Importance-
Performance Map Analysis 448
    Peace Kumah, Ghana Education Service, Accra, Ghana
    Winfred Yaokumah, Department of Information Technology, Pentecost University College,
        Accra, Ghana
    Charles Buabeng-Andoh, Pentecost University College, Ghana

Chapter 25
Unlocking Drivers for Employee Engagement Through Human Resource Analytics 471
    Kanupriya Misra Bakhru, Jaypee Institute of Information Technology, India
    Alka Sharma, Jaypee Institute of Information Technology, India

Chapter 26
Human Resource Information System Use, Satisfaction, and Success 491
    Sonalee Srivastava, Jaypee Institute of Information Technology, India
    Santosh Dev, Jaypee Institute of Information Technology, India
    Badri Bajaj, Jaypee Institute of Information Technology, India

Chapter 27
Research on Human Resource Allocation Model Based on SOM Neural Network 513
    Jing Xu, Department of Economics Management, Shanxi Institute of Technology, Xi'an, China
    Bo Wang, Department of Electrical Engineering, Shanxi Institute of Technology, Xi'an, China
    Gihong Min, Department of Game Engineering, Paichai University, Daejeon, South Korea

Chapter 28
Theory of Constraints and Human Resource Management Applications 526
    Brian J. Galli, Assistant Professor and Graduate Program Director, Master of Science in
        Engineering Management Industrial Engineering, Hofstra University, USA

Volume II

Chapter 29
Instructional Design in Human Resource Development Academic Programs in the USA 545
    Sunyoung Park, Louisiana State University, USA
    Doo Hun Lim, University of Oklahoma, USA
    Minkyoung Kim, University of West Florida, USA

Chapter 30
High-Performance Work Systems in a Cross-Cultural Context: A Comparison Between Sweden
and Brazil 564
    Gislaine Martinelli Baniski, Ponta Grossa State University, Brazil
    Rosana Silveira Reis, Institut Supérieur de Gestion, Paris, France
    Bruno Henrique Rocha Fernandes, Pontifical Catholic University of Parana, Brazil
    Fabricio Palermo Pupo, Positivo University, Brazil

Section 3
Tools and Technologies

Chapter 31
Utilizing Technology to Enhance Human Resource Practices 588
    Kelly M. Torres, The Chicago School of Professional Psychology, USA
    Aubrey Statti, The Chicago School of Professional Psychology, USA

Chapter 32
Innovative Technology and Human Resource Management 606
    Sachin Soonthodu, Garden City University, India
    Susheela Shetty, Brindavan College, Bangalore, India

Chapter 33
The Role of Human Resource Accounting in the Business Environment 619
    Ahmet Özcan, Adana Science and Technology University, Turkey

Chapter 34
Impact of Design Thinking on Human Resources 636
    Helena Boaventura, Polytechnic Institute of Cávado and Ave, Portugal
    Teresa Dieguez, Polytechnic Institute of Cávado and Ave, Portugal
    Oscarina Conceição, Polytechnic Institute of Cávado and Ave, Portugal & DINÂMIA'CET-
        IUL, ISCTE, Instituto Universitário de Lisboa, Portugal & UNIAG, Portugal

Chapter 35
Portal for Employees in the Public Sector: A Tool for Knowledge Management in Human
Resources 659
    Ana Campos Cruz, University of Aveiro, Portugal

Chapter 36
Applicability of Six Sigma in Human Resource Management 680
    Nagaraj Shenoy, Dayananda Sagar Junior Business School, India

Chapter 37
Human Resources and their Tendency to Information Security Crimes Based on Holland
Theory 695
    Mahmoud Mohammad Al-Ajlouni, Northern Border University, Saudi Arabia

Chapter 38

Transformation of Human Resources Management Solutions as a Strategic Tool for GIG Workers
Contracting.. 711
    Malek B. Elayan, Institute of Public Administration, Saudi Arabia

Chapter 39

eHR Cloud Transformation: Implementation Approach and Success Factors 735
    Robert-Christian Ziebell, Universitat Politècnica de València, Valencia, Spain
    Jose Albors-Garrigos, Universitat Politècnica de València, Valencia, Spain
    Martin Schultz, HAW Hamburg, Hamburg, Germany
    Klaus Peter Schoeneberg, Beuth University of Applied Sciences Berlin, Berlin, Germany
    M. Rosario Perello-Marin, Universitat Politècnica de València, Valencia, Spain

Chapter 40

Role of Human Resources, Production Process, and Flexibility on Commercial Benefits From
AMT Investments.. 760
    Jorge Luis García-Alcaráz, Autonomous University of Ciudad Juarez, Mexico
    Emilio Jiménez-Macías, University of La Rioja, Spain
    Arturo Realyvásquez-Vargas, Instituto Tecnológico de Tijuana, Mexico
    Liliana Avelar Sosa, Autonomous University of Ciudad Juarez, Mexico
    Aide Aracely Maldonado-Macías, Autonomous University of Ciudad Juarez, Mexico

Chapter 41

Electronic Media: An Emergent Personality Mining Tool for Attracting and Screening.................. 791
    Sakshi Gupta, Rukmini Devi Institute of Advanced Studies, India
    Neha Yadav, Rukmini Devi Institute of Advanced Studies, India
    Loveleen Gaba, Rukmini Devi Institute of Advanced Studies, India

Chapter 42

Applying ISPAR Model of Service Dominant Logic on Mentoring a Part of Training and
Development Function of HRM Functions... 803
    Taimoor Basharat, University of Management and Technology, Lahore, Pakistan

Chapter 43

A Fuzzy System for Evaluating Human Resources in Project Management 814
    Oladele Stephen Adeola, Department of Computer Science, Federal University of
        Technology, Akure, Nigeria
    Adesina Rafiu Ganiyu, Ladoke Akintola University of Technology, Ogbomoso, Nigeria

Chapter 44

Application of Statistics in Human Resource Management 847
    Roma Puri, International Management Institute Kolkata, India
    Pooja Sengupta, International Management Institute Kolkata, India

Chapter 45

Six Sigma in Human Resources: Application in the Domain Function.. 867
    Sushree Lekha Padhi, Xavier University, India

Section 4
Utilization and Applications

Chapter 46
How the Human Resource Practices of Chinese MNEs in Africa Create Economic Growth and
Livelihood Options 892
Sue Claire Berning, University of Erlangen-Nuernberg, Germany
Judith Ambrosius, University of Erlangen-Nuernberg, Germany

Chapter 47
Augment Human Resource Proximity Plumbing Cybernation 911
Anant Deogaonkar, Shri Ramdeobaba College of Engineering and Management, India
Sampada Nanoty, M. S. University Vadodara, India
Archana Shrivastava, Jaypee Business School, Jaypee Institute of Information Technology, India
Geetika Jain, FMS, Amity University, Noida, India

Chapter 48
HRM Practices in Human Capital-Intensive Firms: An Empirical Study of IBM Corporation 921
Sabrina Loufrani-Fedida, Université Côte d'Azur, France

Chapter 49
The Role of Human Resource Management in Agriculture Sector Enterprises 939
Nemanja Berber, Faculty of Economics in Subotica, University of Novi Sad, Serbia
Agneš Slavić, Faculty of Economics in Subotica, University of Novi Sad, Serbia

Chapter 50
Examination of Vocational Schools as Sustainable Human Resources in Supply Chain
Management: The Case of Turkey and South Korea 962
Bülent Özgür Olgun, Başkent University, Turkey
Güner Koç Aytekin, Ufuk University, Turkey

Chapter 51
Green Human Resources and Sustainable Business Solutions 987
Ibrahim Olanrewaju Lawal, Kwara State University, Malete, Nigeria
Femi Stephen Olawoyin, Kwara State University, Malete, Nigeria

Chapter 52
The Effect of Education on Information Systems Success: Lessons from Human Resources 1001
Richard J. Goeke, Widener University, Chester, USA
Kerri Anne Crowne, Widener University, Chester, USA
Dennis R. Laker, Widener University, Chester, USA

Chapter 53
Analysis of Strategic Human Resource Management Practices in Small and Medium Enterprises
of South Asia 1021
    A. Anjum, Glorious Sun School of Business and Management, Donghua University
       Shanghai, China
    X. Ming, Glorious Sun School of Business and Management, Donghua University Shanghai,
       China
    Lilian Consuelo Mustelier Puig, Glorious Sun School of Business and Management,
       Donghua University Shanghai, China

Chapter 54
A Real-World Exploration of Green Human Resources and Sustainability Education in Hyper-
Connected and Technology-Driven Organizations 1040
    Darrell Norman Burrell, The Florida Institute of Technology, USA
    Roderick French, George Mason University, USA
    Preston Vernard Leicester Lindsay, The University of Maryland, College Park, USA
    Amina I. Ayodeji-Ogundiran, The Chicago School of Professional Psychology, USA
    Harry L. Hobbs, The Florida Institute of Technology, USA

Chapter 55
Human Resources Management and Its Contribution to Colombian SME Sustainability 1052
    Rafael Ignacio Pérez-Uribe, EAN University, Colombia
    María Teresa Ramírez-Garzón, La Salle University, Colombia

Chapter 56
Strategic Human Resources Management: Strategies in Iraq and Jordan.. 1074
    Ahmad Ali Salih, Middle East University, Jordan

Volume III

Chapter 57
The Investigation of Employer Adoption of Human Resource Information Systems at University
Using TAM 1094
    Pınar Göktaş, Süleyman Demirel University, Turkey
    Yakup Akgül, Alanya Alaaddin Keykubat University, Turkey

Chapter 58
Innovations in HRM Practices in Indian Companies: A Review-Based Study................................ 1122
    Minisha Gupta, Quality Cognition Private Limited, India

Chapter 59
Adoption and Use of Human Information System Digital Technology for Organizational
Competitiveness: An Exploratory Study in the Context of Nepal 1132
    Alamuri Surya Narayana, Osmania University, India
    Roshee Lamichhane Bhusal, Kathmandu University, Nepal

Chapter 60
Human Capital in Business: The Case of Overgas 1158
    Marina Stefanova, UNGC Network Bulgaria, Bulgaria

Section 5
Organizational and Social Implications

Chapter 61
Dynamics of Human Resource Strategies and Cultural Orientations in Multinational
Corporations... 1177
    Isaac Idowu Abe, University of KwaZulu-Natal, South Africa
    Ethel N. Abe, University of KwaZulu-Natal, South Africa

Chapter 62
Organizing Human Resources in Family Firms During Generational Succession 1193
    Anna Maria Melina, University Magna Graecia di Catanzaro, Italy
    Concetta Lucia Cristofaro, University Magna Graecia di Catanzaro, Italy
    Marzia Ventura, University Magna Graecia di Catanzaro, Italy
    Rocco Reina, University Magna Graecia di Catanzaro, Italy

Chapter 63
Examine the Factors Influencing Effectiveness of HRM Practices Designed to Improve
Knowledge Transfer: Organizational Experience 1211
    Shanmuganathan Vasanthapriyan, Sabaragamuwa University of Sri Lanka, Sri Lanka

Chapter 64
Enhancing Employee Innovative Work Behavior Through Human Resource Management
Practices 1230
    Nurten Polat Dede, Istanbul Medipol University, Turkey

Chapter 65
The Role of Human Resource Management in Enhancing Organizational Information Systems
Security 1251
    Peace Kumah, Ghana Education Service, Ghana

Chapter 66
Green Human Resource Management Practices and Organisational Sustainability 1278
    Kabiru Ishola Genty, Lagos State University, Nigeria

Chapter 67
Wasta, the Impact of Preferment on Organizational Culture and Human Resource Management ... 1297
    Elizabeth Kassab Sfeir, Université Antonine, Baabda, Lebanon

Chapter 68
Human Resources Information Systems Implementation and Influences in Higher Education:
Evidence From Malaysia 1314
 Ashkan Davarpanah, Universiti Teknologi Malaysia, Malaysia
 Norshidah Mohamed, Prince Sultan University, Saudi Arabia

Chapter 69
Green HRM: Best HR Practices Within an Organization for Reducing Employees' Carbon
Footprint... 1337
 Anupama Lakhera, Delhi School of Professional Studies and Research, India
 Pooja Sharma, Institute of Information Technology and Management, Delhi, India

Chapter 70
Caring for the Caregivers Through Healthy Human Resource Practices: The Caregivers 1344
 Mihir Dilip Kalambi, S.K. Somaiya College of Arts Science and Commerce, Mumbai, India

Chapter 71
The Impact of Electronic Human Resource Management (E-HRM) Strategies on Organizational
Innovation by Knowledge Repository as Mediating Role 1352
 Aysar Mohammad Khashman, The World Islamic Sciences and Education University,
  Amman, Jordan

Chapter 72
Human Resources Management for Sustainable Sea Tourism 1375
 Isabel Duarte, Universidade Lusófona de Humanidades e Tecnologias, Portugal

Chapter 73
Fourth Generation of Rights and Their Reflections on Human Resources Practices in Tourism
Businesses 1390
 Füsun Istanbullu Dinçer, Istanbul University, Turkey
 Gul Erkol Bayram, Sinop University, Turkey
 Ozlem Altunoz, Ankara Haci Bayram Veli University, Turkey

Chapter 74
Friends or Foe? Unravelling the Role of Familiness in Promoting Business Ethics in the
Workplace 1412
 Rosalba Manna, National Institute for Documentation, Innovation, and Educational
  Research, Italy
 Rocco Palumbo, University of Rome "Tor Vergata", Italy
 Massimiliano Pellegrini, University of Rome "Tor Vergata", Italy

Chapter 75
Role of Employee Engagement in Reducing Workplace Deviance 1436
 Jitendra Singh Tomar, Amity University, India
 Ruchi Khandelwal, Amity University, India
 Ruchi Jain, Amity University, India

Chapter 76
The Influence of HRIS Usage on Employee Performance and Mediating Effects of Employee
Engagement in Five Stars Hotels in Jordan 1468
    Rand H. Al-Dmour, The Univeristy of Jordan, Jordan

Section 6
Managerial Impact

Chapter 77
Media and Human Resource Management 1491
    Dimos Savvas Charidimou, Department of Informatics, School of Sciences, Aristotle
        University of Thessaloniki, Greece
    Stylianos Euaggeos Gouloudis, Independent Researcher, Greece

Chapter 78
Human Resources Management in Social Entrepreneurship 1524
    Burcu Kümbül Güler, Dokuz Eylul University, Turkey

Chapter 79
Managing Human Resources in E-Commerce 1549
    Roksana Binte Rezwan, Hiroshima University, Japan

Chapter 80
Law and HRM Challenges in Generational Transition of Family Firms 1578
    Emiliano Marchisio, "Giustino Fortunato" University of Benevento, Italy

Chapter 81
The Influence of SHRM and Organizational Agility: Do They Really Boost Organizational
Performance? 1601
    Nibedita Saha, Tomas Bata University in Zlín, Czech Republic
    Ales Gregar, Tomas Bata University in Zlín, Czech Republic
    Beatrice I.J.M. Van der Heijden, Radboud University Nijmegen, The Netherlands & Open
        University of the Netherlands, The Netherlands & Kingston University, UK
    Petr Sáha, Tomas Bata University in Zlin, Czech Republic

Chapter 82
Understanding Human Resources Needs in Tourism: A Competittive Advantage 1623
    Teresa Dieguez, Polytechnic Institute of Cávado and Ave, Portugal

Chapter 83
Relevance of Strategic Management of Human Resources in Travel Agencies: The Colombian
Case 1644
    Maria Del Pilar Ramirez-Salazar, EAN University, Colombia
    Omar Orlando Ovalle-Mora, EAN University, Colombia
    Carlos Salcedo-Perez, EAN University, Colombia
    Rafael Ignacio Perez-Uribe, EAN University, Colombia

Volume IV

Chapter 84
International Human Resource Management Strategies for Multicultural Organizations 1666
 Neeta Baporikar, Namibia University of Science and Technology, Namibia & University of
  Pune, India

Chapter 85
Importance of ICT in Human Resources Management and Evaluation in Terms of Events 1688
 Pınar Uçar, Antalya AKEV University, Turkey

Chapter 86
Specific Human Resource Practices Towards Middle Managers and Their Effects on Their
Strategic Roles: A Case of Large Tunisian Companies Participating in Industrial Upgrading
Program 1707
 Fakher Moncef Jaoua, College of Economics and Administrative Sciences, Riyadh, Al Imam
  Mohammad ibn Saud Islamic University, Riyadh, Saudi Arabia & University of Sfax,
  Sfax, Tunisia

Chapter 87
How does Leadership Motivate the Innovative Behaviors of Software Developers? 1727
 Youngkeun Choi, Sangmyung University, Seoul, South Korea

Chapter 88
Managerial Ambidexterity and Firm Performance: The Mediating Role of Knowledge
Brokerage 1743
 Ching Seng Yap, Curtin University, Malaysia
 Rizal Ahmad, Bandung Institute of Technology, Indonesia
 Farah Waheeda Jalaludin, Universiti Tunku Abdul Rahman, Malaysia
 Nurul Afza Hashim, Universiti Tun Abdul Razak, Malaysia

Chapter 89
Spiral Management: New Concept of the Social Systems Management 1762
 Justína Mikulášková, Slovak University of Technology in Bratislava, Slovakia
 Miloš Čambál, Slovak University of Technology in Bratislava, Slovakia
 Ľuboš Polakovič, Lotes Centrum s.r.o., Slovakia
 Petra Urbanovičová, Slovak University of Technology in Bratislava, Slovakia

Chapter 90
Management Game: Gamifying Leadership Learning 1783
 Marko Kesti, University of Lapland, Lapland, Finland
 Aino-Inkeri Ylitalo, University of Lapland, Lapland, Finland
 Hanna Vakkala, University of Lapland, Lapland, Finland

Chapter 91
Talent Management as a Part of Sustainable Human Resources Management 1800
    Mária Janošková, Department of Management in Poprad, Catholic University of
        Ružomberok, Poprad, Slovakia
    Iveta Ubrežiová, Department of Management in Poprad, Catholic University of Ružomberok,
        Poprad, Slovakia
    Katarína Čulková, Technical University of Košice, Slovakia

Chapter 92
Approaches and Practices in Strategic Human Resources Management 1823
    Abraham Pius, Arden University, UK
    Husam Helmi Alharahsheh, University of Wales Trinity Saint David, UK
    Saikou Sanyang, Arden University, UK

Chapter 93
The Conceptual Model of Managing Older Employees to Achieve Their Work Engagement 1843
    Maja Rožman, University of Maribor, Slovenia
    Sonja Treven, University of Maribor, Slovenia

Chapter 94
Transferring Japanese Management Practices in Asia and the West 1868
    Hitoshi Iwashita, Faculty of Economics and Management, Vietnamese German University,
        Vietnam

Chapter 95
Strategies for Business Sustainability in a Collaborative Economy: Building the Career Resilience
of Generation Z 1884
    Naomi Borg, RMIT University, Australia
    Christina M. Scott-Young, RMIT University, Australia
    Nader Naderpajouh, RMIT University, Australia

Chapter 96
Digital Era and New Methods for Employee Recruitment 1908
    Elif Baykal, İstanbul Medipol University, Turkey

Section 7
Critical Issues and Challenges

Chapter 97
Reflections of Human Resource Practices in Family Business: A Qualitative Research 1928
    Büşra Müceldili, Yıldız Technical University, Turkey
    Berivan Tatar, Gebze Technical University, Turkey

Chapter 98
HRM in the Tourism Industry: Inferences From Research.. 1944
    Maria Carolina Martins-Rodrigues, CinTurs, University of Algarve, Portugal
    Luciana Aparecida Barbieri da Rosa, Universidade Federal de Santa Maria, Brazil &
        International University of La Rioja, Spain & Federal Institute of Education, Science,
        and Technology of Rondônia, Brazil
    Maria José Sousa, ISCTE, Instituto Universitário de Lisboa, Portugal
    Larissa Cristina Barberi, FESL, Brazil
    Tais Pentiado Godoy, Universidade Federal de Santa Maria, Brazil

Chapter 99
The Role of HRM for Innovation: A Conceptual and Analytical Study... 1965
    Sandra Marnoto, Instituto Universitário da Maia, Portugal & Universidade do Porto, Portugal
    Célio A.A. Sousa, Instituto Universitário da Maia, Portugal

Chapter 100
Adoption and Success of e-HRM in a Cloud Computing Environment: A Field Study................... 1990
    Robert-Christian Ziebell, Universitat Politècnica de València, Valencia, Spain
    Jose Albors-Garrigos, Universitat Politècnica de València, Valencia, Spain
    Klaus-Peter Schoeneberg, Beuth University of Applied Sciences, Berlin, Germany
    Maria Rosario Perello Marin, Universitat Politècnica de València, Valencia, Spain

Chapter 101
e-HRM in a Cloud Environment: Implementation and its Adoption: A Literature Review............. 2022
    Robert-Christian Ziebell, Universitat Politècnica de València, Valencia, Spain
    Jose Albors-Garrigos, Universitat Politècnica de València, Valencia, Spain
    Klaus-Peter Schoeneberg, Beuth University of Applied Sciences, Berlin, Germany
    Maria Rosario Perello Marin, Universitat Politècnica de València, Valencia, Spain

Chapter 102
Human Resources Accounting Disclosure Practices (HRADP): A Review...................................... 2053
    Amit Kumar Arora, KIET Group of Institutions, Delhi-NCR, Ghaziabad, India
    Ankit Panchal, KIET Group of Institutions, Delhi-NCR, Ghaziabad, India

Chapter 103
A Survey of the Literature on Human Capital-Intensive Firms: A Bibliometric Analysis............... 2068
    Cécile Cézanne, Université Côte d'Azur, France
    Laurence Saglietto, Université Côte d'Azur, France

Section 8
Emerging Trends

Chapter 104
An Exploratory Content Analysis of Human Resources Management in Healthcare
Organizations 2092
    Delores Springs, Regent University, USA

Chapter 105
Green Human Resource Management: A Review and Future Directions 2103
  Richard Afedzie, Pentecost University, Ghana
  Richard Brace, Pentecost University, Ghana
  Fidelis Quansah, University of Professional Studies, Accra, Ghana
  James Attah-Panin, Pentecost University, Ghana

Chapter 106
Green Work-Life Balance and Global Leadership in Industry 4.0 2121
  Idris Olayiwola Ganiyu, University of KwaZulu-Natal, South Africa
  Olufemi Michael Oladejo, University of KwaZulu-Natal, South Africa

Chapter 107
Influence of Internal Corporate Social Responsibility on Employee Retention With Special
Reference to the Apparel Industry in Sri Lanka 2138
  A. G. N. K. Fernando, Uva Wellassa University of Sri Lanka, Sri Lanka
  Jayaranjani Sutha, Uva Wellassa University of Sri Lanka, Sri Lanka

Chapter 108
Media Business Literacy in the Digital Age: Changing Industry Trends 2155
  Inci Tari, Arel University, Turkey

Chapter 109
Job Engagement Levels Across the Generations at Work 2179
  Mark E. Brightenburg, University of Dallas, USA
  J. Lee Whittington, University of Dallas, USA
  Simone Meskelis, University of Dallas, USA
  Enoch Asare, Texas A&M University, Texarkana, USA

Chapter 110
The Future of Workforce Planning 2202
  Ayansola Olatunji Ayandibu, University of Zululand, South Africa
  Irrshad Kaseeram, University of Zululand, South Africa

Index xxviii

Preface

As technology develops, policies in organizations tend to accelerate in tandem. This leads to new and innovative practices developing for many departments, especially within human resource departments. As human resource practices develop, many strategies advance as well. It is essential to be knowledgeable about these new advances in human resource practices to have the best practices for running business.

Staying informed of the most up-to-date research trends and findings is of the utmost importance. That is why IGI Global is pleased to offer this four-volume reference collection of reprinted IGI Global book chapters and journal articles that have been handpicked by senior editorial staff. This collection will shed light on critical issues related to the trends, techniques, and uses of various applications by providing both broad and detailed perspectives on cutting-edge theories and developments. This collection is designed to act as a single reference source on conceptual, methodological, technical, and managerial issues, as well as to provide insight into emerging trends and future opportunities within the field.

The *Research Anthology on Human Resource Practices for the Modern Workforce* is organized into eight distinct sections that provide comprehensive coverage of important topics. The sections are:

1. Fundamental Concepts and Theories;
2. Development and Design Methodologies;
3. Tools and Technologies;
4. Utilization and Applications;
5. Organizational and Social Implications;
6. Managerial Impact;
7. Critical Issues and Challenges; and
8. Emerging Trends.

The following paragraphs provide a summary of what to expect from this invaluable reference tool.

Section 1, "Fundamental Concepts and Theories," serves as a foundation for this extensive reference tool by addressing crucial theories essential to understanding modern human resource practices. The first chapter of this section, "Strategic Human Resource Management," by Profs. Zainab Hamid, Muhammad Muzamil, and Shawkat Ahmad Shah of University of Kashmir, India, focuses keenly on the various domains centering around human resource management. Initially, a detailed theoretical background regarding this construct has been presented followed by highlighting the components and objectives of strategizing human resource management. The last chapter of this section, "Identifying Innovations in Human Resources: Academia and Industry Perspectives," by Profs. Amrik Singh and Sanjeev Kumar of Lovely Professional University, Punjab, India, develops a meaningful debate on the innovations in human resource in terms of new ideas, methods, and technology to better meet the evolving requirement of the organization and workforce.

Section 2, "Development and Design Methodologies," presents in-depth coverage of the design and development of human resource practices. The first chapter of this section, "Legal Framework on the Implementation of the Human Resource Management Reforms in the Philippines After the Marcos Era Up to the Duterte Administration," by Prof. Mercia Selvia Malar Justin of Xavier Institute of Management and Entrepreneurship, India; Prof. Perfecto G. Aquino, Jr. of Duy Tan University, Vietnam; and Prof. Revenio C. Jalagat Jr. of Al-Zahra College for Women, Oman, discusses the overview of both the legal reform processes happening in the public sector of the Philippine government and of recent developments and challenges initiated by the Civil Service Commission of the Philippine government as its Central Personnel Agency. The last chapter of this section, "High-Performance Work Systems in a Cross-Cultural Context: A Comparison Between Sweden and Brazil," by Prof. Gislaine Martinelli Baniski of Ponta Grossa State University, Brazil; Prof. Rosana Silveira Reis of Institut Supérieur de Gestion, Paris, France; Prof. Bruno Henrique Rocha Fernandes of Pontifical Catholic University of Parana, Brazil; and Prof. Fabricio Palermo Pupo of Positivo University, Brazil, investigates how high-performance work systems are applied in different cultural contexts and how cultural dimensions affect high-performance work system adaptation.

Section 3, "Tools and Technologies," explores the various tools and technologies that can be utilized to better communications for human resource departments. The first chapter of this section, "Utilizing Technology to Enhance Human Resource Practices," by Profs. Kelly M. Torres and Aubrey Statti of The Chicago School of Professional Psychology, USA, discusses how HR management departments are evolving from the advancement in technology. The last chapter of this section, "Six Sigma in Human Resources: Application in the Domain Function," by Prof. Sushree Lekha Padhi of Xavier University, India, explains that tools and methodologies are paving its way to bring efficient human resource management practices. Six Sigma is one of the tools that is booming into the application space of Human Resource Management. Six Sigma is being considered as a business process and is helping in shaping and improving their bottom line by designing and monitoring various activities to reduce the defects.

Section 4, "Utilization and Applications," describes how human resource practices are used and applied within diverse organizations. The first chapter of this section, "How the Human Resource Practices of Chinese MNEs in Africa Create Economic Growth and Livelihood Options," by Profs. Sue Claire Berning and Judith Ambrosius of University of Erlangen-Nuernberg, Germany, critically analyzes the economic development impact of multinational enterprises (MNEs) in developing countries. The last chapter of this section, "Human Capital in Business: The Case of Overgas," by Prof. Marina Stefanova of UNGC Network Bulgaria, Bulgaria, examines the most important theoretical contributions and basis of the human capital and human capital resource theories. It also covers the practical implications of these concepts in a newborn Bulgarian company which has a vision to transform the society it operates in.

Section 5, "Organizational and Social Implications," includes chapters discussing the impact of evolving human resource practices on many different organizations. The first chapter of this section, "Dynamics of Human Resource Strategies and Cultural Orientations in Multinational Corporations," by Profs. Isaac Idowu Abe and Ethel N. Abe of University of KwaZulu-Natal, South Africa, explains the dynamics behind multinational corporations (MNCs) that seek the market expansions in other developing countries transfer specific advantages and benefits to the emerging markets in order to operate effectively. The MNCs are required by law to comply with the legal obligations, local regulations, and cultural adaptations in the bid to transfer specific advantages. The last chapter of this section, "The Influence of HRIS Usage on Employee Performance and Mediating Effects of Employee Engagement in Five Stars Hotels in Jordan," by Prof. Rand H. Al-Dmour of The Univeristy of Jordan, Jordan, evaluates the role of employee engagement with their work as a mediating factor in the relationship between utilisation of a human resource information system (HRIS) and employee performance in five-star hotels in Jordan.

Section 6, "Managerial Impact," describes the implementation and effects of innovative human resource practices on organizations. The first chapter of this section, "Media and Human Resource Management," by Prof. Dimos Savvas Charidimou of Department of Informatics, School of Sciences, Aristotle University of Thessaloniki, Greece and Prof. Stylianos Euaggeos Gouloudis, Independent Researcher, Greece, explains how animated knowledge acquisition, peer networking, and action-planning have been introduced as managerial educative aspects, along information and entertainment, in the world of broadcasting. The last chapter of this section, "Digital Era and New Methods for Employee Recruitment," by Prof. Elif Baykal of İstanbul Medipol University, Turkey, examines the handling of recruitment functions within human resources management and the digitization process.

Section 7, "Critical Issues and Challenges," presents coverage of academic and research perspectives on challenges to innovating and implementing new human resource practices to organizations. The first chapter of this section, "Reflections of Human Resource Practices in Family Business: A Qualitative Research," by Prof. Büşra Müceldili of Yıldız Technical University, Turkey and Prof. Berivan Tatar of Gebze Technical University, Turkey, performs interviews on three experienced and successful family firm owners and human resource managers. The research findings reveal that family firms have professionalized, formalized, and employee-oriented perspective in their human resource practices. The last chapter of this section, "A Survey of the Literature on Human Capital-Intensive Firms: A Bibliometric Analysis," by Profs. Cécile Cézanne and Laurence Saglietto of Université Côte d'Azur, France, provides a survey of the academic research dedicated to human capital-intensive firms (HCIF) both at a theoretical and empirical level.

Section 8, "Emerging Trends," highlights areas for future research within this field. The first chapter of this section, "An Exploratory Content Analysis of Human Resources Management in Healthcare Organizations," by Prof. Delores Springs of Regent University, USA, provides a detailed analysis of human resources management (HRM) roles that affect employee management changes to explore human resource (HR) accountability, competency management, employee abilities, and organizational capabilities around treatment effectiveness and reduction of errors in healthcare delivery. The last chapter of this section, "The Future of Workforce Planning," by Profs. Ayansola Olatunji Ayandibu and Irrshad Kaseeram of University of Zululand, South Africa, examines the future of workforce planning in contemporary work organisations. Workforce planning is regarded as one of the essential human resource management (HRM) activities in recent times.

Although the primary organization of the contents in this multi-volume work is based on its eight sections, offering a progression of coverage of the important concepts, methodologies, technologies, applications, social issues, and emerging trends, the reader can also identify specific contents by utilizing the extensive indexing system listed at the end of each volume. As a comprehensive collection of research on the latest findings related to human resource practices, the *Research Anthology on Human Resource Practices for the Modern Workforce* provides human resource employees, managers, CEOs, employees, business students and professors, researchers, and academicians with a complete understanding of the applications and impacts of human resource practices. Given the vast number of issues concerning usage, failure, success, strategies, and applications of human resource practices in modern technologies and processes, the *Research Anthology on Human Resource Practices for the Modern Workforce* encompasses the most pertinent research on the applications, impacts, uses, and development of human resource practices.

Section 1
Fundamental Concepts and Theories

Chapter 1
Strategic Human Resource Management

Zainab Hamid
University of Kashmir, India

Muhammad Muzamil
University of Kashmir, India

Shawkat Ahmad Shah
University of Kashmir, India

ABSTRACT

Human resource management has become an integral part of management with the basic aim of maintaining better human relations at work place through the application and evaluation of organizational policies and programs so as to utilize human resources in an optimized and effective manner. In this context, this chapter focuses keenly on the various domains centering around human resource management. Initially a detailed theoretical background regarding this construct has been presented followed by highlighting the components and objectives of strategizing human resource management. Lastly, the models and perspectives pertaining to strategic human resource management have also been discussed considering their application and relevance in modern-day organizations.

INTRODUCTION

All the activities are initiated and completed by human resource, one of the important sources of any organization that needed to be handled and managed carefully by the management professionals. In essence human resource management (HRM) is very important and a very difficult job because of the dynamic nature of human resource as people are responsive, they feel and act, therefore can't be treated and operated like machines (Ganesan, 2014). The researcher further added that human resource management (HRM) is considered with management of the people working in an organization. It's a process that leads the management to think about human as an important work capitals and investment.

DOI: 10.4018/978-1-6684-3873-2.ch001

In other words it's an approach that enables the mangers to fully utilize the human resource in a proper and appropriate way so as to ensure growth and development of organization and protect the interest of its employees. Therefore, human resource management can be defined as a system that lay emphasis on effective management and progress of human resource on the ground of human approach. The basic principle of human resource management (HRM) is treating employees with human dignity while focusing on their skills, knowledge, abilities, capabilities, potentials, achievements, satisfaction and dedication etc. Thus human resource management is very important for the success and prosperity of an organization as it helps the organizations to acquire the services of employees, develop the skills and potentials of workers, increases the motivation of workforce to work with competence, ensuring commitment and dedication of employees, encourage employees to increase their performance and efforts, resolving human conflicts and issues in a reasonable way. In simple terms it helps the organization in achieving its set objectives and goals in a very effective and efficient manner. Human resource management is associated with '*people dimension*' in management and helps in selecting, recruiting, training, assisting and developing members of an organization. Boxall and Purcell (2000) stated that "*human resource management deals with anything and everything related with management of employment relationships in the firm*". Byars and Rue (2004) defined "*human resource management (HRM) as an activity designed to provide for and coordinate of human resources of an organization*". The authors further stated that human resource management is a new terminology for personnel administration or personnel management. As per Westover (2014) human resource management (HRM) is a process of selecting and employing people; training and compensating them; designing policies, programmes and strategies to retain and promote them. Besides, role of human resource management (HRM) is staffing, retention, development of work policies, training and development, compensation and benefiting administration, worker protection and deals with laws and regulations affecting workforce and performance appraisal. For Guest (1987) the key ingredients of human resource management (HRM) is to facilitate employees to remain committed in achieving organizational goals, assist employees to adjust and adapt to change prevailing within the organizational structure, focuses on quality of services of employees, staff members and management personals, and finally integrating human resource strategies into organizational goals (Osibanjo & Adeniji, 2012).

Human resource management have replaced the previous fundamental personal management in an organization. Human resource management (HRM) is relatively a new construct containing range of ideas and practice in managing workforce in an organization (Itika, 2011). Moreover researcher indicated that human resource management (HRM) has became an integral part of management with the basic aim in maintaining a better human relations at work place, application and evaluation of organizational policies and programmes so to utilize human resources in an optimize and effective way. Further, researcher elaborated that it's a process associated with recruitment and selection of employees, development and utilization of skills, assessment and evaluation of employee's performance, providing training and compensation, and motivating employees and maintaining a proper relationship among different members of an organization. Human resource management (HRM) has developed and evolved into different areas and managing people at the organizational level is well documented in the work of Cuming (1985), Munsterberg (1913) and Taylor (1914) cited in Itika (2011). Also the practice of management of human resource can be found in booming *European Economy* of 1900, where a congenial environment were created for managing workers effectively to face the market competition. Besides, Elton Mayo, Kurt Lewin, Abraham Maslow, Deci and Ryan, Armstrong and so on emphasis on improving the working conditions and treating employees as human beings rather than machines are also an important inputs in the development and practicing of human resource management. The British and Harvard School of human resource management and the work of Michael Armstrong, John Storey, Terrington and Hall (1991); Farnham and Pimlott (1992 cited in Itika (2011) have revealed that the philosophy of human resource management is based on six important components via:

- Human resource management has to be owned by top management.
- One of the basic fundaments of human resource management (HRM) is organizational strategy and there should be strategic fit between organizational strategy and human resource strategy.
- In human resource management practices, employees are considered as assets not liability.
- It's a mandatory role of management to get additional value from employees through human resource development and performance management system.
- Role of management is to encourage and enticement employees commitment to organizational missions, targets, objectives and goals in order to get success.
- Sixth is also based on employee commitment which can be stimulated by strong cooperate culture. The important tool to develop cooperate culture includes effective communication techniques, training, coaching, mentoring, performance evaluation etc.

On the basis of above philosophical postulates following are the main objectives of human resource management (HRM) (Itika, 2011):

- First and foremost important objective of human resource management is to achieve organizational goals, mission, targets and values by using people as a valuable human resource.
- Second objective of human resource management (HRM) is to effectively and successfully utilize the potential of employees and the staff capacity.
- Next objective is that the management should ensure organizational commitment and organizational identification in employees.
- Another objective of human resource management (HRM) is the optimal utilization of scare resource in the form of land, labour, capital and entrepreneur.
- One of the essential objective is to focus on wholeness rather sum of the parts. It means human resource management (HRM) emphasis on work together and collectively.
- Last but not least, objective of human resource management (HRM) is to give the weight to innovation, creativity, teamwork, flexible manager and high quality management which are the key sources of organizational success and excellence.

Due to the globalization, change in business environment and highly business competition people witnessed a great development and exploration in the concepts of human resource management from 2000's with more focus on strategic human resource management (SHRM). Etymologically the word strategy is derived from a Greek word *"strategus"*, means *"commander in chief"* or *"long run direction"*. Pertinently in management literature 'strategic' word has replaced a traditional term '*long term planning*', to denote *specific pattern of plans, decisions* and *actions* taken by the top management professional to accomplish organizational ends. In business context the main focus of term '*strategy*' is to help an organization to achieve competitive advantage with its unique capabilities by putting emphasis on present and future direction of the organization (Hassija, 2014).

BACKGROUND

Evolution of Strategic Human Resource Management (SHRM)

From Personnel Management to Human Resource Management (HRM) (Agarwala, 2002)

The Human resource (HR) function has evolved over the period of time. In 1970's human resource management (HRM) emerged as a replacement for personnel management with a huge change in the objectives and boundaries of the function. The main thrust of human resource management (HRM) is the achievement of organizational goals and mission with the help of people. However personnel management is different from HR, where the former is more bureaucratic with high levels of centralization and high level of formalization, with lower levels of flexibility. While, latter is decentralized, more flexible and involves strategic areas of business.

From Human Resource Management (HRM) to Strategic Human Resource Management (SHRM) (Agarwala, 2002)

Early 1980's witnessed an increased use of terminology strategic human resource management (HRM). With adjective *strategic* prefixed to human resource management (HRM), it focuses on relationship of human resource management (HRM) with the strategic management of the organization. Strategic human resource management goes beyond the functional role of human resource management (HRM), ensures organizational effectiveness and performance, modification in structure and culture, alignment of resources to present and future requirements of the firm, enhancement of organizational capability, development of employment relationships and managerial changes etc. One of the main difference between traditional human resource management (HRM) and strategic human resource management (SHRM) is the extent to which human resource management is integrated with the strategic decision making processes that tend to direct organizational efforts to cope effectively with environmental demands. Traditional human resource management (HRM) focuses mainly on physical skills, training on specific tasks and individual efficiency; don't put more emphasis on "people" but rather to "task" (Karami, Analoui & Cusworth, 2004). In contrast strategic human resource management (SHRM) focuses the total contribution of the firm, innovation and creative behaviour of employees, overall effectiveness and cross functional integration of an organization.

As per Hendry and Pettigrew (1986) strategic human resource management (SHRM) comprises the use of planning in human resource management; an integrated approach to design and implement HR systems; matching human resource management (HRM) practices and policies with business strategy of the organization and lastly, it views people as strategic tool and resource for achievement of organizational goals and competitive advantage. Wright and McMahan (1992) have rightly stated that *"strategic human resource management (SHRM) is a pattern of planned human resource activities intended to achieve organizational goals"*. Wheelen and Hunger (1995); Hill and Jones (2001) defined *"strategic human resource management (SRMH) as a set of managerial actions and decisions taken to attain superior and long term performance"*. For Mabey, Salaman and Storey (1998) strategic human resource management (SHRM) involves four main elements i.e. human capability and commitment, strategic importance of human resources, managing human resources by specialists and integration of human resource management into business strategy. According to Bamberger and Meshoulam (2000) strategic human resource management (SHRM) is the process by which organizations seek to link the human, social, and intellectual capital of their members to the strategic needs of the firm. However Itika (2011) and Agarwala (2002) stated that strategic human resource management (SHRM) is more proactive approach of human resource management, concerned with planned and effective utilization of workforce by the organization to achieve competitive advantages, organizational effectiveness and increment in performance. While defining strategic human resource management (SHRM), Kazmi and Ahmad (2001) have provided four approach namely strategy- focused, decision focused, content focused and implementation focussed. As per strategy focused approach, human resource management (HRM) is strategic by its very nature and all its components and elements have strategic linkages with each other (Krishnan & Singh, 2011). While as the decision focused approach encompasses three decision making levels such as operational, managerial and strategic and views human resource management (HRM) at strategic level to be strategic human resource management (SHRM) (Krishnan & Singh, 2011). As far as content focused approach is considered, strategic human resource management (SHRM) emerges when elements of human resource management (HRM) match with the organizational strategy. Lastly, in terms of implementation focused approach, strategic human resource management (SHRM) involves human resource management (HRM) systems that help in the formulation and implementation of business strategies or the alignment of HR policies and practices with business strategies of an organization (Krishnan & Singh, 2011). While for Bjorkman and Xiucheng (2002) there is a positive relation between firm performance and the extent to which the firm adopts and uses a high performance Human Resource Management (HRM) system as well as the degree of integration of human resource management (HRM) with business strategy. Dessler (2008) stated that "strategic human resource management (SHRM) indicates development and execution of human resource (HR) policies and practices to generate workforce competencies and behaviours so to reach strategic goals and aim of a firm". Wei, Liu and Herdon (2011) revealed that strategic human resource management (SHRM) has a positive influence on performance of an individual and positive impact on firm's product innovation and also the relationship is stronger for organization with a developmental culture. According to Hoppas (2013) the integration of human resource management (HRM) and strategic management process lead to strategic human resource management (SHRM) which in turn focuses on "*integration*" and "*adaptation*". Besides, researcher further elaborated that strategic human resource management (SHRM) is different from human resource management (HRM) in that later emphasis on individual performance and strategic human resource management (SHRM) focuses on organizational performance. Second, strategic human resource management (SHRM) considered the role of human resource management (HRM) as a solution to business problems and focus on how human resource management (HRM) system attaches strategic value and significantly contributes to organizational success and effectiveness.

Researcher like Hassija (2014) demonstrated that strategic human resource management (SHRM) is all about systematically linking or connecting people with organization, it's specifically an integration of human resource management (HRM) strategies into corporate strategies and an integration of HR with business and with its environment. In other terms strategic human resource management (SHRM) is an integration of human resource management into business strategy and involves human resource practice to meet environmental challenges. Further Integration between human resource management (HRM) and business strategy in turn contributes significantly in effective management of human resources, improvement in organizational success and performance and ultimately develop organizational cultures that foster innovation, creativity and flexibility. Researcher further elaborated that there are various internal and external factors affecting human resources management. Internal factors affects performance of organizational directly and are controllable such as availability of skilled workforce, leadership styles, attitudes of employees, work ethics and so on; while as external factors are uncontrollable factors affecting organizational strategies and whole environment such as labour environment, changes in political and legal environment. Anyangwe (2017) stated that *"strategic human resource management (SHRM) is a well established plan of an organization to get things done effectively with the help of human capital and development of process capabilities"*.

Providing central and significant role to the *people* in an organization, human resource management (HRM) is becoming more strategic in nature and practice. In other terms, strategic human resource management (SHRM) is related to the association between human resource management (HRM) and strategic management in an organization (Agarwala, 2002). The author further demonstrated that strategic human resource management (SHRM) is basically an approach that deals with the decision regarding the nature of employees' relationship, selection, attracting, recruitment, training, coaching, rewards, developing, and retaining and performance appraisal for the benefit of both employees and the organization. Its application may bring a drastic and desirable change in the workplace and its resources; affect employees in a desirable manner and create strong organization. One of the important issues faced by any organization is a human issues and the strategic human resource management (SHRM) is concerned with the issues, and problems of human resource that affect or are affected by the organizational strategic plan. Strategic human resource management (SHRM) is a continuous process and activity that demands the constant synchronization of the value of the top management, the environment and the resources available. According to Agarwala (2002) there are four important components/ elements of strategic human resource management (SHRM) viz. (1) human resource is a major source of *competitive advantage* of an organization, (2) it's an integrated approach where human resource activities, practice and programmes are the ways and means to make use of work force to gain competitive advantage, (3) there is an alignment between human resource strategy and business/ corporate strategy of an organization, (4) employee activities, plans and programmes are directed to attain organizational goals. Krishnan and Singh (2006) developed a model to divide the strategic human resource management (SHRM) into three stages. First stage is formulation of business strategy such as cost reduction, improving quality of products and so on, and fit it into human resource management (HRM) strategy. Second stage is implementation of human resource management system based on Human resource (HR) strategy. And third stage involves assessment and evaluation of effectiveness and success of human resource management strategy. These three processes of strategic human resource management (SHRM) are dynamic, complex and closely related with each other. While as Daft (2001) highlighted that strategic human resource management includes five important stages. First stage is concerned with mission, target and goals management philosophy. Second stage deals with environment analysis involving both internal and external scan. Next stage is associated with formulation of strategy, then the implication of formulated strategy and final stage deals with evaluation and reviewing of strategy. Strategic human resource management (SHRM) involves HR professional as a partners to design and implement strategies related to human resource planning, recruitment and selection, training and development, performance management, compensation and reward management (Bagga & Srivastava, 2014). The responsibility for execution of strategy is mostly shared between HR professionals and line managers. Uric (1997) has stated that human resource (HR) professionals are strategic partners and planners. There are three level of strategy that HR professionals have to develop. First is *corporate level strategy* associated with general philosophy of growth, development and management of business units. It includes strategies that decide which type of business should be acquires, modified and sold etc. Second is *business level strategy* concerned with planning and actions designed for each business units to make those units more competitive in a market. Third is *functional level strategy* that intended to maximize productivity, efficiency, research and development, marketing and investment and so on. Besides, the formulation of human resource strategy involves five steps i.e. *Analyse* of what are the business needs, problems and issues, *Diagnose* what are the causes of problems, why issues prevail and so on, *Conclusion and recommendation* of analysis and diagnosis, next is *Action Planning* which identifies actions required to implement to overcome the issues and problems, *Resource planning* highlights what resources are required and how to obtain these, and final step is *Benefits* of implementing these actions and proposals. Moreover, success of strategic human resource management (SHRM) depends upon competencies of human factor such as business knowledge, analytical skills, leadership qualities, influence management, achievement motivation and so on, also support of top management, organizational policies, availability of resources, appropriate techniques of measurement, transparency in evaluation process and flexibility of human resource management (HRM) system and so on (Krishnan & Singh, 2006). All these mentioned factors have a direct impact on the success of strategic human resource management (SHRM).

MODE OF STRATEGIC MANAGEMENT

The process of strategic management is usually broken down into five steps (Daft, 2001):

Mission, Targets and Goals: The mission and vision of an organization has to be clear, we cannot proceed on without having a mission. The mission should be in line with the vision. There is a very thin line of difference between vision and mission. Vision is more future oriented and encompasses the main targets or positions or status to be achieved and mission is a set of actions taken in this regard. The mission, targets and goals go hand in hand with each other. All these three components need to be strategized in order to achieve organizational effectiveness.

Environmental Analysis: While strategizing, it needs to be clearly seen that whether the actions taken are in consonance with the prevailing environment, hence environmental analysis is of paramount importance in this regard. If we deny the role of environment in which the organizations are functions, then the planning will be of no use. A number of factors prevailing in the environment may directly or indirectly impact the vision and mission of an organization, and there needs to be a proper mechanism to address the problems that may arise because of these factors.

Strategy Formulation: It involves formulation of a roadmap to achieve particular targets/objectives. While formulation of strategies, we should keep in mind that whether all factors that may impact the achievement of goals, are taken into consideration or not. Strategy formulation must be an objective and rational process and it should be grounded in the knowledge of behavioural science. Pertinent to mention here that behavioural science has a lot to offer in this regard.

Strategy Implementation: No strategy is of any use until it is implemented in letter and spirit. Implementation may be a challenging task, but better managerial skills can prove in a handy while implementation of the plans. Proper planning, controlling, coordinating and allocation of resources in judicious manner are always desirable in this regard. Apart from this the knowledge of organizational behaviour and human resource management can also prove effective in this regard.

Strategy Evaluation: After the strategy has been implemented, it needs to be checked that whether the strategy is helping the organization to be more effective than before. A proper follow up of strategy becomes very important in this regard. In case of any negative impact of the strategy, the managers or administrators of any organization should revisit the strategy. There can be many ways of analysing the impact of the strategy, one way is to go for a prior SWOT (Strengths, Weaknesses, Opportunities & Threats) analysis and compare it with the SWOT analysis carried after the strategy has been implemented over a course of time.

OBJECTIVES OF STRATEGIC HUMAN RESOURCE MANAGEMENT (SHRM)

According to Agarwala (2002) strategic human resource management (SHRM) ensures the availability of skilled, trained, loyal, knowledgeable and highly motivated, committed and dedicated employees of an organization to sustain in competition and also achieve competitive advantage. Next is it helps the organization to meet the needs of both workforce and business. As per Anyangwe (2017) strategic human resource management (SHRM) have been proven to be an effective management style and a worthy mean to provide suitable solution for handling critical issues and effectively handling human capital with the objectives of improving performance and overall success of an organization. Further, while managing people, it focus more on human relation aspect with continue development of resources. Strategic human resource management (SHRM) brings necessary coordination between various units and activities of an organization, creating an optimal utilization of opportunities, attaining goals and objectives and preventing threats (Gilani, Zadeh & Saderi, 2012). Moreover, the researcher indicated that the strategic human resource management creates consistency and harmony between human resource strategy and organizational strategy and at the same time creates synergetic coordination between HR policies and general strategies of an organization. It provides framework to achieve organizational targets and goals and design plans to achieve desirable outcomes, compete with others; and exploit human capital and other resources effectively and efficiently. According to Dessler (2008) objectives of strategic human resource management (SHRM) is to ensure fairness in terms of treatment and job security for every employee. Next is it provides competitive salaries, promotion incentives and build healthy communication channels so to reduce turnover. Besides, strategic human resource management (SHRM) develop and design career management tools, work enrichment strategies, and other beneficial programmes in order to prepare employees for new challenges and curb new opportunities. Further strategic human resource management (SHRM) builds cordial relationship with senior professional and also identify mangers whose value are not people oriented. According to Bagga and Srivastava (2014) strategic human resource management (SHRM) promotes high level of performance and develops organizational culture that flourishes creativity, innovation, flexibility and competitive advantage. In fact now-a-days one of the important way of implementing strategic HR policies, and practices in an organization occurs in the form of E- human resource management (HRM), E – attendance and E- recruitment by removing the chances of frauds (Ganesan, 2014).

IMPORTANCE OF STRATEGIC HUMAN RESOURCE MANAGEMENT (SHRM)

As Fombrun, Tichy and Devanna (1984) had rightly stated *that Strategic human resource management (HRM) is a set of techniques enables intervention to be made within business in order to improve performance.* Karami, Analoui and Cusworth (2004) revealed that strategic human resource management (SHRM) is a key element of organizational success, improves organizational performance and leads to organizational effectiveness. Also strategic human resource management (SHRM) practices are very highly advantageous for the business organization as it plays an important role in the advancement of the degree of team development and team learning among employee (Alharthey & Rasli, 2011). Besides, it fosters the degree of transfer of knowledge among diverse team members with more emphasis on the establishment of collaborative working practices. Strategic human resource management (SHRM) policies and practices are very essential for engaging the diverse employees towards performing integrated roles and responsibilities. Strategic human resource management (SHRM) views human resource as an important source of competitive advantage and when their human resources are managed effectively with human resource policies and practices, it may in turn improve productivity, quality of products, services and financial performance (Caliskan, 2010). According to Brewster, Dowling, Grobler, Holland and Warnich (2000) strategic human resource management (SHRM) is very beneficial to the organization because it contributes in the accomplishment of organizational goals and helps in the survival of the organization. Strategic human resource management (SHRM) supports and helps in implementing business strategies of the firm successfully. Moreover it creates and maintains a competitive advantage for the organization. Besides, strategic human resource management (SHRM) also helps in improving the responsiveness, creativity and innovation capability and potential of the company. It enables in increasing and exploring the number of feasible strategic options available to the company. Further strategic human resource management (SHRM) improves cooperation and connection between human resource management (HRM) department and line managers. Additionally, strategic human resource management (SHRM) impacts performance of an employees and organizational performance positively.

MODELS OF STRATEGIC HUMAN RESOURCE MANAGEMENT (SHRM)

There are three main models of strategic human resource management (SHRM) which are given below:

Control Based Model: This approach is based on the nature of control and how managers direct, monitor and controls employee's performance. According to this model strategy HR is an instrument to direct, monitor and controls all aspects of work to ensure maximum productivity and profitability. Thus this model is results oriented and always focuses on the maximisation of the output, so due care should be taken while adoption of this model because the Hawthorne studies carried out in the 1930's have demonstrated that output should not be the only concern, there are a number of other factors which may impact the functioning of the organization. The studies had manipulated a lot of factors like lighting conditions, supervision etc. To check their impact on productivity. Mass interviews were also carried out and it came to the forefront that the social ties in a group have a lot to do with the productivity and merely reliance on increasing output doesn't work beyond a particular threshold. It was noticed that the workers within a group had set limits for producing a particular level of output to prevent the demands of an increased level of output from the organizations. Thus it is clear that the control based model should be used very judiciously in order to achieve the maximum efficiency.

Resource Based Model: This approach implies the phenomena of reward-effort exchange, where managers perceive and treat their work force as a valuable resource and asset not a liability. Resource based strategic HR emphasis on strategic importance to exploit the competencies, strengths, resources and capabilities of an organization efficiently. Thus here the human resources are given a prime importance and employees are considered as the key agents of growth and development of an organization. As the model believes in reward-effort exchange, every individual in the organization goes beyond the expected level of performance and benefits the organization in the long run.

Integrative Model: It integrates the above two mentioned models with focus on managerial control and reward –effort exchange (Bamberger & Meshoulam, 2000). Thus it is an amalgam of the control and resource based methodology and has the advantage of not only controlling but also getting the maximum from the resources of the organization. Pertinent to mention here, due to a myriad of factors affecting the functioning of today's organizations, integrative models are being increasingly adopted.

FOUR MAJOR PERSPECTIVES OF STRATEGIC HUMAN RESOURCE MANAGEMENT (SHRM)

Contingency Perspective: Contingency perspective of strategic human resource management (SHRM) indicates that fit, interaction or alignment between human resource management (HRM) strategies and organizational strategy have a great effect on effective performance (Hoppas, 2013). The contingency perspective of strategic human resource management (SHRM) investigates directly the link between the strategy adopted by the organization and the human resource management (HRM) practices (Jery & Souai, 2014). Besides, this perspective believes that the firm's performance is enhanced and improved by the adoption of human resource management (HRM) practices which are in line with the type of strategies adopted by the firm. In contrast if human resource management (HRM) practices are not consistent with business strategies and are in conflict with other human resource management (HRM) practices it will create confusion, ambiguity and may also lead to reduction in performance for the employees and the whole organization (Essays, 2013).

Universalistic Perspective: The universalistic perspective is a best practice within HR system and a simplest approach of strategic human resource management (SHRM) (Delery & Doty, 1996). This approach emphasis on a single set of universally applicable human resource management system and to achieve organizational goals and effective performance it focuses on coordination among various HR practices. Development of universalistic approach needs two steps. First, identifying important strategic HR practices and second is the integration of HR practice to organizational performance (Fagerholm, Lorentzson & Moritz, 2010). This approach of strategic human resource management (SHRM) believes that there are certain HRM practices that are better suited than others to improve and increase firm's performance (Hamid, 2013). Universalistic approach is based on three main principles: principle of universality and superiority which emphasis that there are some strategic human resource management (HRM) practices which are more beneficial than others and can be adopted by any organization (Delery & Doty, 1996). Second is principle of selectivity and superior financial performance reading also called best human resource management (HRM) practices that creates higher financial performance (Hamid, 2013). Third is principle of independence and additivity that states that effect of human resource management (HRM) practices on performance is the outcome of the individual effects of each practice with instantaneous use of several other Human resource management practices. The universalistic perspective of strategic human resource management (SHRM) is basically based on two theories i.e. the human capital theory and the strategic resource theory (Hamid, 2013).

Configurational Perspective: The configurational perspectives is one of the complex approach emphasis shared influence of various variables and deals with *patterns* or *configure* of human resource management (HRM) system that determines effective performance (Hoppas, 2013). The configurational perspective combines internal and external fit which is considered as a basis for maintaining and improving performance of individual and the organization (Essays, 2013). Configurational approach of strategic human resource management (SHRM) are different from universalistic perspective and also from contingency approach, as configurational theories are based on holistic principle of inquiry and adopts the assumption of *"equifinality"* (Delery & Doty, 1996). In simple terminology configurational theories deals with how the patterns of multiple independent variables are related to dependent variable instead of how individual independent variable are associated with dependent variable (Delery & Doty, 1996). There are three types of strategies used in configurational approach i.e. prospector, analyser and defender (Essays, 2013). The prospector strategy is applied when strategy is changing frequently and is more suited to market type system. While as defender strategy emphasis on efficiency and quality of products are more suitable in the market that are competitive in nature. The third type of configurational strategy is the analyser which is the middle ground between the defender and prospector and is more appropriate for organizations that are new and have stable product domains.

Contextual Perspective: The contextual perspective is a broader explanation of the relationship between strategic human resource management (SHRM) and its context. In other terms this approach views organization as a social institutions need to integrate in a context in which it operates (Hoppas, 2013). The contextual perspective provides a descriptive and global explanation that goes beyond the organizational level and integrates the function in a macro-social framework with which it interacts (Martin-Alcazar, Romero-Fernandez & Sanchez-Gardey, 2005). As per this approach strategies are not considered through their contribution to the organizational performance but through their impact on the internal aspect of the organization and external environment of the organization. The contextual theories focused on three aspects of strategic human resource management (SHRM) i.e. the nature of human resources, the level of analysis and the actors involved in organizational functions (Martin-Alcazar, Romero-Fernandez & Sanchez-Gardey, 2005).

CHALLENGES IN IMPLEMENTING STRATEGIC HUMAN RESOURCE MANAGEMENT (SHRM)

According to Becker and Huselid (2006) various challenges facing during the implementation of strategic human resource management (SHRM) are mentioned below:

- Challenge of managing the workforce as well as managing HR professionals.
- The challenge of differentiation.
- Appropriate measurement challenge.
- New competencies in workforce management.

CONCLUSION

It can be safely concluded that organizations cannot survive without strategizing human resource management (SHRM), to ensure the same it is of paramount importance to gain an understanding into this construct in light of components, objectives, models and perspectives. However according to Becker and Huselid (2006) one can face various challenges during the implementation of strategic human resource management (SHRM), a few of those include challenge of managing the workforce as well as managing HR professionals, the challenge of differentiation, appropriate measurement challenge and highlighting the new competencies in workforce management. So it is highly recommended for the organizational researchers to speed up the pace of research not only for the sake of understanding strategic human resource management but also the potential challenges in its implementation.

SOLUTIONS AND RECOMMENDATIONS

Every organization wants to be effective in the contemporary world, but a lot of obstacles might come in the way to stay effective. But the experts in the field of organizational psychology & human resource management offer many solutions and recommendations for the same. Efficient planning is very important and highly recommended for strategizing of organization at various levels. In case there is any deficit in planning, then the process of strategizing will not be effective, rather it can prove counterproductive for any organization. Strategizing should involve a rational decision making process and while taking any decision it should be kept into consideration that whether it is grounded in the key aspects of intelligence, choice and design. Besides, strategizing process should be transparent and should be backed by a very dynamic structure of an organization, it is highly recommended that organizations should strategize not only the human resource management aspects, but the same should also reflect in structure & methodology of functioning of the organization.

FUTURE RESEARCH DIRECTIONS

No field is devoid of the attention from researchers, and same holds true for strategizing the human resource management. A plethora of research has always been carried out in understanding the dynamics of strategizing the human resource management. Both qualitative and quantitative enquiries have been made from time to time, however there is further scope of carrying out objective research enquiries in the field. Rigorous methodological techniques in the form of structural equation modelling, path analysis and allied techniques can be used to check the benefits of strategizing. Besides the future research studies should mainly focus on the policy implications of the research process rather than merely relying on the significance levels, managerial implications need to be focused to a more extent.

REFERENCES

Agarwala, T. (2002). Human resource management: The emerging trends. *Indian Journal of Industrial Relations*, 315–331.

Alharthey, B. K., & Rasli, A. (2011). Key role of strategic human resource management (SHRM) in advancing the degree of team learning. *African Journal of Business Management, 5*(26), 10446. doi:10.5897/AJBM11.1663

Anyangwe, X. (2017). Strategic human resource management: a cross-cultural managerial approach. Centria University of Applied Sciences Business Management.

Bagga, T., & Srivastava, S. (2014). SHRM: Alignments of HR function with business strategy. Strategic HR Review, 13(4/5).

Bamberger, P., & Meshoulam, I. (2000). *Human resource management strategy.* London: Published Sage.

Bamberger, P. A., Meshoulam, I., & Biron, M. (2014). *Human resource strategy: Formulation, implementation, and impact.* Routledge. doi:10.4324/9780203075838

Becker, B. E., & Huselid, M. A. (2006). Strategic human resources management: Where do we go from here? *Journal of Management, 32*(6), 898–925. doi:10.1177/0149206306293668

Björkman, I., & Xiucheng, F. (2002). Human resource management and the performance of Western firms in China. *International Journal of Human Resource Management, 13*(6), 853–864. doi:10.1080/09585190210134246

Boxall, P., & Purcell, J. (2000). Strategic human resource management: Where have we come from and where should we be going? *International Journal of Management Reviews, 2*(2), 183–203. doi:10.1111/1468-2370.00037

Bratton, J., & Gold, J. (2017). *Human resource management: theory and practice* (6th ed.). Palgrave, Red Globe Press. Retrieved from http://www.otaru-uc.ac.jp/~js/downloads/SP2005-PDF/SP2005-Chapter2SHRM.pdf

Brewster, C., Dowling, P. J., Grobler, P., Holland, P., & Warnich, S. (2000). *Contemporary issues in human resource management: Gaining a competitive advantage.* Academic Press.

Byars, L. L., & Rue, L. W. (2004). *Human resource management* (7th ed.). Boston: McGraw-Hill.

Çalişkan, E. N. (2010). The impact of strategic human resource management on organizational performance. *Journal of Naval Science and Engineering, 6*(2), 100–116.

Cuming, M. (1985). *The Theory and Practice of Personnel Management.* London: Heinemann.

Daft, R. (2001). *Organization theory and design* (7th ed.). Cincinnati, OH: South-Western College Publishing.

Daft, R. L. (2001). *Essentials of organization theory and design.* South Western Educational Publishing.

Delery, J. E., & Doty, D. H. (1996). Modes of theorizing in strategic human resource management: Tests of universalistic, contingency, and configurational performance predictions. *Academy of Management Journal, 39*(4), 802–835.

Dessler, G. (2008). *Human Resource Management.* Pearson Prentice Hall.

Essays, U. K. (2013). *Universalistic Contingency and Configurational Approaches*. Retrieved from https://www.uniassignment.com/essay-samples/business/universalistic-contingency-and-configurational-approaches-business-essay.php?vref=1

Fagerholm, S., Lorentzson, P., & Moritz, R. (2010). *Strategic Human Resource Management: A study of EWES Stålfjäder AB's HR Strategies alignment to corporate strategies.* Academic Press.

Farnham, D., & Pimlott, J. (1992). *Understanding industrial relations.* London: Cassell.

Fombrun, C. J., Tichy, N. M., & Devanna, M. A. (1984). *Strategic human resource management.* Wiley.

Ganesan, S. (2014). A study on e-attendance system practices of electronic human resource management in organizations at Chennai, India. *International Journal of Business and Administration Research Review, 1*(6), 147.

Gilani, M. H. N., Zadeh, M. S., & Saderi, H. R. (2012). The role of strategic human resource management in creation of competitive advantages (Case study: A commercial organization in Malaysia). *International Journal of Business and Social Science, 3*(16).

Guest, D. E. (1987). Human Resource Management and Industrial Relations. *Journal of Management Studies, 24*(5), 503–521. doi:10.1111/j.1467-6486.1987.tb00460.x

Hamid, J. (2013). Strategic human resource management and performance: The universalistic approach-case of Tunisia. *Journal of Business Studies Quarterly, 5*(2), 184.

Hassija, T. (2014). Strategic Human Resource Management in Changing Environment. International Journal of Reviews, Surveys and Research, 86-99.

Hendry, C., & Pettigrew, A. (1986). The practice of strategic human resource management. *Personnel Review, 15*(5), 3–8. doi:10.1108/eb055547

Hill, C., & Jones, G. (2001). Strategic Management: An integrated approach (5th ed.). Boston, MA: Houghton Mifflin.

Hoppas, C. A. (2013). *Strategic human resource management and oganisational performance: a study of the university administrators in Cyprus.* Academic Press.

Itika, J. (2011). *Fundamentals of human resource management: Emerging experiences from Africa.* Leiden: African Studies Centre.

Jery, H., & Souai, S. (2014). Strategic human resource management and performance: The contingency approach case of Tunisia. *International Journal of Humanities and Social Science, 4*(6), 284–291.

Karami, A., Analoui, F., & Cusworth, J. (2004). Strategic human resource management and resource-based approach: The evidence from the British manufacturing industry. *Management Research News, 27*(6), 50–68. doi:10.1108/01409170410784202

Kazmi, A., & Ahmad, F. (2001). Differing approaches to strategic human resource management. *Journal of Management Research, 1*(3), 133–140.

Krishnan, S., & Singh, M. (2006). Strategic Human Resource Management: Three-Stage Process and Influencing Organisational Factors. *Human Resource Management.*

Krishnan, S. K., & Singh, M. (2011). Strategic human resource management: A three-stage process model and its influencing factors. *South Asian Journal of Management, 18*(1), 60–82.

Mabey, C., Salaman, G., & Storey, J. (1998). *Human resource management: A strategic introduction.* Blackwell Publishing.

Martin-Alcazar, F., Romero-Fernandez, P. M., & Sánchez-Gardey, G. (2005). Strategic human resource management: Integrating the universalistic, contingent, configurational and contextual perspectives. *International Journal of Human Resource Management, 16*(5), 633–659. doi:10.1080/09585190500082519

Münsterberg, H. (1913). *Psychology and industrial efficiency.* Boston: Academic Press. doi:10.1037/10855-000

Osibanjo, O., & Adeniji, A. (2012). *Human Resource Management: Theory and Practice* (1st ed.). Pumark Nigeria Limited. Retrieved from https://accountlearning.blogspot.com/2013/01/concept-and-objectives-of-human.html

Taylor, F. W. (1914). *The principles of scientific management.* Harper.

Torrington, D., Hall, L., & Taylor, S. (2005). *Human resource management.* Essex, UK: Pearson Education.

Ulrich, D. (1997). *Human Resource Champions, the next agenda for adding value and delivering results.* Boston: Harvard Business School Press.

Wei, L. Q., Liu, J., & Herndon, N. C. (2011). SHRM and product innovation: Testing the moderating effects of organizational culture and structure in Chinese firms. *International Journal of Human Resource Management, 22*(01), 19–33. doi:10.1080/09585192.2011.538965

Westover, J. H. (2014). *Strategic Human Resource Management.* HCI Press.

Wheelan, T., & Hunger, J. (1995). *Strategic Management and Business policy* (5th ed.). Addison Wesley Longman.

Wright, P. M., & McMahan, G. C. (1992). Theoretical perspectives for strategic human resource management. *Journal of Management, 18*(2), 295–320. doi:10.1177/014920639201800205

ADDITIONAL READING

Alcázar, F. M., Fernández, P. M. R., & Gardey, G. S. (2005). Researching on SHRM: An analysis of the debate over the role played by human resources in firm success. *Management Review*, 213–241

Andersen, K. K., Cooper, B. K., & Zhu, C. J. (2007). The effect of SHRM practices on perceived firm financial performance: Some initial evidence from Australia. *Asia Pacific Journal of Human Resources, 45*(2), 168–179. doi:10.1177/1038411107079111

Becker, B. E., & Huselid, M. A. (2010). SHRM and job design: Narrowing the divide. *Journal of Organizational Behavior, 31*(2/3), 379–388. doi:10.1002/job.640

Bloom, M., & Milkovich, G. T. (1998). A SHRM perspective on international compensation and reward systems. *CAHRS Working Paper Series*, 124.

Chien, M. H. (2004). A study to improve organizational performance: A view from SHRM. *The Journal of American Academy of Business, Cambridge*, 4(1/2), 289–291.

Cohen, E., Taylor, S., & Muller-Camen, M. (2010). *HR's role in corporate social responsibility and sustainability*. Alexandria: SHRM Foundation.

Inyang, B. J. (2010). Strategic human resource management (SHRM): A paradigm shift for achieving sustained competitive advantage in organization. *International Bulletin of Business Administration*, 7(23), 215–243.

Kaufman, B. E. (2010). SHRM theory in the post-Huselid era: Why it is fundamentally misspecified. *Industrial Relations*, 49(2), 286–313. doi:10.1111/j.1468-232X.2009.00600.x

Krulis-Randa, J. S. (1990). Strategic human resource management (SHRM) in Europe after 1992. *International Journal of Human Resource Management*, 1(2), 131–140. doi:10.1080/09585199000000044

Schoonover, S. C. (1998). *Human resource competencies for the year 2000: the wake-up call!* SHRM Foundation.

KEY TERMS AND DEFINITIONS

Configurational Perspective: The configurational perspectives is one of the complex approach emphasis shared influence of various variables and deals with *patterns* or *configure* of human resource management (HRM) system that determines effective performance.

Contextual Perspective: It is a broader explanation of the relationship between strategic human resource management (SHRM) and its context.

Contingency Perspective: Contingency perspective of strategic human resource management (SHRM) indicates that fit, interaction or alignment between human resource management (HRM) strategies and organizational strategy have a great effect on effective performance.

Human Resource Management: Human resource management (HRM) is an activity designed to provide for and coordinate of human resources of an organization.

Strategic Human Resource Management (SHRM): It is the extent to which human resource management is integrated with the strategic decision-making processes that tend to direct organizational efforts to cope effectively with environmental demands.

Strategy: A particular way of doing something, the word is derived from a Greek word *strategus*, means "commander in chief" or "long run direction."

Universalistic Perspective: The universalistic perspective is a best practice within HR system and a simplest approach of strategic human resource management (SHRM) which emphasis on a single set of universally applicable human resource management system.

This research was previously published in the Handbook of Research on Positive Organizational Behavior for Improved Workplace Performance; pages 260-275, copyright year 2020 by Business Science Reference (an imprint of IGI Global).

Chapter 2
Understanding Green Human Resources in Healthcare

Terrence Duncan
https://orcid.org/0000-0002-5456-6013
Liberty University, USA

Emad Rahim
Bellevue University, USA

Darrell Norman Burrell
https://orcid.org/0000-0002-4675-9544
The Florida Institute of Technology, USA

Brian Hurd
Washington University, USA

ABSTRACT

Human resource management plays an integral role in developing capital for the triple bottom line. In the Fourth Industrial Revolution, human resources now shift their focus to advancing communication and connectivity versus focusing purely on technological advances. As the Fourth Industrial Revolution continues, communicating the effectiveness of human resource management and human capital development should be considered as an essential area of interest. As healthcare practitioners continue to provide treatment and care for those in need, human resource managers need to learn green practices to create a more sustainable environment that contributes socially and economically while adhering to the demands of the international stakeholders. As healthcare continues to be either one of the most significant expenditures or needs for numerous countries, consideration in this field provides potential holistic benefits for stakeholders.

DOI: 10.4018/978-1-6684-3873-2.ch002

INTRODUCTION

The Fourth Industrial Revolution (4IR) features the disruption of the current industrial environment due to the emergence of current and developing technologies. The disruption caused during this revolutionary period redefines work in a dynamic and sophisticated manner. Focus on interconnectivity, unpredictability, and rapid evolution of work processes and practices are inherent traits of the Fourth Revolution requiring numerous industries to recognize change agents and make rapid adjustments. Some of the benefits noted include operational efficiency, innovation, and effective deployment of assets and capital (Park, 2016). These changes not only provide value-added benefits to organizational development, but employees also benefitted from the change as well.

Organizations must contend with technological advances and competing for environmental, social, and financial demands. Known as the triple bottom line, these demands create a framework over the years to become a model for an organization's mission and vision statement. No longer defined by monetary gain, businesses now focus on sustainable solutions that provide direct and indirect benefits to the organizational culture, and the global economy (Fields & Atiku, 2017).

Human resource management plays an integral role in developing social and intellectual capital for the triple bottom line. In the 4IR, human resources now shift their focus to advancing communication and connectivity versus focusing purely on technological advances (Schwab, 2016). Technology continues to remain relevant in the development of human capital (Atiku, 2018; 2020). However, recognizing ways to become more responsive in the global environment while maintaining a strong corporate social responsibility footprint are some of the key elements found within the 4IR.

Green Human Resource Management

Green human resource management (GHRM) is an approach quickly which is gaining recognition as a critical element of the 4IR. GHRM focuses on the performance of human resource functions within organizations from a sustainability perspective. The sustainable use of company resources supports ecology as well as the development of ecological sensitivity in workers (Atiku, 2019; Bombiak, 2019). GHRM generates value for company stakeholders via efficiencies in the social and environmental aspects of human resource processes (Bombiak, 2019). The application of processes in these areas provides additional value to the organizational culture and its global footprint in the environment.

The adoption and implementation of green practices, such as training, recruitment, and training and development, are useful if the staff is hired or trained in competencies related to the principles of GHRM. Those responsible for human capital management considers several functions that are incorporated in the GHRM methodology: job design and analysis, employee selection, developing working discipline, performance evaluation, employee relations, and working conditions (Bombiak, 2019; Fields & Atiku, 2017).

The demand for sustainable solutions in human capital management and development increased from a multi-national perspective. As different industries and economies growing increasingly global, competition for assets, capital, and productivity grew, as well as diversifying business processes to continue to meet such demand. Businesses were required to do more in terms of developing efficient products of value with an emphasis on corporate social responsibility to the environment. The production of goods and services for a business is essential for profitability, yet the foundation of such processes, supply-chain logistics, and delivery of the goods and services are dependent on the framework of the organization's human resources management. Therefore, scholars shifted their focus in the past decade towards researching and understanding how human resources play a critical role in sustainability and the green revolution.

Due to its relatively recent focus on this specialization, there exists a wide variation of interpretation as to what GHRM consist of, and the different types of work processes within the human resource management paradigm that benefits need additional research. Yong, Yusiliza, and Fawehimi (2019) conducted a study which focused on a systematic literature review concerning GHRM from 2007 – 2019. The study found an increase of research and discussions from scholars during the past decade, but there was no consensus towards a way to measure successful objectives and outcomes. For example, some of the literature focused exclusively on methods to implement cleaner production, green employee empowerment, adoption of GHRM, and retention of employees. Despite the different methods of study or discussions through a review of 70 academic journal databases, the topic of GHRM increased and is considered essential to the development of human resource management practices.

GHRM and Healthcare

In the U.S. and across the globe, healthcare continues to be a complex and dynamic industry that features a myriad of challenges. One of the significant challenges involves sustainability within the industry. Governments, globally, continue to focus on innovations that create sustainability and address the needs and demands of their stakeholders. Projects encounter social, economic, environmental, and health-related barriers that impede the growth and application of how these projects deliver hospitals, physicians, staff, and pharmaceuticals. Different patient and global needs necessitate the ongoing commitment to deliver solutions that benefit global health, safety, and welfare.

GHRM contributes to sustainability in several ways if appropriately administered. Employees are encouraged to be more productive if adequately engaged. Green methods to encourage employee empowerment provide opportunities for conscientious consideration of how their work processes affect the environment. Emotional well-being may improve with organizational commitment as an effort to improve social awareness. As one of the largest industries in numerous countries, the direct and indirect benefit of working for a healthcare company provides economic benefits by potentially increasing wages and improving consumer consumption, as well as improved life expectancy and a decrease of illnesses (Du Toit & Millum, 2016).

Lennox, Maher, and Reed (2018) discussed how failing to follow sustainability initiatives create adverse effects for an organization. Wasted investments into human capital and monetary investments detract from the organization's bottom line. Potential profits not received cannot be reinvested within the triple bottom line, and as a result, inefficiencies and structural breakdowns could occur. Staff enthusiasm could decline, and employee turnover rates will increase. Lack of adopting sustainable methods within the healthcare structure will also increase energy consumption and provide other direct and indirect damage to the environment (Lennox, Maher, & Reed, 2018).

Collectively, healthcare faces another threat towards sustainability by the global staffing shortages and challenges related to the connectivity of physical and personnel resources contributing to significant healthcare disparities. Therefore, it is viable for healthcare human resource personnel with the support of organizational leadership to consider proper adoption and implementation of green practices and take advantage of the benefits available.

Modern health care systems are confronted with the task of effectively managing the expertise, information, knowledge, and human resources necessary for improving the health and wellbeing of those they are committed to serving (Smith, 2018).

The human resources department of an organization plays a significant role in the creation of their company's sustainability culture that serves those organizational goals (Ahmad, 2015). Notable procedures at every stage of the talent management are considered powerful tools for aligning employees with a company's corporate social responsibility strategy around sustainability (Ahmad, 2015). GHRM refer to using every employee touchpoint/interface to promote sustainable practices and increase employee awareness and commitments on the issues of sustainability (Ahmad, 2015). GHRM approaches can occur with recruiting messages, recruiting processes, training, employee development, employee rewards, and performance measures that are intentionally focused on the promotion of sustainability and environmentally friendly practices (Ahmad, 2015). For example, human resources can support sustainability through the development and adoption of paperless processes in hiring, benefits, training, and communications where the consumption of paper and the environmental impacts around that paper consumption can be reduced (Ahmad, 2015).

Implementing talent management approaches that promote sustainability and corporate social responsibility implies sound and effective decision making at critical points throughout the entire healthcare organizational system. Contemporary health care systems can be divided into macro-level and micro-levels of decision-making (Gray et al., 2017). Each level has a distinct mandate, but all are linked to contributing to the overall health care system performance and organizational strategy (Gray et al., 2017). Green initiatives within human resources form part of more comprehensive programs of corporate social responsibility. GHRM mostly consist of two major elements namely environment-friendly HR practices and the preservation of knowledge capital (Ahmad, 2015). Hiring approaches that promote messages and programmes that show the organizational commitment to sustainability are a critical part of this process (Ahmad, 2015).

Modern health care systems generate massive amounts of knowledge and information. This is one of its great strengths (Milton & Lambe, 2016). At the same time, this resource and the employee expertise that generates this knowledge and expertise is often not fully leveraged for improving organizational processes (Milton & Lambe, 2016). It is critical for organizations to develop knowledge management systems that allow for information to be shared in a way that promotes green training and development. According to Ahmad (2015) green training and development are activities and initiatives that help employees at all levels gain knowledge and expertise, in the context of their own job roles and duties, of the organization understand the values, processes, and programs around sustainability. Green training and development is a focus on knowledge development, knowledge sharing, and knowledge transfer around the roles employees and the organization can play in waste reduction, energy conservation, recycling, and provide an opportunity to engage employees in environmental business process improvement endeavors that support sustainability (Ahmad, 2015). In order to green training to grow and flourish in the organization, human resources and senior leadership need to support the development of strong knowledge management systems.

The purpose of this proposal is twofold. The first purpose is to contribute to the ongoing and continued need for literature and research related to GHRM. As the 4IR continues, communicating the effectiveness of human resource management and human capital development should be considered as an essential area of interest. The second purpose of this proposal is to address the needs of the healthcare industry, which are many. As healthcare practitioners continue to provide treatment and care for those in need, human resource managers need to learn green practices to create a more sustainable environment that contributes socially and economically while adhering to the demands of the international stakeholders. As healthcare continues to be either one of the most significant expenditures or needs for numerous countries, consideration in this field provides potential holistic benefits for stakeholders.

Sustainability Challenges in Healthcare

Before understanding the need for GHRM practices in healthcare, it is essential to understand the challenges that exist in healthcare. For example, healthcare accounts for 17% of the U.S. gross domestic product (GDP) (Papanicolas, Woskie, & Jha, 2018). GDP is not only high in the U.S., but other wealthy nations as well. According to the Organization of Economic Cooperation and Development (OCED), countries such as Germany, Switzerland, Denmark, and the Netherlands feature high GDP outputs.

Presently, the continued growth and the demand for improved and accessible healthcare by stakeholders raises the prospect of increased waste and inefficiencies of scale. Such waste with adverse impact on the environment, quality of life, financial performance, and human capital creates challenges for those in the industry to deliver premium care without wasted resources. Therefore, the reliance on suitable workers with an understanding of sustainability whether directly or directly holds the key to how the carbon footprint of this planet is affected.

Leadership within the industry has the opportunity to take hold of these challenges and make significant changes to their operations. The resulting benefits include increased operational and financial benefits by meeting the demands of their stakeholders. Embracing significant sustainability provides opportunities to improve overall patient outcomes and public health. Hospitals, clinics, rehabilitation centers, and outpatient centers are real estate entities that consume vast tracts of land. Due to the needs of the general public for availability, energy output and consumption well-exceeds other industries in operation throughout (Mellow, 2019).

Furthermore, in terms of environmental impact, most healthcare-related entities rarely meet 100% capacity, thus resulting in additional waste. Levine (2016) noted that in the U.S. alone, $8 billion annually is spent on energy through nonrenewable sources. Thus, controlling energy consumption and efficient use of resources should be underscored by initial training and ongoing training not only by staff, but for those in healthcare leadership as well.

Human resource management is the central point where business operations begin and sustain over time. Therefore, programs and initiatives requires effective waste management, not just biohazard waste. Energy consumption practices and identifying sources could release chemicals, pathogens, toxins, and other greenhouse gases that could erode the environment from the land, water, and air. Despite this knowledge, similar to the slow adoption of information technology, leadership continues to show signs of slow adoption of significant sustainability initiatives. Despite the researched and known benefits of certain practices such as utilizing renewable energy to pare down costs.

Waste management in healthcare is an underrated and not widely discussed focus of healthcare providers. The challenge is not disposing of waste, which healthcare entities are ethically bound to do, but how the waste is disposed of correctly, efficiently and effectively, thereby minimizing the risk of harm from a sustainable perspective. A continued practice that does not focus within the scope of environmental control results in an undercurrent of a public health crisis that many do not understand. Therefore, it cannot be understated that healthcare leadership should continue to be stewards of the environment and developing organizational strategies with this concept in mind.

Waste management areas to take into consideration could include heating and cooling, energy usage related to lighting, reducing air changes in operating rooms, and water consumption. Although some may not associate the importance of these areas of waste management as a significant operational concern; however, those providers who rely on plant directors, vendors, and even front-line staff are the first wave of stewardship of waste management. Understanding that waste management has a direct impact on operational expenses and potential realized savings should be a continued focus on human capital management and a core focus of the organizational culture.

The challenges of waste management exist in sub-segments in healthcare such as the long-term care industry (LTC) (Mousa & Othman, 2020). As the population continues to age, and more people are required to work, the reliance of a care-based model for loved ones to remain in a nursing home or assisted living facility continues to generate huge demand (Mello, 2019). Responding to the demand, more LTC companies are acquiring land and developing extensive facilities which will produce more waste than a neighborhood of homes. The amount of energy consumption, various types of waste, as well as the concentrated vehicle and foot traffic continue to provide potential harm to the environment.

Many of the facilities feature high percentages of unoccupied rooms and empty halls. However, based on the energy needs of these facilities, increased energy consumption occurs thus accelerating pollutants. High turnover and inadequate training increase the amount of stress and financial waste associated with replacing staff. Although nursing and nursing aides continue to highlight some of the major concerns of the LTC and overall healthcare industry, other personnel contribute to the high production of waste that leadership should consider developing strategies to mitigate against such a threat. Purchasing practices also feature a sustainability challenge as individuals manage who may not comprehensively understand the importance of inventory management make excessive purchases or purchase items that are not necessary.

Human resources managers continue to struggle with the increasing demand for adequate staffing, thus placing less a priority towards educating staff in promoting sustainability initiatives. Even most surveying bodies do not focus on energy consumption or waste by the facility except for regulated concerns and focus more on the quality of care which is a fair number of instances continues to be substandard and inadequate. Despite not being the focus from a political perspective, leadership should consult human resource management about developing sustainability initiatives with the potential for growth throughout numerous departments from a scalability perspective rather than a broader perspective.

Healthcare should be a focal point for sustainability efforts from an operational and a human capital development perspective. With a myriad of sophisticated delivery systems, regulations, and stakeholders, healthcare arguably has the most significant impact on individuals from birth until mortality. Despite its global impact on ecological systems, the industry generally ignores sustainable practices (Mousa & Othman, 2020). Therefore, one may argue that human resources is central in driving sustainability initiatives to improve performance and minimize waste based on activities economic, social, and financial performance.

Sustainability and Human Resource Management

Once perceived as a matter of doing minimum harm, sustainability is now an issue of the greater good that affects individual stakeholders, human resources, and Fortune 500 companies alike (Cooper & Burke, 2006)). In the face of scarce resources, climate change, and population explosion, businesses, governments, and organizations are all realizing the interconnectedness of the various systems in which they operate and the impact those systems have on global, environmental sustainability. As a business professional, the decisions that one makes on behalf of his or her organization will directly impact these critical issues.

The discussion question (DQ) that follows centers around understanding an organization's sustainable options within the context of the ever-changing business or economic environment. As a result, sustainability offers a variety of strategies for transforming or improving an organization in order to cope with and potentially preemptively remedy the socio-economic and political challenges taking place in the ever-evolving business environment.

Globalization is a vital contributor to a rapidly changing world as a result of international economic interdependence. Such interdependence, to some extent, has resulted in for better or for worse situations in various regions of the world. In this context, environmental sustainability is imperative because, for example, global warming or environmental challenges are adversely affecting the ecosystems the world over, as well as resource availability and procurement for individuals of multiple socioeconomic statuses, and various tiers of businesses alike from mega-corporations to independent small businesses.

Several definitions and concepts are associated with sustainability. Nevertheless, the core concept of sustainability is that actions that an organization will take that will enable it to have a long-term survival socially, environmentally, and financially (Epstein, 2008). Also, sustainability is key to making the environment a better place after pollutions and other degradations have taken their toll on it. Further, King (2008) pointed out that the "economics of sustainability must find a way to raise the standards of living of a large number while reducing the negative environmental consequences of economic activity, with priority for the future, so that "future generations have at least the same potential economic opportunities to achieve the welfare of the current generation" (p. 28-29).

The definition of sustainability is the economic development that meets the needs of the present generation without compromising the ability of future generations to meet their own needs (Brundtland, 1987). In the early stages, sustainability was considered as an environmental discourse that sought to preserve as much biodiversity and unspoiled land as possible. However, as Galpin and Whittington (2012) noted, ". . . sustainability requires the full integration of social, economic, and environmental issues into the vision, values, and operation of the organization." From what was initially considered a one-dimensional construct (an environmental discourse), sustainability has become the centerpiece of a long-term organizational strategy.

Some organizations fully embraced sustainability as a means to more efficiently deploy its human and other resources; by engaging in and sponsoring certain civic/social activities; establishing itself as a caring, responsible corporate citizen within the communities that the organization has a presence. One of the more significant changes noted includes hiring practices. Today, prospective employees for sustainability-minded organizations provide examples of their involvement in civic/social activities as a means of attracting individuals who are open to making a positive contribution to society.

According to Epstein (2008), ethics, governance, transparency, business relationships, financial return, community involvement/economic development, the value of products and services, employment practices, and protection of the environment as the nine principles of sustainability performance (p. 37). Organizations shifting to a GHRM framework considers building positive business relationships and adding resources to help sustain performance and maintain viability. Furthermore, organizations can address the level of social responsibility desired by improving more promotion of employment practices in the area of diversity. Employment practices are when "the company engages in human-resource management practices that promote personal and professional employee development, diversity, and empowerment" (Epstein, 2008, p. 37).

In this case, the assumption of society's potential inability to sustain itself in the future is to manage itself socially, economically, and naturally. This assumption is rooted in the belief that a sustainable and ecologically livable environment can be achieved if the social, economic and natural resources are well managed to the benefit of future generations. Environmental sustainability is about the future and the present is where appropriate actions are taken to preserve the environment for future generations.

Consequently, the practical application is sustainable thinking: helping people consider and implement simple choices that can have a positive environmental impact extending to all facets of life. Thus, sustainable behavior becomes a moral and ethical imperative for everybody, not only those concerned, to consciously think about sustainability or sustainable solutions. Moreover, a deep understanding of systems thinking by individuals, groups, or organizations can enhance their motivations to become proactive agents of positive social change for the greater good of society, the economy, and above all, the environment. In this direction, crisis management and total quality management are solution tools that can significantly assist in finding sustainable solutions that will positively affect the welfare of all.

In this situation, systems thinking, sustainable thinking, and social responsibility are interwoven concepts that are incredibly relevant to the discussion of finding sustainable solutions to crises and destructive practices that have the potential to destroy humankind and the environment. To this end, the concept and implementation of corporate social responsibility (CSR) compel all stakeholders to dedicate portions of their resources to the protection of the environment (Atiku, 2019). Firms operating in communities frequently neglect the development of and eventually those communities falter economically, socially, environmentally, and otherwise. Therefore, corporate social responsibility, sustainable thinking, and systems thinking are powerful management and leadership philosophies that can help guide decision-making which results in positive and sustainable solutions that will have a more significant impact on society, economy, and the environment. Sustainability enables organizations to continue beyond the immediate borders of the present without depleting environmental, economic, and social resources in the present (Epstein, 2008).

Sustainability is a significant objective of any business regardless of the product or service that it provides. Even with this as a clear objective, the evolving landscape of business coupled with technological advancements makes operating a business sustainably quite challenging. The values of the culture and organization define the perception and practices used in measuring sustainability. Methods used for immediate gains may be the critical ingredient for destruction in the future. The depletion of environmental resources has ecological consequences just as disregard of the individual values can weaken development. A successful business will have to reposition in order to maintain a viable business that continues to flourish (Senge et al., 2008).

The concept of sustainability applies not only to private industries that are profit-oriented but also to government agencies. An example of this occurs in the collaboration between the Department of Health and Human Services (HHS) and the Environmental Protection Agency (EPA). HHS uses green standards established by the EPA in its procurement requirements for products and services. These requirements frequently occur in the request for proposals for commercial products as a means of protecting our valuable resources and preventing situations such as the tragedy of commons. Although this may not be as prevalent in research and development, there are conditions of awards that govern the use rights of the individuals as well as disposal of hazardous material. The limitation of these measures affects the ability to provide appropriate oversight and monitoring consistently. Regulating compliance can be costly. However, the expansion of our perception of sustainability beyond economics measures, to include factors such as human flourishing, should be the basis of a responsible culture (King, 2008). We are all stakeholders in this endeavor and directly benefit from embracing and perpetuating sustainability.

Green Human Resources in Healthcare

The Institute of Medicine defines healthcare quality as "the degree to which health services for individuals and populations increase the likelihood of desired health outcomes and are consistent with current professional knowledge" (Agency for Healthcare Research and Quality, 2020). More specifically, healthcare is one of many efforts organized by society to protect, promote, and restore the people's health (Last, 1988). The general purpose of the healthcare sector is to foster a healthy environment where individuals and populations realize the opportunity to live longer, healthier lives.

The healthcare sector includes many industries, sub-industries, and a wide variety of companies. Any company involved in products and services related to health and medical care are represented in the healthcare sector and further categorized under six primary industries. These industries include pharmaceuticals, biotechnology, equipment, distribution, facilities, and managed healthcare (Ledesma, McCulloh, Wieck, & Yang, 2012). It should be noted that any health-based organization, including institutions and nonprofits, contribute to the healthcare sector. The healthcare sector accounts for close to one-fifth of the overall U.S. gross domestic product (GDP), making a substantial impact on jobs and local economies.

Healthcare businesses should be open-minded about the more significant aspects of their bottom-line aligned with green sustainability. Green means to protect and enhance natural systems such as the air, water, and land. Green also addresses recreational and open space opportunities to ensure community and social cohesion. Communities desire clean air, water, land, and access to open space and parks for recreation and healthy living. Sustainability occasionally refers to meeting the needs of the present generation without jeopardizing the opportunities of future generations to meet their needs. Sustainability presents the opportunity to provide good jobs, healthy communities, and quality lifestyle choices.

Investments in green sustainable policies and initiatives by the healthcare sector can benefit employees and local communities where they operate. Such policies and initiatives link to a value system of corporate and social responsibility. Local communities benefit from healthcare businesses that address social and physical determinants of health. Social determinants of health can include lack of healthcare access, food insecurity, poverty, mental health, and residential segregation. Physical determinants of health can include blight, dumping and litter, lack of trees, brownfields, lack of open and green space, and substandard housing.

Outcomes of individuals and communities are influenced by many factors, including economic conditions, the built environment, accessibility to healthy products, the behavioral choices people make, and access to and quality of medical care systems. Green sustainability contributes to these factors. Green hiring is an essential dimension within GHRM hiring practices which may improve overall performance, productivity, and morale (Mousa & Othman, 2020).

The healthcare sector must be a leader of community and employee health and wellness. Making up one-fifth of the nation's GDP, the healthcare sector as employers can more naturally connect to their employees around strategies of green sustainability, health, and wellbeing. Further, employers in the healthcare sector can be a significant catalyst for sustained, community improvement and growth of local economies. Healthcare companies and organizations also have the opportunity to galvanize local communities through their employees.

Employees who have the resources and support systems of their healthcare employers that are focused on green sustainability practice will have the knowledge and tools to help make healthier and environmentally sound changes in their life and among family members, friends, and the community. Employees engage with individuals and groups during work hours and outside of work. When employees value and adapt their employer's culture into their way of life, the interactions can be beneficial. Their influence can be in the form of lifestyle changes through the adoption of green sustainability practices at the individual, household, and community levels.

Companies that align green sustainability efforts are often viewed more favorably by the public. Conversely, employees feel more loyal and prouder of their company when the business has closely connected the needs of the local community. Community and social responsibility can lead to attracting top talent and reducing turnover. Green sustainability affects morale, leading to better employee performance. Employees within the healthcare sector can have a more significant impact on society, more specifically, local communities.

Millennials in particular are significant drivers of green sustainability practices. According to the 2016 Millennial Employee Engagement Study by Cone Communications, millennials make up the largest group of employees in the U.S., 50% of the workforce. Further, millennials seek a higher purpose in their company's social responsibility commitments. Key findings from the study included: 64% consider a company's social and environmental commitments when deciding where to work; 64% will not take a job if a company does not have strong corporate and social responsibility values; 83% would be more loyal to a company that helps them contribute to social and environmental issues (vs. 70% U.S. average); and 88% say their job is more fulfilling when they are provided opportunities to make a positive impact on social and environmental issue. Sustainable living is becoming more commonplace and creates a culture for innovation in the workplace.

Business goals and values in the healthcare sector that integrate social responsibility into its strategic organizational framework by serving the community become the responsibility of human resources. Healthcare companies can achieve value by linking green sustainability and human resources. However, it will take a deep dive into understanding how profit-driven healthcare organizations can grow by focusing on mission-driven social innovation and community impact at the local level. Significant advancements in green sustainability are more effective with support from executives. Executives must think more in-depth about their organization's brand and reputation at a more micro level.

Human resources and organizational culture are two critical functions for healthcare companies. Human resources involve the collective capabilities, experiences, and commitment of the company's board, management team, and staff. The culture of a company binds together shared values and common practice. These values and practices should define how healthcare businesses in particular function and define themselves. Human resources are at the heart and forefront for employees. Benefits designed to improve employee skills, health, and wellbeing often fall to human resources.

Human resources can help to integrate and operationalize strategies into the workplace culture. Further, human resources can lead an organization's employees by providing training and development sessions to understand and adopt green sustainability principles and actions; offering incentives and recognition for green sustainable achievements; setting policies that encourage employee cooperation; and involving the company's environmental objectives (MacGuire, 2015). These efforts can support an internal shift that can establish a leadership position within the economy, nationally and locally. Healthcare businesses can also advance building healthier, sustainable, and more equitable local communities.

When healthcare businesses make financial contributions and provide employee volunteer hours to community and civic green sustainability initiatives, these companies can make a significant, positive cultural shift that is not only profit-driven,but can also be socially innovative that is impactful on local communities. For example, volunteer community outreach initiatives can engage all levels of an organization's employees. Recognizing employees' participation in volunteer programs is the most common way that companies involve workers in sustainability (Bates, 2011).

The value of sustainability supported by human resources can provide many vital drivers. These drivers could include: a competitive financial advantage; operational cost savings; contribution to local communities; environmental considerations; and health and safety considerations. Positive outcomes could include improved employee morale; increased employee loyalty; stronger public image; and increased brand recognition. Human resource professionals are essential to leading these drivers and outcomes within their companies.

In many cases, healthcare companies are anchor institutions in local communities, particularly hospitals. They are economic engines that employ thousands of workers, purchase goods and services, attract external income and resources, generate innovations, and incubate new businesses that in turn produce economic benefits (Giloth, 2018). Healthcare companies will need to lead green sustainability initiatives. Their bottom-lines directly link to the quality of protecting, promoting, and restoring the public's health. Moreover, as a sector that makes up one-fifth of the nation's GDP, healthcare businesses are pivotal to embracing green sustainability principles and actions that can improve profits, employee performance, and outcomes of social and physical determinants of health. Profit-driven companies must align value-based green sustainability priorities focused on the health and wellness of individuals and communities. Human resource professionals must be the change agents within their corporate structure to help lead social innovation and impact. Healthcare businesses and their local communities can both do well and be healthy. It will be up to human resources professionals working with executive management in their organizational frameworks to lead a new value-based culture of green sustainability. The time is now to do business unusual with game-changing work and commitment. The effort will take a dynamic, needed shift in organizational strategic thinking and culture.

Knowledge Management Human Resources Systems

Knowledge management is defined as "the process by which an organization creates, captures, acquires and uses knowledge to support and improve the performance of the organization" (Kinney, 1998, p. 2). It can also be understood as the exploitation and development of the knowledge assets within an organization, aimed at furthering the goals and objectives of the organization (Metaxiotis et al., 2005). Knowledge management, therefore, can be said to involve a conscious effort to incorporate strategies and practices that ensure maximum use of knowledge in organizations to advance the goals and objectives of the organization (Dalkir, 2017; Gray et al., 2017; Milton & Lambe, 2016). It is presently recognized that successful organizations are those that create new knowledge, disseminate it widely throughout the organization, and represent it into new technologies and products (Metaxiotis et al., 2005).

Dalkir (2017) identifies explicit and tacit forms of knowledge as the two forms of knowledge used in organizations that should be managed, captured, and leverage as part of the knowledge management process. These two forms of knowledge are currently recognized as the de facto knowledge categorization informing decisionmaking in almost all organizations (Dalkir, 2017; Gray et al., 2017; Milton & Lambe, 2016) According to Dalkir (2016) a large portion of organizational knowledge and intellectual capital is tacit. Knowledge of this type is action-oriented and has a personal quality that often is not documented or written down in organizational processes and manuals (Dalkir, 2017; Gray et al., 2017; Milton & Lambe, 2016) Given the personalized characteristics of such knowledge, for it to be useful there must be mechanisms in place to ensure the transfer of personal knowledge between individuals as well as the transfer of explicit knowledge between individuals and organizations (Dalkir, 2017; Gray et al., 2017; Milton & Lambe, 2016).

Nonanka and Tekeuchi (1995) define knowledge construction progression as a five-step process involving four approaches of knowledge translation. The process starts with the tacit knowledge or specialized expertise of one or several individuals, who share it with others, thus developing a collective understanding (Nonanka &Tekeuchi, 1995). This collective level of comprehension is transferred into explicit knowledge in the form of a concept or an action in the second step of the process (Nonanka & Tekeuchi, 1995). In the third step that concept or action is validated by paralleling and connecting it to other forms of explicit organizational knowledge (Nonanka & Tekeuchi, 1995). In the fourth step the concept is established into a process or approach this is used (Nonanka &Tekeuchi, 1995). In the final step the new knowledge is shared through a knowledge transfer process throughout the organization (Nonanka & Tekeuchi, 1995). Organizations draw on both tacit and explicit knowledge forms in making decisions around strategy and values (Dalkir, 2017; Gray et al., 2017; Milton & Lambe, 2016).

Knowledge management is defined as the process by which an organization creates, captures, acquires, validates and uses knowledge to support and improve its overall functioning (Kinney, 1998). An important analytical tool for understanding knowledge management is the knowledge system conceptual framework, a framework that provides a holistic approach to understanding how knowledge is learned, developed, documented, shared, and constructively leveraged (Dalkir, 2017; Gray et al., 2017; Milton & Lambe, 2016). The knowledge system refers to the institutionalization of knowledge processes that shape behavior and actions in complex environments (Holzner and Marx, 1979). These processes include the creation, organization, distribution and application of knowledge (Dalkir, 2017; Gray et al., 2017; Milton & Lambe, 2016). The knowledge management process involves the activities or initiatives undertaken to provide the enabling conditions that facilitate the utilization of knowledge within organizations (Dalkir, 2017; Gray et al., 2017; Milton & Lambe, 2016).

Human resources play a significant role in the development of practical knowledge management processes that support sustainability in organizational infrastructure through policies and approaches that function as enablers of, or impediments to, effective knowledge management strategies and practices (Ahmad, 2015). The knowledge system concept, therefore, provides a sociological framework for analyzing organizational knowledge management structures and processes (Dalkir, 2017; Gray et al., 2017; Milton & Lambe, 2016). A knowledge system approach offers organizations the opportunity to integrate approaches capable of dealing with all its knowledge resources in the most efficient way (Dalkir, 2017; Gray et al., 2017; Milton & Lambe, 2016).

The conversion of tacit knowledge into explicit knowledge, the transfer of either form of knowledge between individuals or within (or between) organizations, and the application or utilization of such knowledge constitute the primary actions underlying knowledge management from knowledge system perspective (Dalkir, 2017; Gray et al., 2017; Milton & Lambe, 2016). For these activities to be practical, human resources should put into place a knowledge management strategy that promotes sustainable practices (Ahmad, 2015).

Hansen et al. (1999) point to two differing strategies for knowledge management: codification and personalization. According to Hansen et al. (1999) codification strategies focus on explicit knowledge, and involve carefully codifying and storing knowledge in databases, which can then become accessible to all in the organization. According to Hansen et al. (1999) such knowledge management strategies adopt a "people to document approach" by extracting knowledge from those who developed it, making it independent of them, and reusing it for various purposes. Hansen et al. (1999) outline that personalization strategy, on the other hand, focuses on the dialogue between individuals, and involve knowledge that has not been codified, but instead has been transferred from individual to individual through interpersonal encounters such as conversations or brainstorming sessions.

According to Milton and Lambe (2016) an effective knowledge management strategy is always a combination of codification and personalization, but with a stronger emphasis either on the former or the latter. Moreover, the preferred knowledge management strategy should be designed in a manner that enhances the goals and objectives of the organization (Dalkir, 2017; Gray et al., 2017; Milton & Lambe, 2016). Effective execution of a knowledge management strategy requires organizations to examine critically the knowledge forms underlying their decision-making and how that knowledge is used (Dalkir, 2017; Gray et al., 2017; Milton & Lambe, 2016). This is important because knowledge management strategies not commensurate with organizational goals and objectives can derail the growth and development of the organization (Dalkir, 2017; Gray et al., 2017; Milton & Lambe, 2016). Human resources can play a significant role in ensuring that there is alignment between organizational policies and effective sustainability practices (Ahmed, 2015).

A knowledge strategy is simply a plan that describes how an organization intends to better manage its knowledge for the benefit of that organization and its stakeholders (Dalkir, 2017; Gray et al., 2017; Milton & Lambe, 2016). A good knowledge management strategy is closely aligned with the organization's overall strategy and objectives. Selecting the right knowledge management strategy is, therefore, an essential prerequisite for attaining organizational objectives (Dalkir, 2017; Gray et al., 2017; Milton & Lambe, 2016). Hansen et al. (1999) point at two different strategies for knowledge management: codification and personalization. They believe that the best knowledge management strategy is always a combination of the two, but with a stronger emphasis on one (Hansen et al., 1999). While a codification strategy is appropriate for explicit knowledge to thrive, the personalization knowledge management strategy better supports the use of tacit knowledge in organizations (Hansen et al., 1999). Since tacit and explicit knowledge forms are complementary, an organization's efforts towards knowledge management should be focused on instituting the most appropriate strategy or a combination of the two (Milton & Lambe, 2016).

These two knowledge management strategies have distinctive features. The codification knowledge management strategy ensures the re-use of explicit knowledge by capturing, codifying, classifying and making available knowledge to support routine problem solving (Milton & Lambe, 2016). Uniformity in action is ensured since knowledge is recycled to guide decision-making Milton & Lambe, 2016). Questions regarding organizational problems and the usual response to them serve as the primary questions guiding codification strategies in organizations (Milton & Lambe, 2016). For such questions to be resolved, libraries of procedures, policy documents, guidelines, data collection forms, typical cases and outcomes, and risk assessment tools derived from all parts of the organization must be developed and made available to all individuals in the organization (Milton & Lambe, 2016).

The codification knowledge management strategy also thrives on the availability of incentives to encourage staff to engage in the knowledge management process fully (Dalkir, 2017; Gray et al., 2017; Milton & Lambe, 2016). This implies that organizations adopting the codification knowledge management strategy should reward the use of, and contributions to, document databases as recognition of staff adherence to policies. The codification strategy, in general, involves intensive investment justified by multiple knowledge re-use (Dalkir, 2017; Gray et al., 2017; Milton & Lambe, 2016). The codification strategy, stresses the need for technology and its importance in identifying, classifying, categorizing, storing, and retrieving knowledge (Dalkir, 2017; Gray et al., 2017; Milton & Lambe, 2016). The personalization strategy, takes a softer stance on knowledge and acknowledges that knowledge cannot always be formalized and used explicitly, but rather tacitly in an organization's process, actions, and activities through those of the employees (Dalkir, 2017; Gray et al., 2017; Milton & Lambe, 2016).

Promoting organizational communities of practice are examples of an effective personalization knowledge management strategy. Communities of practice are networks capable of nurturing and supporting the development of the personalization strategy of knowledge management in organizations through the sharing of knowledge, expertise, ideas, best practices, and problem-solving approaches around a topic that is important in an organization (Wenger, 2002; Brown & Duguid, 2001). The literature views communities of practice as powerful conceptual tools for pursuing personalization (person-to-person) knowledge management in organizations (Wenger, 2002; Brown & Duguid, 2001). Communities of practice function within not only an organization, but can extend to embrace individuals outside an organization who also share a common passion and interest in an issue or topic (Wenger, 2002; Brown & Duguid, 2001). Human resources can play a significant part in developing, promoting, and organizing the communities of practice process with a focus on sustainability and employee behaviors around sustainability (Ahmed, 2015).

Health care decision-makers rely on the use of information and knowledge in making dynamic decisions (Lengyel, 2018; Johnson, 2016) Understanding the knowledge that underlies health care decision-making, and how that knowledge is acquired, stored, validated, shared and applied, is an essential first step in ensuring effective knowledge management (Lengyel, 2018; Johnson, 2016). Effective knowledge management in health care decision-making requires the coordination of many elements: organizational structure and culture, policies, the extent of individual interactions within organizations, and the use of information and communication technology (Lengyel, 2018; Johnson, 2016). Human resources with their engagement, policies and comprehensive knowledge management approaches can drive organizational sustainability policy and employee behaviors in support of sustainability through green training (Ahmed, 2015; Atiku, 2020).

CONCLUSION

Technology advances help drive the innovation and progress associated with the 4IR. These changes create numerous opportunities for different industries to become more flexible, innovative, and develop operational efficiencies of scale. The advances made in technology gives organizations an ability to produce at a higher rate than ever before, thus requiring more of its workforce.

GHRM involves a set of policies, practices, and systems that promote a more socially responsible environment. Sustainability initiatives now drive the strategic goals of many organizations spanning numerous industries. Such initiatives drive the green behavior of employees and set the tone for recognizing the importance of how actions by an organizational entity may affect its internal and external stakeholders, including the environment.

Healthcare is historically known to be a slow adopter of new innovative practices. From technology adoption to healthcare delivery, waste management, record management, and data security, many providers within the industry continue to lag behind other major industries despite the significance of how the industry affects a country's overall well-being. Such challenges remain true in human capital management within the healthcare industry. Sustainability challenges exist ranging from mental and physical stress, wasting energy and land resources, hiring practices, education, and high turnover rates.

Exhibited by occupying swaths of land that consume many natural resources at a rate that is unsustainable to the environment, healthcare is at a crisis in terms of becoming a more conscientious entity in ensuring that the natural resources are not expended at an accelerated rate that results in developing more waste than necessary. Globalization of healthcare provides more possibilities for healthcare delivery and access; however, the manner that is used by many organizations mirrors a status quo method rather than adopting green practices that do not pose an overall risk to public health.

It is incumbent on researchers and leadership to work simultaneously in developing sustainable initiatives that mitigate risks associated with financial, ecological, and social waste. Ensuring that the appropriate personnel from the line staff to senior leadership practice green initiatives improves awareness of performing tasks that provide positive benefits to the environment. Knowledge management and the sharing of information between organizations that help limit excess greenhouse gases, and less reliance on older systems in the healthcare delivery process can provide financial savings and show that the healthcare industry itself shows value in being a socially responsible industry.

REFERENCES

Ahmad, S. (2015). Green human resources management: Policies and practices. *Cogent Business and Management, 2*(1), 1030817. doi:10.1080/23311975.2015.1030817

Atiku, S. O. (2018). *Reshaping Human Capital Formation through Digitalization. In Radical Reorganization of Existing Work Structures through Digitization.* IGI Global.

Atiku, S. O. (2019). Institutionalizing Social Responsibility through Workplace Green Behaviour. In *S. O. Atiku (Ed's). Contemporary Multicultural Orientations and Practices for Global Leadership* (pp. 183–199). IGI Global. doi:10.4018/978-1-5225-6286-3.ch010

Atiku, S. O. (2020). Knowledge Management for the Circular Economy. In *Handbook of Research on Entrepreneurship Development and Opportunities in Circular Economy* (pp. 520–537). IGI Global.

Atiku, S. O. (2020). *Human Capital Formation for the Fourth Industrial Revolution.* IGI Global. doi:10.4018/978-1-5225-9810-7

Bates, S. (2011). *HR Has Key Role in Sustainability Strategy, Report Finds.* Academic Press.

Bombiak, E. (2019). Green human resources management – The latest trend or strategic necessity? *Entrepreneurship and Sustainability Issues, 6*(4), 1647–1662. doi:10.9770/jesi.2019.6.4(7)

Brown, J. S., & Duguid, P. (2001). Knowledge and organization: A social practice perspective. *Organization Science, 12*(2), 198–213. doi:10.1287/orsc.12.2.198.10116

Cooper, G., & Burke, R. (2006). *Inspiring Leaders.* Routledge.

Dalkir, K. (2017). *Knowledge Management in Theory and Practice*. MIT Press.

Du Toit, J., & Millum, J. (2016). Are Indirect Benefits Relevant to Health Care Allocation Decisions? *The Journal of Medicine and Philosophy*, *41*(5), 540–557. doi:10.1093/jmp/jhw018 PMID:27465773

Epstein, M. J. (2008). *Making sustainability work. Best practices in managing and measuring corporate social, environmental and economic impacts*. Greenleaf Publishing.

Fields, Z., & Atiku, S. O. (2017). Collective Green Creativity and Eco-Innovation as key drivers of Sustainable Business Solutions in Organisations. In *Collective Creativity for Responsible and Sustainable Business Practice* (pp. 1–25). IGI Global. doi:10.4018/978-1-5225-1823-5.ch001

Galpin, T., & Lee Whittington, J. (2012). Sustainability leadership: From strategy to results. *The Journal of Business Strategy*, *4*(33), 40–48. doi:10.1108/02756661211242690

Giloth, R. (2018). The Opportunity Challenge (Advancing Equity Planning Now). Cornell University Press.

Gray, M., Gray, J., Rotenberg, E., Nelson, C., Murgatroyd, P., Armstrong, J., & Hayward, P. (2017). *Knowledge Management (Healthcare Transformation Book 4)*. Ko Awatea.

Hansen, M. T., Nohria, N., & Tierney, T. (1999). What's your strategy for managing knowledge? *Harvard Business Review*, *2*(77), 106–116. PMID:10387767

Holzner, B., & Marx, J. H. (1979). *Knowledge application: The knowledge system in society*. Allyn and Bacon. https://www.shrm.org/resourcesandtools/hr-topics/behavioral-competencies/ethical-practice/pages/sustainabilitystrategy.aspx

Johnston, C. (2016). *Crafting a system of profound knowledge management in long-term care* (Order No. 10252778). Available from ProQuest Dissertations & Theses Global. (1853429854)

King, M. C. (2008). What sustainability should mean. *Challenge*, *51*(2), 27–39. doi:10.2753/0577-5132510204

Kinney, T. (1998). Knowledge management, intellectual capital and adult learning. *Adult Learning*, *10*(2), 2–5. doi:10.1177/104515959901000201

Last, J. M. (1988). *A Dictionary of Epidemiology* (2nd ed.). Oxford University Press.

Ledesma, A., McCulloh, C., Wieck, H., & Yang, M. (2012). *Health Care Sector Overview*. Washington State University.

Lengyel, D. M. (2018). *A critical examination of the relationships between risk management, knowledge management and decision making* (Order No. 10931990). Available from ProQuest Dissertations & Theses Global. (2103990692)

Lennox, L., Maher, L., & Reed, J. (2018). Navigating the sustainability landscape: A systematic review of sustainability approaches in healthcare. *Implementation Science; IS*, *13*(1), 27–17. doi:10.118613012-017-0707-4 PMID:29426341

Levine, L. (2016, September 15). *Why Environmental Sustainability is Important*. http://healthcarehubgreen.com/blog/why-environmentaTsustainability-is-important/

MacGuire, J. (2015). *What is HR's Role in Sustainability Strategy?* Academic Press.

Mello, J. A. (2019). Sustainability in health care organizations: Successes, challenges and opportunities. *Journal of Strategic Innovation and Sustainability, 14*(2), 123–128.

Metaxiotis, K., Ergazakis, K., & Psarras, J. (2005). Exploring the world of knowledge management: Agreements and disagreements in the academic/practitioner community. *Journal of Knowledge Management, 2*(9), 16–18. doi:10.1108/13673270510590182

Milton, N., & Lambe, P. (2016). The Knowledge Manager's Handbook: A Step-by-Step Guide to Embedding Effective Knowledge Management in your. *Organization.*

Mousa, S. K., & Othman, M. (2020). The impact of green human resource management practices on sustainable performance in healthcare organisations: A conceptual framework. *Journal of Cleaner Production, 243*, 118595. doi:10.1016/j.jclepro.2019.118595

National Research Council. (2002). *The Future of the Public's Health in the 21st Century.* The National Academies Press.

Nonanka, I., & Takeuchi, H. (1995). *The knowledge creating company.* Oxford University Press.

Papanicolas, I., Woskie, L. R., & Jha, A. K. (2018). Health care spending in the United States and other high-income countries. *Journal of the American Medical Association, 319*(10), 1024–1039. doi:10.1001/jama.2018.1150 PMID:29536101

Park, H. A. (2016). Are we ready for the Fourth Industrial Revolution? *Yearbook of Medical Informatics,* (1), 1–3. doi:10.15265/IYS-2016-s042 PMID:27830223

Schwab, K. (2016). *The Fourth Industrial Revolution: What it means and how to respond.* World Economic Forum.

Senge, P., Smith, B., Kruschwitz, N., Laur, J., & Schley, S. (2008) *The necessary revolution: How individuals and organizations are working together to create a sustainable world.* Doubleday.

Smith, H. L. (2018). *Working smarter: The case for knowledge management in global health* (Order No. 10937506). Available from ProQuest Dissertations & Theses Global. (2130125996)

Wenger, E. (1998). *Communities of practice: Learning, meaning, and identity.* Cambridge University Press. doi:10.1017/CBO9780511803932

Yong, J. Y., Yusliza, M., & Fawehinmi, O. O. (2019). Green human resource management: A systematic literature review from 2007 to 2019. *Benchmarking, 27*(7), 2005–2027. Advance online publication. doi:10.1108/BIJ-12-2018-0438

KEY TERMS AND DEFINITIONS

Fourth Industrial Revolution: Infusion of technological and digital practices towards advancement of productivity and operational capacity.

Green Human Resource Management: Set of policies and practices designed to stimulate environmentally sensitive, resource efficient, and socially responsible workplace.

Green Sustainability: Pursuit of knowledge and practices designed to improve environmentally, ecological, and social resources.

Knowledge Management: Process of creating, sharing, and using the knowledge and information by an organization.

This research was previously published in Human Resource Management Practices for Promoting Sustainability; pages 38-55, copyright year 2021 by Business Science Reference (an imprint of IGI Global).

Chapter 3
Trends and Issues in Strategic Human Resources Management

Abraham Pius
https://orcid.org/0000-0002-9587-9876
Arden University, UK

Husam Helmi Alharahsheh
https://orcid.org/0000-0002-0194-3700
University of Wales Trinity Saint David, UK

Saikou Sanyang
Arden University, UK

ABSTRACT

The key function of human resources will continue to play a key role in the process of firms' future planning. The chapter has highlighted, discussed, and explored key activities at the strategic levels of human resource management and planning including introductory comments and definitions of current understanding of HRM, the flexible firm, HRM planning and its benefits, HRM planning at the strategic levels, the role of individuals within their wider teams and organisations, and the development of technological advancement and its reflection in the planning process for HRM leading to further embedding of virtual aspects and activities. Furthermore, the chapter also included current practices of outsourcing and different key stages of workforce planning. The chapter aimed to enhance application by providing several practical discussions and case studies reflecting current trends in HRM at a strategic level.

INTRODUCTION

This Chapter is planned and designed to explore strategic human resources (SHR), key terms, activities and requirements in organisations. Using various activities and case studies to support the lines of discussion throughout the chapter. For over a century now, human resource, as a discipline and practice, has progressed into various areas of studies. This, for a time, had been through a process of trial and

DOI: 10.4018/978-1-6684-3873-2.ch003

error – hitherto; using a model that largely relied on the development and testing of various ideas by academics and practice managers. The fundamental forces driving this advancement and growth in the field are profitability, efficiency, sustainability and the quest for the acquisition of new knowledge which supports the utilization of and development of staff as part of several resources organisations have at their disposal. It is highly essential for firms to enhance and management professionals to enhance their understanding and reflection of key trends in the process of planning for HRM activities at a strategic level in both the short and long terms.

The chapter is developed for students, professionals, managers, researchers that already have prior knowledge and experience in the field of HR or other associated field, and positions such as being a line manager for a small or large team, or even running own small firm where the aspects of HRM are highly essential and vital for the development and growth of the firm. The chapter is providing identification, exploration and in depth discussion of key strategic aspects of HRM such as the following:

- Forecasting External Supply
- Job Analysis and Workforce Profiling
- Job Descriptions and Person Specifications
- Competencies
- Job Families (market groups)
- Redundancy

Furthermore, the chapter is supported by key case studies and identification of current trends to enhance understanding of key changes and developments in the field. Also other associated activates are included across different sections of the chapter to enhance classroom discussions and reflection.

Summary of Learning Outcome

- Define and discuss some of the key terminologies and activities of HR
- Explain human resources requirements in organisations.

Chapter Objectives

By the end of this chapter readers should be able to:

- Define and discuss key terminologies and activities of SHR.
- Discuss and apply strategic HR requirements and undertake a job analysis for an identified position.

Before you start, make a note below of objectives you wish to set yourself for this chapter. After completing the chapter, you should hopefully be able to appreciate key terminologies associated with HR as well as the strategic HR requirements that aids managers undertake a job analysis.

Forecasting External Supply

In most organisations, a gap will exist between the demand for staff and the internal supply. This has to be plugged from outside.

Some internal information may be useful for evaluating the potential external supply, in terms of both quantity and quality. This may take the form of the response rates to advertisements, the quality of interviewees and the number of staffs leaving to join other organisations. However, the most useful information will be collected from outside the organisation.

Most labour markets are local, based on a 'travel to work' area (often determined by time, rather than distance, as a motorway or good train service can substantially increase the distance people are willing to commute). It is important for the Human Resource planner to gather several key statistics, including:

- Unemployment rates,
- Population density,
- Number of school leavers,
- Proportion with or in higher education,
- Skill levels,
- Age profile (e.g. seaside towns are often retirement havens).

The question of available skills is an interesting challenge facing organisations starting new plants on 'greenfield' sites. Do they move to an area near to their competitors, so they can 'poach' people who already have the skills they need, or do they start-up in a location without immediate competitors and train the local population? There are pluses and minuses with both:

Case Study Four: DoubleTree by Hilton Hotel

When DoubleTree by Hilton Hotel – some years ago decided to increase its hotel numbers in the UK, buying in existing skills was not a priority. They were less interested in the skills people already had, but rather what type of person they would be. *90% of those recruited had never worked in the industry before.* To give an idea of scale, they received over 35,000 applications, with 9,000 people going through their assessment centre, 5,000 of those being interviewed and 3,000 being appointed.

Another prime value during DoubleTree recruitment process was that although it is important to hire the right people, it is even more important to train them – *'even with the right ingredients, you still need to bake the cake'.* After the initial recruitment exercise, DoubleTree's emphasis switched to improving efficiency. Their HR specialists are told 'do not let anyone leave, as you can't replace them – you'll have to improve productivity'. We will provide more information on the DoubleTree recruitment exercise later in this chapter. Broadly speaking, local labour market information can be obtained from a variety of sources; including government publications, chambers of commerce, local authority and employment agencies. Some useful data sources are featured in Appendix 2 at the end of the chapter.

To bring together what we have examined in this section, the following diagram provides a useful template. It also adds some additional points to consider, such as the commercial factors which influence planning, and reward systems.

Figure 1. Showing different façades of workforce planning

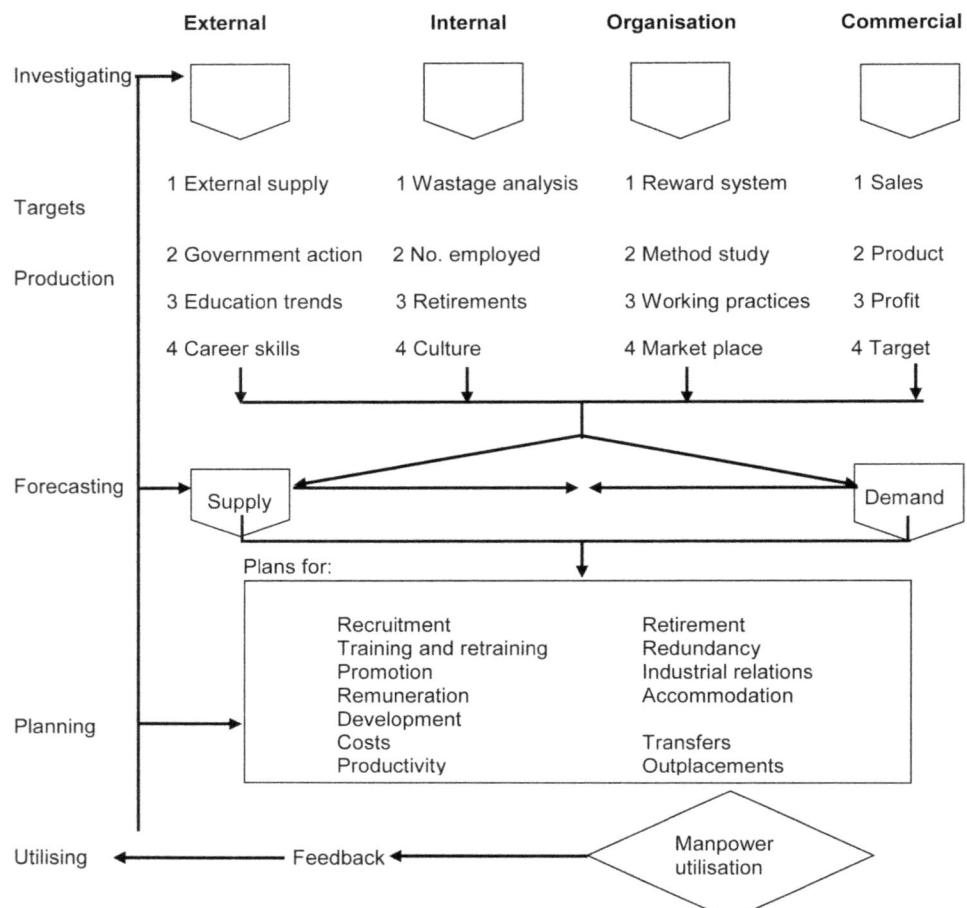

JOB ANALYSIS AND WORKFORCE PROFILING

What Is Job Analysis?

Job analysis can be elucidated as a process aimed at determining and describing the content of jobs in such a way that a clear understanding of what any job is about can be communicated to anyone who might require the information for management purposes. Yet, Shneider and Konz in (1989) argued that sometimes job analysis application techniques place too much emphasis on the implicit notion that information regarding the knowledge, skills and performance requirement of a job, as they exist in the present, will remain the same for the future. Though this may partly hold true for smaller organisations existing in a 'static stable' market environment, for a vast number of organisations, complex and unpredictable market forces (i.e. internal and external) means this may not be the case. Indeed, a job analysis may also be viewed as a performance tool which sets the benchmark for what is to be expected of employees, and once this is achieved, the reward or compensation that follows (Hailemariam et al., 2019; Mira et al., 2019).

You may sometimes hear a job analysis referred to as an *'occupational analysis'*, as noted in the quotation at the foot of this page.

Why Is It Important?

There is a misconception about what a job analysis is made up of. In view of this, Taylor (2002:94) explains a job analysis, in addition to contents of a job and activities it consists of, also *"looks at how each job fits into the organisation, what its purpose is, and at the skills and personality traits required to carry it out"*.

As noted above, a job analysis has a central part to play in Human Resource Planning and on a range of practices within the organisation. It specifically has a central part to play in:

- Recruitment and selection,
- The determination of pay differentials,
- The identification of training needs,
- The setting of performance targets,
- The construction of new organisational structures.

Additionally, without objective, effective job analyses behind them, it can be very difficult for firms to back up actions undertaken in making key decisions – such as to do with:

- Redundancy,
- Promotion,
- Disciplinary action,
- Performance review,
- Changing rates of pay.

So, although it is primarily a technical and administrative tool, it adds value to a range of organisational activities. In view of this, Legere (1985) remarked:

'Occupational analysis is a business investment – it requires considerable expenditure of funds, human effort and time. These costs, however, can be amortised over a period, during which the data can be used to avoid costs, tailor programs, increase efficiency and flexibility, improve quality control, and effect operational change. The data developed during occupational analysis can serve initially to validate existing programs, to document or articulate specific program needs, or to influence almost every aspect of the personal management program within that occupation' (p.1327).

Let us look at the help a job analysis provides to firms:

- **Human Resource Planning.** Organisations must plan the resources required to meet their agreed objectives. We have already seen that this means having the right people in the right places at the right time. This might mean designing totally new jobs or redesigning existing jobs to meet current or future demands. For these activities, it is vital that the organisation has good analytical data about its jobs.

- **Job evaluation.** This is one of the standard reasons for undertaking a job analysis. If the information used is not accurate, it will not produce fair results and could undermine the credibility of the procedure.
- **Selection.** The organisation must have clear information about what skills, knowledge, experience, attitude and personal attributes are needed for each job – otherwise, it cannot properly match potential candidates against these. Job descriptions and person specifications will be drawn up for this purpose.
- **Organisation review.** When structures are being amended, it is necessary to have sound information about the content of jobs. This will ensure that any important tasks are not overlooked, and duplication does not occur.
- **Training and development.** Analytical information allows outputs to be matched to the knowledge, competencies and skills required for each job and, from them, the training and development needs for each individual team.
- **Job design.** We know that organisations are changing very rapidly both in terms of operations and structure. Reallocating duties and redesigning jobs, therefore, have to be carried out quickly. Good information about jobs will allow this to be completed quickly and effectively.
- **Employee rights.** A job description of some kind should be given to each employee so that there is no ambiguity about what each role entails, and the outputs required from it. If this isn't clear, it could lead to issues of performance, discipline and grievance. The job description is a prime part of the contractual relationship between employer and employee – the employer who doesn't clearly state what the job is about could be storing up trouble for the future.
- **Performance management.** To ensure employees are performing their jobs roles with utmost efficiency, and to the benefit of both individuals and the organisation, training and development are comprehensive information is needed. The requirements of the job could then be compared with the extent to which the individual meets those requirements.

Principles of Job Analysis

The principles governing job analysis are:

1. **Jobs, not people** are analysed. The skills, knowledge and experience required for the job itself should not be confused with those of the current post-holder (there may, of course, be a gap between the two). It is always worth remembering that there are a variety of factors that can affect job content, as illustrated below.
2. **Non-judgemental.** The person carrying out the job analysis should not be concerned with how appropriate each part of the job is – i.e. personally, they might think the whole job is a complete waste of time, but it is not their role to comment unless they have been asked to perform some kind of organisational review.
3. **Not a list of tasks.** The analysis should describe the various components of the role and how it relates to the success of the organisation. Simply list individual tasks will only provide a partial picture and will not give the job 'life'
4. **Here and now.** The analysis should concentrate on the job as it is today, rather than anything that may have happened to it in the past, or any potential future changes.
5. **A tool.** Job analysis is a process, a means to an end, not an end.

Figure 2. Showing factors with an effect on job content

Methods of Analysis

There is a variety of approaches to job analysis and we will attempt to introduce you to the popular approaches used here.

What do you think will influence the technique chosen to perform the analysis? Make a note of the approaches you are familiar with

The technique chosen will depend on the type of information being looked for. If training and development are driving job analysis, then the analysis will not just concentrate on individual tasks, but also on the skills and resources likely to be required.

Questionnaires

Collecting data about jobs via a structured questionnaire has the advantages of reducing time and cost. Where large numbers of current job holders are to be consulted, a well-designed questionnaire will generate clear and useful findings. By using a structured questioning approach, a good level of consistency can be obtained.

The *Position Analysis Questionnaire (PAQ)* – one of a number of commercial packages available, gathers six discrete categories of information:

1.   The source of information used to do the job (how and where the employee gets the information),
2.   The kind of mental processes required (reasoning, decision-making, planning etc.),
3.   The output expected and methods used (physical activities performed, tools and equipment used),
4.   The types and levels of relationships with others,
5.   The physical and social environment in which the job is performed,
6.   Additional job characteristics and activities not covered by the above – such as hours and level of responsibility.

As noted earlier in the chapter, this reiterates that job analysis is not just concerned with data on job content, but how each job fits into the organisation, what its purpose is, and the skills and personality traits needed to perform it.

Interviews

With this common method, *trained* analysts talk to the job holder, relevant supervisors and colleagues about the job and how it fits into the organisation. The job holder is encouraged to be open and discuss events they have experienced. What they say is then validated by others.

With this method, what do you think the inherent weakness may be? How might it be overcome? Make a note of this during your independent study.

There is a strong possibility that the interviewee will 'talk up' their work to impress the interviewer (particularly if a re-grading is being considered). They will tend to concentrate on the more interesting aspects and downplay the mundane duties. It is common for people to think they have more responsibility than is the case, particularly if they've had some responsibility delegated to them.

It is often better to interview staff who have been in the job for a relatively short period of time, rather than those have been in it for years. A trained interviewer will, however, be able to 'bring back' the employee to the nitty-gritty details of their work.

A good way of ameliorating this problem is to conduct a group interview of several people in the same role. There is then less chance that one person will exaggerate. As stated earlier, it is important to remind them that it is the job that is being analysed, not the person's performance in it.

Activity 1

Imagine you must conduct a job analysis interview in two weeks' time in a department you don't know much about. What things would you have to do or consider before, during and after the interview? List 10 of these below.

1.
2.
3.
4.
5.
6.

7.

8.

9.

10.

Compare your list against our points in the Appendix.

Several specific job analysis interviewing methods have been developed to strengthen the process. Two of them are:

Critical Incident Technique

Here the job holder is asked only to concentrate on those aspects of the job that make the difference between success and failure. The starting point is objectives, with the interviewer agreeing and recording the main inputs and outputs required in the job to produce the desired performance levels. Once these are established, the next step in the interview process is to get the post holder to describe actual incidents (hence the title) or events that resulted in success or failure in meeting key objectives. They are asked to state specifically what their own contribution to the outcome was.

This technique helps to avoid recording general statements and gives the interviewer a very detailed picture of the role. The behaviours required for success are comprehensively documented.

A variant of the critical incident technique is *hierarchical task analysis*. Jobs are broken down into a hierarchical set of tasks and then into subtasks. These are then described in terms of their inputs, outputs and how they are to be achieved. The process details what must be done, and the standards to attain any specific conditions associated with performing the tasks.

The Repertory Grid

This involves putting together a list of tasks that form part of a job and then comparing each one with all the others regarding the skills and abilities needed for success. Pairs or triads of tasks are chosen at random. These are then analysed by the job holder, supervisor and colleagues to establish new information on the pertinent skills.

The list of tasks and skills are then positioned at right-angles to each other on a grid. This allows each skill to be rated in terms of its significance to the achievement of each task. A five- or seven-point rating scale is normally used, with a score of one meaning that the skill is not relevant to the task and a five or seven meaning that it is crucial.

Table 1. Showing an example of a Repertory Grid in practice

Skills					
Duties	**Assertiveness**	**Accuracy**	**Keyboard Skills**	**Reliability**	**Verbal Fluency**
Make outbound calls	5	2	1	4	4
Record customer details	2	5	4	4	2
Complete sale	4	5	2	4	4
Forward documentation	1	4	2	5	1

A simple example of a telesales agent is given in Table 1.

Table 1 shows a run-down of some of the available options for collecting data to support job analysis.

1. ***Self-reports:*** This approach involves post holders describing their roles and producing job descriptions. It can lead to substantial discrepancies and variations between employees both in content and accuracy (not least because of the differences in writing skills). Thorough training is usually needed to make self-reporting work – particularly if it is to be used as the basis for grading, and hence pay.

2. ***Diaries and logs:*** Here, the post holder is required to keep a full record of what they do each day. It can be a time-consuming approach and is rarely suitable for people in repetitive or predictable jobs. It is again open to a high degree of subjectivity and needs to take place in a non-threatening work environment.

3. ***Checklists:*** These tend to be of most use when there are many jobs with a relatively straightforward task breakdown. A long list of tasks is given to the post holder and/or supervisor and they tick off the ones used in the job.

4. ***Observation:*** Tends to be regarded as one of the most accurate, but at the same time costly, methods of gathering job data. It was at the heart of work study methods, which have now largely disappeared. One serious drawback with observation is that the people observed might well change their behaviour – for many years this has been known as the *Hawthorne effect,* following a series of experiments conducted in the USA at the Western Electric Company.

5. ***Participant observation:*** This involves the analyst performing the job and recording their findings. Naturally, it can only really work for either routine jobs or in a section or department where the analyst already knows the work intimately – otherwise, the technique will quickly fall into disrepute.

Job Descriptions and Person Specifications

The written job description has long been the primary output from a job analysis process. It is at the heart of many Human Resource Planning decisions and processes (such as the production of training plans and determination of rates of pay) and supports organisational processes for managing performance. Forming a key part of the contractual package, job descriptions often provide a key defence in cases of unfair discrimination.

In fact, a job description is a multi-purpose tool. To take this forward, Consider and explore the following question: *What uses does it have in your organisation? Have this been considered from both perspectives of employers and employees?* Make a note in your personal learning log/diary.

Some typical applications of a job description are explored below:

*   *As a tool in recruitment; i.e. t*o help with writing advertisements and briefing applicants.
*   *As a tool in selection.* Decisions about which candidates to appoint can be made with reference to an up-to-date job description to ensure that other factors (e.g. personal bias) do not cloud judgements.
*   *For employment contracts.* Often organisations will refer to job descriptions in their contracts of employment. They can be important if an employee is dismissed for failing to reach the required performance standards. Similarly, if someone resigns and then claims constructive dismissal for

being given work outside their terms of employment, the job description's content can 'make or break' the case.

- *For communicating values.* Information about the organisation's priorities, expectations and rewards can be included to outline what the employee is expected to achieve.
- *As a defence against unfair discrimination.* If someone has been denied employment (or promotion) and feels this is due to discrimination, they may pursue legal action against the employer. If the case reaches an Employment Tribunal, the job description will usually be a critical piece of evidence.

The points above illustrate not only the value of having a job description but of getting it right. If nebulous phrases are used, or ones which are all-embracing (such as 'any other duties deemed suitable by the employer'), the employer's case may be weakened. However, the reverse is true if the requirements in the job description are written clearly, concisely and objectively.

Armstrong (2012;2003) has given some general advice about constructing meaningful job descriptions, as follows:

- Each item contained in the job description should relate to the outputs that the job-holder will be expected to produce.
- The document should make explicit what the job holder can be held responsible for.
- If a component task of the job is to be completed under supervision, this should be made clear.
- If there are deadlines to be worked to, these should be included.

It is important for the language contained in job descriptions to refer to *what gets done*, rather than *what employees do*, so that there is less room for ambiguity (Taylor, 2002). Certainly, there has been a long-held view that the way job descriptions are written by some organisations emphasises on the task requirement and performance requirement as opposed to what employees are responsible for achieving in their job role. This, argued (Taylor, 2019: 136), has prompted some forward-thinking organisations to move toward *'accountability profiles'* or *'role profiles'* which rather places emphasis on achievement. Our view on this is – for this to be efficient, there has to be a clear benchmark or framework sitting alongside the role profile setting out what achievement or success looks like.

Job descriptions tend not to vary a great deal in their main headings from organisation to organisation and usually include:

- Job title,
- Grade/rate of pay,
- Main location,
- Supervisor's name/post,
- Details of any subordinates,
- The main purpose of the job – i.e. a succinct summary of what it consists of,
- List of the principal duties and accountabilities, together with very brief descriptions. These would not normally number more than around ten, or the job description will be going into too much detail. Additionally, the more senior employees will tend to have *objectives* to achieve, rather than *tasks* to carry out.

- Reference to other documents (such as trade union or other collective agreements) that may expand on other items.
- Context – how work is progressed. Where it comes from and goes to, together with any environmental conditions and how it fits into the rest of the organisation.
- Contacts – communications lines, including external people and bodies, and the reasons for them.
- Dimensions – financial or statistical information that helps to illustrate job size.
- Working conditions – particularly if there are special conditions relating to chemical hazards, noise and so on.
- Signatures of post holder and supervisor, plus date – it is surprising how many job descriptions in current use are more than five years old.

Drawbacks of Job Descriptions Include

- The content and quality will depend very much on the job analysis technique used and the skills of the analyst. Weaknesses in either will be transmitted directly to the job description.
- If job descriptions are written too rigidly, they can affect flexibility, with employees retorting: *'I'm not doing that, it's not on my job description'.*
- It is now widely acknowledged that in today's work environment, job descriptions date fast.
- In modern organisations, employees can be used very flexibly, according to their abilities, rather than the specific, itemised, duties they were originally hired to perform.

Person specifications set out the attributes required to perform a particular role. They are used as the basis for short-listing and selection, and normally specify requirement in terms of:

- Skills,
- Knowledge,
- Personality attributes,
- Education and qualifications,
- Experience.

The individual items listed under each of these headings are then commonly divided into 'desirable' and 'essential'.

There are several ways of describing the ideal candidate for a job, with two popular ones being Munro Fraser's Five-Fold Grading System and Alec Rodger's Seven-Point Plan. These are shown in Table 2.

Both models are well-established in HR and their current use needs to be considered against prevailing legislation. For instance, factor one in each model is likely to contravene the European Human Rights Convention (2000), as it may deny freedom of expression and ask unduly intrusive questions of prospective candidates. This is also true for point five of the Seven-Point Plan. Point seven may stray into the area of indirect sexual discrimination, perhaps assuming or implying that a woman with a family may not be able to meet those sorts of requirements.

The skill, qualification and experience requirements have to be those that are strictly necessary for effective performance of the job. If any unnecessary factors are included, they might unfairly discriminate against minority groups.

Table 2.

Five-Fold Grading System
1. *Impact on others* – physical make-up, appearance, speech and manner, 2. *Acquired qualifications* – educational, vocational training, work experience, 3. *Innate abilities* – quickness of comprehension and aptitude for learning, 4. *Motivation* – individual goals, consistency and determination in following them up; the success rate, 5. *Adjustment* – emotional stability, ability to stand up to stress and ability to get on with people.
Seven Point Plan
1. *Physical make-up* – health, appearance, bearing and speech, 2. *Attainments* – education, qualifications and experience, 3. *General intelligence* – intellectual capacity, 4. *Special aptitudes* – mechanical or manual dexterity, facility in the use of words and figures, 5. *Interests* – intellectual, practical, constructional, physical, social, artistic, 6. *Disposition* – acceptability, influence over others, steadiness, dependability, self-reliance, 7. *Circumstances* – any special demands of the job, such as the ability to work unsocial hours, or travel abroad.

Competencies

Some organisations will prefer to emphasize the behavioural competencies needed by the post holder. A popular framework for this is the MSL/McBer competency cluster for managerial jobs as shown below.

Competencies have the advantage of describing observable behaviour, which is helpful in assessing work performance. In many organisations, there is a competency framework in place providing each work role with a set of clear performance standards and a path for development. But competences need to be defined thoroughly to avoid vagueness or ambiguity and, again, indirect discrimination or human rights infringements. Their definitions need to be capable of distinguishing between excellent, acceptable and unacceptable performance.

If an organisation puts in place a competency framework or mechanisms such as performance indicators, it is then able to align the processes of selection, performance, monitoring, reward and discipline designed to bring about and reinforce those behaviours. It is essential that these are aligned properly and that the competencies identified are appropriate to the organisation. If not, a situation could arise where an individual was recruited against one set of criteria, expected to do something else by his/her colleagues, appraised against another list of indicators and rewarded by an unrelated system.

Figure 3. Showing MSL/McBer competency cluster for managerial jobs

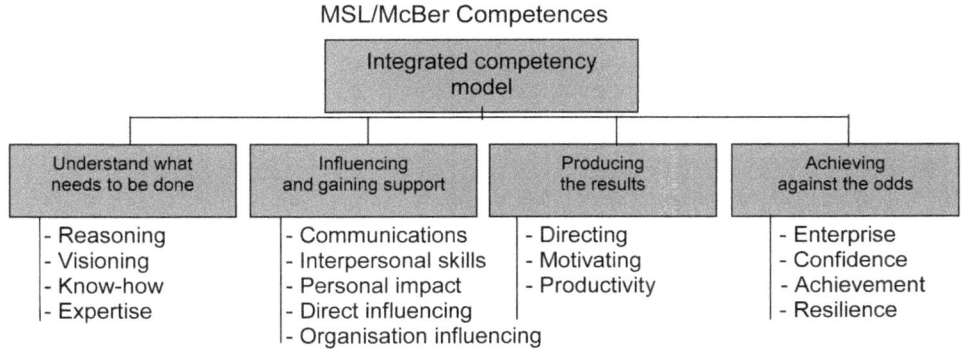

The standard practice is to start with high performers. Here, analysis (perhaps using critical incident or repertory grid) aims to ascertain why they are effective and use that knowledge to create a competency framework reflecting the behavioural strategies used by successful people. Organisations are all different, so they will not all use the same competency template, but there now exists a comprehensive 'menu' of competences from which to choose. The culture and values of an organisation are important in choosing which competences sit in their framework. For example, a traditional accountancy firm may want auditors who are thorough and trustworthy. By comparison, a small care organisation may need people who are compassionate, driven and altruistic.

It is crucial that people within an organisation contribute to producing their own competency framework. Those imported wholesale from outside will feel alien and not part of everyday working life – like a ten-page mission statement written solely by the chairman. On the other hand, a keen awareness of the competencies required to compete in the organisation's environment is crucial. And insularity in devising competences can result in 'cloning' – i.e. the recruitment and promotion of people whose close similarities reduce organisational creativity and flexibility.

It is also important that organisations look forward, not backwards, when drawing up the core competencies. No doubt some of the competencies from the past that have brought success will be valid, but some will be out-dated or marginalised. Competency frameworks are discussed further.

Minimising the Drawbacks of Job Analysis

We have already commented on the negative aspects of individual job analysis techniques. None are perfect and neither are the people performing them.

There are, though, a couple of ways in which we can reduce problems:

- *Regular updating.* Each line manager should be required to update the job descriptions of reporting positions at least once a year. A good time to do this is before the annual appraisal of the current post holder. The content can then be agreed and signed-off as part of that process.
- *Loose job descriptions.* To cope with rapid change, job analysis can be performed on a flexible basis, using less precise language in the job description. For example, instead of saying a job involves writing monthly sales reports and weekly sales updates, it could just state: 'providing sales data when required'. Similarly, instead of saying a healthcare job involves washing and dressing service users daily in an elderly residential home, it could just state: 'implementing Service user care plans related to personal cleansing and dressing'.

Job Families

A job family is a group of jobs in which the nature and objectives of the work are similar, but the work is performed at different levels. Job family definitions are used to identify levels of competence or capacity within a job family as a basis for rewarding people within that family. The Hay Management Consultants' (1996) process of job family modelling involves:

- Identifying the families,
- Analysing and determining levels of work in each family,
- Establishing levels of work between job families by job evaluation,

- Defining pay grades.

Job families can be treated as distinct market groups, with the structure helping career planning, but the system can be divisive and equal pay issues may arise between the families. Where movement between job families is inhibited there is also the danger that people will become 'labelled'.

Jobs within a family may be linked in any of the following ways:

- The nature of the work – e.g. customer services;
- The professional or technical discipline – e.g. engineers or scientists;
- The same job operating at different levels – e.g. secretaries;
- A common function – e.g. sales.
- Branch (or regional) managers – with local conditions reflecting the size of different branches.

An important point relating to the broad-band pay structures associated with job families is that formal analytical job evaluation schemes may not be used at all. If they are used, they may have an essentially supporting role once the band structures have been defined.

Redundancy

It is perhaps not surprising that we may tend to think of recruitment and selection in terms of positive events, such as how to plan recruitment, train the workforce, and cope with expansion. But there are negative elements involved in planning – that is, ensuring that if a problem arises, its impact is minimised, and the people involved are treated fairly and with dignity. Redundancy planning is one such activity.

The three main routes out of an organisation are resignation, retirement and redundancy. Although in this section we will be covering redundancies and practices connected with redundancy programmes, you should bear in mind that 'voluntary' retirements, for employees who have reached a certain age, are often used as an alternative. In reality, pressure is placed on the employee to accept retirement and the associated pension payment as an alternative to a one-off redundancy payment.

We looked at the wide variety of reasons people leave organisations in Activity 4. However, distinguishing between departures initiated by employers and those by employees is not completely straightforward. While some reasons for termination are easy to define, such as dismissal for gross misconduct, or someone resigning to join another organisation, others may have several contributory factors. Common examples of this blurring occur when someone resigns without having another position or when someone must retire at a predetermined age, when perhaps they would have preferred to continue working (current UK legislation is changing this situation, and now organisations are obliged to give employees the option to continue working beyond what was the mandatory retirement age).

What Is Redundancy?

A major point to make is that *jobs are made redundant, not people*. A person's employment may be terminated because their job is disappearing, but strictly speaking the classic comment of 'I am being made redundant' is incorrect – it should be 'my job is being made redundant'. But this semantic distinction will not make much difference to the despondency of the person affected.

The Employment Protection (Consolidation) Act of (1978) stated that a termination due to redundancy occurs due to one of four reasons:

- The employer has ceased or will cease, carrying out the *business* in which the person was employed,
- The employer has ceased or will cease, carrying out the *business* at the *place* where the person was employed,
- The requirement to perform *work* has ceased or diminished, and the person was employed in that work,
- The requirement to perform *work* has ceased or diminished at the *place* where the person was employed.

So, if there has not been a reduction in the overall need for staff in general, or at a location, then, in legal terms, a redundancy has not occurred.

Activity 2

What do you think this means for organisations that are expanding? Does it mean no jobs can be made redundant?

Compare your initial thoughts against our comments in the Appendix.

You may at first feel that the legal definition is rather academic, but it can be critical for several reasons, not least financial. For example, there are minimum guaranteed redundancy payments and the Inland Revenue allows a certain amount of redundancy pay to be paid tax-free. You should remember that redundancies are just one type of dismissal and Employment Tribunals will always look to ensure that proper procedures have been followed and that, as is mentioned elsewhere in this dossier, a *'reasonable' approach is taken.*

Part of the process of examining reasonableness would be to see what steps had been taken to avoid the redundancies, whether the correct procedures had been followed and the relevant redundancy payments made. So, let's look at the practicalities.

Support Materials

Organisations

The Chartered Institute of Personnel and Development stands pre-eminent in the HR world since it is the professional body for those working in the field. It has a comprehensive library (from which textbooks and magazine extracts are available), a website and a legal service. Details are as follows:

CIPD House Tel: 020 8971 9000
Camp Road Fax: 020 8263 3333
London SW19 4UX e-mail: cipd@cipd.co.uk
Website: www.cipd.co.uk

ACAS (Advisory, Conciliation and Arbitration Service) helps organisations prevent and deal with dispute resolution. You can find your local office from the telephone directory or at www.acas.org.uk

The Equal Opportunities Commission, the expert body on equality between men and women, can be contacted at www.eoc.org.uk

Saville & Holdsworth UK is the most well-known ability testing organisation in this country. They are available at www.shlgroup.com

The two leading generalist HR journals currently in the UK are *People Management* (published by the Chartered Institute of Personnel and Development, www.peoplemanagement.co.uk) and *Personnel Today* (www.personneltoday.com).

Other specialist periodicals from a variety of organisations are also regularly available, from *Professional Recruiter* (published by Centurion) to *HR Director* (produced by Arthur Andersen). Some are included in the bibliography.

CONCLUSION

The chapter is developed for students, professionals, managers, researchers that already have prior knowledge and experience in the field of HR or other associated field, and positions such as being a line manager for a small or large team, or even running own small firm where the aspects of HRM are highly essential and vital for the development and growth of the firm. The chapter is providing identification, exploration and in depth discussion of key strategic aspects of HRM such as forecasting external supply, job analysis and workforce profiling, job descriptions and person specifications, competencies, job families (market groups), and redundancy.

Furthermore, the chapter is supported by key case studies and identification of current trends to enhance understanding of key changes and developments in the field. Also other associated activates are included across different sections of the chapter to enhance classroom discussions and reflection.

Based on the key discussions and reflection of current trends in various sections within this chapter, it evident that HRM is a key player in the process of organisational growth and development. Therefore, it is highly essential for firms and managers to recognise the critical role human resources management is playing at the strategic level to further ensure that business needs are met considering the rapidly changing external environment including but not limited to politics, regulations, technology, social, and economic.

REFERENCES

Armstrong, M. (2003). *A Handbook of Human Resource Management Practice.* Kogan Page.

Armstrong, M. (2012). Armstrong's Handbook of Human Resource Management Practice (12th ed.). London: Kogan Page.

Hailemariam, D. A., Shan, X., Chung, S. H., Khasawneh, M. T., Lukesh, W., Park, A., & Rose, A. (2019). Developing an appropriate staff mix for anticoagulation clinics: Functional job analysis approach. *Journal of Industrial Engineering International*, *15*(1), 103–118. doi:10.100740092-018-0267-5

Legere, C. L. J. (1985). *Occupational analysis* (R. Tracey, Ed.). Human Resources Management and Development Handbook.

Mira, M., Choong, Y., & Thim, C. (2019). The effect of HRM practices and employees' job satisfaction on employee performance. *Management Science Letters, 9*(6), 771-786. Available at: https://doaj.org/article/ee4a5ad9589b45369f21e4bdb99ed91c

Schneider, B., & Konz, A. (1989). Strategic job analysis. *Human Resource Management, 28*(1), 51–63. doi:10.1002/hrm.3930280104

Taylor, S. (2002). *People resourcing* (2nd ed.). London: Kogan Page.

Taylor, S. (2019). *Resourcing and Talent Management* (7th ed.). London: Kogan Page.

ADDITIONAL READING

Bramham, J. (1994). *Human resource planning*. London: Institute of Personnel and Development.

Bratton and Gold — Human Resource Management. (2003). *Theory and Practice*. Palgrave MacMillan.

Carbery, R., & Cross, C. (2019). *Human Resource Management* (2nd ed.). London: Red Globe Press. doi:10.1057/978-1-352-00403-8

Kessler, I., Heron, P., & Spilsbury, K. (2017). 'Human resource management innovation in health care: The institutionalisation of new support roles'. *Human Resource Management Journal, 27*(2), 228–245. doi:10.1111/1748-8583.12114

Leap, T., & Crino, M. (1993). *Personnel/human resource management*. New York: Macmillan.

Mullins, L. (2001). *Management and Organisational Behaviour*. Prentice Hall.

Pierson, P. (2004). *Politics in Time: History, Institutions and Social Analysis*. Princeton, NJ: Princeton University Press. doi:10.1515/9781400841080

Rothwell, S. (1995). Human Resource Planning. In J. Storey (Ed.), *Human Resource Management: a critical text*. London: Routledge.

Searle, R. (2003). *Selection and Recruitment: A Critical Text*. Palgrave McMillan.

Ulferts, G., Wirtz, P., & Peterson, E. (2009). Strategic Human Resource Planning In Academia. *American Journal of Business Education, 2*(7), 1. doi:10.19030/ajbe.v2i7.4123

Wood, R., & Payne, T. (1998). *Competency-based Recruitment and Selection*. John Wiley & Sons Ltd.

This research was previously published in Trends and Issues in International Planning for Businesses; pages 17-41, copyright year 2020 by Business Science Reference (an imprint of IGI Global).

APPENDIX

Commentary on Activities

Activity 1

1. Research, as far as possible, the role of the department and the job
2. Prepare a list of questions and place them in a logical sequence
3. Choose an appropriate location for the interview – this should be quiet and free from distraction.
4. You may also wish to visit the person's actual place of work, particularly if, for example, they are using machinery. This will also give a good idea of the working environment.
5. Try to relax the interviewee, as they will often be anxious. The usual route is to engage them in small talk, offer them a tea or coffee and thank them for sparing their valuable time.
6. Inform them that you are only after facts, not opinions.
7. Clarify any general or vague answers with follow-up questions.
8. Ensure the information you are given and note down is not judgemental.
9. Ask *open-ended* questions which prompt people to describe their role.

Examples might be: ' *Tell me about…',*
    'Describe to me…',
    'Give me some examples of…'

10. Avoid *leading* questions, which might suggest what the answer should be.

Examples might be: *'Would you agree that…?'*
    'I'm sure that you must…?'
    'It must be difficult to…?'

11. Try to get specific examples of what the job holder actually does.
12. Let them describe the limits of their authority.
13. Tell them who else you'll be speaking to (supervisors and colleagues – this should help to counter any exaggerations).
14. Take full notes – ask the post holder to slow down if necessary, so that you get all the information you need. It is possible to use a tape recorder, but this can be off-putting to some people.
15. Clarify essential points with them by summarising what they have said.
16. Use closed questions when you only want short, factual answers.

Examples would be: *'How many…?'*
    'How often…?'
    'Who…?'
    'When…?'

17. When the interview is drawing to a close, ask them if there is anything they would like to add, or anything that has not been covered.
18. Explain to them what the next stage in the process will be.
19. Thank them for their time and help.
20. Check and write up your notes *as soon as possible*. Straight away is best – it's amazing how quickly the memory fades, or how notes which seem perfectly clear at the time later look like they've been written by a GP.
21. Write the job description.
22. Check the job description with the post holder and the relevant manager and get both to sign it off.

Activity 2

In most cases, redundancy occurs from a general reduction in business. However, it is perfectly possible for expanding businesses to make jobs redundant if certain *types* or work or skills are no longer required. Large organisations, following best practice and endeavouring to negate the bad publicity (both internal and external) which the dreaded 'R' word brings, will normally try to retain or redeploy the people affected.

Chapter 4
Impact of Psychological Contract on Employees' Performance:
A Review

Geeta Sachdeva

National Institute of Technology Kurukshetra, India

ABSTRACT

The performance of employees defines the competitive advantage of the company in current ferocious competition, and it affects the long-standing growth of the company. If a company inspires its workforce merely by the means of financial contract, then the company will not be in the position to gain the effective and efficient performances from its employees. Because apart from this financial contract, psychological contract also upsets attitudes and performance of the employees at the workplace. The spirit of the firms is the employees, and the implementation of the psychological contract can effectually decrease the turnover rate of employees and consequently increase their efficiency at the workplace. In the current chapter, first of all an attempt has been made to elucidate the concept and development process of psychological contract. After that it is endeavored to highlight the positive impact of psychological contract on employees' performances such as job satisfaction, organizational commitment, job performance, organization citizenship behavior, and turnover intentions.

INTRODUCTION

In the year 1960, there was a time when the word psychological contract was appeared for very first time. Since then investigators and researchers have been discovering this concept incessantly. (Kotter, J. P. 1973., Portwood, J. D., Miller, E. L 1976., & Nicholson, N.,& Johns, G. 1985). Argyris (1960) spoke about the concealed and informal unspoken settlement between the supervisor and workers. Levinson et al. (1962) demarcated psychological contract as an unrecorded contract that factually means a psycho-

DOI: 10.4018/978-1-6684-3873-2.ch004

logical contract between employer and employees without any formal letter contained anticipations. This was used to highlight internal and unseen anticipations, which headed the formation of the relationship.

Schein stated psychological contract as a set of unprinted anticipations amongst organization fellows, and he separated psychological contract into two stages: individuals and organizations. Further, Kotter posited that psychological contract was a concealed contract amongst organizations and persons including about what they were due, what they deserved. These type of philosophies represent that the psychological contract is a type of shared understanding amid employee and employers. The researchers who believed the opinion of two-way anticipations were named as Classical School; in the meantime, all the philosophies in harmony with two-way anticipations were termed comprehensive description of the psychological contract. Rousseau, an American scholar redefined the psychological contract as a type of trust about joint accountability between employees and employer. Further, Robinson stressed out that this type of trust is the promise, understanding and perception on interchange connection between employees' contribution such as hard-work, capability, faithfulness etc. and inducements offered by the employer such as reimbursement, advancement, job security, etc. (Robinson, Kraatz, & Rousseau, 1994). Morrison further recognized this notion. He stated that the psychological contract was generally demarcated as a set of confidences held by personnel about shared accountabilities. These confidences were grounded on making sense of promise, though the organization may not recognize them. Overall, two diverse descriptions of the psychological contract have been given. The comprehensive meaning is the understanding about mutual accountabilities in exchange relationship amongst employer and employees subjectively in harmony with the all types of promises whether written, verbal or under the rules of the company whereas the contracted meaning is a set of confidences that were created under the understanding of company policy, practice and culture or the reinforcement by agents' promises, sometimes the agents might not be conscious.

DEVELOPMENT OF THE PSYCHOLOGICAL CONTRACT

Generally, there are three phase under of psychological contract. The first phase is primarily the theoretic expansion of the notion (Kotter, 1973., Argyris, 1960 & Schein, 1965). These readings propose that workforces' and employers anticipations make the psychological contract. Next phase starts with the redefinition of the concept given by Rousseau's. Rousseau (1989) suggests the contract is merely a worker's anticipations (Rousseau, 1989).Guzzo et. Al., (1994) and Sugalski, (1995) stated the role of psychological contract in employment. As per Rousseau (2004), there are some features of the psychological contract such as volunteer choice, joint accountability on the part of both employees and employers.

The third phase stresses upon the results of psychological contract contentment. For instance, Turnley, (1999), inspected the effect of psychological contract towards the extraction, liberty of speech, faithfulness & neglect behaviors. In the current years, theoretical and experiential studies generally focus on one feature of the subsequent fields such as scrutinize the motives for the break of the psychological contract, investigate the connection amid break & breach of psychological contract & observe the penalties of its violation.

DIMENSIONS OF PSYCHOLOGICAL CONTRACT

MacNeil (1985) proposed two-dimensional structure and contract is separated into two groups such as transactional and relational. Transactional psychological contract is apprehensive about the structure of short-term economic issues whereas Relational psychological contract is employment covers both socio-emotional frankness structure.

Further Robinson, Kraatz, Rousseau (1994) revealed based on his study that there are two important factors such as transactional factor and relational factor. Transactional factor reveals the staff to perform intensely, doing job responsibilities outer the cost, in interchange for good recompense, inducements, learning and career development opportunities, grounded upon contractual relations. Relational factor states the personnel to work for long run, faithful and eager to consent the cost of inner work modification, in interchange for long-term job safety based on emotional exchange based associations. Personnel must take the accountability for their individual opinions and company accountabilities in this procedure.

PSYCHOLOGICAL CONTRACTS MODELS

Psychological contract can be more understood with the help of following models.

Venn Model

This model represents a multifaceted interpretation of the Psychological Contract, comprising outside stimuli, which are frequently overlooked while applying Psychological Contracts philosophy. This is useful in demonstrating all kinds of situations where two or more connected parts interrelate. The following model delivers an easy interpretation of the contents working in Psychological Contract.

Above Diagram represents "vc = visible contract – this is the normal transcribed service responsibilities for employees as well as employers to carry out duties securely and properly in exchange for a good salary, generally holidays also. pc = psychological contract – this is concealed, understood, unprinted, and takes account of the relationship references (r) amid employee and market that comprises other outside factors and also the employer's relationship with the market (also r), and the visible contract (vc)". In this diagram the writing parts is only the visible contract (vc) which is translucent and rest aspects are subject to perceptions until or unless they are being elucidated.

Figure 1. Psychological contract model

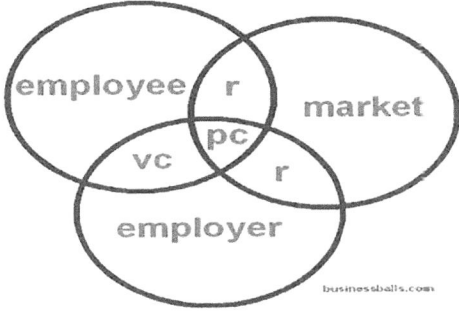

Iceberg Model

Iceberg model is a valuable to exemplify the vital phases and stimuluses inside Psychological Contracts theory. It is also useful for trainers and leaders for elucidating and discovering the concept and its individual sense for persons.

Ninety percent of the model is concealed underneath the water, which states that maximum observations of the contract are unrecorded and concealed. This representation matches the Psychological Contract very well. It is specially so for low-ranking employees in organizations, where shared anticipations usually have little discernibility & lucidity. Hence, in this case we might envisage ninety-five percent or may be ninety-nine percent of the iceberg model is submerged. The Psychological Contract is probable to be more understood & noticeable with profounder inputs and rewards in case of the connection amid the rational employer and its employees, particularly proficient and fruitful workforce. Hence, in this case sixty percent or even seventy percent of the model is submerged. The above discussed percentage are not scientific it just elucidate the manner the model performs. Model spreads expediently so that the 'sky' and the 'sea' embody outside and marketplace forces acting on employee and employer, affecting the balance, and the upsurge or collapse of the iceberg. With the upliftment of the achievement, maturity and knowledge of the employees there will be rise in the iceberg. Gradually higher contributions & recompenses arise from being unseen or muddled perceptions below from the water line, to become noticeable mutual contractual agreement above the water line. This procedure could also function in contrary, though in a healthy situation both parties i.e. employees and employers wish the iceberg to upsurge.

Figure 2. Psychological contracts 'iceberg' model

© Businessballs.com 2010

Left hand of the above figure describes employees' inputs. Employees' inputs are the anticipations and expectations of the employers form their employees. These expectations can be noticeable & contractually settled, or presumed, supposed, inferred, etc., and unrecorded, or possible anticipations contingent on performance and opportunity that not essentially applicable to all employees and employers.

Right hand of the above figure states the different type of recompenses offered by the employers. Employers' rewards are the employees' anticipations that again can be noticeable & contractually settled, supposed or inferred etc. They would usually be unrecorded. These potential inputs not essentially appropriate to all workforces and organization.

"Work and Pay" lies above the water level that signifies the primary service contract i.e. the traditional contract means financial compensation for work. The traditional compensations is same as the "vc" section discussed in the above Venn diagram which is the noticeable service contract which is usually the written responsibilities for both employees and employers. Iceberg model represents the exchange between simple work & pay. However, in reality maximum of the employees are formally accountable for other types of inputs and are allowed for several welfares apart from the pay alone, therefore, in this respect the iceberg here signifies a very simple condition.

Black Arrows in the model signify market impacts at the workplace environment, particularly to the situation that is clear, noticeable, and recognized, etc. These stimuli usually contain particulars likewise market demand of persons who are highly competent to perform the task.

Red arrows signify the propensity of the model to increase along with the development in the job as well as the degree of the victory & maturity of the employer. In case of highly matured, knowledgeable & achievement oriented employees there would be a tendency to perceive their personal icebergs increasing and the concealed contractual factors would become noticeable. Employees usually desire the iceberg to be increased and employers wish to be associated with such type of employees. Employees want that the concealed unrecorded facets of the Psychological Contract that be underneath to be relevant, noticeable and formalized contract wise. An intensifying iceberg indicates increased involvement in the job by the employees towards the company that is usually compensated with progressively profounder recompenses & profits.

Underneath the water line - ninety percent of the iceberg, which is below the surface, contains the concealed insights that intensely affect clarification of the Psychological Contract, particularly held with the employees. These insights associate with the 'pc' part of the Venn model. The place where Psychological Contract is mainly concealed and jointly uncertain, then it can be imagined that the iceberg being more than ninety percent submerged. The place where the Contract is improved and stronger it can be imagined that only sixty-seventy percent of the iceberg is submerged.

The successive list of aspects represented below the water line on left and right side is not conclusive and carry same worth. It offers a direction to the concept, not a systematic list of correspondingly harmonized factors. It gives a wide clue of comparative importance of the aspects in both lists.

Blue arrows signify concealed factors effecting both parties i.e. employees & employers and particularly their views and outlooks towards each other. These perceptions might be noticeable & obviously recognized by one side and not to the other unless exposed & elucidated in a clear cut way. Numerous concealed stimuli are not well recognized by either side. Most of these factors vary erratically, but several are comparatively perpetual and can simply be explained. Some factors are concealed because they are problematic for anyone to realize or forecast. It is a matter of wonder for some employers and leaders that how all these concealed and subjective factors could probably be recognized. Actually, these factors cannot be in complete terms however, they could be made clearer if management attitude & approaches endeavor for good open optimistic teamwork between both the parties.

SIGNIFICANCE OF THE STUDY

Due to the quick fluctuations in the industries, it has become mandatory for the companies to modify, meet and acclimate to these variations that upsurges employees' stress at the workplace. Moreover, due to the quick change in the life styles has also altered the values of employees. Most of the employees desire the good change in their contracts and liberty to numerous additional choices. Due to this, there has been observed the reduction in employees' commitment level and job satisfaction towards the companies that can distract managers of companies. Therefore, it has become essential for the companies to keep healthy relationship with their human assets. Therefore, the psychological contract has become a main apprehension for researchers. Assimilating psychological contract and employee's engagement is a novel direction in knowledge worker management. Due to quick change in the market place and the resulting organizational change have intensely altered the service association between companies and workforces. It shakes the psychological contract between company and workforces. The declining faith and obligation amid company and employees, there is a decrease in the level of job satisfaction and consequently high employee turnover rate has extremely affected the performance of the organizations. Therefore, to retain an effective workforce in this cutthroat competition, organizations need an effective Human Resource management System (HRM). It contains dense contracts amid organization and its workforces, outside the contract which is in writing, stipulating their prospects, principles, abilities, and responsibilities amid employees and employers. Psychological contract deals with the examination of its key features and the identification of its phases of development. This contract are based upon the mental representation, which are based on employees' perception. This type of contract aid the employees and the organizations to avoid a complex employment relationship. Both parties viz. the employees and employers comprehend very obviously about the terms and conditions.

KEY OBJECTIVES OF THE CHAPTER

Over-all objective of the current chapter is to inspect the impact of psychological contract on employee outcomes. Specific objectives are recognized as:

1. To discuss the impact of psychological contract on job satisfaction
2. To discuss the impact of psychological contract on employee commitment
3. To Discuss the Impact of psychological contract on job Performance
4. To Discuss the Impact of psychological contract on Organizational Citizenship Behavior
5. To Discuss the Impact of psychological contract on Turnover Intentions.

LITERATURE REVIEW

Conceptualizing the Psychological Contract

After studying a lot of reviews and interview discussions the word psychological work contract was used to define the reciprocated respect amid employees and employers by the Argyris (1960). Employers reinforced their employees' informal norms, which they had experienced beforehand being elevated to their supervisors positions. Further, Levinson, et al. (1962) also used the word psychological contract to define the perceived association among employers and employees. Levinson et al., (1962) revealed that employees supposed a number of indirect and tacit anticipations from their employer. They demarcated psychological contracts as "a series of mutual expectations of which the parties to the relationship may not themselves be even dimly aware but which nonetheless govern their relationship to each other". Though owning alike characteristics, there were variances between Argyris' (1960) and Levinson et al.'s (1962) conceptualization of psychological contracts (Roehling, 1997). For instance, Argyris observed the contract as an employee group-level phenomenon (i.e., culture) whereas Levinson and colleagues observed that each worker had distinct beliefs concerning the psychological contract. Throughout the succeeding few periods, little consideration was given to the conceptualization of psychological contracts (for two exceptions see Kotter, 1973, and Schein, 1965).

The Effect of Psychological Contract on Employee Performance

Psychological Contract has very positive outcomes towards workplace attitudes, which increase the employee's performance.

Psychological Contract and Job Satisfaction

Oshagbemi, (2003) stated that job satisfaction is an imperative trait that firms wish from their employees. Inner and outer stirring aspects such as influence the amount of job satisfaction: supervision, relationships within group and the amount to which persons prosper or fail at their workplace (Armstrong, 2001). Individuals are encouraged to realize their objectives and would be pleased if they realize these aims. "Job satisfaction refers to the attitude and feelings people have about their work. Positive and favorable attitudes towards the job indicate job satisfaction and negative and unfavorable attitudes towards the job indicate job dissatisfaction" (Armstrong, 2006),

Job satisfaction reveals instant emotional responses to the job and its aspects and these feelings and perceptions are formed after employee join the organization. It grows gradually with the understanding of the job and its aspects, company's objectives and performance anticipations and their significances. The kind of understanding, behind job satisfaction is not instant; it needs introduction to a diversity of company constituent's external of the job itself.

Hoppock (1935, as cited in Jam & Fathima, 2006)) stated, "There is a strong relationship between worker's emotional adjustment (psychological contract) and levels of job satisfaction. Furthermore violation of the transactional obligations such as pay, benefits and promotions of the psychological contract result in decrease in job satisfaction (Anderson & Schalk, 1998)".

Due to the resemblance between the outcomes of job dissatisfaction, and violation of psychological contract, researches furthermore recommended that satisfaction partly arbitrates the association amid violation and commitment (Turnley and Feldman, 2000). Psychological contracts are better understood in case of its violation (Rousseau, 1989). And consequently, it becomes one of the strongest reason for researcher to further investigate psychological contract' breach and violation. As it can meaningfully shake employees' behavior, their approach, level of job satisfaction and obligation towards the company. Theory of Psychological Contract proposes that workforces with family accountabilities might negotiate psychological contracts which contain family- receptive welfares likewise flexible working times. (Rousseau, 1995).

Rousseau & Schalk, (2000) established that employees did not leave the organization especially to the competitor in case when companies provided them safety of the jobs and career development opportunities. Workforces were dutiful and well organized while performing the duties performed well at their respective tasks. In reoccurrence, workforces anticipated the recompense of constancy through continuance of the employment relations, safety of jobs regardless of financial benefits, stability of the career by company and certain recompenses.

Psychological contract can be developed when one's job fulfill one's expectancies and they are being valued and recognized by their employers (Worrell, 2004). With responses to overhead problems, companies were capable to recognize diverse type of contracts & wanted employees'- employers' assistance for optimistic psychological contract.

On the other side job, dissatisfaction can happen amongst employees if there is a violation of psychological contract. In case of any type of inconsistency between the employees and employers promises towards each other leads towards to the retort might result into job dissatisfaction leading towards upsurge in absence and turnover (Morrison and Robinson, 1997 & Griffeth, et al. 2000). If displeased personnel continue in the company, then poor performance, critical buzzes, stealing and disruption of apparatus, nonattendance and turnover can happen by the counterproductive performances of the employees. These unhealthy behaviors end in economic costs to the company in terms of lost output and replacement costs. Spector (1997 stated that strain, nervousness, difficulty in sleeping, weariness, despair and stiffness in muscles and joints can be found in discontented employees. These signifies a very noteworthy price to the psychological and physical wellbeing of the workforces, unplanned economic cost to the company.

Psychological Contract and Organizational Commitment

Strong connections have been found between psychological contract and organizational commitment, since job contract fix the employees and employers to certain accountabilities towards each other. Psychological contract starts to be formed even before joining the organization, through pre-existing anticipations regarding the enterprise. Slowly, these pre-existing anticipations would take the form of supposed responsibilities that constitute the psychological contract. According to Mowday et al. (1979) "Organizational commitment is the expressive attachment towards the organization". It can be measured by the means of absence, employee turnover, illness and absence (Ismail et al. 2011., Khandelwal, 2009 and Meyer and Herscovitch, 2001).It reveals the worker's emotion of intentional contribution in company actions with the increasing unilateral investment in company and the replicates the faith of workforces to joint accountability and commitment amid employees and company. However, there is dissimilarity amid organizational commitment and psychological contract. The concept of organizational commitment is one -way that simply reveals the personnel's' sentiment towards the company however psychological contract includes two- way connection that reveals employees' certainty towards accountabilities and the company assuming accountabilities too. In this procedure, employees would compare and alter the degree of both sides gratifying the contract, in order to get the stable state eventually (Cassar, 2011). Rousseau, (1995) has highlighted that organizational commitment is really the outcome of psychological contract. Employees have different commitment levels that depends on their Singular understanding, assessment of accountabilities of both parties. Psychological contract replicates the employee's subjective belief of the accountability & responsibility among employees and employers. Psychological contract expectations have a significant impact on knowledge workers. With the correct anticipation, the substantial assurance is to offer great level of recompense, compensation for performance, elevation & development. These assurances form organization's side have a great influence on employees decision about whether they would continue in the company and affect their emotional dependence and engrossment in organizations. The relational sustenance and inner development anticipation has connection with long-term work assurance, career development, good interactive environment and social expressive interactions. These facets would affect employees to love for their respective organization, consequently affects whether they stay or not in the organization. Negative but significant relationship between transactional contract and organizational commitment and positive relationship between relational contract with organizational commitment has been observed by Luo and Yu (2013).

Agarwal (2011) investigated the relationship amid psychological contract & organizational commitment. Results exposed that Psychological contract of employees was positively and meaningfully correlated to their organizational commitment. Behery, Paton and Hussain (2012) discovered the significant impact of relational contract on organizational commitment while transactional contract has not any significant relationship with organizational commitment. Furthermore, McDermott, et al., (2013) there is a connection among psychological contracts, organizational commitment & other employment characteristics, outcomes of this result directs that level of perceived obligation in psychological contract impacts contrarily on three sub-dimensions of organizational commitment. Finally, Jabeen et al., (2015) established that both relational and transactional psychological contract is positively & meaningfully connected to transactional leadership and organizational commitment with a decision that rational psychological contract encourages greater amount of organizational commitment.

According to Robinson & Morrison (2000), the break of the psychological contract happens when a staff member observes that the responsibilities that he considers to happen between the both parties have not been achieved. It is an emotive experience of dissatisfaction, obstruction, annoyance & bitterness that may originate from the method the employee understands & perceives about the psychological contract breaches & their conditions.

Cassar & Briner, (2011) and Lapointe, et al (2013) stated that there exists a reverse connection amid breaks in psychological contract and organizational commitment. Shahnawaz & Goswami, 2011; Simosi, (2013) also examined the influence of break of psychological contract and organizational commitment. The main crux of the studies states that with the breach in the psychological contract there is decrease in the organizational commitment of the employees. On the other side, as per Parzefall, (2008) there exists a positive & noteworthy relationship between psychological contract and organizational commitment. Castaing (2006) established a noteworthy association amid psychological contract variables and affective organizational commitment (AOC). AOC is linked to the various organizational results such as organizational citizenship behavior (OCB) and job performance in earlier readings (Meyer et al., 2002).

Figure 3.
Source: Rousseau et al (1998); Agarwal (2014); Rosen et al (2009); Sels, Jansenns and Brande (2004).

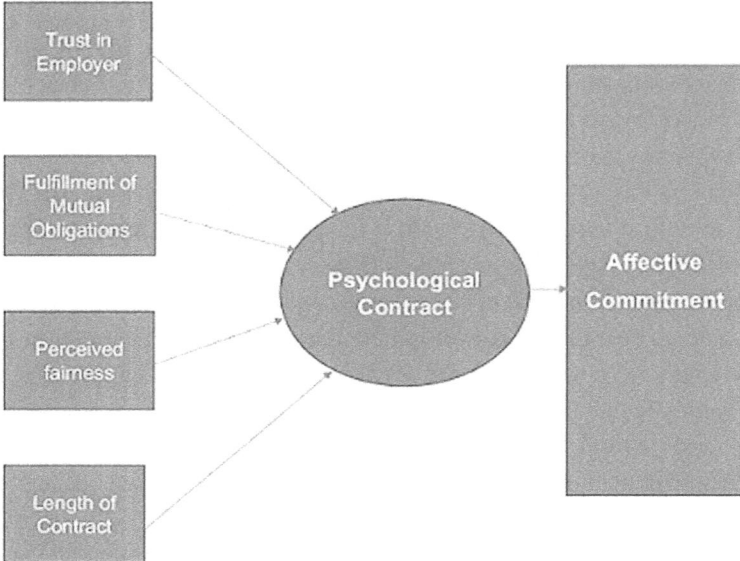

Psychological Contract and Job Performance

Organization performance is dependent upon the performances of the employees' performance carried out in their respective jobs, which further affects existence, & expansion of the organization. In this competitive world, organizations have their own targets, on the other side employees also have their own goals to achieve, and the performance of organization as well as employees jointly decide the company's overall performance. The objectives to be attained by the organization are divided to individually functional department after that functional department divides the tasks to every member of the unit, consequently employees' accomplishment of performance aids the organization to attain company's goal. Some researchers have separated job performance into task performance & environmental performance. As per Wanghui, Li Xiaoxuan, Luo Shengqiang, (2003) there are two parts of job performance such as task performance and contextual performance. As per Muxin, (2014) psychological contract positively and significantly affects the job performance. Greater the level of the psychological contract is, greater will be the job performance. The relationship between psychological contract & job performance differs from dissimilar groups. According to Zhao Sili., (2014) psychological contract has an important positive effect on task performance & innovation performance, but its effect on circumstantial performance is not noteworthy.

Psychological Contract and Organizational Citizenship Behavior

OCB mentions employee's wish to work in a particular organization. It is defined as the workers' behavior & the workers' own option to work outside the anticipations of an enterprise (Organ, 1997; Shahin, et al. 2014 and Williams & Anderson, 1991). It is one of the employee behaviors, that is, individual wish to perform & act out of the job description provided to employees to efficiently attain the company objectives (Organ, 1997). OCB is generally mentioned to perform extra ordinary (Van Dyne et al. 1994), pro-social behavior (O'Reilly & Chatman, 1986), spontaneity (George & Jones, 1997) & circumstantial employee performance (Borman & Motowidlo, 1997).As per Beardwell, et al. (2004); Karagonlar et al., (2016); Low et al., (2016) and Sparrow and Cooper, (1998) Psychological contract generates firmness in the working environs & increase the connection among the enterprise & the workforces. Robinson & colleagues (Robinson, 1996., Robinson and Morrison, 1995) stated that many in-role and extra-role performances of the employees have been associated with the psychological contract and its fulfilment. These performances are such as faith, gratification and intention to continue with the firm.

If company maintains somewhat relaxed and open ended relationship as opposite confined relationship with employees then employees will be predictable to perform extra-ordinary performance (Organ 1990., Rousseau 1995). In this response, employers will can reciprocate as they are there at the employees' discretion and in total incline to upsurge the firm's efficacy and success (Rioux and Penner, 2001). Truly, citizenship behavior contributed by employees in their respective organizations can be vital to the efficient functioning of the firm (Organ, 1998., Podsakoff, Ahearne and Mckenzie, 1997). Robinsson and Morrison (1995) established a strong relationship amid psychological contract fulfilment & the civic virtue form of OCB, while, a negative influence has been observed between the psychological contract and OCB, when there is a breach in the contract (Turnley and Feldman, 1999). However, accomplishment or breach of contract might be significant precursors to workforces' performances. When employees consider that their employer is extremely indulged to deliver a comprehensive variety of obligations, they might be more motivated to involve in a broader variety of citizenship behavior that are beneficial for the organizations. Conversely, when employees consider that their organization is only interested to offer economic exchange then they might not consider to perform extraordinary for their respective organizations. According to Hui, et. al., (2004) relational contract greatly narrates to the citizenship behaviors and the transactional contracts affects the OCB only if mediated by contributory views. As per Kiazad et al., (2014b) and Panaccio et al. (2015) employees will exhibit long-term relationships with the company and exhibit extra performance if they consider that company is capable to ease their anticipations. Psychological contract affects an organization Citizenship Behavior (Chen and Kao 2012); Priesemuth and Taylor 2016). Moreover, Coyle-Shapiro and Kessler (2000) also elucidated that OCB is affected by the relational contracts.

Psychological Contract and Turnover Intentions

Due to increase in the knowledge economy, it has become imperative for the organizations to gain competitive advantage in the form of having best talented people at all levels in the organization (Halawi, et al. 2005). Though, it has become painful situation for those companies which have the lack of talented people. Increased employee turnover do not include only financial losses but also decreases the image of the company, lower down the morale of organizational members. Therefore, it is not favorable to constant and vigorous growth of the organization.

There are some researchers who suppose that psychological contract has a straight influence on the turnover intentions (Turnley & Feldman, 1999), but these researchers had diverse opinions regarding the indirect impact of psychological contract on the turnover intentions of workforces in their respective organizations.

As per Rousseau, there are two parts of psychological contract named transactional contract and relational contract as discussed above. Transactional contract deals with the economic welfares, which include performance, based compensation, high returns, career development opportunities but on the other side relational contract deals with the mutual emotional exchange (Turnley & Feldman, 2000).

In case, there is a breach in the either part of the psychological contract that might lead towards the damage of financial assets & the emotional possessions of an enterprise. If a worker undergoes abundant damage of financial resources and emotional resource due to the break of psychological contract then employees will have the intent behavior to leave the company.

According to Turnley and Feldman (2000), there exists a strong relation amid violation of psychological contract & the worker's intentions to leave the organization. Moreover, Wei Feng (2004) also stated that the psychological contract violation straight impacts the exit of employees form their respective organization. It reflects that there exists a negative relationship between psychological contract and turnover intentions of the personnel at the workplace.

SUMMARY

Psychological contract is a personnel faith in joint responsibilities with their respective organizations. Now a days this contract is the key apprehension for managers, as it could affect workforces' approaches and their behaviors in a manner that effect firms' efficacy and success. In this chapter, author analyzed the association amid the psychological contract and different workplace approaches likewise job satisfaction, job performance, Organizational commitment, organizational Citizenship behavior and Turnover Intentions. Employees' expectations are changing day by day. They are not attracted merely by the traditional allurements i.e. economic employment contract. They have certain expectations from their employers and vice versa. So in this case, adopting psychological contract in organizations can do wonder. Most of the studies discussed in this chapter focuses that psychological contract improves the satisfaction, performance, commitment and organizational citizenship behavior of employees and reduces the turnover rate of the employees in their respective organizations. Therefore, it can be inferred employees' performance and their attitudes towards their work can be improved by adopting psychological contract along with the traditional economic allurements, which is generally the mutual but unwritten expectations from each other.

REFERENCES

Agarwal, P. (2011). Relationship between psychological contract & organizational commitment in Indian IT industry. *Indian Journal of Industrial Relations*, *47*(2), 290–305.

Anderson, N., & Schalk, R. (1998). The psychological contract in retrospect and prospect. *Journal of Organizational Behavior*, *19*(S1), 637–647. doi:10.1002/(SICI)1099-1379(1998)19:1+<637::AID-JOB986>3.0.CO;2-H

Argyris, C. (1960). *Understanding organizational behaviour*. London: Tavistock Publications.

Armstrong, M. (2001). *A handbook of human resource management practices*. London: Kogan Page.

Armstrong, M. (2006). A handbook of human resource management practices (10th ed.). London: Kogan Page Publishing.

Beardwell, I., Holden, L., & Claydon, T. (2004). *Human resource management, a contemporary approach* (4th ed.). Harlow: Financial Times Prentice Hall.

Beherym, Paton, R.A., & Hussain, R. (2012). Psychological contract and organizational Commitment: The mediating effect of transformational leadership. *International Business Journal, 22*(4), 299–319.

Borman, W. C., & Motowidlo, S. J. (1997). Task performance and contextual performance: The meaning for personnel selection research. *Human Performance, 10*(2), 99–109. doi:10.120715327043hup1002_3

Cassar, V., & Briner, R. B. (2011). The Relationship between Psychological Contract Breach and Organizational Commitment: Exchange Imbalance as a Moderator of the Mediating Role of Violation. *Journal of Vocational Behavior, 78*(2), 283–289. doi:10.1016/j.jvb.2010.09.007

Chen, C. H. V., & Kao, R. H. (2012). Work values and service-oriented organizational citizenship behaviors: The mediation of psychological contract and professional commitment: A case of students in Taiwan Police College. *Social Indicators Research, 107*(1), 149–169. doi:10.100711205-011-9832-7

Chen, S. H., Yang, C. C., Shiau, J. Y., & Wang, H. H. (2006). The development of an employee satisfaction model for higher education. *The TQM Magazine, 18*(5), 484–500. doi:10.1108/09544780610685467

Coyle-Shapiro, J., & Kessler, I. (2000). Consequences of the psychological contract for the employment relationship: A large scale survey. *Journal of Management Studies, 37*(7), 903–930. doi:10.1111/1467-6486.00210

George, J. M., & Jones, G. R. (1997). Organizational spontaneity in context. *Human Performance, 10*(2), 153–170. doi:10.120715327043hup1002_6

Griffeth, R. W., Hom, P. W., & Gaerther, S. (2000). A meta analysis of antecedents, and correlation of employee turnover; update, moderator tests, and research implications for the next millennium. *Journal of Management, 26*(3), 463–448. doi:10.1177/014920630002600305

Guzzo, R. A., Noonan, K. A., & Elron, E. (1994). Expatriate managers and the Psychological contract. *The Journal of Applied Psychology, 79*(4), 617–626. doi:10.1037/0021-9010.79.4.617

Halawi, L., Aronson, J., & McCarthy, R. (2005). Resource-Based View of Knowledge Management for Competitive Advantage. *Electronic Journal of Knowledge Management, 2*, 75–86.

Hui, C., Lee, C., & Rousseau, D. M. (2004). Psychological contract and organizational citizenship behavior in China: Investigating generalizability and instrumentality. *The Journal of Applied Psychology, 89*(2), 311–321. doi:10.1037/0021-9010.89.2.311 PMID:15065977

Ismail, A., Mohamed, H. A., Sulaiman, A. Z., Mohamad, M. H., & Yusuf, M. H. (2011). An empirical study of the relationship between transformational leadership, empowerment and organizational commitment. *Business and Economics Research Journal, 2*(1), 89–107.

Jabeen, F., Beherym, & Elanain, H.A. (2015). Examining the relationship between the psychological contract and organizational commitment: The mediating effect of transactional leadership in the UAE context. *The International Journal of Organizational Analysis, 23*(1), 102–122. doi:10.1108/IJOA-10-2014-0812

Jam, F. A., Haq, I. U., & Fatima, T. (2006). Psychological contract and job outcome: Mediating role of affective commitment. *Journal of Management, 4*(2), 13–25.

Karagonlar, G., Eisenberger, R., & Aselage, J. (2016). Reciprocation wary employees discount psychological contract fulfillment. *Journal of Organizational Behavior, 37*(1), 23–40. doi:10.1002/job.2016

Khandelwal, K. A. (2009). Organizational commitment in multinationals: A dynamic interplay among personal, organizational and societal factors. *ASBM Journal of Management, 2*(1), 99–122.

Kiazad, K., Seibert, S. E., & Kraimer, M. L. (2014b). Psychological contract breach and employee innovation: A conservation of resources perspective. *Journal of Occupational and Organizational Psychology, 87*(3), 535–556. doi:10.1111/joop.12062

Kissler, G. D. (1994). The New employment contract. *Human Resource Management, 33*(3), 335–352. doi:10.1002/hrm.3930330304

Kotter, J. P. (1973). T psychological contracts: Managing the joining-up process. *California Management Review, 15*(3), 91–99. doi:10.2307/41164442

Lapointe, E., Vandenberghe, C., & Boudrias, J. S. (2013). Psychological contract breach, affective commitment to organization and supervisor, and newcomer adjustment: A three-wave moderated mediation model. *Journal of Vocational Behavior, 83*(3), 528–538. doi:10.1016/j.jvb.2013.07.008

Levinson. (1962). Organization Diagnosis. Harvard University Press.

Low, C. H., Bordia, P., & Bordia, S. (2016). What do employees want and why? An exploration of employees' preferred psychological contract elements across career stages. *Human Relations, 69*(7), 1457–1481. doi:10.1177/0018726715616468

Luo, J., & Yu, M. F. (2013). A Study of Knowledge Staffs' Loyalty Based on the Psychological Contract. *Journal of Xi'an Shiyou University, 1*, 50–54.

Macneil, I. R. (1985). Relational contract: What we do and do not know. *Wisconsin Law Review, 3*, 483–525.

McDermott, A. M., Heffernan, M., & Beynon, M. J. (2013). When the nature of employment matters in the employment relationship: A cluster analysis of psychological contracts and organizational commitment in the non-profit sector. *International Journal of Human Resource Management, 24*(7), 1490–1518. doi:10.1080/09585192.2012.723635

Meyer, J. P., Stanley, D. J., Herscovitch, L., & Topolnytsky, L. (2002). Affective, continuance, and normative commitment to the organization: A meta-analysis of antecedents, correlates, and consequences. *Journal of Vocational Behavior, 61*(1), 20–52. doi:10.1006/jvbe.2001.1842

Meyer, P. J., & Herscovitch, L. (2001). Commitment in the workplace: Toward a general model. *Human Resource Management Review*, *11*(3), 299–326. doi:10.1016/S1053-4822(00)00053-X

Morrison, E. W., & Robinson, S. L. (1997). When Employees Feel Betrayed: A Model Of How Psychological Contract Violation Develops. *Academy of Management Review*, *22*(1), 226–256. doi:10.5465/amr.1997.9707180265

Mowday, R. T., Steers, R. M., & Porter, L. W. (1979). The measurement of organizational commitment. *Journal of Vocational Behavior*, *14*(2), 224–247. doi:10.1016/0001-8791(79)90072-1

Muxin. (2014). Influences on job performance of psychology contract of new-era knowledge workers: regulating effect of organizational socialization. Industrial and Commercial University of Chongqing.

Nicholson, N., & Johns, G. (1985). The Absence Culture and Psychological Contract-Who's in Control of Absence? *Academy of Management Review*, *10*(3), 397–407.

O'Reilly, C. A., & Chatman, J. (1986). Organizational commitment and psychological attachment: The effects of compliance, identification, and internalization on prosocial behavior. *The Journal of Applied Psychology*, *71*(3), 492–499. doi:10.1037/0021-9010.71.3.492

Organ, D. W. (1990). The motivational bases of Organizational Citizenship Behavior. Research in Organizational Behavior, 12, 43-72.

Organ, D. W. (1997). Organizational citizenship behavior: It's construct clean-up time. *Human Performance*, *10*(2), 85–97. doi:10.120715327043hup1002_2

Organ, D. W. (1998). *Organizational Citizenship Behavior: The Goal Soldier Syndrome*. Lexington, MA: Health.

Oshagbemi, T. (2003). Personal correlates of job satisfaction: Empirical evidence from UK Universities. *International Journal of Social Economics*, *30*(12), 32–1210. doi:10.1108/03068290310500634

Parzefall, M. R. (2008). Psychological contracts and reciprocity: A study in a Finnish context. *International Journal of Human Resource Management*, *19*(9), 1703–1719. doi:10.1080/09585190802295272

Podaskoff, P. M., Ahearne, M., & Mackenzie, S. B. (1997). Organizational Citizenship Behavior and the quantity and quality of work group performance. *The Journal of Applied Psychology*, *82*(2), 262–270. doi:10.1037/0021-9010.82.2.262 PMID:9109284

Portwood, J. D., & Miller, E. L. (1976). Evaluating the Psychological Contract: Its Implications for Employee Job Satisfaction and Work Behavior. Academy of Management Proceedings, 109-113.

Priesemuth, M., & Taylor, R. M. (2016). The more I want, the less I have left to give: The moderating role of psychological entitlement on the relationship between psychological contract violation, depressive mood states, and citizenship behavior. *Journal of Organizational Behavior*, *37*(7), 967–982. doi:10.1002/job.2080

Rioux, S. M., & Penner, L. A. (2001). The causes of Organizational Citizenship Behavior: A Motivational Analysis. *The Journal of Applied Psychology*, *86*(6), 1306–1314. doi:10.1037/0021-9010.86.6.1306 PMID:11768072

Robinson, S. L. (1996). Trust and Breach of the Psychological Contract. *Administrative Science Quarterly, 41*(4), 574–599. doi:10.2307/2393868

Robinson, S. L., & Morrison, A. E. W. (2000). The development of psychological contract breach and violation: A longitudinal study. *Journal of Organizational Behavior, 21*(5), 525–546. doi:10.1002/1099-1379(200008)21:5<525::AID-JOB40>3.0.CO;2-T

Robinson, S. L., & Morrison, E. W. (1995). Psychological Contracts and OCB: The effect of unfulfilled obligations on civic virtue behavior. *Journal of Organizational Behavior, 16*(3), 289–298. doi:10.1002/job.4030160309

Robinson, S. L., & Rousseau, D. M. (1994). Violating the psychological contract: Not the exception but the norm. *Journal of Organizational Behavior, 15*(3), 245–259. doi:10.1002/job.4030150306

Roehling, M. V. (1997). The origins and early development of the psychological contract. *Journal of Management History, 3*(2), 204–217. doi:10.1108/13552529710171993

Rosen, C. C., Chang, C., Johnson, E., & Levy, P. E. (2009). Perceptions of the organizational context and psychological contract breach: Assessing competing perspectives. *Organizational Behavior and Human Decision Processes, 108*(2), 202–217. doi:10.1016/j.obhdp.2008.07.003

Rousseau, D. M. (1989). Psychological and implied contracts in organizations. *Employee Responsibilities and Rights Journal, 2*(2), 121–139. doi:10.1007/BF01384942

Rousseau, D. M. (1995). *Psychological contract in Organizations: Understanding Written and Unwritten Agreements*. Newbury Park, CA: Sage Publications.

Rousseau, D. M. (2004). Psychological contract in the work place: Understanding Ties That Motivate. *Academy of Management Executive Journal, 18*(1), 122–127.

Rousseau, D. M., & Schalk, R. (2000). *Psychological contracts in employment: Cross-National Perspectives*. London: Sage Publications.

Schein, E. H. (1965). *Organizational Psychology*. Englewood Cliffs, NJ: Prentice- Hall.

Sels, L., Janssens, M., & Van Den Brande, I. (2004). Assessing the nature of psychological contract: A validation of six dimensions. *Journal of Organizational Behavior, 25*(4), 461–488. doi:10.1002/job.250

Shahin, A., Shabani Naftchali, J., & Khazaei Pool, J. (2014). Developing a model for the influence of perceived organizational climate on organizational citizenship behavior and organizational performance based on balanced score card. *International Journal of Productivity and Performance Management, 63*(3), 290–307. doi:10.1108/IJPPM-03-2013-0044

Shahnawaz, M. G., & Goswami, K. (2011). Effect of psychological contract violation on organizational commitment, trust and turnover intention in private and public sector Indian organizations. Vision. *The Journal of Business Perspective, 15*(3), 209–217. doi:10.1177/097226291101500301

Simosi, M. (2013). Trajectories of organizational commitment: A qualitative study in a Greek public sector organization. *International Journal of Cross Cultural Management, 13*(1), 111–130. doi:10.1177/1470595812452637

Smith, C. A., Organ, D. W., & Near, J. P. (1983). Organizational citizenship behavior: Its nature and antecedents. *The Journal of Applied Psychology, 68*(4), 653–663. doi:10.1037/0021-9010.68.4.653

Sparrow, P., & Cooper, C. L. (1998). New organizational forms: The strategic relevance of future psychological contract scenarios. *Canadian Journal of Administrative Sciences, 15*(4), 356–371. doi:10.1111/j.1936-4490.1998.tb00177.x

Spector, P. E. (1997). *Job satisfaction application, assessment, causes and consequences.* London: Sage Publications. doi:10.4135/9781452231549

Sugalski, T. D., Manzo, L. S., & Meadows, J. (1995). Resource Link: Reestablishing the employment relationship in an era of downsizing. *Human Resource Management, 34*(3), 389–403. doi:10.1002/hrm.3930340304

Turnley, W. H., & Feldman, D. C. (1999). The impact of psychological contract Violations on exit, Voice, Loyalty, and neglect. *Human Relations, 52*(7), 895–922. doi:10.1177/001872679905200703

Turnley, W. H., & Feldman, D. C. (2000). Re-examining the effects of psychological 48 contract violations: Unmet expectations and job dissatisfaction as mediators. *Journal of Management, 21*, 25–41.

Van Dyne, L., Graham, J. W., & Dienesch, R. M. (1994). Organizational citizenship behavior: Construct redefinition, measurement, and validation. *Academy of Management Journal, 37*(4), 765–802.

Wanghui, L. X., & Luo, S. (2003). Validation of the two-factor model: Task performance and contextual performance. *Management Science in China, 11*, 79–84.

Wei, F. (2004). *A Study on the Breach of Organization-Manager Psychological Contract* (Doctoral Dissertation). Fudan University, Shanghai, China.

Williams, L. J., & Anderson, S. E. (1991). Job satisfaction and organizational commitment as predictors of organizational citizenship and in-role behaviors. *Journal of Management, 17*(3), 601–617. doi:10.1177/014920639101700305

Worrell, T. G. (2004). *School Psychologists' Job Satisfaction: Ten Years Later* (Unpublished doctoral dissertation). University of Polytechnic Virginia.

Zhao, S. (2014). *Empirical study in the influence of psychological contract on job performance of university counsellors.* Anhui University of Finance and Economics. Retrieved from https://www.businessballs.com/building-relationships/the-psychological-contract/

KEY TERMS AND DEFINITIONS

Job Performance: The work-related activities expected of an employee and how well those activities were executed.

Job Satisfaction: It refers to the attitude and feelings people have about their work.

Organizational Citizenship Behavior: It is defined as the workers' behavior & the workers' own option to work outside the anticipations of an enterprise.

Organizational Commitment: It is the expressive attachment towards the organization.

Psychological Contract: It is an unrecorded contract that factually means a psychological contract between employer and employees without any formal letter contained anticipations.

Relational Psychological Contract: It covers both socio-emotional frankness structure.

Transactional Psychological Contract: It is apprehensive about the structure of short-term economic issues.

Turnover Intentions: It is the process through which staff leave a business or organization and that business or organization replaces them.

Chapter 5
Emotional Labor in the Tourism Industry:
Strategies, Antecedents, and Outcomes

Rajat Gera

https://orcid.org/0000-0001-7558-1426
Manav Rachna International Institute of Research and Studies, India

Shilpa Arora

Manav Rachna International Institute of Research and Studies, India

Sahil Malik

Manav Rachna International Institute of Research and Studies, India

ABSTRACT

The chapter reviews the key concepts, definitions, individual and organizational antecedents, and individual and organizational outcomes of emotional labour (EL) in the tourism industry. The application of the concept in research and practice is discussed along with the implications. The theoretical domains of convergence and divergence are identified. key challenges and applications of EL with airlines cabin crew, restaurant service staff, and hotel industry frontline staff are identified and discussed. A systematic review of literature on EL in tourism is undertaken followed by critical appraisal of the implications of EL for HR practices in the tourism and hospitality industry.

INTRODUCTION

Hochschild's (1983) initially conceptualized emotional labor within the theatre metaphor wherein service is envisioned as a "show", service employee as the "actor", customer as the "audience" and the work place as the "stage, " in which the actor (employee) is expected to enact a role according to a script. Emotional labor is highly relevant to service's as they are difficult to evaluate, perishable (which makes it impossible to rectify any mistakes in the service which has been offered), and employee behavior and

DOI: 10.4018/978-1-6684-3873-2.ch005

attitude significantly impact customer emotions, cognitions and behaviors produced during the service encounters Zapf (2002).

Tourism is labor intensive service (Deery & Jago, 2009) with humans at the centre of exchange process (McKercher & Robbins, 1998). Therefore, emotional displays by employees potentially can determine the employee-customer relationship in the service delivery (Julian, 2008; Lee & Ok, 2015). The emotional labor of the service provider is therefore embedded in the tourism product (Olsen, 2002; Sharpe, 2005; Van Dijk & Kirk, 2007).

Employees in hospitality and Tourism Industry are expected to express cheerfulness, enthusiasm, friendliness as mandated and expected by the Organization even if they are experiencing negative emotions (Pizam, 2004; Wong and Wang, 2009). The service providers (employees) may embody the product being offered such as 'adventure', 'excitement', 'intrigue' or 'fantasy' when enacting their role irrespective of the routine nature of the work(Beardsworth & Bryman, 2011;).

The Tourism industry expects the employees to perform by offering emotional labor in addition to the physical and Intellectual labor (Chu & Murrmann, 2006; Sharpe, 2005; Zapf, 2002, Constanti & Gibbs, 2005; Guerrier & Adib, 2003). Employees in the Hospitality and tourism industry are in direct contact with customers of the employing organization and need to enact a role which requires them to perform emotional labor in their encounter with the customer/visitor (Anderson, Provis, & Chappel, 2003). The three types of workers who deliver tourism are Directors and stage managers, performers and intermediaries of cultural performances who embody the attributes of emotional labor and power. Thus for exp., workers who provide 'dancing' as part of hotel evening entertainment have a human capital requirement of 'dancing' but it also has elements of emotional labor as they are expected to have friendly and positive disposition even with irate, demanding or impatient customers .

The most studied jobs in Tourism have at least two of the characteristics specified by Hochschild (1983) for high EL jobs ie frequent interactions with the public (i.e., customers); the expectation of inducing emotions in others, and the management or control of these emotional interactions. From perspective of tourism industry, the jobs most researched are cabin crew, frontline staff of airlines, tour guides and restaurant waiters to some extent.

Tourism focused service providers (employees) provide emotional expressions to service receivers (visitors) to elicit the desired emotional response to the interaction (Sharpe, 2005). The employers manage the same by designing and providing scripts consisting of simple instructions to detailed processes to direct their employees physical and emotional movements. (Erickson and Wharton, 1997).

Hotel service work requires managers to manage their own emotions and those of the service employees (Young and Corsun, 2009) for organizational success. This requires emotion management between the service provider and service receiver in order to meet the desired service quality expectations (Lashley, Morrison, & Randall, 2005). These rules and norms are framed by the hospitality organizations to maximize customer satisfaction and service quality, Kim (2008).

Organizational norms or "feeling rules' are attempts to control the private thoughts or feelings and inner lives of employees. However, scholars later argued that the appropriate term is "display rules" as organizations can only regulate the observable behavior or emotional expressions and had no control over the unobservable inner states (Ashforth & Humphrey, 1993; Rafaeli & Sutton, 1989).

The customers (visitor's) reaction and perception to the experience is partially determined by the service providers adoption of appropriate emotional expressions (Grandey, Fisk, Mattila, Jansen, & Sideman, 2005). Thus service quality may be evaluated adversely if the customer (visitor) does not perceive the emotional expressions and facial and bodily cues as authentic (Ekman, Friesen, & O'Sullivan, 1988;

Grandey et al., 2005; Olsen, 2002). Though the service provider may display false emotions (surface acting) or genuine emotions (deep acting) to enact the experience being offered (e.g. adventure, excitement, fun) (Van Dijk & Kirk, 2008),the emotional expressions perceived as authentic would benefit the organization (Grandey, 2000; Grandey et al., 2005).

There is a debate as the appropriate theoretical framework of EL in Tourism Industry and service Industry in general is still lacking and there is no single framework adopted by the studies. The review of theories and definitions (Table 1.0) also indicates the existence of multiple definitions of EL being adopted in Tourism sector. There is lack of consensus on whether EL is acting, impression management or self regulation of feelings . There is also variance in conceptualization of EL of whether it's a cognitive, emotional or behavioral dominant concept. Though EL is construed as self management of emotions as per role expectation, it's also evaluated as a behavioral (Surface acting) and cognitive (Emotional Intelligence) concept .

Table 1. Theoretical models and definitions

Hothschild (1983)	Hochschild defined the organizationally desired expression of emotions by employees as acting. Surface Acting is when the the employee enacts certain emotions without feeling them ie she is regulating the emotions expressed by her, "just an actor, not sincere" (Hochschild1983). However, Deep Acting is when the employee generates authentic feelings for the role for which she is displaying emotions
Ashforth and Humphrey (1993)	Ashforth and Humphrey (1993) defined emotional labour as "act of displaying appropriate emotions" and observable behavior and they evaluated the affect of EL on task effectiveness as against employee health. According to them, whether Customers perceive the emotions expressed by employees as genuine.or not is important. Employees expressed emotions will become natural over period of time as they identify with the role being played routinely and the organization they are working for.
Morris and Feldman (1996)	Morris and Feldman (1996) defined Emotional Labour as "the effort, planning, and control needed to express organizationally desired emotions during interpersonal transactions" (Emotional Labour has four dimensions (a) interaction frequency (b) interaction Intensity and duration of emotions (c) Variety of emotions expected to be expressed and (d) Emotional Dissonance. (discrepancy between felt and displayed emotions) This model was supported by Hochschild, (1983), Brotheridge and Lee (1998), Grancley (2000) and Zapf et al. (1999)
Brotheridge and Lee (1998)	Brotheridge and Lee (1998)::Emotional Labour defined as "actions undertaken as a means of addressing role demands". According to them, Surface Acting is a indication of Emotional Dissonance
Gross's (1998)	Gross's (1998) model states that Emotion Regulation might occur when individuals regulate the precursors of emotions and modifies the physiological signs of emotions (antecedent focused) and when she modifies her physiological state to express the specific emotional response (response focused similar to surface acting) or suppresses her true emotions.
Grandey (2000)	Grandey (2000) defined emotion regulation as "the processes by which individuals influence which emotions they have, when they have them, and how they experience and express these emotions" The two aspects of antecedent focused regulation are attentional deployment (when person thinks about events that elicit the required emotions) and cognitive change (when person reappraises her personal thoughts about the external situation similar to deep acting). Emotional Labour is influenced by situational variables of interaction expectations (Frequency, Variety, Duration, And Display rules) and positive and negative emotional events. Organizational factors like job autonomy and co worker/supervisor support also influence the way EL is performed. Individual well-being which is likely to affect job satisfaction, and burnout, and organizational well-being and its effect on performance and withdrawal behavior are the long term consequences of EL.
Zapf (2002)	Zapf (2002) used the term Emotional Work as "the psychological processes necessary to regulate organizationally desired emotions." Zapf (2002), argued that EL is the psychological part of work process, and therefore the cognitive processes are linked to work environment and behavior through psychological regulation

Emotional labor strategies: According to Hochschild(1983), EL strategies are of two types: surface acting and deep acting . Surface Acting is enactment of emotions without genuinely feeling them or trying to feel them by regulating the expressed emotionsand sees herself as "just an actor, not sincere" (HochschIld, 1983). However, Deep Acting is when the individual genuinely feels the emotions and consciously tries to feel the emotions being expressed for the role being performed. Later, a third strategy was proposed ie Genuine acting wherein expressed emotions are congruent with the emotions being felt by the employee(Chu, Baker, & Murrmann, 2012).

The individual can regulate emotions at two points, by modifying the situation(antecedent focused regulation) prior to the encounter and by modifying their physiological reactions to the situation (response focused regulation) during the encounter (Gross,1998)

LV et al (2012) categorized emotional labor strategies into five types as surface acting, deep acting (active deep acting or positive consonance), deliberative dissonance acting, negative consonance and automatic emotional regulation (passive deep acting)

Emotional Suppression involves inhibiting ones emotion-expressive behavior (Gross and John, 2003) like displaying a poker face during a card game. Emotional suppression and denial are linked with lower levels of immunity and susceptibility to viral infection and cardio vascular disease (Schaubroeck and Jones, 2000) and result in reduced memory for social information (Sieverding, 2009) and other physiological, social, affective, and cognitive consequences.

Emotional consonance is when individual naturally expresses his/her genuine felt emotions (Yugo, 2009; Zammuner & Galli, 2005b). It is similar to deep acting as the felt emotions are congruent with the expressed emotions.

Emotional labor strategies have also been differentiated based on the extent to which they involve an antecedent-focused or response focused emotion regulation strategy. Emotional regulation involves all conscious and unconscious efforts to manage elements of one's emotions, (Gross,1999). which can be: antecedent –focused and response-focused. The individual evaluates the source of the emotion in case of antecedent-focused (waiter reminding himself to be friendly towards an irate customer) while in response-focused regulation, the individual manipulates her physiology, behaviors, cognition, facial/ bodily expressions when emotional reaction has already occurred (waiter attempting to show positive emotion to a customer who is misbehaving with her), (Coˆteˊ and Morgan, 2002). Gross, (1998) found that the psychological strain is greater in case of response –focused emotion regulation as compared to antecedent-focused strategy and Coˆteˊ and Morgan (2002) found the same pattern in job-related outcomes as response-focused response strategies resulted in lower job satisfaction and higher turnover intentions.

However, emotional consonance has a number of positive effects, including enhanced feelings of personal accomplishment and decreased levels of emotional exhaustion (Na¨ring, Brie¨t, & Brouwers, 2006).

Deep Acting protects the employee from negative moods (Judge et al., 2009; Polletta and Tufail, 2016), and minimizes her emotional dissonance and emotional exhaustion. (Brotheridge and Lee, 2003; Kim and Kim, 2018). Deep Acting negatively impacts personal accomplishment, and can produce conflicting results with surface behavior (Kruml and Geddes, 2000; Brotheridge and Grandey, 2002; Johnson and Spector, 2007). As per the conservation of resources (COR, Hobfoll, 1989) model, individuals attempt to enhance, protect and preserve their psychological resources. According to hospitality and tourism researchers surface acting is negatively associated with job satisfaction, organizational commitment and positively associated with turnover intentions: Deep acting is associated with positive attitudinal outcomes(e.g., Kim & Back, 2012; Wu & Shie, 2017).

Deep acting has positive impact on resources through cognitive effort, by eliminating the gap between internal feelings and displayed expressions leading to a positive interaction (Xu et al., 2017a). It produces a more positive emotional experience (Grandey, 2003) and develops positive resources overtime by resulting in enhanced satisfaction.

Thus, outcomes of emotional labor are dependent on the emotion labour strategy adopted by the employee and the organizational context in which service is performed (Grandey and Gabriel, 2015). Personality and emotional intelligence are the most widely studied individual antecedents of emotional labor (Kim et al., 2012; (Sohn and Lee, 2012; Gursoy et al., 2011; Kim, 2008). Positive and negative affect are linked with emotional dissonance levels Chu et al. (2012) while other antedecents of EL include mindfulness (Li et al., 2017), exhaustion and work-family conflict (Zhao et al., 2014) and national culture (Newnham, 2017)

Organizational antecedents of emotional labor ie organizational support (Lam and Chen, 2012; Hur et al., 2013)., job autonomy Gursoy et al. (2011) and Intensity, variety, frequency, duration, autonomy and the display rules of service interactions moderate the impact of individual factors on the EL strategies (Kim, 2008). Customer orientation culture (Lee et al., 2016), customer misbehavior (Hu et al., 2017; Karatepe et al., 2010) and human resource management practices (recruitment selection, training and empowerment, (Johanson and Woods, 2008) are other organizational antecedents of EL) Hu et al.,2017). Customer misbehavior has negative affect on emotional labor while customer verbal aggression triggers emotional dissonance amongst hospitality employees (Karatepe et al., 2009).

Outcomes of EL

Burnout, (emotional exhaustion, depersonalization and diminished personal accomplishment are the most studied employee outcomes of emotional labor (Chu et al., 2012; Hu et al., 2017; Hur et al., 2013; Kim, 2008; Lee and Ok, 2012; Li et al., 2017; Lv et al., 2012; Newnham, 2017; Rathi et al., 2013. EL is positively linked with emotional exhaustion, and depression (Wharton, 1993), employee stress (Pugliesi & Shook, 1998), and adversely correlated with job satisfaction (Bulan, Erickson, & Wharton, 1997) and organizational citizenship behaviors (Ashkanasy, Hartel, & Daus, 2002).

Surface acting involving "suppression of emotions" (Brotheridge & Lee, 2002) could cause distress in employees when they lose resources and desire to escape or quit the job (Xu et al., 2017a) and is related with negative outcomes of commitment, job satisfaction and turnover intentions while deep acting which involves trying to feel positive internally and positive and authentic display of emotions is positively linked with higher outcomes of job satisfaction, employee commitment and lower turnover intentions (Kim & Back, 2012; Wu & Shie, 2017)

Burnout can affect employees job satisfaction (Rutner, Hardgrave, & McKnight, 2008), physical health (Dormann & Kaiser, 2002; Wegge, Vogt, & Wecking, 2007; Zapf, Vogt, Seifert, Mertini, & Isic, 1999), performance problems (Bakker & Heuven, 2006), work withdrawal, and turnover intentions (Abraham, 1999; Bakker & Heuven, 2006; Karatepe & Aleshinloye, 2009; Rutner et al., 2008).

Some of the negative organizational consequences of burn out are higher turnover, and employees intentions to quit, adverse work attitudes, and lower performance levels (Lee & Ashforth, 1996). Surface acting drains employees' motivational resources and eventually their creativity levels (Shin, Hur, & Oh, 2015) and positively impacts CWB (e.g., service sabotage) in hospitality employees (Lee and Ok, 2014) while deep acting is related to employees ego depletion (Deng, Walter, Lam, and Zhao, 2017).

Moderating Variables: Social support (Abraham, 1999) moderates the impact of emotional dissonance on job satisfaction and organizational commitment. The relationship of EL with positive and negative outcomes (tipping) is moderated by LMX quality (quality of relationship between managers and employees) (Medler-Liraz 2014). Climate of Authenticity has a moderating effect on relationship of surface acting with emotional exhaustion (Li et al., 2017) as employees who engage in surface acting experience less emotional exhaustion within a strong organizational climate . The effect of emotional intelligence on emotional labor is moderated by employee gender and position (deep and surface acting). (Jung and Yoon, 2014) as per their study on hotel employees. However, there is dearth of empirical studies on the effects of gender on emotional labour performance. One relevant study on adventure tour leaders in Australia showed no significant affect of gender on surface and deep acting (Torland, 2011).

Display Rules: Organizations use formal control mechanisms in form of explicit and implied norms to ensure that employees display the emotions valued by customers (Hochschild, 1979, 1983; Leidner, 1999). These norms or standards prescribed by an organization are in form of recommended expressions of emotions and attitudes during service interactions with customers and labeled as "Organizational display rules" (Ashforth & Humphrey, 1993; Hochschild, 1983). Display rules provide guidance to employees in the service encounters with customers as regards which emotions are to be expressed and in what ways and when (Susskind et al., 2007). They are communicated through human resource practices (Xu, 2020).Display rules are reflected through the organizational philosophies, values and culture as core values and mission statements (Ashkanasy, 2002;; Zapf, 2002).

For example, Southwest Airlines' commitment to customer service (i.e., display rules) is reflected in their mission statement: "The mission of Southwest Airlines is dedication to the highest quality of customer service delivered with a sense of warmth, friendliness, individual pride, and Company Spirit" (Southwest Airlines, 2012).

Employees "perceptions of expression of positive emotions" are referred to as positive display rules while "perceptions of suppression of negative emotions" are referred to as negative display rules (Kim, 2008, p. 153). Positive display rules in workplace are associated with deep acting while negative display rules are linked with surface acting Diefendorff, Croyle, and Gosserand's (2005).

Table 2. Antecedents and outcomes of EL

Attributes	Measure of Emotional labor	Source
Antecedents		
Emotional regulation and intelligence	Emotional dissonance and emotive effort	Lee and Ok (2012)
	EL Strategies	Jung and Yoon (2014b)
	EL strategies	Kim et al. (2012)
Personality	EL Strategies	Sohn and Lee (2012)
	Emotional effort and dissonance	Gursoy et al. (2011)
	EL Strategies	Kim (2008)
Mindfulness	Surface acting	Li et al. (2017)
Affect	EL Strategies	Medler-Liraz (2014)

continues on following page

Table 2. Continued

Attributes	Measure of Emotional labor	Source
	EL Strategies	Chu et al. (2012)
Work-family conflict	Faking positive and suppressing negative	Zhao et al. (2014)
Exhaustion	Faking positive and suppressing	Zhao et al. (2014)
National culture	EL Strategies	Newnham (2017)
Organizational support	EL Strategies	Hur et al. (2013)
	EL Strategies	Lam and Chen (2012)
Job characteristics	EL Strategies	Kim (2008)
	Emotional effort and dissonance	Gursoy et al. (2011)
Customer orientation	EL Strategies	Lee and Hwang (2016)
Customer misbehavior	Emotional effort and dissonance	Hu et al. (2017)
	Emotional Dissonance	Karatepe et al. (2009)
Empowerment, recruitment, selection and training		Johanson and Woods (2008)
Supervisor support		Abbas, Mansour, and Elshawarbi (2018)
Harmonious passion, Obsessive passion		Chen et al. (2019)
Affect, Emotional contagion, Emotional concern		Chu, Baker, and Murrmann (2012)
Extraversion, Neuroticism		Gursoy et al. (2011)
Big Five Personality		Hameed (2016)
Age, Work experience, Emotional intelligence		Hur, Moon, and Han (2014)
Perceived organisational support		Hur et al. (2013)
Psychological capital,, Co worker support		Hur, Rhee, and Ahn (2016)
Coworker support		Hwa (2012)
Emotional intelligence Extraversion,		Jeon (2016)
Emotional intelligence		Kim et al. (2012)
Emotional intelligence		Kim et al. (2019)
Outcomes		
Employee Well-being		Sandiford and Seymour (2002)
Employee creativity and job stress	EL Strategies	Geng et al. (2014)
Burnout	EL Strategies	Kim (2008)
	EL Strategies	Newnham (2017)
	Emotional effort and dissonance	Lee and Ok (2012)
	EL Strategies	Hur et al. (2013)
	Emotional effort and dissonance	Hu et al. (2017)
	EL Strategies	Rathi et al. (2013).
	EL Strategies	Lv et al. (2012)

continues on following page

Table 2. Continued

Attributes	Measure of Emotional labor	Source
	Surface acting	Li et al. (2017)
	EL Strategies	Chu et al. (2012)
Job satisfaction		Abbas, Mansour, and Elshawarbi (2018)
Customer Oriented behaviour, Service Performance, Customer Loyalty		Aziza, Najafia, Shamsudinb, and Alshuaibi (2016)
Strain		Beal et al. (2013)
Job satisfaction		Bozionelos (2016)
Tip		Bujisic, Wu, Mattila, and Bilgihan (2014)
Job satisfaction, Service performance		Chen et al. (2012)
Job satisfaction, Emotional Exhaustion		Chen et al. (2019)
Service performance, CW B		Chi & Grandey (2019)
Service performance		Chi & Wang (2018)
Service performance,		Chi et al. (2011)
Tip Job satisfaction, Emotional exhaustion		Chu, Baker, and Murrmann (2012)
Customer satisfaction CWB		Collishaw, Dyer, and Boies (2008)
CWB		Deng et al. (2017)
Customer oriented behaviour		Fu (2013)
Creativity		Geng, Liu, Liu, and Feng (2014
Customer satisfaction		Grandey, Fisk, Mattila, Jansen, and Sideman (2005)
Job satisfaction		Gursoy et al. (2011)
Ervice performance		Hameed (2016)
Tip		Hülsheger et al. (2015)
Organizational Commitment		Hur, Moon, and Han (2014)
Organizational commitment, Turnover Intention		Hur et al. (2013)
Turnover intention		Hur, Rhee, and Ahn (2016)
Emotional Exhaustion		Hwa (2012)
Customer-oriented behaviour		Jeon (2016)
Burnout		Jung & Yoon (2014
Service performance		Kim et al. (2012)
Service performance, Turnover Intention		Kim et al. (2019)
Turnover intention		Krannitz et al. (2015)

Adapted from Lee et al, 2019 and Xu et al., 2020

Most studies have adopted the COR theory (Hobfoll, 1989) for evaluating the individual antecedents and individual, organizational and customer outcomes of EL and adopted the AET (Weiss and Cropanzano, 1996), theory for evaluation of organizational antecedents of EL. AET postulates that affective experiences affect individuals' evaluative judgments of their jobs and work environments (positive and negative emotions).

However, many of the studies (Chu et al., 2012; Kim, 2008; Lv et al., 2012; Newnham, 2017; Rathi et al., 2013; Sandiford and Seymour, 2002; Sohn and Lee, 2012) have lacked a theoretical framework or have used a context-specific theoretical model. Diverse measures of EL which are outcomes of EL but have been employed in Tourism (including emotional dissonance and emotive effort) as measures of EL in many studies (Lee, 2019). Further, very few studies have considered the longitudinal or temporal variation of EL and the contextual or situational effects on EL have not been adequately explored.

EL and Customer Service Performance

Emotional labor is positively linked with performance as emotional expressions are perceived as sincere by customers and have negatively impact on performance (Rafaeli & Sutton, 1987) if viewed as insincere. Grandey, Fisk, Mattila, and Sideman (2002) discovered that customer's can differentiate between faked smiles and authentic smiles of a hotel clerk, and respond positively to authentic smiles. Bærenholdt and Jensen (2009) in their study at Danish tourist attractions found that recognition from visitors was a relished reward for frontline employees for their emotional performance and contributed to their enhanced sense of self-development and self-esteem.

Hence, chances of surface acting being perceived as insincere are higher as the desired emotions are faked, while deep acting has higher probability of being perceived as sincere because the felt emotions and displayed emotions are equivalent (Grandey, 2000). Employees therefore need to adjust their emotional display to each customer and situation depending on the verbal and non vernal cues transmitted by customers.

Display of positive emotions have significant association with organizational objectives of customer delight, return intentions and positive word of mouth (Johanson and Woods, 2008;) which in turn have financial implications. Financial implications of positive emotional display by service employees especially in Hospitality Industry is universally accepted (Fox, 2001; Pugh, 2001). Positive customer consequences are related to deep acting while negative outcomes are linked with surface acting. (Van Dijk et al., 2011).

Psychological research results show that positive displays and authentic expressions are linked with interpersonal outcomes (Frank & Ekman, 1993; Surakka & Hietanen, 1998). Positive emotional displays of greeting customers, having eye contact, and smiling have been found to be related with positive mood, service quality, and positive behavioral intentions (i.e., willingness to recommend and repurchase intentions) (Ford, 1995; Mattila & Enz, 2002; Tsai, 2001). Pugh (2001) and Tsai and Huang (2002) found positive displays by employees are associated with service quality perceptions and positive behavioral intentions which may be mediated by customer affect and perceptions of the employee's friendliness. However, smiling and similar behavioral cues only have been the focus of most studies (e.g., Ford, 1995; Pugh, 2001; Tsai & Huang, 2002).

Sector Specific Studies of EL

While most of the results enumerated above are similar across the different sectors of Hospitality and Tourism, some of the studies results are sector specific. The four most studied roles are Tour operators, airlines cabin crew, frontline staff of Hotels and service staff of restaurants.

The unique aspects of these sectors are as follows

Tour Leader

Tour leader roles have dual role as a service provider to the visitors and a consumer representative to vendors of the group package components. Tour leaders have to display positive and suppress negative emotions inspite of unreasonable and demanding tour participants while at the same time express or fake negative emotions to suppliers to ensure delivery of service quality and problem resolution (e.g., Sutton, 1991). Men have been found to adopt surface acting more often as compared to women and older Tour guides who have spent more years on the job adopt deep acting as they are more successful at internalizing themselves and their emotions.

Cabin Crew (Airlines)

Commercial Airlines have traditionally mandated their staff to adhere to high level of emotional display rules especially as regards cabin crew who are expected to manage the intricacies of surface acting, deep acting and other emotional coping approaches (Hochschild, 1983; Williams, 2003).

Flight attendants experience emotional exhaustion as a result of surface acting (Hur et al. 2013) due to distress or strain from displaying emotions they do not feel (Li et al. 2017) . Flight attendants service conditions of providing service over a long period of time; high pressure in the aircraft cabin and hermetic space; passengers complexity of temperament; disease prone environment; uncertain work hours causing work family conflicts and heavy work loads may induce burnout leading to flight attendants' alienation from work . Flight attendants are prone to emotional exhaustion due to long periods of stressful work environment.

As mentioned by a male cabin crew in one of the studies ; It's fatigue – you're working a harder roster. They throw in an Atlantic, late Europe's, early Europes. I can say I haven't been as tired in the last 15 years as I have been in the last six months that's for sure. They're tightening up the working hours, more productivity, they're maximizing

Frequent misbehaviors by passengers make the staff vulnerable to emotional exhaustion and make them experience higher levels of emotional labor.(Hu et al., 2017).

A cabin crew expressed her situation as "Passengers are just miserable because we are delayed! All I can do is smile when really I want to just tell them all to go home if they don't want to fly with us. Of course I can't really say that to them" (Mary, 2007).

An illustration of display rules of airlines is " Passengers have to be addressed politely and courteously at all times . Flight attendants are expected to be good mannered at all times and make use of "please," "thank-you," "excuse me," "Sir," "Madam," and should address passengers by their names whenever applicable. The following terms "you guys," "Hon," "dear," and "love" are not acceptable".

Restaurant

Restaurant industry employs standardized work practices such as scripts to protect service workers from the psychological costs of depersonalization and alienation from their true feelings. (Leidner,1993). Female workers, are likely to be exposed to gendered emotional labour due to suggestive jokes, undesirable bodily contact and innuendos.

As quoted by one waitress: `If you sell yourself all the time you end up losing your identity. You must hold a part of you back. You don't want to end up being just part of the meal experience. You need to learn to keep respect for yourself. Hence, service workers in standardized roles feel the need to personalize their service to retain their individual character and self identity', whereas those engaged in highly personalised authentic service contexts feel the need to hide their true selves from the customers view through deep acting.

Hospitality

The success of guest services is dependent on employees' displayed hospitality behaviors such as courtesy and full attention, as customer service require's constant face-to-face interaction with customers in an effort to satisfy their varied demands and expectations (Lee, 2002). These employees are mostly required to stand or sit still for long time periods and sometimes maintain awkward postures during the shits of 10-12 hours every day. The job involves displaying the appropriate attitude, with correct level of authenticity, and concern for guests. Employees, in their interactions with customers, are expected to exhibit certain emotional displays such as friendliness, cheerfulness, confidence, warmth, or enthusiasm, for long periods of time

Discourse on Emotional Labour (EL)

The research on EL in Tourism has been bounded by the theatre analogy and it is assumed that EL is only relevant to the performance of the front stage employees and does not have much relevance to the backstage performers or workers at the boundary of front and back stage for example ticket checking staff, customer service representatives, security personnel at airports who may also need to produce EL for effective service experiences. These roles have not been studied or focused on in Tourism industry,

Many organizations are small and medium scale, micro entrepreneurial ventures for example transportation agencies, travel agents and workers who are on contractual basis where HRM departments with specific skills and processes may not be existent. For example owner managed enterprises who engage with service customers. EL has only been considered on employee-employer context and how EL is experienced by owners who are also service providers have not been explored. For example, a taxi driver who is also owner of the taxi provides service to passengers in similar contexts as cabin crew but with different levels of job autonomy and psychological situation.

Most of the studies on EL have been focused on establishing the dyadic linkages of EL with organizational variables and psychological well being of the Individuals. The Cognitive appraisal theories of emotion have predominated the theoretical approach in understanding EL and its effects which raises the question of whether tourism industry needs to manage EL uniquely or management of employee EL is a generic competency. The AET theory states that cognitive interpretations by employees trigger emotional states, which then drive affect-driven behaviors (e.g., emotional displays). However, processes and mechanisms through which emotions influence outcomes at work remain unanswered.

The antecedent, moderating and outcome effects on EL ie job autonomy, emotional intelligence, extraversion, neuroticism, social support, display rules, supervisor support, job satisfaction, emotional exhaustion, burnout have not been studied together. Their concurrent impact has not been understood which makes the results prone to selection bias.

The most correlated outcomes of EL studied in literature are burnout, job satisfaction, depersonalization and emotional exhaustion. Other organizational and individual outcomes such as employee commitment, employee engagement, motivation have been relatively ignored.

There is a dearth of longitudinal studies on EL and culture, EL and gender, EL and different role categorizations. Most of the studies have been undertaken in Europe, USA and Australia. Some of the studies in other parts of the world are of in Japan (Ogino, Tak*gasak'& Inaki, 2004) and China (Shulei & Miner, 2006 and Wu ýi & Cheng, 2006) and are limited to customer contact persons in Hospitality, restaurant, airlines and Tour operators.

There are methodological issues also. Actual turnover has not been measured in these studies as intentions to quit may not reflect the actual behavior. There is dearth of quantitative research on Emotional Labour and Emotional Dissonance (Dormann & Zapf, 2004; Heuven & Bakker, 2003) and many of the studies have used semi structured data collection methods. There is lack of concurrence regarding the conceptualization of EL and theoretical approach to be adopted for evaluating the effects and causes of emotional labor (Brotheridge and Grandey, 2002) and its operationalization (Bono and Vey, 2005). There is a debate on whether researchers should investigate individual differences while attempting to understand the variability in consequences of emotional labor as individual characteristics determine how individuals deliver emotional labor (Diefendorff et al., 2005; Zapf and Holz, 2006).In their review paper (Xu et al., 2020), authors have made an attempt to develop an integrated model of EL.

However, further research is required on the cross cultural differences in EL, group behavior and EL, gender and age effects, the positive emotional outcomes produced in customers through interactional transactions, and whether the results are generalizeable to back stage interactions between employees, and spill-over effects of EL on family life and society

There is lack of clarity on whether the results of investigations on EL predominantly undertaken in the airlines (cabin crew), hospitality (front-line), restaurant (service staff) and Tour leaders can be generalized to other sectors, roles and positions in Tourism. It's also not established whether managers and back stage personnel need to regulate their emotions in their interactions with frontline personnel and service staff and how their interactions with the personnel engaged with customers affect the delivery of service The literature on EL in Tourism has not adequately investigated the positive outcomes of EL and how to leverage deep acting for enhanced customer satisfaction and loyalty.. For example, what job design changes to implement for cabin crew to alleviate the negative outcomes of EL experienced by them over their career. Specific recommendations are non-existent as general observations on higher job autonomy offer little managerial guidance.

Though airlines have become more sensitive to passenger's mis-behaviour with airlines stewardesses post 9/11, the literature does not provide any recommendations for HR practitioners on how to alleviate the emotional exhaustion and stress on account of adverse working environment.

Human Resource Management and Emotional Labor:

Some challenges which HR practitioners are likely to face are: Whether employees can be trained to surface /deep act and how to develop these competencies. How to define and measure the emotional intelligence and personality traits for specific roles and organizational culture? How to implement higher job autonomy in routine jobs? Can deep acting skills be developed over a period of time and how? Whether to offer higher rewards for EL? How to motivate employees in front line roles and adverse working environments for long hours and periods of time in their career? Where to draw the line regarding acceptable customer abuse? Whether positive emotional displays are the appropriate display strategies in all situations? For example, what emotions to display when employees have to undertake leadership roles for example in a crisis?

A functional approach has been adopted to assess the applicability of EL research to HR practices in Tourism. Thus, specific HR functions are examined for EL related practices.

Personality tests can used for selection of employees for frontline positions. By selecting candidates with desirable traits and better person-brand fit, tourism service providers can ensure better emotional performance. Hiring people with higher levels of extroversion and lower levels of neuroticism could lead to behavioral outcomes as a natural consequence of their personality. Certain situational and role play assessments may provide a better evaluation of the emotional dispositions of the potential employee.

Performance appraisal and reward systems can be designed to encourage positive affect and job autonomy? Having more control on various aspects of the job have been found to have positive association with EL. Hence extrinsic rewards can enhance intrinsic motivation by providing meaningful information about self-competence and when employees have discretion on how and when to complete the task .Incentive and reward systems that enhance employee control on their behavior can lead to higher levels of perceived organizational support and lessen the negative impact of EL on self and the organization.

Job design can minimize the need for EL for example in scripted and impersonal performances. However, the impact on self identity needs to be understood and tackled. What level of empowerment would reduce the negative effects of for example surface acting by front-line service staff can be examined.

Employees who need to perform EL can be provided supportive organizational contexts in form of higher perceived organizational support and perceived supervisory support. The organizational rules may be more flexible as regards their behavior and adherence to norms and culture when they are not performing their roles. Training may be given to them on emotional self management and customer management strategies to minimize the negative impact of EL.

A supportive work culture would moderate the ill effects of EL on their health and organizational outcomes. HR practitioners can experiment and develop policies and practices which lead to a supportive work culture for EL performances. For example, an informal work culture in back stage for example in restaurant kitchen could lessen the impact of EL in front stage.

REFERENCES

Abbas, T., Mansour, N., & Elshawarbi, N. (2018). Examining to what extent do employees express emotional labor: An application on front-office department in five-star hotels in Cairo. *Journal of the Faculty of Tourism and Hotels-University of Sadat City, 2*(2).

Abraham, R. (1999). The impact of emotional dissonance on organizational commitment and intention to turnover. *The Journal of Psychology, 133*(4), 441–455. doi:10.1080/00223989909599754 PMID:10412221

Ashforth, B. E., & Humphrey, R. H. (1995). Emotion in the workplace: A reappraisal. *Human Relations, 48*(2), 97–125. doi:10.1177/001872679504800201

Ashkanasy, N. M., Härtel, C. E. J., & Daus, C. S. (2002). Advances in organizational behavior: Diversity and emotions. *Journal of Management, 28,* 307–338. doi:10.1177/014920630202800304

Aziza, N. A., Najafia, B., Shamsudinb, F. M., & Alshuaibi, A. S. I. (2016). *Customer perception of emotional labor of airline service employees and customer loyalty intention.* Paper presented at the ISSC 2016: International soft science conference. doi:10.15405/epsbs.2016.08.86

Beal, D. J., Trougakos, J. P., Weiss, H. M., & Dalal, R. S. (2013). Affect spin and the emotion regulation process at work. *Journal of Applied Psychology, 98*(4), 593–605.

Beardsworth, A., & Bryman, A. (2001). The wild animal in late modernity: The case of the Disneyization of zoos. *Tourist Studies, 1*(1), 83–104. doi:10.1177/146879760100100105

Bono, J. E., & Vey, M. A. (2005). Toward understanding emotional management at work: A quantitative review of emotional labor research. In C. E. J. H€artel, W. J. Zerbe, & N. M. Ashkanasy (Eds.), Emotions in organizational behavior. Mahwah, NJ: Lawrence Erlbaum Associates Publishers.

Borenstein, M., Hedges, L. V., Higgins, J. P. T., & Rothstein, H. R. (2009). *Introduction to meta-analysis.* Chichester: Wiley.

Brotheridge, C. M., & Lee, R. T. (2003). Development and validation of emotional labor scale. *Journal of Occupational and Organizational Psychology, 76*(3), 365–379. doi:10.1348/096317903769647229

Brotherigde, C. M., & Grandey, A. A. (2002). Emotional labor and burnout: Comparing two perspectives of people work. *Journal of Vocational Behavior, 60*(1), 17–39. doi:10.1006/jvbe.2001.1815

Bujisic, M., Wu, L., Mattila, A., & Bilgihan, A. (2014). Not all smiles are created equal: Investigating the effects of display authenticity and service relationship on customer tipping behavior. *International Journal of Contemporary Hospitality Management, 26*(2), 293–306.

Chen, K. Y., Chang, C. W., & Wang, C. H. (2019). Frontline employees' passion and emotional exhaustion: The mediating role of emotional labor strategies. *International Journal of Hospitality Management, 76,* 163–172.

Chen, Z., Sun, H., Lam, W., Hu, Q., Huo, Y., & Zhong, J. A. (2012). Chinese hotel employees in the smiling masks: Roles of job satisfaction, burnout, and supervisory support in relationships between emotional labor and performance. *International Journal of Human Resource Management, 23*(4), 826–845.

Chi, N. W., & Grandey, A. A. (2019). Emotional labor predicts service performance depending on activation and inhibition regulatory fit. *Journal of Management, 45*(2), 673–700.

Chi, N. W., & Wang, I. A. (2018). The relationship between newcomers' emotional labor and service performance: The moderating roles of service training and mentoring functions. *International Journal of Human Resource Management, 29*(19), 2729–2757.

Chi, N. W., Grandey, A. A., Diamond, J. A., & Krimmel, K. R. (2011). Want a tip? Service performance as a function of emotion regulation and extraversion. *Journal of Applied Psychology, 96*(6), 1337–1346.

Chu, K. H., Baker, M. A., & Murrmann, S. K. (2012). When we are onstage, we smile: The effects of emotional labor on employee work outcomes. *International Journal of Hospitality Management, 31*(3), 906–915. doi:10.1016/j.ijhm.2011.10.009

Chu, K. H.-L., & Murrmann, S. K. (2006). Development and validation of the hospitality emotional labor scale. *Tourism Management, 27*(6), 1181–1191. doi:10.1016/j.tourman.2005.12.011

Chu, K. H., Baker, M. A., & Murrmann, S. K. (2012). When we are onstage, we smile: The effects of emotional labor on employee work outcomes. *International Journal of Hospitality Management, 31*(3), 906–915.

Co^ te´, S., & Morgan, L. M. (2002). A longitudinal analysis of the association between emotion regulation, job satisfaction, and intention to quit. *Journal of Organizational Behavior, 23*, 947 – 962.

Collishaw, M. A., Dyer, L., & Boies, K. (2008). The authenticity of positive emotional displays: Client responses to leisure service employees. *Journal of Leisure Research, 40*(1), 23–46.

Constanti, P., & Gibbsm, P. (2005). Emotional labour and surplus value: The case of holiday 'reps'. *Service Industries Journal, 25*(1), 103–116. doi:10.1080/0264206042000302432

Deng, H., Walter, F., Lam, C. K., & Zhao, H. H. (2017). Spillover effects of emotional labor in customer service encounters toward coworker harming: A resource depletion perspective. *Personnel Psychology, 70*(2), 469–502.

Diefendorff, J. M., Croyle, M. H., & Gosserand, R. H. (2005). The dimensionality and antecedents of emotional labor strategies. *Journal of Vocational Behavior, 66*(2), 339–357. doi:10.1016/j.jvb.2004.02.001

Diefendorff, J. M., & Gosserand, R. H. (2003). Understanding the emotional labor process: A control theory perspective. *Journal of Organizational Behavior, 24*(8), 945–959. doi:10.1002/job.230

Ekman, P. (1973). *Darwin and facial expression: A century of research in review*. Academic Press.

Erickson, R. J., & Wharton, A. S. (1997). Inauthenticity and depression: Assessing the consequences of interactive service work. *Work and Occupations, 24*(2), 188–214. doi:10.1177/0730888497024002004

Fu, Y. K. (2013). The influence of internal marketing by airlines on customer-oriented behavior: A test of the mediating effect of emotional labor. *Journal of Air Transport, 32*, 49–57.

Geng, Z., Liu, C., Liu, X., & Feng, J. (2014). The effects of emotional labor on frontline employee creativity. *International Journal of Contemporary Hospitality Management, 26*(7), 1046–1064. doi:10.1108/IJCHM-12-2012-0244

Grandey, A. (2000). Emotion regulation in the workplace: A new way to conceptualize emotional labor. *Journal of Occupational Health Psychology, 5*(1), 95–110. doi:10.1037/1076-8998.5.1.95 PMID:10658889

Grandey, A. A. (2000). Emotional regulation in the workplace: A new way to conceptualize emotional labor. *Journal of Occupational Health Psychology, 5*(1), 95–110. doi:10.1037/1076-8998.5.1.95 PMID:10658889

Grandey, A. A., Fisk, G. M., Mattila, A. S., Jansen, K. J., & Sideman, L. A. (2005). Is "service with a smile" enough? Authenticity of positive displays during service encounters. *Organizational Behavior and Human Decision Processes, 96*(1), 38–55.

Grandey, A. A., Fisk, G. M., Mattila, A. S., Jansen, K. J., & Sideman, L. A. (2005). Is "service with a smile" enough? Authenticity of positive displays during service encounters. *Organizational Behavior and Human Decision Processes, 96*(1), 38–55. doi:10.1016/j.obhdp.2004.08.002

Gross, J. J. (1998). The emerging field of emotion regulation: An integrative review. *Review of General Psychology, 2*(3), 271–299. doi:10.1037/1089-2680.2.3.271

Gursoy, D., Boylu, Y., & Avci, U. (2011). Identifying the complex relationships among emotional labor and its correlates. *International Journal of Hospitality Management, 30*(4), 783–794. doi:10.1016/j.ijhm.2010.10.009

Hobfoll, S. E. (1989). Conservation of resources: A new attempt at conceptualizing stress. *The American Psychologist, 44*(3), 513–524. doi:10.1037/0003-066X.44.3.513 PMID:2648906

Hochschild, A. R. (1983). *The Managed Heart: Commercialization of Human Feeling.* University of California Press.

Hu, H. H. S., Hu, H. Y., & King, B. (2017). Impacts of misbehaving air passengers on frontline employees: Role stress and emotional labor. *International Journal of Contemporary Hospitality Management, 29*(7), 1793–1813. doi:10.1108/IJCHM-09-2015-0457

Hülsheger, U. R., Lang, J. W., Schewe, A. F., & Zijlstra, F. R. (2015). When regulating emotions at work pays off: A diary and an intervention study on emotion regulation and customer tips in service jobs. *Journal of Applied Psychology, 100*(2), 263–277.

Hur, W. M., Moon, T. W., & Han, S. J. (2014). The role of chronological age and work experience on emotional labor: The mediating effect of emotional intelligence. *Career Development International, 19*(7), 734–754.

Hur, W. M., Moon, T. W., & Jun, J. K. (2013). The role of perceived organizational support on emotional labor in the airline industry. *International Journal of Contemporary Hospitality Management, 25*(1), 105–123.

Hur, W. M., Moon, T. W., & Jun, J. K. (2013). The role of perceived organizational support on emotional labor in the airline industry. *International Journal of Contemporary Hospitality Management, 25*(1), 105–123.

Hur, W. M., Rhee, S. Y., & Ahn, K. H. (2016). Positive psychological capital and emotional labor in Korea: The job demands-resources approach. *International Journal of Human Resource Management, 27*(5), 477–500.

Hwa, M. A. C. (2012). Emotional labor and emotional exhaustion: Does co-worker support matter? *Journal of Management Research, 12*(3), 115–127.

Jeon, A. (2016). The effect of pre-flight attendants' emotional intelligence, emotional labor, and emotional exhaustion on commitment to customer service. *Service Business, 10*(2), 345–367.

Johanson, M. M., & Woods, R. H. (2008). Recognizing the emotional element in service excellence. *Cornell Hospitality Quarterly*, *49*(3), 310–316. doi:10.1177/1933965508316267

Johnson, H. M., & Spector, P. E. (2007). Service with a smile: Do emotional intelligence, gender, and autonomy moderate the emotional labor process? *Journal of Occupational Health Psychology*, *12*(4), 319–333. doi:10.1037/1076-8998.12.4.319 PMID:17953492

Jung, H. S., & Yoon, H. H. (2014). Antecedents and consequences of employees' job stress in a food-service industry: Focused on emotional labor and turnover inten:. *International Journal of Hospitality Management*, *38*, 84–88. doi:10.1016/j.ijhm.2014.01.007

Jung, H. S., & Yoon, H. H. (2014). Moderating role of hotel employees' gender and job position on the relationship between emotional intelligence and emotional labor. *International Journal of Hospitality Management, 43*, 47–5.

Karatepe, O. M., Yorganci, I., & Haktanir, M. (2009). Outcomes of customer verbal aggression among hotel employees. *International Journal of Contemporary Hospitality Management*, *21*(6), 713–733. doi:10.1108/09596110910975972

Kim, H. J. (2008). Hotel service providers' emotional labor: The antecedents and effects on burnout. *International Journal of Hospitality Management*, *27*(2), 151–161. doi:10.1016/j.ijhm.2007.07.019

Kim, Y., & Back, K. J. (2012). Antecedents and consequences of flight attendants' job satisfaction. *Service Industries Journal, 32*(16), 2565–2584..

Kruml, S. M., & Geddes, D. (2000). Exploring the dimensions of emotional labor. *Management Communication Quarterly*, *14*(1), 8–49. doi:10.1177/0893318900141002

Lam, W., & Chen, Z. (2012). When I put on my service mask: Determinants and outcomes of emotional labor among hotel service providers according to affective event theory. *International Journal of Hospitality Management*, *31*(1), 3–11. doi:10.1016/j.ijhm.2011.04.009

Lam, W., & Chen, Z. (2012). When I put on my service mask: Determinants and outcomes of emotional labor among hotel service providers according to affective event theory. *International Journal of Hospitality Management, 31*(1), 3–11.

Lam, W., Huo, Y., & Chen, Z. (2018). Who is fit to serve? Person–job/organization fit, emotional labor, and customer service performance. *Human Resource Management, 57*.

Lee, J. J., & Hwang, J. (2016). An emotional labor perspective on the relationship between customer orientation and job satisfaction. *International Journal of Hospitality Management*, *54*, 139–150. doi:10.1016/j.ijhm.2016.01.008

Lee, J. J., & Ok, C. (2012). Reducing burnout and enhancing job satisfaction: Critical role of hotel employees' emotional intelligence and emotional labor. *International Journal of Hospitality Management*, *31*(4), 1101–1112. doi:10.1016/j.ijhm.2012.01.007

Lee, J. J., & Ok, C. M. (2014). Understanding hotel employees' service sabotage: Emotional labor perspective based on conservation of resources theory. *International Journal of Hospitality Management*, *36*, 176–187. doi:10.1016/j.ijhm.2013.08.014

Lee, R. T., & Ashforth, B. E. (1990). On the meaning of Maslach's three dimensions of burnout. *The Journal of Applied Psychology, 75*(6), 743–747. doi:10.1037/0021-9010.75.6.743 PMID:1981064

Lee, S. H. (2002), *A Study on the job Stress of Hotel Employees: Focused on the Deluxe Hotel in Seoul* (Unpublished Doctoral Dissertation). Kyonggi Univ Seoul, Seoul.

Lee, J. J., Ok, C. M., & Hwang, J. (2016). An emotional labor perspective on the relationship between customer orientation and job satisfaction. *International Journal of Hospitality Management, 54*, 139–150.

Lee, J., Ok, C. M., Lee, S. H., & Lee, C. K. (2018). Relationship between emotional labor and customer orientation among airline service employees: Mediating role of depersonalization. *Journal of Travel Research, 57*(3), 324–341.

Leidner, R. (1993). *Fast Food, Fast Talk*. University of California Press.

Li, J. J., Wong, I. A., & Kim, W. G. (2017). Does mindfulness reduce emotional exhaustion? A multilevel analysis of emotional labor among casino employees. *International Journal of Hospitality Management, 64*, 21–30.

Lv, Q., Xu, S., & Ji, H. (2012). Emotional labor strategies, emotional exhaustion, and turnover intention: An empirical study of Chinese hotel employees. *Journal of Human Resources in Hospitality & Tourism, 11*(2), 87–105. doi:10.1080/15332845.2012.648837

Medler-Liraz, H. (2014). Negative affectivity and tipping: The moderating role of emotional labor strategies and leader-member exchange. *International Journal of Hospitality Management, 36*, 63–72. doi:10.1016/j.ijhm.2013.08.010

Morris, J. A., & Feldman, D. C. (1996). The dimensions, antecedents, and consequences of emotional labor. *Academy of Management Review, 21*(4), 986–1010. doi:10.5465/amr.1996.9704071861

Newnham, M. P. (2017). A comparison of the enactment and consequences of emotional labor between frontline hotel workers in two contrasting societal cultures. *Journal of Human Resources in Hospitality & Tourism, 16*(2), 192–214. doi:10.1080/15332845.2016.1202729

Ogino, K., Takigasaki, T., & Inaki, K. (2004). Effects of emotion work on burnout and stress among human service professionals. *Japanese Journal of Phycology, 75*(4), 371–377. PMID:15747559

Pugliesi, K. (1999). The consequences of emotional labor: Effects on work stress, job satisfaction, and well being. *Motivation and Emotion, 232*(2), 125–154. doi:10.1023/A:1021329112679

Rafaeli, A., & Sutton, R. I. (1987). Expression of emotion as part of the work role. *Academy of Management Review, 12*(1), 23–37. doi:10.5465/amr.1987.4306444

Rathi, N., Bhatnagar, D., & Mishra, S. K. (2013). Effect of emotional labor on emotional exhaustion and work attitudes among hospitality employees in India. *Journal of Human Resources in Hospitality & Tourism, 12*(3), 273–290. doi:10.1080/15332845.2013.769142

Rutter, D. R., & Fielding, P. J. (1988). Sources of occupational stress: An examination of British prison officers. *Work and Stress, 2*(4), 291–299. doi:10.1080/02678378808257490

Sandiford, P. J., & Seymour, D. (2002). Emotional labor in public houses: Reflections on a pilot study. *Journal of Hospitality and TourismResearch*, *26*(1), 54–70. doi:10.1177/1096348002026001004

Schaubroeck, J., & Jones, J. R. (2000). Antecedents of workplace emotional labor dimensions and moderators of their effects on physical symptoms. *Journal of Organizational Behavior*, *21*(2), 163–183. doi:10.1002/(SICI)1099-1379(200003)21:2<163::AID-JOB37>3.0.CO;2-L

Sharpe, E. K. (2005). "Going above and beyond": The emotional labor of adventure guides. *Journal of Leisure Research*, *37*(1), 29–50. doi:10.1080/00222216.2005.11950039

Shin, I., Hur, W. M., & Oh, H. (2015). Essential precursors and effects of employee creativity in a service context: Emotional labor strategies and official job performance. *Career Development International*, *20*(7), 733–752.

Shulei, M., & Miner, H. (2006). Emotional Labor; Surface Acting and Deep Acting, Which one is better? [Chinese]. *Acta Psychologica Sinica*, *38*(2), 262–270.

Sohn, H. K., & Lee, T. J. (2012). Relationship between HEXACO personality factors and emotional labour of service providers in the tourism industry. *Tourism Management*, *33*(1), 116–125

Tsai, W. (2001). Determinants and consequences of employee displayed positi%'c emotions. *Journal of Management*, *27*(4), 497–512. doi:10.1177/014920630102700406

Van Dijk, P. A., & Kirk, A. (2007). Being somebody else: Emotional labour and emotional dissonance in the context of the service experience at a heritage tourism site. *Journal of Hospitality and Tourism Management*, *14*(2), 157–169. doi:10.1375/jhtm.14.2.157

Weiss, H. M., & Cropanzano, R. (1996). Affective events theory: a theoretical discussion of the structure, causes and consequences of affective experiences at work. In B. M. Staw & L. L. Cummings (Eds.), *Research in Organization Behavior* (Vol. 19, pp. 1–74). JAI Press.

Williams, C. (2003). Sky Service: The Demands of Emotional Labour in the Airline Industry. *Gender, Work and Organization*, *10*(5), 513–550. doi:10.1111/1468-0432.00210

Wong, J., & Wang, C. (2009). Emotional labor of the tour leaders: An exploratory study. *Tourism Management*, *30*(2), 249–259. doi:10.1016/j.tourman.2008.06.005

Wu, T. Y., & Cheng, B. S. (2006). The Effect of Interactions among Job Involvement, Ability of Regulating Other's Emotion, and Emotional Labor on Emotional Exhaustion. *Chinese Journal of Psychology*, *48*(1), 69–87.

Wu, X., & Shie, A. J. (2017). The relationship between customer orientation, emotional labour and job burnout. *Journal of Chinese Human Resource Management*, *8*(2), 54–76.

Xu, S., Martinez, L. R., & Lv, Q. (2017b). Communication is key: The interaction of emotional labor strategies on hotel supervisors' turnover intentions in China. *Tourism Analysis*, *22*(2), 125–137.

Young, C. A., & Corsun, D. L. (2009). What a nuisance: Controlling for negative affectivity versus personality in hospitality stress research. *International Journal of Hospitality Management*, *28*(2), 280–288. doi:10.1016/j.ijhm.2008.10.002

Zapf, D. (2002). Emotion work and psychological well-being: A review of the literature and some conceptual considerations. *Human Resource Management Review, 12*(2), 237–268. doi:10.1016/S1053-4822(02)00048-7

Zapf, D., Mertini, H., Seifert, C., Vogt, C., & Isic, A. (1999). *Frankfurt Emotion Work Scales—Frankfurter Skalen zur Emotionsarbeit FEWS 3.0*. Department of Psychology, J. W. Goethe-University Frankfurt.

Zhao, X., Mattila, A. S., & Ngan, N. N. (2014). The impact of frontline employees' work–family conflict on customer satisfaction: The mediating role of exhaustion and emotional displays. *Cornell Hospitality Quarterly, 55*(4), 422–432. doi:10.1177/1938965513517172

This research was previously published in the Handbook of Research on Human Capital and People Management in the Tourism Industry; pages 73-91, copyright year 2021 by Business Science Reference (an imprint of IGI Global).

Chapter 6
Human Resource Information System Adoption and Implementation Factors:
A Theoretical Analysis

Sonalee Srivastava

https://orcid.org/0000-0002-8092-9658

Jaypee Institute of Information Technology, Noida, India

Badri Bajaj

Jaypee Institute of Information Technology, Noida, India

Santosh Dev

Jaypee Institute of Information Technology, Noida, India

ABSTRACT

In the modern era, human resource management is accompanied by the information system which is instrumental in managing human resource processes. In the current competitive and challenging environment, organizational success depends on its effective and efficient human resource. Human resource along with IT professionals can create an environment in an organization for successful adoption of human resource information systems. While considering it as a key factor in modern enterprise management, its burgeoning interest has led to the foundation of this article. The study is to delve deep into the literature and to explore the factors responsible for human resource information system adoption and to identify the barriers in its implementation and to provide suggestions to overcome these barriers. The findings reveal that the factors of human resource information system mentioned in literature are important. These factors should be taken into consideration while adopting Human Resource Information System by integrating Technology-Organization-Environment (TOE) framework with Human-Organization-Technology (HOT) framework.

DOI: 10.4018/978-1-6684-3873-2.ch006

INTRODUCTION

A remarkable and constant advancement in technology adopted by various organizations has led to the modification of human resource function and marked its evolution from administrative to strategic domain (Teo, Soon, & Fedric, 2001). With the talented pool of human resource, an organization has been moving toward a knowledge-based economy. Today, organization success widely depends on their talented pool of human resource; they are treated as a strategic asset by an organization and this could be competitively maintained through effective application of Human Resource Information System (HRIS). For generating higher value results, automation of standardized Human Resource Processes is a must have attitude carried by almost every organization. Organizations have been extensively affected by technology (Kossek & Young, 1994) and to overcome the technological impediment, they are adopting the automation of human resource function through the advent of a human resource information system. Correct usage of an information system tends to increase the efficacy and effectiveness of all facets of human resource management like planning, accounting, personnel management, compensation and regulatory analysis (Maditheti & Gomes, 2017).

HRIS facilitates in cost reduction or efficiency gaining. It improves and facilitates client services and enhances employees' productivity by improving its strategic orientation towards human resource management (Broderick & Bounreau, 1992; Kundu, 2012; NishadNawaz, 2012; Ruël, Bondarouk, & Looise, 2004). According to Hendrickson (2003), "A well designed HRIS can serve as the management tool in the alignment or integration of the human resources department goals with the goals of long-term corporate strategic planning." The Human Resource Information System is an indispensable part for most of the organizations (Aggarwal & Kapoor, 2012; Nishad Nawaz, 2013; NishadNawaz, 2012).

With the advent of globalization in the late 1980's many organizations have started relying on the computerized management information system for their day-to-day activities (Bal, Bozkurt, & Ertemsir, 2012). In the mid-1980's HRIS became a major sub-function of Management Information System for many organization. We have applied archival research methodology; the study begins by a literature review of conceptualization of HRIS, its adoption factors and barrier in its implementation. This study has integrated the Technology-Organization-Environment (TOE)with Human-Organization-Technology (HOT)frameworks. To begin with the definitions of HRIS, literature is full of various definitions given by various researchers, some are tabulated in Table 1.

There is plenty of literature on the adoption, implementation, and barriers of human resource information system, but there is dearth/paucity of literature on a comprehensive view towards its totality. This article integrated the Technology-Organization-Environment framework-TOE (Tornatzky and Fleischer, 1990) with Human-Organization-Technology framework –HOT (Yusof et al., 2006), so as to get a complete overview of the factors responsible for HRIS adoption. The objectives of the paper are to study the adoption factors of human resource information system and its benefits and to identify the barriers in HRIS implementation and to recommend some suggestions to overcome the barriers.

Table 1. HRIS definition

DeSanctis, 1986	Kavanagh, Gueutal & Tannenbaum, 1990	Brodericks & Boudreau, 1992	Kovach & Cathcart, 1999	Hendrickson, 2003	Ruel et al., 2011	Rietsema, 2016
"a systematic procedure for collecting, storing maintaining, retrieving & validating data needed by an organization about its human resources personal activities, &organizational unit characteristics"	"as a system used to acquire, store, manipulate, analyze, retrieve and distribute information regarding an organization's human resources"	"an integrated system comprised of the databases, computer applications, hardware, software necessary to collect, record, store manage, deliver, present and manipulate data for a company's human resources function"	"as a systematic procedure for collecting, storing, maintaining, retrieving, and validating data needed by organization about its human resources, personnel activities, and organization unit characteristics"	"an integrated system used to gather, store & analyze information regarding an organization's human resources comprising of databases, computer applications, hardware and software necessary to collect, record, store. manage, deliver, present and manipulate data for human resource function"	"all IT-based information systems and applications either stand alone or networked based information systems and applications either stand alone or networked, for human resource purpose, be it for facilitating HR practices, policies or strategies"	"a suite of software, database & cloud computing which provide an all-encompassing solution for managing every aspect of a workforce"

HRIS Benefits

There is plenty of literature by researchers which shows that organizations have been hesitating in adopting HRIS unless they are convinced of its benefits (Ngai, Law, Chan, & Wat, 2008; Troshani, Jerram, & Hill, 2011). The initial benefits of HRIS are that it reduces the paperwork and error in the data formulation which lead to easy management of the workforce with speedy and accurate information (Bamel, Bamel, Sahay, & Thite, 2014). HRIS reduces cost and time and acts as facilitator for decision makers by analyzing and documenting the employee's and organizational information (Altarawneh & Al-Shqairat, 2014; Bal et al., 2012; Khera, 2012; Kovach & Cathcart, 1999; Yang, Lee, & Lee, 2007). Thus, due to cost-saving and quick access to information, HR employees avail daily support from HRIS (Ngai et al., 2008). Overman (1992) states that HRIS benefits include quick, accurate and prominent information processing along with effective employee communication. Watson and Wyatt (2002) claim that these benefits have a positive impact on employee productivity and return on investment which an organization could accrue while adopting HRIS (Al-Dmour & Al-Zu'bi, 2014). HRIS also supports in strategic decisions (Kundu, 2012) and enhances firm's strategic capabilities through improving the flow of information, utmost use of resources with data integrity (Altarawneh & Al-Shqairat, 2014; Lengnick-Hall & Moritz, 2003). HRIS improves the performance of organization via enhancing the quality of HR functions that lead to organizational excellence by creating a sense of satisfaction among employees (Mbgua, 2015). For overall improvement in the HR functions, HRIS aligns HR practices with the organizational strategies (Shiri, 2012).

According to Beckers and Bsat (2002) companies should use HRIS as it enhances competitiveness by improving HR operations; it produces a variety of HR related reports; it helps in focusing of HR towards strategic HRM; it re-engineers the entire HR functions while making employees part of HRIS (Boateng, 2007). HRIS benefits based on prior studies has been tabulated in Table 2.

Table 2. HRIS benefits based on prior studies

Benefits	Prior Studies
Accuracy, timely & quickly access to information & costs saving	Ngai & Wat, 2008
Administrative purposes that reduce costs & time automation of routine transactions	Kovach & Cathcart, 1999; Kovach et al., 2002
Recording & analyzing employees and organization information & documentation of procedures and safety procedure.	Lee, 2008
Improving HR operations; focused on strategic HRM & re-engineer the HR function	Boateng, 2007
Improves the flow of information & enhanced the firm's strategic capabilities	Lengnick, Hall & Moritz, 2003
Support strategic decision making and daily operations.	Kundu et al., 2012
Control & manage HR costs such as labor and recruitment cost	Khera & Gulati, 2012
Produces more effective and faster outcomes.	Shiri, 2012
HRIS improves employment services	Bamel et al., 2014
HRIS lead to organizational effectiveness	Mbugua, 2015
HRIS reduces overhead expenses by adding greater value to the business, accurate & fast information transmission along with the rate of investment and effective communication.	Rand et al., 2015

All these benefits make HRIS an imperative tool for its adoption. In the modern era with the advent of technology human resource potentialities and capabilities get enhanced (Al Shibly, 2011). Today, organizations automate all its functioning by adopting technology in general and HRIS software in particular (Kossek & Young, 1994). The modification of HR functions is solely due to its technological advancement (Teo et al., 2001). Moreover, with the correct use of information it enhances the efficiency and effectiveness of HRM functions (NishadNawaz, 2012).

Theoretical Background

In this paper, we have integrated the TOE framework and HOT framework in order to fulfill the first objective of this paper. The TOE framework explains three different elements that are the technological, organizational and environmental context. The HOT framework has three different elements that are Human, Organization and Technology factors. Further these factors have been classified into internal and external factors. These internal factors are further sub-divided into organizational and human factors and external factors are divided into environmental and technological factors (Rand Hani Al-Dmour, Love, & Al-Zu'bi, 2013). TOE framework has been shown in Figure 1.

Figure 1. Technology-organization-environment framework

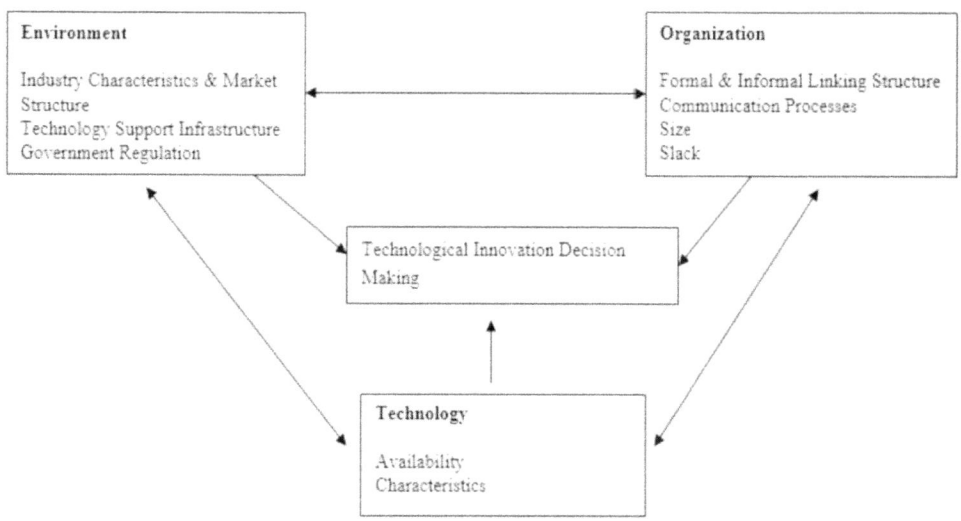

Source: (Baker, 2011). *The Technology-Organization-Environment Framework*

Brief Description of Technology, Organization, Environment and Human Factors

- **Technology factors:** Basically, technology factors include the availability and characteristic of the required technology, which includes technology readiness, existing technology within the organization (IT Infrastructure); data integrity, system usefulness; system integration. Readiness of technology and potential realization of organizational capabilities have played a major role in HRIS adoption (Anitha & Aruna, 2014; Thite & Kavanagh, 2012; Nyeko & Angundaru, 2017; Al-Dmour, 2013). For making HRIS as an integral part, an organization has to build a needed infrastructure (Chakraborty & Mansor, 2013). Prior studies deal with organization technology fit, adoption cost, user-friendliness as an essential requirement for an organization to go with HRIS (Troshani et al., 2011). Institute of Management and Administration (2002) surveyed that it's not only the organizational technology fit which is a prerequisite for any technology to run properly but staff knowledge and skills are also vital requirement for these technologies to be utilized properly (Ngai et al., 2008; Oliveira & Martins, 2010);
- **Organizational Factors:** Organization dimensions comprise organization size, centralization and decentralization; communication process; top management support; data access, security & privacy, capabilities and resources. Organizational factors such as size, centralization, organizational IT structure, and its financial readiness have played a pivotal role in HRIS adoption (Tariq et al., 2017; Al-Dmour, 2013). Studies have acknowledged that the most significant factor for HRIS adoption is organizational size that dictates its affordability and thus has been a clear factor of HRIS adoption (Kundu, 2012; Teo et al., 2001). Previous studies found that smaller organization are unaware about HRIS benefits and due to lack of financial and top management support they are reluctant in its adoption and use (Ngai et al., 2008). Besides organization size, top management commitment and employee involvement showed positive influence on HRIS adoption (Troshani et

al., 2011; Yang et al., 2007). The organization capabilities in respect of both human and technical skills have been equally important besides organizational IT structure (Al-Dmour et al., 2013). Employee structural IT knowledge and their educational level have a positive impact on HRIS adoption. Though financial readiness is an important factor acknowledged by researcher however some researcher failed to establish any significant relationship between financial readiness and HRIS adoption (Yang et al., 2007);

- **Environmental Factors:** Environmental dimensions comprise the Government regulations, environmental readiness, supportive infrastructure and competition intensity or competitive pressure. By competitive pressure authors means the forces that led organizations to adopt these technology extensively for gaining strategic benefits over their competitors. In this globalized world, competitiveness and external pressure have a direct relationship between HRIS adoption and its success (Anitha & Aruna, 2014). Environmental factors that influence HR activities are competition; technological development; HRM state of art; labor market; societal developments and governmental regulation (Ruël et al., 2004). External pressures of the competition have a direct influence on the adoption of HRIS System. For being competitive, organization has to depend on technological advancement and rely on this type of innovative technology for its development;

- **Human Factors:** Human dimension comprises the top management supports and commitment; end user acceptance; organizational units' communication and collaboration; HR Skills and IT expertise. Kossek et al. (1994) suggested that end user perceptions towards new technology have a critical impact on HRIS implementation. Human factors are based on emotional beliefs of employees towards any change in an organization. The perception of end users should be taken into consideration while taking decision regarding HRIS adoption and implementation (Kossek & Young, 1994). These perceptions are based on employees' self-efficacy and anxiety towards any change in an organization. By securing employees' human factor, an organization could easily adopt HRIS or any system change. The success or failure of any system solely depend on the employee perception toward that system (Anitha & Aruna, 2014). Perceptions of new technology, inner satisfaction, and organization employees' efficiency have been critical for the successful implementation of HRIS and this could be easily done by the support of HR leader (Anitha & Aruna, 2014; Kossek & Young, 1994). However, satisfaction with HRIS has been influenced phenomenally by its end-user perception and ease of use associated with HRIS (Kumar & Parumasur, 2013; Bal et al., 2012). Individuals' willingness to explore new technologies and their risk taking abilities has a great impact on HRIS adoption (Al-Dmour et al., 2013; Panayotopoulou & Galanaki, 2007; Voermans & Van Veldhoven, 2007). It is important that the potential users perceive the system to be compatible and fit as per their work requirement (Nah, Tan, & Teh, 2004).

Alam et al. (2016) combined TOE and HOT framework and developed a conceptual framework including Technology, Organization, Environment and Human factors. A conceptual framework based on TOE and HOT frameworks has been shown in Figure 2.

Besides, technological, organizational and environmental factor; human factor is a new facet in the HRIS adoption. By considering all these prominent factors an organization could enhance the likelihood towards adoption of HRIS.

Figure 2. Combined of technology-organization-environment and human-organization-technology framework

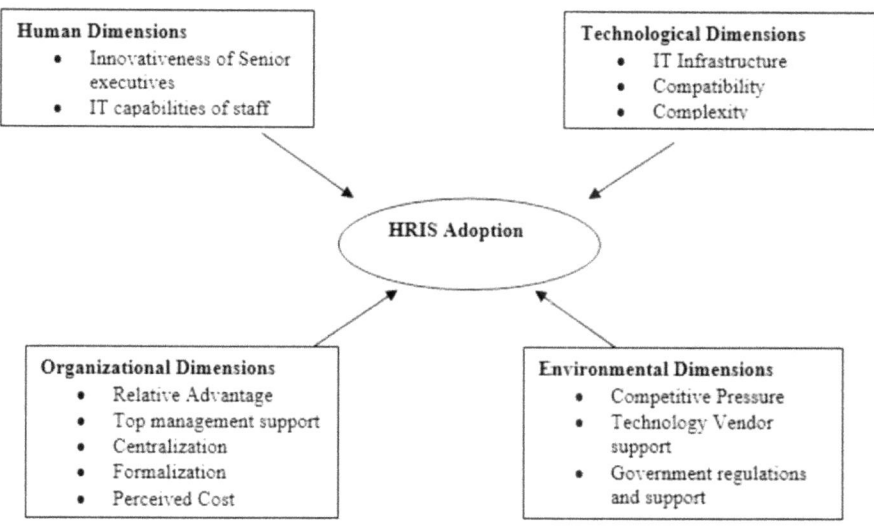

Source: Alam et al. (2016)

Prior studies include CEO characteristics, perceived benefits and barriers along with technological, organizational, environmental and individual characteristics (Alam, Masum, Beh, & Hong, 2016; Awa, Ukoha, & Emecheta, 2016; Bhatti, 2017; Leung, Lo, Fong, & Law, 2015; Pan & Jang, 2008; Ramdani, Kawalek, & Lorenzo, 2009; Thong, 1999; Zhu, Kraemer, & Xu, 2003). On the technological front the most prominent factors of HRIS adoption emerged out to be organizational IT infrastructure and perceived relative advantage. On the organizational front the most prominent factors are top management support, financial readiness and organizational size. Governmental regulation and competitive pressure is the most prominent factor as far as environmental dimension is concern. Besides, these factors the most prominent factors concerning the Human dimension are end user perception and employees IT expertise, which is required to run and do task effectively in these type of technology. If organizations consider all the stated prominent factors while adopting HRIS it would not only enhance their competitiveness but also eliminates the barriers in HRIS implementation. Hence, by consolidating all the adoption factors the authors try to justify the first objectives of this paper.

The lists comprise of technological, organizational, environmental and human context which includes both quantitative and qualitative data have been tabulated in table 3, tick mark denotes factors that were significant predictors of HRIS adoption.

Table 3. Various prior studies along with significant p-values of HRIS adopting factors based on TOE and HOT framework

Authors	Dimensions	Technology	Organization	Environment	Human
Thong, 1999 N=166	Decision maker Characteristics				
	CEO Innovativeness		Π		
	CEO IS Knowledge		Π		
	IS Characteristics				
	Relative Advantage	Π			
	Compatibility				
	Complexity	Π			
	Information Intensity				
	Organizational Characteristics				
	Business Size		Π		
	Environmental Characteristics				
	Competition				
	Individual Characteristic				
	Employee IS Knowledge				Π
Zhu et al., 2003 N=3103	Technology Characteristics				
	Technology Competence	Π			
	Organizational Characteristics				
	Firm Scope (Financial Readiness)		Π		
	Firm size		Π		
	Lack of trading partner readiness				
	Consumer readiness				
	Environmental Characteristics				
	Competitive Pressure			Π	
Teo et al., 2007	Innovation Characteristic				
	Relative Advantage	Π			
	Organizational Characteristics				
	Firm Size		Π		
	Environment Characteristic				
	Competitive Pressure			Π	
	Human characteristics				
	HR & IT Expertise				Π

continues on following page

Table 3. Cotinued

Authors	Dimensions	Technology	Organization	Environment	Human
Ju et al., 2008 Personal Interview 99 Firms	Technological Characteristics				
	IT Infrastructure				
	Technological readiness	Π			
	Organizational Characteristics				
	Size		Π		
	Perceived Barriers		Π		
	Environmental Characteristics				
	Production & operations Improvement			Π	
	Enhancement of products and services				
	Competitive Pressure				
	Regulatory Policy				
Ramdani et al., 2009 Direct Interview Method (logistic regression) N=102	Technological Characteristics				
	Relative Advantage	Π			
	Compatibility				
	Complexity				
	Trialability	Π			
	Observability				
	Organizational Characteristics				
	Top Management Support		Π		
	Organization Readiness		Π		
	IS Experience				
	Size		Π		
	Industry				
	Market Scope				
	Environmental Characteristics				
	Competitive Pressure				
	External IS Support				
Oliveire & Martin, 2010 N=2459 logistic regression analysis	Individual characteristics				
	Perceived Benefits &Obstacles		Π		
	Technology Characteristics				
	Technology Readiness	Π			
	Technology Integration	Π			
	Organizational Characteristics				
	Trading Partner Collaboration		Π		
	Firm Size				
	Environmental Characteristics				
	Competitive Pressure			Π	

continues on following page

Table 3. Cotinued

Authors	Dimensions	Technology	Organization	Environment	Human
Chowdhary, 2015 N=331 Questionnaire Method	Individual Characteristics				
	IT Expertise				
	Employee Individual Attributes				Π
	Technological Characteristics				
	IT Infrastructure	Π			
	Compatibility	Π			
	Complexity				
	Organizational Characteristics				
	Top Management Support		Π		
	Environmental Characteristics				
	Industry Pressure			Π	
Aalm et al., 2016 N=383	Innovative Characteristics				
	Innovativeness of senior executive		Π		
	IT Capabilities of Staff				Π
	Technology Characteristics				
	IT Infrastructure	Π			
	Perceived Compatibility	Π			
	Perceived Complexity	Π			
	Relative Advantage	Π			
	Organizational Characteristics				
	Top Management support		Π		
	Centralization		Π		
	Formalization		Π		
	Perceived Cost		Π		
	Environmental Characteristics				
	Competitive Pressure			Π	
	Technology Vendor Support			Π	
	Government Regulation &Support			Π	

continues on following page

Table 3. Cotinued

Authors	Dimensions	Technology	Organization	Environment	Human
Hart, 2016 N=373	Technological Characteristics				
	ICT Infrastructure	Π			
	Technical know how	Π			
	Perceived Compatibility	Π			
	Perceived Values	Π			
	Organizational Characteristics				
	Security		Π		
	Firm Size		Π		
	Scope of Business		Π		
	Trading partner readiness		Π		
	Environmental Characteristics				
	Competitive Pressure			Π	
	External Support			Π	
	Human Characteristics				
	Subjective Norm				Π
Bhatti, 2017 N=105	Technological Characteristics				
	Relative Advantage	Π			
	Compatibility				
	Complexity				
	Technology Readiness	Π			
	Organizational Characteristics				
	Firm Size		Π		
	Top Management Support		Π		
	Trading Partners		Π		
	Environmental Characteristics				
	Competitive Pressure			Π	
Nyeko et al., 2017 Partial Least Squares Structured Equation Modeling (PLS-SEM) N=91	Technological Characteristics				
	Relative Advantage	Π			
	IT Infrastructure	Π			
	Complexity				
	Organizational Characteristics				
	Organization Compatibility		Π		
	Top Management Support		Π		
	Human Characteristics				
	IT Knowledge				Π

continues on following page

Table 3. Cotinued

Authors	Dimensions	Technology	Organization	Environment	Human
Troshani et al., 2011 Qualitative Analysis-16 interviews across 11 Australian Public sector organizations.	Technological Characteristics				
	Integration	Π			
	User friendliness	Π			
	accessibility	Π			
	efficiency	Π			
	vendor support	Π			
	Organizational Characteristics				
	Human capability		Π		
	Centralization		Π		
	Environmental Characteristics				
	Regulatory Compliance			Π	
Anitha et al., 2013	Technological Characteristics				
	Operationalization of technology	Π			
	potential benefits of technology	Π			
	organization adoption capability	Π			
	organizational Characteristics				
	Size		Π		
	Centralization		Π		
	IT Infrastructure		Π		
	Financial Resource		Π		
	Environmental Characteristics				
	Competitive capability			Π	
	External pressure			Π	
	Impact of Globalization			Π	

continues on following page

Table 3. Cotinued

Authors	Dimensions	Technology	Organization	Environment	Human
Al Dmour, 2013	Technological characteristics				
	Perceived IT innovation	Π			
	Relative Advantage	Π			
	Compatibility	Π			
	Complexity	Π			
	Trialability	Π			
	Observability	Π			
	Organizational Characteristics				
	Top Management Support		Π		
	Centralization		Π		
	Formalization		Π		
	Size		Π		
	Type of business		Π		
	Specialization		Π		
	Environmental Characteristics				
	Competitive pressure			Π	
	Vendor support			Π	
	Governmental regulations			Π	
	Human Characteristics				
	HR Role				Π
	Involvement of HR Leader				Π
	Managerial IT Knowledge				Π
Leung et al., 2015 Qualitative data- Interview 4 Managers	Technological Characteristics				
	Expected/Achieved direct benefits	Π			
	Expected/Achieved indirect benefits	Π			
	Compatibility	Π			
	Expected risk	Π			
	Organizational characteristics				
	Financial Readiness		Π		
	Technological Readiness		Π		
	Top Management Support		Π		
	Environmental Characteristics				
	Perceived pressure from Industry			Π	
	Perceived pressure from partner			Π	
	Perceived pressure from Customer			Π	

HRIS Barriers and its Implementation

Implementation of HRIS is very much essential to convert adoption into a success. According to Kovach & Cathcart (1999), lack of money and top management support plays the biggest barrier to HRIS implementation (Kovach & Cathcart, 1999). Similarly, Beckers and Bsat (2002) come up that cost of setting and maintaining these technologies have the major obstacles and often they come along with reluctant attitude of top management and employees (Al-Dmour & Al-Zu'bi, 2014; Ngai et al., 2008; Nishad Nawaz, 2013).The most significant hurdles in HRIS implementation is the unwillingness of top management and their resistance to change(Rand H. Al-Dmour & Al-Zu'bi, 2014; Bamel, Bamel, Sahay, & Thite, 2014b) .Other factors resisting the implementation of HRIS includes lack of knowledge, culture resistance and changing organization culture along with lack of commitment from top managers and lesser importance given to HR department (Altarawneh & Al-Shqairat, 2010, 2014; Krishnan & Singh, 2012; Theeb, 2018).Participation and support of management and employees have been essential requirement for a successful implementation of HRIS (Hirvonen, 2011). According to Batool (2012), lack of IT expertise, untrained staff and mishandling of HRIS are the most important impediment in the path of HRIS implementation (Batool, 2012). Summary of barriers to HRIS implementation has been tabulated in Table 4.

Table 4. Barriers to HRIS based on prior studies

Lack/Insufficient financial support	Ngai & Wat (2006); Altarawnel & Al-Shqairat (2010)
	Md. Faruk Abdullah (2018)
Organizational Culture	Altarawnel & Al-Shqairat (2010); Arafat Alshaikh Theeb (2018)
Lack of commitment	Altarawnel & Al-Shqairat (2010); Bamel et al. (2014); Al-Dmour & Al-Zu'bi, 2014
Cost of setting and maintaining HRIS	Arafat Alshaikh Theeb, Md. Faruk Abdullah (2018)
Lack of application for HR users	Kovach & Cathcart (1999)
Lack of information technology support	Ngai et al. (2008)
Resistance to change	Al-Dmour & Al-Zu'bi (2014)
Lack of importance and knowledge of HR Department	Krishnan and Singh (2006); Altarawneh & Al-Shqairat (2010)
Lack of skill and expertise, technical problems, Lack of capital, time consumption by the untrained staff	Batool, Sajid, & Raza (2012)

In addition to the above barriers, following are the challenges faced by an organizations in order to implement HRIS successfully (Dery, Grant, & Wiblen, 2009); (Jahan, 2014):

1. A discrepancy between observed and actual attitude of HRIS, results in intricacy of top management commitment towards HRIS;
2. Organization underestimates the complexities involved with HRIS and its impact on the behavioral changes in an organization;

3.   The most important barrier which comes out within a literature is users/employee acceptance and involvement in HRIS adoption and implementation process.

Today organizations are aware of HRIS benefits and its long-term impact on their employees and the role HRIS is playing in achieving organizational goals. So, the need of HRIS should be generated & analyzed for its further adoption and implementation. It is very important that HRIS adoption and implementation process must be seen as a whole so that system cohesiveness would be maintained. Each and every steps of implementation must be cross check to ensure its correctness and feasibility. By managing and upgrading employees skills an organization creates an edge over its competitors. This has been an achievable target only due to organizational embedded with HRIS workflow activities. For better adoption, the employees should be given sufficient training to adopt the new system. The role of HR leaders cannot be neglected as they can motivate employees in enhancing their acceptance level on the one hand and fetch out ways to overcome any barriers in the line of HRIS adoption and implementation process on the other. Proper integration and implementation of HRIS with organization would enhance integration of HR function with organizational objectives. So, it is important for organizations to look on the factors which are necessary for HRIS implementation. In order to take advantage of HRIS, an organization should follow the following steps for its implementation as shown in Figure 3.

Figure 3. HRIS implementation steps

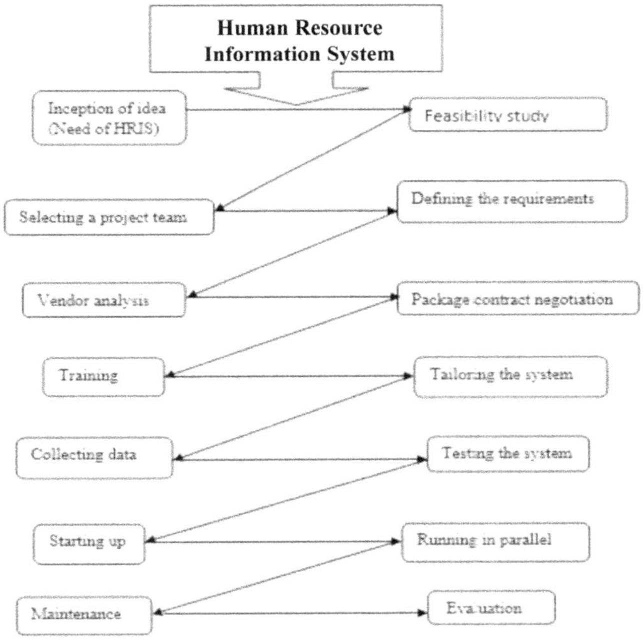

Source: (Jahan, 2014)

Step 1: Initially, organization and top management should realize and must agree upon the needs for HRIS. Top management must be fully aware and recognize that organization needs to automate its HR function and treat HR as a strategic partner in their business.

Step 2: They must treat HRIS as an investment and so its feasibility should be assessed. The feasibility must cover the avenues like the scope of the software, its future benefits and their values to business along with its cost estimation and rate of investment. Consequently, it enhances organization decision making efficacy toward HRIS.

Step 3: For successful implementation, both HR and IT should form a team taking into consideration a specific budget, time and quality. The involvement of top-level management and HR leaders is essentially required at this stage as they create a framework/blueprint for HRIS Implementation.

Step 4: The process that is required to be incorporated in the system need to be analyze at this stage. As organizational needs are different from one another some wants to incorporate payroll module first and other wants leave management module and other wants some other module to be incorporated first. Company's financial readiness and HR requirements should be synchronized properly in order to get benefits of HRIS.

Step 5: Organizational affordability and vendors have been scrutinized while taking their capacity, track record and goodwill into account.

Step 6/7: Subsequently, the organization moves towards package contract negotiation with vendor based on their cost which should include installation, training and maintenance.

Step 8: Further HRIS systems is tailored and only those features and functions are visible on the screens which is require for work assignment, thus accelerate the pace of employee acceptance towards the system.

Step 9: On fulfillment of these basic initial formalities contact is finalized, approved and signed by the different parties.

Step 10/11: Next, data is shared and validated before entering it in the HRIS software. Once, discrepancies are analyzed, final delivery of the software is done while taking user acceptance into consideration.

Step 12/13: To be secure, the organization initially runs it parallel with their existing process for at least one full cycle and meanwhile HRIS maintenance if required is done.

Step 14: This is followed by undertaking software evaluation which is done by investigating the values and differences it has created for an organization.

The most prominent barriers in HRIS implementation are: lack of top management support and poor HRIS needs analysis (Khatri & Raheja, 2013; Krishnan & Singh, 2012; Mohapatra & Patnaik, 2011). Whatever change management strategies are applied by the organizations, they have to ensure that top management is aware and convinced about new technology. Besides this, the employees' skills should be upgraded by providing proper training to them as and when the need arises (Dilu, Gebreslassie, & Kebede, 2017; Krishnan & Singh, 2012; Masum, Kabir, & Chowdhury, 2015; Mohapatra & Patnaik, 2011). Thus, authors have given the answers to the second objective by consolidating the literature of HRIS Implementation. Barriers to HRIS implementation and suggestions have been tabulated in Table 5.

The findings of this paper reveal that the most prominent HRIS adoption factors are organizational IT infrastructure, perceived relative advantage, top management support, financial readiness, organizational size, governmental regulation & competitive pressure and end user perception along with employees IT expertise. Furthermore, the most prominent barriers in HRIS implementation are lack of top management support and poor HRIS needs analysis. In addition to these factors many unexplored factors are

CEO innovativeness, CEO knowledge, Individual attributes, technology vendor support, trade partner readiness, perceived benefits and barriers and market scope.

Table 5. Barriers to HRIS implementation and suggestions

Authors/Year	Barriers to Implementation	Suggestions
Sanjay, 2011 Case Study	Lack of Management Commitment; Satisfaction; inadequate need analysis; Failure to include key people and significant group; Lack of communication.	Upgrading employee skills; Train the trainer approach to save cost; Project timeliness & senior management review; Mapping with organizational objectives; Streamlining business process by reengineering; Stakeholder involvement & communication.
Sandeep Krishnan, 2012 Nine Indian Organization	Lack of knowledge and focus on HR department; Low involvement of user	Proper workforce analysis; user training; Internal capability building; Streamlining of processes & commitment for change management.
Khatri, 2013 Qualitative Study	Poor need assessment; change management; vendor selection; organizational system fit; Data migration; Availability of internal user support; Lack of cooperation; Management Commitment; Human capability and privacy issues.	Change Management along with support from top management.
Chowdhury et al., 2015 N=18 Companies	Unwillingness of Top Management; Lack of IT expertise; Cost of IT Infrastructure; Shortage of IT Expert; Internal Resistance; Privacy & security Issues; Inadequate ROI and more adaptation cost.	Ensure top management awareness, infrastructural development, IT expertise and IT training of HR people; Overcome resistance from employees by protecting their privacy and security.
Dilu et al., 2017 N=288	Internet access; Separate HR department; computer skills; fear of unemployment	Provide basic computer skills with internet access; train the HR employees; create a separate HR department.

CONCLUSION AND FUTURE RECOMMENDATION

The focus of this study has been to gain insights about factors leading to HRIS adoption and its barriers in implementation faced by an organization. The literature clearly demonstrates that HRIS has gained momentum since the advent of technology. The study explores the literature and finds the factors of HRIS adoption. The indubitable benefits of HRIS lead an organization to implement HRIS while ensuring its proper utilization. Organizations now-a-days are aware about the significance of HRIS software and its potentialities (Bondarouk, Parry, & Furtmueller, 2017) as it simplifies HR functions, supports in achieving organizational and employees goals. Apart from organizational and top management support, the employees or ultimate users support & involvement is necessary for making all those internal and external factors relevant for any organization. Technological-fit i.e., required infrastructure and IT expertise and organizational-fit i.e., alignment of organizational needs with its human resource expertise are the indispensable requirements for any new innovation or technology to run successfully. For generating high value results, automation of Human Resource Process is the basic prerequisite, and this can be easily done with the help of HRIS. Thus, both the collaborative efforts of human resource Professional and IT expert team are required for making this technology feasible for any organization. The future researcher should focus on these TOE and HOT framework and do some empirical analysis on the basis of this paper outcome. Longitudinal analysis could be done, and factors could be analyzed while considering implementation phase of HRIS. Further researcher should analyze these adoption and implementation factors in relation to CEO innovativeness, CEO knowledge, Individual attributes, technology vendor support, trade partner readiness, perceived benefits and barriers and market scope.

REFERENCES

Aggarwal, N., & Kapoor, M. (2012). Human Resource Information Systems (HRIS)-Its Role and Importance in Business Competitiveness. *Gian Jyoti E-Journal, 1*(2), 1–13.

Al-Dmour, R.H., Love, S., & Al-Zu'bi, Z. (2013). Factors Influencing the Adoption of HRIS Applications: A Literature Review. *International Journal of Management & Business Studies, 3*(4), 9–25.

Al-Dmour, R.H., & Al-Zu'bi, Z. M. F. (2014). Factors Motivating and Inhibiting the Practice of HRIS in Business Organizations: An Empirical Analysis. *International Business Research, 7*(7). doi:10.5539/ibr.v7n7p139

Al-Dmour, R. (2013). Factors Influencing the Adoption of HRIS Applications: A Literature Review. *International Journal of Management and Business Studies, 3*(4), 9–26.

Al Shibly, H. (2011). Human Resources Information System Success Assessment: An Integrative Model. *Australian Journal of Basic and Applied Sciences, 5*(MAY), 157–169.

Alam, M. G. R., Masum, A. K. M., Beh, L. S., & Hong, C. S. (2016). Critical factors influencing decision to adopt human resource information system (HRIS) in hospitals. *PLoS One, 11*(8), e0160366. doi:10.1371/journal.pone.0160366 PMID:27494334

Altarawneh, I., & Al-Shqairat, Z. (2010). Human Resource Information Systems in Jordanian Universities. *International Journal of Business and Management, 5*(10). doi:10.5539/ijbm.v5n10p113

Anitha, D. J., & Aruna, M. M. (2014). Adoption of human resource information systems in organizations. *Journal of Contemporary Research in Management, 9*(4), 63–74. doi:10.1016/j.sbspro.2013.04.051

Aswanth Kumar, N., & Brijball Parumasur, S. (2013). Managerial Perceptions of the Impact of HRIS on Organizational Efficiency Nikhal. *Journal of Economics and Behavioral Studies, 5*(12), 861–875.

Awa, H. O., Ukoha, O., & Emecheta, B. C. (2016). Using T-O-E theoretical framework to study the adoption of ERP solution. *Cogent Business and Management, 3*(1), 1–23. doi:10.1080/23311975.2016.1196571

Baker, J. (2011). *The Technology-Organization-Environment Framework.* Springer. doi:10.1007/978-1-4419-6108-2

Bal, Y., Bozkurt, S., & Ertemsir, E. (2012). The Importance of Using Human Resources Information Systems (HRIS) and a Research on Determining the Success of HRIS. In *Proceedings of the Management Knowledge and Learning International Conference* (pp. 53–62).

Bamel, N., Bamel, U. K., Sahay, V., & Thite, M. (2014). Usage, benefits and barriers of human resource information system in universities. *Vine, 44*(4), 519–536. doi:10.1108/VINE-04-2013-0024

Batool, Q. (2012). Benefits and Barriers of Human Resource Information System In Accounts Office. *International Journal of Humanities and Social Science, 2*(3), 211–217.

Bhatti, T. (2017). Influences on adoption of cloud-based ERP systems in SMEs: The technological-organizational-environmental framework. *Corporate Ownership and Control, 15*(1), 370–380. doi:10.22495/cocv15i1c2p6

Boateng, A. A. (2007). The Role of Human Resource Information Systems (HRIS) in Strategic Human Resource Management (SHRM). *HANKEN-Swedish School of Economics and Business Administration.*

Bondarouk, T., Parry, E., & Furtmueller, E. (2017). Electronic HRM: Four decades of research on adoption and consequences. *International Journal of Human Resource Management, 28*(1), 98–131. doi:10.1080/09585192.2016.1245672

Broderick, R., & Bounreau, J. W. (1992). Human resource management, information technology, and the competitive edge. *CAHRS Working Paper Series., 6*(351), 7–17. doi:10.5465/ame.1992.4274391

Chakraborty, A. R., & Mansor, N. N. A. (2013). Adoption of Human Resource Information System: A Theoretical Analysis. *Procedia: Social and Behavioral Sciences, 75,* 473–478. doi:10.1016/j.sbspro.2013.04.051

Dery, K., Grant, D., & Wiblen, S. (2009). Human Resource Information Systems (HRIS): replacing or enhancing HRM. Retrieved from http://www.ilera-directory.org/15thworldcongress/files/papers/Track_1/Wed_W3_DERY.pdf

Dilu, E., Gebreslassie, M., & Kebede, M. (2017). Human Resource Information System implementation readiness in the Ethiopian health sector: A cross-sectional study. *Human Resources for Health, 15*(1), 85. doi:10.118612960-017-0259-3 PMID:29262832

Hirvonen, M. (2011). Planning and implementation of HRIS to support change management. Saimaa University of Applied Sciences.

Jahan, S. (2014). Human Resources Information System (HRIS): A Theoretical Perspective. *Journal of Human Resource and Sustainability Studies, 2*(June), 33–39. doi:10.4236/jhrss.2014.22004

Khatri, P., & Raheja, N. (2013). HRIS Implementation in Organizations: Issues & Challenges. In *Proceedings of the National Conference on Information and Communication Technologies (ICT) for Competitive Advantage.* Academic Press.

Khera, D. S. N. (2012). Human Resource Information System and its impact on Human Resource Planning: A perceptual analysis of Information Technology companies. *IOSR Journal of Business and Management, 3*(6), 6–13. doi:10.9790/487X-0360613

Kossek, E. E., Young, W., Gash, D. C., & Nichol, V. (1994). Waiting for innovation in the human resources department: Godot implements a human resource information system. *Human Resource Management, 33*(1), 135–159.

Kovach, K. A., & Cathcart, C. E. Jr. (1999). Human Resource Information Systems (HRIS): Providing Business with Rapid Data Access, Information Exchange and Strategic Advantage. *Public Personnel Management, 28*(2), 275–282. doi:10.1177/009102609902800208

Krishnan, S. K., & Singh, M. (2012). Issues and Concerns in the Implementation and Maintenance of HRIS. *Management and Labour Studies*, *32*(4), 522–540. doi:10.1177/0258042X0703200407

Kundu, S. C., & Kadian, R. (2012). Applications of HRIS in Human Resource Management in India: A Study. *European Journal of Business and Management, 4*(21), 34–41.

Lengnick-Hall, M. L., & Moritz, S. (2003). The impact of e-HR on the human resource management function. *Journal of Labor Research*, *24*(3), 365–379. doi:10.100712122-003-1001-6

Leung, D., Lo, A., Fong, L. H. N., & Law, R. (2015). Applying the technology-organization-environment framework to explore ICT initial and continued adoption: An exploratory study of an independent hotel in Hong Kong. *Tourism Recreation Research*, *40*(3), 391–406. doi:10.1080/02508281.2015.1090152

Maditheti, N. N., & Gomes, A. M. (2017). Human Resource Information System: A Review of Previous Studies. *Journal of Management Research*, *9*(3), 92. doi:10.5296/jmr.v9i3.11488

Masum, A. K. M., Kabir, M. J., & Chowdhury, M. M. (2015). Determinants that influencing the adoption of E-HRM: An empirical study on Bangladesh. *Asian Social Science*, *11*(21), 117–124. doi:10.5539/ass.v11n21p117

Mbgua, C. N. (2015). the Role of Human Resource Information Systems in Organizational Effectiveness: A Case Study of Kenya Commercial Bank. *International Journal of Business and Commerce*, *4*(406), 99–145.

Mohapatra, S., & Patnaik, A. (2011). Sustainability in HRIS implementation through effective project management. *International Journal of Project Organisation and Management*, *3*(1), 78–90. doi:10.1504/IJPOM.2011.038865

Nah, F. F.-H., Tan, X., & Teh, S. H. (2004). An Empirical Investigation on End-Users' Acceptance of Enterprise Systems. *Information Resources Management Journal*, *17*(3), 32–53. doi:10.4018/irmj.2004070103

Nawaz, N. (2013). The usage of human resource information systems in HR processes in select software companies in Bangalore City India. *Information and Knowledge Management*, *3*(12), 102-112. Retrieved from www.iiste.org

Nawaz, M.N. (2012). To assess the Impact of HRIS in Facilitating Information Flow among the select Software Companies in Bangalore, India. *Research Journal of Management Sciences*, *1*(3), 1–8.

Ngai, E. W. T., Law, C. C. H., Chan, S. C. H., & Wat, F. K. T. (2008). Importance of the internet to human resource practitioners in Hong Kong. *Personnel Review*, *37*(1), 66–84. doi:10.1108/00483480810839978

Nyeko, J. S., & Angundaru, G. (2017). Employee Adoption and Use of Human Resource Information Systems (HRIS): Evidence from Ugandan Local Government Perspective. *International Journal of Scientific Research in Science and Technology*, *3*(1), 327–340.

Oliveira, T., & Martins, M. F. (2010). Understanding e-business adoption across industries in European countries. *Industrial Management & Data Systems*, *110*(9), 1337–1354. doi:10.1108/02635571011087428

Pan, M. J., & Jang, W. Y. (2008). Determinants of the adoption of enterprise resource planning within the technology-organization-environment framework: Taiwan's communications industry. *Journal of Computer Information Systems*, *48*(3), 94–102. doi:10.1080/08874417.2008.11646025

Panayotopoulou, L., & Galanaki, E. (2007). E-HR adoption and the role of HRM : Evidence from Greece. *Personnel*, (March). doi:10.1108/00483480710726145

Ramdani, B., Kawalek, P., & Lorenzo, O. (2009). Predicting SMEs' adoption of enterprise systems. *Journal of Enterprise Information Management*, 22(1/2), 10–24. doi:10.1108/17410390910922796

Ruël, H., Bondarouk, T., & Looise, J. K. (2004). E-HRM: Innovation or Irritation. An Explorative Empirical Study in Five Large Companies on Web-based HRM. *Management Review*, 15(3), 364–380. doi:10.5771/0935-9915-2004-3-364

Shiri, S. (2012). Effectiveness of Human Resource Information System on HR Functions of the Organization-A Cross Sectional Study. Retrieved from http://www.davidpublishing.com/davidpublishing/Upfile/11/14/2012/2012111401088443.pdf

Tariq, B., Pangil, F., & Shahzad, A. (2017). Diffusion of innovation theory: Beyond decision stage. *International Journal of advanced and applied sciences*, 4(5), 12–18. doi:10.21833/ijaas.2017.05.002

Teo, T. S. H., Soon, L. G., & Fedric, S. A. (2001). RESEARCH AND PRACTICE Adoption and Impact of Human Resource. *Research and Practice in Human Resource Management*, 9(1), 101–117.

Theeb, A. (2018). The Role of Information Systems in Human Resource Management. In *Management of Information Systems* (pp. 88–98). Intech. doi:10.5772/intechopen.79294

Thite, M., Kavanagh, M.J., & Johnson, R.D. (2012). Evolution of Human Resource Management &Human Resource Information Systems: The role of information technology.

Thong, J. (1999). Management-Informations-Systeme. *Informationssysteme in Wirtschaft Und Verwaltung*, 15(4), 187–214. doi:10.1515/9783111571928-004

Troshani, I., Jerram, C., & Hill, S. R. (2011). Exploring the public sector adoption of HRIS. *Industrial Management & Data Systems*, 111(3), 470–488. doi:10.1108/02635571111118314

Voermans, M., & Van Veldhoven, M. (2007). Attitude towards E-HRM: An empirical study at Philips. *Personnel Review*, 36(6), 887–902. doi:10.1108/00483480710822418

Yang, K. H., Lee, S. M., & Lee, S. G. (2007). Adoption of information and communication technology: Impact of technology types, organization resources and management style. *Industrial Management & Data Systems*, 107(9), 1257–1275. doi:10.1108/02635570710833956

Zhu, K., Kraemer, K., & Xu, S. (2003). Electronic business adoption by European firms: A cross-country assessment of the facilitators and inhibitors. *European Journal of Information Systems*, 12(4), 251–268. doi:10.1057/palgrave.ejis.3000475

This research was previously published in the International Journal of Human Capital and Information Technology Professionals (IJHCITP), 11(4); pages 80-98, copyright year 2020 by IGI Publishing (an imprint of IGI Global).

Chapter 7
How Can Human Resource Management Help the Theory of Constraints

Brian J. Galli

(iD) https://orcid.org/0000-0001-9392-244X

Assistant Professor and Graduate Program Director, Master of Science in Engineering Management Industrial Engineering, Hofstra University, USA

ABSTRACT

Now, more companies consider human resource management (HRM) as part of strategic business management. A critical analysis of The Goal: A Process of Ongoing Improvement by Goldratt as it relates to HRM allows for discussion and evaluation of HRM implications. However, does HRM implementation support achieving a companies' strategic objectives? If so, how is it related to The Goal? This report seeks answering these questions by evaluating HRM in the book's context. This article discusses the role of HRM in companies, HRM principals that impact operations, roles of stakeholders and their value in the Theory of Constraints (TOC), HRM and its impact on the TOC, roles of HRM management and leadership, and the relationship between technology and human resources. Discussing these topics, this article provides an overview of HRM's impact on organizations. The main findings indicate that HRM implementation is a strategic management resource to be implemented by any businesses.

1. INTRODUCTION AND BACKGROUND OF THE GOAL

A company's main resource is its people, who contribute to achieving the company's strategic goal to be a profitable business (Goldratt, 2014; Galli, 2017). Human Resource Management (HRM) is defined as a process of strategic decisions for the benefit of both employees and companies to improve profits and business performance. Further, HRM focuses on management processes such as recruitment, job analysis, training programs, performance appraisals, incentive plans, and health and safety programs with the purpose of increasing motivation and employee engagement (Dessler, 2017). HRM integrates human resource and management strategies to support decision-making and aids companies in effectively

DOI: 10.4018/978-1-6684-3873-2.ch007

overcoming economic challenges that they may face. However, the question is, does implementation of HRM support the achievement of strategic objectives? If it does, how is that related to the book *The Goal* by Goldratt? The book describes how a manufacturing company implements changes to meet its strategic goal (Anderson et al., 2006).

Eliyahu M. Goldratt and Jeff Cox wrote the book, *The Goal: A Process of Ongoing Improvement,* based on an analysis of a manufacturing plant. The first edition was published in 1984, and the story still influences people today about continuous improvement. Goldratt was the pioneer in presenting the Theory of Constraints (TOC) in this story. The TOC is a systemic manner that identifies constraints, or bottlenecks, that impedes the success of a business and the changes needed to eliminate those constraints. Furthermore, this theory encourages companies to achieve their goals through methodologies that can allow them to control strategies in the short and long terms. Overall, the book describes a UniCo manufacturing plant, located in a small factory town called Bearington. This plant experienced a critical financial situation that can occur in other businesses as well, but, thanks to the strategic management and implementation of TOC, it was rescued from being closed down (Anderson, 2014).

This paper discusses and evaluates the HRM implications and moral effects that impact the achievement of strategic goals as they relate to *The Goal.* The paper is organized into two sections. The first section presents a review of the literature on Human Resource Management (HRM), *The Goal: A Process of Ongoing Improvement*, and the Theory of Constraints (TOC). The next section discusses the role of HRM, its principles and their impact on companies, the role of stakeholders and the TOC, the relationship between HRM and TOC, the role of management and leadership in HRM, and the relationship between technology and human resources. This paper ends by providing conclusions and brief suggestions on opportunities for future works.

2. LITERATURE REVIEW

The following section analyzes the concepts of Human Resources Management (HRM), the book *The Goal: A Process of Ongoing Improvement,* and the Theory of Constraints (TOC). It begins with a brief explanation of the HRM concept and its impact on organizations. Following these concepts, a brief review of *The Goal* is conducted. Finally, the selection describes the impact of implementing TOC on the achievement of a company's objectives.

The following section provides literature in the concepts mentioned above.

2.1. Human Resource Management (HRM)

For the development of this paper, it is important to emphasize there is no one common definition of HRM, but it was identified that some researchers share the notion that HRM assumes a significant role in organizations. HRM is considered, in this paper, as the process by which companies manage their main resources, including employees, to achieve objectives (Dessler, 2017). According to Aswathappa (2005), HRM includes the processes that should be implemented by managers such as hiring, motivating, and engaging employees (Atkinson, 1999; Bakker, 2010). In other words, HRM can be considered as management strategies that optimize decision-making processes and improve profitability and performance of a company (Dessler, 2017). HRM impacts management processes, as discussed in the book, *The Goal.*

2.2. The Goal: A Process of Ongoing Improvement

The book was written by Eliyahu M. Goldratt and Jeff Cox, and its first edition was published in 1984. The book describes how a manufacturing plant, with expensive operations can be transformed into a profitable one. The author highlights reasons why the plant was not making profits. The primary reason was the constraints or bottlenecks (Atkinson, 1999; Bakker, 2010; Galli, 2017). These bottlenecks were the result of mistakes such as machinery standing idle, mismanagement of human resources, and poor workflow. All this resulted in delays in delivery of orders, which caused the company to lose clients due to decreased customer satisfaction.

Following the help of a specialist, the plant manager and his team identified bottlenecks and associated reasons for their lack in profit. They implemented new strategies to eliminate and mitigate bottlenecks, which produce profits until the new bottlenecks appeared. After the changes were implemented, the plant manager and his team developed principles to manage all bottlenecks; (1) identify them, (2) decide how to fix them, (3) make them a priority, (4) prevent their recurrence, and (5) use the resolution process for the next bottleneck. These principles support any business in identifying and addressing constraints, which improves profitability.

The main characters of the story were Alex Rogo, the plant manager, Jonah, Rogo's college professor, Herbie, a boy scout who represented the bottlenecks, Bill Peach, the division vice-president, and Lou, Stacey, Bob Donovan, and Nakamura, all part of the plant management team.

The following section describes the Theory of Constraints (TOC) as explained by Goldratt during the story.

2.3. Theory of Constraints (TOC)

The Theory of Constraints (TOC) was first introduced by Goldratt in the afore-mentioned book. The purpose of TOC is to identify, in a systemic manner, the constraints or bottlenecks and mitigate or eliminate them (Kumar, 2011). Goldratt (2014) also describes three key performance indicators: throughput - the "rate at which the system generates money through sales," inventory - which represents "the money that all the system has invested in purchasing things which it intends to sell," and operating expense - which is "all the money the system spends to turn inventory into throughput" (Goldratt, 2014, p. 67) . He affirmed the purpose of any company is to increase throughput by reducing inventory and operating expenses. As a result, meeting strategic goals is feasible, which makes for a profitable business.

Based on the review of literature presented in this section, the following section discusses HRM as it relates to *The Goal*.

3. DISCUSSIONS

3.1. The Role of HRM

People are a company's main resource and most valuable asset. Thus, the role of HRM is to advise companies on how to manage that resource. The purpose of HRM is to create benefits for both company and employees, to improve productivity and profitability. Moreover, HRM provides companies with strategies and processes such as recruitment, training, performance appraisals, communication methods, and incentive programs to generate a positive impact on the company (Atkinson, 1999; Bakker, 2010). Recruitment and training programs lead to hiring people that fit the job requirements and preparing them to develop tasks with the best performance possible. Performance appraisals provide a clear understanding of the job expectations, which supports execution of the objectives with the best efforts possible (Bazeley, 2007). The development of effective communication channels and incentive programs help maintain a healthy and safe work environment. For these reasons, employees stay motivated, and consequently, improve their performance (HRE, 2017). Overall, management of human resource strategies impacts companies in such a way that all the processes get integrated to accomplish the strategic goal of being profitable.

In the story described by Goldratt, HRM played a supporting role in the development of changes the plant required. Based on the story, two situations were identified from the HRM viewpoint. When Rogo, the production manager, received the ultimatum from Bill Peach, the division vice-president, to get the plant up and running again, the employees seemed to lack the knowledge about the plant status, strategic objectives, and importance of keeping up to date with the delivery of orders (Bradley, 2010; Breese, 2012). An indication that HRM was not integrated with the company's management. However, during the implementation of changes and assessment of TOC, HRM started to play its supporting role in the identification, evaluation, and mitigation of the constraints that impeded on the success of the company processes (Bradley, 2010; Breese, 2012).

When Rogo, with Jonah's help, identified that the machine NCX-10 represented a bottleneck in the production process, meeting with all his production team and managers to communicate the impending changes the process required and the reason they were implementing change, was a clear example of implementing human resource strategies (Bradley, 2010; Breese, 2012). As a change agent, Rogo, and his team, assigned one person to do quality control of the bottleneck. This demonstrated the training and communication strategies used to implement changes. Another example was when Rogo and his team agreed with the union to modify employee rest times, demonstrating how the company was interested in balancing the production effectiveness and well-being of employees. The implementation of these strategies gave them the opportunity to optimize the production time of the machine by mitigating the lost time in the bottleneck. Overall, without the engagement and motivation of employees, the change implementation would not have been as effective (Bryman, 2008).

The next section reviews HRM principles and their impact on performance.

3.2. HRM Principles

The main purpose of HRM is to accomplish goals of a company and manage its employees so both parties profit. There are several HRM principles that could be applied to improve the operations of the UniCo manufacturing plant in the book (Kohli & Grover, 2008; Lycett et al., 2004). The following are some examples:

- **Job Evaluation Method:** Rogo and his team could have developed job designs for the operators with the purpose of identifying critical responsibilities, desired knowledge, and required abilities and skills. This would be especially true for jobs around the bottlenecks. This strategy could have had positive implications such as improving the workflow, minimizing labor turnover, decreasing defective products, and meeting the orders' lead-time. However, for this strategy to be successful, Rogo and his team would have had to share the strategy with employees and inform them about the process and how they would be impacted.

- **Programs for Training and Developing Employees:** The purpose of this HR strategy is to develop employees' learning, enhance skills and knowledge, and minimize the impact of the required training time on production workflow. Further, companies must ensure the skills and knowledge of employees are continually updated to maintain and improve productivity. Rogo and his team decided to implement training programs after they identified the bottlenecks in the production flow and the high number of quality problems. They wanted the new production model to be successful and ready for future challenges so, for these reasons, they created a detailed training program to mitigate quality issues and improve productivity.

Alternatively, creating a career development plan for its employees could have provided a continuously improved system for employees' skills and knowledge, while simultaneously enhancing professional development (Kohli & Grover, 2008; Lycett et al., 2004; Galli, 2016). In sum, this HR principle could have helped increase productivity, reduce supervision time, minimize errors, and, be beneficial in improving quality, enhancing employees' satisfaction, developing teamwork, and optimizing the use of resources. All of which would have incentivized employees and garnered major improvements to help the plant meet its strategic goal (Kohli & Grover, 2008; Lycett et al., 2004).

- **Employee Compensation Plan:** Major reasons for compensation is to benefit and encourage employees concerning their jobs, improve employees' retention and motivation, and be competitive in the employment market (Chanda, Krishna, & Shen, 2007). Further, compensation includes different forms of pay or rewards for work done, according to the job evaluation per role.

According to Goldratt (2014), the traditional manufacturing system was based on an incentives program calculated from production performance. Although Rogo and his team identified the bottlenecks and implemented changes in the quality checkpoints, that was not enough to send the priority orders on time. Employees were motivated enough to have the orders ready to deliver, but the production capacity was their constraint. Rogo mentioned to Bob, his production manager, that they needed to look at their incentives (Goldratt, 2014, p. 135). This indicates that, even though the employees worked as hard and efficiently as they could, there were other changes that needed to be made to improve the orders' delivery time (Kohli & Grover, 2008; Lycett et al., 2004; Galli, 2016).

Goldratt explained the new way that companies should create their incentive plans to align with the company's strategic objective to make money. Then, he described the TOC and how the three variables - throughput, inventory, and operational expenses - can be measured when the company is making money. Based on this analysis and development of that theory, Goldratt explained how companies can develop an appropriate incentive model for their employees that can also enable the company to meet its strategic goal (Kohli & Grover, 2008; Lycett et al., 2004).

An employee compensation plan can improve productivity, if it is based on a strategic performance and reward system. Additionally, an appropriate compensation plan can improve the position of businesses by enhancing employee recruitment and retention, which is translated to a reduction of expenses in recruitment and training (Melville et al., 2004; Money, 2006; Galli, 2017). This performance and reward system should be based on business constraints and, as Goldratt suggested, take into consideration that throughput relation between machines and employees should remain low, which ensures low levels of inventory and operational expenses.

- **Performance Management and Appraisal:** According to Dessler (2017), the performance appraisal is based on the evaluation of performance standards compared to the employees' performance history. It includes three steps: (1) determine work standards, (2) compare the current performance of employees against the standards, and (3) provide feedback for future improvements. The purpose of the performance appraisal is to benefit both companies and employees. This evaluation provides employees with an overview of the importance of their job contribution to the achievement of objectives. As a consequence, employee morale increases, which enhances productivity of both the company and employees.

The lack of an accurate performance appraisal was one starting point that Goldratt used to explain the plant's inefficiencies and how TOC plays a role in improving operations. As Jonah said to Rogo, "productivity is meaningless unless you know what your goal is" (Goldratt, 2014, p. 38). For that reason, Goldratt explained how important it was for the plant to understand that its goal was to make money and change the way it measured productivity (Melville et al., 2004; Money, 2006). It was not enough to just improve performance of employees. It was also necessary to consider the three variables of TOC: throughput, inventory, and operational expenses. Once the company measured and developed its strategies around the improvement of these variables, after a year of implementation, the company was seeing profits (Melville et al., 2004; Money, 2006).

Overall, performance appraisals involve management and employees to obtain benefits regarding productivity. This methodology could be spread in all departments to benefit the plant. It was not enough to implement in the production plant because they also depended on the selling department to equilibrate constraints in the production processes (Rowe, 2012). For that reason, to improve employee productivity and support achieving the strategic goal, all parties needed to be involved.

- **Communication Programs:** The most valuable resource that companies have is their employees. Communication programs are one way to build positive employee relations and engagement. For that reason, it is important to communicate, to establish a clear overview of expectations versus results. Effective communication can mitigate the occurrence of errors and, therefore, the decrease of productivity. When employees have knowledge of the company's strategic goal and how they can contribute to achieving it, they increase engagement within the company and, thereby, improve their productivity.

After Rogo and his team detected the changes required, the company used different communication methods to inform its personnel. Some media used were (1) newsletters, to briefly explain the reasons and context for changes; (2) internal promotion, to tell employees about the implementation of color tags and their purposes, and (3) bulletin posters, to keep plant operators informed about goals, progress, and new procedures (Goldratt, 2014). The plant used these communication techniques as a short-term strategy to improve production methodologies. Langston, the quality control manager, mentioned setting up "training sessions so people can learn those procedures" (Goldratt, 2014, p. 182). This was an indication that a training program is the next essential step to improving communication within a company (Rowe, 2014).

Lack of communication can lead to employee frustration and as a result, impact performance and productivity. The case of Rogo's plant is a clear example that a company must ensure its employees have sufficient knowledge about changes to be made and their roles in the achievement of strategic goals. Through effective communication management and evaluation of the productivity variables addressed in TOC, companies can pursue the right path to achieve strategic goals with an appropriate management of human resources.

The following section discusses the role of stakeholders and their value in TOC.

3.3. The Role of Stakeholders and TOC

HRM focuses on achieving a company's strategic goal by developing, implementing, and enhancing HR strategies. These strategies involve two key ideas, which are company planning and stakeholder value creation (Dessler, 2017). Stakeholders are parties that influence the company's strategic goal and are also impacted by the company. They include employees, direction management, suppliers, unions, and even the government (Science of Business, 2017). Some stakeholders can represent constraints in achieving a company's goal derived from productivity and quality issues. Here, TOC plays a key role because it focuses on the constraints, or bottlenecks, to improve profitability by measuring throughputs, inventory, and operational expenses. Also, it emphasizes identifying and eliminating obstacles that impede the system from working as a whole (Schryen, 2012).

The key stakeholders described in the book allowed the TOC to be implemented. For that reason, they played a key role in improving the operation and quality of the finished product. The book mentioned several stakeholders, but the key ones were internal, such as Alex Rogo, the manufacturing plant manager and the main character; Jonah, Rogo's college professor who made the suggestions about changes; Bill Peach, the division vice-president; and the production management team (Shenhar & Levy, 1997; Smyrk & Bakker, 2014). Regarding external stakeholders, the book described Rogo's family, and their influence on employees' performance. It also focused on the plant's customers, who influenced the variation of sales demands because they were not satisfied with the delay in order delivery. All stakeholders reflected ways in which their roles impacted the achievement of the company's goal (Shenhar & Levy, 1997; Smyrk & Bakker, 2014).

To implement the TOC, stakeholders influenced the management of constraints, such as resources and policies. An example of resource management included the actions taken the production team the machine NCX-10 and how they used older machines to increase capacity of the process performed. This represented one of the critical paths in production. Regarding policies, during one of Jonah's visits to the plant, Rogo and his team identified that a change had to be made in union policies. Rogo explained to Jonah that a union's clause "stipulates there must be a half-hour break after every four hours of work" (Goldratt, 2014, p. 153), but after the bottlenecks were identified, the clause was revised to allow employees to take breaks only when the machines that represent bottlenecks were turned off. The stakeholder management described in the book used management skills such as team building, effective communication, conflict resolution, and empowerment to reflect an engagement with primary stakeholders (Shenhar & Levy, 1997; Smyrk & Bakker, 2014; Galli, 2017).

Based on stakeholder values, the following section discusses how HRM impacts TOC.

3.4. HRM and TOC

HRM impacts the development of TOC in such a way that it influences the company's decision-making process. Companies can identify their constraints and evaluate HR strategies, such as training programs, compensation plans, and job analysis to mitigate those constraints.

The best example of constraints analysis was explained in the book with 'Herbie,' the Boy Scout that Rogo met during a hike. Herbie was the slowest kid in the troop, and his remarkable performance was the reason Rogo used him for his constraint analysis. Rogo compared the hike performance to his plant (Soderlund, 2011). Each Boy Scout represented a station process in the plant. In his analysis, he discovered that no matter how fast the troop hiked, they would never complete that hike if the Herbie's performance and constraints were not assessed. Rogo affirmed that he "used Herbie to control the troop during the hike" (Goldratt, 2014, p. 140) and used the same theory to analyze bottlenecks and resource management at the plant.

Furthermore, the other troop members represented different scenarios and machines in the plant. Based on this, Rogo identified the bottlenecks in his plant's production process, after which, he worked with his team to implement HR strategies that assessed the changes to be made (Soderlund & Bakker, 2014). These changes required implementing training programs, changes in working hours and breaks, retention and motivational programs, incentive plans, and using communication tools to integrate all parties (Soderlund & Bakker, 2014).

This highlights the connectivity between HRM and TOC. Once companies assess their constraints, they can implement different HR strategies that help them create a better environment for employees. There may be some resistance to those changes, but the purpose of HR strategies is to evaluate how companies and their employees can benefit from change. In the end, the purpose of the assessment of both HRM and TOC is to achieve the company goal, which is to make money (Soderlund & Bakker, 2014).

The next section reviews the role that management and leadership have in HRM.

3.5. Management and Leadership in HRM

The Human Resource Society defined leadership as one of the competencies that human resource managers need to influence developing strategies and policies for companies (Dessler, 2017). Leaders are those who become "a role model for the behaviors required for the change," (Dessler, 2017, p. 54) and for that reason, more companies that want to improve require managers with strong leadership skills. That is where HRM plays a key role because, through HR methodologies, companies can ensure the development of leadership skills in their employees. In most cases, when companies identify the need for change, they implement HR strategies to improve their personnel's skills, such as programs of leadership development training, 360-degree assessments, and empowerment roles (MSG, 2017). Although the results of these strategies are reflected in the long run, companies must be sure to assign the right leaders to motivate and encourage employees to meet strategic goals. Now, more than ever, HRM is a significant component of companies' development regarding profitability. For that reason, leadership and management skills should be assessed to support improvements that companies may need (Svejvig & Anderson, 2015; Galli, 2017).

At the end of the book, Alex Rogo concluded that a manager, which is his prototype of a leader, must answer three basic questions: "What to change? What to change to? And how to cause the change?" (Goldratt, 2014, p. 343). He explained that a good manager is one who can create solutions without generating problems. The role then, of HRM, is to develop those skills of analyzing and thinking about the company's environment. This will allow employees to identify changes that should be made to improve the profitability of the company. Further, leadership programs should not focus on just the management level, but also involve all parties to align them with strategic objectives. Leadership should also contemplate incentive programs to motivate employees to collaborate more. For those reasons, the development of management and leadership are main competencies that should be considered in HRM to enhance the companies' bottom line (Soderlund & Bakker, 2014).

The following section discusses the relationship between technology and human resources.

3.6. Technology and HR

Nowadays, most companies use technology as the main tool to meet business strategies. The implementation of technology has the highest impact on human resource strategies, such as recruitment, training, and performance management (Thorgren et al., 2010). The development of those strategies supported by technology tools can improve processes, productivity, and efficiencies within companies. However, the human resource factor is an important driver because the technology by itself does not create any improvement. For that reason, an appropriate management, performed by people, is the key success factor in incorporating technology, which provides advantages in efficiency and effectiveness.

According to Goldratt (2014), the companies' goal is to make money. He explained how the old business models supported the idea that implementation of technology ensured the optimization of productivity and revenues. As the author expressed, "a system of local optimums is not an optimum system at all; it is a very inefficient system" (Goldratt, 2014, p. 217). One interpretation of this quote is that the implementation of sophisticated robots is not the only key to optimizing processes. Through TOC, the author explained how evaluating three performance indicators could support developing strategic business goals by improving throughputs while inventory and operational expenses decrease. Based on those indicators, Rogo and his team identified that some machines represented bottlenecks, and through the process of on-going improvement, they evaluated the capacity of the machines, machinists, and inputs and outputs of inventory to improve performance in those bottlenecks (Zwikael & Smyrk, 2012). In sum, the team made all analyses to explain how the system was impacted by the implementation of technology. They identified that analysis of all the factors involved in the production process was key to achieving the goal of being profitable (Tranfield et al., 2003; Galli, 2016).

Overall, well-used and integrated technology in HR strategies can represent a key advantage for businesses. In the book, the use of machines or robots represented constraints for the production process. Rogo and his team analyzed in real-time different scenarios that allocated resources differently every time until they optimized the system. The advantage of technology is that tools such as simulation software help to identify bottlenecks (Vom Brocke et al, 2009; Ward & Daniel, 2012). The HR department can interact with the allocation of resources in bottlenecks through this software, and then they can obtain information on different scenarios. Based on those results, they can identify which option is the most convenient and creates the best improvements. For that reason, the optimum use of technology in HR strategies can create a high impact in achieving company objectives (Winter et al., 2006a; Webster & Watson, 2002; Galli, 2017).

4. FINDINGS

Several findings were highlighted at the conclusion of this study. They are listed below.

- HRM plays a supportive role in the performance of the UniCo plant described in the book and other businesses.

- The implementation of HR processes such as job analysis, programs for training and employees' development, compensation plans, performance management and appraisal, and communication programs can enhance the motivation and engagement of employees around continuous improvement of the company.
- HRM and the implementation of TOC are related in such a way that employees identify constraints and assess resources needed for their mitigation or elimination. Their purpose is to change whatever is needed, but in an effective manner that increases productivity and profitability.

4.1. Relevance and Implications for Management and Project Environments

Based on the acquired skills and management strategies from the research, there is a need to utilize human resources in conducting business projects and in project management. This can be achieved by ensuring a well-functioning human resources, where distinct skills are combined to create a team that envisions and realizes the company's or project's ultimate goals. In this case, there is a need to invest substantially in human resources before thinking of the mode of technology to use in the project or management. The findings from this research study of *The Goal* helps to identify several managerial implications. More specifically, these results highlight the importance of a top-down and bottom-up approach to leadership and strategic planning, especially with regards to elements of operations management and process improvement. The results of this study highlight the criticality of integrating human resource principles into the leadership styles and tools used by leaders to manage their human resources.

The findings from this study also highlight the importance of human resources throughout all aspects of an organization; obviously HRM is one element in an organization's business model, but this study shows that the human resource element directly impacts many other elements of an organization. Management and leadership of any organization need to have the training and skill sets to, not only manage their human resources, but to effectively do so. This study has shown that many of the current-state issues seen within the factory of *The Goal* stemmed from the leadership's lack of effectively leading and managing their employees. If the leadership is equipped with the tools and knowledge to effectively manage their human resources instead of focusing on the bottom line (i.e. profits and costs), then the performance of an organization will improve and, as a result, the profits and costs will also improve. Highlighted in this study is that business leaders tend to focus mainly on the financial elements of their business, at the expense of ignoring or minimizing the human resource element. This might work in the short term, but the factory in *The Goal* shows that it is not a good long term strategy. Over the long term, leadership must have a multi-faceted approach where they manage operations, human resources, financials, performance, and strategy from one overarching understanding that all of these elements are critical, and they are all related. By understanding this view, a business leader will be better equipped to lead a successful company in both the short term and long term.

5. CONCLUSION

5.1. Limitations

The study and results are somewhat restricted due to a few research limitations that should be discussed. The main limitation was the fact that the study had a limited sample size (i.e. one book) and it only studied key factors from this sample. The limitation of sample size introduces some potential bias and validity behind the findings and conclusions identified in the study, all of which could be alleviated by executing the study with a larger sample. Another limitation was that this study only examined the key factors and their relationship in terms of a project environment; therefore, the conclusions and analyses are specific to project environments and the findings cannot necessarily be extrapolated to other arenas such as supply chain management, operations management, or strategic management. This is a limitation since the conclusions and analyses are specific; this limitation makes it difficult to argue that the findings from this study could be deployed and used in other industries or managerial settings.

5.2. Recommendations for Future Research

This report finds that the implementation of HRM strategies such as training, recruitment, and safety programs build effective teamwork. Performance appraisal may also improve the performance of businesses because employees can feel more motivated and engaged with the company. As a result, the company's profit can increase, which is the main goal of every company. After all, "The company exists to make money" (Goldratt, 2014, p. 46), as it is described in *The Goal*.

This paper recommends companies to follow the five steps of thinking of TOC. They are: (1) identification of constraints, (2) address and fix the constraints, (3) prioritize management of the constraints, (4) prevent its occurrence, and (5) be prepared for the next bottlenecks and go back to step one to repeat the process. This process will support companies in improving their performance and profitability. Also, the author strongly recommends for future researchers to include more strategies from Goldratt's other book *The Theory of Constraints*. This book can expand the viewpoint of HRM as an integral part of companies.

Future research should explore a few different arenas. For example, future research could investigate the HRM-TOC relationship, but in the context of other industries and managerial settings. In these settings or contexts, it would be interesting to study the strength of these variables and the relationship, as well as the factors that impact them. Another avenue of research could be to explore these strategies and their relationship from different perspectives, such as an organizational, strategic, or cultural point of view. This would shed further light into the how this relationship is perceived across many different views and further understand the depth of the impact that factors such as culture, strategy, human resources, operations have on the key variables and their relationship.

5.3. Conclusion and Contribution

Many researchers agree that organizations have a high likelihood of improving their business profitability when they promote and implement TOC. TOC is developed by the companies' human resources through strategies of continual improvement. However, it would be advisable for companies to follow the five steps of the thinking process of TOC. Based on the analysis of *The Goal*, much can be derived about the need for proper management skills that boost the company's production and profitability. Good management should be based on the fact that, for a company to achieve the ultimate goal of profit maximization, there is a need for well-established coordination that ensures both the human capital and technology are adequately used. Human capital should be nurtured to foster performance at the most efficient and optimal levels. There is also the need to ensure the company produces the product that will create and maintain customer loyalty. In this case, the quality of the product must be taken into consideration throughout all processes and decision-making. This quality can only be ensured through standards set by the human resource and proper planning on the step-by-step strategies to be employed. The book, therefore, demonstrates the management techniques that engage the human resource in achieving the goals of a company.

Review of the literature shows that there is limited research that explored the concepts and their relationships. Therefore, this study sought to further analyze these concepts and the relationships between them in general. In an effort to fill a void in the research identified earlier on this study and alleviate previously preconceived risks and uncertainty.

The results of this research study contributes to several different fields of research and topics, including: human resource management, theory of constraints, project management, and process improvement. By performing this study, the results help to enhance and evolve these fields of research and topics since this study, not only built on existing research, but attempted to expand and fill a gap in the research that was identified earlier on this study. By more thoroughly understanding these concepts and their relationships, we can understand their advantages and disadvantages, which in turn should help improve their effectiveness.

This study also contributes, since it introduces new ideas and avenues for future research in each of these fields of research and topics. This study not only sought to explore different concepts and their relationships, but it also sought to understand the relationships and identify new ways of thinking about the variables under study. The results of this study were also valuable from a practitioner perspective, since the understanding of these variables and relationships helped to introduce ideas and strategies that a practitioner can deploy to be more effective in their profession. The results from this study help a practitioner to understand the relationships and variables but also the implications related to these variables and relationships.

6. REFERENCES

Andersen, E. S. (2014). Value creation using the mission breakdown structure. *International Journal of Project Management*, *32*(5), 885–892. doi:10.1016/j.ijproman.2013.11.003

Andersen, E. S., Birchall, D., Jessen, S. A., & Money, A. H. (2006). Exploring project success. *Baltic Journal of Management*, *1*(2), 127–147. doi:10.1108/17465260610663854

Aswathappa, K. (2005). Human Resource and Personnel Management: Text and Cases (4th ed.). McGraw-Hill.

Atkinson, R. (1999). Project management: Cost, time and quality, two best guesses and a phenomenon, it's time to accept other success criteria. *International Journal of Project Management*, *17*(6), 337–342. doi:10.1016/S0263-7863(98)00069-6

Bakker, R. M. (2010). Taking stock of temporary organizational forms: A systematic review and research agenda. *International Journal of Management Reviews*, *12*(4), 466–486. doi:10.1111/j.1468-2370.2010.00281.x

Bazeley, P. (2007). *Qualitative Data Analysis with NVivo*. London: Sage Publications Ltd.

Bradley, G. (2010). *Benefit Realisation Management: A Practical Guide to Achieving Benefits through Change* (2nd ed.). Farnham: Gower.

Breese, R. (2012). Benefits realisation management: Panacea or false dawn? *International Journal of Project Management*, *30*(3), 341–351. doi:10.1016/j.ijproman.2011.08.007

Bryman, A. (2008). *Social Research Methods* (3rd ed.). Oxford: Oxford University Press.

Chanda, A., Krishna, S., & Shen, J. (2007). Strategic Human Resource Technologies: Keys to Managing People. *Sage (Atlanta, Ga.)*.

Dessler, G. (2017). *Human Resource Management (15 to* (G. Edition, Ed.). Pearson.

Galli, B. (2016). A Shared Leadership Approach to Transformational Leadership Theory: Analysis of Research Methods and Philosophies. *International Journal of Strategic Decision Sciences*, *7*(3), 1–42. doi:10.4018/IJSDS.2016070101

Galli, B. (2017). Applying Strategic Analysis to Quantify Investor Risk: Case Study of Pfizer. *International Journal of Risk and Contingency Management*, *6*(3), 1–13. doi:10.4018/IJRCM.2017070101

Galli, B. (2017). How To Truly Win in Business With Leadership – A Case Study Report. *Middle Eastern Journal of Management*, *4*(3), 235–245. doi:10.1504/MEJM.2017.086426

Goldratt, E. (2014). *The Goal. A Process of Ongoing Improvement* (4th ed.). Great Barrington, MA: The North River Press Publishing Corporation.

Human Resource Excellence (HRE). (2017, January 20). *The importance of Human Resource Management*. Retrieved from http://www.humanresourceexcellence.com/importance-of-human-resource-management/

Kohli, R., & Grover, V. (2008). Business value of it: An essay on expanding research directions to keep up with the times. *Journal of the Association for Information Systems*, *9*(1), 23–28, 30–34, 36–39. doi:10.17705/1jais.00147

Kumar, R. (2011). Theory of Constraints (TOC) Gaining Better Project Control. *Project Perfect*. Retrieved from http://www.projectperfect.com.au/white-paper-theory-of-constraints.php

Lycett, M., Rassau, A., & Danson, J. (2004). Programme management: A critical review. *International Journal of Project Management*, *22*(4), 289–299. doi:10.1016/j.ijproman.2003.06.001

Melville, N., Kraemer, K., & Gurbaxani, V. (2004). Information technology and organizational performance: An integrative model of IT business value. *Management Information Systems Quarterly*, *28*(2), 283–322. doi:10.2307/25148636

Money, A. H. (2006). Exploring project success. *Baltic Journal of Management*, *1*(2), 127–147. doi:10.1108/17465260610663854

Management Study Guide (MSG). (2017). *The role of Human Resource Management (HRM) in Leadership Development*. Retrieved from http://www.managementstudyguide.com/role-of-hrm-in-leadership-development.htm

Rowe, F. (2012). Toward a richer diversity of genres in information systems research: New categorization and guidelines. *European Journal of Information Systems*, *21*(5), 469–478. doi:10.1057/ejis.2012.38

Rowe, F. (2014). What literature review is not: Diversity, boundaries and recommendations. *European Journal of Information Systems*, *23*(3), 241–255. doi:10.1057/ejis.2014.7

Schryen, G. (2012). Revisiting IS business value research: What we already know, what we still need to know, and how we can get there. *European Journal of Information Systems*, *22*(2), 139–169. doi:10.1057/ejis.2012.45

Shenhar, A. J., & Levy, O. (1997). Mapping the dimensions of project success. *Project Management Journal*, *28*, 5–13.

Smyrk, J., & Zwikael, O. (2011). *Project Management for the Creation of Organisational Value*. Springer London.

Söderlund, J. (2011). Pluralism in project management: Navigating the crossroads of specialization and fragmentation. *International Journal of Management Reviews*, *13*(2), 153–176. doi:10.1111/j.1468-2370.2010.00290.x

Söderlund, J., & Bakker, R. M. (2014). The case for good reviewing. *International Journal of Project Management*, *32*(1), 1–6. doi:10.1016/j.ijproman.2012.11.007

Svejvig, P., & Andersen, P. (2015). Rethinking project management: A structured literature review with a critical look at the brave new world. *International Journal of Project Management*, *33*(2), 278–290. doi:10.1016/j.ijproman.2014.06.004

The Science of Business. (2017). *What Is Theory Of Constraints (TOC)?* Retrieved from http://www.scienceofbusiness.com/home/what-is-theory-of-constraints-toc/

Thorgren, S., Wincent, J., & Anokhin, S. (2010). The importance of compensating strategic network board members for network performance: A contingency approach. *British Journal of Management*, *21*(1), 131–151. doi:10.1111/j.1467-8551.2009.00674.x

Tranfield, D., Denyer, D., & Smart, P. (2003). Towards a methodology for developing evidence-informed management knowledge by means of systematic review. *British Journal of Management*, *14*(3), 207–222. doi:10.1111/1467-8551.00375

Vom Brocke, J., Simons, A., Niehaves, B., Riemer, K., Plattfaut, R., & Cleven, A. (2009). Reconstructing the giant: On the importance of rigour in documenting the literature search process. *ECIS 2009 Proceedings. Paper*, *161*, 1–13.

Ward, J., & Daniel, E. (2012). *Benefits Management: How to Increase the Business Value of Your IT Projects*. West Sussex, UK: Wiley. doi:10.1002/9781119208242

Webster, J., & Watson, R. T. (2002). Analyzing the past to prepare for the future: Writing a literature review. *Management Information Systems Quarterly*, *26*, xiii–xxiii.

Winter, M., Andersen, E. S., Elvin, R., & Levene, R. (2006a). Focusing on business projects as an area for future research: An exploratory discussion of four different perspectives. *International Journal of Project Management, 24*(8), 699–709. doi:10.1016/j.ijproman.2006.08.005

Zwikael, O., & Smyrk, J. (2012). A general framework for gauging the performance of initiatives to enhance organizational value. *British Journal of Management, 23*, S6–S22. doi:10.1111/j.1467-8551.2012.00823.x

This research was previously published in the International Journal of Strategic Engineering (IJoSE), 2(1); pages 1-13, copyright year 2019 by IGI Publishing (an imprint of IGI Global).

Chapter 8
Human Resource Management in Indian Microfinance Institutions

Richa Das
IMS Unison University, India

ABSTRACT

Over the years, microfinance has assumed a great importance all over the world. The reason behind the increasing importance of microfinance in poverty alleviation is considered a prime objective in all developing and underdeveloped countries. Traditionally, MFIs did not have a defined HR policy or structure, since the size of the organization was always very small. The last few years have seen an upswing in the size of the organizations and also in the margins generated by MFIs. The purpose of this chapter is to analyze the human resource management issues and challenges faced in microfinance industry in India.

INTRODUCTION

About 238 million people in India live below the poverty line with the per capita income of less than one dollar per day. Since independence, policy makers and practitioners have been trying to improve the lives of these poor and fight against poverty. This got reflected in the successive five-year plans, which had the objectives of "growth with equity" and "social justice". The planners, however, realized that rapid growth did not bring about "trickle down" effect, particularly so in rural areas. This realization led to the restructuring of institutions and schematic lending to facilitate better accessibility of credit for the underprivileged. Thus, initiatives in this regard were taken by building an institutional framework through nationalization of banks and creation of regional rural banks. Hence, the tasks of microfinance are the promotion of greater financial inclusion and, in the process, improve the social and economic welfare of the poor

Microfinance is defined as an "attempt to improve access to small deposits and loans for the poor households neglected by banks" (Schreiner and Morduch, 2001). Morduch (1999) explains Microfinance Institutions as specialized financial institutions, consolidated under the banner of microfinance, sharing

DOI: 10.4018/978-1-6684-3873-2.ch008

the responsibility to work for financial inclusion. The main objectives of Microfinance Institutions are financial inclusion, poverty reduction, women empowerment and sustainability.

Over the period of time Indian Microfinance Sector has shown an impressive growth in terms of client coverage. Microfinance sector is a labor intensive sector. Human resource is the backbone of any MFIs. However, finding and retaining skilled manpower, to manage its growth is among the major challenges of the Indian Microfinance sector. There are several reasons for failure to attract competent personnel in microfinances sector by the MFIs. Firstly, different organizations such as banks, welfare organizations, NGOs and financial organizations have entered in this sector and have implemented diverse business models to run the show (Basargekar, 2013). Creating a leading MFI takes more than charging the right price and knowing how to design a financial offering. Secondly, indicators to measure the performance of human resources is varied, and it takes into consideration social performance along with profitability, which does not give clear picture of the industry to the bystander (Basargekar, 2013).

Workforce diversity encompasses race, gender, ethnic group, age, personality, cognitive style, tenure, organizational function and education of the employees in the organization. Understanding how HR responsibilities change during growth, communicating effectively with the expanding workforce, finding best people to join team, providing training opportunities, supporting staff performance and transferring institutional culture to establish work expectations and values are important in supporting a MFI's growth. Supporting diverse workforce in MFIs creates a powerful and sustainable tool for economic growth. According to Ikeayibe (2010) inappropriate Human Resource may serve as major havoc to the sustenance of MFIs and argued that staff of MFIs is fundamentally relevant towards the success or otherwise of MFIs.

This chapter presents a brief overview of the Microfinance Industry its Objectives, and current status of Microfinance Industry in India. The chapter also explores key issues and challenges faced by Microfinance Institutions (MFIs) in India. Finally, this chapter discusses Human Resource Management, and its present scenario in Indian MFIs.

A BRIEF OVERVIEW OF MICROFINANCE

United Nations Millennium Goals state that by 2015 the number of people living in extreme poverty should be half of what it was in 2000 (World Bank, 2000). Over the time researchers have shown that those underprivileged are creditworthy (Ahmed et al., 2006; Coleman, 2006; Hiatt and Woodworth, 2006). Microfinance has established itself as an integral part of financial sector policies of emerging and developing countries in the past decade for underprivileged population. Microfinance spans a range of financial instruments including credit, savings, insurance, mortgages, and retirement plans, all of which are denominated in small amounts, making them accessible to individuals previously shut out from formal means of borrowing and saving. The majority of microfinance is aimed at the estimated 2.8 billion people who live on less than $2 a day in the developing world.

Hubka, and Zaidi (2005) defined Microfinance as a credit methodology, which employs effective collateral substitute for short-term and working capital loans to micro-entrepreneurs. According to Otero (1999) Microfinance is "the provision of financial services to low-income poor and very poor self-employed people". Robinson (2001) defines microfinance as 'small-scale financial services–primarily credit and savings provided to people who farm or fish or herd; who operate small enterprises or microenterprises where goods are produced, recycled, repaired, or sold; who provide services; who work for wages or commissions; who gain income from renting out small amounts of land, vehicles, draft animals, or machinery and tools; and to other individuals and groups at the local levels of developing countries, both rural and urban'.

In India, microfinance gained momentum during the mid-1990s with the emergence of Basix India, SHARE, and SNF as major players in the field of microfinance Between 2000 and 2003, a number of new players, primarily Spandana and SKS, with innovative business models emerged on the microfinance radar of India. The spectacular returns and scalable business models adopted by these firms attracted the attention of commercial banks like ICICI Bank, HDFC Bank, and ABN AMRO Bank. Most of these banks syndicated an exclusive microfinance lending cells and started looking for microfinance as a business opportunity rather than a section of their priority sector obligation. Microfinance gained further momentum after 2003 and the sector started growing at a pace of more than 100% from every year The commercial banks started aggressively considering national and international equity funds in India and microfinance rose as a business opportunity. Riding on this new wave, a number of new Micro Finance Institutions (MFIs) like Ujjivan, Swadhar, Sonata, Bandhan, Arohan and KAS Foundation came into existence (Alok, 2006).

OBJECTIVE OF MFIS

The main objectives of MFIs are as follows:

1. **Financial Inclusion:** According to United Nation Capital Development Fund (2006) microfinance aims to produce a well-functioning financial system, which is more comprehensive in nature.
2. **Poverty Reduction:** The primary goal of microfinance is to reduce poverty in developing countries by providing poor with basic financial services that will enable them to earn more, accumulate assets, and protect themselves from unexpected setbacks (Orrick et al, 2012). Otero (1999) stressed that MFIs address major constraint of the poor, i.e., shortage of material capital. Many researcher advocates MFIs reduce vulnerability of poor and enhance their quality of life (Gibbons & Meehan 2002; Bakhtiari 2006).
3. **Women Empowerment:** Few studies from Uganda suggest that there is status upliftment of women within the family and gains control in the family business as an impact of microcredit (Wakoko, 2004; Lakwo, 2006). According to United Nations Fund for Women (2001) the objective of women empowerment complements MFIs aim of poverty alleviation.
4. **Sustainability:** MFIs highlight the need for financial sustainability of all the participants in the business. According to Rhyne (1998) sustainability is not an end, but a mean to create improved benefit through financial outreach to poor.

CURRENT STATUS OF MFIS IN INDIA

Inadequacies in access to formal finance have led to the growth of Microfinance in India. In India, Microfinance operates through two main channels: a) banking system through self-help groups and b) lending through Microfinance Institutions.

MFIs have evolved into a vibrant segment of the financial sector exhibiting a variety of business models in recent years. According to Sa-Dhan's "Bharat Microfinance Report 2015" MFIs currently operate in 28 states, 5 union territories and 568 districts of India. The reported MFIs have a client base of 37 million with an outstanding portfolio of Rs.48882 crore. The average loan outstanding per borrower stood at Rs.13162 and 80% loans were used for income generation purposes. Outreach grew by 13% and loan outstanding grew by 33% over the previous years. The southern region of India has the highest share of both outreach and loan outstanding, followed by Eastern region. The proportion of urbane clientele increased from 44% in 2013-14 to 67% in 2014-15. Women borrowers constitute 97% of the total clientele of MFIs, SC/ST borrowers constitute 28% and minorities constitute 18% of total clients (Bharat Microfinance Report 2015).

As per MFIN Annual Report 2015-16, data lending by MFIs exhibited a growth with 50% jump in loans disbursed consecutively in the last three years from Rs. 23682 Crore during 2013-14 to Rs. 37599 Crore and further to Rs. 61860 Crore during 2015-16 (MFIN Annual Report 2015-16). NABARD Report of 2015-16 states that the total loan to MFIs by banks and financial institutions increased by over 36.90% during 2015-16 as against 47.73 during the previous year. During 2015-16, refinance to the tune of Rs. 2300 Crore have been distributed to 17 MFIs. NABARD expended a sum of Rs. 52.92 Crore from Women Self Help Group Development Fund and Financial Inclusion Fund. During 2015-16 more than 5100 training programmes were conducted and about 1.81 lakh participants were trained by NABARD. Village level Programmes on MFIs were sponsored by NABARD with support of banks in 13 priority states (NABARD Report of 2015-16).

In a short span of 30 years microfinance has transformed itself from a credit-based rural development scheme that has claimed to reduce poverty and empower poor women, to a $70 billion financial industry. In the process, the traditional NGO-led model has given way to the commercialized institutions, resulting in an increased emphasis on profit making. Though MFIs unconventional group-lending model has the potential to mitigate risk and facilitate financial intermediation at the bottom of the pyramid, it has one major challenge associated with it—high intermediation costs. To cover the high intermediation costs by generating a surplus from its operations and remain operationally self-sustainable are a daunting task for MFIs.

According to a report published in Live Mint on 30th January 2017, India's microfinance industry is showing signs of overheating in a possible reminder of the crisis that hit micro lenders in Andhra Pradesh in 2010. Around 1.26 million microfinance borrowers had received top-up loans over and above their existing loan amounts as on December 2016 end. Further, Crif High Mark has defined top-up loans as those with a ticket size of less than Rs10,000 and where customers have at least two active loans. Typically, such a loan is taken for a period up to nine months. It has also been found that 70% of these borrowers have at least three loans running at the same time, while Reserve Bank of India guidelines mandate that not more than two microfinance Institutions (MFIs) can give loan to the same borrower simultaneously.

KEY ISSUES AND CHALLENGES OF MFIS IN INDIA

Access to financial services to all have been recognized as a human right and has been part of millennium goal. Microfinance provides access to various financial services like savings, credit, and insurance to economically poor section of the population. However, the MFIs in India face certain issues and challenges which are discussed in the following sub-sections:

Low Outreach

In India, MFI outreach is only 8% as compared to 65% in Bangladesh (Nasir, 2013). Also, it has been observed that MFIs in India focus more on women clients than men which further decreases the outreach of MFIs.

High Interest Rate

The interest rates charged by MFIs in India range between 18% to 30%, which poor population find it difficult to pay. This again decreases the outreach of MFIs in the country.

Client Retention

Client retention in Indian MFIs is restricted to around 28% (Nasir, 2013) due to lack of awareness, education and information regarding MFI services.

Loan Default

Around 73% of loan default has been identified in Indian MFIs. Loan default derails the growth and expansion of MFIs. Reasons of loan defaults can be attributed to crop failure or fall in commodity prices.

Lack of Information

Due to low level of education among poor and language barrier, it is difficult to pass on information to the clients by MFIs. Also getting credit information from poor clients is difficult to obtain because of their reliance on informal lenders such as sahukars and zamindars.

Weak Regulatory Framework

The Government is yet to develop and pass a legal and regulatory framework conducive to MFIs, which makes the operation of MFIs more difficult.

High Transaction Cost

The volume of transactions in MFIs is very small, whereas the fixed cost involved in those transactions is very high. If the producer's fixed cost in proportion of his total cost is higher, the element of risk in business increases in same proportion. Moreover, if the demand for the product falls or the marginal cost increases, it becomes very difficult for the producer to adjust the cost by cutting output.

Lack of Access to Funding

Requisite financial support is not being provided to MFIs by concerned agencies. 68% MFIs report that government doesn't support them to meet the funds requirement.

HUMAN RESOURCE MANAGEMENT: A BRIEF INTRODUCTION

Human Resource Management (HRM) has been defined as the "mobilization, motivation, development, and deployment of human beings in and through work" (World Health Organization, 2007). HRM handles the design of formal systems in an organization to ensure effective and efficient use of human talent to achieve organizational goals (Ahmadreza et al, 2014). Human Resource Management deals with essentially subjective quantities of human being like "skill" and "promo ability" (Li, Chen, 2010).

Recent studies proved that organizations are identifying that their employees are their most valuable assets (Stambor, 2006). Combs et al (2006) studied the process of regulation of human resource for increasing productivity. Today organization doesn't consider their employee as a cost factor, but as an important asset to the organization (Golding, 2010).

Sar et al. (1972) observed that with the shift of focus from manufacturing industry to service and with increasing technological changes, human resource has become the ingredient to the nation's well-being and in service oriented industry like banks and hospitals especially, it has become more important. The human resources need to be treated with great care and human resource issues require special attention of decision makers at the strategic level (Som, 2007).

HR ISSUES AND CHALLENGES OF MFIS

Over the period of time Indian Microfinance Sector has shown an impressive growth in terms of client coverage and outstanding portfolio. However, finding and retaining skilled manpower to manage its growth is the major challenges to the Indian Microfinance sector.

Issues related to manpower planning were ranked in first five in 2008 survey and fourteenth in 2012 survey conducted by The Centre for the Study of Financial Innovations (CSFI) Survey of Microfinance. The survey conducted by Microfinance Insights (2008) states that more than 51 percent of MFIs in India consider human capital issues as the most pressing issue in comparison to financial issues, technical issues and turnover issues. In managing human capital, recruitment of qualified staff is considered to be the utmost important challenge (32% organizations considered it most important) followed by preventing turnover (28%) and training and capacity building (24%). It is estimated that with this growing rate, the requirement of skilled manpower in this sector is likely to increase to 2.5 lakh in next decade, out of which nearly 20,000 will be required at middle level management and 1,50,000 will be required as loan officers or area/ programme leaders (Sector Report- Microfinance India, 2009). In practice more than 55% of the development of an employee occurs through on-the-job experience followed by 15% through job relationship and regular feedback mechanism (Mbeba, 2007). As per Sa-Dhan, one of the leading MFI in India, there are less than 25 institutes which are involved in imparting training and development activities in the field of microfinance. This number is grossly inadequate as compared to present as well as future needs of the MFIs.

Jha and Singh (2015) examined the human resource (HR) issues faced by the microfinance institutions (MFIs) in India. They identified HR issues faced by MFIs are high attrition rate, over burden of work, low compensation, and informal hiring. Selvaraj (2012) focused his research on the importance and challenges of HR department in MFIs. He found most of the HR functions are being carried out on ad-hoc basis in MFIs and proposed HR department requires strong support from the board as well as senior management. Raghav (2012) found communication gap between top and operational staffs, lack of MFI experience, overload of work are the reasons for high attrition rate in MFIs in India. Batra (2012) recognized high turnover, lack of training as common HR issues faced by MFIs. Ikeanyibe (2009) stated that one of the crucial reasons behind slow growth of microfinance in Nigeria is poor human resource management in this sector. Alok (2006) in his work compared two microfinance institutions in India regarding HR planning, recruitment and deployment policies. Schreiner et al. (2001) put forward MFIs need to train staffs in financial domain and professional information management to improve their efficiency. They also proposed MFIs should focus on formulation of effective incentive plans for their staff members, if they want to explore new markets. Churchill (1997) classified HR challenges in MFIs as sectoral level, organizational level, and individual level.

The important problems faced by MFIs are discussed in the following sub-sections.

Recruitment and Retention of Qualified Staff Members

The requirement of manpower in microfinance has been rising from 4000 in the year 2002 to 45,000 in the year 2009 in India (Alok, 2006). Cook and Jaggers (2005) stated the importance of staff retention policies for MFIs as they account for the direct cost of high turnover in terms of lost productivity, new recruitment cost, training and development cost, etc. Raghav (2012) cited examples of few cases where MFIs in South India have used innovative tools to control high attrition of field workers and branch officers by hiring local people after doing ground verification of the candidates and grooming field officers and loan officers to become branch officers in the long run

Overburdening of Staff Members

MFIs have large base of borrowers availing very small loans (Hulme and Mosley, 1996). These large numbers of borrowers overburden the staffs working in MFIs by increasing the ratio of borrowers to total staff in MFI and thereby decreasing the productivity of each staffs (Rashid et al., 2013).

Training and Development of Staff Members

Mubarik (2008) discusses the critical role of training and development in microfinance industry and states it acts like a multiplier if implemented properly. It also requires variety of training which is continuously evolving and aligning itself with changing needs and objectives of MFIs (Krumm, 2007). Churchill (1997) states that foundation of any microfinance organization lies at the locus of interaction between the organization and its clients. The role of front line staff or loan offices, area leaders is very significant in building this relation. In such case training can act as a multiplier.

Compensation and Benefits Plans

Studies show that compensation and benefits system in many MFIs is not attractive. The compensation and benefit plans need to be structured scientifically to develop productivity based incentives and structure based on accounts/ clients load per credit officer and loan recoveries (MFIs in India: An analytical study of its financial, Human Resource and Managerial aspects of selected institutions).

Human Resource Planning and Policies

Women's World Banking report on development of competency based human resource management (2007) states that microfinance organizations today cannot wholly rely on leadership qualities and capabilities of their leaders, because as a growing organization it is required that development of capabilities of all the personnel in the organization must take place.

Performance Management System

Performance Management system is not very well defined in the Indian MFIs leading to high attrition rate in the industry. Prevailing performance Management system needs to be relooked at from the point of suitability and relevance to each of the grades rather than the same system for all the grades (Shastry, 2014).

Lack of Female Employees

Female borrowers constitute the major part of total borrowings of any MFIs (Armendariz & Morduch, 2010). But there is severe scarcity of female employees and their participation in the management of MFIs. Analysis shows that the attrition rate is low in organization employing more women.

Staff Grievance Redressal Systems

Very few of the MFIs in India have staff grievance redressal systems in their organization. Lack of awareness among staff of such systems and where aware, unwillingness to invoke the system needs to be tackled (Shastry, 2014).

Challenges of MFIs in Growing Stage

According to Helmuth, Parrot & Cracknell (2004), key challenges faced by growing MFIs is to control the high performance of human resources, because HRM system comes under stress during high growth stage. Pityn & Helmuth (2007) proposed a tool kit to develop HRM system in MFI based on its size and stage of development such as small size having up to 20 staff, medium size having 20 to 49 staff and large MFI having more than 50 staff members.

RESULT

Human Resource challenges that MFIs face are similar to that of mainstream organization like hiring the right people, finding the organization fit and retaining employees. While the host of changes has been seen in the HR policies of MFI sector over the period of time, there are critical areas that need immediate attention like working hours of employees, training and development programs, performance management system and staff redressal mechanism.

CONCLUSION

The topics covered in this chapter were overview of microfinance, current status of MFIs in India, key issues and challenges faced by MFIs in India, overview of Human Resource Management, and HRM issues and challenges of MFIs. Due to high customer - employee ratio in MFIs, human resource management needs to be given priority for proper functioning of the organization. One of the problems of human resource management is manpower planning, which mainly involves hiring, promotion, and exit of employees.

One of the reasons behind the failure of MFIs is the inexperience of management in handling the kind of market. The human resources who are mostly recruited from the banking industry have problems in generating demand, serving clients, meeting performance objectives. Their decisions have not been able to provide the desired result for the industry. Hence, it becomes necessary to on the part of MFIs to have a defined HR policy. The policies generated will ensure better performance for the MFI. The discussion suggests the decision makers to choose appropriate policies for minimizing the current and future shortage of employees in the industry.

REFERENCES

Ahmadreza, I., Ebraza, A., & Afsar, K. M. A. (2014). Analysis of different HRM policies Effect on Organization Knowledge Level. *Research Journal of Recent Sciences, 3*(3), 12–22.

Ahmed, S. M., Petzold, M., Kabir, Z. N., & Tomson, G. (2006). Targeted intervention for the ultra poor in rural Bangladesh: Does it make any difference in their health-seeking behaviour? *Social Science & Medicine, 63*(11), 2899–2911. doi:10.1016/j.socscimed.2006.07 024 PMID:16954049

Armendáriz, B., & Morduch, J. (2010). *The economics of microfinance*. MIT Press.

Bakhtiari, S. (2006). Microfinance and poverty reduction: Some international evidence. *International Business & Economics Research Journal, 5*(12).

Basargekar, P. (2013). Can Human Resource challenges halt the growth of Microfinance in India. *Indian Journal of Management Science, 3*(1).

Batra, V. (2012). The State of Microfinance in India: Emergence, Delivery Models and Issues. *Journal of International Economics, 3*(1).

CGAP. (2009). *Microfinance and the Financial Crisis*. Retrieved from http://www.cgap.org/gm/document1.9.7439/CGAP%20Virtual%20Conference%202008%20Summary.pdf

Churchill, C. (1997). Managing growth: The organizational architecture of microfinance institutions. *USAID Microenterprise Best Practices Project Paper, 7*, 26–81.

Coleman, B. E. (2006). Microfinance in Northeast Thailand: Who benefits and how much? *World Development, 34*(9), 1612–1638. doi:10.1016/j.worlddev.2006.01.006

Combs, J., Liu, Y., Hall, A., & Ketchen, D. (2006). How much do high-performance work practices matter? A meta-analysis of their effects on organizational performance. *Personnel Psychology, 59*(3), 501–528. doi:10.1111/j.1744-6570.2006.00045.x

Cook, M., & Jaggers, T. (2005). Strategies for staff retention. *Exchanging Views Series, 3.*

Cooper, K., & Lee, G. (2009). Managing the dynamics of projects and changes at Fluor. *Conference of the System Dynamics Society. In Proceedings from the 27th International Conference of the System Dynamics Society,* 1-27.

Deepak, A. (2006). *HR Planning, recruitment and deployment: challenges related to recruitment policies, HR policies and practices.* Available at http://m2iconsulting.com/wp-content/uploads/2014/12/HR-Issues.pdf

Gibbons, D. S., & Meehan, J. W. (2002). *Financing microfinance for poverty reduction.* Retrieved from http://www.microcreditsummit.org/papers/financing.pdf

Golding, N. (2010). Strategic human resource management. In *Human Resource Management A Contemporary Approach* (6th ed.; pp. 30-82). Person Financial Times/Prentice Hall.

Gu, L., & Chen, S. (2010). A System Dynamics Approach to Human Resource Mangement. In *International conference on Management and Service Science.* IEEE.

Helmuth, J., Parrot, L., & Cracknell, D. (2004). *Human Resource Management for Growing MFIs.* MicroSave Briefing Note – 53. Available at http://www.Microsave.org

Hiatt, S. R., & Woodworth, W. P. (2006). Alleviating poverty through microfinance: Village banking outcomes in Central America. *The Social Science Journal, 43*(3), 471–477. doi:10.1016/j.soscij.2006.04.017

Hubka, A., & Zaidi, R. (2005). Impact of Government Regulation on Microfinance. World Development Report: Improving the Investment Climate for Growth and Poverty Reduction, 1.

Hulme, D., & Mosley, P. (1996). Finance Against Poverty (Vol. 2). Psychology Press.

Ikeanyibe, O. M. (2009). Human resource management for sustainable microfinance institutions in Nigeria. *Global Journal of Social Sciences, 8*(1), 119. doi:10.4314/gjss.v8i1.48915

Insights, M. (2008). Human Resource Challenges and Solutions in Microfinance: Survey Report. New Delhi: Academic Press.

Jha, J. K., & Singh, M. (2015). Human resource (HR) & social challenges faced by microfinance in India: A framework. *Indian Journal of Industrial Relations, 50*(3), 494–505.

Krumm, D. (2007). *Open and Distance Leaning in Microfinance, Planet Finance, Morocco.* Available at http:// www.microfinancegateway.org/p/site/m//template.rc/1.9.29005 accessed on 27/12/2016

Lakwo, A. (2006). *Microfinance, rural livelihoods, and women's empowerment in Uganda* (Ph.D. thesis). Radboud Universiteit, Nijmegen.

Lascelles, D., Mendelson, S., & Rozas, D. (2012). *Microfinance Banana Skins 2012. In The CSFI survey of microfinance risk.* London: Centre for the Study of Financial Innovation.

Mbeba, R. D. (2007). *MFI Internal Audit and Controls Trainer's Manual*. Available at http://www. meda. org

Morduch, J. (1999). The microfinance promise. *Journal of Economic Literature, 37*(4), 1569–1614. doi:10.1257/jel.37.4.1569

Mubarik, Z. A. (2008). *Human Resource development in Microfinance Institutions*. Available at: www. microfinance gateway.org/gm/document-1.9.30202/23.pdf

NABARD. (2015). Status of Microfinance in India National Bank of Agriculture and Rural Development. Mumbai: NABARD.

Nasir, S. (2013). Microfinance in India: Contemporary issues and challenges. *Middle East Journal of Scientific Research, 15*(2), 191–199.

Orrick, Herrington & Sutcliffe. (2012). *Microfinance legal guide*. Author.

Otero, M. (1999). Bringing Development into Microfinance. *Journal of Microfinance, 1*(1), 8–19.

Pityn, K., & Helmuth, J. (2007). *Human Resorce Management: Toolkit*. Microsaves.

Raghav, N. (2012). A study of qualified HR practices among micro finance institution in Northern states in India. *Asian Journal of Research in Social Sciences and Humanities, 2*(4), 8–31.

Rashid, A., & Twaha, K. (2013). Exploring the determinants of the productivity of indian microfinance institutions. *Theoretical and Applied Economics, 18*(12), 83–96.

Rhyne, E. (1998). The yin and yang of microfinance: Reaching the poor and sustainability. *MicroBanking Bulletin, 2*(1), 6–8.

Robinson, M. (2001). *The microfinance revolution: Sustainable finance for the poor*. World Bank Publications. doi:10.1596/0-8213-4524-9

Sa-Dhan. (2015). *Bharat Microfinance Report-2015*. New Delhi: The Association of Community Development Finance Institutions.

Sar, A. L., Garth, L. M., & Ray, M. (1972). *Human resources and labour markets*. New York: Horper and Row Publishers.

Schreiner, M., & Morduch, J. (2001). *Replicating microfinance in the United States: Opportunities and challenges*. Washington, DC: Fannie Mae Foundation.

Schreiner, M., & Morduch, J. (2001). *Replicating microfinance in the United States: Opportunities and challenges*. Washington, DC: Fannie Mae Foundation.

Sector Report- Microfinance India: 2009. (2009). Available at http://www.microfinanceindia.com

Selvaraj, S.N. (2012). Challenging tasks of human resource department in Microfinance Institutions. *A Journal of Economics and Management, 1*(5).

Shastry, V. (2014). *Human Resource Management Practices among MFI's in India*. Available at http:// indiamicrofinance.com/human-resource-management-mfi-india.html

Som, C. V. (2007). Exploring the human resource implications of clinical governance. *Health Policy (Amsterdam)*, *80*(2), 281–296. doi:10.1016/j.healthpol.2006.03.010 PMID:16678293

Stambor, Z. (2006). Employees: A company's best asset. *Monitor on Psychology*, *37*(3), 28.

United Nations, Department of Economic and United Nations Capital Development Fund. (2006). Building inclusive financial sectors for development. United Nations Publications.

Wakoko, F. (2004). *Microfinance and women's empowerment in Uganda: A socioeconomic approach* (Doctoral dissertation). The Ohio State University.

World Bank. (2013). *Historic Goals to End Extreme Poverty: Endorsed by World Bank Governors*. Press Release. Available at http://www.worldbank.org/en/news/press-release/2013/04/20/historic-goals-to-end-extreme-poverty-endorsed-by-world-bank-governors accessed on 07/08/2016

World Health Organization. (2007). *Knowledge Management Strategy*. World Health Organization Press.

This research was previously published in Management Techniques for a Diverse and Cross-Cultural Workforce; pages 297-311, copyright year 2018 by Business Science Reference (an imprint of IGI Global).

Chapter 9
International Human Resource Management:
How Should Employees Be Managed in an International Context?

Mar Bornay-Barrachina
Pablo de Olavide University, Spain

ABSTRACT

Nowadays, internationalization is key for the survival of firms. Internationalization of a firm involves an internationalization of all the functional areas of the firm, of which international human resource management (IHRM) is one of the most relevant. In an international context, managers should make decisions about what human resource practices are best suited to the firm's international operations. Being aware of the differences between domestic and international human resource management will help readers and managers to establish operational mechanisms to deal with country differences in terms of industrial labor, culture, and firm practices. Therefore, after reading this chapter, readers should be able to deal with aspects like adaptation or standardization of HR practices, international staffing, and relevant issues around expatriation and repatriation.

INTRODUCTION

International Human Resource Management (IHRM) has for many years been established as an important area in management studies, and one which is critical for organizations. Currently, firms take part in a process of globalization or internationalization that obliges them to be competitive in a world market. To maintain competitiveness, firms must innovate and develop a greater capacity for reaction than that of their competitors. In this sense, appropriate people management can endow firms with the indispensable capacities needed to achieve survival and differentiate themselves from their competitors.

DOI: 10.4018/978-1-6684-3873-2.ch009

A company's internationalization means having to adopt an international orientation in all the functional activities of the company, such as finance, marketing, production or human resource practices. As an example, in the Human Resource (HR) department, HR managers will have to ask themselves questions such as:

- If the company goes international, what type of employees do they need to hire? Employees from the home country (expatriates), or local employees? How will we choose whether to send expatriates or use local employees?
- How can we know how HR practices are conducted in other countries? Is the recruitment and selection process the same in the country or countries the company wants to operate in?
- How do we manage knowledge across geographical and cultural distances? etc.

Knowing how to manage and deal in an effective way with all the issues involved in IHRM is critical to the success of the company. This chapter will cover key issues in IHRM, and after reading this chapter, the reader should know about differences between domestic and international HRM, the impact of culture in IHRM, alternatives for international staffing, and issues related to expatriation and repatriation. The treatment of "international" in the management of employees in an organization gives it a certain degree of complexity which makes studying it very relevant.

BACKGROUND

IHRM is a complex area which has usually been approached in the literature from three different perspectives (Adler, 1997; Brewster & Hegewisch, 1994):

1. **Cross-Cultural Management:** This focuses on the differences between nations in values and attitudes. Each nation has a set of values and beliefs which makes them unique, and that are reflected in the way in which societies operate, in the manner in which the economy operates, and in how employees are managed. According to this premise, when HR is managed, it must be considered that HR practices such as recruiting, reward, or performance appraisal are usually affected by values in host-countries. For example, when a culture or society is characterized by high levels of masculinity (i.e. material possession and assertiveness are emphasized), HR practices like compensation or rewards are affected by those values, and need to be high in order to motivate employees, or for the recruitment of new employees. In this sense, it is important for managers to understand such cultural differences, so that it is possible to understand the differences in human behavior within organizations in an international context.
2. **Comparative Human Resource Management:** This explores the extent to which HRM differs between countries. It specifically comes from the study of the comparison between industrial relations in different countries. It is not about cultural differences, but differences in terms of labor markets (size, composition, ages or training), educational systems, or different employment laws and trade unions. In the main, this perspective on IHRM sustains that industrial relations are different between countries and that, therefore, employees must also be treated differently.
3. **International Human Resource Management (IHRM):** This perspective studies the way in which MNCs manage and deal with their employees in different international contexts. It consists of the

study of how companies develop and design their own HR systems worldwide. International organizations have to manage their employees in different institutional, legal and cultural circumstances. Therefore, they need to develop effective management practices from a strategic and a cost-efficient point of view. IHRM activities cover the management of employees in different locations and, in particular, those who work internationally (expatriation). The IHRM perspective deals with to what extent a MNC should standardize its politics and HR practices to all the countries in which the company operates.

The last perspective is probably the broadest of the three, and the one on which this chapter will be focused. The study of how a company standardizes or adapts its HR functions around the world, involves taking into account the culture (cross-cultural management perspective) and the specifics on industrial relations (comparative HRM) of each of the countries. As is shown in Figure 1, there is a certain overlapping between the three approaches.

Figure 1. Inter-relationship between IHRM approaches
Source: Dowling & Welch, 2004

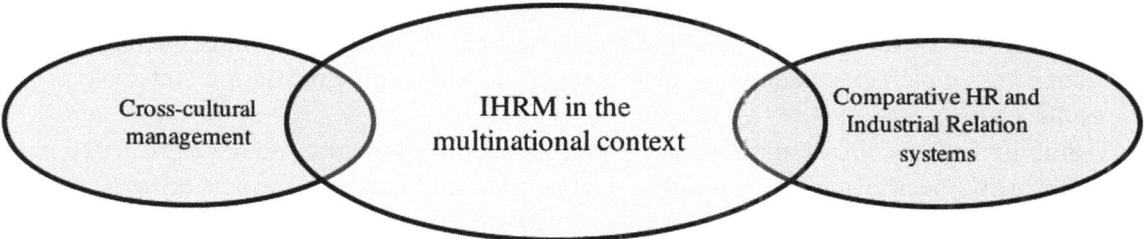

DOMESTIC HUMAN RESOURCE MANAGEMENT VS. INTERNATIONAL HUMAN RESOURCE MANAGEMENT

HR management refers to those activities which organizations use to effectively and efficiently manage their employees (Dolan et al., 2007). These activities include, for example, HR planning, recruitment and selection, training, performance appraisal and compensation, among others. Among the most important processes which HR departments develop are:

- **HR Planning:** Which, setting out from the aims and the strategy that the organization has established for a specific time horizon, means determining what the need for and availability of present and future staff are.
- **The Analysis of the Job Position:** Where the aim is to know both what the job involves and what is required to correctly carry it out.
- **Recruitment and Selection:** Of staff for organizations, through which internal and external processes are set up to find candidates for jobs.

- **Training and Career Management:** By which the organization increases the human potential and develops the individual through training and the opportunity of promotion and development within the organization.
- **Performance Appraisal and Remuneration:** By which organizations measure the performance of individuals and design the most appropriate systems of compensation for motivating and retaining valuable employees.

The issue is that when we consider International Management, all of these activities become more complex (Dolan et al., 2007) and others could also be added. For example:

- **Recruitment and Selection:** The HR departments must take into account that the contracting needs of MNCs are different from those of firms which only act nationally. For instance, questions arise such as whether to select people from the host country or expatriates, or what should be the appropriate recruitment sources based on the location, among others.
- **Performance Appraisal:** An international firm's performance appraisal system must take into account the competency of the employees, but it also has to consider intercultural personal skills, sensitivity toward foreign norms and values, and the capacity to adapt to new environments. Therefore, when appraising the managers of MNCs, there must be a simultaneous consideration of global performance and the results of the subsidiary. There may be factors, such as work legislation and/or market conditions, among others, which hinder the measuring and comparison of results.
- **Training:** The function of training for international HR departments also has a greater complexity. Normally, the decisions about training and improvement are taken based on the firm's degree of internationalization. For example, a firm in an export phase tends to cover its specific needs with external staff or professionals. In the regional activity phase, the firm should consider the cultural and geographic differences to create training strategies. The training of managers of global firms tends to be oriented to increasing their capacity to process and exchange social, technological and market tendency information, among other skills.
- **Remuneration:** The design of a globally appropriate remuneration policy is one of the greatest challenges HR departments are faced with. To design and administer an appropriate remuneration policy requires a thorough knowledge of the legislation, the customs and the employment practices of many countries. The industrial systems and relations are very relevant to this function. The economic climate changes quickly and firms must create remuneration proposals for their employees that are competitive. The aim is not to design global remuneration policies but rather for them to be equitable, fair and uniform for all the contexts within the organization.

The complexity of international HR could be attributed to different factors, such as more HR activities (international taxation; international relocation and orientation; administrative services for expatriates; host-government relations; and language translation services), more involvement in employees' personal lives (housing arrangements, cost-of-living allowances, etc.), or broader external influences (type of government, the state of the economy, etc.).

Taking into the account the noted differences between domestic and international HRM, a manager from a domestic company must consider the greater complexity of HR practices when the company goes abroad.

CONVERGENCE VS. DIVERGENCE: THE IMPACT OF CULTURE

A question that all HR managers should ask themselves is whether the organization should implement similar policies in all the countries in which it operates (*convergence or standardization*) or, on the other hand, whether each subsidiary should adopt its own HR policies, adapting or at least modifying the general policies of the parent company to suit local requirements (*divergence or localization*). This is not a new question, and numerous authors have helped to answer it. In this line, studies such as Brewster et al. (2002) pointed out that the dilemma for those in charge of MNCs' HR is often centered on achieving a balance between international consistency and local autonomy. In this respect, authors such as Festing & Eidems (2011) suggest that firms tend not to standardize an entire HR system but center on specific practices in an individualized manner and try to adapt them to each context. On other hand, the convergence or divergence of HR policies is also associated respectively with the centralization and decentralization of the practices, although there are differences (Armstrong & Taylor, 2014) between them. *Centralization* is the concentration of authority and responsibility for decision making in the hands of the top managers. *Decentralization* implies that the authority and responsibility for decision making is dispersed among lower levels. Both concepts, centralization and decentralization, have major implications for decision making, for the degree of autonomy and for the organizational structures. Convergence tends towards a concentration of decision making in the parent company and divergence tends towards the decentralization of functions and of decision making, granting the subsidiaries greater autonomy.

In addition, culture is identified in the literature as a key factor in determining the degree of convergence or divergence, centralization or decentralization of HR practices. In general, the impact which culture has on international relations and on business is recognized as one of the most important elements to achieve successful internal businesses. Particularly, culture has a significant impact on the establishing of HR policies and practices. Organizations are "culture-bound" and management practices are heavily influenced by collectively shared values and belief systems. Specifically, the literature indicates that cultural values shape the conduct of HRM through the following mechanisms (Sparrow & Hiltrop, 1997):

- Attitudes and definitions. For example, how an effective manager is defined in different countries. Western managers tend to be defined in terms of efficiency, while Eastern managers are defined in terms of collaboration and loyalty.
- Differences in concepts such as distributive justice, social security payments, individualistic versus collectivistic rewards, among others. For example, in collectivistic societies, relationships are said to be relational, in that people expect their group to care for them in exchange for unwavering loyalty. Therefore, HR practices to retain key employees should be based on trust more than money.
- Expectations of the employee's behaviors, manager-subordinate relationships, employee's performance or motivational incentives. There are cultures in which the opportunity to cover spiritual needs (Indians; Arabs) is a greater motivating factor than increases in salary.
- The way of communicating feedback, face-to-face, differences in levels of power distance, and their implications for recruitment, selection processes, negotiation or participation processes. For example, Australia, Germany, the UK and the US, have large gender role differences, lower equality and a high level of individual freedom.
- The mindsets used to think about resolving problems or organizational dynamics (ranging from more to less impulsive styles).

The number of studies on culture increased noticeably from the 1960s (Urteaga, 2009), and in the 80s interest in this topic soared due fundamentally to the attempt to understand the elements that had led to Japan having a prime place in the world economy, as well as the relationship between culture and performance inside the firm.

From this increasing interest in understanding the influence that culture has in IHRM, it could be said that, in general, there are two strands of thought with respect to the role played by culture in current society and in businesses (Al Ariss & Sidani, 2016):

- **Convergent Strand:** This maintains that the world will converge toward what we know as Western culture, due in part to the globalization process. From this perspective, HRM practices are standardizable worldwide, irrespective of the country and the culture which is concerned. Friedman (2005) follows this line of thought and distinguishes three events in the course of history which have contributed to convergence:
  - Globalization 1.0 or globalization of countries (1492 to 1800). This begins with the discovery of America and is characterized by the powers which seek riches through new conquests.
  - Globalization 2.0 or globalization of MNCs, (1800 to 2000). Caused by the appearance and development of the major companies and unified markets (EEC, NAFTA, etc.). The most important industrial advances appear in this period.
  - Globalization 3.0 or globalization of people, (2000 until now). This period is characterized by the advance of information technologies capable of connecting people (and firms) from anywhere in the world.
- **Divergent Strand:** This maintains that there will continue to be a diversity of cultures in the world due mainly to the influence of numerous religions (such as Islam). Its followers do not agree that the same set of HR practices is applicable regardless of the international context. -

To a manager wanting to internationalize his or her company, or wanting to manage their employees, it is important to understand how culture influences IHRM, and if culture follows a convergent or divergent path.

Jackson (2002) provides a reference framework to explain how culture affects HRM. Specifically, he proposes the concept of "locus of human value" which means the management's perceptions of the value of people in the organization[1]. According to Hofstede & McCrae (2004, p. 58), culture is characterized by: being collective and not individual; it is externalized through behaviors; and it is common for many people, but not for everyone. Following these authors, it is established that culture is made up of certain values, symbols, beliefs and attitudes which help to differentiate the ways of thinking and acting of a group of people. Being born in a specific country or region also determines the way in which people react to certain events, and culture explains in part these variations in behavior and helps to make clear a person's or a group's way of acting. An important question which many of the studies in this field tackle is how it is possible to discover the cultural differences between countries and how to elaborate a tool which enables the measuring of a specific culture. Its recognition and measurement would allow the establishing of orientations and guidelines for decision making in terms of HR policies and practices, among other matters. In this respect, one of the most relevant and generally accepted works is that of Hofstede and its cultural dimensions.

In the 70s, Geert Hofstede identified and quantified four dimensions of national culture which explained differences in response and that he called "cultural dimensions." These are:

1. *Power distance* (the degree to which societies accept that the power in institutions and organizations is unequally distributed); when a society scores high in power distance, people accept power inequality without question; people tend to value concepts like tradition, and organizations tend to be highly hierarchical. The power distance cultural dimension determines the way in which people prefer to be managed, and the way in which they make decisions, for example, in a more or less participative managing style.
2. *Individualism* (the degree to which people are integrated into groups or put their interest before that of the group). Individualism is the cultural belief that the individual comes first. In individualistic countries, people are concerned about themselves and their families, rather than others. At the other extreme, collectivist cultures value the overall good of the group. People subordinate their own interests to those of the group. In highly individualistic societies, people are oriented to self-achievement.
3. *Masculinity* (the degree to which the dominant values of a society are assertiveness, acquiring material goods, and not caring for others). The other extreme is femininity. When a country scores high in femininity, nurturing roles are emphasized, and equal roles between men and women are evident. Societies scoring high in femininity tend to build a health system which is free and accessible to all the population.
4. *Uncertainty avoidance* (the degree to which a society prefers certain events and avoids risk). Countries with strong uncertainty avoidance prefer more structure, resulting in explicit rules of behavior. Spain is an example of a country which scores high in this dimension.

According to Hofstede (1980), a cultural dimension is a mental program which distinguishes those who make up a group, due to their having been exposed to similar experiences and having the same education. These conditioners affect the behavior of societies but also that of organizations and are characterized by being persistent over time.

Hofstede's dimensions are used to establish the cultural distance between countries. This cultural distance is measured using the average difference between the origin country and the destination country (see Hofstede, 1980, 2001; House et al., 2004). In this framework, "cultural distance" can also be defined as "the distance perceived between the home country and the host country, in terms of culture, economic system and business practices" (Hill et al., 1990, p. 122). Hofstede's work showed that there are cultural groups which revolve around the cultural dimensions at the geographical level. This researcher developed a method to identify the cultural patterns of each group. This is done in such a way that each culture finds a pattern defined for each of the dimensions and each culture is defined in terms of the values attained in each of these dimensions. Yet, the interpretation of the cultural dimensions is carried out in relative terms and in comparison, with other cultures. For example, the Spanish culture obtains an average value in power distance, but in comparison to Sweden it could be said that the power distance in Spain is much greater than it is in Sweden. HR practices can be standardized or adapted to each cultural characteristic from each country. Such a decision will depend upon whether the firm goes with the same HR policy worldwide or not (always in coherence with the general business strategy).

INTERNATIONAL STAFFING

As mentioned in the introduction to this chapter, when a company operates internationally, managers should make decisions about the internationalization of all the functional areas (finances, marketing, or HRM, among others) of the firm. They should make decisions about where and how to carry out their specific activities. Should these activities be done in the home country? For example, Should the recruitment or selection process be carried out in the home country or in the host country? Should the company externalize their HR activities? or Should international assignments be covered by employees from the home country? Should local employees be hired?

One of the activities of IHRM revolves around how to fill international vacancies or how to staff internationally. IHRM has traditionally centered on the study of "expatriation" –international assignments of employees who stay abroad for a significant period of time (Harris & Brewster, 1999). At the level of managers, it is increasingly common to be expected to relocate during an international career, and there are many firms which these days have part of their staff installed in or semi-permanently relocated to other countries in the world. These employees are among the most expensive human resources of the organizations which operate internationally. They have issues and problems which go beyond those of most other employees. Therefore, the study of the practices of expatriation is very relevant for the business world.

There are four main approaches to staffing in multinationals (MNCs) (Perlmutter, 1969):

- **Ethnocentric Orientation:** This is based on the presumption that the parent company's professionals, functions and approaches to management are better than the subsidiaries'. All the top positions in the host country's firm are covered by expatriates. Fundamental decisions are made at the headquarters and foreign subsidiaries have little autonomy. Among the business reasons for pursuing an ethnocentric staffing policy is the perception that there is a lack of qualified professionals in the host country.

- **Polycentric Approach:** The management is based on staff contracted from the country where the subsidiary is deployed, endowing it with authority and power to make decisions. The top positions are occupied by local employees. This approach assumes that the cultures are different, and that headquarters may find the people in the host country difficult to understand. Therefore, the organization considers that the local people are better placed to make decisions about what happens in each location. From a management point of view, the headquarters has financial power, but the subsidiary units work as quasi-independent centers. The headquarters considers subsidiaries as independent entities and autonomy is granted to a great extent.

- **Geocentric Approach:** This approach has been defined by Perlmutter (1969) as a concept oriented at the world; that is to say, nationality is not regarded as the basis of superiority. Management, in this case, is based on the search for the most suitable person to solve a problem or do a job, regardless of their nationality. The aim of such an approach is to achieve an international image, both in the headquarters and in the subsidiary. The subsidiaries do not function as independent satellites, but together contribute to the identity of the multinational organization. The aims of each business unit are both local and global, each one of them offering a unique contribution based on a unique competence. This approach requires a great effort of collaboration between all the units (headquarters and subsidiaries).

- **Regiocentric Approach:** In this case, international vacancies are filled by people whose personal profile fits the specific host region. Staff may move outside their countries but only within the particular geographic region. Here subsidiaries are interconnected and regulated by a regional center. Regional managers are not usually promoted to headquarter positions. For example, a US-based firm can create three different regions, Europe, South America and Asia. Managers from Europe can be moved through Europe (from Madrid to Brussels) but will rarely be moved to the Asian region or to the headquarters in the USA.

According to Collings & Scullion (2012), it is important to nuance that these approaches are mainly focused on the policies and practices of hiring staff for key posts in the MNCs and, therefore, they are centered on top posts both in the headquarters and in the subsidiaries. Moreover, the firms do not tend to follow a specific pattern derived from a corporate policy. Experience leads the firms to deploy elements of the various approaches simultaneously.

Who takes part in the IHRM activities? The country categories involved in IHRM activities are (1) the *host country* where a subsidiary may be located, (2) the *home country* where the firm is headquartered, and (3) "other" countries that may be sources of labor, finance and other inputs –*third countries*. And, who are the employees who take part in IHRM? The three categories of employees of an international firm are (1) host-country nationals (HCNs), (2) parent-country nationals (PCNs) and third-country nationals (TCNs).

Making decisions involving all of these parties is not easy. A review of the advantages and the disadvantages of employing different categories of employees can help to clarify the applicability of distinct selection policies. Table 1 details the advantages and the disadvantages of using PCNs, HCNs and TCNs.

Table 1. Advantages and disadvantages of using parent, host and third country national

	Advantages	**Disadvantages**
PCNs	• Greater control of operations with the subsidiaries. • Familiarity with the goals, aims, policies and practices of the headquarters. • Cultural similarity with the headquarters, assuring the transfer of business policies. • Greater effectiveness in the communication with the headquarters. • Higher technical and managerial qualifications.	• High cost. • Problems of family adjustment, especially if partners of managers are unemployed. • Potential difficulties adapting to the foreign language and the social, economic and political-legal environment. • Do not trust the host-country employees.
HCNs	• Greater knowledge of the local economic and political conditions. • Lower costs than the use of PCNs. • Provide local employees with promotion opportunities, improving the acceptance of the firm in the locality.	• Greater difficulty controlling of the operations of the subsidiaries. • Difficulties transferring specific business policies and practices. • Hinder the balance between local demands and international strategies.
TCNs	• Assure the correct balance between technical skills and managerial experience. • Help to develop a reserve of international managers. • Normally involve lower costs than the use of expatriates.	• Represent less opportunities for international development for local employees. • Host-country's sensitivity with respect to nationals of specific countries.

Source: Own elaboration

In addition to the advantages and disadvantages of using expatriates and locals, it should also be taken into account that there are specific situations in which the use of expatriates is more frequent. Following Gómez-Mejías et al. (2016) the following situations are noted:

- The political situation is unstable. In these cases, firms tend to send expatriates to the subsidiaries because they can better defend the company's interests (for example, in the case of terrorist attacks or general strikes).
- The cultural differences between the parent-country and the host-country are very marked. When two countries have marked cultural differences, the firm may send expatriates to ensure communication of the know-how and organizational culture of the home country.
- There is a lack of qualified staff in the host-country.
- The company's business strategy involves the building of a global image.
- The international subsidiaries and the national activities are highly independent.

Considering the possibility of a combination of employees (expatriates and locals), it is useful to know what types and classifications of international employees can be found.

Types of International Employees

The terms expatriate manager and global manager tend to be used as synonyms, but in fact reflect different concepts (Bastida, 2007). Expatriate managers take on leadership posts in countries and cultures distinct from their own, while global managers (also called transnationals) are executives assigned to posts abroad who are characterized by their comprehension of international business and their capacity to work among different countries and in different functions. In this way, global managers can have been expatriates or not, and not all expatriates are global managers.

In general terms, an expatriate is an employee who is temporarily working and residing in a foreign country. According to Reiche & Harzing (2011), although the term expatriate may refer to any employee working outside his/her home-country, it is generally reserved for the group of Parent Country National employees.

Traditionally, the basic types of cross-border career moves are those involving mainstream expatriates and so called "flexpatriates." However, there is a wider list of international workers (Table 2). We mainly mention four types: expatriates, flexpatriates, inpatriates/impatriates and those on short-term assignments.

Focusing on the expatriates (mainstream) and heeding the possible effect of the expatriate's performance on the firm's global functioning, expatriates can be classified as (Bonache & Stirpe, 2012):

- **Star:** Posts in which a poor performance is not too critical for the firm, but a good performance is excellent. These are managers who head a subsidiary that does not depend significantly on the headquarters, where the essential question is the development of new projects highly adapted to the work market.
- **Guardian:** Posts in which an exemplary performance would not be of great importance for the firm's success, but in which a poor performance would be disastrous. An expatriate on a guardian work post would represent the firm in the home-country's delegations, the reputation of the firm being a valuable asset.

- **Foot Soldier:** Posts in which neither a star performance nor a poor one has a significant impact on the firm's general functioning. In the international area, foot soldiers are young expatriates assigned abroad with the objectives of learning and development.

Table 2. Types of international movements

Type	Features
Expatriation (mainstream)	• Initiated by the employer or by the employee. • Assignment to a subsidiary of the firm in a different country. • Substantial time period (usually ranging from 3 to 5 years.
Expatriation – flexpatriates	• Perform short-term assignments (sometimes a few days). • "global traveller" – "frequent flyers." • Tend to be firm's lawyer, negotiator.
Expatriation – Inpatriates/impatriates	• Inpatriation is the practice of developing host-country or third-country managers via a transfer to the headquarters. • Reflects an investment on a long-term basis. • To develop a future reserve of managers. • Inpatriates are foreign nationals hired for a fixed-term temporary employment. • Inpatriates are subsidiaries' staff sent for periods to work at the parent company.
Short-term assignments	• From 3 months to 1 year. • It usually involves a family move, house, car, among others. • It can have severe implications for the work-family balance.
Others: Secondments overseas Off-shore transfer Globetrotting Immigration (legal) Immigration (illegal) Asylum Immigration (temporary) Cross-border (commercial) Government –diplomatic services Government –armed services Non-governmental organizations Work experience, voluntary work, internships Students/traineeships Sabbaticals Virtual global employees	For a full description, see Dickmann & Baruch (2011)

Source: Own elaboration

EXPATRIATION

Why carry out an expatriation? Various motives lead a firm to carry out an international assignment and it is important to understand them, as they can have a direct impact on the firm's results. Edström & Galbraith (1977) identified three main reasons which drive an international assignment:

1. To work in a specific and qualified job when people from the host-country are not available;
2. For the development of the manager, when the firm wants a person to develop global competences and;

3.   As a means of organizational development; that is to say, to transfer knowledge between subsidiaries and to modify and maintain the organizational structure and the decision-making process.

For Harzing (2001), the reasons for an international assignment are centered on identifying control roles for the expatriates, and she calls them: the *bear*, the *bumble-bees* and the *spider*. According to this author, the *bears* act as a substitute for the centralized decision makers and are a direct means of supervision over what happens in the subsidiaries. Their degree of dominance over the operations there is high. The *bumble-bees* "fly from plant to plant and create cross-pollination between the various offshoots" (Harzing, 2001, p. 369). These expatriates can be used to control the subsidiaries through socialization. Finally, the *spiders* control by means of an informal communication network in the multinational. The work of Harzing (2001) is important not only because it explains why expatriates are necessary, but because it introduces the question of whether their roles are equally important in diverse situations.

To sum up, expatriates are a necessary option when short visits to the subsidiary are not enough for the optimum development of the business in the host-country. MNCs need people capable of interacting with other cultures for the benefit of the headquarters. This facilitates the adaptation to the local market and thus assures the corporation's success.

Types of International Assignments

Another key issue is what types of jobs will be carried out in the host-country. International assignments can be classified based on the work to be performed in the host-country. Specifically, Caligiuri (2006) distinguishes four categories:

- **Technical Assignments:** This type of assignment is increasingly more common as organizations are expanding their *technical expertise* globally. For example, when a company is interested in the implementation of a new technical production system. It is supposed that the work done will not be significantly different to that performed in the home country, and significant relations with the nationals of the host country are not expected.
- **Development or High Potential Assignments:** This type of assignment tends to be consistent with the general plan of strategic management of HR and many organizations use these assignments in the context of their manager development programs. They often require rotations, one of them being a stay abroad. Personal development is the aim of the assignment. For example, when a company wants to develop a pool of top international managers, it sends managers on international assignments to gain experience and develop their competences.
- **Strategic or Executive Assignments:** In this case, the assignments are covered by people who are being developed for top posts in the future. They tend to have high profiles, such as managers or vice-presidents, and the experience is understood both from the development and the strategic point of view, as they tend to be sent to fill a specific need in the host-country, such as the opening of new markets, developing a base in a new area, being the manager of a subsidiary, etc.
- **Functional or Tactical Assignments:** This type of assignments is similar to technical ones, with the difference that success in the mission requires a high degree of interaction with the host-country's nationals. It can be focused on covering a technical or managerial gap and it is the most common of the international assignments.

However, this is not the only classification of international assignments that we can find. Stahl et al. (2009) also suggests a classification, this time distinguishing between two types: functional and developmental. The former is those driven by the market demand (demand-driven assignees or functional assignees) which usually involve tasks of coordination, control, training of local staff, problem solving, etc. The latter are those done in order for the candidate to develop a series of professional competences (learning-driven or developmental assignees).

Expatriation Failure

Reiche & Harzing (2011) summarize the success criteria of an international assignment in terms of individual benefits and organizational benefits.

- **Individual Benefits:** In short-term assignments, the carrying out of tasks, the development of skills, learning and knowledge, adaptation and a greater degree of work satisfaction are understood as the main individual benefits. In the case of long-term assignments, these are continuous development, attractive future assignments, development of contacts with key people, possibilities of promotion, and broadening of responsibility.
- **Organizational Benefits:** In short-term assignments, the achievement of fulfilling organizational tasks and the attaining of the organization's key aims (control, coordination, knowledge transfer) stand out. In the case of long-term assignments, the retaining of repatriated workers, the use of new experience, experience transfer, the stimulus among colleagues in favor of international mobility, and the wish to adopt new and future international missions are pointed out.

Yet, not all international assignments turn out to be successful. The majority of studies on expatriation equate "failure" with a premature return. That is to say, if the expatriate remains abroad for the established time period of the assignment, it is considered that the experience has been successful. However, this definition is clearly insufficient. The *Global Mobility Survey* report (2014) indicates that 31.7% of firms directly taking part in their study did not at any moment measure the success of the international mission. Of the rest that did measure the success of the international assignment, 57.1% considered the performance during the assignment abroad, and only 21.8% contemplated the subsequent retention of the worker in the firm as a sign of the success of the mission.

Among the main problems which explain the failure of expatriates, the literature points out (Bonache & Stirpe, 2012; Gómez-Mejías et al., 2016; Harzing, 2001):

- **Family:** Many of the failures of expatriates are related to family problems; that is, the inability of the family to adapt to the new cultural environment. Many firms do not foresee and do not anticipate the issues related to the candidate's family. In general, these questions could be taken into account in the initial recruitment process and candidate selection through interviews (at least with the partner of the candidate), in which the firm could gather information for instance about the couple's work state and/or the need for specific training (language).
- **Blocking the Professional Career:** At the beginning of the international assignment, the expatriates are excited about the experience and the new destination. Nevertheless, as time passes, they feel that the headquarters has forgotten about them and think that their professional career has

been blocked, while they note how colleagues who remained at the headquarters continue being promoted in the organization.

- **Lack of Transcultural Training Prior to Leaving:** Few multinational firms offer any type of training concerning cultural diversity and those that do only offer short, simple courses that do not cover the employee's needs. This is a problem because employees need to know how to deal with the new culture and to develop their capacity for cultural sensitivity.

- **Excess of Technical Qualifications:** Normally firms select highly qualified staff for international assignments - employees with a profile of very high performance in the firm and who have an impressive work record. However, the consideration of these qualities in the candidates for international assignments has led to many failures, given that the firm has given more importance to these qualifications than to other skills, such as cultural sensitivity or the capacity for cultural adaptation.

- **Culture Shock:** The lack of adaptation to the cultural environment of the host-country. Instead of learning to work in the new culture, the expatriate tries to impose his/her values or those of the headquarters on the local employees. This factor is called lack of "cultural intelligence" or incapacity to relate to people of different cultures. Firms can help employees avoid culture shock by selecting candidates with a greater cultural sensibility and who speak the local language.

- **Use of the Assignment to Avoid Conflicts:** In many firms, expatriations are used as a means of getting rid of managers who have problems in the headquarters. By sending these employees abroad, the firm assumes the risk of the failure of international assignments, given that the selection of the candidate has not been made in relation to the qualities and skills required, but in response to the need to solve an internal conflict in the headquarters.

Irrespective of the motive or circumstances which have caused the failure of the international experience, the costs that the firm assumes are worth considering. Ashamalla (1998) determined that the direct cost (relocation, remuneration and training) ranges from 200,000 dollars to 1.2 million dollars, to which other possible losses would have to be added such as the damage caused to the company's image, the loss of market share and business opportunities, as well as a decrease in productivity. It is estimated that, when the total cost of an expatriation package is taken into consideration, the investment in an expatriate is three times as high as the investment in an employee in the headquarters. The failure of the expatriation means not obtaining any benefit from this investment. It has also been found that the average remuneration package of expatriates is between twice and five times what locals receive in developing countries, which are often the host countries of international assignments. Indeed, the high costs entailed by an expatriation can even affect its authorization, thus the need to consider the remuneration and the associated costs in the firm's framework of internationalization strategy.

Given the high disbursement that starting up an international assignment involves, the literature contributes distinct ways for firms to be able to reduce, and even eliminate, some of the factors which make the assignment difficult:

- **Selection Initiatives:** Expatriate only the most essential staff. Organizations should develop selection processes in a way which assures that only those who are interested in experiencing an expatriation are assigned to posts abroad. The bonuses for services abroad, the bonuses for hardship, and the adjustments to the cost of living would be paid only to those who accept an international mission in undesirable or dangerous host countries. In this selection process, the members of the candidate's immediate family should be included.

- **Initiatives of career Planning:** Another alternative is to require that managers have international experience as a criterion for promotion to top posts in the organization. Thus, it is possible to request that the youngest workers undertake an international experience if they wish to climb the ladder. In this way, they renounce short-term gains in exchange for long-term benefits. This is more difficult in the case of older managers.

- **Shorter Assignments:** In the case that these are feasible, they can be a cheaper alternative. It might be possible to send an individual for a shorter period, e.g. for 6 months, instead of sending him/her for 1-2 years. A shorter assignment period can help the employee to adapt to the new culture, reducing the potential for failure and the costs associated with it.

Once firms are aware of the costs of this type of assignment, the investment in the repatriation stage begins to be considered important. Even though the cost of a repatriation program is much less than the investment made during the stay abroad.

As well as the economic perspective, the intangible contributions that a repatriate offers are also important aspects to consider, for example, a global viewpoint and comprehension of the firm, the transfer of information and knowledge, a greater capacity for coordination, and/or an inter-organizational network which favors the firm's globalization. The literature has shown that MNCs whose managers have significant international experience obtain better results than those who do not have staff with these characteristics. These skills can fall into the hands of the competition if the repatriate leaves the company.

In this sense, repatriation can be seen as an important part in the definition of the failure of an international assignment and therefore the following section tackles the main questions about the problems of repatriation.

REPATRIATION

An international assignment does not finish when the expatriate returns to his/her home-country. Rather, it is then that a last phase, called repatriation, begins. The literature points out that in spite of the importance of this phase, many firms are still not aware of it (Gross, 2002; Larson, 2006; Lee, 2007; Tyler, 2006), and some do not even consider repatriation as part of the international assignment process. Expatriation and repatriation are not separate processes: expatriation is the beginning and repatriation the end of the same process. In general terms, the literature has centered on the study of the keys to a successful expatriation and not so much on the end of the process, repatriation. However, for a manager tasked with expanding the company internationally, it is an aspect that should not be forgotten.

Despite the huge benefits that an international assignment can bring both for the firm and for the worker, there are problems associated with the return of the expatriate to the headquarters after an international assignment:

- **Impossibility of Transmitting Skills Learnt:** The literature has pointed out this factor as a problem that repatriates face on their return to the headquarters. In many organizations, the information and skills which the expatriate has learnt in the international assignment are unappreciated by the colleagues and supervisors in the headquarters. Nonetheless, this has of late been changing.

Firms such as "General Electric" or "HP" want the services of veteran managers who have international experience.

- **Loss of Status:** When the expatriate returns to the headquarters, he/she often suffers from a loss of privileges, prestige, power, independence and authority.
- **Poor Planning of the Return to the Headquarters:** The uncertainty of the repatriation. The employees frequently do not know what their post is going to be in the headquarters or what options there will be for professional growth.
- **Reverse Culture Shock:** As the time the worker spends abroad increases, his/her adaptation to the home country after repatriation will become more difficult, given that he/she will have, to a greater extent, adopted the host country's cultural values. To this must be added the countless changes which have taken place in the home country and which the worker will have to face on his/her return.

Regarding all these questions about the problems suffered by the employees on their return from their international assignment, along with the economic and operational problems caused by bad management of the repatriates, IHRM suggests:

- **Necessary Integration of the Selection, the Performance Management and the Repatriation System:** The low rates of retention of repatriates are not surprising, considering that international assignments have not, until now, been understood as a component of professional development. That is, they have not been integrated into the general career planning program. However, these components of professional development cannot occur in an isolated manner after repatriation. Selection for the international mission must be part of a wider career development plan. The performance of the expatriate has to be measured based on the competences desired for his/her development during the international assignment and, then, the repatriate can also return with a greater knowledge of what his/her career plan will be after repatriation.
- **Certain Departures after Repatriation are Operable:** The relocation in the company is difficult and many receive a job which means a loss of the privileges and rights that they had. An explanation of this is the lack of strategic integration of the international assignment, and another is that, in reality, some multinationals do not want or do not need all the expatriates to return.
- **Different International Assignments Require Different Repatriation Strategies:** Considering the classification of the international assignments mentioned beforehand, suggested by Caligiuri (2006), the literature suggests different considerations:
  - **Technical Assignments:** For the repatriation strategy to be successful, the firms will have to take into account the extent to which they need the technical skills of the repatriated employee once the international mission has been completed. In many firms, these are required throughout the organization, therefore they are in high demand, although not necessarily in the headquarters. That is, the experts may see themselves in the situation of stringing together different international destinations. For example, a manager that had just landed in the country as the CEO of a company in Tokyo but, a few years ago, had moved to London where he/she was setting up home. In other organizations, this "experience" is only necessary for a specific period of time, so once the project is finished, the contract with the firm also ends and this is how it must be set out.

- ○ **Development of High Potential Assignments:** This type of assignment is often made up of a series of very structured experiences. Therefore, the repatriate's subsequent assignment tends to be clearly understood well before the culmination of the period abroad. In this case, the repatriation is simple and predetermined by the rotations set out in the manager development program.

- ○ **Strategic or Executive Assignments:** The repatriation in these cases tends to be well thought out and is part of the organization's general planning. The repatriates tend to be in the know that they are being prepared for a given post. An important issue will be to ensure the use of the skills developed during the international mission. The repatriates should be endowed with a sufficient level of autonomy and freedom, as if these profiles leave after the repatriation, this will be highly harmful for the firm.

- ○ **Functional or Tactical Assignment:** These are profiles more inclined to leave and the strategy of repatriation should primarily be based on determining whether the skills acquired are necessary in the company. If they are, they have to be recognized and rewarded and their use has to be made possible, considering all this as an investment in human capital. On the other hand, if the skills are not necessary, the expatriate has to be informed as soon as possible. This is also the case when the company's intention is to replace this international post stringing together new recruitments.

- • **Individual Career Motivations Differ:** As occurs in the case of other professional profiles in high demand, on occasions not even the best program of repatriation will be able to prevent the employee leaving. International experience is currently a very valuable asset that substantially increases employability. Some workers will opt for other employment alternatives, either for reasons which have to do with the post, or for economic reasons, and they will not perceive leaving as a negative career move. Retaining repatriated staff is a real challenge in these cases, where some considerations take on special relevance, such as recognition, stimulus, praise, professional growth opportunities, remuneration, corporate communication, flexibility and stock options.

Briefly, and to sum up, with respect to the repatriation phase, a repatriation is successful given three conditions: that the repatriate obtains an appropriate job on his/her return, that the difficulties of cultural re-adaptation are minimal, and that there is little or no intention of leaving (O'Sullivan, 2002).

Models for Repatriation Management

As an example, we will now explain one of the models that the literature recognizes for expatriation-repatriation processes, developed by Caligiuri & Lazarova (2001), as this is one that is generally accepted.

Model of Caligiuri & Lazarova (2001)

Caligiuri & Lazarova (2001) carried out a theoretical study in which they provide proactive recommendations for a strategic repatriation. According to the authors, many MNCs are concerned about the high leaving rates of repatriates. This is why the study firstly analyzes the four causes of the problem and how this reflects on the repatriation management. As well as the recommendations, the authors present a program which has 11 management practices applicable "to almost all expatriates" (Table 3) (Caligiuri & Lazarova, 2001, p. 254).

Table 3. Recommendations for a strategic repatriation

Informative session prior to the move about what to expect during repatriation
Career planning sessions
Guarantee and agreement indicating the type of position to be held after repatriation
Tutorials during the stay abroad
Reorientation program about changes which have taken place in the company
Training seminars about the emotional response of repatriation
Financial and tax assessment and advice
Help with respect to daily life and assessment concerning probable changes after repatriation
Continuous communication with the headquarters
Visible signs that the company values international experience
Communication with the headquarters about the details of the repatriation process

Source: Own elaboration

The model supports the idea that organizations have to make an effort to manage expectations about repatriation, given that this will help to reduce uncertainty on return. Firms should provide informative instructions or sessions detailing what to expect on return, for example, through using former expatriates.

The model considers career planning as a critical element in retaining the repatriates. This has to begin between six and twelve months before the end of the international assignment. MNCs must offer multiple sessions to discuss the expatriates' worries about, for example, the aims of their post and their functions. The intention is to offer a feeling of security about their future in the company. This planning must involve the HR team, the manager of the business unit and the expatriate. For the sake of reducing uncertainty about the expatriate's future in the organization, another relevant aspect is that of offering certain guarantees in writing or repatriation agreements, indicating the post to be held on return.

A popular practice according to the authors of the model is the use of the figure of a tutor to keep the expatriate in the know about what is happening in the organization during his/her absence and as a guide concerning his/her career.

In addition, Caligiuri & Lazarova suggest that firms must offer reorientation programs about changes in the company related to new policies, staff and strategies immediately after the return, when the repatriate goes back to work. This training should be accompanied by seminars which respond to the emotional worries caused by repatriation, not only for the worker but also for his/her family.

The offer of financial and tax assessment and help is also considered an important element for an appropriate expatriation-repatriation. As an example, some organizations offer bridging loans or loans with low rates of interest for buying a home or helping with the mortgage. Others are willing to cover the costs of private schools in the return country to provide continuity in the children's education. Moreover, financial assessment related to the life style is also beneficial for the worker and his/her family. Some alternatives in this sense may be payment to belong to a club of expatriates, entrance to private schools, among others. Another recommendation is to understand that expatriates need time to readapt, without additional pressure from the organization. This could be assured through reducing travel time, or lengthening vacations, among other actions. During the stay abroad, firms should also provide opportunities to communicate with the headquarters through visits, sending reports by email, maintaining contact with colleagues, etc.

Lastly, the organization must offer visible signs that it values the international experience, for example through promotions, maintaining the prestige and status linked to the post, or additional remuneration. The model shows the importance of being clear in the communication of the details of the repatriation process.

REFLECTIVE QUESTIONS

- What is the difference between domestic and International HRM?
- Discuss in class: Is the world moving toward a convergence in terms of business policies?
- Discuss in class: Is it true that a company following an Ethnocentric orientation is highly concerned with cultural differences?
- Is it possible for a company to mix different approaches when staffing internationally?
- What are the advantages of using host-country nationals vs. using third-country nationals?
- When (in what situations) is the use of expatriates more appropriate?
- Explain what "Technical Assignments" consist of?
- What are the main recommendations for avoiding host-country problems for expatriates?
- What does IHRM suggest in order to improve the repatriation processes?

REFERENCES

Adler, N. J. (1997). *International Dimensions of Organizational Behavior*. South Western: College Publishing.

Al Ariss, A., & Sidani, Y. (2016). Comparative international human resource management: Future research directions. *Human Resource Management Review*, 26(4), 352–358. doi:10.1016/j.hrmr.2016.04.007

Armstrong, M., & Taylor, S. (2014). *Armstrong's Handbook of human resource management practice*. London: Ediction. Kogan Page Limited.

Ashamalla, M. H. (1998). International Human Resource Management Practices: The challenge of expatriation. *Competitiveness Review*, 8(2), 54–65. doi:10.1108/eb046368

Bastida, M. (2007). El capital humano internacional como fuente de ventaja competitiva. *Boletín Económico de ICE*, 59-73.

Bonache, J., & Stirpe, L. (2012). Compensating global employees. In *Handbook of Research in International Human Resource Management* (2nd ed.; pp. 162–182). Cheltenham, UK: Edward Elgar Publishing Limited.

Brewster, C., Harris, H., & Sparrow, P. R. (2002). United Nations. *People Management*, 8(14), 32–34.

Brewster, C., & Hegewisch, A. (1994). *Policy and Practice in European Human Resource Management: The price Waterhouse Survey*. London: Routledge.

Caligiuri, P. M. (2006). Performance measurement in a cross-national context. In *Performance Measurement: current perspectives and future challenges* (pp. 227–243). Laurence Erlbaum Associates, Inc.

Caligiuri, P. M., & Lazarova, M. (2001). Strategic Repatriation Policies to Enhance Global Leadership Development. In *Developing Global Business Leaders: Policies, Processes, and Innovations, cap. 14* (pp. 243–256). Greenwood Publications Group Inc.

Collings, D., & Scullion, H. (2012). Global Staffing. In Handbook of Research in International Human Resource Management (2nd ed.). Cheltenham, UK: Edward Elgar Publishing Limited. doi:10.4337/9781849809191.00014

Dickmann, M., & Baruch, Y. (2010). *Global Careers*. London: Routledge.

Dolan, S. L., Valle-Cabrera, R., Jackson, S. E., & Schuler, R. S. (2007). *La gestión de los recursos humanos. Cómo atraer, retener y desarrollar con éxito el capital humano en tiempos de transformación.* Madrid: McGraw Hill.

Dolan, S. L., Valle-Cabrera, R., & López-Cabrales, A. (2014). *La gestión de personas y del talento. La gestión de los recursos humanos en el siglo XXI.* Madrid: McGraw Hill Education.

Dowling, P. J., & Welch, D. E. (2004). *International Human Resource Management. Managing People in a Multinational Context* (4th ed.). Thomson Learning.

Edström, A., & Galbraith, J. R. (1977). Transfer of managers as a coordination and control strategy in multinational organizations. *Administrative Science Quarterly*, *23*(2), 248–263. doi:10.2307/2391959

Festing, M., & Eidems, J. (2011). A process perspective on transnational HRM systems--A dynamic capability-based analysis. *Human Resource Management Review*, *21*(3), 162–173. doi:10.1016/j.hrmr.2011.02.002

Friedman, T. (2005). *The World is Flat: The Globalized World in the Twenty-first Century*. London: Penguins Books.

Global Mobility Survey. (2014). *Global Mobility: Strategic or Tactical?* Harvard Business School Publishing.

Gómez-Mejías, L. R., Balkin, D., & Cardy, R. (2016). *Gestión de Recursos Humanos (8ᵗʰ ed.).* Pearson Education.

Gross, L. (2002). The right way to bring expats home. *Workforce*, *81*(7), 40–44.

Harris, H., & Brewster, C. (1999). The coffee-machine system: How international selection really works. *International Journal of Human Resource Management*, *10*(3), 488–500. doi:10.1080/095851999340440

Harzing, A. W. (2001). Of bears, bumble-bees, and spiders: The role of expatriates in controlling foreign subsidiaries. *Journal of World Business*, *36*(4), 366–379. doi:10.1016/S1090-9516(01)00061-X

Hill, C. W. L., Hwang, P., & Kim, W. C. (1990). An eclectic theory of the choice of international entry mode. *Strategic Management Journal*, *11*(2), 117–128. doi:10.1002mj.4250110204

Hofstede, G. (1980). *Culture's Consequences*. London: Sage Publications.

Hofstede, G. (2001). *Culture's Consequences: Comparing Values, Behaviors, Institutions and Organizations across Nations* (2nd ed.). Sage Publications.

Hofstede, G., & McCrae, R. (2004). Personality and Culture Revisited: Linking Traits and Dimensions of Culture. *Cross-Culture Research: The Journal of Comparative Social Science, 38,* 52–88.

House, R. J., Hanges, P. J., Javidan, M., Dorfman, P. W., & Gupta, V. (2004). *Culture, leadership and organizations: The GLOBE study of 62 societies.* SAGE Publications.

Jackson, T. (2002). *International HRM. A cross-cultural approach.* London: SAGE Publications Ltd. doi:10.4135/9781446280089

Larson, D. A. (2006). Here we go again: How a family's cross-cultural and repatriation adjustment relates to the employee's receptivity to future international assignments. *S.A.M. Advanced Management Journal, 71*(2), 46–57.

Lee, H. W. (2007). Factors that influence expatriate failure: An interview study. *International Journal of Management, 24*(3), 403–413.

O'Sullivan, S. L. (2002). The protean approach to managing repatriation transitions. *International Journal of Manpower, 23*(7), 597–616. doi:10.1108/01437720210450789

Perlmutter, H. V. (1969). The Tortuous Evolution of the Multinational Corporation. *The Columbia Journal of World Business, 4,* 9–18.

Reiche, S., & Harzing, A. W. (2011). *International Assignments. In International Human Resource Management* (3rd ed.). London: Sage Publications.

Sparrow, P. R., & Hiltrop, J. M. (1997). Redefining the field of European human resource management: A battle between national mindsets and forces of business transition? *Human Resource Management, 36*(2), 201–219. doi:10.1002/(SICI)1099-050X(199722)36:2<201::AID-HRM3>3.0.CO;2-0

Stahl, G., Chua, C. H., Caligiuri, P., Cerdin, J. L., & Taniguchi, M. (2009). Predictors of turnover intentions in learning-driven and demand-driven international assignments: The role of repatriation concerns, satisfaction with company support, and perceived career advancement opportunities. *Human Resource Management, 48*(1), 89–109. doi:10.1002/hrm.20268

Tyler, K. (2006). Retaining repatriates: Pre-assignment planning, ongoing communication and mentoring help retain valuable repatriates. *Human Resource Magazine, 51*(3), 97–104.

Urteaga, E. (2009). Orígenes e inicios de los estudios culturales. *Gazeta de Antropología, 25,* artículo 23.

ENDNOTE

[1] Jackson's work (2002) moves on to a discussion of the impact of culture on leadership and management styles.

This research was previously published in Managerial Competencies for Multinational Businesses; pages 174-194, copyright year 2019 by Business Science Reference (an imprint of IGI Global).

Chapter 10
Key HRM Challenges and Benefits:
The Contributions of the HR Scaffolding

John Mendy
University of Lincoln, UK

ABSTRACT

Whilst HRM is responding to organizational challenges, HRM tutors have to deal with avoiding labour imposition (Mather et al., 2007) and ensuring that their students are well prepared for society. The chapter's findings involve linkages between people, HR systems and the workplace in an HR Scaffolding that is argued to contribute to resolving the challenges caused by 'the black box' of organizational performance (Becker & Huselid, 2006). Four steps of research extrapolate lessons to be learnt.

INTRODUCTION

Important issues require attention in our society, for example the recent banking scandal, potentially social disasters like Brexit, problems of immigration and ethnic diversification. At the organisational level HRM has been dealing with fundamental challenges, amongst which whether HR adds value to organizational processes, whether HR should be an agent or administrator of work practices, the alignment between work practices, HRM systems and functions (e.g. recruitment and selection, performance appraisals etc) and whether the teaching of the subject should focus on the functional aspects of what HR professionals do or whether a more critical exploration is required. Whatever the future may hold for the subject area, HRM is currently faced with the dilemma of how it can contribute to or enhance organizational performance. The ways such a challenge has been dealt with by tutors and scholars seem to create more confusion than the anticipated resolution of the challenges posed. The chapter identifies the nature of the challenges and what needs to be done. To help deal with the challenges the author has chosen to focus on research, i.e. especially on ways to recognise social/people resources that may provide the necessary help. It is anticipated such type of scholarship will help students to become persons in society who are able to change it for the better and from within.

DOI: 10.4018/978-1-6684-3873-2.ch010

Part of the challenges being faced by HR stems from the argument that HRM seems to be taught and practised as if it is comprised of and should be practised as a set of prescriptions (advice, decisions, imperatives). It is anticipated that when carried out these would boost Organizational Performance. Whether it does is still questionable. This deficit has provided a counter-argument which is to conduct research on performance. Over the decades the studies carried out have focused on intermediate variables to explain whether HRM practices do have an impact on performance. It is in this type of challenge that the author wishes to focus the current chapter to see what can be added to the 'black box' (Becker and Huselid, 2006) or gap between what HRM does (i.e. its practices, systems, functions) and organizational performance. Based on the research and the literature three categories could be found and these are referred to as theoretical, methodological and empirical. The debates in each of the categories are polarised and help to add to the confusion of whether what HRM does as a function improves an organization's performance. Under the theoretical challenge, Fleetwood and Hesketh (2005) lamented the 'under-theorised' nature of the area. The survey-based approach, short-term empirical work has also not succeeded in capturing the full breadth of the performance related issues as anticipated (see Wright, Gardner, Moynihan and Allen (2004); Huselid, 1995). The author uses empirical data from four organizations that he researched within a six year period in the UK to demonstrate how the linkages between people, HRM systems and the workplace can, in a small but important part, provide a solution to the extent to which HRM/working practices contribute to organizational but also employees' performance. The findings are used to provide lessons on what needs to be done to address the under-theorised, the methodological and empirical challenges HRM and HR tutors continue to face in the area of performance management.

The author explores the seminal works of leading scholars in the area such as Bowen and Ostroff (2004), Guest (2011), Goddard (2004), Lepak and Snell (1999) and Becker and Huselid (2006) amongst others to see what can be added to the 'black box'. The author categorises the theoretical framework within two major strands of discussion; the first labelled as 'content' and the second as 'process.' Their exploration has helped to identify aspects of the challenges to see what the chapter's proposed HR Scaffolding has to offer. Under content theories the author examines the HRM practices, policies and procedures which together could be seen as part of bundles of functional HRM (a set of advice or prescriptions). Under the process theories, the author explores the ways via which employees make sense of the actions of managers when they use the HRM systems and practices to bring about organizational performance. As the challenges are still ongoing, the chapter proposes research that provides a linkage between the various elements (people, HR systems and workplace) in what is referred to as an HR Scaffolding. From the empirical data, this concept shows what has been missing in the discussions; that is 'why' is it that people – i.e. employees as well managers might wish to perform well and thereby strengthen their organization's HRM/working practices, policies and procedures especially as they respond to challenges such as labour imposition (Mather et al, 2007) and the threats of the recent banking scandal. From the fieldwork, four research steps and the concept of The HRM Scaffolding are added to help explain and resolve challenges posed by the 'black box' of organizational performance and an extension of the works of Bowen and Ostroff (2004), Lepak and Snell (1999), Guest (2011) and Becker and Huselid (2006).

The author combines the HR challenges and proposes some benefits in the form of lessons as has hitherto not been attempted (see Goddard, 2004). To find out whether HR practices contribute to performance the author looked at what employees and managers did when their organizations were challenged to address performance issues under four pressurized environments. Such an exploration is timely and necessary.

The aims and objectives for this chapter can therefore be summarised as follows:

1. Provide some evidence to demonstrate that HRM is confronted with the key challenge of performance
2. Show what key benefits and opportunities could be achieved
3. Draw lessons for HRM tutors, scholars and practitioners.

The second section looks at the content and process theories and critiques the linkages and causality debates between HRM practices and organizational performance and the third provides the four organizational settings that gave rise to the performance pressures. This is followed in the fourth and fifth sections by the research pathway and the data presentation. The discussions are featured in the sixth section followed by conclusions and future research.

KEY CHALLENGES AND BENEFITS

Numerous academics, HR professionals and students continue to be intrigued by whether working practices do contribute and have contributed to enhancing performance, organizationally and individually. Resolving the challenge is no mean achievement as previous attempts have not succeeded. Part of the problem here is that HRM ends up being portrayed as a function that advises practitioners and aspiring professionals what employment practices they should carry out as a set of prescriptions to maximise performance rather than doing research that helps to alleviate the problem. In the latter, the question is whether intermittent variables between HRM working practices and performance management can be explained such that the confusion becomes clarified. In essence the fundamental question here is 'How can HRM show that it is its employment/working practices that have contributed and continue to contribute to organizational performance?' Has the latter happened by chance or can we do research to explain the relationship? The author adopts the latter approach to see what can be contributed.

Firstly, the author categorises the challenges under two areas: 'content' and 'process' in line with the literature (see Bowen and Ostroff, 2004; Guest, 2011; Sanders, Shipton and Gomes, 2014). A central aspect in this is an examination of Lepak and Snell's (1999) 'HR Architecture' model. These include Human Capital and the Resource Based View of the Firm to see whether there is even a relationship between HRM and Performance. The benefits of having High Performance Work Systems within organizations are critiqued with the aim of challenging the causality between the HRM systems on organizational performance. The empirical data from four organizations is used to proposing a new framework that brings together people, HRM/working practices and the workplace in an HRM Scaffolding. Its aim is to show that contrary to the literature which has examined the necessary elements in isolation, this chapter shows that there is a linkage between a combined set of HRM practices, the workplace and the contributions of people to organizational performance, elements which are treated as if in isolation in the literature. Key challenges are presented as follows.

Under-Theorisation: HR Theories, HRM Practices, and Organizational Performance

In this section, the author will show how the under-theorising in this topic has added to the challenge. In their seminal work Lepak and Snell (1999) started a research trend to examine whether HRM practices have a direct impact on organizational performance. They proposed the 'black box' (Becker and Huselid, 2006; Sanders, Shipton and Gomes, 2014) as a way to show the causality between the under-theorised nature of HRM practices and organizational performance. They examined how effective HRM Systems have contributed in this area by Human Capital theory, the Resource Based View (RBV) of the Firm and transaction cost economics in order to develop the Human Resource Architecture (HRA) model (also see Bowen and Ostroff, 2004)). Lepak and Snell claim the architecture can be used to examine modes of employment, relationships and configurations to see how competitive an organization can be within its market environment. They recognised the limitations of organizational talent acquisition both internally and externally and fell short of addressing how these skills can be linked and channelled. As skills' identification and management are crucial towards performance, the final word had not been said as vital elements remain missing.

Huselid (1995) and Gerhart and Trevor (1996) earlier looked at a combination of HR practices on employees and whether their application/implementation triggered similar or varying performance and employment outcomes. Goddard (2004) advocated for commitment and engagement so as to enable a high performing work environment alternatively referred to in the literature as High-Performance Work Systems. However, the nature of the commitment from employees and its various characteristics/elements as a mediating variable has eluded scholarly and HR clarification over the past thirty years. In essence, anything could be used to explain the missing link. Something else is required. Fleetwood and Hesketh (2006) buttressed Bowen and Ostroff's 'strength' within the HR System as a panacea to the limitations. These limitations still abound and exacerbate the challenges. Resolving these would entail looking at the nature of 'content' and 'process' theories.

Lepak and Snell's (1999) and Becker and Huselid's (2006) works are examined to see what else can be added to the debates and discussions as follows.

Content Theories: The HR Architecture

In their attempt to resolve the problem of under-theorisation Lepak and Snell (1999) used Human Capital to shed light on the different employment modes and relationships. They claim that some of the characteristics are 'static' whilst others are 'dynamic' (p. 33) as organizations use the Architecture as a way to help them achieve competitive advantage. It is claimed that achieving the necessary employee skills can help organizations manage staff internally, save on employment costs and boost productivity. Part of the difficulty arises when skills cannot be sourced from within. This had been identified earlier to help resolve an organization's future productivity and value (see Barney's, 1995 Resource Based View (RBV) of the Firm)). However the costs associated with training, management and administrative time, amongst others, are downplayed whilst the benefits of value, the creation of knowledge workers and competitive advantage are overplayed (see Porter, 1996). Also underplayed is the centrality of people who provide the necessary talent for RBV. It is also claimed that Human Capital acquisition would bring about commitment as a result of having HR Systems in place (Arthur, 1994). Such 'configuration' (Lepak and Snell, pp. 39, 42) is expected to yield the effectiveness organizational performance required (see Becker and Huselid, 2006). Both sets of scholars tended to emphasize on the alignment between the HR Architecture, an organization's strategic capacities and strategy implementation to bring about successful outcomes. Again the emphasis is on the functional aspects rather than on what people can contribute to it.

We now need to go beyond what the architecture promises to deliver to looking at both what the organization, its HR systems as well as its employees can contribute to add to and explain the 'mediating variables' of the 'black box'. The value of each employee and how they are managed and treated is therefore dependent on their skills, what they are willing to contribute as part of their capabilities and how they become beneficial to the organization. The latter two aspects need to be further developed as an extension of Lepak and Snell's HR Architectur. So, the more strategic and unique an employee's skills and capabilities are, the greater his/her value to the company and therefore the greater the role of HR. However, not all companies are the same and no single strategic environment in which a company operates in is the same and sustaining such a value-laden position may be problematic (Prahalad and Hamel, 1994). Strategies do not also necessarily deliver the types of functional performance outcomes as propounded in the literature on the fit between HRM practices and performance (Barney, 2001; Bowen and Ostroff, 2004; Wright et al, 2004; Stanton et al, 2010).

In recognition of what is missing Wright et al (2001) called for the use of dynamic capabilities whilst Siggelkow (2002) advocated for the 'connecting' capabilities within an implementation strategy. Makadok (2001) identified that a company's resources (both tangible and intangible assets) should be embedded within a company and serve as part of the intermediate variable. An organization's resources and capabilities are viewed as part of its practical processes to bring about strategic competitive advantage (see Eisenhardt and Martin, 2000; Ray et al, 2004). To bring about differentiation to earlier proponents, Becker and Huselid (2006) advocated a focus on the job and not the employee skills. They proposed two types of HR Architectures: A and B both of which are designed to provide the human attributes needed for business effective. That which is expected to be improved included performance behaviours although this has not yet been the case judging from developments in the literature.

Process Theories: How to Conduct HRM

In this section, the author argues that Becker and Huselid's (2006) proposition to focus on strategy implementation to boost financial performance only helps in adding to the challenges faced by HRM. It is argued that by looking at those aspects with high scores of human capital to bring about strategic difference, the authors of this seminal piece only highlighted practical implementation issues rather than focusing on what people are willing to and can contribute to its success. They recognised the challenges associated with the repositioning of the debate as proposed. Part of this involve the validation of outcome measurements on each organization where the proposal is being implemented. There is a problem though and that is who determines at what point that the validation is robust and that it will generate the anticipated effectiveness. One thing that is most needed is case study research to add to the debates although we have to be mindful of data omission or leaving out employees' contributions or attempting to show linkage or causality.

Relationship: Linkage or Causality?

The issue of linkage or causality between HRM practices and performance has been addressed in relation to research constraints rather than as part of the theoretical, methodological and empirical considerations. In their two-year study of forty five business units from a large food business in the US and Canada, Wright, Gardner, Moynihan and Allen (2004) looked at the extent to which HR practices and commitment impacted on profitability and productivity, amongst others. Interestingly, they found that attempts to control past and current performance tended to dampen the longer term linkage. It is therefore not surprising that survey-type questions focus on the shorter term. Even though Stanton, Young, Bartram and

Leggat (2010) carried out interviews, presentations, discussions and focus-groups with participants on a five-year research into Australian hospitals interestingly the adoption of a consistent HRM message at various organizational levels sounded more like a plea for the adoption and integration of HRM practices. When such integration failed employees' resistance rather than their contributions is emphasized (see Boxall and Purcell, 2007; Mayrhofer, 2004 and Harris, Cortvriend and Hyde, 2007 for similar research).

Most empirical studies show a link between HRM and firm performance (see Guzzo, Jette and Katzell's (1985) study on training, productivity and organizational performance, and Gerhart and Milkovich's (1992) link between reward, training and organizational profits and Harter et al's (2002) research that linked employee engagement, turnover, productivity and customer satisfaction. Koys (2991) noted employee satisfaction, customer satisfaction and profits. Limited studies have shown causality (see Scnheider et al, 2003 and Wright et al (2004). When this is the case, the emphasis is on skills, talent and HRM systems not people. The totality of HRM systems is often emphasized (see Huselid's (1995) 'High Performance Work Practices' (HPWPs). Such advocacies have not resolved the challenges posed by performance. Currie and Proctor (2001) and Renwick (2003) reminded us of the constraints of devolving HR responsibilities and line management's difficulties in carrying out the HR function (see McGovern and Stiles, 1997) or claims to symbiotic relationships between HR and line management (see Purcell and Hutchinson, 2007). Combining theory, method and empirical data as part of a new proposition remains problematic partly due to the issues earlier experienced by Lepak and Snell (1999) and bemoaned by Fleetwood and Hesketh (2006).

Benefits

However an over-emphasis on the challenges has led to more challenges as argued. This section seeks to address the imbalance and help resolve part of the difficulties in a small way. It is advocated that combining HRM practices and their impacts on performance could deliver positive outcomes for organizations as well as individuals. This resolves motivation, knowledge management, performance and best practice issues (see Guest and Peccei, 2001). Such developments have been referred to in the literature as the High Performance Paradigm (HPP) as an alternative. Examples of the HPP include functional aspects such as job enrichment, job rotation, quality circles and work teams and it is assumed that aligning these to a strategy will deliver the anticipated outcomes (Hoque, 1999; Pfeffer, 1998). However, we are reminded that the required outcomes might still elude us (Becker and Huselid, 1997). It is generally argued by HPP proponents that HRM practices or 'bundles' of practices when combined in the matching model serve to boost effective performance (Pfeffer, 1998). The benefits to be accrued are identified and critically examined in line with the data in the fifth section.

Guest (1999) found some positive relationship between HPP and management-employee trust and commitment as well as the 'psychological contract'. Such a claim stands to be contested as elements such as making work 'interesting' could be considered outside of the HPP frame. Measuring variables such as motivation and satisfaction is no mean feat especially when participants have their individual biases, interpretations, intentions and contributions. White and his colleagues (2003) found some relationship between the use of appraisals within an HPP frame and work-life balance although Ichiniowski et al (1997) found some differences in the HR and HPP bundles. The instruments focus on mainly HRM ones rather than what people contribute.

Other studies are more critical of the 'bundling' method and its benefits. Although Appelbaum and his colleagues (2000) found some relationship between HPP and trust they could not verify a similar trend for stress. The fact that belonging and contributing to team work might not necessarily have any significant impact on HPP's outcomes throws the argument for HPP and the bundles of employment practices off the HRM and performance course. On the contrary research conducted by Cappelli and Neumark (2001) found some damning results on HPP including a hike in employment-related costs and no direct impact on performance effectiveness (see also Guest et al (2003) for similar research results). The chapter proceeds to look at the interviews that were held with employees and managers to see what was done to improve the fortunes of four private organizations whose managers and employees felt challenged to contribute to pressures faced during the economic downturn. The author attempted to find a suitable frame to make comparisons of domains of data as people, HRM systems and workplaces were challenged to boost their workplace performance. This process has been referred to as abstraction, examples of which include critical evaluations of what employees' experiences or stories (see Alvesson and Skoldberg, 2000).

ORGANIZATIONAL CONTEXTS

The study was started to find out what happens when employees and management are challenged to improve their performance. It was decided to collect empirical data from four organizations that were having to deal with challenges which included lack of productivity, employee disengagement and de-motivation leading to poor performance. All four UK-based organizations operate in Lincolnshire and Nottinghamshire, while some have branches internationally. All four are small to medium sized companies which employed different nationalities.

Longhurst Housing Association ran a group of organizations that provided housing that may be rented for a shorter contracted time or sold. Longhurst faced challenges to modernize their services and to provide additional affordable homes to clients. Employees came under increased scrutiny.

Bakkavor-Laurens Patisserie, the UK's largest cake manufacturer, produces cream cakes for national supermarkets and also caters for smaller private events. The organization needed to expand and integrate into its new parent company, the Bakkavor Group, with headquarters in Iceland. They were facing an increasing demand of their products.

Eden Enhanced Housing provided care and housing services to approximately a hundred and fifty people with learning and other disabilities as well as with health problems. The company aimed to expand and this entailed employees having additional responsibilities to boost performance.

Lagat provided educational support, career advice and counselling services to students. The challenges included extreme market pressures, a fast increase in customer demands for a better service and dwindling government's financial support – hence an increase in staff or redundancies. This meant employees and managers had to restructure operations and increase productivity.

Research Pathway

To find out the nature of the challenges two sets of interviews were conducted. The first set centred on finding out what the challenges were, whether these involved having to change working practices and the ways people reacted in their roles as managers and employees. During the second set the author sought to understand how the companies dealt with the challenges, what strategies they implemented and whether employees felt challenged to improve their performance. In the first series 68 interviewees were interviewed (2004/2005) with 17 interviewees per organization. In Bakkavor-Lauren's Patisserie - 10 employees and 7 management staff, in Longhurst Housing - 10 employees and 7 management staff, in Eden Housing - 10 employees and 7 management staff and in Lagat -10 employees and 7 management staff were interviewed. A fair representation of managers and non-managers, nationalities, age and gender was achieved. Companies waived anonymity.

In 2011 a second set followed, with 17 interviewees (with four interviews per company with the exception of five at Bakkavor). The second saw a more equal distribution of management and employee interviewees. The author was made aware that all four companies wanted to improve their performance levels in response to customer demands and economic pressures. In both interview rounds each of the roles were provided the opportunity to follow-up or clarify issues where they felt challenged to performance. Some made additions, others did not. The responses were taken to refer to the way participants chose to contribute to the challenges of performance. .

From the responses, the author checked the emerging common themes from each company and for both roles. The themes were checked, re-checked before being agreed with a different researcher. Participants were asked again when both researchers appeared to disagree on some themes. These we then reflected as part of the themes in participants' contributions. Analyses were performed subsequently. The respective company themes were combined where they showed similarities and reported elsewhere where differences emerged.

Responses were compared as part of a process of finding a suitable frame to make comparisons of employees' and managers' contributions based on the data. This process has been referred to as abstraction, examples of which can be fused into emerging themes (Alvesson & Skoldberg, 2000). The results were presented into four stages (showing the four themes) reflecting people's contributions to their performance.

Research Data From Four Organizational Cases

The results from the four companies showing what people did in response to the challenges are presented in this section. The benefits are also shown from the interviewee responses. The latter were anonymised and what people did (on the basis of their responses) was abstracted. The statements are presented in 4 stages and these are followed with 4 steps of research to show how this can be used as a guide for teaching research to address the challenges. Each of the four stages presented hereunder is supported by employees and managers' statements and the emerging story shows what could be done when people, HRM systems and workplace issues are combined. Their combination is linked to the HR Scaffolding as part of the chapter's contribution.

Stage 1: Managers Initiate New Working Practices

At the introduction of new working practices managers start to impose strict discipline. Employees were expected to collaborate in joint tasks and where performance fell short of expected standards, initiated punishment. A senior manager at Lagat said: 'management put up an away day to break barriers between teams; we also arrange weekly then monthly meetings for people to see what others are doing, it's about improving things, understanding other people's jobs.' Another Manager in the same company added 'we are involved in the quality of the delivery of career services throughout the company. I also develop programmes as government funding and opportunities arise, working in partnership with organization s to maximise opportunities (e.g. Lincoln College, Action for Employment (A4e), Jobcentre Plus, in providing training and employment skill], we work with community groups (e.g. Catch 22 and Leap both of which are for homeless people)...we are trying to respond to government's 'big society' work in jobcentre, we support people looking for jobs'.

The Business Advisor said 'we have regular communication, operations meetings to rectify communication blockage...we used to work independently whereas everybody has talents we can pool together in a team to contribute to targets'. A Senior Training Officer mentioned 'some management are also Internal Verifiers for various courses and they work with employers, we also go out and have Lagat Days and we talk about the company training plan, the company business plan and so on... All new staff are encouraged to do the key skills they require. Several of them want to branch out'.

At Eden the HR Manager remarked 'we are growing what's called Eden Enhanced; we are working with people with more complex needs, we are growing geographically with an ambitious growth plan while managing the cost plan, so doing more with less resources, introducing new projects in certain strategic places every nine months; each of those projects is multi tasked, for example the Health Care Manager and Team Managers are managing staff and delivering frontline support. Whereas they used to be full time managers or team leaders, now they have to deliver front line care services, a lot of managers are having to work round the clock, regional managers have to pick up one to one (i.e. supervision) with staff, changes will ensure we are leaner and more efficient...'

An employee at Lagat remarked 'there's a lot of cross working, a lot of cross function work that goes on in departments around disciplinary issues, staff training and quality support.'

The Head of Construction at Longhurst said 'there is a policy for every manager to meet staff once every month; it's a download session really, they talk about jobs on site, with end users, how they are working, if it doesn't work we think of alternatives, to get the best solution, good to download now and again so you are not in your box.'

The Quality and Information Manager at Longhurst noted 'the degree to which we can change would come under scrutiny; we might be separate entities in the next 3-5 years but there will be more conflating of work. This is not all bad. We try to be more effective. Previously we were separate such that the last 2 companies had 2 IT systems. When Friendship Care and Housing joined, they had separate IT systems, part of the amalgamation joined with Spire. One of the benefits is the recognition to make all of this more cost effective. We have just finished upgrading Friendship ICT and to build on that platform. There have been some good bits but there are some areas to cover. These will benefit the company because there will be better returns on investments on the IT results.

Another employee at Longhurst said 'until recently we have been financially stable but there's increasing recognition we have to compete, to be cost effective and to be able to grow. Government grant aid has been cut, so the only way to grow is to be leaner and meaner so that we can borrow more and build more. There has been a cultural shift at the same time as there has been a fiscal shift.'

The Systems Manager at Bakkavor noted the following changes in working practices: 'The change was driven by becoming leaner, to measure ourselves, train personnel and a need to drive down labour costs to make maximum profits... The previous management team has been scrapped. In a similar vein, the way we quantify all the processes have changed. For example information and manufacturing processes have changed, technical staff [Technical Assistants] have been increased, factory operatives have decreased, but there has been more management staff, more quality assistants, additional health and safety staff. Therefore, services to manufacturing have increased.'

Stage 2: Additional Working Structures Are Introduced

Managers started to identify additional resources by creating social networks, friendships and other collaborations when they realised their mistake in formalising relationships with non-managers. Everyone realises the urgency to contribute in boosting their performance in innovative and creative ways.

The HR Director at Longhurst said 'so we get social media champions for people who understand it. When you have changes in people coming into a company HR staff get involved, training gets involved, ICT gets...its' like spider's web...'.

The Systems Manager at Bakkavor said the following: 'In the old performance matrix, supervisors/line managers did service customer-needs; now they are asked to service the order whilst doing so at the right quality while looking after people in a financially viable way We are asking for lots more...it is to make sure we have processes to make more money from informed decisions because we are not making money at the moment...My personal agenda is to do a good job, befriend people and be promoted to the most senior financial role on site...'

Stage 3: Communication Is Improved to Boost Performance

Employees engaged colleagues as ways of improving their performance and develop traditional initiatives for collective benefit. This stage also witnessed the introduction of quality checking mechanisms such as quality teams and customer service schemes. Management thought their introduction will enhance the quality of employees' contributions and their collaboration with management.

The Quality Manager at Longhurst said 'We have residents' scrutiny panel who look at our customer service, our performance. Residents are engaged and quite involved in retendering contracts and that has been good' (i.e. in improving our services).

Another employee said 'we have always had housing officers who engage with the local community. When I first came here there has always been the expectation to engage with people. As part of the amalgamation (with other companies), there were big consultations with Grimsby, senior management spent a lot of time and engaged with Grimsby community. We were commended by the Homes and Communities Agency [HCA] on how we consulted on changes; we had really good feedback on that. When we had really difficult things to deal with all directors in their garments are prepared to get out there and face some difficult things'.

The Systems Manager at Bakkavor remarked 'Efficiencies in how we make our products are a big variable in performance. At the moment we are talking about how we decide how many people come in, how we manage people out of the business and how we review all of that...'

Stage 4: Employees Encourage Collaborative Contributions

Employees started to interpret tasks in their own way and to make their contributions cohere and thereby more valuable to each other. They did not report their initiatives to the managers, but stimulated their collectives to do what they consider beneficial to their company rather than to themselves.

Employees said the following 'I want to have responsibility on the way things are going. If I need help I ask for help. It winds me up if someone tells me what to do. I manage my function and I get on with it... I would like to see myself at the next level within next couple of years, being the most senior person and develop towards a broader role as head of finance and then have more strategic role or equivalent in another Bakkavor site…'

Others mentioned 'Learning to appreciate the work demands on each other's role through support for each other. We are struggling to be where we want to be; we are not there because people have to fill gaps…We have been forced to do things that we should have done a while ago. Some of the capacity we had is long gone, in terms of people; now in terms of the capacity of being able to do things, we are struggling.'

An employee at Eden remarked 'it's about developing a positive attitude, enhance team working across departments and develop core care values 'it's a very 'can do' approach. There's a lot of cross working, a lot of cross function work that goes on… Cross departmental working is always appropriate in staff training and the delivery of quality support…'

Another employee said 'it's all about learning to balance between performing one's role and doing additional administrative/paperwork. You hear the odd comment: 'my day job has gone through the window' and I've been personally involved in TUPE. Recently, I've been doing my job again. With TUPE consultations, you struggle to get jobs done.'

Another employee at Eden remarked 'more is expected; managers are less visible, because they have more work to do; now investors want to know whether managers are going to achieve action points, by when and how you are going to achieve them; as an employee I used to go to people and say 'can I help with something', I can't do that now because am now working to capacity.'

FOUR STEPS TO TEACH RESEARCH INTO HRM/ WORKING PRACTICES AND PERFORMANCE

What follows next is a reinterpretation of four items from the research process described earlier. From the methodology that follows, the aim is to solve the problem of lack of performance in the four organizational contexts. From the previous four sets of issues from the four-stage story, four steps (i.e. following a research methodology) are developed. What is presented here is part of a methodology to support what people do when they are challenged in practice thereby responding to the methodological challenge that has partly been responsible for the under-theorised nature of the topic. The methodology demonstrates a way for individuals to add to their resources (i.e. the contributions of other employees as well as management) and hence to better improve their performance. The methodology is part of a process whereby people implement what they prefer to implement despite the organization's pressures, the working practices and the structures. The studies examined earlier pay emphasized HRM structures, working practices and competencies. What the findings from the four organizations point to is that we need to focus on people and what they do to boos performance.

The first step is to identify and bring a number of people and companies with similar characteristics and properties together (those who are challenged to restructure their working practices). The second step is to identify and initiate forms of engagement that could enhance performance. The third step is to improve the interactions via research. The aim here is twofold: firstly that a collective task of survival can be achieved when groups of people agree to improve their performance and secondly that individuals contribute to the task. This implies that the collective becomes able to defend the implementation of that task against external challenges as they simultaneously cooperate from within to contribute to organizational performance. The fourth step is to ensure that the three earlier steps are continued i.e.

improve the way individuals and collectives collaborate to achieve coherence on tasks. Having to contribute to resolve challenges such as performance and workplace disengagement can still be achieved not through the further creation of the very workplace structures against which people resist. Teaching such a topic can be done by identifying people's collective preference through the four steps here. This is very much like research. It has the same structure and follows a process: observing what individual employees do in one case, bringing individuals into a collective who are able to interact in the other. This implies that both the approach that recognises and teaches HRM as a set of functional pieces of advice/prescriptions and the one that wants to research into the intermediate variables between HRM and organizational performance are researched and their objectives achieved. Therefore the challenge that had bedevilled the teaching, research and practice of HRM and performance for the past thirty years can be resolved by examining the ways people who are affected by the challenges and what they said are their performance preferences.

The research argument follows like this. The decision to initiate a new set of working practices that forces each individual employee and teams of people within a company to contribute and to make those contributions cohere will be taken within the framework of the existing organization - and hence were based on behaviours that were appropriate in the company's past. This means that measures like constantly monitoring and supervising staff's performance and punishing them might be justified in ways that are difficult to fight (if one cannot change and thereby improve the company's collective task to improve their performance and hence survive). The data suggest that what people seemed to deplore most keenly is the loss of individual power and the loss of their performance as a result of managers' initiation of the bundles of HR/employment practices. The problem to be resolved is another one, however – as argued. It is the loss of the ability to help make individual and collective preferences cohere, which is precisely the ability that following the four steps is intended to strengthen and to resolve the challenges posed by organizational performance. One possibility of doing so would be for the company to attempt to identify new tasks and new challenges for staff. Another possibility would be that employees initiate tasks (and engage those willing to contribute). This may make it possible to contribute to the development of a new company structure as well as to resolving the company's past, current and potentially future difficulties.

It is also reported, following the literature, that workers tended to become entrepreneurial in their contributions (see stage 4) and were able to show responsible behaviour. The results of the study show something additional; they echoed statements that demonstrated that employees preferred to contribute to organizational performance rather than followed what managers dictated to them. In the case of the current chapter, employees show creativity in recreating workplace contexts that had previously been attempted to be abolished by their managers through the latter's introduction of what employees would see as draconian working practices.

The research data and the literature the process involved seems to follow a different frame from that proposed by Becker and Huselid (2006) or even Bowen and Ostroff (2004) or proponents of HPP (see Goddard, 2004; Guest, 2011). Here, what is being proposed follows the injunctions of what people wanted to contribute once these have been recognised from the data and acted upon via research (see the 4 research steps). This implies that the organization as a collective becomes more competent to deal with the difficulties of restructuring and its performance issues. Although the original managers had more authority, they eventually failed in increasing the collective performance (Argyris and Schon, 1996). It might be advised to have managers become aware of the 4 steps and the potential damages that might be caused by following functionalist HRM practices advocated by Stanton et al (2010). Isolating themselves as suggested by the existing organizational structures seemed to work out negatively. Managers might have attempted to expand the company's business as a way to counteract the need to combat lack of productivity or an increase in performance, cut budgets and induce an increase in employee contributions. As indicated, such attempts would have been supported by preference research rather than research that tended to look at the correlation (linkage/causality) between HRM practices or High-Performance Practices (HPPs) and organizational performance.

The benefits of such a research methodology are that it resolves the two problems which are lack of performance and therefore a signal of employee disengagement from their and organizational context and their goals. The methodology achieves two objectives the individual and organizational/company/collective. Firstly, it addresses the level of the collective – i.e. the company where decisions to force people to contribute to keep their companies afloat amidst the challenges as part of a process of management to induce people to improve their performance; secondly it attempts to deal with the level of people where the effects of being forced to adopt unfavourable and stiffer working practices is keenly felt as they have to find alternative ways of contributing or else be punished (e.g. via sackings, suspensions, extra supervisions and monitoring, disciplinary activities etc); thirdly, it recognises the role of government or quasi-governmental bodies and attempts to deal with this level of operation that often regulate the activities of management and organizations but do so in a more coordinated and people-centred-manner; fourthly it brings out the interactions and linkages between people, HR practices instantiated by line managers and workplace contexts. The combination of these elements is linked to the HRM Scaffolding. The concept shows what can be achieved when elements that impact on performance are combined holistically (i.e. bringing data, theories and methodology in a process of research).

DISCUSSIONS

In this section the author identifies key areas emerging from the literature and the findings from the four case studies to see what might have been added. The first strand looks at the key challenges in relation to HRM and these are as follows: theoretical, methodological and empirical challenges. For the study and teaching of HRM practices and organizational performance to benefit, it is crucial that these challenges are recognised and dealt with through a process of research that supports people.

Following the literature Fleetwood and Hesketh (2005) bemoaned the 'under-theorisation' and the challenges scholars have faced when they tried to address organizational performance. The 'content' and 'process' based approaches have not resolved the issues as argued as follows. Scholars who have looked at the intermediate variables have ended up emphasising HRM as a bundle of prescriptions in a functionalist and standardised way. This treats people as things onto whom working procedures and systems are applied (see Huselid, 1995; Appelbaum et al, 2000; Lepak and Snell (1999)). The HR Architecture is a crystal example of this. Even though Becker and Huselid (2006) later recognised the 'significant' role of organizational, contextual variables this area is underdeveloped. This chapter contributes towards that development in a small way. This chapter has considered what is lacking in both the 'content' and 'process' theories and used a combination of essential elements such as HRM practices and systems, workplace contexts and people and their combination is linked to the HR Scaffolding. It brings together and recognises that contributions to organizational performance are multi-dimensional and do not necessarily come from what managers and organizations do at the higher level. The name 'scaffolding' was chosen as it firstly denotes the holding together of both human (people) and non-human elements (HRM/workplace structures, systems, procedures) and secondly it acts as a symbol of the support needed during the implementation of performance improvement initiatives. It contributes to the debates started by Lepak and Snell (1999) and links HR with vital elements, whose totality of treatment, enhances workplace performance. People are central in these debates on organizational performance.

From a methodological stance, it has been shown that limitations of previous work, most of which are short, survey-type studies, are reported. The shortcomings instantiated the emergence of the four steps which are derived from the data. It is argued that these could be used by academics and students as a way of researching and teaching the relationship between HRM/working practices and organizational performance. It is anticipated the HRM Scaffolding contributes to the 'under-theorisation' recognised by Fleetwood and Hesketh (2005) and that its identification goes beyond the reporting of HRM messages as bundles of advice and prescriptions in terms of how to do HRM (see Stanton et al, 2010). The story-like presentation of the findings has evidenced some of the challenges faced by HRM practitioners as well as identified benefits via research (the latter by uses the 4 steps).

CONCLUSION

It has been demonstrated that organizations in general and HRM in particular are increasingly having to deal with challenges. Tutors are increasingly having to keep up with these challenges and where possible help to resolve the challenges. However, both tutors and research done in the area are constrained as shown from the literature. Where attempts are made to address the constraints caused under-theorisation, methodological deficit and the lack of empirical sophistication abound.

The chapter has addressed all the three core challenges. Doing so requires conducting a type of research that focuses on what people contribute to achieve the chapter's core research aims and objectives. These are as follows:

1. Provide some evidence to demonstrate that HRM is confronted with the key challenge of performance
2. Show what key benefits and opportunities could be achieved
3. Draw lessons for HRM tutors, scholars and practitioners.

In order to achieve the first research aim the author has looked at the nature of the challenges that HRM has faced and critiqued the theoretical arguments from a 'content' and 'process' perspective. It is anticipated that such examination will enable HRM students to turn out to be sources of good for society and for business to avoid resorting to standardized HR practices, parts of which led to the banking and corporation scandals before and subsequent to the 2008 global financial crash.

With the exception of Hoque (1999), Pfeffer (1998) and Ichiniowski (1997), the majority of research seems to over-emphasise the challenges faced and downplay benefits. This chapter has addressed that deficit. More work is needed on the potential benefits of studying the linkage or causality between HRM practices and organizational and employee performance and moreover, teaching the latest research in this growing area to students and aspiring HRM practitioners. Dealing with the challenges through the adoption of the appropriate HRM/workplace mechanisms and methods is one thing. Recognising and harnessing the opportunities from the benefits presented to HRM is another. Identifying a way of teaching research such that the challenges posed by organizational performance as a result of HRM/working practices is yet another. It is anticipated this chapter has addressed these issues and contributed in a small way.

An area that needs more attention is to develop pedagogies and teaching and research methods that harness from both the challenges and benefits of HRM and performance and presenting these to academics and practitioners alike so as to inform new ways of thinking and practising HRM in an ever-changing world of work and business. A good starting point is what has been done in this chapter which is that if HRM and the world of work is to profit from new thinking and practice, it has to begin to acknowledge that forms of employee and management experiences require a form of teaching research that captures and presents both the challenging nature as well as the opportunities that the field of HRM stands to gain from the link between HRM practices and performance. Using the experiences in this emerging area of research provides participants, those that they engage with in trying to enhance organizational performance and the HRM practices that are designed to facilitate such engagement with a direct link to HRM as a practice. This is where people, HRM practices and the world of work intersect in what has been proposed as the new 'HRM Scaffolding' as it brings the three key elements together as well as recognising the support needed by people. The literature examined to date treat the elements as if one is impacting on the other without due recognition of what such an impact could generate or create not only at an organizational level but also at an individual, employee level. It was shown in the four-stage story of the findings that it is at the personal, employee level that perceptions about HRM practices and performance are crystallised and enacted upon in the form of what people do. It was also shown that at the fourth stage employees begin to interpret the organizational procedures, including the employment and HRM practices in ways that they considered beneficial for themselves and other participants given their awareness of the existence of other people's actions and what they could contribute.

In order to capture the complexity of the types of behaviours emanating from employees when they are challenged to enact HRM practices as part of a process of improving their performance, something more special than is currently presented in the literature and HRM teaching circles is required. The fourth stage of empirical data capture and analysis is required: this is the stage where employees begin to interpret and use the contributions of other participants in order to address organizational problems such as those related to performance and collective survival. It is shown through the data and the challenges posed from the literature that collective, organizational survival is also dependent on an appreciation of the task by those formulating the HRM policies, those who are expected to identify the challenges posed and clarify the confusions in their teaching but more importantly those students (just like the employees) who should be supported or as referred to in the concept need 'scaffolding' such that they contribute to the wellbeing and progress of society. It is argued to be useful and timely to emphasise the role of the HRM Scaffolding in bringing together the key players to make this happen.

FUTURE RESEARCH

From the theoretical discussions, the analysis and the findings from the current study, this chapter does highlight a couple of areas where the research conducted could open up new research questions and methods to look at developing further insights into HRM practices and performance. Among other things, these include, but are not restricted to the following areas that need further developments, answers and clarifications. Further work could look at developing policies and structures for dealing with the challenges to organizational performance within multicultural and multinational organizations. The question to be asked here is 'Has research identified how HRM policies and practices are able to provide the best support to create environmentally-positive institutions?' In what way might further research benefit the

HRM Scaffolding? The work continues in this vital area for tutors, practitioners and other HRM-affiliated people…It is anticipated that further research will generate lessons that will be used to enrich theories, data and methodologies on the linkages between HRM practices and organizational performance.

REFERENCES

Alvesson, M., & Skoldberg, K. (2000). *Reflexive Methodology: New Vistas for Qualitative Research.* London: Sage.

Appelbaum, E., & Batt, R. (1994). *The New American Workplace.* New York: Cornell University Press.

Barney, J. B. (2001). Is the resource-based 'view' a useful perspective for strategic management research? Yes. *Academy of Management Review, 26*(1), 41–56.

Becker, B. E., & Huselid, M. A. (2006). Strategic Human Resources Management: Where Do We Go From Here? *Journal of Management, 32*(6), 898–925. doi:10.1177/0149206306293668

Bowen, D. E., & Ostroff, C. (2004). Understanding HRM-Firm Performance linkages: The Role of the 'Strength' of the HRM System. *Academy of Management Review, 29*(2), 203–221.

Boxall, P., & Purcell, J. (2003). *Strategy and Human Resource Management.* Basingstoke, UK: Palgrave Macmillan.

Cappelli, P., & Neumark, D. (2001). Do 'high-performance' work practices improve establishment level outcomes?. *Industrial & Labor Relations Review, 54*, 737–776.

Currie, G., & Proctor, S. (2001). Exploring the Relationship between HR and Middle Managers. *Human Resource Management Journal, 11*(7), 53–69. doi:10.1111/j.1748-8583.2001.tb00045.x

Dany, F., Guedri, Z., & Hatt, F. (2008). New insights into the link between HRM integration and organizational performance: The moderating role of influence distribution between HRM specialists and line managers. *International Journal of Human Resource Management, 19*(11), 2095–2112. doi:10.1080/09585190802404320

Eisenhardt, K. M., & Martin, J. A. (2000). Dynamic capabilities What are they? *Strategic Management Journal, 21*(10-11), 1105–1121. doi:10.1002/1097-0266(200010/11)21:10/11<1105::AID-SMJ133>3.0.CO;2-E

Fleetwood, S., & Hesketh, A. (2006). HRM Performance research: undertheorized and lacking explanatory power. *International Journal of Human Resource Management, 17*(12), 1977 – 1993.

Gerhart, B., & Milkovich, G. T. (1992). Employee Compensation: Research and Practice. In M. D. Dunnette & L. M. Hough (Eds.), *Handbook of Industrial and Organizational Psychology* (Vol. 3, pp. 481–569). Consulting Psychology Press.

Gerhart, B., & Trevor, C. (1996). Employment variability under different managerial compensation systems. *Academy of Management Journal, 39*(6), 1692–1712. doi:10.2307/257075

Goddard, J. (2004). A Critical Assessment of the High-Performance Paradigm. *British Journal of Industrial Relations, 42*(2), 349–378. doi:10.1111/j.1467-8543.2004.00318.x

Guest, D. E. (1999). Human Resource Management: The workers verdict. *Human Resource Management Journal, 9*(3), 5–25. doi:10.1111/j.1748-8583.1999.tb00200.x

Guest, D. E. (2011). Human Resource Management and Performance: Still searching for some answers. *Human Resource Management Journal, 21*(1), 3–13. doi:10.1111/j.1748-8583.2010.00164.x

Guest, D. E., & Peccei, R. (2001). Partnership at work: Mutuality and the balance of advantage. *British Journal of Industrial Relations, 39*(2), 207–236. doi:10.1111/1467-8543.00197

Guzzo, R. A., Jette, R. D., & Katzell, R. A. (1985). The effect of psychologically based intervention programs in worker productivity: A meta-analysis. *Personnel Psychology, 38*(2), 275–291. doi:10.1111/j.1744-6570.1985.tb00547.x

Hamel, G., & Prahalad, C. K. (1994). *Competing for the future.* Boston: Harvard Business School Press.

Harris, C., Cortvriend, P., & Hyde, P. (2007). Human Resource Management and Performance in Healthcare Organization s. *Journal of Health Organization and Management, 21*(4/5), 448–459. doi:10.1108/14777260710778961 PMID:17933375

Harter, J., Schmidt, F., & Hayes, T. (2002). Business-unit-level relationship between employee satisfaction, employee engagement and business outcomes: A meta-analysis. *The Journal of Applied Psychology, 87*(2), 268–279. doi:10.1037/0021-9010.87.2.268 PMID:12002955

Hoque, K. (1999). Human Resource Management and Performance in the UK Hotel Industry. *British Journal of Industrial Relations, 37*(3), 419–443. doi:10.1111/1467-8543.00135

Huselid, M. A. (1995). The Impact of Human Resource Management Practices on Turnover, Productivity and Corporate Financial Performance. *Academy of Management Journal, 38*(3), 635–872. doi:10.2307/256741

Ichiniowski, C., Kochan, T., Levine, D., Olson, O., & Strauss, G. (1996). What works at work. *Industrial Relations, 35*(3), 299–333. doi:10.1111/j.1468-232X.1996.tb00409.x

Koys, D. (2001). The effects of employee satisfaction, organizational citizenship behaviour and turnover on organizational effectiveness: A unit-level longitudinal study. *Personnel Psychology, 54*(1), 101–114. doi:10.1111/j.1744-6570.2001.tb00087.x

Lepak, D. P., & Snell, S. A. (1999). The Human Resource Architecture: Toward A Theory of Human Capital Allocation and Development. *Academy of Management Review, 24*(1), 31–48.

Makadok, R. (2001). Toward a synthesis of the resource-based and dynamic capability views of rent creation. *Strategic Management Journal, 22*(5), 397–401. doi:10.1002mj.158

Mayrhofer, W., Muller-Carman, M., Ledolter, M., Strunk, J., & Ellen, C. (2004). 'Devolving Responsibilities for Human Resources to Line Management?' An Empirical Study about Convergence in Europe'. *Journal for East European Management Studies, 9*(2), 123–146.

McGovern, P., & Stales, P. (1997). Human Resource Management on the Line? *Human Resource Management Journal*, *7*(4), 12–29. doi:10.1111/j.1748-8583.1997.tb00286.x

Pfeffer, J. (1994). *Competitive Advantage through People*. Harvard Business School Press.

Porter, M. (1996). What is strategy? *Harvard Business Review*, *74*, 61–78. PMID:10158474

Purcell, J., & Hutchinson, S. (2007). Front Line Managers as Agents in the HRM-Performance Causal Chain: Theory, Analysis and Evidence. *Human Resource Management Journal*, *17*(1), 3–20. doi:10.1111/j.1748-8583.2007.00022.x

Renwick, D. (2003). Line Manager Involvement in HRM: An Inside View. *Employee Relations*, *25*(3), 262–280. doi:10.1108/01425450310475856

Sanders, K., Shipton, H., & Gomes, J. F. S. (2014). Is the HRM Process Important? Past, Current and Future Challenges. *Human Resource Management*, *53*(4), 489–503. doi:10.1002/hrm.21644

Schneider, B., Hanges, P., Smith, B., & Salvaggio, A. (2003). Which comes first: Employee attitudes or organizational financial and market performance? *The Journal of Applied Psychology*, *88*(5), 836–851. doi:10.1037/0021-9010.88.5.836 PMID:14516248

Siggelkow, N. (2002). Evolution toward fit. *Administrative Science Quarterly*, *47*(1), 125–159. doi:10.2307/3094893

Stanton, P., Young, S., Bartram, T., & Leggat, S. G. (2010). Singing the same song: Translating HRM messages across management hierarchies in Australian hospitals. *International Journal of Human Resource Management*, *21*(4), 567–581. doi:10.1080/09585191003612075

White, M., Hill, S., McGovern, P., Mills, C., & Smeaton, D. (2003). High-Performance Management Practices, Working Hours and Work-Life Balance. *British Journal of Industrial Relations*, *41*(2), 175–196. doi:10.1111/1467-8543.00268

Wright, P. M., Dunford, B. B., & Snell, S. A. (2002). Human Resources and the Resource-Based View of The Firm. *Journal of Management*, *27*(6), 701–721. doi:10.1177/014920630102700607

Wright, P. M., Gardner, T. M., Moynihan, L. M., & Allen, M. R. (2004, January). *The Relationship between HR Practices and Firm Performance: Examining Causal Order*. Centre for Advanced Human Resource Studies Working Paper Series.

Chapter 11
The Role of E–HRM Practices on Digital Era

Nurten Polat Dede

ⓘ https://orcid.org/0000-0002-9952-4642

Istanbul Medipol University, Turkey

ABSTRACT

The changes brought about by trends such as globalization, technological developments, and knowledge-based economy, and the speed of these changes are forcing the enterprises to create more innovative ways of doing business and business processes. This rapid change has also affected and altered human resources departments' way of business. In this chapter, the changes in human resources management functions and applications with the effect of technology during this time have been explained. In addition, the electronic human resources management process and its applications, which have been more important as a result of developed human resources technology, are examined and presented in this chapter.

INTRODUCTION

The increasing competition with globalization in today's business world and the developments in communication technologies push the enterprises to develop effective working styles and to adapt rapidly to the changes. Changes in company strategies and business practices created by globalization, supply and demand situation of labor force, current labor force situation, developments in technology, HRM practices of competitors, economic developments, changes in legislation, changes in employee expectations, cost reduction expectations, mergers and acquisitions have created the need for the restructuring of HRM processes and it became necessary fort he HRM units to undertake more strategic HRM roles (Cook, 1999; Bondarouk & Ruel, 2009; Marler, 2009).

The changing roles of HR managers foresee a transition from the realization of traditional operational activities to the realization of long-term strategic activities. The HR managers are increasingly taking advantage of the expertise and opinions of the senior management in strategic decisions, providing support function instead of being excluded from the strategic decisions of the organization (Barney & Wright, 1998). On the other hand, the strategic and traditional roles of the HR manager cannot coexist.

DOI: 10.4018/978-1-6684-3873-2.ch011

For this reason, it is envisaged that traditional roles will be carried out by creating integrable HR service centers or by external sources (Ulrich, 1996; Caldwell, 2003).

As a result, the responsibilities of the HR manager are narrowed in scope; however, they have more strategic and higher responsibilities. In other words, it is important that the HR manager's main roles in the personnel management period are separated from the changing current roles; It is envisaged that the HR manager will be valued in a position closer to the top management and in a more strengthened position and will be able to identify and identify the organization with the strategy and the desired values (Legge, 1989; Ulrich, 1998).

The efforts to restructure the HRM processes to provide added value to the operational results have revealed restructuring efforts involving the inclusion of information technology in the processes (Iqbal, Ahmad, Raziq, & Borini, 2019). Accordingly, HR departments are focused on reducing the intensity of the transaction volume by using information technology.

In this process, information technologies and human resources management experts worked together to create software and systems that transfer human resources information and decision-making systems from personnel files to computers, and played an important role in implementing E-HRM applications by restructuring HRM processes (Hall & Moritz, 2003).

In the Human Resources Management (HRM) processes, computers and internet has made it possible for human resources departments to assume more strategic roles to contribute to the operational results. Recruitment, success assessment, in-house transfers, remuneration, work security, personnel affairs, training and development, performance measurements, rewarding and punishment management processes were transferred to electronic systems, and it was possible to manage these processes with a holistic approach. In addition, the bureaucracy in the management of the human resources processes in enterprises has been reduced and instead of the manual methods that are performed inadequately, with more efficient HRM processes time and cost savings have been ensured. This has made it easier for business managers and HR experts to spend more time concentrating on strategic issues than on routine jobs (Cook, 1999; Ulrich & Lake,1990; Snell, 1994).

In the following sections of the study, the concept, scope and importance of electronic human resources management, the characteristics of electronic human resources management, the role of electronic human resources in HRM processes, the important effects of human resources management departments in assuming more strategic roles, the advantages and disadvantages of electronic human resources management in terms of enterprises will be explained extensively.

THE CONCEPT AND CONCEPT OF ELECTRONIC HUMAN RESOURCES MANAGEMENT

The concept of E-HRM was first used in the late 1990s with the concept of e-commerce, which became widespread in order to carry out commercial transactions (Hall and Moritz, 2003). E-HRM is defined as the effective use of internet technology-based systems in designing and implementing the human resources strategies, policies and practices of the enterprise (Sylvester, Bamidele & Oluyemi, 2015). In other words, e-HRM can be defined as the transfer of human resources systems to the computer environment by using communication technologies. E-HRM concept, is expressed as the implementation of the human resources management systems via the Internet, intranet and networks, or directly through the use of these channels (Ruël, Bondarouk, & Looise, 2004).

The main aim of E-HRM is to create more favorable conditions for harmonizing the organizational strategies and objectives and HRM targets and strategies. When we look at the previous studies in this field, it is seen that the concept of E-HRM is expressed in the literature with different concepts and it is not agreed on a common concept. Examples include web-based HRM, human resource information system (HRIS), virtual HRM and business-to-employee (B2E) systems (Strohmeier, 2007). These concepts are close to each other but point to separate functions.

Virtual HRM refers to networks that mediate the delivery of human resources activities within the business and to external actors in a virtual environment, without individuals in the Human Resources (HR) departments. E-HRM refers to the implementation of human resources activities through the internet and human resources department and includes less advanced technological applications (Lepak & Snell, 1998). Web-Based HRM is a concept that emphasizes direct internet networks. E-HRM is integrated with internet networks as well as additional technologies such as systems like ERP, LOGO etc. (Ruël, Bondarouk & Looise, 2004).

The Human Resources Information System (HRIS), the sub-system of E-HRM, is a special form of information system established for the need of human resource management and is one of the first systems that can be seen as a form of Electronic Human Resource Management in an organization. It is expressed as a systematic procedure for collecting, storing, maintaining, receiving and verifying the data that an organization needs for human resources management (Venterink, 2017). The users of HRIS are mostly human resources department personnel. The HRMS system aims to improve the business processes of the human resources department and to achieve more efficient results in business processes. E-HRM is designed for the personnel who are outside the human resources department and the employees and managers of the organization. (Ruël et al., 2004). Briefly, E-HRM enables human resources applications to be used by organization employees without having any place and time limit outside the organization (Celep & Fındıklı, 2018).

Human resource information systems (HRMS) and e-HRM are different from each other. HRMS is mainly directed to the HR department itself. The users of these systems are HR professionals. This type of system aims to improve the processes within the HR department. Processes such as payment of wages, storage of employees' work contracts and registration of necessary files for web sites are covered by HRMS. The contribution of HRMS to the objectives of business units is indirect. With this feature, e-HRM refers to a technological structure. HRMS is not a technology on its own, but the integration of HR processes with information and communication technologies. From this point of view, e-HRM, web-based HRM and IT-based HRM practices can be considered as development and stages that facilitate the functioning of HRMIS (Ruël, Magalhães, & Chiemeke, 2011).

Finally, B2E deals with HR practices for internal actors of the organization, such as department managers and HR experts. The E-HRM includes practices that are open to all relevant actors, such as job applicants, HR consultants, other than the employees of the institution (Huang, Jin, &Yang, 2004).

E-HRM after the explanations of the differences between similar concepts frequently used in literature related to E-HRM; In particular, information technology can be defined as the application of at least two individual or more users to both network and support systems to enable them to perform HR activities on a shared platform (Stronhmeier & Piazza, 2011).

The inclusion of human resources information technologies in HRM processes and issues within the scope of traditional human resources management can be solved in a shorter time and with less effort in electronic environment. Quick access to the right data can be provided.

E-HRM PURPOSE

It is seen that most of the e-human resources management activities are carried to the web environment in order to provide effective and productive human resource applications for the employees and provide the information needed for the organization. Thanks to E-human resources management activities, it is at the forefront of features such as reducing stationery, saving time and reducing costs (Güler, 2006).

The strategic benefits of e-human resources for businesses are as follows (Ruël, Bondarouk, & Looise, 2004; Öğe, 2004; Güler, 2006; Nivlouei, 2014):

- Providing organizations with effective and efficient human resources applications and communicating the expected information about the organization.
- Providing the appropriate environment for human resources employees in order to create and implement strategic human resources service.
- Using motivators such as e-mails, greeting messages to make employees feel special and valuable through electronic systems to improve the motivation and talents of the employees within the organization.
- Increasing the quality of services offered.
- Increasing the communication within the organization with employees provides an increase in the possibility of producing and implementing new ideas.
- Reduce internal cost and administrative procedures.
- Employees share their ideas and suggestions with their colleagues in the organization, for example due to the use of internal blogs. Providing an increase in the information shared in the organization and creating a basis for human resources within the organization.
- Reducing the number of employees and human resources department employees in E-Human Resources, as it creates an alternative to meet the needs of the employees in the intranet.
- E-HR, human resource management in human resources development and support to members of the organization in the career planning process and to provide new opportunities.
- In this new model, we contribute to the separation of the organizational practices from the centralization in the classical understanding and to enable the creative and the subordinates to act together in accordance with the organisation's objectives.
- International organizations to manage those who work in different geographical locations using the same system in a universal way.
- Ensuring the institutionalization of enterprises at higher levels.
- Harmonizing the skills of employees within the organization in line with the needs of the organization and providing organizational flexibility.
- Designing the trainings to be given to the employees according to job descriptions and skill requirements of individuals.
- Ensure that more informed decisions are taken.
- Ensuring the active participation of employees in applications through EHRM and thus increasing employee satisfaction.
- Being able to focus on the issues that create value through e-HRM activities without depending on the location and time zone, without disrupting the routine work processes of the organization.
- Providing information about the important human resources events of the organization and the news in the organization.

- Minimization of response time for human resources applications.
- Establishing a flexible human resources model to adapt to the globalizing world and labor needs.

E-HRM STAGES

Nowadays, in the changing economy with technology, human resources management develops electronic solutions through some stages (LeTart, 1998). These stages are as given below:

Information Sharing: The first step of human resources is sharing information within the organization. The activities at this stage are the one-way transfer of information within the organization to the employee within the organization. Most commonly used applications in information sharing; The organizational chart of the organization, employee's job description and responsibilities, areas of activity, organizational history, organizational policies, organizational news and bulletins, employee lists and contact information.

Database Creation: It is a database that includes staff's information such as demographic information, working area and working hours, duties and responsibilities, date of employment, premium and salary increase, health records and retirement status.

Basic Human Resources Transactions: It is the activity of transferring the internal information to the electronic environment and updating the changes in full time. These activities include the renewal of personal information of the personnel and the transfer of changes such as new assignments of the personnel to the database.

Complex Human Resources Transactions: Analysis of the responsibilities of personnel, evaluation of data, investigation of compliance of business processes, classification of multidimensional operations and applications according to various variables within this scope.

Network-Based Human Resources Transactions: The staff and managers of the organization are provided with the opportunity to use human resources processes via computer without using paper or administrative support. When integrated with in-house networks and non-organizational networks, the scope of human resources management expands as well

With the rapid development of technology, Cloud-Based applications yıl applications have been used since 2010. With the transition to the cloud-based information system, there is an increase in the use of mobile applications and social media by organizations. For example, shifting the choice of potential elements to an electronic election field with the increasing use of social media (Johnson, Lukaszweski, & Stone, 2015).

The types of e-HRM applied by organizations are related to some factors. The examples of these factors are like organizations having technology experts who can apply and design information technology systems specific to the organization, having human resources specialists who can do special application and design in the organization, number of employees who have personal computers and the level of computer literacy of the employees within the organization (Hall & Moritz 2003).

Some organizations choose an evolutionary process from simple to complex E-HRM types, while some organizations prefer to switch to transformational E-HRM with sudden changes (Ruël, Bondarouk, & Looise, 2004).

In previous studies, E-HRM has been shown to be separated by three main categories (Rajalakshmi & Gomathi, 2016).

Operational E-HRM: It is the e-HRM application that performs administrative functions such as salary and payroll management. The most significant goal of operational e-HRM is to increase the efficiency and efficiency of human resources management with automation and supports.

Relational E-HRM: The function of the organizational process in the organization deals with organizational functions such as employment, staff performance management and training and development activities. Relational E-HRM aims to improve the relations of its stakeholders and service delivery. In addition, it aims to support the business process through training, employment and performance management.

Transformational E-HRM: Includes the strategic function of human resources. It aims to improve organizational support and strategy management of E-HRM such as information management and strategic redirection.

HUMAN RESOURCES MANAGEMENT PROCESSES AND ELECTRONIC APPLICATIONS

The functions carried out by E-HRM under this heading will be discussed in detail.

E-Organization Structure, Business Processes and Document Tracking

In the process of E-HRM, an enterprise-specific HRIS needs to be developed in order to carry out the organizational structure, business processes and the follow-up of the documentation. In MIS, all information about the organization should be defined first. This information should be defined in the organization's departments, tasks, employee titles, work places and positions, organizational chart, process flows, approval mechanisms, flows that may require documents. In addition, positions should be established for the organization based on these jobs defined to HRMS and the personnel with the position characteristics specified for the positions created should be indicated. All information required to be kept in HRIS should be kept historically. The organization chart of the organization should be formed in line with all these structures. Since all the hierarchical structures created will be kept on the historical basis in the system, the changes and developments within the organization over time are also open to analysis (Daud, 2010).

In line with the rules and procedures set out in the organization, there can be a definition of flow for each work process and document requirements for each phase.

E-Workforce Planning

The organizational prediction that aims to use the best available human resources of the organization and to determine the quality and quantity of human resources for the future is called 'Human Resource Planning' (Şimşek & Öge, 2011). These activities carried out under E-HRM are transferred to electronic environment. In the electronic applications developed, each classification shows the number of personnel required at each level of the work. All analyzes and evaluations, actions and plans made during the human resources planning process are kept electronically. In this way, human resources specialists can reach the required information at the required time, and the presence of existing plans in electronic environment facilitates their control at any time. In addition, these systems provide some benefits in the operational sense via the electronic operation. The work processes that require intensive work of human resources are made to be transferred to electronic environment faster (Emmerichs, Marcum, & Robber, 2004). The number of personnel, reserve and additional personnel that will be required can be determined and the calculations such as total work rate, labor turnover rate, continuity analysis are made more accurately and faster by means of computers, by the system. In addition to the calculations, the information and data obtained can be kept in electronic environment and it is also possible to see the periodic changes and the comparisons (Doğan, 2011).

E-Recruitment System

Nowadays, many companies prefer electronic hiring methods instead of traditional hiring methods due to their advantages such as cost, time and efficiency. In the traditional recruitment process, while interdependent chaining steps are followed, e-recruitment processes are simultaneous online processes. The relationship of the candidate pools with the internet applications of the enterprises has made the electronic recruitment activities more integrated. The benefits of integrated recruitment systems have been accepted and widely used by enterprises (Sylva & Mol, 2009). Electronic recruitment is the use of electronic tools which efficiently fill open positions within the company (Lee, 2005). Using corporate websites, companies can create unlimited job vacancies for the employees they need and create a candidate pool with low cost. The recruitment process decreased by 75% compared to previous periods and the costs decreased by 95% (Cappelli, 2001).

E-recruitment process stages (Lee, 2005):

- Definition of open positions.
- Notification and approval of job vacancies on career portals.
- Announcement of the job on the internet.
- Announcement of the need for open position to potential candidates in electronic environment.
- Enabling current announcements to be seen by job seekers.
- Job seekers evaluating themselves whether or not the position is suitable for them.
- The applicant's application via system who intends to apply for a job.
- The HRM department's evaluation of the pool in the virtual environment.
- Job interview by human resources authorities.
- Job offers and contracts.

Electronic hiring seems to be an effective process where some activities are performed simultaneously, compared to the traditional recruitment method. (Lee, 2005).

Business advertisements that companies announce through their corporate websites provide low cost for companies and provide easier access within job seekers (Körfez, 2008).

Companies can create a corporate resume pool in a single database by taking recruitment processes from different sources such as consultancy firms, career sites, other than corporate websites. The data such as interviews, examinations, interviews and evaluations with the candidates to be hired can be monitored historically. Companies are able to follow in-house evaluations via electronic media with features such as reporting and scoring according to the open position criteria on the candidate pools they create. The candidate pool can be taken into the register for further positions in the future. In electronic recruitment, collection of resume data in a virtual pool provides productivity with labor, time and cost savings (Barber, 2006).

The employees who want to apply to positions of which the companies hire through their websites should consider well whether they meet the criteria in the job description. If the processes carried out to save time, are not evaluated well, there is a risk of not selection the the appropriate candidate. If the appropriate employee is not selected, it is necessary to repeat these processes (Bonti & Cori, 2004).

Looking at the rapid change, it is estimated that electronic recruitment will be used more widely in the years to come and the competition will increase among the human resources sites. It is clear that e-recruitment seems to be an effective solution when it is taken into consideration that businesses want to provide the labor force that will provide them with added value in a short time (Körfez, 2008).

E-Personal Information, Payroll Accounts, Leaves and Exit Procedures System

Payroll and personnel transactions from the activities that form the basis of Human Resources Management have been transferred to the electronic environment within the scope of E-HRM. In this respect, firstly, each personnel defines personal registration numbers and all human resources processes related to the person are monitored with this number. Personal information of the personnel, education details, contact information, demographic details like date of birth etc, address information, work experiences, foreign language information, family and child information, driver's certificates, official institutions are included in the personal information of the records. In the same way, the demands of the personnel regarding the excuses, paid and unpaid leaves, and the right of permission are made through electronic information systems. However, in the classical permission management applications, all registries like including employee's leave of absence requests written by hand and other details were kept kept in the personnel files.

With the electronic application system, employees can easily follow their entitlements in electronic environment according to the labor law, and they can send their leave of absence like vacation requests to the system by entering the location and time information. It is easily seen on the electronic information system by the managers of the unit when they request for vacation leave etc, at what date they are allowed to use and how much unused permissions they have. Time and paper savings were ensured along with the electronic permission application, and the managers started to make their business plans more effective and the problems caused by keeping the employee's permit/vacation information in the personnel files were eliminated (Sylva & Mol, 2009; Allahverdi, 2006).

E-Job Evaluation and E-Remuneration System

With the development of human resources management information technologies, wage management and business valuation processes of enterprises have been transferred to the electronic environment. E-Pricing; it means collecting, storing, processing, analyzing and using the information and data required for the establishment of the compensation systems of the organization on electronic media. The electronic environment provides both time and cost advantages to businesses in collecting the data analysis data that form the basis of wage systems and other HRM systems. For example, if the business prefers to use the survey method as a business analysis, the questionnaires are easily delivered to all operating personnel and the employees' answers about the business information can be obtained more quickly. HRM departments can analyze and summarize the data they have obtained and finally prepare job descriptions for all positions in the enterprise.

Moreover, the e-remuneration system also facilitates the conversion of business analysis data into job evaluation points. The fee research information obtained from the web pages of different institutions and organizations can be easily integrated with the job evaluation points. Thus, these data are used to determine wage degrees and to create wage systems of companies (Dulebohn & Marler, 2005). HRM departments can design and manage wage systems efficiently and effectively using web-based software systems with e-pricing. HRM departments can provide more effective services and provide necessary information to employees in electronic environment.

The e-remuneration system allows businesses to process all kinds of fees faster. It can be solved without any problems in the system such as installment payments, personnel with special insurance, advance transactions as well as wage transactions. According to the legislation in force, information requested by social insurance institutions, tax offices, employment agencies or electronic forms are automatically generated by the system. All forms and reports are established in accordance with the standards set by the institutions. The data related to the salary payroll of the personnel can be obtained from the regional offices and mobile workers in a safe way via internet.

E-remuneration also offers advantages in terms of providing fair wages for employees in the same positions in business and other businesses. The benefits such as pension, insurance and health services provided to the personnel can be managed more effectively in electronic environment.

Through the use of information technologies, it is possible to identify the needs of employees by obtaining the opinions of the employees and to offer personalized, flexible side benefits to the employees. Personalized benefits increase employees' commitment to business and increase their motivation. One of the most important components of HRM practices, which is expressed as high commitment work practices, increases employee loyalty and performance, is the wage systems of firms.

E-Performance Management System

Performance management is a goal-oriented process to maximize the efficiency of organizational processes, employees, teams, and ultimately the organization. Each employee's efforts in performance management should focus on the achievement of strategic objectives. In recent years, performance management has become the biggest contributor to organizational effectiveness. An effective performance management system should be the responsibility of everyone in the organization, starting with the chairman of the executive committee; because an organization ignoring the performance system can not progress, can not develope. Performance evaluation is an official system for the examination and evaluation of task performance as an individual or as a team (Mondy & Mondy, 2012).

Developing information technologies enable performance management and evaluation applications to be realized in electronic environment. Thanks to electronic performance evaluation systems, all data on performance interviews, reconciliations, standards, objectives, performance problems and evaluation results are kept in electronic data centers, and it has provided time to human resources professionals in terms of accessing data and time. For the transparent and objective decision-making and implementation of the performance development process, both the employee and the manager should start with these data. The use of information technologies enables the performance evaluation system to ensure traceability, impartiality and continuity in a fast and easy way (Karcıoğlu & Öztürk, 2009).

Electronic Performance Management Systems (e-PMS) facilitate performance measurements by keeping records of certain data such as completed work quantities, error rates, time spent on tasks. E-PMS facilitates managers to give quick feedback to the employees. For example, in multi-assessments or 360-degree evaluations through intranet networks in enterprises, all assessors are asked to perform an online performance assessment of the person to be assessed by e-mail. Afterwards, the evaluation data are combined to provide feedback to the evaluated person and enable them to improve their performance (Stone, Stone-Romero, & Lukaszewski, 2003). E-performance is an application that is adapted to the needs of institutions and provides a fast and effective solution to the performance evaluation process. In this system, evaluations are made by keeping privacy and security in the foreground.

Electronic performance is an application that is adapted to the needs of the company and provides an effective and fast solution to the performance evaluation system. In this system, evaluations are made in a virtual environment by taking into consideration the security and confidentiality criteria.

Organizational performance with E-PMS improves employee loyalty and loyalty, increases efficiency, exceeds communication barriers, explains accountability and provides cost advantages. Explains employees' expectations, self-assessment opportunities clarify job responsibilities and contribute to performance improvement, clearly define career paths and improve job satisfaction. Administrators receive immediate feedback on performance and draw attention to the performances of individual employees. Furthermore, there is no need for performance contracts to be rewritten every year. Simply, it can be loaded from the previous period and can be edited (Celep, 2017).

E-Performance management systems enable employees to monitor their developmental levels and to make plans for the future as a result of their knowledge and skill levels, the current status of their work performance and their training. One of the important objectives of E-Performance management systems is the matching of individual and business competencies. The integration of system performance management systems with other HRM systems, it is possible to ensure that the appropriate job-suitable candidate to be placed, and that the development of the competencies of the employees according to the positions to be employed in the future is correctly planned and developed accordingly. In addition, the potential candidate or the current employee's competencies to determine the job, to ensure compliance with the job-person are faciliated. The competencies required for the job are divided into two as compulsory and optional, and the level of compliance of the individuals with the competencies can be determined and statistical comparison can be made. The business and job specific competency inventory can establish the measurement standards of these competencies, and the competence levels of the individual can be compared at the organizational and business level. Thus, the development process of the person is monitored and a competency-based performance evaluation, backup and career planning system is created. Competency data include competence, level of competence, time interval during which competence is achieved, the method where competence is obtained, and the next date to be evaluated (Ghazzawi & Accoumeh, 2014; Daud, 2010).

E-Training and Development

Training and development are initiatives and efforts to improve the current and future performance of employees within the organization by increasing their ability to work. Distance education is the realization of the educational function, which is one of the functions of human resources, independent of time and space. Electronic learning, which is a subset of distance education, consists of processes and applications that involve digital based and virtual spaces. With the support of e-learning information and communication technologies, educational content is realized by transferring the contents of the internet to the electronic media via multimedia tools such as internet, intranet and extranet as well as audio, videotape, interactive television broadcast and CD-ROM (Schank, 2002).

The main difference between distance education and electronic learning is learning through a web network. Electronic learning is the structure in which materials (video, audio, text, multimedia) are used together. These different materials, which are used, adopt being oriented towards employees whose learning styles change. The harmonious use of electronic learning with traditional education methods facilitates the development of the competencies of employees when effectively designed with the support of the right computer technologies (Yazıcı, 2004).

E-training and development activities can be provided at a lower cost than the traditional training and development practices (Schank, 2002). In addition, it improves the quality and effectiveness of training and by making training suitable for the job requirements, learning by applying and accessing information in a timely manner. In addition, personalized learning content increases the motivation of employees with the sense that employees are valued by their institutions and ensures the retention of talented individuals.

Although e-learning has so many benefits to enterprises and employees, staff who are accustomed to training in physical environment may be prejudiced against electronic education, they may experience adaptation problems. Despite such disadvantages, the benefits of electronic training and development cannot be ignored. It is seen that if the changing structure of education is planned well together with technological developments, visionary enterprises can not be indifferent to electronic learning (Aydın, 2016).

E-Career Management and Talent Management

Career is the advancement of an individual in any field of work, gaining experience and skills (Tunçer, 2012). Corporate career management refers to policies and practices that are deliberately designed by institutions to increase the career effectiveness of their employees (Seema & Sujatha, 2013). Career management is the development of the career plan of the people with the career development tools of the enterprise. The main goal of the career management of the company is to increase the productivity of the enterprise and to ensure the development and improvement of the employees in the business, and to plan and shape them in order to meet the needs of the qualified employees in the future (Atay, 2006). Nowadays, employees are analyzing their situation in their businesses and other businesses and making their own career plans. In this case, businesses are giving too much importance to career management.

E-HRM practices provide various tools for employees to manage their careers. Employees can obtain information about the internal and external job opportunities in the system they enter with their personal accounts and benefit from different training opportunities. In this way, E-HRM practices create an environment where employees can receive self-education to acquire new skills (Esen, 2011). Businesses can provide e-career services to their organization employees through their own corporate web pages, as well as other web sites created for the same purpose. The HR portals created by the enterprises benefit from the training and development opportunities for the employees to manage their career ladders, to obtain data for the job opportunities in and out of the company.

With e-career planning, businesses can reach the results of trainings, competencies, career goals and performance measurement obtained by their employees. In this direction, promotions can be made among the candidates who have the required competencies according to the labor force gap within the enterprise (Aydın, 2016).

The career planning model developed in electronic environment and the qualifications of the employees included in the career planning system are evaluated. As a result, the opportunities for promotion and progress within the enterprise are determined and the backup lists of the employees providing the necessary conditions are established (Dündar, 1995).

E-mentoring

E-mentoring method is a system in which the employees of the enterprise can be supported with their problems with their organization and career development. This method allows the interaction between the employee and the client to be realized over the Internet. Expert advisors can advise and support the employees in different positions, job changes, personal development and similar issues. For example, like the "Ask the employer" web site and similer web sites, are web sites where professional specialists in network-mentoring units answer questions and suggests about the career planning to the employees (Allahverdi, 2006).

E-Administrative and Support Services System

The electronic environment can also be created in a more advanced manner by using different human resources data. These reports are updated after each new information entry. For example; personnel attendance control systems control the employees' entry and exit. New employees are provided with identification numbers and personnel ID cards. In the event that the personnel cards are read to the card readers during the entry and exit, all data is collected through the terminals. After measuring the entry-exit movements of the employees of this program during the day, the payroll data which constitute the actual payroll are arranged according to the contract conditions. Statistics and analysis reports are then produced for all users. In many enterprises, electronic applications are widely used which contribute to the rapid execution of administrative and support services at lower costs.

E-Worker Health and Safety System

Companies are obliged to minimize the risk factors when dealing with the security and health conditions of the existing human resources. The company is trying to take precautions against health and security problems from human resources issues that cause job loss. Regular records should be kept on which approach to choose and use in all health and safety related activities (Robson, Clarke, Cullen, Bielecky, Severin, Bigelow, & Mahood, 2007).

It prepares reports for the management of occupational health and occupational safety from records such as monitoring occupational diseases with occupational health and safety systems of the enterprises, keeping records about injuries and occupational accidents. In addition to this, it is necessary to prepare the information of the employees who may be faced with the chemicals, the inventories and the distribution within the company. The safety training received by the employees is classified according to the type of education they receive.

Businesses can submit their legal documents that they are obliged to do by means of the internet, for example, by sending them electronically. Employees in the company can make examinations about occupational health and safety online and can give motivation to employees who have succeeded at the end of the exam. Employees can be asked online about their current safety importance in their workplace (Doğan, 2011).

E-Industry Relations

The organizational structure is changing the employer relations and the nature of the work in a way that information technologies will not be restored (Armstrong, 2011). Businesses provide their employees with dialogue with the opportunities offered by technology. The companies' surveys, communication contacts, recalls and solutions for problems can be applied on the internet.

The software is carried out in an electronic data-based manner in order to decide on the problems that may arise in industrial relations and to determine these problems in their managers. This software can be found in software that responds to issues such as laws without applying to a lawyer or consultant (Doğan, 2011).

Social and Cultural Services System

Different activities are carried out in order to increase the requests of the employees within the Company. Cultural activities and social responsibility projects are carried out with employees through internal communication departments. The company also supports hobbies for various employees. Activities, business greeting dinner, sports, picnics during the year, social responsibilities are carried out periodically. In addition to these, meetings are organized in order to support corporate internal communication within the institution, in order to provide information about magazines, spelling and information during the year. On the whole, all these activities are planned by the human resources department, and the personnel can be reported to the personnel by giving authority and responsibility. In terms of feedback, it is possible to answer the questions directed to the people in a virtual environment with the help of a survey conducted to the personnel (Bondarouk, Ruël & Kees Looise, 2011).

SOLUTIONS AND RECOMMENDATIONS

In human resources, it is believed that the use of electronic systems will increase productivity. In order to realize this idea, it is not enough to transfer the human resources fields of activity to the electronic environment. Companies also need to redesign human resource management practices and processes. The success of E-HRM practices requires a transparent environment in a constantly learning, renewed, open-to-development organizational culture, discipline and reward policies. Alignment of E-HRM and organizational culture is another important factor which determines success in this process. In the transformation of organizational culture, senior management, other department managers and HRM managers must cooperate.

FUTURE RESEARCH DIRECTIONS

The study aims to explain extensively the ways in which HRM applications can be used in HRM processes and contribute to the literature. In this study, it is tried to emphasize that the ultimate aim of the departments of human resources management is to develop applications that affect the financial performance of enterprises and to restructure the HRM processes in a way to achieve strategic results.

HRM departments that want to create added value for organizational outputs need to restructure HRM processes. It is stated in some studies that E-HRM applications increase the efficiency of HRM applications by increasing the quality of the employees (Iqbal, Ahmad, Raziq, & Borini, 2019; Ramezen et al., 2013; Wahyudi & Park, 2014). The quality of E-HRM applications is also stated to affect the quality and perception of HRM services. (Meijerink et al., 2016; Iqbal, Ahmad, Raziq, & Borini, 2019; Ruel & Kapp, 2012). In some studies, it is claimed that HRM practices lead to higher operating performance with e-HRM (Bondarouk and Ruel, 2006; Meijerink et al., 2016). On the other hand, Nivlouei (2014) defines as the labor force commitment, high competence, cost efficiency, and positive effects on institutionalization level.

The number of empirical studies investigating the effects of electronic human resources management on operational performance and results should be increased in the literature. In addition, it is recommended to increase the research studies of the relationships between the perceptions of company employees about the effectiveness of E-HRM practices and the perceptions of the quality of the services provided by HRM departments.

Besides, although the enterprises use significant budgets for E-HRM applications, the effect of business culture on the process of adaptation of E-HRM applications in enterprises should be investigated.

CONCLUSION

Through the increasing focus on transformational outcomes over the last decade, the role of the HR professional has evolved from an administrative character to a more strategic structure (Gardner, Lepak, & Bartol, 2003). Therefore, the strategic role of HRM in the changing role of an HR expert has become increasingly important (Ruël Bondarouk and Looise, 2004). E-HRM practices help organizations create a more effective and strategically focused HR function in organizations. It provides a fast and accurate interpretation of information technology-based data, thus providing a competitive advantage in aligning qualitative and quantitative data for human resources with business strategies (Lazazzara & Galanaki, 2018).

In addition, HRM has recently turned into a concentration on information sharing and strategic workforce analysis and has increasingly become an important contributor to organizational strategic management (Troshani & Jerram & Rao, 2011). E-HRM ensures compliance of IT tools with organizational objectives and strategies. Therefore, the main objective of E-HRM is to create conditions to balance the goals of the organization and HR objectives and strategies (Sadegh, Kohansal, & Haghshenas, 2016).

There is a need for the support of senior management for the use of electronic human resource management practices in organizations. The costs for the first establishment of electronic human resources management in the organization may be slightly higher. Senior management, who will accept these costs and encourage the use of electronic human resources management practices by managers and employees in the organization, will be able to increase the advantages to be achieved through the use of these practices.

The biggest problem in the implementation of E-HRM systems is the adaptation of E-HR management to the organization. When implementing the adaptation, the organization should work with an expert team and the HRM departments should train their employees in this field and take an active role in the process. In addition, E-HRM practices should be accepted and used correctly by all employees. It is not possible for an E-HRM system that is not properly used and implemented. It also has the disadvantages of not having a face-to-face communication because the system interacts in a virtual environment. Not having a face-to-face communication may in some cases reduce collaboration between employees.

Another important disadvantage of E-HRM applications is the safety of information. Businesses that do not take a high level of security measures may be at risk of cyber attack within or outside the organization (Gueutal, 2003).

The impacts of E-HRM and its employees on both organizational and employee performance will continue to be important in the future together with the ever-developing information technology.

REFERENCES

Allahverdi, M. (2006). *Elektronik İnsan Kaynakları Yönetimi ve Türkiye'deki Uygulamalarına Yönelik Bir Araştırma*. Konya: Selçuk Üniversitesi Sosyal Bilimler Enstitüsü Yüksek Lisans Tezi.

Armstrong, M. (2011). Armstrong's handbook of strategic human resource management. London, UK: Kogan Page Publishers.

Atay, Ş. (2006). *Kariyer Yönetiminin Örgütsel Bağlılığa Etkisi*. Afyon Kocatepe Üniversitesi, Sosyal Bilimler Enstitüsü, Yüksek Lisans Tezi, Afyon.

Aydın, K. (2016). *Elektronik İnsan Kaynakları Yönetimi Uygulamaları ve İnovasyon Performansı*. İstanbul, Turkey: Bahçeşehir Üniversitesi, Sosyal Bilimler Enstitüsü, Yüksek Lisans Tezi.

Barber, L. (2006). *E-recruitment Developments*. Brighton, MA: Institute for Employment Studies.

Barney, J. B., & Wright, P. M. (1998). On Becoming A Strategic Partner: The Role Of Human Resources İn Gaining Competitive Advantage. Human Resource Management: Published in Cooperation with the School of Business Administration, *The University of Michigan and in alliance with the Society of Human Resources Management, 37(1),* pp. 31-46.

Bondarouk, T., Ruël, H., & Kees Looise, J. (Eds.). (2011). Electronic HRM in theory and practice. Bingley, UK: Emerald Group Publishing Limited. doi:10.1108/S1877-6361(2011)8

Bondarouk, T. V., & Ruel, H. J. M. (2009). Electronic Human Resource Management: Challenges in the digital era. *International Journal of Human Resource Management, 20*(3), 505–514. doi:10.1080/09585190802707235

Bonti, M., & Cori, E. (2004). The Communication of Company Values and Internetland empirical evidence. In Information, Knowledge and Management: Re-assessing the Role of ICTs in Public and Private Organization.

Caldwell, R. (2003). The changing roles of personnel managers: Old ambiguities, new uncertainties. *Journal of Management Studies, 40*(4), 983–1004. doi:10.1111/1467-6486.00367

Cappelli, P. (2001). Making the most of on-line recruiting. *Harvard Business Review, 79*(3), 139–148. PMID:11246921

Celep, M. (2017). *Elektronik İnsan Kaynakları Uygulamalarının Örgütsel Çıktılar Üzerindeki Etkileri: Türkiye'de Yabancı İştirakli Sigorta Şirketlerinde Bir Araştırma.* İstanbul, Turkey: Bahçeşehir Üniversitesi Sosyal Bilimler Enstitüsü Yüksek Lisans Tezi.

Celep, M., & Fındıklı, M. A. (2018). Elektronik İnsan Kaynakları Uygulamalarının Örgütsel Çıktılar Üzerindeki Etkileri: Türkiye'de Yabancı İştirakli Sigorta Şirketlerinde Bir Araştırma. *Bilgi Ekonomisi ve Yönetimi Dergisi, 13*(1), 63–77.

Cook, M. F. (1999). *Outsourcing Human Resources Functions: Strategies For Providing Enhanced HR Services At Lower Cost.* New York, NY: American Management Association.

Daud, K. İ. (2010). *İnsan Kaynakları Yönetim Süreçlerinde Bilgi Teknolojilerinin Kullanımı ve E-İK Uygulamaları.* İstanbul, Turkey: İstanbul Teknik Üniversitesi, Fen Bilimleri Enstitüsü, Yüksek Lisans Tezi.

Doğan, A. (2011).. . *Elektronik İnsan Kaynakları Yönetimi ve Fonksiyonları, İnternet Uygulamaları ve Yönetimi Dergisi, 2*(2), 51–80.

Dulebohn, H., & Marler, J. H. (2005). E-Compensation: The Potential to Transform Practice? In *H. G. Gueutal, & D. L. Stone (Eds.), The Brave New World of eHR: Human Resources Management in the Digital Age* (pp. 166–189). San Francisco, CA: Jossey Bass.

Dündar, İ. G. (1995). *Stratejik İKY'de İK Bilgi Sistemleri'nden Yararlanılması ve Kariyer Yönetimi Sistemine İlişkin Bir Model Önerisi.* İstanbul, Turkey: İstanbul Üniversitesi, Sosyal Bilimler Enstitüsü, Yayınlanmamı Doktora Tezi.

Emmerichs, R. M., Marcum, C. Y., & Robbert, A. A. (2004). An operational process for workforce planning. Santa Monica, CA: Rand Corporation.

Esen, M. (2011). *Bireysel Ve Kurumsal Hazır oluşun Teknolojik Kabulüne Etkisi: Elektronik İnsan Kaynakları Yönetimi (E-İKY).* Alanında Ampirik Bir Araştırma, Kocaeli Üniversitesi Sosyal Bilimler Enstitüsü, Doktora Tezi, Kocaeli.

Gardner, S. D., Lepak, D. P., & Bartol, K. M. (2003). Virtual HR: The Impact of Information Technology on the Human Resource Professional. *Journal of Vocational Behavior, 63*(2), 159–179. doi:10.1016/S0001-8791(03)00039-3

Ghazzawi, K., & Accoumeh, A. (2014). Critical success factors of the e-recruitment system. *Journal of Human Resources Management and Labor Studies, 2*(2), 159–170.

Gueutal, H. G. (2003). *The Brave New World of E-HR: Advances in Human Performance and Cognitive Engineering Research.* USA: Emerald Group Publishing Limited.

Güler, E. Ç. (2006). İşletmelerin E-İnsan Kaynakları Yönetimi ve E-İşe Alım Süreçlerindeki Gelişmeler. *Ege Akademik Bakış Dergisi, 6*(1), 17–23.

Hall, M. L., & Moritz, S. (2003). The Impact of e-HR on the Human Resource Management Function. *Journal of Labor Research, 14*(3), 365–379. doi:10.100712122-C03-1001-6

Huang, J. H., Jin, B. H., & Yang, C. (2004). Satisfaction with Business-to-Employee Benefit Systems and Organizational Citizenship Behavior: An Examination of Gender Differences. *International Journal of Manpower*, 25(2), 195–210. doi:10.1108/01437720410535990

Iqbal, N., Ahmad, M., Raziq, M. M., & Borini, F. M. (2019). Linking e-hrm practices and organizational outcomes: Empirical analysis of line manager's perception. *Revista Brasileira de Gestão de Negócios*, 21(1), 48–69. doi:10.7819/rbgn.v21i1.3964

Johnson, R., Lukaszweski, K. M., & Stone, D. L. (2015). The Evolution of The Field of Human Resource Information Systems: Co-Evolution of Technology and HR Processes. *Communications of the Association for Information Systems*, 38(28), 533–553.

Karcıoğlu, F., & Öztürk, Ü. (2009). İşletmelerde Performans Değerleme ile İnsan Kaynakları Bilgi Sistemleri (İKBS) Arasındaki İlişkisi-İstanbul İlinde Bir Araştırma. *Atatürk Üniversitesi Sosyal Bilimler Enstitüsü Dergisi*, 13(1), 343–366.

Körfez, E. P. (2008). *Elektronik İse Alım ve Seçimin İnsan Kaynakları Yönetimi Açısından Yeri ve Önemi ve Bir Uygulama*. İstanbul, Turkey: Yıldız Teknik Üniversitesi, Sosyal Bilimler Enstitüsü, Yüksek Lisans Tezi.

Lazazzara, A., & Galanaki, E. (2018). E-HRM Adoption and Usage: A Cross-National Analysis of Enabling Factors. In C. Rossignoli, F. Virili, & S. Za (Eds.), *Digital, Technology and Organizational Change: Reshaping Technology, People, and Organizations Towards a Global Society*. Lecture Notes in Information Systems and Organisation. doi:10.1007/978-3-319-62051-0_11

Lee, I. (2005). The Evolution of E-Recruiting: A Concent Analysis of Fortune 100 Career Web Sites. *Journal of Electronic Commerce in Organizations*, 3(3), 57–68. doi:10.4018/jeco.2005070104

Legge, K. (1989). Human resource management: a critical analysis. New perspectives on human resource management. In J. Storey (Ed.), New Perspectives on Human Resource Management. Abingdon, UK: Routledge, pp. 19-40.

Lepak, D. P., & Snell, S. A. (1998). Virtual HR: Strategic human resource management in the 21st century. *Human Resource Management Review*, 8(3), 215–234. doi:10.1016/S1053-4822(98)90003-1

LeTart, J. F. (1998). Virtual HR, HR Magazine, p. 62.

Marler, J. H. (2009). Making human resources strategic by going to the Net: Reality or myth? *International Journal of Human Resource Management*, 20(3), 515–527. doi:10.1080/09585190802707276

Mondy, R. W., & Mondy, J. B. (2012). *Human Resource Management*. London, UK: Pearson Education.

Nivlouei, F. B. (2014). Electronic Human Resource Management System: The Main Element in Capacitating Globalization Paradigm. *International Journal of Business and Social Science*, 5(2), 147–159.

Öğe, S. (2004). *Elektronik İnsan Kaynakları Yönetimi (E-HRM)'nde İnsan Kaynakları Enformasyon Sistemi (HRIS)'nin Önemi ve Temel Kullanım Alanları. 3* (pp. 109–117). Ulusal Bilgi, Ekonomi ve Yönetim Kongresi.

Rajalakshmi, R., & Gomathi, S. (2016). A review on E-HRM: Electronic human resource management. *Indian Journal of Research*, 5(8).

Ramezen, M., Nazari, Y., & Ahmadi, M. M. (2013). The effect of electronic human resources management on quality of services provided by human resources in the insurance industry (case study: Iran Insurance Company in Khorramabad City). *Journal of Social Issues & Humanities*, 1(7), 223–232.

Robson, L. S., Clarke, J. A., Cullen, K., Bielecky, A., Severin, C., Bigelow, P. L., ... Mahood, Q. (2007). The effectiveness of occupational health and safety management system interventions: A systematic review. *Safety Science*, 45(3), 329–353. doi:10.1016/j.ssci.2006.07.003

Ruël, H., Bondarouk, T., & Looise, J. K. (2004). E-HRM: Innovation or Irritation. *Management Review*, 15(3), 364–381.

Ruël, H., Magalhães, R., & Chiemeke, C. C. (2011). Human Resource Information Systems: An Integrated Research Agenda. In Electronic HRM in Theory and Practice (pp. 21–39). Binkley, UK: Emerald Group Publishing Limited. doi:10.1108/S1877-6361(2011)0000008006

Ruël, H., & van der Kaap, H. (2012). E-HRM Usage and Value Creation: Does a Facilitating Context Matter? *Zeitschrift für Personalforschung*, 26(3), 260–281.

Ruel, H. J., Bondarouk, T. V., & Van der Velde, M. (2007). The contribution of e-HRM to HRM effectiveness. *Employee Relations*, 29(3), 280–291. doi:10.1108/01425450710741757

Sadegh, T., Kohansal, M. A., & Haghshenas, M. (2016). E-HRM: From acceptance to value cretion. *Journal of Information Technology Management*, 27(1), 18–27.

Schank, R. C. (2002). Designing world-class e-learning: How IBM, GE, Harvard Business School, and Columbia University are succeeding at e-learning.

Seema, A., & Sujatha, S. (2013). Conceptual work on career management strategies from an organization perspective. *International Journal of Management, IT and Engineering*, 3(7), 184.

Şimşek, M. Ş., & Öge, H. S. (2011). İnsan Kaynakları Yönetimi, *Eğitim Akademi Yayınları*. Baskı, Yayınevi Sertifika, (14824).

Snell, N. (1994). Virtual HR: Meeting New World Realities. *Compensation and Benefits Review*, 26(12), 35–37. doi:10.1177/088636879402600606

Stone, D. L., Stone-Romero, E. F., & Lukaszewski, K. (2003). The functional and dysfunctional consequences of human resource information technology for organizations and their employees. In Advances in human performance and cognitive engineering research (pp. 37–68). Binkley, UK: Emerald Group Publishing Limited.

Strohmeier, S. (2007). Research in e-HRM: Review and Implications. *Human Resource Management Review*, 17(1), 19–37. doi:10.1016/j.hrmr.2006.11.002

Strohmeier, S., & Piazza, F. (2011). "Web Mining" as a Novel Approaching e-HRM Research. In Electronic HRM in Theory and Practice (pp. 41–53). Binkley, UK: Emerald Group Publishing Limited. doi:10.1108/S1877-6361(2011)0000008007

Sylva, H., & Mol, S. T. (2009). E-Recruitment: A study into applicant perceptions of an online application system. *International Journal of Selection and Assessment, 17*(3), 311–323. doi:10.1111/j.1468-2389.2009.00473.x

Sylvester, E. O., Bamidele, A. D., & Oluyemi, O. S. (2015). Implementing E-HRM System in Developing Countries: Challenges and Prospects. *International Journal of Applied Information Systems, 9*(8), 38–41. doi:10.5120/ijais2015451452

Troshani, I., Jerram, C., & Rao, S. (2011). Exploring the Public Sector Adoption of HRIS. *Industrial Management & Data Systems, 111*(3), 470–488. doi:10.1108/02635571111118314

Tunçer, P. (2012). Değişen İnsan Kaynakları Yönetimi Anlayışında Kariyer Yönetimi. *Ondokuz Mayıs Üniversitesi Eğitim Fakültesi Dergisi, 31*(1).

Ulrich, D. (1996). Human resource champions: The next agenda for adding value and delivering results. Brighton, MA: Harvard Business Press.

Ulrich, D. (1998). A New Mandate For Human Resources. *Harvard Business Review, 76*(1), 128. PMID:10176915

Ulrich, D. L. (1990). *Organizational Capability: Competing From the Inside/Out* (pp. 78–94). New York, NY: John Wiley & Sons.

Venterink, J. H. (2017). *Practical Future Developments in e-HRM, HR SSC's and Employee Involvement.* (Master thesis, University of Twente).

Wahyudi, E., & Park, S. M. (2014). Unveiling the value creation process of electronic human resource management: An indonesian case. *Public Personnel Management, 43*(1), 83–117. doi:10.1177/0091026013517555

Yazıcı, S. (2004). *E-Öğrenme: İnsan Kaynakları Eğitiminde Stratejik Dönüşüm.* İstanbul, Turkey: Alfa Basım.

KEY TERMS AND DEFINITIONS

Electronic Human Resources Management (E-HRM): It means electronic human resources management system including practices that are open to all relevant actors, such as job applicants, HR consultants, other than the employees of the institution

Electronic Performance Management Systems (E-PMS): Electronic performance management system consists of partially e-HRM and HR information system. Via information technology integration of strategies, policies, practices and performance management process was enabled.

Electronic Recruitment Systems: To collect candidates with their characteristics in a pool in the electronic system and then to recruit personnel with related characteristics or information in this pool for the recruitment of vacant positions.

Electronic remuneration (E-remuneration): is a system that refers to the organization collecting, storing, processing, analyzing, using and distributing data and information related to the remuneration over the web system.

Employee Self Service (ESS): Employee Self-Service (ESS) is seen in the service tools. Employee self-service is a whole networked application that allow all managers and employees to create, record and correct personnel information about themselves

Human Resource Information Systems (HRMS): HRMS is mainly directed to the HR department itself. The users of these systems are HR professionals.

Intranet: Intranet is a person-specific or organizational specific state of the Internet. While anyone can access web sites on the Internet, only those who are authorized have to access the intranet created on the web. The authorized users require user name and a password to enter.

This research was previously published in Tools and Techniques for Implementing International E-Trading Tactics for Competitive Advantage; pages 1-20, copyright year 2020 by Business Science Reference (an imprint of IGI Global).

Chapter 12
Digitalization of Human Resources:
e–HR

Elif Baykal

İstanbul Medipol University, Turkey

ABSTRACT

Recent decades brought about astonishing technologies that affected organizations in several ways. With the latest developments, organizations earned the capabilities to carry out their functions more efficiently and rapidly. Having several tasks affecting both interior and exterior customers, human resources departments also benefited from these technological developments. Owing to the digital revolution, e-HR emerged as a new way of practicing HRM activities with the latest web-based and computer-based tools and applications. These applications eased the work of HR professionals and served them the opportunity to focus on their core work, namely strategic human resources activities rather than procedural paperwork of the department. With a holistic and integrative approach, this digital transformation in HRM has been dispersed among all services in human resources including recruitment, career management, training and development, performance management, and compensation.

INTRODUCTION

Latest technological and competitive developments in the markets enabled the creation of real-time, knowledge-based, self-managed and interactive business atmosphere. This knowledge based interactive work atmosphere was impossible to believe throughout most of the twentieth century. After 1990s digitalization in all spheres of life have become prominent. Latest developments in web based technologies have given birth to production of large bulks of online data varying from social media posts to digitalized libraries. This new body of knowledge and data provided a significant source of data complimenting classical quantitative and qualitative data and allowing individuals to unravel sound patterns regarding managerial and social phenomena (Platanou, Mäkelä, Beletskiy, & Colicev, 2018). The creation of

DOI: 10.4018/978-1-6684-3873-2.ch012

huge online data sets, namely Big Data has also grown significantly recently owing to the astonishing developments in data storage Technologies and digital monitoring mechanisms. This "Big Data" can help individuals understand collective patterns of events, behaviors, perceptions, and attitudes better and easier than other methods (Hannigan, 2015). And its use disseminated in a considerable wide scope of managerial functions including even human resources management.

In fact, use of technology is a new realm of study in management literature. When the related literature is examined as Orlikowski and Scott (2008) suggest there are two streams regarding use of technology in organizations. The first stream explains technological determinism reflecting an underlying positivist approach wherein technology can be conceived as a independent qualitative variable predicting organizational consequences. The second stream considers technology as a new construct evolving over time reflecting a more post-positivist perspective. In the first stream, technology is an entity interacting with different organizational aspects (Orlikowski & Scott, p. 439). It is considered as an independent variable that have a quiet noteworthy number of impacts in organizational life at various analysis levels including individual level, group level, enterprise level, and inter-organizational level. Moreover, it is effective on various organizational outputs when considered as an independent variable including effectiveness, agility, resilience, profitability, etc. (Orlikowski & Scott, 2008). This approach has a rather deterministic perspective, since it views technology as a causal factor which can create assessable, theoretically-determined results. For example, the number of IT projects accomplished in a certain organizations, the number and quality of technical tools used, the qualifications of IT personnel etc. can all be conceived as independent variables in the kind of researched that exist in this first stream of research. The second main stream of studies regarding technology which is prominent in management literature is the stream known with its focus on dynamic interactions between people factor and technology factor over time. This approach can be considered as less deterministic compared to the first one. It views technology as a component of complex process wherein organization of the structure can be accomplished. However, today technology should not be understood with a limited perspective. It is no longer a discrete entity. That is why it cannot be conceived as a quantifiable independent or dependent dimension. In fact, technology is emergent and cannot be determined fully. There are many factors, complicated relationships and grey areas in understanding effects of technology in organizational setting. That is why, Strohmeier (2009) explains the second stream of studies as studies of moderated organizational imperatives wherein there multiple actors interact with the aim of creating an outcome which is in fact cannot be predicted entirely.

In practice, although latest digital technologies have been utilized in HR information systems since 1980s, it was a different application when compared to e-HR. HRISs was focusing on automating HR systems that were used by HR department's itself, namely its sole 'customer' was HR professionals themselves. Moreover, HRISs were not successful in creating the ideal internal virtual value chain. On the other hand, e-HR is more about the application of the internet, including use of social media, and mobile communications technologies are important in changing the nature of interactions among HR professionals, managers and employees. Its aim was changing these relationships from a pure face-to-face relationship to a technology-based one (Martin and Redington, 2010). Nonetheless, HRISs can be accepted as the first step before transition to e-HR.

In technology research the term "e-HR" first emerged after 1990s. Emergence of the term "e-commerce" namely electronic commerce was the antecedent of the term. E- HR is a way of implementing HR activities, strategies and policies through a conscious and directed support of latest technology (Ruël, Bondarouk, & Looise, 2004). E-HR can be explained as a way of conducting HR strategies in companies through a willing, conscious and directed support of full use of internet-based technologies (Ruel et al.;

2004). As in the case in the term e-commerce, e-HR refers to conducting human resources transactions with the help of internet. The use of Internet ensured human resources function with the ease to reach and use information in any time when needed and wanted. (Lengnick-Hall & Moritz, 2003).With the help of e-HR, organizations and employees can administer their own information. E-HR gives them the opportunity to update records and make decisions easily using this records (Lengnick-Hall & Moritz, 2003). E-HR is positively related with both efficiency and effectiveness. Efficiency is possible through reducing the required time for processing paperwork. It also increases accuracy of the data obtained and stored. Moreover, it reduces the time human resource employees spend for their daily activities. On the other hand, effectiveness is also another product of e-HR. With latest technologies and newly adopted know- how to these Technologies companies using E-HR can administer their activities more effectively. Since e -HR improved the capabilities of organizations and organizational members in making more satisfying, more timely and more meaningful decisions (Lengnick-Hall & Moritz, 2003).

In order to understand e-HR, it is necessary to first understand the nature of HR activities.Thite and Kavanagh (2009) grouped human resources management functions into three basic groups: transactional activities, involving daily transactions and record keeping; traditional human resources management activities, encompassing activities like recruitment, selection, HR planning, training and development, compensation and performance appraisal; and transformational activities, activities adding value to the company, like organizational development, talent management and organizational learning. Recently, a shift occurred in the delivery of transactional human resources activities which are often labour in-tensive to the more technology-intensive activities such as e-recruitment, e-coaching, e-mentoring etc. (Florkowski & Olivas-Lujan, 2006). E-HR has become more pervasive after companies adopted this new more technology-based form of doing business. The introduction of e-HRM had significantly reduced the traditional transactional workload of the HR professionals (Parry & Tyson, 2011). And it increased transformational outcomes like more transparent and detailed information or more time available to human resources practitioners (Parry & Tyson, 2011). Moreover, the use of a common technological system led to more consistent HR processes, contributing to higher levels of standardization (Parry & Tyson, 2011). E-HR seems to be more involved in this standardization and homogenization process within larger, more bureaucratic and mostly international companies (Ruel et al., 2004).

In fact, e-HR development has been seen in three main forms. The easiest and most common way to implement e-HR is to publish information. This first form is known as the simplest form of e-HR involving one-way communication in the organization that has a top-down flow, namely top managers or owners tend to disclose information for the use of employees. In this form of e-HR companies mostly prefer to use intranets as the main source information delivery. Earliest examples of this e-HR method encompass some generic content information publishing such as company policies, service directories, informing employees about daily events etc. The second mainstream use of e-HR involves the automa-tion of HR processes and transactions. In this e-HR form it is preferred to use intranets with extranets simultaneously. This form combines different digital applications. In this HR mode, paperwork is mostly replaced by digital input. In the third, and most developed form of e-HR we can talk about transformation of HR functions almost to a fully electronic mode. In this journey, from information to automation and from automation to transformation, e-HR has gone beyond its traditional focus to a more modern and digitalized mode. And through this transformation, e-HR liberated HR from being operational-focused and has been redirected towards being a more strategic function. On the other hand, while some compa-nies embrace a more evolutionary approach to implementing e-HR, others can prefer embracing more radical ways in directly to transforming the HR activities (Lengnick-Hall & Moritz, 2003).

BENEFITS OF E-HR

First of all, e-HR is a cost saving way of conducting HR processes. In organizations that wherein e-HR is used, fewer human resource professionals and lower working hours are required due to the fact that e-HR eliminates the need for HR middleman. Besides reducing costs and increasing efficiency, use of e-HR also can create new revenue sources. Human resources professional earn the ability to direct their energy to new realms in doing their business more effectively and professionally after they have met with e-HR. But, establishing direct and objective methods to measure benefits of these new ways of conducting HR functions are difficult to achieve. For instance, e-HR can increase employee productivity, motivation and can speed up decision-making processes but these issues are difficult to measure (Lengnick-Hall & Moritz, 2003). Moreover, in companies using e-HR, transactions are held with a higher speed, lower levels of information errors are seen, and tracking and control of human resource functions are handled more professionally. Thus, with the help of e-HR companies can improve their HRM service delivery (Lengnick-Hall & Moritz, 2003).

On the one hand, costs can also occur linked with using an e-HR system. For instance, using high technology in HR process may make it necessary to buy expensive technological devices for each personnel that carry on these processes (Lengnick-Hall & Moritz, 2003). For example, making online meetings with HR account managers from other geographies makes it necessary to buy high-tech cameras and computers in each geographical location of the company. On the other hand, variation in e-HR activities, creates variations in organizational capabilities supporting increasingly coordinated and automated HR processes encompassing those kinds of activities such as data processing and stocking, internal and external communication and conducting HR operations using internet-based technologies (Marler & Parry, 2015). In fact, use of e-HR is a planned strategic activity regarding provision of HRM services through modern technologies (Marler & Parry, 2015)

Today, most prominent e-HR systems often include enterprise resource planning software systems, automated HR operations, interactive voice responses (IVR) of HR call centers, web applications of career portals that are used in applications, and most pervasively interior employee portals (Lengnick-Hall, & Moritz, 2003). Using these systems e-HR systems increase efficiency and ensure a change in HR that shifts to a more strategic level (Parry & Tyson, 2011). By the help of these systems, organizations can be successful in attaining five probable goals including e-HRM-efficiency, high-quality service delivery, long-term strategic orientation, more-empowered employees and standardisation in HR processes (Parry & Tyson, 2011).

When considered with a different perspective, e-HR is found to be more pervasive in those kinds of companies wherein a more sophisticated and complex HR functioning is prominent. In this point, Voermans and van Veldhoven (2007) claims that in those kinds of organizations wherein in there is a system of HR strategic partnership, it is more likely to see an inclination towards e- HRM. In HR partnership system, HR professionals are considered as strategic partners of business units or geographical subunits of the main organization. In this system HR professionals are considered as HR account managers in their own strategic business unit. They have intimate contact with the business unit they are responsible for. And they are often working in the location their business unit is located rather than in HR Office that is why the HR department needs using electronic communication and information sharing tools in getting in touch with these professionals.

As mentioned before, researchers like Thite and Kavanagh (2009) divide HR function into two main activities: transactional activities, involving day-to-day activities, daily transactions and record keeping; such as recruitment of new employees, selection, training and development, wage management and performance management; and rather more transformational activities, including organisational development, career management, performance appraisal, mentoring and talent management. In the practice we see that organizations preferring a more strategic HR management tend to engage in e-HR systems (Voermans & Veldhoven, 2007). It is more advantageous to carry on human resources functions through online portals and technological communication tools. It makes HR function more effective on multiple stakeholders such as potential candidates, existing employees, middle and top managers and line managers. In such organizations, a negative possible result of E-HR is losing personal contact with HR professionals. In fact, personal contact with human resources agents is one of the strongest needs when in strategic human resources management, where the human resources professional has employee champion role for HR (Voermans & Veldhoven, 2007). Thus, e-HR is expected to confer many advantages on organizations, such as a more efficient and strategically-oriented HR function and an increased competitive advantage (Lazaaara & Galanaki, 2018).

ANTECEDENTS OF E-HR ADOPTION

Extant literature shows that companies operating in technology-intensive sectors tend to embrace IT tools in order to enhance their external image (Teo, Lim, & Fedric, 2007). But this is a contagious perception for most contemporary companies. Today even those companies that has little to do with technology prefer to use technological tools and mechanisms to create a more modern image. In the digital age human resources professionals started to prefer online domains more frequently, wherein they can learn about the latest trends in the field, they can share their experiences and best practices, and they can embrace in carrying out their daily activities. Of course, there are many reasons underlying the preference of companies and human resources professional regarding the usage of e-HR technologies.

In fact, the task characteristics in an organization or in an industry, that is to say the inclination or necessity to have more or less clerical or stationary tasks is useful in predicting technological adoption, and without doubt e-HR adoption. Sometimes too much clerical work, sometimes disjointed geographical organization structure and sometimes excessive levels of recruitment and selection may result in more frequent use of e-HR. Companies having too many bureaucratic tasks prefer to follow-up their daily routine through web-based applications. Again companies having complicated recruitment, career management or performance management processes prefer to use technological tools to carry on their task more effectively and efficiently.

Moreover, organizational size also effective on the use of technological tools in HRM functions. Namely, number of people working in the organization, span of control, number of departments and organizational structure are all important in designating the use of e-HRM adoption. More crowded companies having too much employees and several hierarchical levels and myriad managers are compelled to embrace web-based e-HR processes in order to ease the complicated and exhausting task of HR professionals dealing with several people and procedures simultaneously. Workload of human resources professionals are heavier the bigger the size of the company. And this necessitates mechanisms and tools for making the job easier for human resources professionals.

Furthermore, the kind of companies that are actors in global competition, namely, international companies tend to engage in e-HRM more frequently. The need to collaborate with their partners and subunits in different geographies and the higher educational levels of their employees are effective on e-HRM adoption. In those kind of companies we can come across lower levels of failure in e-HR adoption since employees are well educated and the characteristics of the tasks that are carried out are proper for web-based procedures (Lazazzara & Galanaki 2018). On the one hand, isomorphic pressures at the industry level namely, the pressured applied by the other competitors in an industry to resemble each other effects the use of e-HR. If in an industry most companies prefer to engage in use of web-based HR tools, rest of the companies also start to engage in a e- HR with the aim of achieving organizational legitimacy. Without doubt employees working in these companies and all the other stakeholders will compare their company with the other companies using e-HR and this will create a pressure on the company to engage in e-HR.

After a company decides on engaging in e-HR, the company decides on the kind of activities that the company should benefit from e-HR. In some companies all e-HR functions are carried out with the help of e-HR, and in some cases, companies prefer to adopt and use e-HR in a limited manner, that is to say only in some functions of e-HR. This id sometimes a preference and sometimes a requirement. In some cases as a strategic decision, companies prefer a limited or a generalized use of e-HR, or in some cases financial limitations end up with a more limited use of e-HR. Nevertheless, technology proponents claim that, the IT possibilities for human resource management are endless: in principal all human resources functions can be supported by technology (Ruël, Bondarouk, & Looise, 2004). In the next part of this chapter, most prominent human resources functions that are benefiting from web-based technologies will be discussed.

E-RECRUITMENT

E-recruitment systems have become quiet popular in the last few years due to its advantages in allowing HR professionals to target a great number of candidates at a small cost (Faliagka, Tsakalidis, & Tzimas, 2012). E-recruitment is carrying out recruitment functions through web-based Technologies. E-recruitment implies publishing job posts, namely open positions in a compony online, having an online fill-in form available for applicants and a web-based database existing to store the resumes of applicants (Brandão, Silva, & dos Santos, 2019). Using e-HR systems companies can be seen in myriad career portals and can attract the attention of astronomic number of candidates with various qualifications. In most e-recruitment processes, companies use an automated system wherein candidates are ranked by using a set of objective and credible criteria, that are easy to apply for companies (Faliagka, Tsakalidis, & Tzimas, 2012). And they use an online career portal in reaching their applicants. By the help of digital Technologies these criteria are applied to all candidates that make a job application through company's internet portal or a common recruitment portal. E-recruitment starts with candidates intend to apply for a job in a certain organization. During this process, in case a new position opens, the human resources professional creates a job post in the internet portal of the company or in a web-based career portal. Predetermined selection criteria and weights of that criteria is used in determining the suitability of each candidate. Selection criteria and position requirements are posted by the recruiter through the job post. The recruitment process starts when the candidates apply for an open position at the e-recruitment portal (Faliagka, Tsakalidis, & Tzimas, 2012). In fact, e-recruitment allows candidates to have contact with more job opportunities and reach a greater flow of information (Sylva & Mol, 2009). In e-recruitment candidates upload their resumes to the system that should be examined by an HR expert in the organization (Faliagka, Tsakalidis, & Tzimas, 2012). And the applicant can get information from the company about his process through the web-based recruitment portal or through the internet site of the company. There are some additional applications in e-recruitment system. For instance, specialized selection tests such as knowledge tests and personality tests can be applied through internet which provide online feedback to the recruiters and the applicants about the qualifications of the candidates. And in e-recruitment, various preliminary online procedures can be applied through internet enabling the elimination of applicants that do not fit the position (Brandão, Silva, & dos Santos, 2019). If their process is negative, namely if after the resume is examined, the evaluation about the resume is negative, the candidate is directly informed about the negative evaluation via the web-based portal. Companies can also use their organizational website in informing their potential applicants regarding new job opportunities, but they mostly prefer to have a permanent recruitment portal for receiving applications of new candidates even when there is not an urgent need for new candidates (Brandão, Silva, & dos Santos, 2019). In fact, organizational websites are communication channels between companies and job seekers (Araújo & Ramos, 2002). Sometimes companies merely use their corporate websites to attract new applications. Whether the tool for receiving applications is their corporate website or a recruitment portal is not important. In both cases their aim That is why companies prefer to have a pool of candidates attracted and collected via their web-based portal that are stocked for a certain period of time that are ready to be evaluated in case there occurs an urgent need. However, it is an inevitable fact that only a small number of overall applicants are selected and receives a call for a job interview (Faliagka, Tsakalidis, & Tzimas, 2012). And this can make the company notorious among applicants if their applicant hiring/applicant stocking rate is too low.

On the one hand, there are also some disadvantages of e-recruitment especially for candidates. Specifically, privacy can be perceived as a problem by the candidates. In their empirical study Petre et al. (2016) found that while applying to online job posts, applicants sometimes perceive a certain privacy risk. They can become anxious about sharing their personal information. They may be suspicious about the possibility that the information they shared in their resumes may be shared by third parties without their permission. Moreover, some people are not accustomed to using technological tools and they may avoid making applications via internet due to their technology bias. That is to say, in e-recruitment candidates' reactions to the online system and job advertisements in this system are influenced by the perceived efficiency and user-friendliness, namely, if or not the applicant views the job advertisement easy to conceive and apply for (Sylva & Mol, 2009).

E-TRAINING

E-training can be considered as a way of distance training through the use of web-based Technologies encompassing either Internet or Intranet that provide individuals with the required knowledge on specific selected themes or a specific specialty, with the help of the computer-based technologies, sound tracks, videos, multimedia messages, e-books, emails, and discussion groups (Amara, & Atia, 2016). In e-training, the use of technology to educate is prominent (Mohsin & Sulaiman, 2013). This kind of training can be either in the form of face to face education or in the form of distance mediated or pure online education. Origins of this term e-training goes back to the 1980s, as in the case with emergence of the term online training. There are various terms indicating e-training such as distance training; virtual training; online training or web-based training (Amara & Atia, 2016). And E-training systems encompass myriad tools including writing technologies, communication technologies, visualization, and storage (Aparicio, Bacao, & Oliveira, 2016). Furthermore, e-training activities are not bounded merely using a computer or we-based technology as an artifact in the training process. Students can be individual students or company employees that prefer using these modules in congruent with the development policies of their employees (Aparicio, Bacao, & Oliveira, 2016). Some organizations embrace knowledge management and virtual collaboration in their e-training strategies, broadly including any system generating and disseminating information and improving organizational and individual performance (Welsch et al., 2003).

E-learning is also a pervasive term used in e-training processes. E-learning is the implementation of Internet-based technologies with the aim of delivering a satisfactory number of alternative solutions enhancing knowledge acquisition (Esterhuyse & Scholtz, 2016). And it seems sound to companies due to its ability to ensure cost-effective training. Moreover, e-learning is also useful for ensuring consistency in learning materials and learning techniques. Each people benefiting from a certain learning material reach the same kind of content. It also ensures flexibility in the time period that the learner prefers to benefit from the learning material, it provides ease of access, it is capable of just- in-time delivery, have low costs, and high customer value (Esterhuyse & Scholtz, 2016). In fact, we can talk about six main elements of e-learning encompassing; computer that have an access to internet, utilization of the system by both the learner and the HR, curriculum development by the HR professionals, content creation by the educator (often a specialist in the topic), content management that is mostly carried out by the related HR professional, learning management, delivery of the education program and development of the program (Riahi, 2015). These processes are mostly carried by HR department of the company with the help of a special institute or education company that is specialist on the related subject.

Companies prefer e-training to decrease their costs of education they spend for training their person-nel. Considering the cost of training employees working in different geographies, it is an important solu-tion to get rid of both waste of time and travel costs. In fact, different from the traditional face-to- face training techniques, e-training techniques help companies reach a considerably large number of educa-tion contents with low costs (Jackson et al., 2018). It is a more egalitarian way of educating employees when compared to classical methods of education, owing to the greater number and quality it serves to employees from various hierarchical levels and geographies. In the table below a good summary of the differences between classical face to face training and web-based digital e-training can be found.

E-MENTORING

E-mentoring is a specific kind of mentoring that get use of technology-based programmes in providing flexibility in time management and scheduling. E-mentoring is helpful in decreasing problems caused by geographical barriers. People that cannot otherwise get mentoring benefit from mentoring opportunities thanks to e-mentoring. In this mentoring style mentor and mentee do not experience adversities related to scheduling. Pairs are not bounded by constraints like a proper place or a proper time to meet, if they can access to a proper computer and the Internet. Mentoring is easier and more comfortable through e-mentoring for the kind of people who are unable to access this service previously (Kasprisin, Single, Single, & Muller, 2003).

Table 1. Training vs. E-Training

Traditional training	E-training
-The trainer is the main source of knowledge	-The trainer is a kind of facilitator and mentor of in the training process
- One-way, from trainer to trainee, flow of knowledge	-Interactive training process
-The trainee receives or takes knowledge from the trainer	-Flexible and more self-involving learning process
-Inflexible and routine processes	-Developing and flexible content
-Static content	-Relatively low cost
-High cost	-Emphasis on individual differences
-Ignorance of individual differences	

Source: Omar Ahmad El-Kabir, Distance training in the context of evolving techniques of training, National symposium on education and vocational e-training, General People's Committee for Workforces, Training and Employment, Tripoli, 2006, P. 7.

In classical mentoring, organizations appoint higher rank employees or managers having more experience or higher performance as mentors to the ones with lower ranks, less experience or lower performance levels. Unfortunately, this can give way to some discomforting feelings on the side of mentee. E-mentoring can lower this discrepancies and unequal power relationship, since in e-mentoring status symbols are often unidentified. That is why, although a bit discomforting for individuals that are not comfortable with digital communication, it is more equalitarian way of mentoring (Kasprisin, Single, Single, & Muller, 2003).

Moreover, unlike classical mentoring programmes encompassing face-to face mentoring relationships, e-mentoring makes it possible for huge organizations design large-scale programmes encompassing many mentor-mentee pairs from different locations (Kasprisin, Single, Single, & Muller, 2003). Individuals can be matched with various alternatives which creates prosperity regarding alternatives. Companies can match mentors and mentees more freely without considering geographical obstacles, financial matters and fear of spending too much time in making peers come together.

E-CAREER MANAGEMENT

Computer-based and web-based career management mechanisms are important tools in identifying and putting across the necessities required for the employee's development. And, these mechanisms ensures the facilities in comparing the knowledge and capabilities hold by employees with the skills and competences necessary for the existing or future tasks and positions (Rothwell et al., 2005, pp. 122-124). E-career management is one of these mechanisms making HR function work profoundly more effective. In classical career management programs HR professionals try to understand properties and potentials of employees and mostly group them according to their performance, potential and career plans. And there occurs a huge data related to all that information that should be stocked and analyzed year by year for a long period of time, which is really a burdensome and exhausting task. With the help of e-career management this difficult and tiring task can be accomplished more easily through computer-based and we-based technologies.

Moreover, with the help of e-career management, employees can follow their own career processes. They can store their own personal data, they can make updates about change in their tasks, roles or positions. Moreover, they can even make decisions on their own, getting help from HR professionals only if they need help. For instance, an individual making a retirement plan can plan it by using the Internet (Lengnick-Hall & Moritz, 2003). Or they can develop their technical capabilities or soft skills that are needed for a promotion through web-based learning modules. And by using intranet they can search open positions in their organizations that can pave the way for a promotion if they are found suitable. Moreover, with the help of e-career management tools human resources professional can also draw career maps of individuals in their organizations comfortably. They can store the necessary data for each employee and can reach the necessary data when creating a pool for candidates for certain position.

E-COMPENSATION

E-compensation can be described as the use computer-based and web-based technologies for planning employees' compensation (Swaroop, 2012). Dulebohn and Marler (2005) explains e-compensation as the use of web-based software applications in allowing managers' effective administration and disclosure of information regarding compensation and benefits procedures and information in an organization. In fact, payroll administration can be considered as one of the earliest forms of e-HR processes. (Lengnick-Hall & Moritz, 2003). After 1990s, growth in integrated human resources information systems ensured administration of several human resources functions simultaneously and resulted in more sophisticated human resources management and reporting opportunities. These technological developments enabled companies to provide their employees and managers access to real-time and trustworthy information. Thus, these technological self-service systems gave organizational members the opportunity to manage HR processes. Organizational members can use these systems in updating their records, and HR Professional can use them for accommodating wages and fringe benefits and managers can use generate reports to develop plans (Stone & Dulebohn, 2013). Most importantly, bureaucratic tasks are conducted by e-compensation mechanisms with the help of real-time data. Web-based technologies ensures more updated, quick and reliable workflows.

The use of e-compensation mechanisms helps HR professionals and line managers access to higher levels of data that can contribute to more effective and accurate compensation initiatives. Having the necessary information whenever needed HR professional can also serve the paperwork needs of employees easily without making them wait for tedious time periods. On the other hand, e-compensation decreases the levels of error regarding compensation function of HR. For example, companies embracing e-compensation experience lower level of errors about wages or other kinds of payments made to the employees.

Moreover, e-compensation can also be beneficial for maintaining wage equality (Dulebohn & Marler, 2005, pp. 166-167). Giving the opportunity to control and report all the wages in an organization simultaneously and giving the change to make analysis on this huge data, a fair HR team can take steps to provide wage equality comfortably with the help of e-compensation. Inequalities made before can be seen and corrected easily. During daily processes if a subordinate makes a mistake regarding compensation function for example if they send wrong payroll to the wrong employee, it can be easily detected by the HR manager and corrective action can be taken quickly.

E-PERFORMANCE APPRAISAL

E-performance systems can be explained as the mechanisms using company's web-based portals and applications in order to conduct an evaluation of the employees' potential, knowledge and performance through internet (Swaroop, 2012). In e-performance appraisal systems all the processes are online. HR Professional do not waste time with paperwork. They can trace the performance evaluation process via web-based performance management tools. All the stakeholders of performance appraisal system, namely the employee whose performance is evaluated, the line manager who is one of the evaluators and the HR professional who is responsible of the success of the process can all benefit from the comfort and easiness of the system.

In e-performance appraisal, all the stakeholders of performance management have access to the online performance module. Namely, the employee whose Performance is evaluated, the line manager evaluating the Performance and the HR Professional coaching the process can reach to the related workflow, but each one can only see and control the part related to his own task in the process. For example, the employee whose Performance is evaluated can see his latest records and his updated situation regarding his performance goals bur cannot change approved performance grades he had earned before. Similarly, a line manager cannot change previous years' performance grades of his staff after they have been approved by the related HR professional.

E-HR GOALS

By embracing e-HR, companies direct their HR function to a more systematized, mode digitalized and more convenient state. It often results in an improvement in HR'S strategic orientation, namely by the help of e-HR, HR function can better accommodate itself with the higher strategies of their organization more comfortably. For example, with the help of using e-performance appraisal systems even huge organizations can cascade their organization's strategic goals and can appoint goals to the people working even in the lowest hierarchical levels. And this goal can be traced by multiple stakeholders in the performance appraisal system including the employee's himself, line manager and the HR account manager. By this way all activities in the organization can be directed towards the highest goal, towards the strategic goal. Moreover e-HR results in cost reductions in the organization. Having their most functions computerized and automated after e-HR adoption, most HR departments start to need less people working in their services. A quieted significant part of the activities are held by computers. The bulk of paperwork's diminishes. On the other hand, most routine tasks no longer take as much time as they took before. So, e-HR can be accepted as a time saving way of doing business in HRM department. Furthermore, it is a comfortable way of doing business when HR account managers are in different geographies or external stakeholders such as new applicants are from various different geographies. In huge companies having different HR services in different strategic business units or in different geographies, most spontaneous communication is ensured via web-based applications such as corporate intranet, corporate messaging applications and e-mails. And most communication from external stakeholders are again ensured via emails, voicemails, video conferences and online meetings. For example, an international bank attracting applicant from all over the world can prefer to make their job interviews in the form of online interview. It will be both time and cost saving method of doing an interview.

On the one hand, according to Ruel et al. (2004) e-HR also creates more committed employees and HR professionals. Experiencing newest technologies in their daily organizational life, both subjects and objects of HR processes benefit from more rapid, more effective and more satisfying HR processes which leads to more committed organizational members. For instance, in a company using e-career management portals, being aware of the fact that his career data is being stocked and administered objectively and securely in e-HR portals, an employee can feel trust for the career management mechanisms in his organizations and can feel secure regarding his future in the organization which will lead to organizational commitment. In the digital age most employees are millennium children that are below their 30s which means that they like technology and they like doing business with the help of latest technological tools and mechanisms. Having HR applications designed with highest technology, employees feel that their organization is technology-friendly, and it creates the perception that they are working in an open-minded organization. On the other hand, the next generations and Z generations, are also even more prone to use technological devices in their daily life and coming across digitalized processes and tools make job more enjoyable for them.

CONCLUSION

As mentioned before, e-HRM or e-HR can be conceived as a concept involving the use of internet and Web-based technologies in the provision of human resources services in organizations. E-HR is the conceptualization of the application of web-based and internet-based strategies, procedures, policies and implications in human resources management function (Ruel, Bondarouk, & Looise, 2004). In 1990s Internet entered the lives of people as an important phenomenon in the digitalization business life. Emergence of internet facilitated previously non-existing spontaneous and cheap two-way communication among people. It was a revolutionary step in creating instant worldwide information that can be easily disseminated with considerably low costs. After 1990s, Web-based started to be used for the benefit of human resources management function. Similar technologies used in managerial functions and e trade has been replicated and acidulated to the human resources. From then on human resources software programs became more congruent with Internet architecture. In the early 2000s, this novel trend ensured centralization of all human resources and administrative data for the use of Web browsers, namely organizational members whenever and wherever they want (Stone & Dulebohn, 2013). After digitalization of HR functions, HR data has become more available and disseminated in organizations.

With the help of electronic human resources management practices, various stakeholders in organizations such as employees, HR agents and managers can access to organizational data and human resources data timelier and easily (Berber, Dordevic, & Milanovic, 2018). E-HR speeds up HRM activities and contributes to more accurate and transparent transactions. In e-HR we can talk about full support and full reliance on web-based technologies in organizational setting. It is not merely the use of internet or computer in carrying out HR activities but also designing tasks and procedures incompatible with latest technologies. After e-HR adoption most companies reevaluate their task designs and processes and embrace more updated versions of their procedures that makes e-HR adoption easier and convenient. E-HR usage ensures more simplistic and more encompassing processes on all over organizations. After e-HR adoption many tools and portals are shared with various stakeholders that somehow has something to do with HR activities. For example, in order to share resumes collected from online e recruitment portal and online job posts with the related line managers. Online accounts are opened for each line manager in the organization. Having their own accounts and these line managers can filter applicants, can evaluate their short lists and can share their comments on these resumes with the related HR account manager. Or they can learn about new applicants quickly without getting any help from the related HR account manager. Thus, this fastens daily activities of both HR department and the other functional departments.

Moreover, e-HR can result in more dedicated and more satisfying HR professionals with considerable heightened customer focus (Ruel et al., 2004). This heightened focus is mostly seemed to be valid for internal customers, namely organizational members. After embracing e-HR, human resources professionals earn the opportunity to act as internal coaches or consultants to the departments that they are responsible for. Being available each time an organizational member wants to reach, being more transparent and informing, an HR agent would create the perception of a friendly strategic partner that can act as an interior consultant. As it is known by almost all HR professionals having a close contact with employee and being in touch with them constantly will make the HR agent more reliable in the eyes of organizational members. Good relationships with the rest of the company will empower HR agents and will make it easy for them to get information from different segments of the organization. The information obtained through good relationship with organizational members will create a mutual understanding between the parts and will lead parties to act in accordance with each other's interests. Both the HR professional and the employees will cooperate in doing business in order to benefit from their mutually nourishing relationship.

Automating human resources management function is about transforming the classical paper-and-pencil, labor-intensive human resources function, into more efficient, more fast-response and more effective functions enabling organizations to expect and benefit from environmental changes creating competitive advantage (Olivas-Lujan, Ramirez, & Zapata-Cantu, 2007). That is to say, human resources function is converted to a strategic tool making organizations more adaptable, flexible and competitive structure benefiting from highest human resources technologies, web based human resources applications and computer programs. These applications are helpful in accommodating daily routines to strategic goals of the organization in a user-friendly manner. By adapting newest Technologies to human resources management function, companies learn and embrace more about latest improvement in human resources realm and they can successfully integrate these improvements to the other functions in the organization. For example, a modern recruitment system will market the company better candidates more quickly compared to their rivals and sophisticated orientation and training modules will make these new employees better adopt to the organizational realities and processes which will make the organization more successful in the long run.

Moreover, e-HR is also effective on the development of capabilities of human resources professional in the organizations that embraced it. In this point, Bell, Lee, & Young (2006) applied a study on senior HR professionals from 19 Fortune 500 companies with the aim of examining the relationships between eHR and the reshaping of HR professionals' competences. Results of the study showed that, e-HR adoption necessitates higher skills in adapting HR practices and strategic competence to the organization. These requirements create a synthesis of HR professionals' expertise in Human resources functions and their business knowledge regarding their organizations' business. Moreover, latest e-HR tools necessitate technical knowledge and some technological knowhow in order to be able to benefit from them. An HR professional that does not know how to get use of this technological applications and tools cannot be successful in carrying out his daily tasks.

Moreover, e-HR is effective on individual productivity in organizations. Generally, companies utilize HRM technologies with the aim of boosting employee productivity (CedarCrestone, 2013). Since, e-HRM creates possibilities of enhancing individual's capabilities in organizations, giving way to improved employee productivity (Bissola & Imperatori, 2013). For example, in a company using e-career management module, everyone should learn the technical details of the system in order to get benefit from it. Or in an organization wherein e-coaching system is prevalent, more organizational members can benefit from the coaching service compared to the case that is seen where classical coaching methodologies are embraced. e-HRM has the potential to boost productivity by increasing automation and by changing low-value processes with high value-added tasks (Marler & Parry, 2016). This increase in productivity also comes about through quick, updated, and reliable data that managers can get from the system in order to make appropriate decisions. Specifically, operational e-HRM tools increase productivity of companies by streamlining classical HR practices, speeding up processes and reducing headcounts (Parry, 2011). In fact, e-HRM has the potential to reduce costs and save organizational members' time by letting them carry out more transactions with fewer fixed costs" and, thus, improving employee productivity (Hendrickson, 2003). Supporting this view Ruel, Bondarouk, and Van der Velde (2007) applied a study. In their study in the Ministry of Internal Affairs in The Netherlands, wherein e-HR was used Ruel, Bondarouk, and Van der Velde (2007) examined whether e-HRM is useful for organizations. Results of their study showed that HRM perceived as technically and strategically effective. Especially perceived quality of the e-HR Services and the structure of e-HR applications have found to be perceived effective by individuals.

SOLUTIONS AND RECOMMENDATIONS

As discussed above, e-HR has the potential to lower Human resources transaction costs thus, the number of people working in human resources department. For instance, by supplying human resources information to several people on a basis e-HR is conceived as an economic way of doing business in HR department. It is a good alternative for re-using information on an infinite number of occasions at little costs. For instance, by e-training large numbers of people can benefit from a specific learning module or training program. Once the company pays for that program in the beginning afterwards many people can use it with little costs. Or once a career portal is established all the personnel can benefit from the portal without creating an expense for the HR department. Furthermore, with the help of e-HR companies may build effective customer relationships both with the internal and external customers (Martin & Reddington, 2010). It increases the frequency and richness of both internal and external communication with the related parts. These improved flows of information are mostly witnessed during e-recruitment process, e-career development and e-performance appraisal. Moreover, e-HR can change the strategic focus of the HR department. With e-HR transformation of classical HR approach to a business model that is more value-focused is possible. E-HR creates more strategic HR departments supporting flexible organizational structures, remote working opportunities, holistic performance management systems and strategic goal tracing.

Organizations with considerably challenging strategic goals, often require unique HR functions privileging transformational goals that spare time for human resources personnel to address strategic issues. Through e-HR transformation, human resources department can provide the necessary means for changing its business model. These attempts range from extending human resource functions to reach all over the organization with the aim of creating a sense of corporateness. This can be achieved by internal integration through human resources portals. On the one hand, the use of more sophisticated recruitment tools, utilizing deep learning through online interactions with potential candidates; increasing the organizational IQ through organizational learning; using technology-based communication tools and creating higher levels of work–life balance through remote and virtual working can ease e-HR integration and make e-HR usage easier (Florkowski & Olivas-Lujan 2006).

According to Schalk et al. (2013), for e-HR to be successful regarding strategic goals, strategic considerations should be considered in HRM decision-making processes. All the goals regarding e-HR should be compatible with the strategic goals of the organization. For example; in a company wherein a cost-reduction strategy has been embraced, adopting new career portals with huge costs would be unmeaningful. It would be more strategy-friendly if the human resources department can solve this requirement with the inner sources like their own IT department. In fact, strategy alignment should be on all over the company especially encompassing critic departments such as human resources management that has very important strategic goal on the lives of employees and managers. Many decisions taken in HR department can create considerable changes in the lives of organizational members. For instance, a company that embraced a strategic orientation towards internalization may prefer to adopt new recruitment that necessitates hiring new candidates that knows more than two foreign languages and giving importance to the knowledge of foreign language in promotions.

On the one hand, e-HR implications can also contribute to the creation of a learning organization. Feeling compelled to keep pace with latest technologies in e-HR companies can become more outwitted, more open-minded and more learning focused structures. Moreover, once the organization adopt a certain e-HR module, routine trainings and routine updates are needed in order to use the tool efficiently. So, companies, send their HR agents to trainings in order to make them benefit from the tools better. Or sometimes companies learn how to update and revise the tools on their own, which necessitates a serous learning process. Once organizations learn how to use and update these e-HR applications, users in the organizations start to teach the usage of this applications to the newcomers and make the learning process continuous. After a certain time, organizational members do not need any more external support regarding the usage of these computer-based tools.

To sum up, E-HR enables HR employees to focus on more strategic, value-added activities. With e-HR adoption, less administrative and paperwork lets the human resources staff to develop other, more strategic functions regarding their jobs. And through self-service, e-HR increase the involvement of employees and line managers in human resources practices (Moran & Anan, 2018). E-HR usage transform some routine tasks from human resources professionals to functional departments and their managers, making it unnecessary to hold too much staff in human resources department. Specifically, sharing operational tasks with related departments would lower the workload of human resources department. Thus, the human resources professionals can earn the opportunity to focus on more differentiated strategic tasks and becomes more and more professional in time.

FURTHER RESEARCH

Although we can talk about a growing body of literature regarding e-HR, it is still an under-theorized and under-explored realm of study (Strohmeier, 2007). And there is a scarcity of empirical study in this topic. This study attempted to have a contribution in filling this gap. In this study, the term e-HR has been explained in details and the use of e-HR in each HRM function has been handled separately with the aim of understanding its positive functional outputs. Moreover, the advantages of e-HR on the effectiveness and efficiency of HRM have been analyzed with a technology-based perspective. However, it will be meaningful to add an empirical research to this study in further studies will be more explanatory in making our assumption clearer regarding the use of e-HR in increasing positive HRM outputs and organizational outputs.

REFERENCES

Agrawal, A. (2017, March). *HRM Effectiveness through E-HRM*. In National Conference on "Contemporary Issues in Management & Entrepreneurship", jointly organized by The Confederation of Indian Industry.

Amara, N. B., & Atia, L. (2016). E-training and its role in human resources development. *Global Journal of Human Resource Management*, *4*(1), 1–12.

Aparicio, M., Bacao, F., & Oliveira, T. (2016). An e-learning theoretical framework. *Journal of Educational Technology & Society*, *19*(1), 292–307.

Araújo, S., & Ramos, A. (2002). *Recrutamento On-line: Estudo da Percepção de Utilização da Internet em Empresa de Consultoria de Recursos Humanos* [Online recruitment: Study of the perception of Internet use in a human resources consulting firm]. Curitibia, Brasil: ENEGEP.

Bell, B. S., Lee, S. W., & Yeung, S. K. (2006). The impact of e-HR on professional competence in HRM: Implications for the development of HR professionals. Human Resource Management: Published in Cooperation with the School of Business Administration, *The University of Michigan and in alliance with the Society of Human Resources Management*, *45*(3), 295-308.

Berber, N., Đorđević, B., & Milanović, S. (2018). Electronic human resource management (e-HRM): A new concept for digital age. *Strategic Management*, *23*(2), 22–32.

Bhatnagar, J., & Sharma, A. (2005). The Indian perspective of strategic HR roles and organizational learning capability. *International Journal of Human Resource Management*, *16*(9), 1711–1739.

Bissola, R., & Imperatori, B. (2013). Facing e-HRM: E consequences on employee attitude towards the organisation and the HR department in Italian SMEs. *European Journal of International Management*, *7*(4), 450–468.

Brandão, C., Silva, R., & dos Santos, J. V. (2019). Online recruitment in Portugal: Theories and candidate profiles. *Journal of Business Research*, *94*, 273–279.

Chen, H., & Tseng, H. (2012). Factors That Influence Acceptance of Web-Based E-Learning System for the in-Service Education of Junior High School Teachers in Taiwan. *Evaluation and Program Planning*, *35*(3), 398–406. PMID:22321703

Dulebohn, J. H., & Marler, J. H. (2005). E-Compensation: The Potential to Transform Practice. In Greutal, & Stone (Eds.), The Brave New World of e-HR (166-189). San Francisco, CA: Jossey-Bass.

Esterhuyse, M., & Scholtz, B. (2016). The Intention to Use e-Learning in Corporations. In CONF-IRM (p. 12).

Faliagka, E., Tsakalidis, A., & Tzimas, G. (2012). An integrated e-recruitment system for automated personality mining and applicant ranking. *Internet Research*, *22*(5), 551–568.

Florkowski, G. W., & Olivas-Luján, M. R. (2006). The diffusion of human-resource information-technology innovations in US and non-US firms. *Personnel Review*, *35*(6), 684–710.

Hannigan, T. (2015). Close encounters of the conceptual kind: Disambiguating social structure from text. *Big Data & Society*, *2*(2), 1–6.

Hendrickson, A. R. (2003). Human resource information systems: Backbone technology of contemporary human resources. *Journal of Labor Research*, *24*(3), 381–394.

Iqbal, N., Ahmad, M., Raziq, M. M., & Borini, F. M. (2019). Linking e-hrm practices and organizational outcomes: Empirical analysis of line manager's perception. *Revista Brasileira de Gestão de Negócios*, *21*(1), 48–69.

Jackson, C. B., Quetsch, L. B., Brabson, L. A., & Herschell, A. D. (2018). Web-based training methods for behavioral health providers: A systematic review. *Administration and Policy in Mental Health*, 1–24. PMID:29352459

Kasprisin, C. A., Single, P. B., Single, R. M., & Muller, C. B. (2003). Building a better bridge: Testing e-training to improve e-mentoring programmes in higher education. *Mentoring & Tutoring*, *11*(1), 67–78.

Lazazzara, A., & Galanaki, E. (2018). E-HRM Adoption and Usage: A Cross-National Analysis of Enabling Factors. In *Digital Technology and Organizational Change* (pp. 125–140). Cham, Switzerland: Springer.

Lengnick-Hall, M. L., & Moritz, S. (2003). The impact of e-HR on the human resource management function. *Journal of Labor Research*, *24*(3), 365–379.

Marler, J. H., & Parry, E. (2016). Human resource management, strategic involvement and e-HRM technology. *International Journal of Human Resource Management*, *27*(19), 2233–2253.

Martin, G., & Reddington, M. (2010). Theorizing the links between e-HR and strategic HRM: A model, case illustration and reflections. *International Journal of Human Resource Management*, *21*(10), 1553–1574.

Mohsin, M., & Sulaiman, R. (2013). A Study on e-Training Adoption for Higher Learning Institutions. *International Journal of Asian Social Science*, *3*(9), 2006–2018.

Olivas-Lujan, M. R., Ramirez, J., & Zapata-Cantu, L. (2007). e-HRM in Mexico: Adapting innovations for global competitiveness. *International Journal of Manpower*, *28*(5), 418–434.

Omran, K., & Anan, N. (2018). Studying the impact of using E-HRM on the effectiveness of HRM practices: An exploratory study for the internet service providers (ISP) in Egypt. *International Journal of Academic Research in Business and Social Sciences*, *8*(4), 458–492.

Parry, E. (2011). An examination of e-HRM as a means to increase the value of the HR function. *International Journal of Human Resource Management*, *22*(5), 1146–1162.

Parry, E., & Tyson, S. (2011). Desired goals and actual outcomes of e-HRM. *Human Resource Management Journal*, *21*(3), 335–354.

Petre, A., Osoian, C., & Zaharie, M. (2016). Applicants' perceptions on online recruitment. *Managerial Challenges of the Contemporary Society*, *9*(1), 63–67.

Platanou, K., Mäkelä, K., Beletskiy, A., & Colicev, A. (2018). Using online data and network-based text analysis in HRM research. *Journal of Organizational Effectiveness: People and Performance*, *5*(1), 81–97.

Riahi, G. (2015). E-learning systems based on cloud computing: A review. *Procedia Computer Science*, *62*, 352–359.

Rothwell, W. J., Jackson, R. D., Knight, S., & Lindholm, J. (2005). *Career Planning and Succession Management: Developing Your Organization's Talent-for Today and Tomorrow*. Westport, CT: Greenwood Publishing Group.

Ruël, H., Bondarouk, T., & Looise, J. K. (2004). E-HRM: Innovation or irritation. An explorative empirical study in five large companies on web-based HRM. *Management Review*, 364–380.

Ruel, H. J., Bondarouk, T. V., & Van der Velde, M. (2007). The contribution of e-HRM to HRM effectiveness: Results from a quantitative study in a Dutch Ministry. *Employee Relations*, *29*(3), 280–291.

Schalk, R., Timmerman, V., & Van den Heuvel, S. (2013). How strategic considerations influence decision making on e-HRM applications. *Human Resource Management Review*, *23*(1), 84–92.

Stone, D. L., & Dulebohn, J. H. (2013). Emerging issues in theory and research on electronic human resource management (eHRM).

Strohmeier, S. (2007). Research in e-HRM: Review and Implications. *Human Resource Management Review*, *17*, 19–37.

Strohmeier, S., & Kabst, R. (2009). Organizational adoption of e-HRM in Europe: An empirical explanation of major adoption factors. *Journal of Managerial Psychology*, *24*(6), 482.

Swaroop, K. R. (2012). E-HRM and how it will reduce the Cost in Organization. *Asia Pacific Journal of Marketing & Management Review*, *1*(4), 133–139.

Sylva, H., & Mol, S. T. (2009). E-recruitment: A study into applicant perceptions of an online application system. *International Journal of Selection and Assessment*, *17*(3), 311–323. doi:10.1111/j.1468-2389.2009.00473.x

Teo, T. S. H., Lim, G. S., & Fedric, S. A. (2007). The adoption and diffusion of human resources information systems in Singapore. *Asia Pacific Journal of Human Resources*, *45*, 44–62.

Thite, M., & Kavanagh, M., & Johnson, R. D. (2009). Evolution of human resource management and human resource information systems: the role of information technology. In M. Thite, M. Kavanagh, & R. D. Johnson (Eds.), *Evolution of human resource management and human resource information systems*.

Voermans, M., & van Veldhoven, M. J. P. M. (2007). Attitude towards E-HRM: An empirical study at Philips. *Personnel Review*, *36*(6), 887–902.

Welsh, E. T., Wanberg, C. R., Brown, K. G., & Simmering, M. J. (2003). E-learning: Emerging uses, empirical results and future directions. *International Journal of Training and Development*, *7*(4), 245–258.

Zainab, B., Awais Bhatti, M., & Alshagawi, M. (2017). Factors affecting e-training adoption: An examination of perceived cost, computer self-efficacy and the technology acceptance model. *Behaviour & Information Technology, 36*(12), 1261–1273.

KEY TERMS AND DEFINITIONS

E-Compensation: The use computer-based and web-based technologies for planning employees' compensation.

E-HR: Electronic Human Resources, Use of web-based computer technologies in carrying on HRM tasks.

E-Mentoring: The kind of menoring method wherein mentor and mentee meet through internet.

E-Performance Appraisal: Pursuing the necessary steps of performance appraisal process on online performance portals.

E-Recruitment: Using online portals for selection and recruitment, attracting applicants through online career portals or corporate websites.

E-Training: Using online learning modules for training staff.

This research was previously published in Tools and Techniques for Implementing International E-Trading Tactics for Competitive Advantage; pages 268-286, copyright year 2020 by Business Science Reference (an imprint of IGI Global).

Chapter 13
Identifying Innovations in Human Resources:
Academia and Industry Perspectives

Amrik Singh

(iD) https://orcid.org/0000-0003-3598-8787
Lovely Professional University, Punjab, India

Sanjeev Kumar
Lovely Professional University, Punjab, India

ABSTRACT

HR is evolving into a more technology-based profession because organizations needs to streamline HR processes and reduce administrative burden, reducing administrative cost; compete more effectively with global talent; improve services and access data to the employees and managers; provide real-time metrics in order tom on spot decisions for the decision makers; and manage the workforce more effectively and enable the HR to transform so it can play more strategic role in the business and operations. The purpose of this chapter is to develop a meaningful debate on the innovations in human resource in terms of new ideas, methods, and technology to better meet the evolving requirement of the organization and workforce. Anticipating and exploring the future needs and circumstances rather than simply finding some responses to the situation, this chapter highlights challenges and prospects related to innovations in HR.

INTRODUCTION

To maintained the long relationship and survive in the globe new innovations should bring in the organization for the development of new culture and traditions. Creativity plays an important role of competitive advantage of business organization. Researchers suggested, for long term survival organization creativity makes an important role to organizational effectiveness, because it prepare to organization achieve a competitive advantage in a rapidly changing environment. It is the prime duty of HR department to build up healthy relationship with employee in term of creativity and achieve the organizational goal. Hr

DOI: 10.4018/978-1-6684-3873-2.ch013

department using various new tool and software where they can store all the details of employees and give excess to their employee where employee get the information without wasting the time and that time can be utilized in the operations to increase the output of the organization. The local government fulfills the requirements of the society and increasing the value of life, Organization play an important role of creativity bringing life through inventive, customer desires creating job for contributing to the economy (Ambardar & Singh, 2017). HR applies more effective practices and cut down the problems. These are the three dimension of innovative Human Resource Practice (IHRPs). (Ambardar & Singh, 2017; Ruël, Bondarouk, & Looise, 2004). The term Human resource management (HRM) is used widely but defined very slackly. HRM have different policies related to employee benefits and increase the employee commitment, Quality of work, flexibility and organizational integration. Furthermore some of the UK organization applies to this model and many are moving slowly to apply this model for example policies of employee involvement. Robotic Process Automation (RPA) grows up to 200 billion US Dollar in next four year, because more than fortune 1000 companies adopting it (Papageorgiou, 2018) . Human opted for innovation and improvement since the beginning time and progress was slow until the Industrial revolution. When each industry breach was adopted by others, the first attempt at automation was started.

Innovation Tool Used by HRM

According to Homer, "Inspiration is a muse, and innovation seeds can often be found in the most unexpected places." forward to 2018.Today many innovations like information technology (IT), artificial intelligence (AI), machine learning, chatbots and RPA. Innovation speed, variety and volume continuous changing across the world and interact each other professionally. But these changes have not supported to human resources benefits function. In business digitalization process HR is once in lifetime opportunity to be strategic and integrating the business. Changing the workforce to purpose based employment, which is task and skill based employment in past (Geer Jr, Tumblin, & Solomon, 2001; Papageorgiou, 2018; Schraft & Schlaich, 1988). Automation technology depends on use, misuse, disuse and abuse.

Advance Bio-Metric machines use for the marking of attendance which will help to cut the time of HR department which provide accurate data and up to date information. The factor of human use of automation can improve effective training method, system design and judicious policy linking automation use (Parasuraman & Riley, 1997; Sheridan, 1992) . Customers support centers reliance on our agents who acquire skills for that is being delivered. There are many skill requirements in call centre like good speech of that language which is speaking on telephone. Other skill is knowledge of computer i.e. knowledge of keyboard, monitor and internet and other electronic devices. When receiving the call customer support agent speak language well, perform the assign task, giving the right information and speaking sound delightful when speaking customer. A method for screening applicants, the customer is asked, via the company web page, to giving responses to a set of question customized to the screening body and responses to the queries are stored and the process of meeting with customer and support is started on telephone and computer (Schalk, Stovall, & Brooks, 2011).

Challenge Faced by HRD

These are the challenge of twenty-first century management. The first challenge to structure companies that can "change as fast as the world around us" says Hamel and Denial, the lack of capacity to innovation of new options which is planned and shares strongly. The second challenge were hardly distributed to ability of innovation instead of old mental method and inadequate respect for testing, are seen as major barrier. The third challenge are "too much management, too little discretion", "too much hierarchy, too little community" and "too much exhortation, too little purpose." These three challenges are mutually dependent. The third challenge is solving to key the other challenge. A latest survey of 8600 employee in different organization found less than 15 percent of employee engaged in their job and quarter was totally disengaged, prompting the researcher to offer "hierarchy of human capabilities". Value creation in terms of contribution is ascending order these are intellect, creativity, diligence, obedience and passion, these are obedience, diligence, intellect, initiative, creativity and passion. Later it is find out intellect, diligence and obedience, is fast becoming global commodities, while company differentiate capabilities with the greatest potential like initiative, creativity and passion, benefit give or withhold to employee day to day and moment by moment. These process are creating a kind of organizational model that will deserve gifts is critical management challenge. For better results organizational apply new management principal in any organizational model. It is not complete example of future best practices. But this is a leading effort at Whole Food Markets, Google and WL Gore. Food retailing sector is one of the fast growing market in USA. USA company give proposal to customer that people give high price for organic and locally food. It is difficult to find 3 companies to offer these products, In this situation company its own way is a modern management pioneer. Taken together they help to underline how radical deviations from management orthodoxy can have a significant commercial impact.

There are 3 key principal to improve the chance of achieving radical management system by Hamel

- For finding the new long standing management approach that restrict creative thinking to adopting a disciplined approach
- Management give power to apply new idea, and
- Capitalizing on insights drawn from the practices of "positive deviants".

Management is a science; it is defining that "positions us toward new truths." Hamal says "Modern management is based on hierarchy, specialization, planning standardization, control, goal and alignment". These are maximizing operational competence in huge scale organization and this is "modern management is fully competent to address. "When it comes to the challenge of how to create organizations that are highly adaptable and appealing, these philosophies are "insufficient and often toxic." So management look new option? According to Hamel there are five subject and literature i.e life, market, faith, democracy, and cities. Life refers to principal of diversity, from market approach refers to flexibility, democracy built up activism, faith gives meaning and cities approaches furnish providence. New Urbanists thinker like Richard Florida and Jane Jacobs, how great cities contribute to generation of "new pools of economic use" through enabling different man to meet and find out opportunities to trade information, goods and ideas, and how, at least in part, cities are "able to reinvent themselves because they make it easy for individuals to reinvent themselves." Great cities also explain us how to arrange for serendipity. Few have dedicated to reinventing their management process while businesses have worked vast to reinventing their HR process. The exception is General Electric, Procter & Gamble and Whirlpool, but it is true internet, the "most flexible, innovative and engaging thing that human beings have created" and in several ways "the new technology of management" because it distribute the path of creativity widely, ideal allow to race on equal track, decentralize everything, freedom of voice to everyone and encourage resources to follow opportunities (Andresen et al., 2002; Hamel, 2008; Noe, Hollenbeck, Gerhart, & Wright, 2017; Panigrahy & Pradhan, 2015; Papageorgiou, 2018; Schraft &

Schlaich, 1988; Walke, 2013). HRM practices power to do financial performance positively; there is a certain reason for expectant them to positive innovation performance. We examine the empirical model through its all hypothesis using 1900 business firms which survey conducted by Danish using principal component analysis. We find out two HRM systems which are conductive to innovative. Researcher examine 9 variables, first variable is equal for the ability to innovative. Second variable is firm internal and firm external training. We have correlate with first system to observing four manufacturing sectors and seconds are five wholesale trade and to the ICT intensive service sectors correlate with the second systems (Laursen & Foss, 2003).

REVIEW OF LITERATURE

Strategic human resource management (SHRM) focuses on to build up strong relationship among individual motivation and their performance.(Schuler, 1992) Various study were conducted on innovation in performance where academia and industry perspective point of view HR expand too much of efforts, time, resources and money. There are number of business theory has been adopting (Jussani, Krakauer, & Polo, 2010). As mentioned in the study that different types of innovation are applicable for different environments (Damanpour & Gopalakrishnan, 1998). In industry point of view HR department create different opportunities and competitive (Chan Kim & Mauborgne, 2005) as per 'Blue Ocean Strategy' it creates different innovation in the field of Academia. In the "Blue Ocean Strategy" which provides new market place, the chance of competition should be less which HY may be explores their idea in term of new innovations which create positive environment in the work place New strategic followed in innovation by the HR give positive results and make organization profitable (Jussani et al., 2010) Invention itself create a positive environment in the organization which have high impact on economic (Serafim, 2011) Today's HR focus on corporate culture in the university and create positive environment among the staff and stakeholders (Araújo & Garcia, 2009) Integration and implementation of Corporate Education e.g promotional activities in the university and their work culture. HR brings various new innovations by giving training and development in the respected areas to meet the objective of the organization to provide positive direction towards the skills, abilities and attitude.(EBOLI, 2006) There are number of new applications of innovation Technologies introduced by the human resources management which can improve the quality and efficiency of the HR department. By introducing the new innovation practices in the academia and industry must get some advance internal and external information with their unique features in term of technologies (García-Carbonell, Martín-Alcázar, & Sánchez-Gardey, 2015) HRD focus on education sector by implementation of new trends followed by the Human Resource in term of recruitment of new staff and their orientation programme. Human Resources Management (HRM) performed various function in term of recruitment, training, remuneration and compensation, and legal issues (Joseph & Ezzedeen, 2009) Human resource management focus on modern techniques and latest trends in HR management practices for better results and performance system (Thom, Ritz, & Masiulis, 2004) A tremendous change has seen in the technology development and their smooth operations in globally. e-HRM's concepts introduced in the academia and industries which will help to reducing the number of task, solving the problems, cut down the administrative cost and increase the efficiency of the work and bring the quality work where manager and employees become fully satisfied.(Analoui, 2007) "Improving organizational performance, managers and decision makers should make their HRM systems more visible, understandable, legitimate and relevant"(Katou, 2015) HR experts believes that it fulfill the needs of employees and these new innovation can also helps in administrative efficiency work, knowledge improving and better results which can build up the confidents (García-Carbonell et al., 2015) Researcher focus on the benefits of e-HRM (Ruël et al., 2004) improving the orientation of HRM, cut down the daily cost, increase the effectiveness, improvement in services and reduce the pressure of managers and employers.(Kavanagh & Johnson, 2017) The key criteria that must be taken in to account for successful innovation through business environment and capacity building analysis (Navin, Navimipour, Rahmani, & Hosseinzadeh, 2014)

In the globalization era, HR must be artistic and promote the culture of creativity by tapping the competency. Different studies proved that creativity makes an important contribution to increase the effectiveness of the organization. Human Resource act as a middleman to facilitate and communicate and achieve the objectives of organization. In a dynamic environment with rapid globalization and advances in science & technology, "creativity" & "innovation" play an important role for long-term development and sustainability (Vveinhardt & Andriukaitiene, 2016) Innovation requires managing flexibility-control tensions. Today innovation found one of the important significant tools which increase the efficiency of the work (Panigrahy & Pradhan, 2015)

Employee behavior leads the organization in the positive direction and to show the involvement in day to day activities (Hartmann, 2006) Organizational culture consider one of the major component which can stimulate the behavior of employee in the organization (Nacinovic, Galetic, & Cavlek, 2009) Creative Innovation help the supportive cultures which will fulfill the expectation of employee and their moral (Khazanchi, Lewis, & Boyer, 2007) "The intentional introduction and application of ideas, processes, products or procedures which are new and benefit to the job, the work team or the organization" (Ying, 2006) innovation have different steps which includes different idea in term of evaluation, development, tasks orientation and their growth (Panigrahy & Pradhan, 2015) Creativity in the innovation provide new direction to organization which fulfill demand of the employer (Woodman, Sawyer, & Griffin, 1993). HR automation always facilitates the processes and procedure in any organization. Every organization use variety of software such as ECM (Enterprise Content Management) which reduces the time taken for completion of tasks. An organization uses this software to capture, store, retrieve and secure information. Followings are the some HR tasks which are rapidly moving toward automated:

1. **Employes Record Management:** Retaining employees records as per government regulations in the depository.
2. **Employee Recruitment:** Automatically store application submitted through online forms into ECM repository and assigning them to a recruiter for review.
3. **Employee Onboarding:** Send some confidentiality agreements, waivers and other forms to new hires and once completed send them to corresponding folder.
4. **Benefits:** Track when employees become eligible for benefits.
5. **Health and Safety:** Sending emails to floor monitors when employees leave the organization or move to the other floor.
6. **Tax Forms:** Facilitate the distribution of W2s employees and other tax documents with employees email reminders.

Increasingly technology has a profound impact on HRM. As technology evolves it will also reforms to take new contours in both its processes and practices. HRIS also emerged as in response to the need of change to be carried out in most fruitful way considering the improved accuracy the quick access to information, the increased competitiveness and efficiency and re-engineer of the HR functions. In this fast changing competitive globalized market place innovation has become the essential factor for any organization to achieve success.

THE CHALLENGES AHEAD

Changing Role of HR

To meet the requirements of the organization the HR professionals need to play variety of roles. Traditionally the HR department had limited involvement in the organizational affairs and goals. The functioning is limited with making staffing plans, providing job training programs, running appraisal programs and payrolls. They only focus on the short term and day to day needs of the human resources. But this situation changed and the growing importance of the HR function to the success of the business made them to be more involved in the business process. And the roles of HR department increased the involvement to the longer term and strategic directions of the organization. The changing roles of HRM are like, strategic role, monitoring role, innovator role, facilitator role, enabler role etc (Richard Wolfe, Patrick M . Wright, And Dennis L . Smart (2006); Rosalie L. Tung, Yongsun Paik, Johngseok Bae (2011); Rothwell, R. (1992); Rousseau, D.M. and Wade-Benzoni, K.A. (1994)

Strategic Role

The HR department and their professionals will get involved in the broader decision making process which will provide overall direction about the organization. And they need to understand the business direction in clear and act accordingly in order to achieve the strategic HRM. SHRM is proactive management technique for the people. This requires thinking ahead, and planning the ways for the organization to meet the needs of the employees, and for the employees to meet the needs of the organization. This can affect the way of HR department functioning by improving everything from hiring practices and employee training programs to assessment techniques and discipline (Richard et. al, 2006; Rosalie, 2011)

Monitoring Role

Reviewing and evaluating the strategic plan implemented by the organization to enhance the organizational capabilities will be the major role to the HR department in future. Were there will be more responsibilities to them regarding strategic monitoring and evaluate the process and diagnose the problems in it and determine the reasons for deficiencies. Then revised action plans with all changes will be implemented.

Innovator Role

The organizations are asking their HR department for innovative approaches and solutions to improve productivity and the quality of work life of the employees in order to overcome all uncertainties in the work place. In this changing world innovation become a necessity for all the organization to achieve their competitive advantage. HR departments face demands same as their organizations. In order to achieve their success they must continually update their operations and redesign the work environment. The HR department review & evaluate the expenses then implements incremental changes to become efficient and stay lean. Flexible HR departments forcefully seek to be liberated and setting an example for other departments and line organizations.

Facilitator Role

It is necessary for the organizations to adopt new technologies, change in organizational structures, business processes, work cultures, and procedures to meet the demands of the customers. HR department has the responsibility to provide skilled labors to facilitate organizational change, and maintain organizational flexibility and adaptability. The HR department plays a significant role in organizational change. And they should guide the discussion, flow of knowledge, information and learning throughout the organization in order to achieve success.

Enabler Role

HR policies and procedures are fully realized by the professional and they will act as the enabler to the employees and helps them to acquire knowledge and skills about the new technologies and processes, so that the employees can easily adapt to the change and make themselves more capable towards the organizational capabilities.

- **The War for Talent:** The talent will be corporate resource in future. Smart, sophisticate and technologically sharp employees will be top priority of any organisation. The traditional work force planning will be replaced by the talent strategies and the skill gap analysis. When the gap analysis is made then the HR department will have knowledge about the need of training and accordingly training can be given to the employees in order to enhance them technically efficient. And the HR department will follow the recruitment strategies like employment branding, nurturing relationships, referrals, competency fit etc. to acquire talented employees to the organization.

Future HR Innovations

In the globalisation era, to compete and sustain in a long run, a business establishment must be creative and foster the culture of creativity by tapping the competency of human resources. And in this business of uncertainty, risk and volatility, creativity plays an important function towards creating a competitive advantage for organizations (Panigrahy, Nrusingh & Pradhan, Rabindra. (2015).

- **Outsourcing of HR Functions:** The HR professionals are expected to deliver values in areas like strategic compensation activities, succession planning for employees, talent acquisition, risk mitigation, employee effectiveness and these are the key expectations by the top management. The reasons behind HR outsourcing is to reduce cost, focus more on the organizational functioning, regulatory compliance (legal risks are transferred to outsourcer and helps in obtaining expertise in specialized regulatory), access to best technologies and scarce of internal resources.
- **Healthy Workplace:** There is a link between work environment, employee's health and well being. When the employees are sick and stressed out the organization cannot achieve its competitive advantage. The goal of healthy workplace development is not only for employees but also for

the organizational health and success. To achieve healthy workplace development the essentials drivers are, healthy leadership, planning the actions, employee focus and healthy outcomes. And the organization should focus on the employee's health in order to improve their performance the main factors to be considered are, physical, emotional, spiritual, mental and social feelings of the employees.

Diverse Workforce

Diversity in workplace has a reputation for acceptances of employees were they are different in religions, culture, beliefs, languages, customs and traditions. Diversity in workplace is a business strategy. Were the futures of workplace will be complex collection of employees and all with different needs and wants. Diversity is good because an organization with a broad variety of people with a diverse range of perspectives is better able to do business with a variety of people, to solve a variety of problems and to make a variety of decisions.

Technology Driven

Technology provides a great impact on the personal and professional lives. The technology is necessary for all the organization which travels towards success and those measures should reduce employee resistance to new technology and processes and ensure that steps are taken to provide support and education of the staff to cope with the underlying changes. The future of HRM will have drastic change in the process and approach to it. The concept of HRIS (Human resource information system) will be vanished and the organizations will develop their information system to improved employee relationship management.

Leadership Development

Leadership styles are not built through courses. It is an in born quality of the people which qualifies their character. But it needs some process to be followed for further development. Through "action learning" we can develop the leadership among the employees. Action leadership involves group of executives from various background who has strategic interests to solve the issues in the organization. Through enhancing the leadership among employees it helps in encouraging them and rewarding in risk taking. The vertical development (earned through individuals) should be focused well in order to increase their leadership efficiency. The challenges for organizations that wish to increase the vertical development of their leaders and cultures. And it helps in implementing the developmental concepts in the workplace.

Succession Planning

Succession planning will be focused more in future to identify and develop the internal employees to the top leadership positions of the organizations. It helps in increase the availability of the experienced and capable employees to the organization to achieve success. In simple terms succession planning will be focused on talent management concept which helps in identifying talented people for the job. The HR department will change to talent department in future which focus on getting young and new talents to the organization.

HRM Innovation in Context to Academia

The success of any educational institution is believed to rely mainly on the quality of its human resources and its consideration of human resource management as the heart of the educational administration (Jones & Walters, 1994). Higher education is an instrument for improving the social life of a nation. The quality of a civilization depends basically on the character of human being not on the physical equipment or the political machinery. The main task of education, especially higher education, is the improvement of this character. Higher education institutions have become more interested in implementing human resource management as a full strategic partner in their operations. Work life Report (1994) listed some factors that make human resource management a successful strategic partner. Some of the innovative trends identified in educational or higher institutions are:

1. **Employee Benefits:** Takes into account the benefits associated with health, dental, prescription medications, workers compensation, and other benefits related to the wellbeing of employees.
2. **Diversity and Respectful Workplace:** Includes policies, programs, and activities that promote a harmonious environment in the workplace, and show respect for individuals and their roles at the institution regardless of their distinguishing characteristics.
3. **Global Human Resources:** Complying with the rules and laws of the U.S. Immigration and Customs Enforcement Agency, as well as those in any country where an ex-patriot may reside.
4. **Human Resource Management:** Includes practical policies and processes on applicant selection and recruitment, development and training, employee relations, general management and records retention, and legal factors.
5. **Performance Metrics:** Includes comprehensive range of metrics in main human resource programme areas where data should be collected and analysed to explore trends and performance measures.
6. **Recruitment/Selection/Termination:** Includes procedures for acquiring, interviewing, and recruiting of quality employees, in addition to assuring minority recruiting. Moreover, procedures and policies for terminating the dismissal of employees (Jones & Walters, 1994).
7. **Risk Management, Safety, and Health:** Includes providing advices in occupational health, environmental protection, the areas of safety and risk management.
8. **Wage and Salary Administration:** Includes developing and adopting criteria for regulating compensation in a reasonable equitable manner (Jones & Walters, 1994).
9. Employee Compliance – Legal Matters – Includes assuring the compliance with all corresponding laws regulating the recruitment, management, and termination of employees.
10. Employee Relations – Labour Issues – Includes handling legal concerns of employees' contracts and negotiations, along with the establishing negotiation team and strategies (Jones & Walters, 1994).
11. **Information Systems and Technology:** Includes providing human resources focused technology to enhance the quality of services when recruiting, while maintaining compliance and empowering professional development and retention.
12. **Employee Leave and Holiday**: Includes non-work activities of employees by allowing paid or unpaid leisure, whether required by policy or designed by the employer.
13. **Payroll:** Includes the determination of compensation.
14. **Retirement:** Includes providing plans for retirement comprising analysis of plans and implementation procedures (Jones & Walters, 1994).

15. **Training and Development:** Includes providing training and development programmes that meet the employees' needs.

In an attempt to identify the best practices, human resource professionals, and experts have spent a lot of efforts for validating human resource strategies and policies. The best practices of human resource management could be defined as those functions that evidently promote human and financial performances (Hafford & Moore, 2005). The purposeful cycle of development of information technology as innovation implementation can lead to the effective application of information technology (Bilevičienė, Bilevičiūtė & Paražinskaitė, 2015).

CONCLUSION

Many researchers have suggested that creativity makes an important contribution to organizational effectiveness for the long-term survival of organizations, because it enables organizations to remain competitive in a rapidly changing environment and achieve a competitive advantage. Thus, encouraging and fostering creativity is a strategic choice of every successful organization. In this competitive business world every organization whether academia or industry is in the need of develops their operational activities in order to sustain in the market. There are emerging trends or innovations to be followed in HRM to improve their efficiency in providing innovational activities in the organization. So HR department increasingly adopt open innovation models and engage with external knowledge sources and they want to bring new groups into the innovation process. This leads for dedicated training of employees, new performance indicators, new rewards, new ways of communicating with and between employees etc., The HRM innovations followed in the organization will have positive influence on the innovation performance among the employees and brings great impact in development. By 2050 the business world will have drastic changes in its functioning. The changes in the technology, global economy, increasing ability scrutiny, threatening talent crisis and the mental illness of the employees are drastically affecting the workplace. These changes will have great impact on the business environment. The best organizations with the sustained innovation derive success towards the competition.

REFERENCES

Ambardar, A., & Singh, A. (2017). Quality of Work Life Practices in Indian Hotel Industry. *International Journal of Hospitality and Tourism Systems, 10*(1), 22.

Analoui, F. (2007). *Strategic Human Resource Management, Thomson Learning.* Ashgate.

Andresen, J., Baldwin, A., Betts, M., Carter, C., Hamilton, A., Stokes, E., & Thorpe, T. (2002). A framework for measuring IT innovation benefits. *Journal of Information Technology in Construction, 5*(4), 57–72.

Araújo, L. C. G. d., & Garcia, A. A. (2009). Gestão de pessoas: estratégias e integração organizacional. Academic Press.

Bilevičienė, T., Bilevičiūtė, E., & Paražinskaitė, G. (2015). Innovative Trends in Human Resources Management. *Economia e Sociologia*, *8*(4), 94–109. doi:10.14254/2071-789X.2015/8-4/7

Chan Kim, W., & Mauborgne, R. (2005). *Blue Ocean Strategy: How to create uncontested market space and make the competition irrelevant*. Harvard Business Review Press.

Damanpour, F., & Gopalakrishnan, S. (1998). Theories of organizational structure and innovation adoption: The role of environmental change. *Journal of Engineering and Technology Management*, *15*(1), 1–24. doi:10.1016/S0923-4748(97)00029-5

EBOLI. (2013). Educação Corporativa Desenvolvendo a Excelência Profissional e Organizacional. *AGANP Proceedings, Goiânia*.

García-Carbonell, N., Martín-Alcázar, F., & Sánchez-Gardey, G. (2015). Determinants of top management's capability to identify core employees. *BRQ Business Research Quarterly*, *18*(2), 69–80. doi:10.1016/j.brq.2014.07.002

Geer, D. E., Jr., Tumblin, H. R., & Solomon, E. M. (2001). Enabling business transactions in computer networks. Google Patents.

Hafford, J. C., & Moore, J. E. (2005). *Sourcing Best Practices in Human Resources*. SHRM white paper.

Hamel, G. (2008). The future of management. *Human Resource Management International Digest*, *16*(6), hrmid.2008.04416fae.001. doi:10.1108/hrmid.2008.04416fae.001

Hartmann, A. (2006). The role of organizational culture in motivating innovative behaviour in construction firms. *Construction Innovation*, *6*(3), 159–172. doi:10.1108/14714170610710712

Joseph, R. C., & Ezzedeen, S. R. (2009). E-government and e-HRM in the public sector. In Encyclopedia of Human Resources Information Systems: Challenges in e-HRM (pp. 272-277). IGI Global. doi:10.4018/978-1-59904-883-3.ch041

Jussani, A. C., Krakauer, P. V. C., & Polo, E. F. (2010). Reflexões sobre a estratégia do oceano azul: Uma comparação com as estratégias de Ansoff, Porter e Hax & Wilde. *Future Studies Research Journal: Trends and Strategies*, *2*(2), 17–37.

Katou, A. A. (2015). The mediating effects of psychological contracts on the relationship between human resource management systems and organisational performance. *International Journal of Manpower*, *36*(7), 1012–1033. doi:10.1108/IJM-10-2013-0238

Kavanagh, M. J., & Johnson, R. D. (2017). *Human resource information systems: Basics, applications, and future directions*. Sage Publications.

Khazanchi, S., Lewis, M. W., & Boyer, K. K. (2007). Innovation-supportive culture: The impact of organizational values on process innovation. *Journal of Operations Management*, *25*(4), 871–884. doi:10.1016/j.jom.2006.08.003

Laursen, K., & Foss, N. J. (2003). New human resource management practices, complementarities and the impact on innovation performance. *Cambridge Journal of Economics*, *27*(2), 243–263. doi:10.1093/cje/27.2.243

Nacinovic, I., Galetic, L., & Cavlek, N. (2009). Corporate culture and innovation: Implications for reward systems. *World Academy of Science, Engineering and Technology, 53*, 397–402.

Navin, A. H., Navimipour, N. J., Rahmani, A. M., & Hosseinzadeh, M. (2014). Expert grid: New type of grid to manage the human resources and study the effectiveness of its task scheduler. *Arabian Journal for Science and Engineering, 39*(8), 6175–6188. doi:10.100713369-014-1256-7

Noe, R. A., Hollenbeck, J. R., Gerhart, B., & Wright, P. M. (2017). *Human resource management: Gaining a competitive advantage.* McGraw-Hill Education New York.

Panigrahy, P., & Pradhan, K. (2015). *Creativity and innovation: Exploring the role of HR practices at workplace.* Paper presented at the Presentation of Paper at National Conference organized by Ravenshaw B-School, Cuttack.

Papageorgiou, D. (2018). Transforming the HR function through robotic process automation. *Benefits Quarterly, 34*(2), 27–30.

Parasuraman, R., & Riley, V. (1997). Humans and automation: Use, misuse, disuse, abuse. *Human Factors, 39*(2), 230–253. doi:10.1518/001872097778543886

Rothwell, R. (1992). Successful industrial innovation: Critical success factors for the 1990"s. *R & D Management, 22*(3), 221–239. doi:10.1111/j.1467-9310.1992.tb00812.x

Rousseau, D. M., & Wade-Benzoni, K. A. (1994). Linking strategy and human resource practices: How employee and customer contacts are created. *Human Resource Management, 33*(3), 436–489. doi:10.1002/hrm.3930330312

Ruël, H., Bondarouk, T., & Looise, J. K. (2004). E-HRM: Innovation or irritation. An explorative empirical study in five large companies on web-based HRM. *Management Review*, 364–380.

Schalk, T. B., Stovall, J. L., & Brooks, W. P. (2011). *Multi-modal automation for human interactive skill assessment.* Google Patents.

Schraft, R.-D., & Schlaich, G. (1988). A survey of the assembly of wire harnesses in industry. *Assembly Automation, 8*(1), 29–32. doi:10.1108/eb004230

Schuler, R. S. (1992). Strategic human resources management: Linking the people with the strategic needs of the business. *Organizational Dynamics, 21*(1), 18–32. doi:10.1016/0090-2616(92)90083-Y

Serafim, L. (2011). *O Poder da Inovação: a experiência da 3m e de outras empresas Inovadoras.* Saraiva.

Sheridan, T. B. (1992). *Telerobotics, automation, and human supervisory control.* MIT press.

Thom, N., Ritz, A., & Masiulis, K. (2004). Viešoji vadyba: inovaciniai viešoji sektoriaus valdymo metmenys. Verlag der Rechtswissenschaftlichen Universität Litauen.

Tung, R. L., Paik, Y., & Bae, J. (2011, January). Korean HRM in the global context. *International Journal of Human Resource Management, 22*(2), 481–482. doi:10.1080/09585192.2011.543315

Vveinhardt, J., & Andriukaitiene, R. (2016). Model of establishment of the level of management culture for managerial decision making with the aim of implementing corporate social responsibility. *Transformations in Business & Economics*, 15.

Walke, S. G. (2013). *Critical study of agritourism industry in Maharashtra*. Academic Press.

Wolfe, R., Wright, P. M., & And Dennis, L. S. (2006, Spring). Radical Hrm Innovation And Competitive Advantage: The Moneyball Story. *Human Resource Management, 45*(1), 111–145. doi:10.1002/hrm.20100

Woodman, R. W., Sawyer, J. E., & Griffin, R. W. (1993). Toward a theory of organizational creativity. *Academy of Management Review, 18*(2), 293–321. doi:10.5465/amr.1993.3997517

Ying, S. (2006). *Creating Supportive Environment for Innovation: A Conceptual Model Study*. Academic Press.

This research was previously published in Transforming Human Resource Functions With Automation; pages 104-120, copyright year 2021 by Business Science Reference (an imprint of IGI Global).

Section 2
Development and Design Methodologies

Chapter 14
Legal Framework on the Implementation of the Human Resource Management Reforms in the Philippines After the Marcos Era Up to the Duterte Administration

Perfecto G. Aquino, Jr.
Duy Tan University, Vietnam

Revenio C. Jalagat Jr.
https://orcid.org/0000-0002-8878-3825
Al-Zahra College for Women, Oman

Mercia Selvia Malar Justin
Xavier Institute of Management and Entrepreneurship, India

ABSTRACT

This study is aimed at filling the gap and will discuss the overview of both the legal reform processes happening in the public sector of the Philippine government and of recent developments and challenges initiated by the Civil Service Commission of the Philippine government as its Central Personnel Agency. This chapter will cover the years commencing 1986 up to the present dispensation of the Duterte administration where the primary goal is to study and suggest the approaches to reforming the Civil Service system and its decision-making process. It also outlines the discourses on the reform of public service among educators and public officials in the Philippines. Then, it elaborates on the laws and institutional measures introduced for an effective public personnel administration system in the country. A documentary analysis on the successful practices of public personnel administration will be used to evolve on the possible steps/strategies to further enhance the delivery of personnel services of the government sector workforce in the Philippines.

DOI: 10.4018/978-1-6684-3873-2.ch014

INTRODUCTION

Understanding the Asian civil service system is still limited according to the study of Moon and Hwang (2013) where they focus their research in the Asia-Pacific countries taking into consideration the legal frameworks, size, recruitment, and supervision. These countries include industrialized countries such as Japan, Korea, Singapore, and Taiwan; Southeast Asian developing countries with Malaysia, Indonesia, Thailand, and the Philippines; and the socialist transitional countries that include China, Vietnam, and Cambodia. Their findings revealed that new initiatives were evident in socialist transitional countries and in Southeast Asian developing countries which include the country Philippines (Berman, 2010; Cheung, 2005; and, Kim, 2010). Moreover; the civil service system primarily ensures the application of the procedural features of human resource management such as performance management, recruitment, selection, compensation, professionalism, career development, requirement, culture, and ethics (Moon and Hwang, 2013).

Anchored on the status of the civil service system in the Asia Pacific countries, the culmination of the Civil Service Commission (CSC) can be traced back to 1900 under public law no. 5 known as an "Act for the establishment and maintenance of an efficient and honest civil service in the Philippine island" by the Second Philippine Commission. The first composition of the commission's structure was anchored on the civil service board of a chairperson, a secretary, and a chief examiner where it administered the civil service examinations and set the standards for the government service appointment. Previously, the commission was named Bureau of Civil Service which later converted in 1959 through the Republic Act (RA 2260) into CSC that transformed the structure from a bureau to a department. However; the 1973 constitution ratification was done to convert the commission into a constitutional body in 1975 whose function is to pioneer the commission as the central Human Resource (HR) agency of the government.

Since then, the CSC continuous to serve as a premier human resource institution that aspires to become a center of excellence globally for strategic resource and organizational development that constitutionally upholds integrity, efficiency, morale, progressiveness, responsiveness, and courtesy in civil service. Accompanying this vision is to showcase the commission's purpose of making every civil servant as servant hero along with its core values of love for God and country, integrity, and excellence. Today, CSC as a constitutional body is governed by three dignitaries: chairperson and two commissioners stationed at the central office, 16 regional directors assigned in 16 regions, and over one hundred field offices all over the country (Civil Service Commission, 2018). The main goal of this chapter is to investigate the present status of the legal frameworks governing the implementation of HRM reforms from Marcos Era to the Duterte Administration and to come up with viable and concrete solutions to reforming the civil service system and its decision-making processes. The sequence of this chapter starts with the legal reform process in transition from 1986 to the Duterte administration and followed by the documentary analysis on the Remarkable Achievement of CSC Law, Measures, Plans, and Programs, then strategizing the CSC's Human Resource Management for better personnel administration, and the conclusion of the chapter.

BACKGROUND

The year 1984 was crucial for the country Philippines as it was the end of the Marcos regime and the onset of Philippine democracy where her Excellency President Corazon Aquino was installed on February 25, 1986. Subsequently, the 1987 constitution provides CSC the mandate under Article IX-B and through Executive Order No. 292 known as the administrative code series of 1987 to give the right of government employees to self-organization and collective negotiation. This mandate has been instrumental in transitioning from the formerly dictatorship leadership to democratic leadership wherein freedom is emphasized including the public service sector. The gradual improvement had been experienced which can be termed as a paradigm shift in the services of the government sector in terms of efficiency and in dealing with the citizens' given excellence, accountability, and transparency. On the other hand, the drive to eradicate corruption was already considered a furious battle by the government since the creation of the Presidential Complaints and Actions Committee (PCAC) in 1950. However; efforts paved the way when PCAC has become a baseline and benchmark for service delivery improvement initiatives through the program called "Citizens First" in 1994 and, the "Public Service Delivery Audit" (PASADA) in 2003 to foster courtesy culture and response effectiveness between the government and the public.

The program often called in the Filipino language "*Mamamayan Muna, Hindi Mamaya Na*" (MMHMN) aimed to immediately respond to the problems encountered by citizens or clients pertaining primarily to the dissatisfaction of the services to any government agencies through complaints while instituting rewards to government employees who have demonstrated excellence in the service based from clients' report of very satisfactory service experience. The ultimate goal is to ensure customer satisfaction in everything that the government employees and officials do with a sense of responsibility and accountability as a call of duty. The MMHMN program which was later renamed as *Mamayan Muna* Program (MMP) through CSC Circular No. 6 dated February 17, 2006, has three major components which are: incorporating mechanisms that emphasized following daily work standards in public dealings, providing quick incentives or rewards for government employee service that upholds superior courtesy and dispatch, and, quick resolution to grievances against government employees who commit violations such as involvement in red tape, discourtesy, failure to respond clients quickly, etc.

On the other hand, PASADA is one of the government's responses to bureaucratic reforms of the CSC which aimed at evaluating the performance of frontline government employees systematically by undercover auditors who are deployed to test the quality of public services provided by government employees to the public. Also, the audit seeks to take into consideration the optimum performance and suggest methodologies and techniques to improve the level of frontline services based on the problems identified. It is for the best interest of the public and building public trust that PASADA was implemented and that the government units' operational efficiency will also improve.

The year 2007 marks the signing of the Republic Act No. 9485 known as the "Anti-Red Tape Act (ARTA) which is primarily designed to speed public service delivery as well as responding to the citizens' clamor for efficient and fast public service (RA 9485, 2007). The implementation of this act provides the power of the CSC to spearhead the transformation of public service by the government employee frontlines. Highlights of the provisions include the establishment of the citizen's charters to showcase the specific services of frontline government offices along with their work timelines; step-by-step procedures; fees and tariffs for services; documentary requirements; anti-fixer campaign; setting up of special lanes for pregnant women, elderly, persons with disabilities; and, observance of "no noon-break". To ensure quality implementation, CSC has directed the use of the Report Card Survey (RCS) and Client Satisfaction Survey (CSS) to all government agencies to evaluate their performance and gather sufficient evidence of curving red tape and business process streamlining. Those agencies with their employees who have met the criteria with excellence will be awarded the center seal of excellence. Government service offices also establish public assistance and complaint desks nationwide with the "*Contact Center*

Ng Bayan" which served as the ARTA feedback mechanism for client suggestions, complaints, queries, and recommendations.

After the implementation of the ARTA from 2007 to 2017, the RA 9485 was later amended into RA 11032 known as "Ease of Doing Business and Efficient Government Service Delivery (EODB-EGSD) Act of 2018" that requires all government agencies and offices that also include the government-owned or controlled corporations (GOCCs) and local government units (LGUs) to formulate simplified systems and steps to speed up government transactions and lessen the cases of red tapes. This has opened a new avenue for reforms in the delivery of services. It highlights the processing time of government transactions into a platform of 3-7-20 days processing. This mandate should be strongly enforced with the aid of the Department of Information and Technology through government technology utilization the observance by all government agencies and offices the completion of transactions of 3 working days for simple transactions, 7 working days for complex transactions, and 20 working days for highly technical applications.

Moreover; the implementation of the EODB-EGSD Act primarily supports the CSC human resource management platforms and programs towards the aim to further promote the efficient and effective delivery of public services by government employees at all levels and regardless of the agencies or offices employed. Initial steps taken by CSC to ensure implementation of this act is the conduct of Anti-Red Tape Unit at CSC central and regional offices by utilizing the RCS (Report Card Survey) outcomes to further improve the present utilization of human resource programs and systems toward service delivery efficiency in terms of immediate response over complaints, non-compliance with regulations, and other related information. Dissemination of the rules and regulations were jointly made with the Department of Trade and Industry is conducting 16 public consultations nationwide with both private and public representatives to elicit views, comments, comments, and suggestions.

LITERATURE REVIEW

Human Resource Management and Public Sector Performance

In the study of Boselie et al. (2019) cited that few papers have practically addressed the impact of HRM on public sector performance. However; reshaping the HRM in the context of government austerity measures, governmental cuts, institutional constraints and pressures, and organizational reforms have proved to directly impact public sector performance. Likewise, New Public Management (NPM) initiatives and the political agenda of countries significantly influence HRM in the government sector (Gooderham et. al., 2018). Nonetheless, considering the scarcity of available studies and the performance measures to assess the outcomes of HRM application to the public sector, Osborne (2017) stressed that most of the studies on HRM impact individual-level performance in the private sector. Hence, in this study, the focus deals on a factual account of the HRM reforms that transcend from Marcos Era to Duterte Administration by discussing narrative and document analysis of outcome rather than quantifying the performance of the said reform.

Human Resource Management: Civil Service System Reforms

The concept of reforms in the civil service system had already been investigated in some studies. For example, the study of Moon and Hwang (2013) shed light on these reforms through a comparative study on the state of civil service reforms in four categories of countries namely: Western countries, Asian industrialized countries, Southeast Asian developing countries, and Socialist transitional countries wherein, findings showed that performance management has been applied across all these groups indicating global diffusion of performance management initiatives. This is in line with Van Waeyenberg et al. (2016) finding where they strongly argued that consistent application of performance management system according to the organization's strategic goals reduces the workers' plans to leave.

Furthermore, in Southeast Asian countries were found most initiatives in the aspect of ethics and transparency, compensation reform, and recruitment reforms over the socialist transitional countries. The recruitment reforms primarily dealt with recruitment, selection, and classification of civil servants in most Asian and Pacific countries. The earlier definition of recruitment according to Frederickson (1996) states that it is a process of finding and attracting job applicants based on certain criteria set while McGregor and Solano (1996) define selection as the process of taking the best person for the job vacancy. Recruitment can be closed or open system wherein a closed system is utilized for entry-level jobs while the open system is applicable for the lateral entrance to all civil service positions.

Zhang and Zhou (2010) have concluded the importance of an open system of recruitment to allow outsiders to be selected to reduce if not eliminate nepotism and corruption. In the Philippines for instance, incidences of corruption and red tapes are prevalent that involve civil servants at all levels and regardless of their ranks or positions. Table 5 shows that 2.14 percent of the citizens' complaints were caused by extortion (Civil Service Commission, 2018). Employees receive money in exchange for quicker service that has been embedded in the government system. However, in the case of Philippine CSC, it has gone a milestone of success in its efforts to improve its services over the years. To provide highlights of such achievements, the succeeding sections will document some of the evidential accounts from the documents gathered and analyzed as the main data gathering tool in this paper. The sequential description of the event will be shown in succeeding paragraphs.

Public Service Delivery Audit (PASADA) 2003

Since the implementation of PASADA in 2003, a pilot implementation was conducted in the National Capital Region which covered forty-five (45) agencies and ninety-eight (98) frontline services (CSC, 2018). The excellent rating was garnered by the business permit and licensing office of Marikina City as well as the CSC Seal of Frontline Service Excellence. Specifically, eleven frontline services rated very good and, recipient of CSC certificate of recognition. This act has allowed the government service to reward and reform top-performing frontlines through recognizing best systems and practices, solutions, while also providing interventions technically, and development initiatives to meet their needs as identified. However; the effectiveness of implementation was considered short-lived and clamors continued especially in the aspect of countering the bureaucratic red tape and corruption. Hence; a law was passed to amend this act to the ARTA under Republic Act No. 9485 of 2007.

The Extent of Implementation of MMHMN/MMP Program

The modified program called MMP previously known as MMHMN has been instrumental in attaining quick response to public service complaints and client dissatisfaction. CSC has instituted the 3 major program components by imposing daily work standards in public dealings, rewards and incentives for superior service, and quick response to complaints of any kind. As evidenced of achievement, the 11-year implementation of the program was able to act on feedbacks/reports totaling 55,297 wherein it has broken down to request and assistance with 23,908 (43%); requests for assistance, 17,988 (33%); and, complaints with 13,401 (24%). These outcomes have helped CSC to determine and evaluate the concerns of all agencies and their clients in the implementation of the program (See Table 1).

Table 1. The outcome of 11-year MMP implementation

Reports/Feedbacks	Frequency	Percentage
Request for Assistance	23,908	43.00
Complaints	17,988	33.00
Commendation Reports	13,401	24.00
Total	55,297	100.00

Source: ARTA: A Decade of Improving Public Service Delivery. www.csc.gov.ph

Further, the program has shown the government's concern through the CSC in reaching out to the public and hearing out their voice and concerns as a way to improve the current public service provision by all government agencies and offices. These initiatives were not possible without the support of partners and counterparts such as the *Bilis Aksyon* Partners (BAP) with 3,722 assigned by respective heads of agencies and the 2,134 government officials and employees who received the *Gantimpala Agad* Awards for their efficient and prompt service. Also, its remarkable mark extends to successfully offering the avenue to resolve the perennial problem of discourteous employees of the government and partially address the increasing concern on red tapes. The CSC has contributed a strong awareness to the public that the government as a whole has expressed its seriousness in improving the public service delivery although it also honestly iron out that the drive against red tape is still a major issue that remains unsolved.

A Decade of Success of ARTA (RA 9485) 2007-2017

One of the most considered success efforts of the government spearheaded by the CSC was the implementation of the ARTA under RA 9485. Highlighted in the CSC report of 2017 and 2018, the 10-year accomplishment reports were publicized in detail. The main emphasis of the ARTA implementation is the creation of a citizen's charter wherein all services provided by government agencies become transparent to the citizens and the general public. The charter has transformed agencies into front-line service transparency, speedy service, and eradication of fixers discouraged corruption and red tapes and setting up of public assistance and complaints desk. In 2011, Administrative Order (AO) No. 2011 was established to form the Inter-Agency Task Force (IATF) chaired by the Department of Budget and Management (DBM) and co-chaired by the Office of the President. The members are comprised of the Presidential Management Staff (PMS), National Economic and Development Authority (NEDA), Department of Finance (DOF), CSC, etc. The success of the Citizen's Charter compliance was evident in 2012 through 2017 in different government agencies (See Table 2).

Table 2. Citizen's charter compliance rate, 2012-2017*

Agencies	2012	2013	2014	2015	2016	2017**
Departments	100%	100%	100%	96%	100%	91%
Constitutional Offices	100%	100%	100%	100%	100%	80%
Other Executive Offices	94%	94%	100%	100%	100%	92%
State Universities and Colleges	86%	96%	98%	99%	99%	86%
GOCCs under DBM	85%	87%	100%	100%	100%	93%

*Data from Office of Strategy Management as of October 15, 2018

**The 2017 agencies' compliance rate will still improve upon validation of agencies' submitted Certificate of Compliance (deficiencies addressed after validation) within 2018.

Clearly, Table 2 shows the high rate of compliance from 2012 to 2017, and the highest compliance was experienced in 2016 which was few months shy of President Rodrigo Duterte's installation as 16th President of the Philippine Republic. This is indeed a remarkable success of the government's fight against red tape and other corruption-related activities. In affirming the quality implementation of the Integrated ARTA Program, Report Card Survey was implemented with direct supervision of CSC to evaluate the extent of the government agencies and offices in battling red tape and in streamlining the business process as previously mentioned. Pieces of evidence from the drive to strongly lessen if not eliminate the red tape were documented and acted based on the data gathered. The conduct of RCS was done through Inspection Checklist (20%) and the Survey Questionnaire (80%) by the CSC through its Regional Offices for a period specified on yearly basis after review and approval by the Philippine Statistics Authority (PSA) of which modifications were made in 2014, 2016, and 2017.

Observable achievement by the survey resulted from an interview of 170,292 Filipino citizens who were recipients of the governments' frontline services in a span of eight years of implementation. Based on RCS compliance criteria, the remarkable achievement was demonstrated in the government sectors in the ARTA implementation in 2010-2017 with the identification of Top 5 Service Offices per Sector. The five government sectors were covered namely: Government-Owned or Controlled Corporations (GOCCs); Local Government Units (LGUs); Local Water Districts (LWDs); National Government Agencies (NGAs); and, State Universities and Colleges (SUCs). The numerical ratings of these Top 5 performing sectors were good and excellent respectively (See Table 3).

As seen in Table 3, GOCCs have topped the list and followed by LGUs while LWDs occupied third place. The NGAs placed in fourth while the SUCSs have taken the last spot. These results showed that the government with CSC leadership had achieved overwhelming success in the effort to fight corruption and red tape at the highest level possible. Most notably, the LGUs. LWDs, and SUCs have demonstrated the effectiveness of their service in 2016 where President Rodrigo Duterte resumed his presidency. On the other hand, the CSC initiative of establishing the "*Contact Center Ng Bayan*" was instrumental in hearing out the public's concerns, complaints, feedback, and suggestions. The Filipino people were able to contact directly the CSC through the center to voice their views and opinions on the quality of service provided by all government agencies and offices. The evidence of the effectiveness of the program can be seen in Table 4 that reveals the identification of Top 10 agencies with the most cases of ARTA-related reports in 2013-2016 for immediate response and further actions.

Table 3. Top 5 Service Offices per Sector, 2010-2017

Sector	Survey Year	Agency	Region	Service Office	Numerical Rating	Descriptive Rating
GOCC	2014	SSS	3	SSS San Ferando, Panpanga	97.76	Excellent
	2013	LBP	3	LBP Meycauayan	97.23	Excellent
	2015	Philhealth	ARMMMMM	PHIC Regional Office ARMM	96.93	Excellent
	2014	Philhealth	7	PHIC LHIO Tagbilaran City, Bohol	96.82	Excellent
	2017	SSS	3	SSS Balanga Branch, Bataan	96.79	Excellent
LGUs	2016	Barangay	2	Calao West Santiago City	96.55	Excellent
	2016	City	2	Santiago City	94.45	Excellent
	2016	Barangay	ARMM	Madaya, Maguing	96.00	Excellent
	2011	City	11	Tagum	95.84	Excellent
	2016	Barangay	5	Barangay 57, Dap-dap, Legaspi City	95.81	Excellent
LWDs	2016	LWD	6	Silay City Water District	92.92	Excellent
	2016	LWD	3	Concepcion Water District	92.84	Excellent
	2016	LWD	5	Casiguran Water District	92.70	Excellent
	2016	LWD	6	Metro Kalibo Water District	92.59	Excellent
	2016	LWD	ARMM	Isabela City Water District	92.35	Excellent
NGAs	2012	DTI	3	Cabanatuan City	98.48	Excellent
	2012	LTO	8	Baybay Extension Office	98.13	Excellent
	2013	DSWD	ARMM	DSWD Lanao del Sur	98.11	Excellent
	2014	LTO	3	Meycauayan District Office	97.89	Excellent
	2013	DOH	ARMM	Luuk District Hospital, Sulu	97.60	Excellent
SUCs	2016	SUC	6	West Visayas State University	87.70	Good
	2016	SUC	1	Mariano Marcos State University	85.70	Good
	2016	SUC	6	Central Philippine State University	85.63	Good
	2016	SUC	6	Aklan State University	85.38	Good
	2016	SUC	6	UP-Visayas	85.27	Good

Source: ARTA: A Decade of Improving Public Service Delivery. www.csc.gov.ph

Table 4. Agencies with most ARTA-related reports 2013-2016

Rank	2013	2014	2015	2016
1	Land Transportation Office	Land Transportation Office	Land Transportation Office	Social Security System
2	Social Security System	Social Security System	Social Security System	Land Transportation Office
3	Government Service Insurance System	Land Registry Authority	Bureau of Internal Revenue	Local Government Units
4	Bureau of Internal Office	Bureau of Internal Office	Land Registry Authority	Provincial Government Offices
5	Professional Regulation Board	Home Development Mutual Fund	Home Development Mutual Fund	Bureau of Internal Revenue
6	Land Registry Authority	National Bureau of Investigation	Department of Foreign Affairs	Department of Foreign Affairs
7	Home Development Mutual Fund	Department of Health (Hospitals)	Philippine Health Insurance Corp.	Home Development Mutual Fund
8	National Statistics Office (PSA)	Government Service Insurance System	National Bureau of Investigation	Land Registry Authority
9	Philippine Health Insurance Corp.	Philippine Statistics Authority	Philippine Statistics Authority	Government Service Insurance System
10	Department of Foreign Affairs	Professional Regulation Board	Land Bank of the Philippines	Philippine National Police

Source: ARTA: A Decade of Improving Public Service Delivery. www.csc.gov.ph

Table 4 further indicates that, within the four years of implementation under the 10-year accomplishment report, these agencies proved to be showing complaints and perceived cases of red tapes, corruption, and other concerns which were identified in detail in Table 5. Based on the findings, the most concern that accounts for 57.48% was the government's "slow process" and followed by "unclear procedures" with 8.18%. The third concern was "discourtesy" (7.54%) while the least concern was "bribery". Anchored on one of the objectives of ARTA which is to speed up the government service, the program is trying to address these concerns while upholding integrity, dedication, and commitment to serve the general public.

Highly commendable success was reported with the ARTA implementation especially in fighting red tape (See Table 5). The results of these efforts can be enumerated for the 10 years: Presence of citizen's charter for government offices; full observance of no-noon break policy; application of modernized facilities for frontlines with special lanes; shorter processing time; lessened documentations and eliminate redundant documentation; the success of *contact center ng bayan*; establishment of public assistance and complaint desks to all government agencies and offices; lesser anti-fixing cases; encourages citizen participation; and, improved ease of doing business based from RCS outcomes (Saguin, 2012). In 2017, the waiting time of processing government transactions have significantly reduced from 48 days in 2007 to only 28 days in 2017 that have made the country the rank of 99th place out of 190 countries which were contrary to 126th place out of 175 countries in 2007 thereby, a tremendous achievement (Center for Public Impact, 2018). This success has led to the implementation of RA no. 11032 amending RA No. 9485 which is called the "EODB-EGSD" in 2018 that focused on streamlining business processes and further countering red tape with implementing rules and regulations jointly crafted by the CSC and DTI. However; this act is still in earlier phases of implementation and is expected to pass through rigid test and filtering process to measure the effectiveness of its implementation and thus require joint efforts not only CSC but all other sectors of the government including GOCCs, LGUs, LWDs, NGAs, and SUCs.

Table 5. Nature of ARTA-related concerns 2012-2016

ARTA Concerns	Count	Percentage
Slow Process	15,446	57.48%
Unclear Procedure/s	2,197	8.18%
Unattended Hotline Number	2,027	7.54%
Discourtesy	1,460	5.43%
Failure to Act on Request	1,343	5.00%
Failure to Attend to Clients during Office Hours	792	2.95%
Poor Facility	627	2.33%
Extortion	576	2.14%
Fixing Activities	504	1.88%
Imposition of Additional Cost	371	1.38%
Imposition of Additional Requirements	332	1.24%
Non-issuance of Official Receipt	324	1.21%
No Noon Break	309	1.15%
No Response to Letters	185	0.69%
Non-observance of Queuing Systems	140	0.52%
Appreciation for Service Quality	131	0.49%
No Special Lane for SC, PW, PWD	77	0.29%
No Citizens Charter	19	0.07%
Absence of Easy to Read Identification (Frontlines)	9	0.03%
Bribery	3	0.01%

Source: ARTA: A Decade of Improving Public Service Delivery. www.csc.gov.ph

Strategizing the CSC's Human Resource Management for Better Personnel Administration

Various programs had already been implemented by the CSC primarily to enhance government service and in dealing with clients in the course of its operations. This had been directed to all government agencies and offices. Out of these programs, the researchers gathered evidence to highlight the significant contributions of CSC in the continuous improvement of the human resource system as well as the challenges faced during its implementation. Purposely, excerpts from the panel discussion by National Assembly of Education Leaders on September 25, 2019, and the keynote message from Dr. Alex B. Brillantes during the conference with the theme "Public Administration and the Future: Challenges and Opportunities in Realizing the Sustainable Development Goals and Directions for Reform and Capacity Building" last May 22, 2019. These were also supported by the ARTA Report, and the 2017 and 2018 CSC annual report (Brillantes, 2019).

Excerpt From Panel Session with the theme "Challenged Leaders: Embracing the Future, Braving the Changes" – National Assembly of Education Leaders

The chairman of CSC Hon. Alicia dela Rosa-Bala addressed the educational leaders about the CSC's platform on the role of the government and public servants in meeting goals and vision and in consonance with the 119th Philippine Civil Service Anniversary with the theme "Upholding Integrity and Building a High-Trust Society". Firstly, she emphasized the importance of change as a primordial concern in serving for the better. The key points narrated were the views which are: change shaping HRM towards technological advancement and globalization; improvement towards online and paperless technology as major changes towards management, peers, and government-client transactions; emphasis on 4th industrial revolution introducing the concepts of the Internet of Things (IoT), Robotics, Virtual Reality (VR), and Artificial Intelligence (AI); and the HR outlook of being ahead of the game through access to knowledge, tools, and resources (Civil Service Commission, 2019).

The term "Internet of Things" refers to the day to day coding and interacting of things to condense separately observable and machine-readable objects through the internet (Butler, 2020). Concerning this, the commission is gearing towards the full adoption of the internet of things in the operations and in communicating effectively the organizational vision, goals, and objectives. Likewise, amidst the industrial revolution is the transformation from traditional means of operation into virtual reality applications. Many authors identified the recent applications of virtual reality in various fields such as education, architectural design, gaming, social skills training, etc. (Alexander et al., 2017; Englund et al., 2017; Meldrum et al., 2012; Schmidt et al., 2017; and, Song et al., 2017). However; at Civil Service Commission this application is considered new and still on the verge of adoption hence; the commission has directed the 4th industrial revolution as its main challenges. Meanwhile, in the aspect of robotics and artificial intelligence, scholars stressed that there are still no public data sets on the usage or implementation of artificial intelligence and robotics in both the micro and macro-levels as well as in the academic community in general (McElheran, 2019; Raj and Seamans, 2018). This means that pieces of evidence on the implementation of artificial intelligence and robotics are yet to be seen in companies and organizations both the private and public sectors.

In the context of CSC as the human resource institution of the Philippine government, the agency maintained its mandate to promote integrity, morale, responsiveness, efficiency, courtesy, and progressiveness as its call of duty and as essential aspects of civil service. True to its mandate, the CSC has responded the call to uphold in strategizing the HR system that aims to be at par with global HR standards to serve as a primary contributor to the achievement of the Philippine Development Plan 2017-2022 that ensures a clean, people-centered, and efficient governance and the 2040's goal of building a high-trust society through the plan called *"AmBisyon Natin 2040"*. However; these goals will not be achieved without facing challenges which according to the CSC, three main challenges that will be stressed in succeeding paragraphs. The first challenge faced is on pursuing customer satisfaction. Satisfying customers are not confined with the mastery of the government employees to address the needs but rather on how to meet the changing and varying needs of citizens and all stakeholders in a changing society that may require change policies and programs. She narrated that, "sole reliance on the code of conduct and ethical standards for public officials and employees (RA no. 6713, 1989) may become outdated in terms of service delivery and performance, hence; the improvement has become an urgent concern". The government has responded to this challenge by implementing the ARTA of 2007 and the EODB-EGSD" in 2018 to mention a few.

The second challenge is raising HR maturity levels. The CSC puts prime emphasis on employees as its strongest assets and committed to upholding global standards of HR management. To respond to this call, the agency launched an initial implementation of the program called "PRIME-HRM" or the Program to Institutionalized Meritocracy and Excellence in Human Resource Management in 2012 as a strategy to empower agencies and develop individuals in the Philippine Government which covers all levels of the workforce. It is best known for assessing, assist, and award. HR process in this program is categorized into four core practices such as recruitment, selection, and placement; performance management; learning and development; and rewards and recognition. Moreover; maturity levels of HR classification were identified as Level 1 for Transactional HRM; Level 2, Processed-Defined HRM; Level 3, Integrated HRM; and, Level 4 for Strategic HRM. The challenge is on how to rise from one level to another which requires major action on the part of agencies with a wider understanding of linking HR excellence to service excellence. And, the third challenge dwelt on promoting inclusivity and diversity. The fight against gender issues has received unparalleled attention that continuously raises problems on discrimination involving ethnicity, religion, race, social class, and disability. However; CSC has proved to appropriately address the challenge with successful advocacies for over 30 years since the implementation of the Anti-Sexual Harassment Act of 1995 to the Magna Carta of Women in 2009. Recent laws and regulations were expanded such as the signing of the 105-day Expanded Maternity Leave Law on February 20, 2019. But one of the major challenges is the SOGIE Bill (Sexual Orientation and Gender Identity and Expression Equality Bill) which was re-filed in 118th Congress pending approval. Besides, dignity and identity of gender have gained wider and deeper concern that resembles the challenge. To truly benefit the people, consultation of stakeholders before creating a program or policy is paramount consideration to ensure the success of every effort.

Excerpt From 2019 Annual Conference of Asian Association for Public Administration

The conference with the theme "Public Administration and the Future: Challenges and Opportunities in Realizing the Sustainable Development Goals and Directions for Reform and Capacity Building" has highlighted the "*Ambisyon 2040*" that was embodied in the Philippine Development Plan 2017-2022 that emphasized Excellence in HR Management in the public sector. CSC has been known for its employee-first culture which assumes that gaining success in dealing with clients begins first with taking good care with employees to attain sound human resource programs and policies that equal a competent and highly motivated employee. Furthermore, CSC believed that organizational development worked side by side with the individual worker's development. Towards this end, there are six (6) HRM practices that were considered of top priorities for CSC and these are Prime-HRM; Performance Management System; Recruitment, Selection, and Placement System; Competency-Based Learning and Development; and, Rewards and Recognitions (Civil Service Commission, 2014).

The Prime-HRM's focus is to transform HR practices from transactional day to day management into strategic result-oriented practices that assert the improvement of quality service delivery to the people and the public. It is complemented by the performance management system which deals with the performance-based assessment and incentive system where it showcased the adherence of individual worker's performance to the vision, mission, and strategic goals of the organization. In terms of the recruitment, selection, and placement system, the agency has adopted CBRQS which is the competency-based recruitment and qualification standards that do not only examine the qualification in terms of education, experience, eligibility, and training but also competencies for a specific vacancy. It also lays the premise that hiring good people will enable organizations to have a credible, highly-performing, and highly competent workforce. The fourth practice is the competency-based learning and development programs that CSC put premium consideration through training program offerings by the Civil Service Institute (CSI). This practice aimed not only developing the present workforce but also preparing them to become future leaders to bridge competency gaps. Leadership programs and symposiums were also provided to ascertain future leadership roles. Last but not least is rewards and recognition that emphasized the provision of incentives and rewards for an excellent performance of employees at all levels in both agency level and national level. Specifically, it highlights rewards for excellent performance by executives, individuals, groups, and various programs of CSC aside from the usual loyalty awards for the longevity of service.

FUTURE RESEARCH DIRECTIONS

This chapter focuses on the narrative account of the extent of implementation of HRM during the Marcos Era up to Duterte Administration and sources were primarily taken from secondary sources and information. Thus, the outcome was based on the analysis of the evidence gathered from the Civil Service Commission and other related literature. Researches, therefore, acknowledged the exclusivity of the analysis on the information collected which they believed that the results can be expanded and quantified. Future studies can be undertaken to benchmark the CSC and the country's state of implementation of HRM to other countries to acquire the success points and factors for application. It is also recommended that the CSC will conduct a quantitative research survey directed to citizens and other stakeholders to determine and assess the extent of HRM implementation regularly in consonance with the recent changes brought about by external forces such as political, economic, socio-cultural, technological, legal, and environmental forces.

CONCLUSION

This chapter highlights the transition of CSC human resource development from 1986 to the present and under the presidency of His Excellency President Rodrigo Duterte. Remarkable changes and improvement of the government service in transition were noted starting from the creation of Executive Order 292 empowering government employees for self-organization and collective negotiation. It was followed by the program "Citizens First" in 1994 and later the PASADA of 2003 for service delivery improvement. The MMP was another milestone improvement of CSC that values work standards, rewarding, and responsiveness. The government's merited effort to combat corruption and red tape has realized with the passage of ARTA in 2007 being considered as a breakthrough in showcasing 10 years of successful efforts. The ability of the government through the leadership of CSC is one of the proofs that corruption can be lessened if not eradicated with leaders' strong will to counter this considered perennial problem. This success was further strengthened with the amendment of ARTA into EODB-EGSD of 2018 to further demolish red tape and corruption. In terms of strategizing the human resource management system, CSC has highlighted the six (6) HR practices under the Philippine Development Plan 2017-2022 and following the "*AmBisyon Natin 2040*".

Based on these findings, CSC has shown significant improvement in shaping the HR system strategically and the readiness to compete globally in terms of HR global standards with open-mindedness to embrace change and reform agenda citing the changing society, technological advancements, and globalization. While challenges are inevitable, the program plans of the agency are resilient to the growing needs and demands of the public service and are perceived as a continuous call for exemplary service in the long-term perspective. However; CSC has faithfully acknowledged that there are still areas for improvement and these are: change shaping HRM towards technological advancement and globalization; improvement towards online and paperless technology as major changes towards management, peers, and government-client transactions; emphasis on 4th industrial revolution introducing the concepts of the Internet of Things (IoT), Robotics, Virtual Reality (VR), and Artificial Intelligence (AI); and the HR outlook of being ahead of the game through access to knowledge, tools, and resources.

REFERENCES

Alexander, T., Westhoven, M., & Conradi, J. (2017). Virtual environments for competency-oriented education and training. In *Advances in Human Factors* (pp. 23–29). Business Management, Training and Education. doi:10.1007/978-3-319-42070-7_3

Berman, E. (2010). *Public administration in Southeast Asia: Thailand, Philippines, Malaysia, Hong Kong, and Macao.* CRC Press.

Boselie, P., Harten, J. V., & Veld, M. (2019). A human resource management review on public management and public administration research: Stop right there…before we go any further…. *Public Management Review*, 1–18. Advance online publication. doi:10.1080/14719037.2019.1695880

Brillantes, A. (2019). *Public Administration and the Future: Challenges and Opportunities in Realizing the Sustainable Development Goals and Directions for Reform and Capacity Building* [Paper Presentation]. *2019 Annual Conference of Asian Association for Public Administration*, Manila, Philippines.

Butler, D. (2020). Computing: Everything, Everywhere. *Nature, 440*(7083), 402–405. doi:10.1038/440402a PMID:16554773

Center for Public Impact. (2018). *The Anti-Red Tape Act in the Philippines.* https://www.centreforpublicimpact.org/case-study/anti-red-tape-act-philippines/

Cheung, A. (2005). The politics of administrative reforms in Asia: Paradigms and legacies, paths and diversities. *Governance: An International Journal of Policy, Administration and Institutions, 18*(2), 257–282. doi:10.1111/j.1468-0491.2005.00275.x

Civil Service Commission. (2014). *PRIME-HRM.* http://www.csc.gov.ph/2014-02-21-08-16-56/2014-02-21-08-17-24/2014-02-28-06-36-08.html

Civil Service Commission. (2017). *CSC Annual Report 2017.* http://www.csc.gov.ph/41-transparency-seal-all/transparency-seal-r4/153-ii-annual-report.html

Civil Service Commission. (2018). *CSC Annual Report 2018.* http://web.csc.gov.ph/39-transparency-seal-all/transparency-seal-r2/139-ii-annual-report.html

Civil Service Commission. (2018). *ARTA: A Decade of Improving Public Service Delivery.* https://contactcenterngbayan.gov.ph/images/Manuals/artaphotobook.pdf

Civil Service Commission. (2019). *Challenged Leaders: Embracing the Future, Braving the Changes Association of the Department of Educators.* http://csc.gov.ph/phocadownload/userupload/paio-cabanawan/reporter%203%202019%20(DIGITAL%20VER)%20OCT%2017.pdf

Englund, C., Olofsson, A. D., & Price, L. (2017). Teaching with technology in higher education: Understanding conceptual change and development in practice. *Higher Education Research & Development, 36*(1), 73–87. doi:10.1080/07294360.2016.1171300

Fredericksen, P. W. (1996). *Human resource management: The public service perspective.* Houghton Mifflin.

Gooderham, P. N., Mayrhofer, W., & Brewster, C. (2018). A Framework for Comparative Institutional Research on HRM. *International Journal of Human Resource Management, 30*(1), 5–30. doi:10.1080/09585192.2018.1521462

Kim, J. (2010). Strategic Human Resource Practices: Introducing Alternatives for Organizational Performance Improvement in the Public Sector. *Public Administration Review, 70*(1), 38–49. doi:10.1111/j.1540-6210.2009.02109.x

McElheran, K. (2019). *Economic measurement of AI* (NBER Working Paper). https://scholar.google.com/scholar_lookup?title=Economic%20measurement%20of%20AI&publication_year=2019&author=McElheran%2CK

McGregor, E., & Solano, P. (1996). Data requirement and availability. In H. Bekke, J. Perry, & T. Toonen (Eds.), *Civil service systems: In comparative perspective* (pp. 42–66). Indiana University Press.

Meldrum, D., Glennon, A., Herdman, S., Murray, D., & McConn-Walsh, R. (2012). Virtual reality rehabilitation of balance: Assessment of the usability of the nintendo Wii fit plus. *Disability and Rehabilitation, 7*, 205–210. doi:10.3109/17483107.2011.616922 PMID:22117107

Moon, M. J., & Hwang, C. (2013). The state of civil service systems in the Asia-Pacific Region: A Comparative Perspective. *Review of Public Personnel Administration, 20*(10), 1–19. doi:10.1177/0734371X13484831

Osborne, S. P. (2017). Public Management Research over the Decades: What are We Writing About? *Public Management Review, 19*(2), 109–113. doi:10.1080/14719037.2016.1252142

Raj, M., & Seamans, R. C. (2018). AI, Labor, Productivity, and the Need for Firm-Level Data. In A. Agrawal, J. S. Gans, & A. Goldfarb (Eds.), *NBER Economics of Artificial Intelligence.* University of Chicago Press.

Republic Act No. 6713. (1989). *Code of Conduct and Ethical Standards for Public Officials and Employees.* https://www.researchgate.net/publication/325724839_An_Assessment_Of_Governmental_Services_In_The_Philippines_From_Spanish_To_Contemporary_Times

Republic Act No. 9485. (2007). *An Act to Improve Efficiency in the Delivery of Government Service to the Public by Reducing Bureaucratic Red Tape, Preventing Graft and Corruption, and Providing Penalties Therefore, Philippine Congress.* https://www.researchgate.net/publication/325724839_An_Assessment_Of_Governmental_Services_In_The_Philippines_From_Spanish_To_Contemporary_Times

Saguin, K. I. C. (2012). *Critical Challenges in Implementing the Citizen's Charter Initiative: Insights from Selected LGUs, Policy Research Office, and Center for Governance, and Development Academy of the Philippines.* https://www.researchgate.net/publication/325724839_An_Assessment_Of_Governmental_Services_In_The_Philippines_From_Spanish_To_Contemporary_Times

Schmidt, M., Beck, D., Glaser, N., & Schmidt, C. (2017). A prototype immersive, multi-user 3D virtual learning environment for individuals with autism to learn social and life skills: a virtuoso DBR update. In *Proceedings of International Conference on Immersive Learning.* Springer. 10.1007/978-3-319-60633-0_15

Song, H., Chen, F., Peng, Q., Zhang, J., & Gu, P. (2017). Improvement of user experience using virtual reality in open-architecture product design. *Proceedings of the Institution of Mechanical Engineers. Part B, Journal of Engineering Manufacture*, 232.

Van Waeyenberg, T., Decramer, A., Desmidt, S., & Audenaert, M. (2016). The Relationship between Employee Performance Management and Civil Servants' Turnover Intentions: A Test of the Mediating Roles of System Satisfaction and Affective Commitment. *Public Management Review*, *19*(6), 747–764. doi:10.1080/14719037.2016.1209230

Zhang, M., & Zhou, W. (2010). Civil service reforms in Mainland China. In E. Berman, M. J. Moon, & H. Choi (Eds.), *Public administration in East Asia: Mainland China, Japan, South Korea, and Taiwan* (pp. 145–163). CRC Press. doi:10.1201/EBK1420051902-c7

ADDITIONAL READING

Armstrong, M., & Taylor, S. (2009). *Armstrong's handbook of human resource management and practice* (11th ed.). Color press Ltd.

Ayee, J. R. A. (2012). Improving the Effectiveness of the Public Sector in Africa through the Quality of Public Administration. In K. T. Hanson, G. Kararach, & T. M. Shaw (Eds.), *Rethinking Development Challenges for Public Policy. International Political Economy Series* (pp. 83–116). Palgrave Macmillan., doi:10.1057/9780230393271_4

Biswas, B. (2016). Composition of Public Service Commission in three developing countries in South Asia: Bangladesh, India, and Pakistan. *International Journal of African and Asian Studies*, *22*, 14–22.

Cebu Normal University. (2019). CNU *President speaks in National Assembly of Education Leaders.* http://www.cnu.edu.ph/cnu-president-a-leader-in-education/

Demmke, C. (2010). *Civil Services in EU of 27 Reform Outcomes and the future of civil service.* http://aei.pitt.edu/29755/1/20101022095936_Eipascope_2010_2_Article1.pdf

Hashimi, S. H., & Lauth, G. (2016). *Civil Service Reform in Afghanistan: Roles and Functions of the Civil Service Sector.* https://www.refworld.org/pdfid/590701744.pdf

Owusu, F., & Ohemeng, F. L. K. (2012). The Public Sector and Development in Africa: The Case for a Developmental Public Service. In K. T. Hanson, G. Kararach, & T. M. Shaw (Eds.), *Rethinking Development Challenges for Public Policy. International Political Economy Series* (pp. 117–154). Palgrave Macmillan., doi:10.1057/9780230393271_5

Tzur, R., & Cohen, N. (2018). The Ongoing Israeli Civil Service Reform: Comparing Current Achievements to Past Attempts. *Revue française administration publique, 168*(4), 943-956. DOI:. doi:10.3917/rfap.168.0943

KEY TERMS AND DEFINITIONS

Anti-Red Tape Act 9485: Is a program of the government that aims at eradicating corruption and red tape in the government service.

Artificial Intelligence: The government's aim to respond to the call for implementation of the Artificial Intelligence as challenge to governance.

Civil Service Commission: The central personnel agency of the Philippine government and is responsible for the policies, plans, and programs concerning all civil service employees.

Competency-Based Recruitment and Qualification Standards: Are standards that do not only examine the qualification in terms of education, experience, eligibility, and training, but also competencies for a specific vacancy.

Contact Center Ng Bayan: A center where citizens can voice their views and opinions on the quality of service provided by all government agencies and offices.

Ease of Doing Business and Efficient Government Service Delivery: An act that requires all government agencies and offices that also include the government-owned or controlled corporations (GOCCs) and local government units (LGUs) to formulate simplified systems and steps to speed up government transactions and lessen the cases of red tapes.

Human Resource Management Reforms: Reforms enforced by the Civil Service Commission from the Marcos Era up to Duterte Administration.

Internet of Things: The day to day coding and interacting of things to condense separately observable and machine-readable objects through the internet.

Mamamayan Muna Hindi Mamaya Na or Mamamayan Muna Program: Is a program that aims at serving people first which has 3 major program components by imposing daily work standards in public dealings, rewards and incentives for superior service, and quick response to complaints of any kind.

Philippine Development Plan 2017-2022: A long-term plan that ensures a clean, people-centered, and efficient governance and the 2040's goal of building a high-trust society through the plan called "*AmBisyon Natin 2040*".

Program to Institutionalized Meritocracy and Excellence in Human Resource Management: A strategy implemented in 2012 that empowers agencies and develops individuals in the Philippine Government which covers all levels of the workforce.

Public Service Delivery Audit: A program implemented in 2003 to foster courtesy culture and response effectiveness between the government and the public.

Sexual Orientation and Gender Identity and Expression Equality Bill: Is a pending bill or act prohibiting discrimination on the basis of sexual orientation, gender identity, or expression.

This research was previously published in the Handbook of Research on Global Challenges for Improving Public Services and Government Operations; pages 348-365, copyright year 2021 by Information Science Reference (an imprint of IGI Global).

Chapter 15

Implementation of an Intelligent Model Based on Machine Learning in the Application of Macro-Ergonomic Methods in a Human Resources Process Based on ISO 12207

Edgar Cossio Franco
Universidad Enrique Díaz de León, Mexico

Jorge Alberto Delgado Cazarez
Universidad de Guadalajara, Mexico

Carlos Alberto Ochoa Ortiz Zezzatti
Universidad Autónoma de Ciudad Juárez, Mexico

ABSTRACT

The objective of this chapter is to implement an intelligent model based on machine learning in the application of macro-ergonomic methods in human resources processes based on the ISO 12207 standard. To achieve the objective, a method of constructing a Java language algorithm is applied to select the best prospect for a given position. Machine learning is done through decision trees and algorithm j48. Among the findings, it is shown that the model is useful in identifying the best profiles for a given position, optimizing the time in the selection process and human resources as well as the reduction of work stress.

DOI: 10.4018/978-1-6684-3873-2.ch015

INTRODUCTION

Nowadays, the success of many companies is priority. Among the important aspects and factors that impact on the success of companies is the active human. This means that employees should be comfortable in their workplace, this includes have an appropriate work area center for it can be adequately performed; lighting, ventilation, a comfortable chair or similar artifact to sit, the correct distance between the view and the monitor so you do not get tired and have enough tools. In relation with these specific tools, it is important that the worker has access and control of the elements that allow him to carry out their work. If industrial engineers, ergonomists, designers and managers take the elements described previously, they will be focusing about macroergonomics. The goal of this research is centered in the proposal of a specific model that allows to optimize the process of a company dedicated to the hiring of staff, and according to Lear (2011), a good way to reduce the stress in a job is with the automation of the tasks and process to save time. The process by which the companies in this field go through is eventually stressful and should be avoided. As established in (Palferman, 2011), the consequence of not avoiding this workload can be psychological damage. The scenario under which a situation of stress could happen is the following: applications or vacancies that are offered on a normal day may exceed the rate at which they can be evaluated, especially if the number of team members is reduced with respect to the number of candidates for each vacant. In this case, a bottleneck in which the profiles of the company are requested as soon as possible, the company does not have the names for when it is required. In this case, there is work pressure. For the improvement process in the human recourses area, the present work focuses in the ISO 12207 standard in the block of organizational processes. The proposal is applying a model described in two blocks. The first step is capturing the applicants and analyze them, using a tool developed in the Java language that implements an algorithm to making decision under uncertainty. Once the results are obtained, the second step is sending the data to a tool for automatic learning which implement the j48 selection algorithm in WEKA.

The Appendix shows the terminology presented in this work.

Macroergonomics

The goal of macroergonomics is create a pleasant environment in the workplace where intervene social aspects, but also technological (Hendrick, 1991). As established in Montero (2000), the socio-technical systems are characterized by their composition in 4 aspects as shown in Figure 1.

Each aspect shown in Figure 1 represents an axis that must be covered by Macroergonomics in order to guarantee productivity and quality in employees' life (Realyvásquez & Maldonado, 2018). In addition to the socio-technical aspects, Macroergonomics originates from Ergonomics, that is a field where takes care of three aspects: the healthy environment in the workplace, safety and efficiency. Figure 2 shows the areas to derive from Ergonomics.

Machine Learning

Learning is a process through which an agent receives information from their environment, that is processed and applied (Možina, 2018). In the present research, the knowledge that HR people have, although extensive, is insufficient when it is about to evaluating candidate by candidate for a job position; since there is not enough time. This is the reason why machine learning is used to optimize time and resources.

By means of machine learning it is possible provide knowledge to a computer by algorithms media and based in that knowledge to be able to process a bigger number of candidates in less time. Machine learning offers the algorithms automation to classify data (Arcila-Calderón et al., 2017) and based on this, it is possible to predict scenarios. The most basic and important concept is machine learning; it is a given representation to the process in general that computers work using algorithms. Machine learning has been applied to security systems, power, marketing, sales, medical diagnostics (Langley, & Simon, 1995), and in general, where it is possible to identify future scenarios through prediction (Goodfellow, Mcdaniel & Papernot, 2018). The prediction is achieved thanks to supervised and unsupervised algorithms. In supervised algorithms, it is applied to known information and in unsupervised algorithms the result is unknown, only the input data is known. In the study of Kononenko (2018) it is demonstrated that applying machine learning in complex processes and uncertainty it is possible to improve the accuracy. In other words, computer works better than humans do.

Figure 1. Socio-technical systems' aspects
Source: Montero (2000)

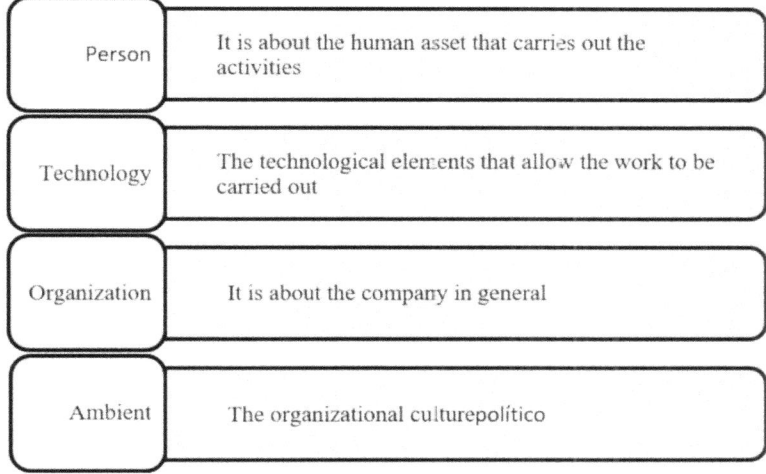

Figure 2. Areas of Ergonomics
Source: Silva, Nickel and dos Santos, 2018

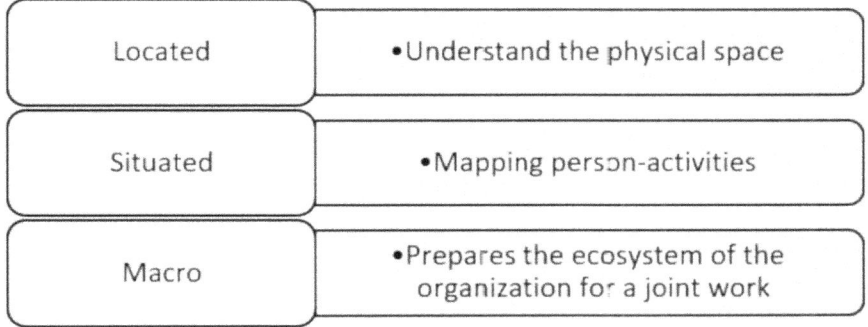

A Specific Standard to Process

In the international organization for standardization (ISO) there is a specific standard in its division of the International Electro-technical Commission (IEC) that is responsible for the life cycle of the software development process: the ISO 12207. This standard establishes a macro-process by which sub-processes are identified (main processes, organizational, support and adaptation processes) strategically direct to the areas that give life to the company (Baldassarre, Piattini, Pino & Visaggio, 2009). Table 1 shows the software life cycle processes according to ISO 12207, as well as the sub-processes that compose it (Piattini et al., 2007). The present research is focused on the human resources (HR) process, identified in Table 1, which provides the organization with adequate human resources and maintains the competence, consistent with the needs of the company. In this process, it is possible to identify the best profiles for a given position. Each company uses its own mechanisms to identify the best profiles. In next section it will be explained the problem that represents for any company the lack of a strategic hiring.

Table 1. Software life cycle processes according to ISO 12207

Main Processes	Support Processes
Acquisition	Documentation
Supply	Configuration management
Development	Quality assurance
Maintenance	Check
Organizational processes	Validation
Management	Review attached
Infrastructure	Audit
Improvement	Management of problem solving
Human resources	Usability
Asset management	Product evaluation
Reuse management programming	Management of exchange requests
Domain eEngineering	Adaptation processes

Problem Description

One problem that the Recruitment Company's Selection Department has is related to decides who is the candidate to choose for a specific job position. Said problem is modeled on the well-known problem of the secretary (Szajowski & Tamaki, 2016), which consists of what has been previously established. The more candidates are profiled to a diffuse job position, the problem becomes exponential in the strict sense to know what variables or characteristics the company requires for that position. It should not generate any problem when dealing with no more than 5 candidates who are only asked for a Java Senior certification. In this sense, the complexity is minimal. The problem arises when about 100 candidates are requested per day to different job positions for 20 companies and the profile or HR analysis team are only 10 people. At this point, the problem is in an advanced complexity. In previous scenarios, if a company does not have a solid strategy through which it is possible to optimize human resources and time, the problems will come automatically and will be reflected in a brief period of time. Several times, when the candidate is already hired, the problem is expressed in diverse ways, for example, the profile was not adequate, the candidate does not have the necessary experience, he has bad behavior and disposition to work like a team, among others. The optimization of human resources is aimed at the productivity of the recruitment company where the current scenario is that a group of people evaluates the candidates through an application of exams, review, interviews, and studies. What happens if the HR team has only 10 people and the profiles to evaluate are 100 in a day? It should be considered that these 100 profiles must be submitted to the process of exams, review, interviews, and studies. The answer is chaos; the HR team will not have enough time to sit down and review each and every one of the profiles. Then, in order to comply with the review, the HR team will hire candidates who do not know the profile. This happens frequently. The worst scenario is when the candidate is fired for not complying with the profile and it involves spending time like a process is triggered insomuch as the cycle must be closed and a new profile started. It has been shown that it is possible to attack this problem by applying strategies, as shown in Broder et al. (2009), who applied Lake Wobegon strategies and the well-known case of Google where started in a garage and that day only the best are hired, a strategy to hire someone who is above average. The proposal in this chapter is to optimize time and resources and avoid scenario discussed previously. Through the application of this proposal, it will be possible to identify, in less time, the best profiles based on artificial intelligence and ideal profiles according to the request of the applicant companies. The proposal is described below.

Organization of This Chapter

The present research is composed of the following sections: INTRODUCTION, where the problem and the basic concepts are directed. The following section is METHODOLOGY, which is a design of the material and algorithms used to solve the problem. The section of RESULTS is related to the statistical analysis and to the results of the application of the algorithms. The sections of CONCLUSIONS and FUTURE RESEARCH contains the conclusions and researches derived from the present investigation.

METHODOLOGY

The methodology proposed in the present Research is divided into two blocks; First: the information analysis will be done in Java and then with machine learning. Figure 3 shows the methodology.

The proposed methodology is formed by three ways (user, algorithm and machine learning) and in each of them a process is carried out interacting with the others. The process starts in the algorithm way, because the processing of the tasks by which the CSV file is received and executed, the chronometer is started, criteria are assigned and, in general, the user interacts with the machine learning. The user's way feeds the CSV file. CSV is a simple file format used to store tabular data, such as a spreadsheet or database. The machine learning way applies artificial intelligence (AI) algorithms. The following sections explain the implementation of the methodology in detail.

Figure 3. Proposed methodology
Source: The authors

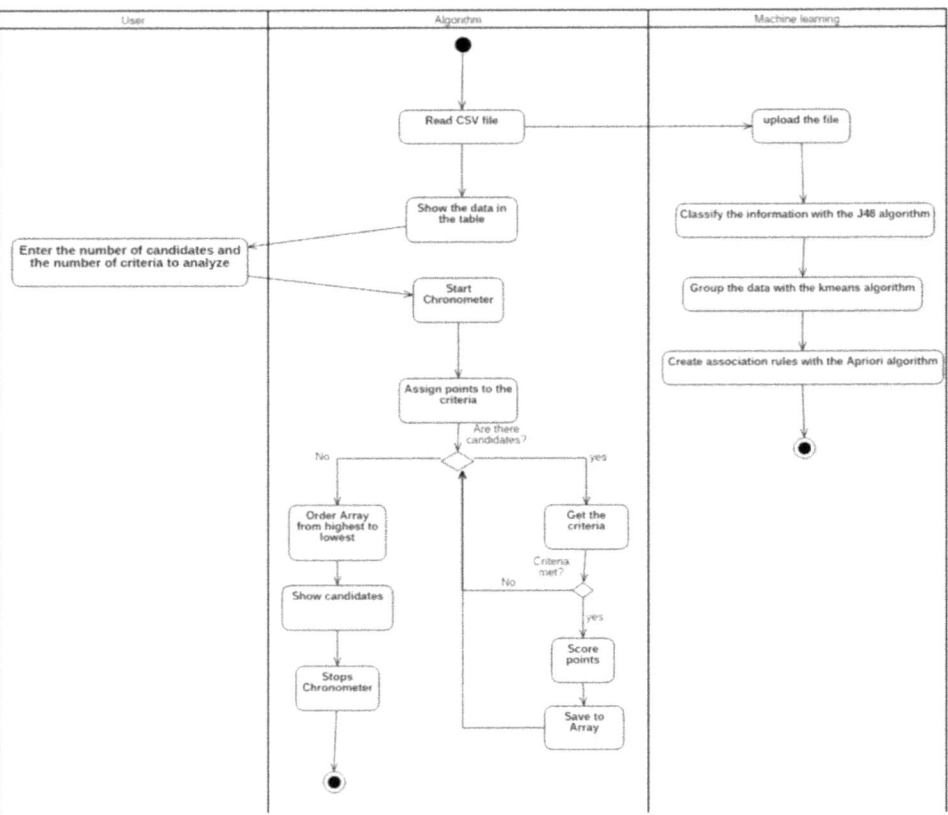

Java Application

Design of the Algorithm

For the Java application, the flowchart is shown as well as code segments in Figure 4. It is the design of the algorithm.

As specific software was built, the class diagram is shown in Figure 5.

Implementation

Following figures show code segments that make up the software in Java. This software was implemented with JAVA (JFrame) because it is fast, secure, reliable and stable. From laptops to data centers, from game consoles to supercomputers, from cell phones to the Internet, Java is everywhere. Figure 6 shows the main view of the proposed Java application. When starting with the software, a CSV (comma-separated values) file is read, it is a text file that stores the data in the form of columns, separated by a comma and the rows are distinguished by line breaks. This file contains all the information of all candidates for evaluation. As shown in Figure 7, seeing in code, the file is read, the name of the columns is obtained, the information of the candidates and it is shown in the table of the software for the visualization of the user. Code for each line in Figure 7 are explained below.

Line 62: Candidates read by the CSV are obtained by means of the ReadCsv function
Line 63: Function where it fills the table with the data obtained from the file.
Line 64: Call the CreateTableResult () function; just create the columns to visualize the result.
Line 65: The Only Checkbox is marked.

Figure 4. Design of the algorithm
Source: The authors

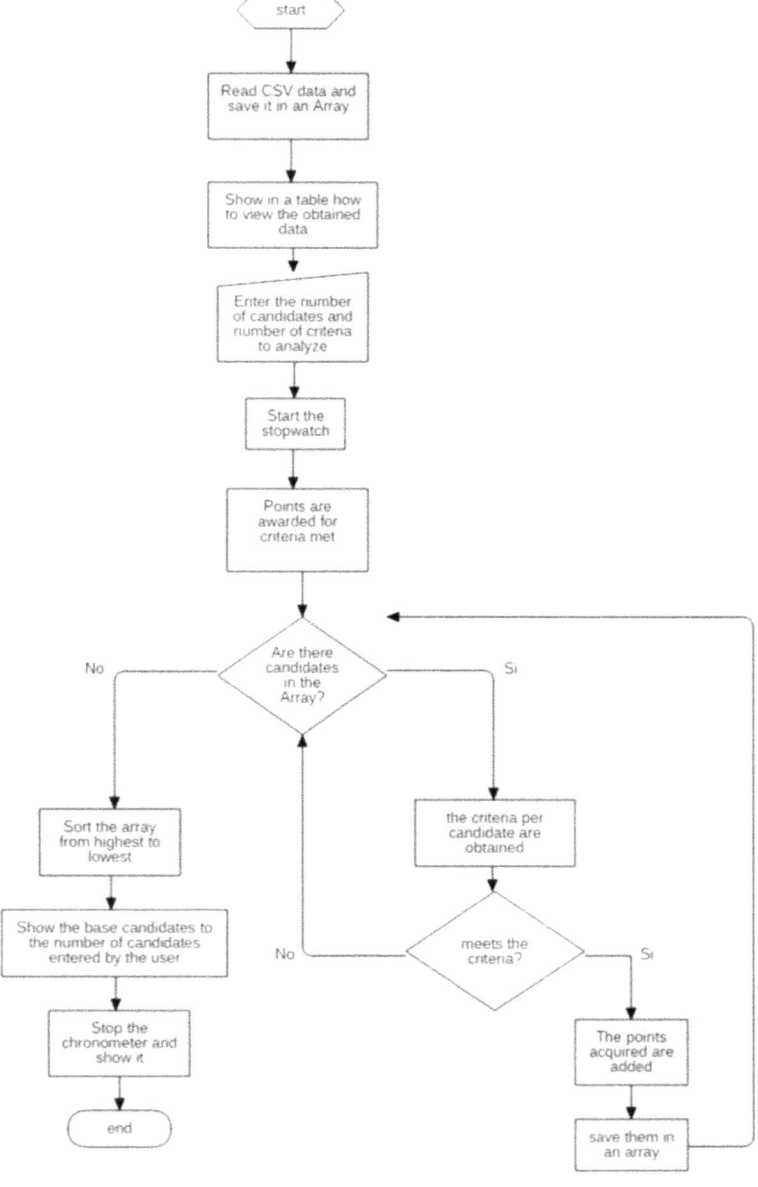

Figure 5. Class diagram
Source: The authors

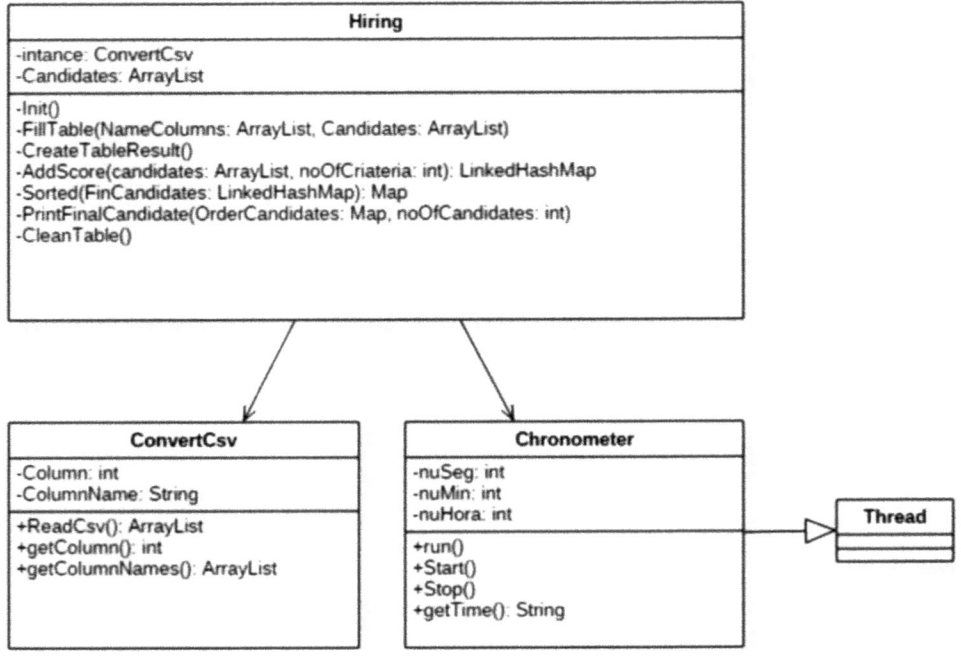

Figure 6. Main view of the proposed Java application
Source: The authors

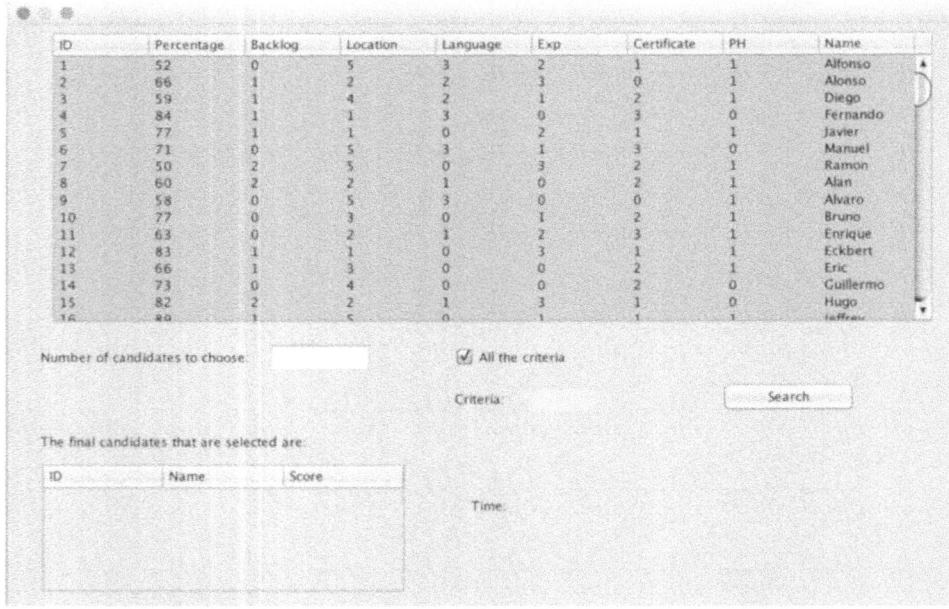

Figure 7. Function to read the candidates
Source: The authors

```
60      private void Init() throws IOException{
61
62          Candidates = data.ReadCsv();
63          FillTable(data.getColumnNames(), Candidates);
64          CreateTableResult();
65          CheckCrite.setSelected(true);
66      }
```

The function shown in Figure 8 is very important because it is the obtaining of all the information about the candidates to be evaluated.

Each criterion is obtained, the qualification and the name of the person.

Line 35: The number of columns that the file has is obtained.

Line 36: The name of the columns is obtained.

Line 38 to 42: Take a tour to obtain all the criteria of the candidates and save them in an ArrayList. This data structure was used because it is much easier to keep information in list form, mining and handling of such information is more efficient.

The items are added to the list in the order they are inserted.

Figure 9 shows the separation of the names of the columns with the information of the candidates to be able to create the table and show it. It is done through a loop that interacts with each column and each evaluation criterion.

Line 36: Create the Model for the interaction of the table, where the candidates will be shown.

Line 38 to 40: The name of the columns crossing the array is added to the Model.

Line 42 to 44: The candidate data is added to the model to going through the array.

Line 47: The model is added to the view table.

Figure 10 shows the event where the user already requires searching the most suitable candidate for the desired needs. The parameters that the user needs to find their candidate are obtained, for example, the number of candidates that they need to search with the skills require, in the same way can be strict and search for the candidate who know all the criteria or only that know certain criteria, that will depend on the user.

Line 323 and 324: It makes the instance of the class of the Chronometer and starts it.

Line 326: Function to clean the results table.

Line 328: Get the number of candidates you want to search.

Line 334 to 338: Condition to check if "All criteria" was selected or enter a number of criteria to evaluate.

Line 340: Function to evaluate the criteria by the candidate.

Line 342: Function to sort by scores from highest to lowest of the candidates that approved the criteria.

Line 344: Function that shows the candidate (s) already ordered in the results table. It only shows the number of candidates who entered by the user that you want to search. (Line 328).

Line 349 and 350: Clean the fields.
Line 352 and 353: Stop the chronometer and show the time.

Figure 11 shows the candidate qualifies, reviews each criterion and depending on the qualification sought by the user, adds his score.

Figure 8. Function to read the CSV file separated by comma
Source: The authors

```
24      public ArrayList ReadCsv() throws IOException{
25
26          BufferedReader br = null;
27          ArrayList list = new ArrayList();
28
29          try {
30
31              br =new BufferedReader(new FileReader(Read));
32
33              String line = br.readLine();
34
35              Column = line.split(",").length;
36              ColumnName = line;
37
                while (null != line) {
39                  line = br.readLine();
40                  if(!line.equals(""))
41                      list.add(line);
42              }
43
44          } catch (Exception e) {
45
46          } finally {
47              if (null!=br) {
48                  br.close();
49              }
50          }
51
52          return list;
53      }
```

Figure 9. Function where data are obtained from the fileSource: The authors

```
34      private void FillTable(ArrayList NameColumns, ArrayList Candidates){
35
36          DefaultTableModel model = new DefaultTableModel();
37
38          NameColumns.stream().forEach((Name) -> {
39              model.addColumn(Name);
40          });
41
42          Candidates.stream().forEach((Data) -> {
43              model.addRow(Data.toString().split(","));
44          });
45
46          TblCandidates.setBackground(Color.LIGHT_GRAY);
47          TblCandidates.setModel(model);
48      }
```

Figure 10. Event to looking candidates
Source: The authors

```
321   private void BtnSearchActionPerformed(java.awt.event.ActionEvent evt) {
322
323       Chronometer crono = new Chronometer();
324       crono.Start();
325
326       CleanTable();
327
328       int NumCandidates = Integer.parseInt(TxtNumCand.getText());
329
330       try {
331
          int NumCriateria = 0;
333
334          if(CheckCrite.isSelected()){
335              NumCriateria = data.getColumn() - 2;
336          }else{
337              NumCriateria = Integer.parseInt(TxtCriterios.getText());
338          }
339
340          LinkedHashMap finalCandidates = AddScore(Candidates, NumCriateria);
341
342          Map OrderCandidates =  Sorted(finalCandidates);
343
344          PrintFinalCandidate(OrderCandidates, NumCandidates);
345
346       } catch (Exception ex) {JOptionPane.showMessageDialog(null, ex.toString());}
347
348
349       TxtNumCand.setText("");
350       TxtCriterios.setText("");
351
352       crono.Stop();
353       lblTime.setText(crono.getTime());
354
355   }
```

Line 70 to 76: Certain points are added to the criteria that will be evaluated by the candidate.

Line 82 to 125: The criteria of the candidate are reviewed and analyzed one by one if it is fulfilled, a certain score is given depending on what was assigned by criteria (Line 10 to 76).

Line 127 to 129: If the criteria were approved, it is saved in the array together with the score obtained.

Figure 12 shows the code for the ranking from highest to lowest and shows the candidate (s) suitable for the user. A data structure, "Map" is used because it allows the value to store with a key and it is much easier to find the desired value. In this case, it is easier to find the name of the candidate who obtained the best score in the evaluation.

Figure 13 shows the suitable candidates who were ordered, go through this function, where it shows in a table the name and the score obtained from the candidate that was the most suitable under the sought criteria. Similarly, if the user enters that he/she requires to search more than one candidate, this function will show the number of candidates with the highest score.

Line 155: The model of results table is obtained to be able to use it.

Line 158 to 168: It obtains an Id, name and the score of the candidate adding to the model of the table to be able to visualize it.

Line 166: The cycle process is interrupted as long as the number of candidates that the user entered to view has already been saved.

Line 170: The model sends results to the table.

Figure 11. Function where add the scores to criteria
Source: The authors

```
68    private LinkedHashMap AddScore(ArrayList candidates, int noOfCriateria){
69
70        int Porcentaje = 25;
71        int AcumTrabajo = 10;
72        int Ubicacion = 10;
73        int Lenguajes = 20;
74        int Experiencia = 10;
75        int Certificados = 20;
76        int Discapacidad = 5;
77
78        LinkedHashMap passedcandidates = new LinkedHashMap();
79        int score = 0;
80        int passedCriterias = 0;
81
82        for (Object rows : candidates) {
83            String [] row = rows.toString().split(",");
84
85            //PERCENTAGE
86            if (Integer.parseInt(row[1]) > 60){
87                score += Porcentaje;
88                passedCriterias += 1;
89            }
90
91            //BACKLOG
92            if (Integer.parseInt(row[2]) == 0){
93                score += AcumTrabajo;
94                passedCriterias += 1;
95            }
96
97            //LOCATION
98            if (Integer.parseInt(row[3]) < 4){
99                score += Ubicacion;
100                passedCriterias += 1;
101            }
102
103            //LANGUAGES
104            if (Integer.parseInt(row[4]) > 1){
105                score += Lenguajes;
106                passedCriterias += 1;
107            }
108
109            //EXPERIENCE
110            if (Integer.parseInt(row[5]) > 0){
111                score += Experiencia;
112                passedCriterias += 1;
113            }
114
115            //CERTIFICATION
116            if (Integer.parseInt(row[6]) > 0){
117                score += Certificados;
118                passedCriterias += 1;
119            }
120
121            //PH
122            if (Integer.parseInt(row[7]) < 1){
123                score += Discapacidad;
124                passedCriterias += 1;
125            }
126
127            if (passedCriterias >= noOfCriateria){
128                passedcandidates.put(rows, score);
129            }
130
131            score = 0;
132            passedCriterias = 0;
133
134        }
135
136        return passedcandidates;
137    }
```

Figure 12. Code for ordering candidates
Source: The authors

```
142      private Map Sorted(LinkedHashMap<String, Integer> FinCandidates){
143
144          Map<String, Integer> Order = new LinkedHashMap<>();
145          FinCandidates.entrySet().stream()
146              .sorted(Map.Entry.<String, Integer>comparingByValue().reversed())
147              .forEachOrdered(x -> Order.put(x.getKey(), x.getValue()));
148
149          return Order;
150      }
```

Figure 13. Candidates who approved the criteria
Source: The authors

```
152      private void PrintFinalCandidate(Map OrderCandidates, int noOfCandidates){
153
154          int cont = 1;
155          DefaultTableModel model = (DefaultTableModel) TblResult.getModel();
156
157          Iterator<Map.Entry<String, Integer>> it = OrderCandidates.entrySet().iterator();
158          while (it.hasNext()) {
159              Map.Entry<String, Integer> pair = it.next();
160
161              String [] Pair = pair.getKey().split(",");
162              String ID = Pair[0];
163              String Nombre = Pair[8];
164              model.addRow(new Object[]{ID, Nombre, pair.getValue()});
165
166              if(cont++ == noOfCandidates)
167                  break;
168          }
169
170          TblResult.setModel(model);
171
172      }
```

Screen *Shots*

Figure 14 shows all the candidates with their criteria read from the CSV file so be able to evaluate them.

Figure 15 shows the field where the number of candidates must be written to know the most optimal.

Figure 16 shows the selection criteria. If deactivate "All the criteria", the user must enter the number of minimum criteria to evaluate.

Figure 17 shows two candidates that were evaluated with all the criteria.

Necessarily, the user must comply with the seven criteria for this case.

Figure 18 shows the duration in which it casts the candidates. The format of the time is: Hours: Minutes: Seconds.

Figure 19 shows an example: the date was entered with five candidates and only three criteria to evaluate. In this option, it evaluates all the criteria of the candidate but only approves if the candidate exceeds the number of criteria entered by the user. Example: There are a total of seven criteria to evaluate; the user enters a minimum of three criteria to approve. If a candidate has more than three criteria, he is a final candidate, if he does not fulfill minimum 3, he is rejected.

Figure 14. Results from the CSV file
Source: The authors

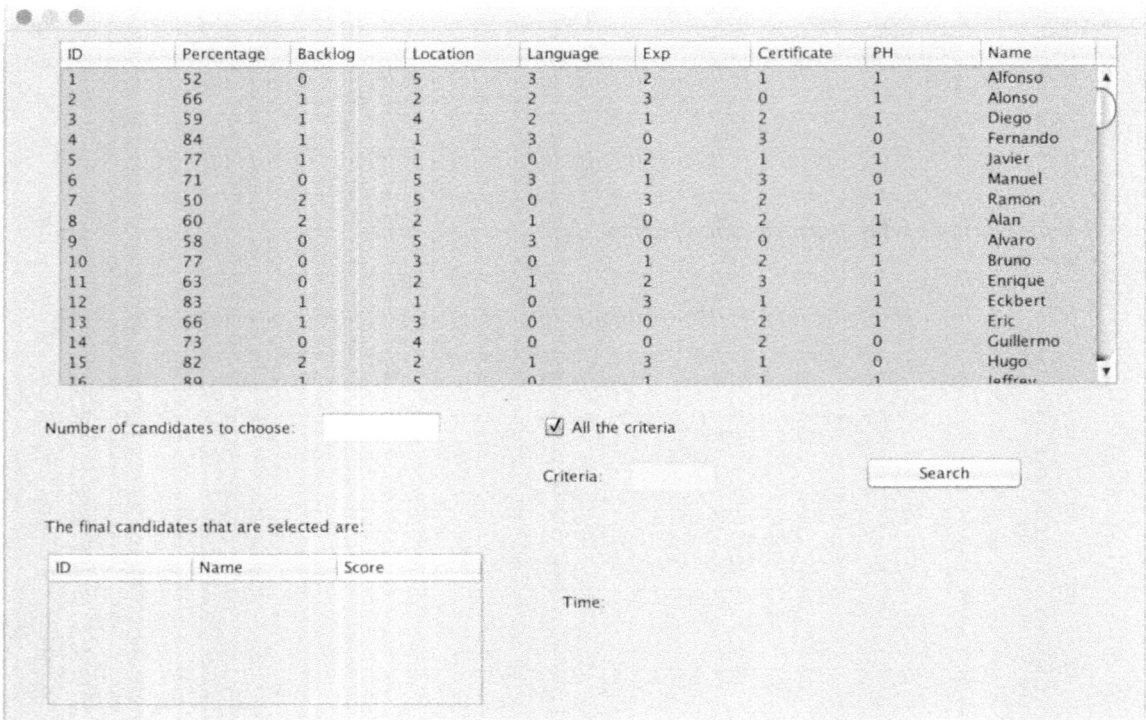

Figure 15. Selecting the number of candidates
Source: The authors

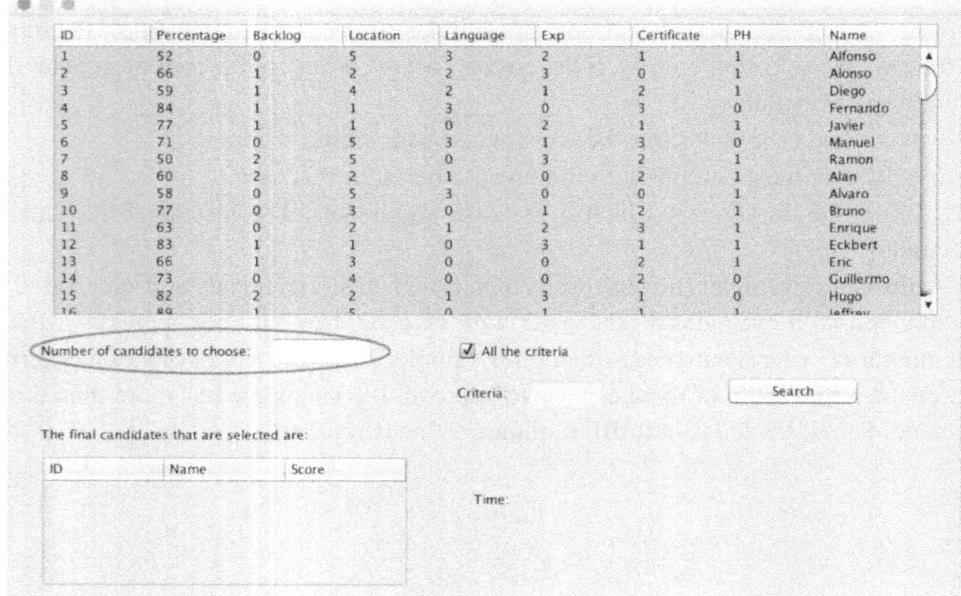

Figure 16. Choose criteria
Source: The authors

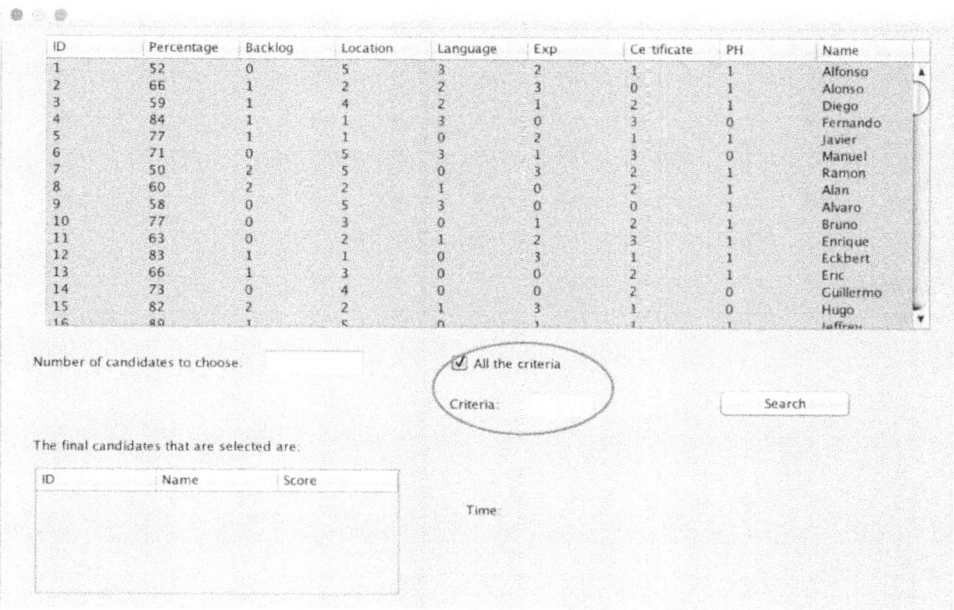

Figure 17. Results of the evaluation
Source: The authors

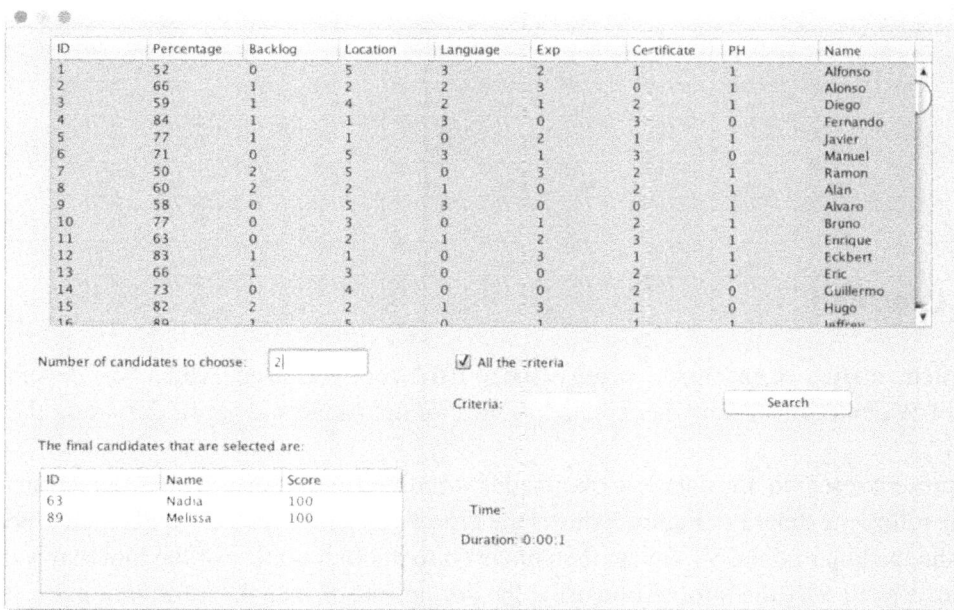

Figure 18. Timer
Source: The authors

The final candidates that are selected are:

ID	Name	Score
63	Nadia	100
89	Melissa	100

Time:

Duration: 0:00:1

Figure 19. Example
Source: The authors

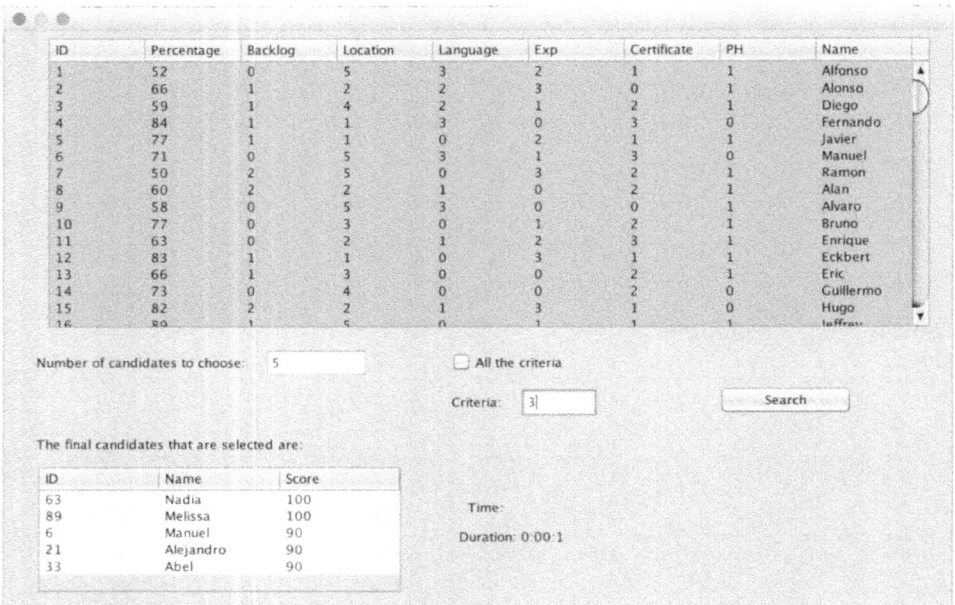

Machine Learning

For the implementation of machine learning, the WEKA tool was used, which was developed by the University of Waikato. It is a software created in Java for data analysis. Figure 20 shows the process of the analysis.

For the present research, the database obtained is submitted to the software to perform an analysis, as shown in the following diagram. Figure 3 shows the process by which the transformation is performed. It starts with the loading of the CSV file, to then move on to the first section of the tool that is the process. The next step is to classify the information using the j48 algorithm, then the information is grouped using the k-means algorithm and finally the association with the a priori algorithm is performed. J48 algorithm is a derivation of C4.5 algorithm, and its purpose is to construct decision and grouping threes in the field of data mining (Tello, Eslava & Tobias, 2013). The k-means algorithm is a grouping algorithm that is applied to the analysis for the prediction of scenarios (Reena & Selvi, 2016). The a priori algorithm is used to apply to learn in the operation rules of a data set (Randhir, Gupta & Selokar, 2013).

Figure 20. Analysis process

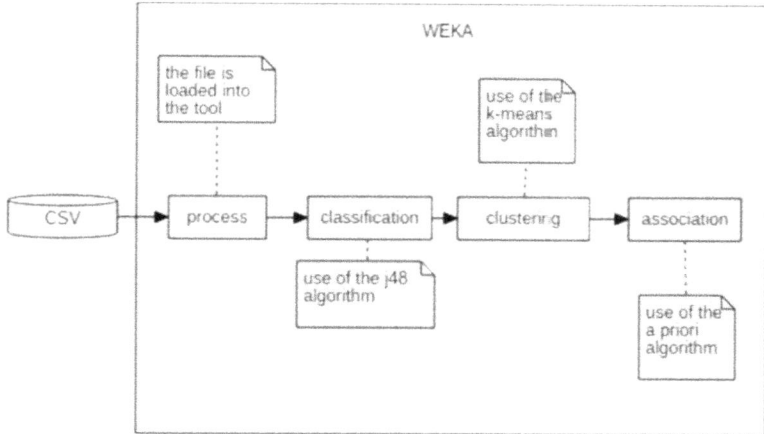

Process

The structure of the CSV file is composed of 100 records, and 7 criteria, as explained in the previous section. The metadata that makes up the structure is location; for the specific case of the present work, the case study is the city of Guadalajara, Mexico, which is divided into 7 zones: Downtown, Minerva, Huentitán, Oblatos, Tetlán, Technological and Industrial. The languages considered are Spanish, English, French and Chinese. The experience is of vital importance for the hiring of a prospect for a position. Respect the software, Java, c #, python, and ruby are the 4 technologies requested, the certificates support the experience of the supporter; it is evaluated how many it has, finally it is considered some possible physical impediment and if it is male or female. The model explained is shown in Figure 21.

The distribution of the age variable is shown in Table 2. It can be seen that most people who apply live in Tetlán zone and those who are less interested in applying live in Oblatos zone. From the total of candidates, it is observed that 47 are men and 53 women, also observed that of the required experience, 36 know ruby, 12 c #, 26 python and 26 java; as is shown in Table 3. Of the languages, it is observed that the majority of people speak Spanish and only the minority speaks Chinese or another language, as is shown in Table 4.

Figure 21. Analysis scheme
Source: The authors

```
@attribute Location {centro,tecnológico,industrial,tetlán,minerva,huentitán,oblatos}
@attribute Language {spanish,french,chinese,english}
@attribute Exp {ruby,c#,python,java}
@attribute Certificate_binarized {0,1}
@attribute PH_binarized {0,1}
@attribute Sex {man,woman}
```

Table 2. Location distribution

Number	Zone	Count
1	Centro	19
2	Tecnológico	16
3	Industrial	11
4	Tetlán	23
5	Minerva	9
6	Huentitán	14
7	Oblatos	8

Source: The authors

Table 3. Distribution of experience

Number	Label	Count
1	ruby	36
2	c#	12
3	python	26
4	java	26

Source: The authors

Table 4. Distribution of languages

Number	Language	Count
1	Spanish	31
2	French	22
3	Chinese	21
4	English	26

Source: The authors

RESULTS

The results of the present research are described in two moments; first, the performance of the application of the algorithm is shown according to the loads of candidates and evaluation criteria. The loads range from one hundred to one million candidates and from two to seven criteria. The result is shown in Table 5. The second moment is described by showing results of the analysis by applying machine learning.

Table 5. Performance of the algorithm with different data

Candidates	Criteria	Time
100	2	25 Milliseconds
100	5	26 Milliseconds
100	7	28 Milliseconds
1,000	2	31 Milliseconds
1,000	5	31 Milliseconds
1,000	7	32 Milliseconds
1,000,000	2	2 Seconds
1,000,000	5	3 Seconds
1,000,000	7	3 Seconds

Source: The authors

Classification of Information

The j48 algorithm is used to construct a decision tree which has two approaches: construction and pruning (Muralidharan, & Sugumaran, 2013). The j48 algorithm is an implementation of the C4.5 algorithm that was proposed by Quinlan in 1993 and it is used to identify target values of a data set. The predicted values are the dependent variables (Ibrahim, Yazin, Udzir & Abdul, 2016). For classify the information, the j48 algorithm was applied to construct a tree for the analysis, the result is shown in Figure 22. It is observed that the algorithm performs information crossings with all the variables.

Figure 22. Result decision tree
Source: The authors

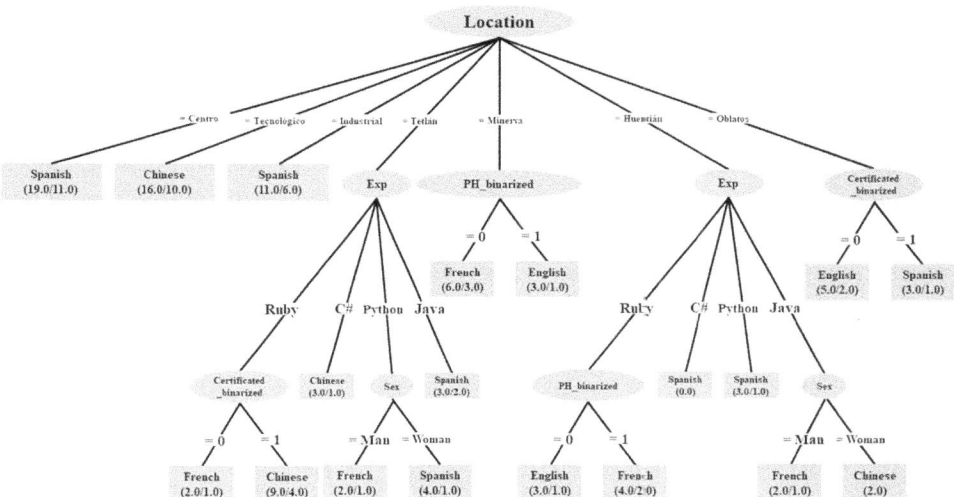

Clustering

The k-means calculation divides the data set into subsets or groups (M_1, M_2, M_3, ... M_k). A group (M_i) is a group of vertices and centroids (μ_i) where i is an integer between 1 and k. The same vertex is not shared. By applying Equation (1), it is possible to minimize the distance of the centroids (Rezaei, & Gunpinar, 2018).

$$\min \sum_{i=1}^{k} \sum_{x \in M_i} || x - u_i ||^2 \tag{1}$$

The algorithm is used, which shows as a result that the information is grouped into two segments, in cluster 0 the highest percentage is concentrated with the 55 of the information where the men in the technologic zone know python and are certified, while in the 1 the 45 of the information is concentrated where women in the Tetlán zone known java and speak French. Figure 23 shows the result.

Figure 23. Clusters
Source: The authors

Attribute	Full Data (100.0)	Cluster# 0 (55.0)	1 (45.0)
Location	tetlán	tecnológico	tetlán
Language	spanish	spanish	french
Exp	ruby	python	java
Certificate_binarized	1	1	1
PH_binarized	1	1	0
Sex	woman	man	woman

Association

The basis for the association rules was born in IBM in 1993 by R. Agrawal at Almaden research center. Originally, they were raised to identify a set of client operations in a database. The association rules have been applied to physical activities, business, finance, and medicine, among others. The association algorithms are distinguished in two moments; support and confidence. The support means the frequency with which an element appears in a list and is defined according to the Equation (2).

$$Support(A \Rightarrow B) = P(A \cap B) \tag{2}$$

The confidence consists of the generation of the association rules according to the Equation (3) (Li et al., 2017):

$$Confidence(A \Rightarrow B) = P(A \mid B) \tag{3}$$

For the association rules, the apriori algorithm was used, through which it was possible to build rules from the given information. The result is shown below and in Figure 24:

1. The men who are in the center are certified.
2. People who speak Chinese and have a disability are certified.
3. Men who speak Chinese are certified.
4. The people of the industrial zone are certified.
5. The women of Huentitán are certified.
6. The experience in python is certified.
7. Men who know java are certified.
8. Men with some disability who know ruby are certified.
9. The Chinese language is certified.
10. Disabled people who know ruby are certified.

In Figure 24, the rules are shown with the degree of confidence

Figure 24. Association rules and the level of trust
Source: The authors

```
1.  Location=centro Sex=man 12 ==> Certificate_binarized=1 12    <conf:(1)> lift:(1.28) lev:(0.03) [2] conv:(2.64)
2.  Language=chinese PH_binarized=1 12 ==> Certificate_binarized=1 11    <conf:(0.92)> lift:(1.18) lev:(0.02) [1] conv:(1.32)
3.  Language=chinese Sex=man 12 ==> Certificate_binarized=1 11    <conf:(0.92)> lift:(1.18) lev:(0.02) [1] conv:(1.32)
4.  Location=industrial 11 ==> Certificate_binarized=1 10    <conf:(0.91)> lift:(1.17) lev:(0.01) [1] conv:(1.21)
5.  Location=huentitán Sex=woman 11 ==> Certificate_binarized=1 10    <conf:(0.91)> lift:(1.17) lev:(0.01) [1] conv:(1.21)
6.  Exp=python PH_binarized=1 11 ==> Certificate_binarized=1 10    <conf:(0.91)> lift:(1.17) lev:(0.01) [1] conv:(1.21)
7.  Exp=java Sex=man 11 ==> Certificate_binarized=1 10    <conf:(0.91)> lift:(1.17) lev:(0.01) [1] conv:(1.21)
8.  Exp=ruby PH_binarized=1 Sex=man 11 ==> Certificate_binarized=1 10    <conf:(0.91)> lift:(1.17) lev:(0.01) [1] conv:(1.21)
9.  Language=chinese 21 ==> Certificate_binarized=1 19    <conf:(0.9)> lift:(1.16) lev:(0.03) [2] conv:(1.54)
10. Exp=ruby PH_binarized=1 20 ==> Certificate_binarized=1 18    <conf:(0.9)> lift:(1.15) lev:(0.02) [2] conv:(1.47)
```

CONCLUSION

It is possible to reduce the stress levels of the personnel in charge of applying the surveys and analyze the results for a given position. This is achieved through the application of the model presented in the present work; using the algorithm we identify the best profiles. Through the application of artificial intelligence techniques, it is possible to predict behavior and group the profiles according to the results of the application. The importance of having information prior to the application of surveys allows visualizing scenarios for decision making.

FUTURE RESEARCH

As part of the future work of the present work, the development of a tool is contemplated through which it is possible to apply the surveys to the candidates for a job in and that the results are stored in real time through a mobile application.

REFERENCES

Arcila-Calderón, C., Ortega-Mohedano, F., Jiménez-Amores, J., & Trullenque, S. (2017). Análisis supervi-sado de sentimientos políticos en español: Clasificación en tiempo real de tweets basada en aprendizaje automático. *El Profesional de la Información*, 26(5), 973–982. doi:10.3145/epi.2017.sep.18

Baldassarre, M. T., Piattini, M., Pino, F. J., & Visaggio, G. (2009). Comparing ISO/IEC 12207 and CMMI-DEV: Towards a mapping of ISO/IEC 15504-7. In *2009 ICSE Workshop on Software Quality* (pp. 59-64). ICSE. 10.1109/WOSQ.2009.5071558

Broder, A. Z., Kirsch, A., Kumar, R., Mitzenmacher, M., Upfal, E., & Vassilvitskii, S. (2009). The hiring problem and Lake Wobegon strategies. *SIAM Journal on Computing*, 39(4), 1233–1255. doi:10.1137/07070629X

Goodfellow, I., Mcdaniel, P., & Papernot, N. (2018). Making Machine Learning Robust Against Adversarial Inputs. *Communications of the ACM, 61*(7), 56–66. doi:10.1145/3134599

Hendrick, H. W. (1991). Ergonomics in organizational design and management. *Ergonomics, 34*(6), 743–756. doi:10.1080/00140139108967348

Ibrahim, H., Yasin, W., Udzir, N. I., & Abdul Hamid, N. W. (2016). Intelligent Cooperative Web Caching Policies For Media Objects Based On J48 Decision Tree And Naïve Bayes Supervised Machine Learning Algorithms In Structured Peer-To-Peer Systems. *Journal Of Information & Communication Technology, 15*(2), 85–116.

Kononenko, I. (2018). Early Machine Learning Research in Ljubljana. *Informatica, 42*(1), 3-6.

Langley, P., & Simon, H. A. (1995). Applications of Machine Learning and Rule Induction. *Communications of the ACM, 38*(11), 55–64. doi:10.1145/219717.219768

Lear, C. (2011). How can system administrators reduce stress and conflict in the workplace? *ACM Queue; Tomorrow's Computing Today, 9*(1), 1–10.

Li, Q., Zhang, Y., Kang, H., Xin, Y., & Shi, C. (2017). Mining association rules between stroke risk factors based on the Apriori algorithm. *Technology and Health Care, 25*, S197–S205. doi:10.3233/THC-171322 PMID:28582907

Montero, R. (2000). *Un paso hacia el futuro: el desarrollo de la Macroergonomia, en Factores Humanos*. Academic Press.

Možina, M. (2018). Arguments in Interactive Machine Learning. *Informatica, 42*(1), 53-59.

Muralidharan, V., & Sugumaran, V. (2013). Selection Of Discrete Wavelets For Fault Diagnosis Of Monoblock Centrifugal Pump Using The J48 Algorithm. *Applied Artificial Intelligence, 27*(1), 1–19. doi:10.1080/08839514.2012.721694

Palferman, D. (2011). Managing Conflict and Stress in the Workplace: Theory and Practice. *Legal Information Management, 11*(2), 122–125. doi:10.1017/S1472669611000417

Piattini Velthuis, M., García Rubio, F., & Caballero Muñoz-Reja, I. (2007). *Calidad de sistemas informáticos*. Alfaomega.

Randhir, H. N., Gupta, R., & Selokar, G. R. (2013). Extract Knowledge and Association Rule from Free Log Data using an Apriori Algorithm. *International Journal Of Advanced Computer Research, 3*(12), 191–196.

Realyvásquez, A., & Maldonado-Macías, A. (2018). Measuring the Complex Construct of Macroergonomic Compatibility: A Manufacturing System Case Study. *Complexity, 2018*, 1–10. doi:10.1155/2018/7374307

Reena, R., & Selvi, R. T. (2016). Analyzing software defect prediction using k-means and expectation maximization clustering algorithm based on genetic feature selection. *Journal on Software Engineering, 11*(1), 28-36.

Rezaei, M., & Gunpinar, E. (2018). A k-means clustering based shape retrieval technique for 3d mesh models. *Selcuk University Journal of Engineering, Science & Technology, 6*(1), 114-128. doi:10.15317/Scitech.2018.119

Silva, L. D., Nickel, E. M., & dos Santos, F. A. N. V. (2018). Evaluation of Macroergonomic Methods for the Application of Organization Analyzes in Startups. In F. Rebelo & M. Soares (Eds.), *Advances in Ergonomics in Design. AHFE 2017. Advances in Intelligent Systems and Computing* (Vol. 588). Cham: Springer.

Szajowski, K., & Tamaki, M. (2016). Shelf life of candidates in the generalized secretary problem. *Operations Research Letters, 44*(4), 498–502. doi:10.1016/j.orl.2016.05.002

Tello, M. L., Eslava, H. J., & Tobías, L. B. (2013). Análisis y evaluación del nivel de riesgo en el otorgamiento de créditos financieros utilizando técnicas de minería de datos. *Visión Electrónica, 7*(1), 13–26.

KEY TERMS AND DEFINITIONS

AI: Artificial intelligence.

Array List: In Java it is a dynamic storage structure that allows to store data in memory, this has the similarity to a list.

C#: Microsoft object-oriented programming language.

Clustering: Grouping technique according to distance or similarity.

Csv: File separated by commas. Commonly used to manage data in an open data environment or to share non-native information between different software packages.

Data Structure: It is a particular way of organizing data in a computer so that they can be used efficiently.

Decision Tree: Intelligent model based on rules and used to predict.

ISO 12207: Standard for the life cycle specification system development of the International Standardization Organization.

J48 Algorithm: Algorithm that generates decision trees based on rules to classify.

Java: Set of computer programs. Also known as programming language or software.

Jframe: It is a graphic library to generate windows on which to add different objects with which you can interact with the user.

Loop: Also known as a cycle, it is a statement that executes a piece of code repeatedly, until the condition assigned to that loop is no longer fulfilled.

Machine Learning: Branch of artificial intelligence that allows computers to learn.

Macroergonomy: A field that takes care of three aspects: the healthy environment in the workplace, safety, and efficiency.

Map: Data structure that allows to store "key/value" pairs; in such a way that for a key we only have one value.

Object: Entity in the memory of the computer that has properties (attributes or data about itself stored by the object) and specific available operations (methods).

Object-Oriented Programming: Programming paradigm that uses objects and their interactions to design applications and computer programs.

Python: Interpreted programming language.

Ruby: Mixed programming language between interpreted and object-oriented.

Weka: Software for managing information that has to do with machine learning.

This research was previously published in Advanced Macroergonomics and Sociotechnical Approaches for Optimal Organizational Performance; pages 261-285, copyright year 2019 by Business Science Reference (an imprint of IGI Global).

APPENDIX

Table 6. Extract of 19 of the 100 Records in the Database

ID	Percentage	Backlog	Location	Language	Exp	Certificate	PH	Sex	Age
1	52	0	Centro	Spanish	ruby	2	1	Man	20
2	66	1	Tecnológico	French	c#	3	1	Woman	30
3	59	1	Industrial	Spanish	python	3	1	Man	23
4	84	1	Tetlán	French	ruby	0	0	Man	24
5	77	1	Tetlán	Chinese	c#	2	1	Woman	28
6	71	0	Minerva	Chinese	java	2	0	Man	19
7	50	2	Huentitán	Chinese	java	1	1	Woman	24
8	60	2	Minerva	Spanish	java	0	1	Man	18
9	58	0	Tetlán	Spanish	java	0	1	Woman	34
10	77	0	Huentitán	Spanish	python	2	1	Woman	34
11	63	0	Tetlán	French	java	0	1	Woman	23
12	83	1	Centro	French	ruby	1	1	Man	22
13	66	1	Centro	English	ruby	3	1	Woman	21
14	73	0	Minerva	Spanish	python	1	0	Man	20
15	82	2	Tetlán	Spanish	python	0	0	Woman	28
16	89	1	Minerva	English	python	3	1	Woman	20
17	90	1	Industrial	Spanish	ruby	3	0	Woman	31
18	49	1	Centro	English	ruby	3	1	Man	27
19	83	1	Tetlán	Chinese	ruby	2	1	Man	26

Chapter 16
Human Resource Management in Agile Scrum Processes

Matthew Zingoni
University of New Orleans, USA

ABSTRACT

The value agile scrum process can generate is not guaranteed simply by mere adoption. Rather the process creates an opportunity for improvement in the development process. Mismanagement of the approach by an organization can reduce the potential added value or in extreme situations have a negative impact. Therefore, appropriate management procedures are necessary to realize the full potential of the agile scrum approach. This chapter focuses on the human resource challenges the agile scrum approach creates for an organization. The dynamic pace, cross-functional composition, and self-directed team approach requires special consideration in the development of most human resource functions. In particular, the authors will review changes to the employee selection, performance management, and learning and career development processes. These changes will better align these functions with the values and principals of the agile scrum approach and help organizations manage this sometimes chaotic approach to innovation without constraining it.

INTRODUCTION

The benefits of an Agile Scrum process have been well established in the software development field (Rigby, et. al., 2016) and other organizations have taken notice. Today an Agile Scrum process approach can be seen applied to fields beyond information technology such as marketing and financial (Oprins, et al., 2019; Sherman, et. al., 2017). Essentially an Agile Scrum process approach is increasingly being applied to situations where innovation is needed to respond to rapidly changing customers' demands (Rigby, et. al., 2018). This creates a challenge to organizations to not only implement an agile scrum approach but to also create processes and procedures to manage the Agile Scrum process and also cultivate the proper organizational climate needed to realize its full benefit in a sustainable manner (Mahajan, 2013; Rigby, et. al., 2016).

DOI: 10.4018/978-1-6684-3873-2.ch016

Like previous process innovations such as total quality management, the Agile Scrum approach offers an opportunity for a competitive advantage but not a certainty. In what has been described as a chaotic approach to innovation (Rubin, 2012) the Agile Scrum approach to development generates several challenges for organizations to overcome. Just like a sailor cannot control the wind but instead must try to direct and harness it, managers must direct Agile Scrum teams without containing the sometimes-chaotic process of innovation. This chapter will address some of the human resource challenges an organization must overcome to successfully implement the agile scrum approach to innovation and other dynamic endeavors in a sustainable manner. Specifically, this chapter reviews and offers recommendations for an organization to consider in the areas of talent acquisition and management, which are vital to implementing an Agile Scrum approach effectively (Gilles & van der Meer, 2017).

Human resource management addresses who works for an organization and how work gets done. In particular human resource processes (i.e. employee selection, performance management, talent deployment, and employee career development) play an essential role in the acquisition and cultivation of the main raw material needed to utilize the agile scrum approach, which is the individual. The Agile Scrum approach requires a cross functional team to self-navigate a demanding, fast pace, dynamic environment (Beck, et. al, 2001; Rubin, 2012; Rigby, et. al., 2016). The Agile Scrum approach has a set of values and principles that human resource functions need to be aligned with to be successful. Specifically, agile processes are built around people over process and tools, emphasize working prototypes over excessive debate, respond to change than follow a plan, and focuses on customer collaboration instead of structured contracts (Beck, et. al, 2001; Rigby, et. al., 2016). It is important that organizations have human resource practices that reflect these values and principals so the Agile Scrum approach can be effectively managed but not constrained. However, human resource practices have traditionally been slow to involve (Cappelli, 2015) at the organizational level so it is important that organizations make adjustment to the procedures used to manage employees directly involved in the Agile Scrum approach to innovation. This will allow the organization to maximize the benefit of the Agile Scrum approach and develop human resources practices that may be suited to be expanded company wide. In short organizational level human resources changes may be slow to evolve but if companies can successfully create human resource practices to accommodate their Agile Scrum involved employees it could lead to a more agile approach to human resources at an organization wide level.

This chapter will review the major aspects of human resources that will need to be adjusted to accommodate the Agile Scrum approach. First, it will review adjustments needed to the hiring process for employees who will directly participant in work utilizing the Agile Scrum approach. Next, it will review how changes to the performance management procedures an organization uses will be necessary for employees to make the corrective changes in their work behavior that is required by such a dynamic process. This in turn will transition to a discussion on talent deployment which is how an organization should determine what Agile Scrum team an employee should be involved with next. A review of the changes to how an organization handles career development of their Agile Scrum involved employees will then follow. Lastly. it will discuss how adjusting human resource practices used to manage Agile Scrum involved employees will assist in the evolution of a more agile approach to human resources at the organizational level. During these discussions examples not only from the technology field but also other innovation focused industries such as the entertainment industry and fashion industry will be used.

Employee Selection in an Agile Scum Context

All aspects of human resources are interdependent and therefore equally important. However, employee selection is the human resource function that gets the most attention as it directly determines who joins an organization. Due in part to this attention, employee selection procedures have greatly evolved from the days of solely relying on a single job interview. This evolution has included organization trying to assess applicants fit at multiple levels such as, person-job, person-group, and person-organization (Kristof-Brown, et. al., 2005) and the increased use of psychological assessments and situational judgements test (Chamorro-Premuzic, 2015). When selecting employees to work in an agile scum approach a radical departure from these advancements is not necessary but adjustments, particularly to how each selection tool is weighted in the hiring decision and who should be involved in the selection process, is needed (Gilles & van der Meer, 2017). Furthermore, the qualities desired in an employee are difficult to directly measure so organization need to take steps to utilize multiple selection tools to indirectly measure these qualities in candidates.

The job interview has always been and will continue to be the cornerstone of employee selection in business. In particular, the structure interview approach, where a predetermined set of questions are developed to measure desired qualifications and are consistently asked across all applicants, is vital to any selection process. This of course remains true for employee selection for positions that will have a role in an agile scrum approach. However, during the question development process an emphasis on measuring not only technical knowledge but also person-group fit, emergent leadership, and broad competencies is important.

Focus on fit between an employee and a potential job, group, and or organization is vitally important to all hires (Kristof-Brown, et. al., 2005). However, due to the cross functional team composition of the Agile Scrum process group-fit becomes a priority. Group-fit focuses on the match between and individual and their work group (Kristof-Brown, et. al., 2005). In an interview setting a panel interview with existing team members is considered a best practice. However, due to revolving number of team memberships a new employee will be part of in an agile scrum approach, team members will not be a constant. Therefore, a panel interview with experienced proven members of ongoing agile scum process should be conducted. Even though these panel members will not always directly work with the applicant their perspective and input will be valuable. For example, GE utilize a cross functional team to assist in all hiring requisitions (Cappelli & Tavis, 2018).

Although not specifically established in the "fit" literature it would be valuable to try to measure person-approach fit. That is does the applicants competencies match the unique demands of the Agile Scrum approach. This is particularly true if the applicant does not have previous experience working on an Agile Scrum development team. In fact, a lack of experience is one of the most significant challenges in implementing the Agile Scrum approach (Cappelli & Tavis, 2018). For example, the dynamic nature of Agile Scrum work creates a level of uncertainty that may be uncomfortable for some employees. Uncertainty has a significant negative relationship with performance for both students and professionals (Taipalus, et. al., 2018). Therefore, assessing an applicant's tolerance for ambiguity (Frenkel-Brunswik, 1948) would be valuable. Tolerance of ambiguity is often used to indicate how comfortable someone is with change. Furthermore, tolerance for ambiguity has been found to have a significant relationship to creativity (Zenasni, et. al., 2008) Tolerance for ambiguity is the combination of three factors (Budner, 1962). First factor is novelty, which is how comfortable someone is with new information and processes. Second is complexity, which is how comfortable some is with complex problems that change often. The last component is insolvability, which is how comfortable people are working on problems that do not have a clear or perfect solution. Overall, these components reflect agile scrum processes and therefore someone high in tolerance for ambiguity will likely be a better fit for the agile scrum approach.

In addition to the panel interview, contextual questions such as situational judgement test should be utilized as well. Situational judgement questions are a selection tool that presents an applicant a relevant challenging situation they are likely to encounter (Chamorro-Premuzic, 2015). Often the applicant is then given several choices of action to which they are to select what they feel is the most effective approach. Having an applicant complete a series of situational judgement questions and then discuss their responses with a panel would be the best course of action for hiring potential Agile Scrum team members.

A focus of the structure interview and situational judgment tests should be if the applicant reflects an emergent leadership style. In a New York Times article Google executive stated that emergent leadership and humility are more valuable the traditional leadership traits in a dynamic environment (Friedman, 2014). Emergent leadership does not only include the ability and motivation to step up and lead a group when the situation calls for it but also the ability to take a step back and let others lead when appropriate (Anderson & Wanberg, 1991). This is vital in a self-managed team like the ones used in Agile Scrum process because as objectives change during each sprint it is important for employees to be able to lead at times but also be a good follower at other times. Emergent leadership is a form of contingency or situational leadership models that are found to be the most useful in self-managed teams such as agile scrum teams (Anderson & Wanberg, 1991; Przybilla, et. al., 2019).

The use of assessments as a selection tool has steadily increased over the past decade. To the point where fortune 500 companies use assessments for over half of their entry level positions and almost three quarters of their upper management positions (Chamorro-Premuzic, 2015). These assessments offer another means to measure qualities we attempt to gauge in the structured interview process. As situational judgement test with a panel interview, as described above, can help measure person-group fit. Assessments could further this examination by assessing other traits and abilities valuable for dynamic team-based work. For example, certain dimensions of the Big Five personality dimensions as described below may be valuable.

- **Extroversion**: Sociable and outgoing
- **Neuroticism**: Stability in emotions
- **Openness to experience:** Being flexible and curious
- **Agreeableness**: Being courtesy and caring
- **Consciousness**: Detailed and achievement oriented

Specifically, of the Big Five personality dimensions agreeableness, being courtesy and caring, is vital for person group fit. Furthermore, openness to experience, being flexible and curious, also vital for a dynamic team structure particularly one that requires constant learning and adjusting (Barrick & Mount, 1991). In addition, emotional intelligence would be another important assessment to utilize in the selection process. Emotional intelligence is one's ability to be aware their emotion and keep them under control. Along with recognizing emotions in others and responding appropriately. Emotional intelligence is a vital ability for employees to not only respond to feedback appropriately but also giving feedback to others (Chamorro-Premuzic, 2015). Furthermore, emotional intelligence has been found beneficial in agile processes particularly regarding the dynamic nature and resulting time compression (Wilding, 1999).

In summary the selection process for employees needs to be refocused if the employee is going to be part of an Agile Scrum development team. The use of panel interviews, a focus on group-fit, and supporting assessments (i.e., agreeableness, openness to experience, emotional intelligence) are useful in most if not all hiring situations. However, these qualities are more relevant to the Agile Scrum process and therefore greater emphasis and weighting should be place on these selection tools.

Performance Management

Performance management is a systematic evaluation to ensure that employee's behavior is align with assigned responsibilities and organizational goals. Changes in performance management have been slower to evolve than that of other aspects of human resources. The traditional approach to performance management consist of an annual review, where a formal evaluation is conducting and discussed with the employee. In addition, corrective action is discussed along with any compensation decisions. This annual meeting is supported by shorter less formal coaching sessions throughout the year. Recently there has been movement away from this approach towards a more flexible process (Cappelli & Tavis, 2018). However, for employees participating in Agile Scrum development teams breaking away from this traditional approach is vital.

Performance management for employees involved in the Agile Scrum approach to development needs to take three major questions into consideration.

- **How often?** Focus on frequency and timing
- **Who to involve?** Stakeholders and information sources
- **Where it takes place?** Not location but organizational climate

First focus is on the "how" that is how often performance management should be conducted. When managing an Agile Scrum development teams, the timing and frequency of performance management efforts need to reflect the flow of work and not a predetermined day on the fiscal calendar. Specifically, once a project is completed a formal evaluation should be done to discuss the employee's contributions during the project and future assignments. Therefore, this conversation is not only serving a performance management purposes but also addresses deployment and development issues as well. Second, is the "who", that is who should be involved in the performance management process. When managing an Agile Scrum development teams, feedback needs to be conduct in a 360-degree format, with an emphasis on team member input. Due to the interdependent nature of Agile Scrum work it is challenging to determine individual contributions, so team member input is vital. Third is the "where", that is the environment or culture the feedback is given in. A culture of learning and improvement through effort is needed to avoid employees becoming defense and ensure employees are receptive to feedback (Murphy & Dweck, 2010).

Changing the timing and frequency of performance evaluation to match the flow of work is a change that is starting to be adopt in the greater business community. This approach can now be seen in fields that specialize on project-based work like business consulting and the entertainment industry. The approach's value can be best seen through the lens of Reinforcement Theory of motivation (Skinner, 1953). Reinforcement theory is a theory on how to change behavior and essentially discusses how an individual learns how to behave and not behave. According to reinforcement theory consequence for behavior dictates individual's future behavior in either a positive or negative direction. If an individual receives a positive consequence (i.e. reward) after a behavior the behavior will be repeated. If an individual receives a negative consequence (i.e., punishment) after a behavior the behavior will not be repeated. A key tenement to reinforcement theory is the timing of the consequence. The closer the consequence, either positive or negative (i.e., punishment or reward), to the behavior the stronger the directed influence will be on future behavior (Luthans, & Stajkovic 1999). Therefore, according to reinforcement theory, if a project is completed in June but the employee does not receive a full evaluation till the annual designated time in January the evaluation is less effective than one done immediately afterwards in July.

As reinforcement theory informs us on how to best time performance conversation it also holds true for compensation as far as pay for performance decisions. Performance conversation and compensation need to be aligned for both to be effective. The rewards aspect of receiving positive feedback is much strong if any financial reward is also given at the same time (Rigby, et. al., 2018). Therefore, any adjustment to the timing of performance conversations should have a corresponding adjustment to compensation decisions (Cappelli & Tavis, 2018). Also in regards to compensation, organizations need to focus on group level pay for performance policies not just individual level as agile scrum employees are producing a product or service that requires an interdependent group (Darrell, et. al., 2016; Rigby, et. al., 2018).

Frequency of feedback is also important to the performance management of employees participating in an agile scum approach to development. Frequent feedback during a project serves two major purposes. The first is it allows for the opportunity for corrective action by the employee. This approach reflects the workflow of Agile Scrum, which is incremental improvement of a series of iterations or sprints. Therefore, in an Agile Scrum approach the outcomes is constantly being incrementally improved so must the employee behavior who is directly producing the outcome. The second benefit of frequent performance conversations is managing expectations. It is natural for employees to have a positive bias in their perception of their own work contributions leading to inaccurate expectations of their performance level. This can be true about their intangible contributions and interpersonal behavior, which are better viewed from the eyes of team members. Realistic expectations about their performance level is vital to the success of the post project evaluation session. Employee are less defensive when personal information is predictable or anticipated and therefore more responsive to feedback.

Of course, having frequent performance management conversations and timely formal evaluation sessions can be a heavy time burden for any manager regardless of their good intentions. This is particularly true when incorporating feedback from all team members in a 360-degree fashion. In theory, frequent feedback from all stakeholders sounds great. However, the time burden makes it a daunting if not impossible task. Even if an Agile Scrum team accomplished this feat the time committed to it and away from directly working on their project could lead members to resent the performance management process and disengage from it. To avoid this fate, it is important that the performance management process be not only effective but efficient. This is especially true for feedback conversations that take place during an ongoing project.

Creating an efficient and effective performance management process is not solely about forms and procedures but also reflection of team and organizational culture and environment. A company's culture not being aligned with the values of the agile scrum approach is often seen as the most significant challenge to effectively implementing the agile scrum approach (Cappelli & Tavis, 2018). Therefore, discussion about performance need to be routine and a natural part of the organizations culture. For example, at the company Netflix feedback discussion are done frequently and are project driven, like recommended above. The frequent feedback conversations are done in person in a group setting. The conversation is a simple three statement approach about each team member. Please *start* doing this.

Please *stop* doing this. Please *continue* doing this (McCord, 2014). This "start, stop, continue" approach is efficient and predictable for employees and not difficult to make a requirement. However, team and organizational culture must reflect a respectful and forgiving environment also referred to as a learning culture (Murphy & Dweck, 2010). Creating an organization and team with a learning culture is the real challenge to using this approach and the right people go a long way in creating it.

Netflix contributes having this such environment to their rigorous selection process. Simple stated if you hire the right people implementing progressive human resource policies are possible (McCord, 2014). As recommended early in the chapter incorporating potential team members into the selection process in the form of panel interviews sets the right tone for the development of a learning culture. Having potential teammates involved in the selection process signals to an applicant that teammates are a valuable source of information and their feedback is respected.

Of course, creating a learning culture requires more than hiring the right people and involving them in the process. This alone handle the "who" part of human resource management, but steps still need to be taken to address the "how" question. The above recommendation of efficient quick feedback conversation addressing the "start", "stop", and "continue" questions are a significant step towards addressing the "how". However, supplying training that briefly describes how to formulate an effective feedback message is particularly important even in brief exchanges. Focusing on the behavior and subsequent problem not the person is essential. Behavior and problems are controllable where personal characteristics are harder to change and, in some cases, not possible at all. There is a big difference between saying "Stop being stupid because it is creating a problem" and "stop this stupid behavior because it is creating a problem".

Essentially a learning environment focus on improvement through effort (Murphy & Dweck, 2010). This approach is referred to as reflecting a growth mindset and is vital for innovation. Innovation and learning inherently involve mistakes and corrective action but always moving forward through effort and the desire to improve. When feedback focuses not on effort and process but instead on solely just the outcome produced it cultivates what is called a fixed or entity mindset (Dweck & Leggett, 1988). This type of mindset creates an environment that is less forgiving and therefore instills a fragile sense of confidence. Innovation natural involves mistakes and setbacks so when the inevitable setback occurs those with a fixed mindset respond poorly. Specifically, they will become defense and not be receptive to feedback. On the other hand, those with a growth mindset, who view effort to improve future performance, will be more resilient in the face of setbacks and more receptive to feedback (Dweck & Leggett, 1988). The Agile Scrum approach to development is focused on consistent incremental improvement in response to customer's feedback. This is best executed when the employees are also focused on making consistent incremental improvements to their own behavior in response to team member's feedback.

This growth mindset is not only valuable for employees in their response to feedback about themselves but also in the way they give feedback and coach others. Specifically, managers with a more growth mindset, more accurately recognized a change in employees' performance, both positive and negative, from an initial performance level (Heslin, et. al., 2005). Furthermore, managers with a growth mindset, engage in more extensive developmental coaching of their employees, compared with, managers with a fixed mindset (Heslin et al., 2006). This increase in coaching behavior, along with the more accurate performance appraisals mentioned earlier, has led to managers with a growth mindset to also be viewed as more procedural just or fair, by their employees (Heslin & VandeWalle, 2010). Thankfully, research has shown the growth mindset can be cultivated in employees with the proper training (Heslin, et. al., 2005) or presenting them with the proper evidence (Aronson, et. al., 2002).

A culture that is aligned with the values and principals of the Agile Scrum process is important to achieve the highest level of performance (Cappelli & Tavis, 2018). A learning culture, which is one that focuses on effort and incremental improvement (Murphy & Dweck, 2010), is an important component of an aligned organizational culture. Another component an organization should consider is the feedback environment they create. Originally feedback environment just referred to the perceived availability of feedback by employees (Herold & Parson, 1985). However, this concept has been expanded on to include several dimensions supplied by both supervisors and coworkers. These dimensions include, but are not limited to, feedback source and availability, feedback quality and delivery, and promoting feedback seeking behavior (Steelman, et. al., 2004). The recommendations in this chapter positively influence all these components. By directly involving team member in the feedback process both informally and formally on a frequent basis improves both feedback source credibility and source availability. Focusing feedback on effort and controllable behaviors will improve both feedback quality and feedback delivery. Finally, cultivating a learning environment will promote feedback seeking behavior (see Kluger & DeNisi, 1996 for summary of feedback findings). Taken together, these recommendations would improve the feedback environment leading to stronger Agile Scrum team output.

In summary, in an Agile Scrum context an organization needs to address three major characteristics to properly implement effective performance management. First is the question of how and specifically "how often". Moving away from a formal evaluation given at a designated day on the fiscal calendar is necessary. Instead formal evaluations at the time of project completion is the more effective approach. In addition, smaller informal feedback conversation should occur which will allow for corrective action and better manage employee's performance expectations. Furthermore, focusing on effort and controllable behavior will decrease the chances of employees being unreceptive and defensive to feedback. Regarding who, it is important that all team members contribute to the informal feedback conversations in person and give input to the formal evaluation session conducted at project completion. Finally, the "where" question focuses the attention on the environment and team/organizational culture where the feedback is given in. Cultivating a learning/growth culture not only at the team level but also company level will in time create a more resilient agile scrum team that will not only focus on incremental improvement on team outcomes but also incremental improvements in their own actions and behaviors. All these recommendations will positively affect the feedback environment leading to more effective performance management and high-quality outcomes from agile scrum teams.

Learning, Deployment and Career Development

Career advancement opportunities are essential for employee's engagement particularly for talented employees likely to be a part of Agile Scrum development team. Organization need to establish procedures and strategies to reduce employee turnover and cultivate a strong internal labor supply. The traditional components of a development program are job experience, education, and interpersonal relationships. These components are organized to move people up a define career path commonly referred to as the corporate ladder. Where the corporate ladder reflects career progress as a ridged progression directly up the corporate hierarchy. While this approach has been effective for years and still commonly used today it is not appropriate for Agile Scrum team members. The corporate ladder approach is not appropriate for Agile Scrum team members because job titles have less significance and hierarchical levels are fewer (Rigby, et. al., 2018). Instead for Agile Scrum team members these same components must be combined in a different manner that better reflects the dynamics of the Agile Scrum approach to work. Specifically companies need to view career advancement as developing an Agile Scrum members competencies so they can better expand their influence and increase their recognition (financial and non-financial) all while increase their value to an organization (Rigby, et. al., 2018) .

The learning component needs to be more customized to the individual employee's needs with a focus on the competencies required to be an effective Agile Scrum team member. This is achieved through direct coaching conversations with a manager along with self-directed education opportunities. As described above a performance management process that reflects the workflow of Agile Scrum development teams is important. These processes should include formal evaluation at the completion of a project and frequent performance conversation along the way that allows for corrective action. This performance management approach plays an important role not only for employee's performance on current projects but also assist employees in being better prepared for their next assignment. It is important that there is a distinction in these conversation about evaluation of past performance and a development conversation on how to be better equipped for future assignments.

When it comes to learning opportunities, it is vital that the subject matter reflects the unique demands of the Agile Scrum approach to development. To be an effective member of an Agile Scrum development team you need to have more than just technical knowledge but also the competencies that meet the demands created by cross-functional self-directed teams (Fernandez-Araoz, 2014). Therefore, training topics such as conflict resolutions and suppling critical feedback are essential for developing Agile Scrum team members.

All employees have different developmental needs, but this is particularly true for Agile Scrum team members. It is important that the training opportunities are flexible to reflect the unique background of Agile Scrum members. Flexible training programs that empower employees are becoming more popular, being used by companies such as AT&T (Donovan, & Benko, 2016), on a companywide basis. Regarding Agile Scrum employees IBM offers a good example as they have a long history of effectively using Agile Scrum teams. Their success is partially due to the well-developed learning and training program for their Agile Scrum members. The training interface reflects how information is more commonly consumed today. Diane Gherson, IBM's head of human resources, describes there learning and development interface as "tailored by role, with intelligent recommendation's that are continually updated. It is organized like Netflix, with different channels" (Burrell, 2018). The intelligent recommendations are unique to each Agile Scrum team member's developmental needs. These needs are identified not only through each employee's formal performance evaluation but also frequent "spot checks" by team leaders regarding each team member. These "spot checks" replace time consuming skill inventories that were traditionally utilized (Burrell, 2018). Overall, this process allows for employee empowerment in learning decisions that is informed by input from a variety of stakeholders through the team leader. This allows for an optimal level of customization and a shared feeling of accountability.

Job experience is another component of employee development that often reflects career advancement as well. As mention above the corporate ladder approach is not effective for members of an Agile Scrum development team due to its unidirectional conception of career advancement. In an Agile Scrum context career advancement is not a unidirectional ladder but a multiple directional lattice where career progress can be achieved in a variety of ways. This is a new challenge regarding Agile Scrum development but has been a long-standing challenge for industries that rely on innovation for a sustainable competitive advantage. One such industry is the fashion industry and their management of talent in their design department (Shipilov & Godart, 2015). The fashion industry has moved away from predefined career path due to the need for innovation, unique employee skill set, and lack of hierarchical levels. All these characteristics are like that found in an agile scrum team environment. To address this fashion industry has no set career path as the inherent structure could constrain innovation. In fact, career development strategies are often not disclosed to employees even if selected for development. Instead once an employee is identified as having potential worth development the organization will use experience through job rotation to cultivate experience and verify potential (Shipilov & Godart, 2015). This allows the organization to identify a more natural fit between employee's talents and future assignments. Employees in fashion industry using this approach realize career progress not by steps in a formal program but the fashion brands (i.e., customer) they are assigned to, prestige of location of work, and scope of project.

Organizations utilizing Agile Scrum teams could benefit from using a similar approach to that of the fashion industry. A traditional formal development program requires predicable advancement steps to be achieved over time. This stability does not exist in Agile Scrum teams. Instead Agile Scrum team member are constantly reassigned, often referred to as deployed, to new teams after project completion based off current customer needs and not steps in the employee handbook. In an Agile Scrum environment team assignment becomes an important step in employee development and in turn career advancement. This process of deployment should be guided by employees' current competencies along with customer needs. Furthermore, it should incorporate team member's input from their previous teams.

The company Netflix utilize a project team approach to their content development projects. In addition, their performance management process reflects the one described above. That is evaluation on project completion that incorporates feedback from all team members. In addition to the "start doing this"; "stop doing this"; and "continue doing this" approach to performance evaluation they also ask, "Would you select this employee for your next team and why? (McCord, 2014)" This feedback on deployment reflects a source, their former team members, which has the best perspective to evaluate not only their knowledge but their ability to be a good team member. Of course, this approach is only effective if an organization selection process is effective enough to identify not only strong technical talent but individuals that also have the team orientated competencies required to be an effective Agile Scrum team member.

A sense of career progression is important and without defined steps in career development advancement might not be clear to an Agile Scrum team member. Once again, like the fashion industry, the customer may be the best indirect source to signal this to an employee. There are two customer driven indicators that employees may be sensitive to. First, is regarding the customer's image or reputation. In client-based project importance of a project is derived from the value the client relationship has to the organizations business strategy. This value can be financial assessed or based of the client's reputations. Simply put some clients may be perceived as more important because of who they are. The second indicator will be derived from the substance of the work in the form of complexity or novelty. An Agile Scrum employee assigned to a client who requires a complex outcome or an outcome that is unique may view the assignment with greater importance and in being part of the team tasked to complete the assignment as career progress.

In summary, establishing processes for employees' learning, deployment, and career development present some significant challenges in an agile scrum team context. Although the components are the same as in more traditional systems these components need to be combined and used in a different fashion to be aligned with the dynamics of the Agile Scrum approach. The coaching conversations outlined earlier in the chapter establish an important foundation of continuing improvement. User friendly training programs that focus on both technical knowledge and the competencies need for Agile Scrum work helps build on this foundation. Customized suggestions based off the input of team leaders allows for a directed freedom that encourages engagement and accountable on the part of the employee. Finally, a strategic approach to team deployment allows for an organic multidirectional career path to emerge.

CONCLUSION AND THE FUTURE OF AGILE HUMAN RESOURCES

As described in this chapter human resources do not have to be completely recreated to accommodate the Agile Scrum approach. The main components of human resources (i.e., selection, performance management, and learning and development) remain the same as do their objectives. However, how these components are carried out need to be modified to accommodate the Agile Scrum approach. In this chapter I have offered suggestions on how to modify these components of human resources to help manage but not constrain the Agile Scrum approach.

The selection process should involve potential Agile Scrum team members, not only in a panel interview but also in the development of the job posting and structure interview question formation. A focus on broad competencies not just task specific skills is important. The unique competencies demanded by Agile Scrum work should be assessed to determine not only person-group fit but also person-approach fit. These competencies such as emotional intelligence and tolerance for ambiguity can me measure not only through structured interview question but also psychological assessments and situational judgement tests.

Regarding performance management organizations must modify the "how", "who", and "where" aspects. That is how often feedback is given, who is involved in the process, and where the feedback is given about team climate. Specifically, feedback should be given more frequently and timed with Agile Scrum team's workflow. The focus of feedback should be effort and controllable behavior and generated in a 360-degree manner. Furthermore, cultivating a learning or growth mindset and culture will not only help employees respond to feedback but also improve their ability to give feedback to their team members. All these factors will help cultivate a positive feedback environment that will improve overall team performance.

Learning and development will build on the foundation of performance management utilizing customized learning systems. These learning systems should offer guidance based on specific feedback and performance evaluations but still allow the employee to self-direct to a degree to improve engagement and accountability. Most important, due to the lack of hierarchical levels and less significance of positional titles, a multidirectional view of career advancement is needed. Specifically companies need to view career advancement as developing an agile scrum members competencies so they can expand their influence and increase their recognition (financial and non-financial) all while increase their value to an organization (Rigby, et. al., 2018).

These modifications are needed to effectively manage Agile Scrum team members and should be done when the agile approach is used. However, in today's business environment companies are increasing relying on innovation and rapid response to customers' demands to create their sustainable competitive advantage. Therefore, a more agile approach to human resources in general is likely needed in the future (Cappelli, & Tavis, 2018). It is possible to change over significant organizational operations to an agile approach all at one time like ING did in 2015 (Barton, et. al., 2018). However, this drastic approach is hard to successfully achieve and therefore a slow transition to agile work overtime is more common. This allows the organization to completely understand the principals and values of the agile process and determine where in the organization the agile approach is appropriate (Rigby, et. al., 2018). This chapter hopefully not only assist organizations with the immediate need of managing Agile Scrum teams but also get a head start on the long-term evolution of human resources to a more agile approach.

REFERENCES

Anderson, S. D., & Wanberg, K. W. (1991). A convergent validity model of emergent leadership in groups. *Small Group Research*, *22*(3), 380–397. doi:10.1177/1046496491223006

Aronson, J., Fried, C., & Good, C. (2002). Reducing the effects of stereotype threat on African American college students by shaping theories of intelligence. *Journal of Experimental Social Psychology*, *38*(2), 113–125. doi:10.1006/jesp.2001.1491

Barrick, M. R., & Mount, M. K. (1991). The big five personality dimensions and job performance: A meta-analysis. *Personnel Psychology*, *44*(1), 1–26. doi:10.1111/j.1744-6570.1991.tb00688.x

Barton, D., Carey, D., & Charan, R. A. M. (2018). One Bank's Agile Team Experiment "How ING Revamped its Retail Operation. *Harvard Business Review*, *96*(2), 59–61.

Beck, K., Beedle, M., Van Bennekum, A., Cockburn, A., Cunningham, W., Fowler, M., ... & Kern, J. (2001). *The agile manifesto*. Academic Press.

Budner, S. (1962). Intolerance of ambiguity as a personality variable. *Journal of Personality*, *30*(1), 29–50. doi:10.1111/j.1467-6494.1962.tb02303.x PMID:13874381

Burrell, L., & Gherson, D. (2018). Co-creating the Employee Experience: A Conversation with Diane Gherson, IBM's Head of HR. *Harvard Business Review*, *96*(2), 54–58.

Cappelli, P. (2015). Why we love to hate HR… and what HR can do about it. *Harvard Business Review*, *93*(7/8), 54–61.

Cappelli, P., & Tavis, A. (2018). HR goes agile. *Harvard Business Review*, *96*(2), 46–52.

Chamorro-Premuzic, T. (2015). Ace the assessment. *Harvard Business Review*, *93*(7/8), 118–121.

Donovan, J., & Benko, C. (2016). AT&T's talent overhaul. *Harvard Business Review*, 68–73.

Dweck, C. S., & Leggett, E. L. (1988). A social-cognitive approach to motivation and personality. *Psychological Review*, *95*(2), 256–273. doi:10.1037/0033-295X.95.2.256

Fernández-Aráoz, C. (2014). 21st Century Talent Spotting. *Harvard Business Review*, *92*(6), 46–56. PMID:25051855

Frenkel-Brunswik, E. (1948). Intolerance of ambiguity as an emotional perceptual personality variable. *Journal of Personality*, *18*(1), 108–143. doi:10.1111/j.1467-6494.1949.tb01236.x

Friedman, T. L. (2014). How to get a job at Google. *The New York Times*, 22.

Gieles, H., & van der Meer, W. (2017). *Talent management as the beating heart of an Agile Organization*. Academic Press.

Hastie, S., & Engineer, C. K. (2004). The Agile Mindset: what does it take to make this stuff work? Software Education Associates Ltd.

Hayat, F., Rehman, A. U., Arif, K. S., Wahab, K., & Abbas, M. (2019, July). The Influence of Agile Methodology (Scrum) on Software Project Management. In *2019 20th IEEE/ACIS International Conference on Software Engineering, Artificial Intelligence, Networking and Parallel/Distributed Computing (SNPD)* (pp. 145-149). IEEE.

Herold, D. M., & Parsons, C. K. (1985). Assessing the feedback environment in work organizations: Development of the job feedback survey. *The Journal of Applied Psychology*, *70*(2), 290–305. doi:10.1037/0021-9010.70.2.290

Heslin, P., Latham, G., & VandeWalle, D. (2005). The effect of implicit person theory on performance appraisals. *The Journal of Applied Psychology*, *90*(5), 842–856. doi:10.1037/0021-9010.90.5.842 PMID:16162058

Heslin, P., Vandewalle, D., & Latham, G. (2006). Keen to help? Managers' implicit person theories and their subsequent employee coaching. *Personnel Psychology*, *59*(4), 871–902. doi:10.1111/j.1744-6570.2006.00057.x

Heslin, P. A., & VandeWalle, D. (2010). Performance appraisal procedural justice: The role of a manager's implicit person theory. *Journal of Management*, *12*, 1201–1214.

Kluger, A. N., & DeNisi, A. (1996). The effects of feedback interventions on performance: A historical review, a meta-analysis, and a preliminary feedback intervention theory. *Psychological Bulletin*, *119*(2), 254–284. doi:10.1037/0033-2909.119.2.254

Kristof-Brown, A. L., Zimmerman, R. D., & Johnson, E. C. (2005). Consequences of Individuals'' Fit at Work: A Meta-Analysis of Person–Job, Person–Organization, Person–Group, and Person–Supervisor Fit. *Personnel Psychology*, *58*(2), 281–342. doi:10.1111/j.1744-6570.2005.00672.x

Lei, H., Ganjeizadeh, F., Jayachandran, P. K., & Ozcan, P. (2017). A statistical analysis of the effects of Scrum and Kanban on software development projects. *Robotics and Computer-integrated Manufacturing*, *43*, 59–67. doi:10.1016/j.rcim.2015.12.001

Luthans, F., & Stajkovic, A. D. (1999). Reinforce for performance: The need to go beyond pay and even rewards. *The Academy of Management Perspectives*, *13*(2), 49–57. doi:10.5465/ame.1999.1899548

Mahajan, A. (2013). *The importance of HR in agile adoption*. Scrum Alliance. https://www.scrumalliance.org/community/articles/2013/january/the-importance-ofhr-in-agile-adoption

McCord, P. (2014). How Netflix Reinvented HR: Trust People, Not Policies. Reward Candor and Throwaway the Standard Playbook. *Harvard Business Review*, *90*(3), 71–76.

Murphy, M. C., & Dweck, C. S. (2010). A culture of genius: How an organization's lay theory shapes people's cognition, affect, and behavior. *Personality and Social Psychology Bulletin*, *36*(3), 283–296. doi:10.1177/0146167209347380 PMID:19826076

Oprins, R. J., Frijns, H. A., & Stettina, C. J. (2019, May). Evolution of Scrum Transcending Business Domains and the Future of Agile Project Management. In *International Conference on Agile Software Development* (pp. 244-259). Springer. 10.1007/978-3-030-19034-7_15

Preston, G., Moon, J., Simon, R., Allen, S., & Kossi, E. (2015). The relevance of emotional intelligence in project leadership. *Journal of Information Technology and Economic Development*, 6(1), 16.

Przybilla, L., Wiesche, M., & Krcmar, H. (2019). Emergent Leadership in Agile Teams--an Initial Exploration. *SIGMIS-CPR '19*.

Rigby, D. K., Sutherland, J., & Noble, A. (2018). Agile at scale. *Harvard Business Review*, 96(3), 88–96.

Rigby, D. K., Sutherland, J., & Takeuchi, H. (2016). Embracing Agile. *Harvard Business Review*, 94(5), 40–50.

Rodríguez, G., Soria, Á., & Campo, M. (2016). Measuring the impact of agile coaching on students' performance. *IEEE Transactions on Education*, 59(3), 202–209. doi:10.1109/TE.2015.2506624

Rubin, K. S. (2012). *Essential Scrum: A Practical Guide to the Most Popular Agile Process*. Addison-Wesley.

Sherman, M., Edison, S., Rehberg, B. & Danoesastro. (2017). *Taking agile way beyond software*. Boston Consulting Group. https://www.bcg.com/enau/publications/2017/technology-digital-organization-taking-agile-way-beyondsoftware.aspx

Shipilov, A., & Godart, F. (2015). Luxury's talent factories. *Harvard Business Review*, 93(6), 98–104.

Skinner, B. F. (1953). *Science and Human Behavior*. Macmillan.

Steelman, L. A., Levy, P. E., & Snell, A. F. (2004). The feedback environment scale: Construct definition, measurement, and validation. *Educational and Psychological Measurement*, 64(1), 165–184. doi:10.1177/0013164403258440

Taipalus, T., Seppänen, V., & Pirhonen, M. (2018). Coping with uncertainty in an agile systems development course. *Journal of Information Systems Education*, 29(2).

Wilding, R. (1999). The Role of Time Compression and Emotional Intelligence in Agile Supply Chains. *Supply Chain Practice*, 1(4).

Zenasni, F., Besancon, M., & Lubart, T. (2008). Creativity and tolerance of ambiguity: An empirical study. *The Journal of Creative Behavior*, 42(1), 61–73. doi:10.1002/j.2162-6057.2008.tb01080.x

KEY TERMS AND DEFINITIONS

Deployment: The assignment of employees to new assignment-based employees' capability to meet the future demands of the assignment.

Feedback: Communicating to an employee how a stakeholder views their work behavior.

Learning Mindset: A belief that improvement is possible though increase effort.

Performance Management: Process of informed evaluation and feedback of an employee's work behavior and its alignment with organizational goal.

Person-Group Fit: How a person's values and attitude match with those of a work group.

Person-Job Fit: How a person's skills and abilities match the demands of a job.

Talent Acquisition: The process of identifying, recruiting, and hiring of highly qualified employees.

This research was previously published in Agile Scrum Implementation and Its Long-Term Impact on Organizations; pages 132-146, copyright year 2021 by Engineering Science Reference (an imprint of IGI Global).

Chapter 17
Sustainable and Green Human Resource Practices

Mitali Dohroo
Amity Business School, Amity University, Noida, India

Taranjeet Duggal
Amity Business School, Amity University, Noida, India

ABSTRACT

Two topics, circular economy and human resource practices, have been in separate baskets. However, recent studies have shown that both have a major impact either directly or indirectly on each other. Human resource management or human management is largely associated with a behavior of an economy. It has been largely debated and accepted that human resource management has a major role in creating sustainable organizations. Human resource management as a function involves a lot of postulates of sustainability in the scope of an organization. We all understand that the role of human resources has widened throughout time, and there is a need for more innovations in better management with various stakeholders and employees to create HR as a more solution-based function.

For the longest years the two topics circular economy and Human Resource Practices has been in separate baskets and never thought of bringing both together. However, the recent studies has shown that both has a major impact either direct or indirect on each other.

Human Resource Management or Human management is largely associated with a behavior of a economy. It has been largely debated and accepted that Human Resource Management has a major role in creating sustainable organisations.

The transition is taking place in many organizations where the practices are largely affected through the concepts of circular economy as it helps in optimum utilization of resources or gaining more value from the employees and providing better experiences and outputs to the stakeholders. Human Resource Management as a function involves lot of postulates of sustainability in the scope of a organistion. (Vickers, 2005). We all understand that the role of Human Resource has widened throughout the time

DOI: 10.4018/978-1-6684-3873-2.ch017

and there is a need of more innovations in better management with various stakeholders and employees to create HR as a more solution-based function.

To develop this chapter we have reviewed 53 research and empirical papers along with 15 articles referring to Green HRM and Sustainability along with focused discussions with HR professionals of leading think tanks working on Sustainability. The research gave as an understanding of relationship between Green HR practices, Sustainability and employee development along with the outlook on potential areas to be explored in future to meet the developing needs.

The chapter presents the concepts highlighted in research and adaptation of various Sustainable Human Resource Practices in organisations widely along with the development of the human potential by implementing the relevant practices.

While the widely discussed parameters of Economic, Social and Environmental focus in regard to sustainability are addressed, the chapter takes closer look in developing and applying the same to enrich employee development and providing a Green Work environment to the staff.

INTRODUCTION

Over the years Human Resource function of organisations has evolved from becoming felicitator to a Strategic arm of developing organisations. Since 1980's there had been numerous debates on better management of humans or employees in the organisations and tremendous research shows us direct and positive relationship between Human Resource Management Practices and Organisation Performance.

With the urgent requirements of increasing environmental and sustainability issues around the world, organisations are developing and introducing relevant strategies to focus and address the same.

Research shows that the focus of organisations is growing in terms of demonstrating their commitments to sustainability.

The Think Tanks, Government and other stakeholder bodies are making certain conscious attempts to make these changes through corporate consultative groups and bring a radical change.

We understand that to make Human Resource Practices more sustainable, the functions shall work around economic performance, social performance, and environment performance.

- Economic Performance here means that we analyse the appetite of the organisation to be more innovative in terms of its functions and Products.
- Social Performance would mean effectiveness to manage diversity of resources and human potential.
- Environment Performance is to introduce functions and processes which are more environment friendly and help in providing the conducive work environment to the staff.

Sustainable Human Resource Management has been tried to define through various research studies and the recent rising interest on the topic has shown varied definitions of the same.

Sustainable HRM can be defined as the adoption of HRM strategies and practices that enable the achievement of social, financial and ecological goals by creating an impact inside and outside of the organisation and over a long term time horizon while controlling for the unintended side-effects and negative feedback. (Michel, Muller-Camen, 2016)

The above definition highlights two vital points:

1. The recognition of multiple, potentially contradictory, socially, economic, ecological and social goals such as human sustainability (Dorchery, Kira and Sherry, 2009)
2. Complex Interrelations between HRM systems and impact on internal and external environments with the long term impact on resources and externalities.(Mariappandar, 2003)

"Sustainable human resource management (SHRM) refers to the concept which combines the idea of sustainability with the soft approach to human resources. This approach promotes basing an HRM strategy on fostering a culture of trust and cooperation and on developing employee involvement, one component of which is loyalty to one's employer. The soft approach to HRM aims to achieve adequate financial results, but through the policy of building a good "employer–employee relationship." A soft strategy – according to the research – is effective in retaining an employee for a longer period of time in an organization and encouraging them to share knowledge, work more productive, act with passion and commitment, generate creative ideas in order to achieve the business goals" (Smaliukienė et al., 2017; Ogbeibu et al., 2018; Kim and Shin, 2019; Meier et al., 2019).

"sustainable HRM is the pattern of planned or emerging human resource strategies and practices intended to enable organizational goal achievement while simultaneously reproducing the HR base over a long-lasting calendar time and controlling for self-induced side and feedback effects of HR systems on the HR base and thus on the company itself"(Ehnert I., Parsa S., Roper I., Wagner M., Muller-Camen M. Reporting on sustainability and HRM: a comparative study of sustainability reporting practices by the world's largest companies. Int. J. Hum. Resour. Manag. 2016;27:88–108. doi: 10.1080/09585192.2015.1024157)

Green HRM is defined that socially responsible human resource management function in an organisation helps in building employee-oriented practices which increases overarching sustainability goals in terms of employee retention, performance, and measurement and all other valid HRM Practices. (*Dyllick T., Muff K. and López-Fernández M., 2016*)

The Green or Sustainable Human Resource Practices are not focussed only around the representation of environment and social concerns but also developing a trustworthy culture which helps in providing a conducive and productive workplace environment to the employees.

In the diverse pool of HR principles and sustainability, development of HR is one of the basic elements of the function (Gladwin,1985).

With the growing awareness of the organisation in sustainability, lot of organisations are reporting their social, economic and ecological standards(Schaltegger & Wegner,2006) and the same are further reported in Global Reporting Initiative (GRI).

Sustainability and Human Resource Management are further studied and analysed in relation to gather practices and strategic decisions for implementing Sustainable practices in corporates and organisations (Chen-Taylor, Muller-Camen, 2012).

In this relation it was further found that key role of Sustainable Human Resource Management and Green practices contribute to sustainable business organisations economically, socially and ecologically and evidently making HRM system more sustainable (Enhert & Harry, 2012)

The conclusion of a diverse research and literature review quotes and confirms that Sustainability and HR are not two different directions but a spoon and fork of a same dish. The principles defined by different authors can be put into separate buckets as to the development of concept of the sustainability and specific or intentional practices which can be functioned and adopted by HR in the organisations for employees.

With the changing world, we have understood that how vital is to make an organisation sustainable in nature which is very clear that the function shall be such that it caters the current generation without affecting the resources for future. To develop a more sustainable HRM it is important to bring in more ethical and strategic Human Resource Management. Human Resource Management is a biggest stimulator to bring sustainability in organisation through innovation.

The sustainability in Human Resource Management to understand the social behaviors at large around the world and strategically implementing decisions as a part of process and management of Human Resource within our organisations.

The below given table articulates principles widely and the translation to development of HRM practices.

Table 1.

Social Issues	Human Resource Policy
Freshers or Inexperienced employees who are vulnerable to layoffs	Re-design junior jobs to enable employees to be expected variety of tasks that involve complexity.
Skill differentiation by Gender, Age, Caste and Orientation	Reform policies to accept more diversity. Be inclusive in forming a culture
Inequity related to progression and succession plans	Periodic review of individual needs of training linked to their development plan and career paths.
Employee Participation and Empowerment	Involvement of Employees in Decision Making and providing right platforms
Long Term Perspective and addressing social exclusion of Marginal Employees	Developing Employee Competencies through training and development and Regular Training, Learning and Development for the employees to increase a competency base.
Flexibility	As future of work and to build more conducive culture, the contemporary organisations must encourage flexibility. Flexibility offerings to organisations and individuals as well.
Fair and Equal Opportunities	Reaching to the Unreachable and provide equal opportunities to employees and people reaching out to your respective organisations.
Protection of Human Resources	Employee Retention and Regeneration of your staff in order to take care of people associated with you.
Environment Protection	HRM designs the policies and practices and communicate the same to all employees in order to design and work on initiatives of protecting ecological environment.
Partnership with outer world	To bring collective actions in the atmosphere and environment, organisations must partner with external world and stakeholders.

(Stankevičiute Ž., Savanevičiene A. Designing Sustainable HRM)

Sustainability cannot ignore the important component of Profitability; literature cites that more sustainable principles in practice will bring longevity and profitability to the organisations.

In the further section we are going to analyse vital Human Resource Practices bucketed in different section and how they implement sustainability or learning from circular economy in the function.

1. **Human Resource Planning:** To bring sustainability in organisation through innovation, the practices followed shall be such which makes employees to think, create and reflect. The Employee behavior shall foster the following:

   a. High Degree of Creativity- Organisations shall focus on bringing more creativity in terms of sustainability of the organisation. Sustainability is not just focused on the longetivity of the organisation but also the approach and functionality. Sustainability talks about bringing more green approach. As a HR function it holds the right to develop a culture which focusses on the creativity in sustainability. For example- There are organisations which are making it a part of the policy to not use papers or prohibiting the use of paper in digital era which brings both efficiency and sustainability.

   b. Long Term of Focus – The planning should be taking into consideration the longetivity of the organisation in changing times and era. There should be an increased attention to sustainable development and green organisations in managerial plans (Gonzalez-Benito & Gonzalez-Benito, 2006). The main purpose of sustainable development is to integrate economic, social and environmental objectives to optimaly maximise the benefits and provide welfare to Human capital of the organisation.

   c. High Level of cooperative and interdependent behavior- To bring any change and also in terms of sustainability it is important to conduct a cocperative and interdependent behavior towards the practices, process and people.

   d. High Degree of risk-taking appetite – Sustainability is being explored from various angles recently and also Green HRM, there are changes which may impose risk on the organisations, it is vital to plan the financials and processes in such a manner so that organisations can bear any risk if there is any.

   e. High tolerance to unpredictability- Business Environment is highly unpredictable in nature. Therefore, in terms of changing environment and adaptability of ecological friendly practices is giving birth to many concepts and research which are pot to practice.

2. **Talent Acquisition and Retention:** With the introduction various technological functions in place there is more suitability and means to maintain the whole cycle of employment from acquisition to retention. The technological solutions with the regular update on the functionality are more sustainable in nature, though there has been numerous debates around the same but still Technological innovations and Artificial Intelligence Systems are more effective in implementing sustainability in the process. The manual procedures are more time taking and also effect the Turn Around Time. While we are doing a Human Resource Planning, keeping the circular economy impacts in mind following are expected;

   a. Creating a balanced skill mix in the teams to achieve efficiency.
   b. Opportunities for Voluntary team assignments
   c. Placing right people at the right job.

3. **Talent Development:** Talent Development is one of the key function of Human Resource Practices. To make your employees more efficient and effective at the workplace, it is of utmost importance to invest on your employees. As sustainability is a central theme of circular economy, the talent development not only makes employees equipped to match the market trends and need of the economy but also helps in succession planning.

4. **Performance Management:** Human Resource Management function while focusing on the performance management and performance appraisals, they foster encouragement to take risks,

Employees shall themselves demand innovation in the processes, Making the workforce open to generation and adoption of new ideas, Continuous peer evaluation, frequent evaluations and auditing of innovation practices.

5. **Reward and Recognition:** The practices are evolving and to recognise and reward the employees in context of factors of circular economy and encourage them to more sustainable ideas, the reward and recognition system has to be planned strategically where following shall be covered majorly;
   a. Freedom to employees to do research and bring their ideas into the practice
   b. No Judgements on the failure of ideas which are put into testing
   c. Employees shall form teams as per their own will and ideas; such freedom shall be encouraged
   d. The Pay parity shall be taken as utmost serious agenda and bringing pay and pride in action
   e. Developing dual career tracks
   f. Promoting from within which shall have a consensus to the promotion and equal motivation leading to higher employee quotient factors
   g. Recognition and Rewards shall be continuous in nature.
   h. Maintaining the balance of team and individual rewards

To bring sustainability in the nature of functioning of Human Resource Practices, the function has to be evolved and bring postulates of social performance in the strategy.

a) The performance Management systems shall be developed more on the basis of equity, distributive justice, autonomy and respect.
b) Organizations shall ensure they take care of employees both physical and Mental Health at the workplace.
c) One must ensure there is transparency in the systems and respect towards each other.

Building Green Cultures

The above also articulates how organisations through their evolving practices are developing Green Cultures. One of the important point which appeared with consultation amongst the think tanks and corporate groups is to promoting and sensitizing human resources on forming green organisation cultures through deliberate and responsive attempts in employee behavior.

This all begins with first stage of recruitment and comes down the employee development where you define the green culture of organisation in your talent acquisition process and train the staff further on implementing the same.

The goal by which circular economy runs is the environment. Most of the organisations re now adopting Green Human Resource Practices to become more environmentally inclined. Human Resource policies which make the culture of the organisation greener and environment friendly shows their sustainability in the longer run.

With the change in times and urgency at our environment due to depletion of natural resources, it is of primary importance to imply environment friendly Human Resource Practices. The result of the same can be seen in the kind of benefits organisations are reaping out of it. There are more attraction of environment friendly consumers and making more in house or national productions which result in cost deuteriations.

The literature and researches shows that to have a successful Environment Management System at place, it is of vital importance that the same shall be supported by strategic Human Resource Management System.

Therefore all the Practices as listed above shall have the environment backing to it. The organisations shall focus on the principles and strategies as listed below:

1. **Talent Recruitment and Onboarding:** Recruitment of people is done on the basis where people are environment friendly.

On the onboarding organisation may gift a sapling to take care of during their entire tenure with the organisation. They can plant the same as tree in the organisation campus or take along with them as a sign of farewell when they leave the organisation.

Environmentally motivated activities can bring major impact to their engagement and relation with organisation. The organisarions shall put into practice the concepts of using public transport and less and also fuel less vehicles to reduce pollution and help the environment. This in terms halps in making practice more green and sustainable.

The question arises how is HR doing the same or can make it Green, HR can commit to green practices through virtual or telephonic screening of candiadtes than holding Face to Face interviews. The range of this effort can include simple methods such as using Skype for initial screening interviews, and even more complex electronic methods for the purposes of undertaking group interviews and expansive virtual business exhibitions (Rokos et al., 2012).

2. **Talent Development:** Promote and give more and more trainings on environmentally friendly practices they can conduct in the organisations. The employees can receive environment credits for the same and some reward for the maximum rewards earned.

The concepts must focus on bringing Financial performance and environmental balance. This study was given by (Daily & Hung, 2001; O'Donohuea et al., 2016).

HR must guarantee that preparatory programs in the early stages of recruitment will include information regarding organization's green goals and methods as well as the manner of employees' participation in voluntary and environment improvement programs (Bauer et al., 2012)

The training and development shall not only hold green environment trainings but also focus on building the methodologies to provide such trainings such as reducing paper and transportation.

3. **Reward Management:** Engage your employees in more environment friendly activities and link the same to performance and reward management. HR chas the rights to persuade managers where employees could be drawn towards environment friendly goals. Such goals could be marked as special achievements and foster the culture of sustainability in the organisation. Green Award and Compensation Mechanisams shall be fostered in the organisation where the culture of Green and sustainability could be amplified.

4. **Environmental Team Meets-** As an employee engagement activities try to coordinate and arrange more and more environment talks and open interactions so the synergy remains there. the management must try to establish a workplace in which the employees are able to freely express their opinions regarding green issues because it's them who are really in charge of realization of ethical

guidelines in the routine life of the organization (Collier & Esteban, 2007). A study on 214 British organizations shows that managers' support and employees' possibility of participation result in interest in the environment as the most prevalent encouragement methods (Ahmad, 2015).

In addition to the above practices, it is of immense importance to work on the full structure of organisation. While quoting this we mean catering to Management Development and Leadership and increasing knowledge base on Green Leadership.

Management and Leadership Development

Human Resource Management function is not just a gatekeeper of the organisation functions but a developer and a strategic force to make sure the correct implementation of the same to bring effective results.

It is a key aspect to pay our details on enforcing changes, which are primarily driven through leadership. The green and sustainable practices define that we must consciously attempt to not make any negative reinforcement as they might result in creating dis-engagement and hostile environment for employees, whereas we can make attempt in environmentally educating the employees and connecting the sustainable practices to employee life cycle.

Let us try to understand more functions of Human Resource and its relation to make it Green.

A. **Job Analysis**- While we do the analysis the most important thing which we focus on the responsibilities and dimensions of particular employment and job. In addition to that it is of prime importance to consider green competency as special component of recruitment and job analysis.

B. **Recruitment**- Environmental Criteria's and focus of the organisation towards the same shall be brought up in the recruitment notices.

C. **Selection**- The candidate selection shall not be just restrictive to job specifications but also look at the awareness of the candidate about environment. The candidate shall be focused and aware about the green issues in their job and also take into consideration their complete behavior being green consumers in personal lives as well.

D. **Socialisation** – HR shall focus on informing their employees about the organisation's green initiatives and development upon the same. Building a culture which promotes green citizenship could be done by arranging more socializing events for the employees.

E. **Training and Performance Evaluation:** As discussed earlier, programs on promoting knowledge and skill regarding green roles could be developed and allocated to employees. The goal designing of employees shall include the green goals and the parameters to study their progress on the same should be assessed to allocate a specific training program to employees. The green goals should be studied and developed for all the levels of the organisation.

F. **Reward Management:** Recognizing and rewarding employees who has gone an extra mile in setting and achieving the green goals. Both financial and non financial rewards could be designed for the employees such as introducing them as green employees.

G. **Management of Discipline and Procedures:** Development and Compilation of the green rules and procedure for every employee to adhere for. The induction trainings of the new employees shall have a major session on green practices so as to ensure sustainability throughout in their behaviors.

Green Initiatives that Organisations can build upon: Future of Green HRM

Human Resource being a backbone of a organisation, play an important role from talent acquisition, talent development to exit of an employee. Organisations being socially responsible and moving towards creating ecological friendly policies brings HR at a position to be more responsible in creating a culture and policies in the organisation which are green in nature.

The future of Green HRM bring sustainability in approach and looks promising and with bright future. The practices will prove beneficial for everyone from a researcher/academician to a practitioner.

Though the future is promising we still need to focus more on the academic front on Green HRM practices. Organisations are still working on various policies to bring Green HRM in practices as organisations are focussing more on environment and are designing such practices to meet the same.

Hence we need to bridge the gap between professional and academic front to bring immense parity and understanding in the practices.

Table 2.

Recycling of products and Sustainability Workshops: Encouraging staff to recycle the products and run continuous sustainability workshops to embibe the practice and behaviour which is continuous in nature. This is also encouraged by asking employees to create sustainable practice goals.
Promotion of using public transport: More and more organisations are encouraging to use public transport and reduce the carbon footprint. The same is supported by providing Public Transport Allowances. **Car pooling:** Car pooling is new cool collaboration, it brings different teams and people together from their neighbourhoods and support environment. Organisations are encouraging by announcing Car Pool Champions.
Green Manufacturing: Industries are making conscious efforts to do green and sustainable manufacturing whether it is cloth industry or products. The conscious efforts are made by using more sustainable available resources.
Online training: Technology is a blessing where we can make a conscious effort of reaching to unreachable and developing online content and delivering the same. Training is widely seen as the most effective method of making employees aware about sustainable and environment friendly approach. The staff can be trained on how to collect waste data, build eco literacy. The well trained employees help in bringing radical and effective change sin the organisations over a period of time.
Telecommuting and Teleconferencing: Communication is the key to effectiveness and constant engagement helps in building better performances. The emerging technologies cover the organisations from missing any communication and help in maintaining constant clear communications.
Energy Efficient Office Spaces: As a practice organisations shall look into the physical spaces in order to maintain Green environment. Organisations shall foster on creating energy efficient spaces with sensing electricity, water saving technology, sustainable utensils and No food waste policy initiatives.
Green Office Furniture: Many organisations at present are opting for more sustainable spaces and providing green office furniture's.
Green Work Culture: This is an interesting work area where lot of work has already been quoted and there is still a scope to explore the subject more. Green Work Culture defines the spaces not only physically environment friendly but also the practices which are deliberate to provide conducive work environments to staff. For an instance; Transparent functions, Pay Parity, Employee Friendly policies, Inclusive Decision Making and many more.

Green HRM not only promoted sustainability but has also been ecological, economical and practical at the same time.

We have highlighted some of the initiatives organisations has taken into account to count their practices as green.

With the above mentioned points, it clearly brings out numerous opportunities and ways for organisations to develop Green Human Resource and Sustainable Management practices.

CONCLUSION

The above has been derived from the methodological studies of articles and papers published in the reputed journals and presented in the conferences. The chapter shreds the extensive capacity of Human Resource Management functions for making organizations, operations and employees practices green in nature. We have tried to cover all functions from job design to employee relations. HR professionals in this era of environment fostered economy towards circular sustainability are facing a major challenge to study the depth and scope of green HRM practices in transforming or developing organisations as green entities. More efforts into strategizing the same is leading to make better environmental performance of the organisation. The creation, practice and maintainence of green human resource practices and foster environment lead innovative behaviours of employees coupled with right perceptions and attitudes towards building organisations as green entity, the green HRM practices hold a critical place.

Existing Human Resource Practices, Environment Management and sustainable practices literature suggest that employee behaviors and practices contribute majorly to the goals of a organisations towards sustainability and Green Entity resolutions.

It has been proved and understood that employees only contribute and enjoy to the goals when they feel that it adds to their value profile and certainty. Studies proved that 86% of the employees feel more engaged when they are more related and responsible towards environment practices and understand their organisation fosters a behaviour and practices which is more environmentally aligned and sustainable in nature of functioning.

Green HR contributes to organization building in positive steps and approach to develop organisation reputation, the green practices also promote in developing high degree of engagement of employees and eliminating their negative environment impacts. the Chartered Institute of Personnel and Development (CIPD) thinks that "a green employer may improve employer branding, company image and is a useful way to attract potential employees who have environmental orientation" CIPD(2007).

Green HRM practices contribute in making organisations and their operations green. The green recruitment practices, performance, attitude, and green competencies of human resource management can be designed by following and adapting green HRM practices. Talent Acquisition and Talent Inductions are the first stages of creating green awareness among all the employees working for organisations and making green entities. Such adaptations lead to causes of environmental degradation. The awareness among the talent and practices can lead to green movements, green programs and practices and also retention of resources for future generation.

The Green Human Resource Practices develop inspiration and commitment of employees to contribute their ideas and efforts for the awareness and implementation of Green Human Resource Management Practices in their respective organisation.

These practices result in increased efficiency, cost feasibility, less wastage, sustainable use of resources, improved work life balance as their would be more use of technology for communication and efficiency. The world should eventually move towards Green HRM practices with the change in world towards environment efficiency and sustainability.

We have also discussed about how organisations apart from taking Green HRM responsibility can turn green in various ways. The world is strongly moving towards more sustainable practices and yes, the approach of organisations and HR would play a major role in bringing the behavioural change amongst employees and people.

REFERENCES

Ambec, S., & Lanoie, P. (2008). Does it pay to be green? A systematic overview. *The Academy of Management Perspectives*.

Bashford, S. (2008). *Brownie points for green workers*. Human Resources.

Beardwell, I., & Holden, L. (1997). *Human Resources Management. A Contemporary Perspective*. Pitman Publishing.

Blanco, T. M. (2014). The meaning of employability in the new labour relationships between company-employee: A model of training in companies. *Procedia: Social and Behavioral Sciences*, *139*, 448–455. doi:10.1016/j.sbspro.2014.08.039

Davies, A., Fidler, D., & Gorbis, M. (2020). *Future Work Skills*. University of Phoenix Research Institute.

Eccles, R. G., & Serafeim, G. (2013). The performance frontier: Innovating for a sustainable strategy. *Harvard Business Review*.

Egri, C. P., & Herman, S. (2000). Leadership in the North American environmental sector: Values, leadership styles, and contexts of environmental leaders and their organizations. *Academy of Management Journal*.

Ehnert, I. (2009). *Sustainable Human Resource Management*. Springer.

Fernandez, E., Junquera, B., & Ordiz, M. (2003). Organizational culture and human resources in the environmental issue. *International Journal of Human Resource Management*.

Fryxell, G. E., & Lo, C. W. H. (2003). The influence of environmental knowledge and values on managerial behaviours on behalf of the environment: An empirical examination of managers in China. *Journal of Business Ethics*.

Green Human Resource Management: A Review and Research Agenda. (2012). *International Journal of Management Reviews*.

Gupta, B. (2011). *A comparative study of organizational strategy and culture across industry*. Benchmark Int. J.

Human resources development as an element of sustainable HRM – with the focus on production engineers. (2021). *Elseiver- J Clean Prod.*

Innovation and growth: how business contributes to society. (2010). *Acad. Manag. Perspect.*

Kramar, R. (2014). Beyond strategic human resource management: Is sustainable human resource management the next approach? *International Journal of Human Resource Management.*

Mael, F., & Ashforth, B.E. (1992). Alumni and their alma mater: a partial test of the reformulated model of organizational identification. *Journal of Organizational Behaviour.*

Marcus, A., & Fremeth, A. (2009). Green management matters regardless. *The Academy of Management Perspectives.*

Milliman, J., & Clair, J. (1996). Best environmental HRM practices in the U.S. Academic Press.

Pfeffer, J. (2010). Building sustainable organizations: The human factor. *The Academy of Management Perspectives.*

Philpott, J., & Davies, G. (2007). *Labour Market Outlook.* CIPD/KPMG.

Ramus, C. A. (2002). *Encouraging innovative environmental actions: What companies and managers must do. Journal of World Business.*

Redman, T., & Snell, S. (Eds.), *The Sage Handbook of Human Resource Management.* Sage.

Russo, M., & Harrison, N. (2005). Organizational design and environmental performance: Clues from the electronics industry. *Academy of Management Journal.*

Singh, S.K., & Singh, A.P. (2019). Interplay of organizational justice, psychological empowerment, organizational citizenship behavior, and job satisfaction in the context of circular economy. *Manag. Decis.*

The Gallup Organization. (2010). Employers' Perception of Graduate Employability. Author.

The greening of Euro-pean management education. (n.d.). InWehrmeyer, W. (Ed.), *Greening People: Human Resources and EnvironmentalManagement* (pp. 289–300). Greenleaf Publishing.

UNEP. (2014). International Declaration on Cleaner Production: Implementation Guidelines for Facilitating Organizations. UNEP.

Wagner, M. (2004). Sustainable reporting? The link of environmental reports and environmental performance. *Corporate Environmental Strategy.*

Wilkinson, A., Hill, M., & Gollan, P. (2001). The sustain-ability debate. *International Journal of Operations and Production Management, 21,* 1492–1502.

Chapter 18
The Role of Awareness in Designing Human Resources Management Practices in Family Firms:
A Configurational Model

Giulia Flamini
University of Rome Tor Vergata, Italy

Luca Gnan
ⓘ https://orcid.org/0000-0002-5247-7498
University of Rome Tor Vergata, Italy

ABSTRACT

The chapter aims to develop a theoretical configurational model of HRM practices for family firms based on the construct of awareness. The typology of ideal HRM practices configurations the authors developed grounds on are 1) two organizational factors (awareness of the internal and external environment and organizational awareness) and 2) two dimensions of organizational awareness (the need for explicit and implicit coordination mechanisms). The first dimension refers to the need for mechanisms explicitly adopted by a family firm to manage task or communication interdependencies. The second one relates to those requirements for mechanisms that are available to family firms from shared cognition, which enable them to explain and anticipate task statuses and individuals' collaborative behaviors, thus helping them in managing task interdependencies. The authors combined these results in four configurations of HRM practices (administrative, shared, professional, and integrated configurations) and developed seven propositions.

DOI: 10.4018/978-1-6684-3873-2.ch018

INTRODUCTION

Managing people in organizations asks for a bundle of practices/policies, called Human resources management (HRM) systems (Ulrich et al., 2013), that influences competencies, behaviors, and performances of employees (Noe et al., 2010). Consequently, in generating and maintaining a sustainable competitive advantage, the HR function may perform a strategic role (Zakaria, 2011; Karami et al., 2008). Nonetheless, only recently, the managerial practice and scientific literature recognized the role of the HR function in the strategic management of organizations, coping with growing pressure from both internal and external environmental dimensions.

The recognition of the strategic role of the HR function implies a shift from a deterministic and mechanical approach to the study of organizations to a more psychological and organic one. Huselid (1995), proving a significant relationship between the sophistication of HR practices and the market value per employee, played a critical role in this recognition process. Afterward, scholars developed a considerable bulk of studies to promote the test of positive relationships between HRM and performance (Almajali et al., 2016; Alfes et al., 2013; Buller & McEvoy, 2012).

Literature gives prominence on the influence of different sets of HRM practices, e.g., recruitment and selection, compensation, performance appraisal, training and development, workforce planning, career planning management, job design, and internal communication, on a likewise varied collection of performance outcomes (Combs et al., 2006). Accordingly, a firm should coherently shape its own HRM system to warrant a long-term survival. Family firms do not make any exception to such considerations valid for any organization. By the way, the family business literature on HRM mainly focuses on the formality and informality of specific practices, exploring the possible advantage of adopting different practices in family firms (Reid et al., 2002).

For instance, family firms appear adopting less sophisticated HRM practices (HRMP) than those of non-family firms (De Kok et al., 2006). Nevertheless, literature has recognized some gaps (e.g., Reid et al., 2002) and theory enrichment from time to time fails in agreeing the required settings for allowing validity to the supposed relationships between constructs/variables (Bacharach, 1989). Hence, it seems that it is the right time for the structuring of the prevalent schemata adopted (Ferraro & Marrone, 2016; Gersick, 2015; Le Breton-Miller & Miller, 2014; Botero & Litchfield, 2013; Berrone et al., 2012; Stewart & Hitt, 2012).

The chapter presents a model for building HRMP configurations in family firms grounded on the construct of awareness that family businesses need to make strategic and organizational choices to achieve positive performances. How do they shape their human resources to endure their performance? The chapter tries to address such a question, and it concerns whether and how HRMP complement each other in family firms' performance in facing strategic and organizational changes.

HRMP needs to fit environmental dimensions (Huselid, 1995). Saridakis et al. (2017) find that a bundle of integrated, mutually reinforcing HRMP has a stronger influence on firm performance than HRMP individually. The already cited bulk of the research investigated relationships between HRM and performance (Batt, 2002; Guthrie, 2001; Huselid, 1995) and between HRM and a sustainable competitive advantage (Othman, 2009; Gooderham et al., 2006; Wright et al., 2005; Collins & Clark, 2003; Guest et al., 2003; Huselid, 1995). Outcomes recommend considerable benefits from managing human resources, while several interrogations remain unanswered (Delery, 1998).

Conversely, family business literature (Kidwell & Fish, 2007; Barnett & Kellermanns, 2006; Moshavi & Koch, 2005) investigates HRMP looking at their dissimilarities and arguing how different practices (Jaskiewicz et al., 2018) might have distinctive effects on managing people. Carlson et al. (2006) show that HRMP are crucial to growth in family firms. Tsao et al. (2009) reveal that HRMP affects significantly firm's performances. A few studies study the possible benefit of implementing different combinations of practices in family firms (Reid & Adams, 2001; Huselid, 1995) as suggested by Saridakis et al. (2017).

The chapter offers advice and suggestions about possible future lines of research in exploring how awareness affect decision-making processes on configuring bundles of HRM practices in family firms. Moreover, it suggests a conceptual model as a potential base for theoretic enhancements within the family business' literature and an interdisciplinary platform where scholars, coming from different backgrounds, can devote their focus on family businesses.

THE HRM LITERATURE

To generate and maintain a sustainable competitive advantage, Porter (1985) states that HRM represents an organizational variable for designing support activities in value creation. Accordingly, HRM shows its relationships with the organizational performance (Zakaria, 2011; Zheng et al., 2009; Chang & Chen, 2002). In the last twenty-five years, due to an increase on the environmental pressure, the HR function moved from a mere administrative role to a real spot of distinctive competencies in gaining a sustainable competitive advantage (Zakaria, 2011; Karami et al., 2008; Analoui, 2002). Organizations should develop effective HRMs to organizational performance (Kehoe & Wright, 2013; Hitt et al., 2001; Grant, 1996).

Sustainable competitive advantages come from a continuous accumulation of distinctive competencies in managing HR (Shaw et al., 2013; Coff & Kryscynski, 2011; Ployhart et al., 2006; Coff, 2002; Prahalad, 1983) through multiple relationships connecting performance and HR practices (Almajali et al., 2016; Alfes et al., 2013; Buller & McEvoy, 2012; Georgiadis & Pitelis, 2012; Lawler et al., 2011; Bjorkman & Lervik, 2007; Sun et al., 2007; Combs et al., 2006; Wright et al., 2005; Batt, 2002; Huselid, 1995).

RBV (Barney, 1991) is the primary theoretical reference, linking HRM and performance (Buller & McEvoy, 2012; Beltran-Martin et al., 2009; Phan et al., 2005; Barney, 1991). Resources are sources of competitive advantage if they are: a) value producing, b) rare, c) imperfectly imitable, and d) without strategically equivalent substitutes (Barney, 1991). Only human resources present these four characteristics (Ogunyomia & Bruning, 2015; Marler & Fisher, 2013; Wright et al., 2001), being a strategic resource for performance (Naz et al., 2016; Karami et al., 2008; Harney & Dundon, 2006; Stavrou & Brewster, 2005; Kaman et al., 2001). HRM nurtures processes in implementing a successful firm strategy (Buller & McEvoy, 2012; Noe et al. 2010; Wright et al., 2001; Hitt et al., 2001; Boxall, 1998).

THE FAMILY FIRMS' HRM LITERATURE

Family firms' HRM literature is a quite popular and growing topic (Ferraro & Marrone, 2016; Botero & Litchfield, 2013; Cruz et al., 2011). Herewith, we review the main results and approaches adopted so far, and highlight limitations too. Firstly, family firms' scholars are likely to assume theories and conceptual backgrounds not strictly embedded in the traditional HRM research, such as Agency Theory (Xianga et al., 2014; Schulze et al., 2003) and Stewardship Theory (Combs et al., 2010; Eddleston et al.,

2008). Only some contributions referring to RBV (De Kok et al., 2006; Dyer, 2006; Poza et al., 2004) and Socio-Emotional Wealth (SEW) (Achleitner et al., 2014; Cruz et al., 2014, 2011; Berrone et al., 2012) show some relationships with consolidated HRM streams of research.

Secondly, the family firms' HRM literature proposes a "patriarchal" family model (Cruz et al., 2011; Dale et al., 2008) in defining relationships with employees. Succession planning and the nurturing of a successor are the most critical decisions taken by the patriarch (Cruz et al., 2011; Le Breton-Miller et al., 2004). The patriarchal model involves job security in exchange for family loyalty, substituting the need for incentives. Such a model, however, acknowledges a unique, sole, decision maker, e.g., the founder, reducing the likelihood to explore circumstances that are more complex where different family members share the decision-making power (Haberman & Danes, 2007). In addition, within such an assumption, some HRM's theoretical streams, such as utility theory and compensating wage theory, are too heavily adapted to the context of family firms and this may alter their original goal (Levie & Lerner, 2009; De Kok et al., 2006; Schulze et al., 2003).

Thirdly, most contributions (Kidwell & Fish, 2007; Barnett & Kellermanns, 2006) investigate HR practices in family firms without considering the heterogeneity of this peculiar form of organizations. Family firms are neither equal nor similar (Nordqvist et al., 2014), for example, about size, i.e., large versus small and medium-sized family enterprises. Heterogeneity asks for adopting perspectives of theories and indications of the HRM practices in leading sense-making processes about how to interpret different internal and external environments.

Fourthly, a debate on the formality and informality of HRM practices in family firms emerge. The resistance of the family managers to formality exists (De Kok et al., 2006) since they search for a flexible approach to cope with higher levels of environmental uncertainty (Holten & Crouch, 2014). Informality helps in developing a feeling of teamwork and strong social relationships and in increasing workers' motivation (Marlow & Patton, 2002). Employees may also feel that they can negotiate work responsibilities, hours, and secure personal loans or other forms of aid within such informality (Marlow & Patton, 2002). Conversely, employees' perceptions of fairness are essential in developing their commitment (Reid et al., 2002). However, when grievance and discipline matters arise, people may perceive informal practices as an arbitrary and unfair choice. Facing these tensions, balancing both formal and informal practices becomes one of the most significant challenges for family firms, despite the paucity of studies on this balance in adopting formal and informal practices (Reid et al., 2002).

HRM AND PERFORMANCE: FOUR APPROACHES

HRM literature shows an exponential growth (Marler & Fisher, 2013; Kehoe & Wright 2013; Collins & Clark, 2003; Batt, 2002; Cappelli & Neumark, 2001) in investigating connections between HRM and performance. Four different approaches explain the connections between HRM and performance: the universalistic, the contingency, the configurational, and the contextual one (Zakaria, 2011).

Accordingly, with Human capital theory (Wiesner & Innes, 2010; Martín-Alcázar et al., 2005), the universal perspective focuses on a linear connection between progressively implementing all the possible HRMP and performance (Harney & Dundon, 2006). Firms with high-performance work practices, as recruitment and selection, extensive employees' involvement, training and development, and performance appraisal, present higher levels of employees' retention, and financial performances (Chandler & McEvoy, 2000; Huselid, 1995) aligned with their strategy (Lepak et al., 2006).

The contingency approach adopts a heuristic and an iterative model, where internal and external variables moderate how HRM relates with performance, neglecting the existence of a universal one best way of HR practices. Four different contingency dimensions appear (Martín-Alcázar et al., 2005): HR practices themselves (Martín-Alcázar et al., 2005), organisational variables (size, technology, or structure) (Jones, 1984), and external environmental factors (competitive, technological, macro-economic, and labour contextual dimensions) (Boxall, 1998).

The configurational approach describes HRM as a system of practices, differently combined to achieve consistent internal configurations with the environmental and the organizational variables (Kepes & Delery, 2007). Configurational models present nonlinear relationships with organizational performances, since the interdependence multiply (or divide) the combined effect. HRM practices can be analyzed only as a complex and interactive system.

The contextual approach, finally, looks at social, environmental factors (Williamson & Cable, 2003). This perspective opens perspectives of practice and research toward a network of social and institutional stakeholders and political forces (Innes & Wilsner, 2012). HRM leads the managerial interplay with these forces.

A MODEL OF HRMP FOR FAMILY FIRMS

The chapter proposes a theoretical configurational model of HRMP for family firms, starting from the environmental dimensions that might affect awareness on which HRMP fit a strategic and organizational change and help to preserve a positive performance (Huselid, 1995). An interesting question is how precisely do family firms ideally align different configurations of HRMP?

We propose that specific combinations of HRMP enable family firms to attain goals, granting higher performances than the sum of the particular practices (De Kok et al., 2006; Carlson et al., 2006; Reid & Adams, 2001). We suggest a conceptual model for configuring HRMP in family firms, as reported in Figure 1.

Figure 1. A configurational model of HRMP for family firms

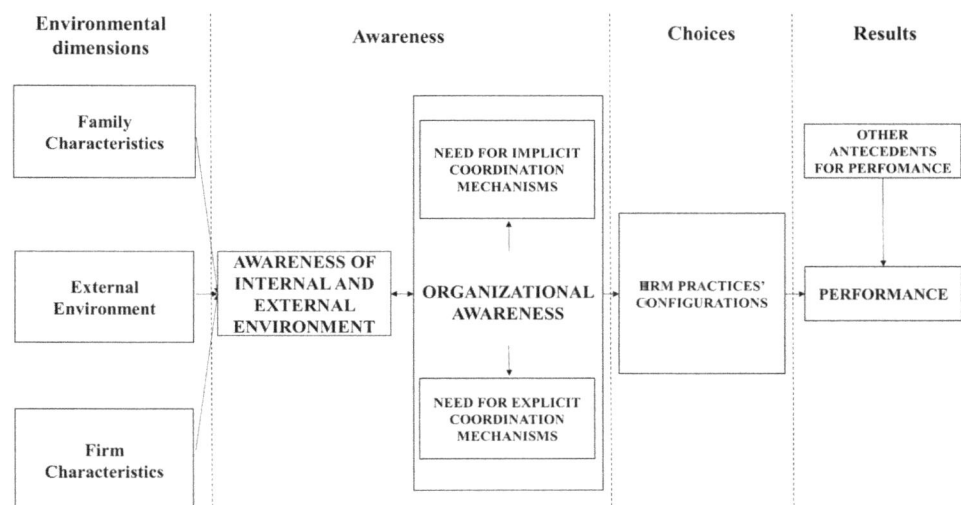

We assume family firms differ in their awareness of the internal and external environment (Woodall, 2000) and how these dissimilarities reflect their view and interpretation of strategic and organizational changes and the possible performance achievable. A strategic and organizational change is a critical change of the bundle of resources and routines that a firm uses to compete. Attaining long-term survival needs competencies to lever resources for emphasizing effectiveness, while preserving flexibility to change the strategic direction (Thompson, 1967). By retrieving, accumulating, orchestrating, and managing resources and routines to fit with the dynamic environment, family firms identify and exploit opportunities, gaining and sustaining competitive advantage (Hitt et al., 2002, 2001). Family firm's environmental dimensions paint the 'place' where entrepreneurial and managerial choices occur and provide inputs for developing meanings for actions to take place.

ENVIRONMENTAL DIMENSIONS

Family firms' entrepreneurial and managerial decisions reflect their awareness on environmental dimensions (Dyer, 2003; Upton et al., 2001; Woodall, 2000). Few scientific contributions show how family firms become aware of the actual dynamic environment. Little is known about the strategic and organizational behavior of family firms facing environmental dimensions changes (Dyer, 2003; Upton et al., 2001). This contingent approach has a long tradition in the strategic and organizational analysis, and the realm of family firms can benefit from it (Thompson, 1967). Catching the awareness of the internal and external environment may help literature in highlighting the many classifications of environmental dimensions (Dess & Rasheed, 1991). We propose that family firms' dimensions influencing their awareness are the external environment (Porter, 1985; Bain, 1968), the firm characteristics (Budhwar & Debrah, 2001), and the family characteristics (Gagné et al., 2014; Zellweger & Sieger, 2012; Baron, 2008; Astrachan & Jaskiewicz, 2008; Gómez-Mejía et al., 2007; Arregle et al., 2007; Eddleston & Kellermanns, 2007; Kellermanns & Eddleston, 2006; Sharma & Irving, 2005; Zahra, 2005; Roca-Puig et al. 2005; Kellermanns, 2005; Kellermanns & Eddleston, 2004; Salvato, 2004; Zahra et al., 2004; Sirmon & Hitt, 2003; Wiklund & Shepherd, 2003; Lumpkin & Dess, 1996).

External Environment

Contingency theory affirms that there is no a universal, best, way in defining organizational variables. Organizational fit relies on external contingencies (Donaldson, 2001). After considering the different alternatives, allowing for external contingencies, firms can take the most efficient choice (e.g., Craig & Dibrell, 2006). Following a strategic fit thinking, organizations might improve their performance by fitting their strategic and organizational choices and the particular external environmental contexts (Katsikeas et al., 2006).

We propose that family firms' HRMP performance depends on an external fit. The external fit represents a normative construct in strategy formulation processes. Miles and Snow (1994) reveal a positive influence between the external fit and performance. The external fit characterizes how HRMP in family firms affect performances. Adopting an external fit logic defines simultaneous multiple positive relationships between HRMP and performances.

Consistent with the external environmental dimensions, we take on the industrial organization understanding of Bain (1968) and Porter (1985). We propose the PEST dimensions: Political environment, Economic cycle, Social issues, and Technology and, the Competitive environment dimensions expressed by Porter's Five-forces model. External dimensions are typically beyond the scope of firms' control, such as industry dynamism and industry growth (Chadwick et al., 2013), local industry-specific unemployment rate (Schmidt et al., 2016), and national culture of the host country (Rabl et al., 2014).

Firm Characteristics

The model we propose reflects the role of firm characteristics (mostly consisting on features such as size, organizational variables, professionalization, firm life cycle, and past performances) on framing the strategic and organizational needs of a family firm. The real integration of business needs and HRMP asks for continuous and systematic consideration, despite the possible dynamics of the environment. Budhwar and Debrah (2010, 2001) explore how different bundles of cultural, institutional and business dynamics influence the effect of contingencies on HRMP. Schuler and Jackson (1987) note that, as organizations change strategies, they are likely to change their HRMP bundles.

Family Characteristics

Family firms differ from non-family firms (Gagné et al., 2014). Family firms show strong, peculiar characteristics. Accordingly, we suggest six dimensions: 1) generation, 2) leadership, 3) culture, 4) emotional attachment, 5) entrepreneurial orientation, and 6) goals. We are aware that family business literature proposes several classifications of family characteristics, such as F-PEC scale (Astrachan et al., 2002), FIBER scale (Berrone et al., 2012), and so on. Nevertheless, they all focus on exploring the sources of heterogeneity of family businesses, disregarding direct relationships with organizational choices.

As per the generation dimension, family members and kinship ties affect interests and values in modeling their choices about orchestrating resources. They display a long-term strategic orientation related to the generational involvement (Eddleston & Kellermanns, 2007; Gómez-Mejia et al., 2007; Kellermanns & Eddleston, 2006; Zahra, 2005). Each generation gives stimuli to decision-making processes and outcomes (Gómez-Mejía et al., 2007; Sharma & Irving, 2005; Kellermanns & Eddleston, 2004; Salvato, 2004). Each generation stretches a peculiar priority to non-financial goals (Baron, 2008; Gómez-Mejía et al., 2007) and outcomes (Gómez-Mejía et al., 2007; Sharma & Irving, 2005).

Family firms' leadership influences organizational norms, including how and when family and non-family members participate in the business. Next, family firms show a collective identity, a unique social context, an emotional attachment, and a commitment to survival (Zellweger & Sieger, 2012; Arregle et al., 2007; Sirmon & Hitt, 2003) that frame the orchestration of their human resources. Moreover, family firms embrace strong and enduring cultures. They affect strategy (Roca-Puig et al., 2005), investment decisions (Astrachan & Jaskiewicz, 2008), resource accumulation (Kellermanns, 2005), and entrepreneurial orientation (Zahra et al., 2004; Wiklund & Shepherd, 2003; Lumpkin & Dess, 1996).

Lastly, family firms are goal-directed (Kappes & Schmid, 2013; Chrisman et al., 2005; Klein et al., 2005; Miller & Le Breton-Miller, 2005). They endure specific goals, as they wish to pass the firm to the next generation (Gómez-Mejía et al., 2007), and those peculiar goals commonly foster specific strategic and organizational behaviors.

THE AWARENESS CONSTRUCT

Organizations survive adapting their strategies and organizational variables to environmental dimensions (Porter, 1985). In framing the environment, family firms consider different choices at various generational stages (Hoy, 2006) or life cycle phases (Moores & Mula, 2000). Consequently, family firms develop an awareness about the need for making strategic and organizational changes. When environmental dimensions change, current resources and routines become old or non-fitting ones, performance deteriorates, and goals remain at stake. Family firms experience a growing sense of urgency (become aware) for change and risk-taking (Murphy, 2005). They formulate growth strategies to avoid the decline and loss of the family business, to foster continuity and family unity, and to save jobs and wealth creation (Upton et al., 2001). Performance increases the most when the magnitude, timing, and direction of strategic and organizational changes fit environmental changes (Zajac et al., 2000) and family firms are aware of them (Zellweger, 2013).

At the strategic and organizational level, awareness refers to the concept of firms as social systems (Parsons, 1951), where cognitive meanings emerge from social interactions of individuals (Mezirow, 1985). Building firm awareness equals the process of creating shared meaning, with the individual developments yielding cognitive, psychosocial, and behavioral effects and aligning them within the individuals belonging to the same organization. The awareness concept refers to psychological literature. As individuals become aware of the need of their assumptions on themselves and the organizational context, they develop a change in their behaviors. Nevertheless, individuals facing similar change concerns manifest different perceptions of the organizational context due to their meaning schema (Schon, 1987). Consequently, awareness represents a change in meaning schema.

Knowledge as cognitive learning and experience on change represent fundamental processes in awareness building and sharing. The speed of awareness building and sharing processes relies on individuals' characteristics and organizational features. The higher will be the concern for a potential future crisis, the bigger will the effort in defining new schema. We can describe a crisis as a twofold phenomenon. On one side, it represents a psychological development opportunity.

On the other hand, it reveals itself as a potential psychological loss. Not addressing a crisis means stagnation in awareness building and sharing and emerging organizational resistance to change. Five revolving stages (pre-developing, rationalization, meeting, enabling, and consensus) shape awareness building and sharing processes on change. Significant differences in addressing the five steps appear in different organizational contexts. Integrating processes with respect similar changes does not mean that similar firms will behave similarly.

Consistently, different family firms will act differently, and they will adapt themselves coherently only if a new schema is developed and shared. A repeating cycle occurs. Each step enacts cognitive and psychological enhancements in the awareness building and sharing processes. Each step grounds in change and learning processes. Cook and Yanow (1996) suggest that change and learning processes rely on environmental scanning, promoting, or developing new interpretative schema through the adoption of sensitive and transmitting tools, and the amount of the group interactional work. Behaviors have not to change to perform organizational learning. Outputs of learning processes are relatively permanent changes in organizational behaviors. An ongoing debate investigates differences in learning processes between individuals and organizations, revealing differences between individual and organizational learning (Schwandt & Marquardt, 2000). This chapter addresses both individual and organizational learning in awareness building and sharing in family firms. Manifesting little experience with a change concern and revealing no cognitive, emotional, behavioral experience with it, family firms are at the pre-developing step of awareness building and sharing. Family firms have no perception of the concern regarding the self or other organizations. Family firms have not experienced it or recognized it about other organizations.

From a contingency perspective, a change concern is out of the organizational context. Accordingly, a family firm may be not aware of it, while others might be. Therefore, within the pre-developing stage, family firms may show different levels of consciousness concerning other organizations on the change concern. Cognitive development begins as the family firm's situation starts reflecting the concern. Family firms move to the rationalization stage (the second phase of awareness building and sharing), showing emotional and cultural connections with the change itself. The rationalization phase will include some single loop learning processes revealing the development of some form of intellectual narrative about the change concern. When in a cognitive development existing routines and mental models drive a single loop learning process, they support self-reinforcing patterns, weakening the discovery of new approaches in framing concerns (Argyris, 1982). A single loop learning approach influences both the family firm and the first-order organizational change. The convergent dimensions of the latter nurture firm's reliability through systems, processes, and structures' changes (Newman, 2000). Resilience on adapting schema and routines appears, developing change behaviors without learning (Cook & Yannow, 1996). The cognitive approach to organizational learning shapes the rationalization step, revealing that leveraging knowledge does not imply learning.

Moving from the rationalization step to the meeting one, family firms develop experiences about the change. Several patterns may depict the movement, from unforeseen immediate exposure to a critical event to a gradual one. Within this continuum, family firms show different emotional attachments, resulting in threats and fears. Usually, the meeting step shows ambivalent emotions, power, and powerlessness, gain and loss of coordination, shaping the awareness building and sharing process. The need for coordination appears. The need for coordination represents an essential mechanism for organizational effectiveness.

Organizational effectiveness denotes an organization able to behave coordinated in achieving the desired results. In the meeting step, family firms realize that their organizational effectiveness has diminished, due to their full involvement in the concern change, and something inhibits in further improvement in their awareness building and sharing. Family firms may enter the meeting step for a crisis or a critical unforeseen event or a progressive lowering of performances.

To contrast organizational resilience, family firms start (enabling step) searches for alternatives that can assure enough decisional power for approaching change while dismantling organizational resistance. In the enabling step, family firms suspend adverse judgment and start thinking. Family firms adopt discretion rather than rationality. During the enabling phase, they reconcile the feelings of the absence of control and loss of coordination produced during the meeting step. Within the enabling step, family firms start to become aware of the extent of coordination they have, and they need. Individuals embedded in the awareness building process search for a shared agreement, adopting cooperative mechanisms, as networks or mentors. The feedback-learning loop with cooperative mechanisms accomplishes the need for coaching individuals in the enabling step. In the enabling step, a discourse or dialogue feedback ask for a strategy to use. The feedback-learning loop represents an organizational making-meaning effort, enabling the addressing of frustration, anger, and misperception of individuals, characterizing the meeting step. Mezirow (1985) suggests that organizations socially develop their making meaning, focusing and handling social information as an initial phase in the change process. The making meaning of social systems fosters the reconnecting of individuals after the isolation experienced during the meeting step.

Consensus, the fifth stage of awareness building and sharing signifies "being whole." In family firms, individuals recover their feeling of coordination. All the negative feelings emerged during the meeting step dissipate. Family firms realize the "what" and "why" they act because of the cognitive and psychological advance occurred during the preceding steps. Family firms are now able to be effective in their change efforts. For a family firm, moving from the enabling phase to the consensus one represents a growth step. During the consensus step, family firms look for strategies and behaviors to address the change concern, stirring out from the crisis that triggered the meeting step. We can refer to the consensus step as a social-oriented intelligence effort where individuals share experiences and knowledge about the environment. In the awareness building and sharing process, the consensus step presents similarities with the double loop learning proposed by Argyris (1982). Adopting new points of view symbolizes the first change in how organizations look at their environment (Mezirow, 1985; Schon, 1987). Moving into the consensus step represents a perspective renovation in framing with respect the specific change concern, implying an organizational transformation (Newman, 2000) through an enduring organizational change. Sensemaking (Murphy, 2005), develops the link between how family firms make sense of information and knowledge about contingent dimensions and how they act to influence their organizational outcomes. The consensus step transforms family firms' abilities to address competitive challenges coming from environmental changes. From decisions taken in the enabling step, the consensus phase activates double-loop learning (Argyris & Schon, 1978) or second-order learning, through the exploration of new routines and schema, since the old routines are obsolete or the old schema do not match with the changed environment.

Awareness of Internal and External Environment

Environmental dimensions affect how family firms' frame reality and, therefore, influence their awareness (Lumpkin & Dess, 1996). Awareness about environmental changes leads strategic and organizational changes (Tsai et al., 2005; Fiedler, 2010). As firms increase their awareness of environmental dimensions, they can better handle them. The higher is awareness of environmental aspects of a family firm; the more consistent are their strategic and organizational choices (Nóbrega & Hoffmann, 2014). In sense-making processes (Thomas et al., 1993), family firms need to: i) Spot the need for change; ii) Understand it as a relevant drift that requires action, and iii) Make choices about how to change. Poor decisions mean a more mechanical response, while rich choices imply the thoughtful employment of human activity. A mechanical reaction indicates a limited awareness of the environmental conditions, asking the firm itself to handle them. An aware answer shows an understanding of the internal and external environment, and the ability to overcome or to exploit it.

The construct of awareness of the internal and external environment defines the sense-making of the problem-setting of strategic and organizational choices. Strategic and organizational choices for family firms may be different. They can adopt new business models, organizational configurations, management models, and managerial tools. Therefore, these differentiate them from their competitors (Acquaah, 2013; Upton et al., 2001; Moores & Mula, 2000) and lead to process or product innovation. Few contributions investigate the strategic sense-making processes in family firms regarding environmental dynamics (Dyer, 2003; Upton et al., 2001). Family firms presenting entrepreneurial orientation and particular family goals develop proactive management decisions (Kellermanns et al., 2012; Craig & Dibrel, 2006; Zahra, 2005). Little is known about the role of the family influence (Aldrich & Cliff, 2003) in these strategic sense-making processes. Aldrich and Cliff (2003) suggest integrating the family influence into exploring sense-making processes on both opportunity recognition and exploitation. Reflecting on strategic decision quality, Mustakallio et al. (2002) show the importance of implicit mechanisms and the role of family influence. Family social interaction relates to a shared family vision, a collectivistic awareness of the reality, linked to strategic decision quality.

Organizational Awareness

Family firms must additionally be aware of organizational variables that can affect their performance (Thomas et al., 1993). Family firms need to infuse a broader, organizationally rational perspective into their practices (Jaskiewicz et al., 2018). Miller and Le Breton-Miller (2006, 2005) show how family firms shape their priorities in the configuration of resources (Kellermanns & Floyd, 2005; Kellermanns, 2003) and routines. Family firms have their own culture, as a set of values, norms, guiding beliefs, and understandings that are shared by family and non-family members, and taught to new members as the correct way to think, feel and behave (Kirst-Ashman & Hull, 2015). The family culture includes expectations for many tangible and objective actions, such as expectations for behaving and communication, but also involves many symbolic dimensions as well. Family structure and culture affect family firms' awareness to accumulate and shed resources (Sharma & Manikutty, 2005; Kellermanns, 2005). Conversely, the organizational climate describes the general atmosphere of the workplace, including stress, energy, and intensity levels as well as general morale and affect (Jaskiewicz et al., 2018) in family firms. To exploit their entrepreneurial orientation and achieve their goals, family firms adopt a specific configuration of the organizational variables.

Organizational variables are the organizational structure (Tolbert & Hall, 2009), the coordination mechanisms, and the power dynamics (Brunninge et al., 2007; Gersick et al., 1990). Here, we focus our attention on coordination mechanisms since they refer to those HRMP that 'keep co-specialized assets in value creating co-alignment' (Helfat et al., 2007). In an organization, when individuals, tasks, and resources act independently, the need for coordination is an insignificant one. Conversely, when they should synchronize one each other in performing a task, the need for coordination is high. The successful integration of organizational variables into the family firm is contingent on the awareness of being able to anticipate, and not just respond to, the internal and external environmental dimensions. Organizational awareness arises from repeated interactions between individuals and close-knit groups, who identify themselves with a more extensive collective that can better develop that awareness. We adjusted the original model presented by Shockley-Zalabak (2006) to describe the three dimensions of organizational awareness in family firms. The first dimension, the fit competency, involves the family firm's ability to recognize and interpret the fit between organizational variables and its internal and external environmental dimensions. The second dimension is the sensitivity competence, which defines the ability in sense-making about the need for a change of organizational variables. The third dimension is a values competency and requires commitment and dedication to the family culture and the internalization and valuing of its goals. Organizational awareness is a prerequisite in the development of skills for choices (Kirst-Ashman & Hull, 2015; Kellermanns & Floyd, 2005; Sharma & Manikutty, 2005; Kellermanns, 2005, 2003) to get a higher level of collaborative behaviors in family firms in achieving their goals. While the designing of the organizational structure grounds on bounded rational organizational theories and power dynamics are contingent on different generational stages (Hoy, 2006) or life cycle phases (Moores & Mula, 2000), coordination mechanisms are mainly responsible for achieving collaborative behaviors in an organization.

Coordinated family firms manage interdependencies using both explicit and implicit coordination mechanisms. Family firms coordinate themselves explicitly using task mechanisms (e.g., schedules, programs, plans, rules, procedures, and so on) or by communicating (e.g., orally, in writing, formally, informally, interpersonally, in groups). We call the need for these mechanisms "explicit" since family firms use them purposely to coordinate. However, family firms may prefer to coordinate "implicitly" (i.e., without deliberately trying to coordinate) through cognition. Cognition grounds on shared knowledge and values about goals, tasks, and about each other. Shared knowledge and values help family firms realize what is going on, and anticipate what is going to happen next, and which actions are likely to be taken, thus supporting them to become more coordinated. Implicit coordination is crucial for family firms to ensure a value-creating co-alignment among individuals, whereby relational conflicts are mitigated while task conflicts are encouraged, meanings are shared, and collaboration is supported. Therefore, implicit coordination mechanisms focus on fostering collaborative behaviors.

Consequently, it is crucial that we understand how needs for explicit and implicit coordination mechanisms complement and relate to each other. We propose a twofold theoretical framework to study the effects of organizational awareness on coordination in family firms. The framework includes both the need for explicit and implicit coordination mechanisms, which, as we discuss later on, ask to be jointly recognized because they may complement, influence, or interact with each other in framing the choice for HRMP in family firms. We begin by defining the need for a coordination construct, which is the central element of the framework. We then propose how the need for implicit and explicit coordination mechanisms influences the configuration of HRMP in family firms.

Need for Coordination

The need for coordination is the requirement for efficient management of interdependencies among tasks, resources, and people (Helfat et al., 2007; Marks et al., 2001; Thompson, 1967). The ultimate goal of coordination is to develop collaborative behaviors (Bedwell et al., 2012; Morgeson et. al., 2010; Griffin et al., 2007; Marks et al., 2001; Podsakoff et al., 2000; Hinsz et al., 1997) in an organization that shape performance outcomes.

Coordination mechanisms define the tools or organizational provisions that let individuals coordinate (Jarzabkowski et al., 2012; Okhuysen & Bechky, 2009). Coordination mechanisms support the coordination process that individuals apply to manage interdependencies (Simon, 1957). Literature reveals how different coordination mechanisms can influence performance (Sherif et al., 2006; Willem et al., 2006) or be affected by environmental dimensions (Mani et al., 2014; Bailey et al., 2010).

Coordination in family firms can be achieved adopting task mechanisms (such as programs, plans, procedures, policies, and rules), or communication mechanisms (such as verbal, written, formal, informal, interpersonal, group ones). Task and communication mechanisms represent "explicit" coordination mechanisms since family firms intentionally adopt them. Conversely, without an intentional aim, family firms may coordinate themselves with cognition. Cognition grounds on the integration of shared knowledge and values. Through shared knowledge and values, family firms understand the actual situation and appreciate the future one. Moreover, with shared knowledge and values, family firms recognize which strategies and behaviors they could adapt to be more coordinated. The adoption of "implicit" coordination mechanisms significantly affects the value-creating co-alignment of individuals. Implicit coordination mechanisms reduce relational conflicts and stimulate task conflicts, activating collaboration among individuals. Therefore, implicit coordination mechanisms focus on fostering collaborative behaviors. We adopt six critical collaborative behaviors' definition (Bedwell et al., 2012). They include: (1) adaptation (Griffin et al., 2007), (2) extra-role (Podsakoff et al., 2000), (3) information processing (Hinsz et al., 1997), (4) leadership (Yukl, 2006), (5) sense-making (Morgeson et al., 2010), and (6) task execution. We adopt this perspective about the need for coordination from the viewpoint of managing interdependencies to enlighten how different elements of the proposed framework fit together in nurturing collaborative behaviors. Accordingly, we define how the needs for implicit and explicit coordination mechanisms influence the configuration of HRMP in family firms.

Need for Explicit Coordination Mechanisms

Classical organizational literature reveals that organizations adopt specific task and communication coordination mechanisms when the routine aspects of a task present more predictable interdependencies and more addressable with a programmed approach. Organizations adopt explicit coordination mechanisms that pre-defined how, when, and with whom to coordinate information via routinized processes (Simon, 1957). In these cases, plans, programs, procedures, and rules manage coordination (Okhuysen & Bechky, 2009) and frequently relate to controlling communication. We refer to this as explicit coordination mechanisms.

Need for Implicit Coordination Mechanisms

Conversely, we define implicit coordination as coordination activities not pre-defined by routinized processes, but driven by emerging characteristics of the environment and defined by the actor(s) involved. They are evocative of coordination mechanisms labelled as organic (Andres & Zmud, 2001), mutual adjustment and feedback (Thompson, 1967) or having features of improvisation (Harrison & Rouse, 2014; Bechky & Okhuysen, 2011). Implicit coordination happens in circumstances where actors have the autonomy to make decisions about how coordination takes place. According to organizational cognition literature, the more individuals interact with each other and share expertise in performing a joint task, the more they become aware of the task and in coordinating themselves implicitly. Such a need for implicit coordination refers to the perception of synchronization of individuals' actions based on unspoken assumptions about what others are likely to do. The individual–organization relationships literature (Rhoades & Eisenberger, 2002) argues that organizations' leaders, i.e., in family firms, the founders, and owners, are the most potent influencers of employee mental models at the workplaces (Barsade, 2002). They can positively influence their organizational identity and affective commitment (i.e., the desire to follow a course of action; Sharma & Irving, 2005) creating conditions under which family firms may reduce their reliance on explicit coordination mechanisms. Randall et al. (1990) show that affective commitment contributes significantly to developing the need for implicit coordination mechanisms between organizational members. Herscovitch and Meyer (2002) state that higher levels of affective commitment relate to successful organizational changes. Organizational identity and commitment are most strongly related to implicit coordination mechanisms, such as extra-role, discretionary contributions of employees (Riketta, 2002). Higher levels of organizational identity and commitment raise the likelihood that individuals will subsidize effort on behalf of the family firms, even in the absence of active supervision or strict rules and procedures (explicit coordination mechanisms). Employee organizational identity and commitment are particularly valuable under dynamic environmental dimensions (Eddleston et al., 2008), fostering collectivist awareness through collaboration, rapid knowledge sharing, adaptability, and helpfulness (Collins & Smith, 2006). Nahapiet and Ghoshal (1998) show the importance of a common system of meanings (e.g., regarding language, words, expressions, or even body movements), which enables the common understanding of collective goals and proper ways of acting in concert.

The need for implicit coordination mechanisms represents those requirements offered to family firms from shared knowledge and values. Family firms presenting strong and enduring cultures smooth their awareness of the need for explicit coordination mechanisms (Zahra et al., 2004). Implicit coordination mechanisms let family firms understand and anticipate task issues and individuals' behaviors. We refer to these needs for coordination mechanisms as implicit since they are not consciously employed for coordinating. While explicit coordination mechanisms may be most appropriate in stable competitive settings, for family firms facing significant environmental changes, uncertainty, or risk, involvement, commitment, trust, and stewardship may contribute more positively to higher levels of awareness of the need for implicit coordination mechanisms. To understand how family firms coordinate themselves, we propose the integration of the classical organizational view of family firms' need for coordination (i.e., need for explicit coordination) with the view from organizational awareness research (i.e., need for implicit coordination). Family firms in familiar and routine tasks may benefit more from task organization mechanisms (i.e., plans, schedules, programs, tools, and so on). Family firms in less frequent and unstable conditions may be more aware of the need for coordinating via communication. The observation that family firms account for a very heterogeneous population of organizations indicates that their differences in innovativeness, proactiveness, risk-taking, autonomy, competitive aggressiveness and organizational flexibility can be used to distinguish between different types of family firms, which are more or less aware. We propose that the choice of a set of HRMP depends on the organizational awareness developed of the need for implicit coordination mechanisms and the need for explicit coordination mechanisms consistent with the awareness of the internal and external environment.

HRM PRACTICES' CONFIGURATIONS

To exploit the roles of complementarity, congruence, and synergy, we describe the firm's HRMP choice from a configurational perspective (Chadwick, 2010). The focus of this perspective reflects a direct connection between the performance and a specific HRMP configuration (Sheehan, 2014; Akhtar et al., 2008). The positive relationship depends critically on assembling the right combination of practices such that all of them separately fit together, support each other, and develop the maximum attainable synergy. The performance effects of HRMP choice are multiplicative rather than additive, implying low returns if all but one or two of the practices fit together, but a consistent package might assure high returns if organizations successfully implement all of them (Zhang & Morris, 2014; Lepak & Shaw, 2008). The configurational perspective lends a systemic viewpoint from which to project HRMP composition (Kaufman, 2010) and claims that the positive performance evolves from a bundle of interrelated HR practices (Meuer, 2016) which together form an internally consistent whole (Colbert, 2004).

In building an HRMP configuration, literature indicates that the potential strategic practices are: 1) Recruitment and selection (Khan, 2010; Katuo & Budhwar, 2006; Ahmad & Schroeder, 2003; Chiu et al., 2002); 2) Compensation (Ahmad & Schroeder, 2003; Chiu et al., 2002); 3) Performance appraisal (Khan, 2010; Chang & Chen, 2002); 4) Training and development (Khan, 2010; Katuo & Budhwar, 2006; Ahmad & Schroeder, 2003; Chang & Chen, 2002); 5) Workforce planning (Mathis & Jackson,

2004; Chang & Chen, 2002); 6) Career planning management (Schein, 1996); 7) Job design (Morgeson & Humphrey, 2006); 7) Internal communication (Oladipo & Abdulkadir, 2011; Osman et al., 2011).

We propose that the choice of a particular complete HRMP configuration depends on the organizational awareness developed of the need for implicit coordination mechanisms and the need for explicit coordination mechanisms consistent with the awareness of the internal and external environment.

Four Configurations of Human Resources Practices

Combining the two sets of needs of coordination mechanisms leads to four configurations of aligned HRMP, described as the Administrative, the Shared, the Professional, and the Integrated one (see Figure 2). Family firms frame their HRMP composition according to their financial capabilities, strategic focuses, and development priorities to avoid potential mismatches between HRMP (Toh et al., 2008). Therefore, the desired synergy generated by the HRMP portfolio will be able to support the formation of valuable and inimitable resources (Barney, 1991) to create competitive advantages for the organization (Chadwick, 2010).

Figure 2. Four configurations of HRMP
Source: Authors

Shared (High)	**Integrated**
Dynamic and complex environmental dimensions	Complex and highly dynamic environmental dimensions
Organizational identity and affective commitment	Family firm orientation, consistent with strategy
Mutual long-term exchange relationships	Development of environmental and cultural scanning
Personal relationships and collaborative behaviors	Emphasis on both efficiency and effectiveness
Practices related to motivation, results-oriented appraisal	Information and communication
Practices related to opportunity	Long-range issues related to employees and organizational variables
Internal communication and flexible in compensation, benefits, training	Organizational identity and affective commitment
Emphasis on effectiveness	Personal relationships and collaborative behaviors
Required knowledge, skills, and abilities are uncertain and changing	Efficiency of the functions or of the divisions
Resource-based approach	Both a resource-based and a control-based approach
Administrative	**Professional**
Simple and not dynamic environmental dimensions	Relative stable and complex environmental dimensions
Managing human resources through few rules and procedures	Many rules, complex procedures, articulated plans, standardization of processes and efficiency
Standardization of processes and efficiency	Efficient organizational environment where family firms manage the functions or the divisions
Family firms are not aware, or are aware of the environmental dimensions, but they do not incorporate them in the personnel management	Emphasis on efficiency
Aware of the administrative role of HRM practices, realized through basic salary and benefit administration	Transaction-based HRM practices with individual short-term exchange relationships
Basic record-keeping via manual employee profile	Development of managerial skills
Nonexempt hiring	Stable set of tasks
(Low)	Control-based approach

(Vertical axis: Need for implicit mechanisms — Low to High. Horizontal axis: Need for explicit mechanisms — Low to High.)

The Administrative configuration refers to an organizational awareness of low levels of both the need for implicit and explicit coordination mechanisms. It denotes simple and not dynamic environmental dimensions. Few rules and procedures manage human resources (Kaman et al., 2001). The aims are the standardization of processes and efficiency. Family firms are aware of these simple environmental dimensions, but they do not integrate them into the people management. They are aware of the administrative role of HRMP, realized through basic salary and benefits administration, essential record keeping via manual employee profiles, and non-exempt hiring.

The shared configuration presents an organizational awareness about a high level of the need for implicit coordination mechanisms and a low level the need for explicit coordination mechanisms. It refers to dynamic and complex environmental dimensions. Family firms search for organizational identity (Zellweger & Sieger, 2012; Arregle et al., 2007; Sirmon & Hitt, 2003) and affective commitment (Sharma & Irving, 2005; Randall et al., 1990). Commitment-based HRMP are implemented, emphasizing mutual long-term exchange relationships (Guchait & Cho, 2010; Williams & Mohamed, 2010; Sun et al., 2007; Collins & Smith, 2006; Batt, 2002). The ultimate goal is to build an organizational environment where family firms manage the personal relationships of individuals and where employees work together displaying collaborative behaviors (Bedwell et al., 2012). Collaborative behaviors emerge, thanks to shared meanings and values (Wheeler et al., 2010; Bergiel et al., 2009; Holtom et al., 2006; Giosan et al., 2005). Creating a culture and network of relationships supports an effective strategy implementation. Family firms display awareness through a cooperative and involved managing of employees. The shared configuration embraces interdependent work structures, clan fostering initiatives, and broader skill development. Family firms implement practices related to motivation, including results-oriented appraisal, and practices related to opportunity, such as employee participation programs. Policies foster internal communication, and new employees' plans are added to flexibly respond to business needs in compensation, benefits, and training (long-range programs). The emphasis is on effectiveness in direct response to business needs. Since not being related to stable tasks and processes, shared configurations are unable to attain high degrees of formalization. In unstable situations, much of the work is ad hoc, devoted to performing unique and unprecedented tasks. Job descriptions are improvised as fresh challenges appear. Required knowledge, skills, and abilities are uncertain and changing. Performance appraisal is equally vague and of limited value when selecting people for future, different, ad hoc tasks. In these circumstances, the use of stable, complex and articulated HRMP may be counterproductive, delaying timely action and consuming resources. With limited periods to reap their value, they are unlikely to pay back the resources put into their development. Recruitment, development, and retention practices are fundamental HRM policies in the shared configuration in fostering strategic capabilities and creating competitive advantage. HRM adopts a resource-based approach to the measurement of high-performance practices (Combs et al., 2006).

The Professional configuration presents an organizational awareness about a high level of the need for explicit coordination mechanisms and a low level of the need for implicit coordination mechanisms. It applies to relatively stable and complex environmental dimensions. The professional configuration asks for managing people through rules, complex procedures, articulated plans, aiming at the highest standardization of processes and efficiency. The ultimate goal is to build an efficient organizational environment where family firms manage the functions, or the divisions of the organizational structure, in direct response to business needs. Family firms adopt interdisciplinary HRMP directed to achieve functional/divisional goals. Transaction-based HRMP are implemented, highlighting individual short-term exchange relationships (Tsui et al., 1995). The professional configuration consists of hard work structures, result-based initiatives, and trans-specialist development. Employees' succession planning is a central concern. The professional configuration provides professionalization in functions/divisions and tries to incorporate and develop managerial skills. The management of the personnel function grounds on control and measurements, evidencing more sophisticated compensation and benefits policies and devoting a great effort to designing job positions and profiles. With a relatively stable set of tasks, family firms can design and describe an enduring set of jobs. People can be recruited, selected, compensated, and trained for and selected into them, though effective data collection. A bundle of formalized procedures can be adopted to run these standardized processes in a transparent, efficient and effective way. In configuring HRMP practices, an increase in benefits leads the adoption of formal practices, rather than ensuring conformity about what family firms perceive as best practices. Integrating HRM systems within the set of managerial systems should generate synergistic results in increasing the family firm's value. Consequently, configuring structured HRMP practices requires a cost-benefit approach. A structured approach raises costs related to less flexibility, fewer financial resources, higher organizational rigidity, while it increases benefits in matching legal standards, keeping records for supporting eventual future litigations, and rising efficiency.

The Integrated configuration presents an organizational awareness about a high level of the need both for implicit and explicit coordination mechanisms. It applies to complex and highly dynamic environmental dimensions. The management of the personnel function strives for family firm orientation, consistently with the strategic business direction. HRMP aim at developing a high environmental and cultural scanning, and long-range planning tension. The emphasis is on both efficiency and effectiveness in direct response to business needs. Information and communication are consistent with the adoption of planning, research, and analysis tools. Long-range and "what if" questions connect to employees and organizational variables. Family firms search for organizational identity and affective commitment, creating an integrated environment where they manage both the personal relationships of individuals' working together, showing collaborative behaviors, and the functions or the divisions of the organizational structure. HRM adopts both a resource-based and a control-based approach to the measurement of commitment-based HRMP (Batt, 2002; Huselid, 1995).

The four proposed configurations consist of a unique combination of aligned HRMP (see Figure 3). The four configurations may all be effective ways of managing human resources practices in family firms.

Figure 3. Aligned HRM practices in the four configurations

	Shared	**Integrated**
High	Recruiting and selection Compensation Training and development Internal communication	Recruiting and selection Compensation Training and development Internal communication Performance appraisal Workforce planning Career planning management Job design
	Administrative	**Professional**
Low	Recruiting and selection Compensation	Recruiting and selection Compensation Training and development Performance appraisal Workforce planning Job design

Need for implicit mechanisms (vertical axis, Low to High)

Low — Need for explicit mechanisms — High

Lastly, we suggest the saturated conceptual model for configuring HRMP in family firms, as reported in Figure 4.

Figure 4. The saturated configurational model of HRMP for family firms

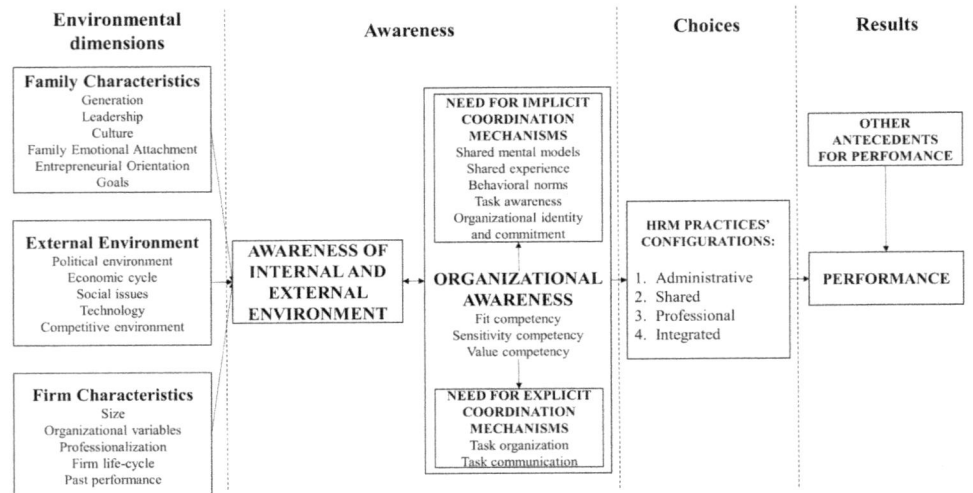

In line with the configurational approach to HRM, such aligned combinations of practices that reflect what a family firm perceive as needed in terms for coordination mechanisms are expected to be effective (Chadwick et al., 2013). Thus, the first proposition we make is that family firms are aware that the 'fit' is perceived correctly.

Proposition 1: Family firms present HRMP' configurations that reflect any of the proposed combinations for the needs of implicit and explicit coordination mechanisms.

Thus, researchers have the chance to discover how complementary HRMP come together and reflect HRMP framing in family firms (Perry-Smith & Blum, 2000). As Kepes and Delery (2007) show, HRMP work synergistically, providing positive organizational results. A frame connected to an internal fit is embedded in HRMP bundles. Internal fit aims to extend the HRM systems' alignment of decisional criteria. Regarding different combinations of HRMP, internal fit asks for complementing practices in attaining equifinality and positive work-related results (Kepes & Delery, 2007).

The second proposition refers to the effectiveness of the fit. Family firms presenting the proposed configurations will perform better than family firms adopting different bundles of HRMP will.

Proposition 2: Family firms with the proposed configurations of HRMP outperform family firms adopting HRMP that do not show any fit.

Different HRMP configurations lead to different results through different means. The shared and integrated configurations enforce commitment to compliance. The two configurations foster employees' extra-role behaviors, going beyond as specified in formal contracts. Shared and integrated configurations aim to develop competencies and motivate family and non-family employees to apply discretionary time and flexible efforts in executing tasks. Lai and Saridakis (2013) suggest that recruiting and selection, training, and development practices increase the workforce's competencies, while compensation and performance appraisal practices stimulate employees' extra-role behaviors.

Proposition 3: Family firms adopting HRMP shared and integrated configurations will be more likely to present extra-role's behaviors by employees than family firms with HRMP that do not fit these configurations.

According to Proposition 2, the administrative and professional configurations present higher levels of effectiveness. Nevertheless, the two configurations will show lower levels of employees' retention due to their high emphasis on regulations, norms, rules, procedures, and sanctions. Conversely, family firms with HRMP configurations that insist on commitment and organizational identity will show higher levels of employees' retention.

Proposition 4a: Family firms whose HRMP reflect administrative and professional configurations will show higher levels of employee turnover than family firms with HRMP that do not fit these configurations.

Proposition 4b: Family firms whose HRMP reflect shared and integrated configurations will show lower levels of employee turnover than family firms with HRMP that do not fit these configurations.

HRMP influence family firms' innovativeness. Some configurations enhance the environmental features of creativity, change, and innovation. A psychological safe workplace environment fosters employees' behaviors toward innovative risk-taking efforts (West & Altink, 1996) and collaborative learning (Edmondson, 1999). Commitment-based HRMP configurations will nurture workplaces environments more favorable to innovation, while configurations based on explicit coordination mechanisms, enhancing formalization and centralization structural characteristics, will present lower levels of innovation.

Proposition 5a: Family firms whose HRMP reflect the administrative configuration will show lower levels of innovativeness.

Proposition 5b: Family firms whose HRMP reflect shared and integrated configurations will show higher levels of innovativeness.

DISCUSSION AND CONCLUSION

This chapter aimed to develop a theoretical configurational model of HRMP for family firms facing strategic and organizational changes based on the concept of awareness. Here, we discuss the conceptual challenges, researchers and practitioners might meet when adopting such an approach. The typology of typical HRMP configurations we developed is grounded on i.) two organizational factors: awareness of the internal and external environment and organizational awareness; and ii.) two dimensions of organizational awareness: the need both for explicit and implicit coordination mechanisms. The first refers to the need for mechanisms explicitly adopted by a family firm to manage task or communication interdependencies. The second relates to requirements offered to family firms from shared knowledge and values. These implicit coordination mechanisms support them in understanding and anticipating task issues and individuals' behaviors. The combination of the two needs for coordination mechanisms results in four ideal configurations of HRMP (administrative, shared, professional, and integrated).

The four proposed configurations consist of unique combinations of aligned HRMP. The four configurations may all be effective ways of managing HRMP in family firms. Therefore, we developed seven propositions to sustain the theoretical enhancement of the model. We adopted three assumptions in our approach: (1) that the sum of each HRMP is more significant than its parts; (2) that the configurations of HRMP are additive rather than multiplicative; and (3) that one key aspect, awareness, of HRMP, is needed (Guest, 1997). The assumptions ground on emphasizing that the complete set of relationships or associations between different parts affect behaviors and performances (gestalt theory - Wolfgang, 1947).

The configurational model proposed is close to the "fit-as-gestalt" approach of Guest (1997), based on which, an additive configuration of HRMP for a family firm might explain a superior performance. The idea behind the model is that, to yield performance when facing strategic and organizational changes, a family firm may adopt a specific configuration of HRMP. More accurately, a particular configuration of HRMP helps to confer a potential competitive advantage on a family firm. Under this assumption, a successful family firm is expected to configure all the HRMP and link each one to all the others in a systematic manner.

For many family firms, the dynamics and complexity of the environmental dimensions have increased. Therefore, the effective responsiveness to the required strategic and organizational changes is a crucial concern. Responsiveness relates to the existence and pervasiveness of rules and procedures. Family firms showing more rules and regulations standardize behaviors and may stress for responsibility for results. Such family firms tend to be more organization-centered showing bureaucratic features and less strategic flexibility.

Conversely, family firms less regulated positively empower their employees in responsibility for results. From a control perspective, bureaucratic family firms showing rules and direct supervision enforce compliant behaviors and output control. The control of behaviors asks for managerial competencies about cause-effect relationships that let family firms design and evaluate correct behaviors. Running an output control requires clear and measurable results and standards of performance. If this is the case, family firms may use rewards in reinforcing the achievement of defined performance targets. Dynamic environments may cause ambiguity and change on desired behaviors and performance standards, negatively influencing the effectiveness of coordination efforts with predetermined rules and procedures.

There are two principal reasons why we adopted our theoretical model in the attempt to investigate HRMP configurations-performance relationships in family firms. First, we want to contribute ongoing debate about the two different typologies of HRMP, respectively named "high commitment work practices" (HCWPs) and "high-performance work systems" (HPWSs). Both typologies may jointly contribute to higher performance (Cappelli & Neumark, 2001; Godard, 2001), but we offer a different perspective. Second, family business literature has long argued that success has primarily been a matter of family firms' unique ways of managing human resources.

Committed employees' relationships, investments in training and development, and quality oriented HRMP are crucial sources for competitive advantages in family firms. For these reasons, our paper proposes a model for explaining how different HRMP could be configured together to exert an influence on family firms' performance.

Our model aims to supply a contribution to the ongoing discussion about the HRMP configurational perspective for family firms. We examined a particular construct (awareness) by which each configuration of HRMP is presenting internal alignment in family firms. We based it on the vast bulk of literature both from HRM and family business, with a focus on understanding how a family firm can cope with strategic and organizational changes by leveraging the adoption of an aligned bundle of HRMP. Despite this possible contribution, the model presents limitations that necessitate caution when interpreting it.

LIMITATIONS

Have we considered an exhaustive or at least comprehensive list of environmental dimensions? Strategic management and organizational theory disciplines reflect on how firms connect with their environment. Nevertheless, the construct 'environment' still presents ambiguity and a loose definition, generating three concerns. First, there is a weak agreement on relevant dimensions defining it. Second, a lack of consensus still exists on measures about environmental dimensions. Third, general uncertainty affects how different environmental dimensions affect strategic and organizational awareness.

How do we measure awareness (Timmermans & Cleeremans, 2015)? Even though literature presents some tentative efforts in measuring awareness (Sitt et al., 2014; Casali et al., 2013), very few attempts have been made in developing a methodology for measuring awareness (Seth et al., 2008). An 'awareness meter' will help in understanding relationships between environmental dimensions, family firms' experience in environmental dimensions, and their decisions about HRMP configurations.

NEXT STEPS OF THE RESEARCH

We intend to support the proposed ideal-typical configurations through an investigation developed in a two-step process: first, we want to invest in an assessment undertaken by a panel of experts on the various variables considered in the model. To test our operationalized model with the four HRMP configurations, we will adopt a panel of experts, limiting the likelihood of measuring random configurations. Next, we will empirically measure the distance between the four advanced configurations and the actual ones in a significant sample of family firms.

REFERENCES

Achleitner, A., Gunther, N., Kaserer, C., & Siciliano, G. (2014). Real Earnings Management and Accrual-based Earnings Management in Family Firms. *European Accounting Review*, *23*(3), 431–461. doi:10.1080/09638180.2014.895620

Acquaah, M. (2013). Management control systems, business strategy and performance: A comparative analysis of family and non-family businesses in a transition economy in sub-Saharan Africa. *Journal of Family Business Strategy*, *4*(2), 131–146. doi:10.1016/j.jfbs.2013.03.002

Ahmad, S., & Schroeder, R. G. (2003). The impact of human resource management practices on operational performance: Recognising country and industry differences. *Journal of Operations Management*, *21*(1), 19–25. doi:10.1016/S0272-6963(02)00056-6

Akhtar, S., Ding, D. Z., & Ge, G. L. (2008). Strategic HRM practices and their impact on company performance in Chinese enterprises. *Human Resource Management*, *47*(1), 15–32. doi:10.1002/hrm.20195

Aldrich, H., & Cliff, J. (2003). The pervasive effects of family on entrepreneurship: Toward a family embeddedness perspective. *Journal of Business Venturing*, *18*(5), 573–596. doi:10.1016/S0883-9026(03)00011-9

Alfes, K., Truss, C., Soane, E. C., Rees, C., & Gatenby, M. (2013). The relationship between line manager behaviour, perceived HRM practices, and individual performance: Examining the mediating role of engagement. *Human Resource Management*, *52*(6), 839–859. doi:10.1002/hrm.21512

Almajali, D., Mansour, K., & Maqableh, M. (2016). The Impact of Electronic Supply Chain Management Usage on Firm's Performance. International Journal of Communications. *Network and System Sciences*, *9*(06), 280–293. doi:10.4236/ijcns.2016.96025

Analoui, F. (2002). *The Changing Patterns of Human Resource Management*. Aldershot, UK: Ashgate.

Andres, H., & Zmud, R. (2001). A contingency approach to software project coordination. *Journal of Management Information Systems*, *18*(3), 41–70. doi:10.1080/07421222.2002.11045695

Argyris, C. (1982). *Reasoning, learning, and action: Individual and organizational*. San Francisco: Jossey-Bass.

Argyris, C., & Schon, D. A. (1978). Organizational learning: A theory of action perspective. Reading, MA: Addison-Wes ley.

Arregle, J. L., Hitt, M. A., Sirmon, D. G., & Very, P. (2007). The development of organizational social capital: Attributes of family firms. *Journal of Management Studies*, *44*(1), 73–95. doi:10.1111/j.1467-6486.2007.00665.x

Astrachan, J. H., & Jaskiewicz, P. (2008). Emotional returns and emotional costs in privately held family businesses: Advancing traditional business valuation. *Family Business Review*, *21*(2), 139–149. doi:10.1111/j.1741-6248.2008.00115.x

Astrachan, J. H., Klein, S. B., & Smyrnios, K. X. (2002). The F-PEC scale of family influence: A proposal for solving the family business definition problem. *Family Business Review*, *15*(1), 45–58. doi:10.1111/j.1741-6248.2002.00045.x

Bacharach, S. B. (1989). Organisational Theories: Some Criteria for Evaluation. *Academy of Management Review*, *14*(4), 496–515. doi:10.5465/amr.1989.4308374

Bailey, D. E., Leonardi, P. M., & Chong, J. (2010). Minding the Gaps: Understanding Technology Interdependence and Coordination in Knowledge Work. *Organization Science*, *21*(3), 713–730. doi:10.1287/orsc.1090.0473

Bain, J. S. (1968). *Industrial Organization*. New York: John Wiley.

Barnett, T., & Kellermanns, F. W. (2006). Are we family and are we treated as family? Nonfamily employees' perceptions of justice in the family firm. *Entrepreneurship Theory and Practice*, *30*(6), 837–854. doi:10.1111/j.1540-6520.2006.00155.x

Barney, J. B. (1991). Firm resources and sustained competitive advantage. *Journal of Management*, *17*(1), 99–120. doi:10.1177/014920639101700108

Baron, R. A. (2008). The role of affect in the entrepreneurial process. *Academy of Management Review*, *33*(2), 328–340. doi:10.5465/amr.2008.31193166

Barsade, S. G. (2002). The ripple effect: Emotional contagion and its influence on group behavior. *Administrative Science Quarterly*, *47*(4), 644–675. doi:10.2307/3094912

Batt, R. (2002). Managing customer services: Human resource practices, quit rates and sales growth. *Academy of Management Journal*, *45*(3), 587–597.

Bechky, B. A., & Okhuysen, G. A. (2011). Expecting the Unexpected? How Swat Officers and Film Crews Handle Surprises. *Academy of Management Journal*, *54*(2), 239–251. doi:10.5465/amj.2011.60263060

Bedwell, W. L., Wildman, J. L., Diazgranados, D., Salazar, M., Kramer, W. S., & Salas, E. (2012). Collaboration at work: An integrative multilevel conceptualization. *Human Resource Management Review*, *22*(2), 128–145. doi:10.1016/j.hrmr.2011.11.007

Beltran-Martin, I., Roca-Puig, V., Escrig-Tena, A., & Bou-Llusar, J. C. (2009). Internal labor flexibility from a resource-based view approach: Definition and proposal of a measurement scale. *International Journal of Human Resource Management*, *20*(7), 1576–1598. doi:10.1080/09585190902985194

Bergiel, E. B., Nguyen, V. Q., Clenney, B. F., & Taylor, G. S. (2009). Human resource practices, job embeddedness and intention to quit. *Management Research News*, *32*(3), 205–219. doi:10.1108/01409170910943084

Berrone, P., Cruz, C., & Gomez-Meja, L. R. (2012). Socioemotional wealth in family firms: Theoretical dimensions, assessment approaches, and agenda for future research. *Family Business Review*, *25*(3), 258–279. doi:10.1177/0894486511435355

Bjorkman, I., & Lervik, J. E. (2007). Transferring HR practices within multinational corporations. *Human Resource Management Journal*, *17*(4), 320–335. doi:10.1111/j.1748-8583.2007.00048.x

Botero, I. C., & Litchfield, S. R. (2013). Exploring human resource management in family firms: a summary of what we know and ideas for future development. In K. X. Smymios, P. Z. Poutziouris, & S. Goel (Eds.), *Handbook of Research on Family Business* (2nd ed.; pp. 371–405). Cheltenham, UK: Edward Elgar.

Boxall, P. (1998). Achieving Competitive Advantage through Human Resource Strategy: Towards a Theory of Industry Dynamics. *Human Resource Management Review*, *8*(3), 265–288. doi:10.1016/S1053-4822(98)90005-5

Brunninge, O., Nordqvist, M., & Wiklund, J. (2007). Corporate governance and strategic change in SMEs: The effects of ownership, board composition and top management teams. *Small Business Economics*, *29*(3), 295–308. doi:10.100711187-006-9021-2

Budhwar, P. S., & Debrah, Y. A. (Eds.). (2001). *Human Resource Management in Developing Countries*. New York: Routledge.

Budhwar, P. S., & Debrah, Y. A. (2010). Rethinking comparative and cross-national human resource management research. *International Journal of Human Resource Management*, *12*(3), 497–515. doi:10.1080/713769629

Buller, P. F., & McEvoy, G. M. (2012). Strategy, human resource management and performance: Sharpening line of sight. *Human Resource Management Review*, *22*(1), 43–56. doi:10.1016/j.hrmr.2011.11.002

Callahan, J. L. (2000). Emotion management and organizational functions: A case study of patterns in a not-for-profit organization. *Human Resource Development Quarterly, 11*(3), 245–267. doi:10.1002/1532-1096(200023)11:3<245::AID-HRDQ4>3.0.CO;2-J

Cappelli, P., & Neumark, D. (2001). Do "High Performance" Work Practices Improve Establishment-Level Outcomes? *Industrial & Labor Relations Review, 54*(4), 737–775.

Carlson, D. S., Upton, N., & Seaman, S. (2006). The impact of human resource practices and compensation design on performance: An analysis of family-owned SMEs. *Journal of Small Business Management, 44*(4), 531–543. doi:10.1111/j.1540-627X.2006.00188.x

Casali, A. G., Gosseries, O., Rosanova, M., Boly, M., Sarasso, S., Casali, K. R., ... Massimini, M. (2013). A theoretically based index of consciousness independent of sensory processing and behavior. *Science Translational Medicine, 5*(198), 98–105. doi:10.1126citranslmed.3006294 PMID:23946194

Chadwick, C. (2010). Theoretic insights on the nature of performance synergies in human resource systems: Toward greater precision. *Human Resource Management Review, 20*(2), 85–101. doi:10.1016/j.hrmr.2009.06.001

Chadwick, C., Way, S. A., Kerr, G., & Thacker, J. W. (2013). Boundary conditions of the high-investment human resource systems-small-firm labor productivity relationship. *Personnel Psychology, 66*(2), 311–343. doi:10.1111/peps.12015

Chandler, G., & McEvoy, G. (2000). Human Resource Management, TQM and Firm Performance in Small and Medium-sized Enterprises. *Entrepreneurship Theory and Practice, 25*(1), 43–57. doi:10.1177/104225870002500105

Chang, P. L., & Chen, W. L. (2002). The effect of human resource management practices on firm performance: Empirical evidence from high-tech firms in Taiwan. *International Journal of Management, 19*(4), 622–638.

Chiu, R. K., Luk, V. W. M., & Tang, T. L. (2002). Retaining and motivating employees: Compensation preferences in Hong Kong and China. *Personnel Review, 31*(4), 402–431. doi:10.1108/00483480210430346

Chrisman, J. J., Chua, J. H., & Sharma, P. (2005). Trends and directions in the development of a strategic management theory of the family firm. *Entrepreneurship Theory and Practice, 29*(5), 555–575. doi:10.1111/j.1540-6520.2005.00098.x

Coff, R. W. (2002). Human capital, shared expertise, and the likelihood of impasse in corporate acquisitions. *Journal of Management, 28*(1), 107–128. doi:10.1177/014920630202800107

Coff, R. W., & Kryscynski, D. (2011). Drilling for microfoundations of human capital-based competitive advantages. *Journal of Management, 37*(5), 1429–1443. doi:10.1177/0149206310397772

Colbert, B. A. (2004). The complex resource-based view: Implications for theory and practice in strategic human resource management. *Academy of Management Review, 29*(3), 341–358. doi:10.5465/amr.2004.13670987

Collins, C. J., & Clark, K. D. (2003). Strategic human resource practices, top management team social networks, and firm performance: The role of human resource practices in creating organizational competitive advantage. *Academy of Management Journal, 46*(6), 740–751.

Collins, C. J., & Smith, K. G. (2006). Knowledge exchange and combination: The role of human resource practices in the performance of high technology firms. *Academy of Management Journal, 49*(3), 544–560. doi:10.5465/amj.2006.21794671

Combs, J., Liu, Y., Hall, A., & Ketchen, D. (2006). How much do high-performance work practices matter? A meta-analysis of their effects on organizational performance. *Personnel Psychology, 59*(3), 501–528. doi:10.1111/j.1744-6570.2006.00045.x

Combs, J., Penney, C. R., Crook, T. R., & Short, J. C. (2010). The impact of family representation on CEO compensation. *Entrepreneurship Theory and Practice, 34*(6), 1043–1182. doi:10.1111/j.1540-6520.2010.00417.x

Cook, S. D. N., & Yanow, D. (1996). Culture and organizational learning. In M. D. Cohen & L. S. Sproul (Eds.), *Organizational learning* (pp. 430–459). Thousand Oaks, CA: Sage.

Craig, J., & Dibrell, C. (2006). The natural environment, innovation, and firm performance: A comparative study. *Family Business Review, 19*(4), 275–288. doi:10.1111/j.1741-6248.2006.00075.x

Cruz, C., Firfiray, S., & Gomez-Mejia, L. R. (2011). Socioemotional wealth and human resource management (HRM) in family-controlled firms. *Research in Personnel and Human Resources Management, 30*, 159–217. doi:10.1108/S0742-7301(2011)0000030006

Cruz, C., Larraza-Kintana, M., Garcés-Galdeano, L., & Berrone, P. (2014). Are family firms really more socially responsible? *Entrepreneurship Theory and Practice, 38*(6), 1–22.

Dale, M. C., Shepherd, D., & Woods, C. (2008). Family models as a framework for employment relations in entrepreneurial family businesses. *New Zealand Journal of Employment Relations, 33*(1), 55–73.

De Kok, J. M. P., Uhlaner, L. M., & Thurik, A. R. (2006). Professional HRM practices in family owned-managed enterprises. *Journal of Small Business Management, 44*(3), 441–460. doi:10.1111/j.1540-627X.2006.00181.x

Dess, G. G., & Rasheed, A. (1991). Conceptualizing and measuring organizational environments: A critique and suggestions. *Journal of Management, 17*(4), 701–710. doi:10.1177/014920639101700404

Donaldson, L. (2001). *The contingency theory of organizations*. Thousand Oaks, CA: Sage Publications. doi:10.4135/9781452229249

Dyer, W. G. Jr. (2003). The family: The missing variable in organizational research. *Entrepreneurship Theory and Practice, 27*(4), 401–416. doi:10.1111/1540-8520.00018

Dyer, W. G. Jr. (2006). Examining the 'Family Effect' on Firm Performance. *Family Business Review, 19*(3), 253–273. doi:10.1111/j.1741-6248.2006.00074.x

Eddleston, K. A., & Kellermanns, F. W. (2007). Destructive and productive family relationships: A stewardship theory perspective. *Journal of Business Venturing*, *22*(4), 545–565. doi:10.1016/j.jbusvent.2006.06.004

Eddleston, K. A., Kellermanns, F. W., & Sarathy, R. (2008). Resource configurations in family firms: Linking resources, strategic planning and technological opportunities to performance. *Journal of Management Studies*, *45*(1), 26–50.

Edmondson, A. (1999). Psychological Safety and Learning Behavior in Work Teams. *Administrative Science Quarterly*, *44*(2), 350–383. doi:10.2307/2666999

Ferraro, H., & Marrone, J. (2016). Examining employment relationship activities in family business research. *Journal of Family Business Management*, *6*(3), 210–224. doi:10.1108/JFBM-01-2016-0001

Fiedler, S. (2010). Managing resistance in an organizational transformation: A case study from a mobile operator company. *International Journal of Project Management*, *28*(4), 370–383. doi:10.1016/j.ijproman.2010.02.004

Gagné, M., Sharma, P., & De Massis, A. (2014). The study of organizational behavior in family business. *European Journal of Work and Organizational Psychology*, *23*(5), 643–656. doi:10.1080/1359432X.2014.906403

Georgiadis, A., & Pitelis, C. N. (2012). Human resources and SME performance in services: Empirical evidence from the UK. *International Journal of Human Resource Management*, *23*(4), 808–825. doi:10.1080/09585192.2011.561236

Gersick, K. E. (2015). Essay on practice: Advising family enterprise in the fourth decade. *Entrepreneurship Theory and Practice*, *39*(6), 1433–1450. doi:10.1111/etap.12176

Gersick, K. E., Lansberg, I., & Davis, J. A. (1990). The impact of family dynamics on structure and process in family. *Family Business Review*, *3*(4), 357–374. doi:10.1111/j.1741-6248.1990.00357.x

Giosan, C. H., Holtom, B. C., & Watson, M. R. (2005). Antecedents to job embeddedness: The role of individual, organisational and market factors. *Journal of Organisational Psychology*, *5*(1), 31–44.

Godard, J. (2001). High Performance and the Transformation of Work? The Implications of Alternative Work Practices for the Experience and Outcomes of Work. *Industrial & Labor Relations Review*, *54*(4), 776–805. doi:10.1177/001979390105400402

Gómez-Mejía, L. R., Haynes, K. T., Núñez-Nickel, M., Jacobson, J. L. K., & Moyano-Fuentes, J. (2007). Socioemotional wealth and business risks in family-controlled firms: Evidence from Spanish olive oil mills. *Administrative Science Quarterly*, *52*(1), 106–137. doi:10.2189/asqu.52.1.106

Gooderham, P., Nordhaug, O., & Ringdal, K. (2006). National embeddedness and calculative human resource management in US subsidiaries in Europe and Australia. *Human Relations*, *59*(11), 1491–1513. doi:10.1177/0018726706072843

Grant, R. M. (1996). Prospering in dynamically-competitive environments: Organizational capability as knowledge integration. *Organization Science*, *7*(4), 375–387. doi:10.1287/orsc.7.4.375

Griffin, M. A., Neal, A., & Parker, S. K. (2007). A new model of work role performance: Positive behavior in uncertain and interdependent contexts. *Academy of Management Journal*, *50*(2), 327–347. doi:10.5465/amj.2007.24634438

Guchait, P., & Cho, S. (2010). The impact of human resource management practices on intention to leave of employees in the service industry in India: The mediating role of organizational commitment. *International Journal of Human Resource Management*, *21*(8), 1228–1247. doi:10.1080/09585192.2010.483845

Guest, D. E. (1997). Human Resource Management and Performance: A Review and Research Agenda. *International Journal of Human Resource Management*, *8*(3), 263–276. doi:10.1080/095851997341630

Guest, D. E., Michie, J., Conway, N., & Sheehan, M. (2003). Human resource management and corporate performance in the UK. *British Journal of Industrial Relations*, *41*(2), 291–314. doi:10.1111/1467-8543.00273

Haberman, H., & Danes, S. M. (2007). Father-daughter and father-son family business management transfer comparison: Family FIRO model application. *Family Business Review*, *20*(2), 163–184. doi:10.1111/j.1741-6248.2007.00088.x

Harney, B., & Dundon, T. (2006). Capturing complexity: Developing an integrated approach to analysing HRM in SMEs. *Human Resource Management Journal*, *16*(1), 48–73. doi:10.1111/j.1748-8583.2006.00004.x

Harrison, S. H., & Rouse, E. D. (2014). Let's Dance! Elastic Coordination in Creative Group Work: A Qualitative Study of Modern Dancers. *Academy of Management Journal*, *57*(5), 1256–1283. doi:10.5465/amj.2012.0343

Helfat, C. E., Finkelstein, S., Mitchell, W., Peteraf, M. A., Singh, H., Teece, D. J., & Winter, S. G. (2007). *Dynamic capabilities: Understanding strategic change in organizations*. Malden, MA: Blackwell.

Herscovitch, L., & Meyer, J. P. (2002). Commitment to organizational change: Extension of a three-component model. *The Journal of Applied Psychology*, *87*(3), 474–487. doi:10.1037/0021-9010.87.3.474 PMID:12090605

Hinsz, V. B., Tindale, R. S., & Vollrath, D. A. (1997). The emerging conceptualization of groups as information processors. *Psychological Bulletin*, *121*(1), 43–54. doi:10.1037/0033-2909.121.1.43 PMID:9000891

Hitt, M. A., Ireland, R. D., Camp, S. M., & Sexton, D. L. (2001). Strategic entrepreneurship: Entrepreneurial strategies for wealth creation. *Strategic Management Journal*, *22*(6-7), 479–491. doi:10.1002mj.196

Hitt, M. A., Ireland, R. D., Camp, S. M., & Sexton, D. L. (2002). Strategic entrepreneurship: Integrating entrepreneurial and strategic management perspectives. In M. A. Hitt, R. D. Ireland, S. M. Camp, & D. L. Sexton, (Eds.), Strategic entrepreneurship: Creating a new integrated mindset (pp. 1-16). Oxford, UK: Blackwell Publishers.

Holten, A. L., & Crouch, C. (2014). Unions in small and medium-sized enterprises: A family factor perspective. *European Journal of Industrial Relations*, *20*(3), 273–290. doi:10.1177/0959680113519639

Holtom, B. C., Mitchell, T. R., Lee, T. W., & Tidd, S. (2006). Less is more: validation of a short form of the job embeddedness measure and theoretical extensions. Paper presented at the Annual meeting of the Academy of Management, Atlanta, GA.

Hoy, F. (2006). The complicating factor of life cycles in corporate venturing. *Entrepreneurship Theory and Practice*, *30*(6), 831–836. doi:10.1111/j.1540-6520.2006.00154.x

Huselid, M. A. (1995). The impact of human resource management practices on turnover, productivity, and corporate financial performance. *Academy of Management Journal*, *38*(3), 635–672.

Innes, P., & Wiesner, R. (2012). Beyond HRM intensity: Exploring intra-function HRM clusters in SMEs. *Small Enterprise Research*, *19*(1), 32–51. doi:10.5172er.2012.19.1.32

Jarzabkowski, P. A., Le, J. K., & Feldman, M. S. (2012). Toward a Theory of Coordinating: Creating Coordinating Mechanisms in Practice. *Organization Science*, *23*(4), 907–927. doi:10.1287/orsc.1110.0693

Jaskiewicz, P., Combs, J. G., Shanine, K. K., & Balkin, D. B. (2018). Making Sense of HR in Family Firms: Antecedents, Moderators, and Outcomes. *Human Resource Management Review*, *28*(1), 1–102. doi:10.1016/j.hrmr.2017.05.001

Jones, G. (1984). Task Visibility, Free Riding, and Shirking: Explaining the Effect of Structure and Technology on Employee Behaviors. *Academy of Management Review*, *9*(4), 684–695. doi:10.5465/amr.1984.4277404

Kaman, V., McCarthy, A. M., Gulbro, R. D., & Tucker, L. T. (2001). Bureaucratic and High Commitment Human Resource Practices in Small Service Firms. *HR Human Resource Planning*, *24*(1), 33–44.

Kappes, I., & Schmid, T. (2013). The effect of family governance on corporate time horizons. *Corporate Governance*, *21*(6), 547–566.

Karami, A., Jones, B. M., & Kakabadse, N., (2008). Does strategic human resource management matter in high-tech sector? Some learning points for SME managers. *Corporate Governance: The International Journal of Business in Society*, *8*(1), 7–17.

Katsikeas, C. S., Samiee, M., & Theodosiou, M. (2006). Strategy fit and performance consequences of international marketing standardization. *Strategic Management Journal*, *27*(9), 867–890. doi:10.1002mj.549

Katuo, A., & Budhwar, P. (2006). Human resource management systems and organizational performance: A test of a mediating model in the Greek manufacturing context. *International Journal of Human Resource Management*, *17*(7), 1223–1253. doi:10.1080/09585190600756525

Kaufman, B. E. (2010). SHRM theory in the post-Huselid era: Why it is fundamentally misspecified. *Industrial Relations*, *49*(2), 286–313. doi:10.1111/j.1468-232X.2009.00600.x

Kehoe, R. R., & Wright, P. M. (2013). The Impact of High-Performance Human Resource Practices on Employees' Attitudes and Behaviors. *Journal of Management*, *39*(2), 366–391. doi:10.1177/0149206310365901

Kellermanns, F. W. (2003). *Strategic consensus on resource accumulation decisions* (Unpublished Dissertation). University of Connecticut.

Kellermanns, F. W. (2005). Family firm resource management: Comments and extensions. *Entrepreneurship Theory and Practice, 29*(3), 313–319. doi:10.1111/j.1540-6520.2005.00085.x

Kellermanns, F. W., & Eddleston, K. A. (2004). Feuding families: When conflict does a family firm good. *Entrepreneurship Theory and Practice, 28*(3), 209–228. doi:10.1111/j.1540-6520.2004.00040.x

Kellermanns, F. W., & Eddleston, K. A. (2006). Corporate entrepreneurship in family firms: A family perspective. *Entrepreneurship Theory and Practice, 30*(6), 809–830. doi:10.1111/j.1540-6520.2006.00153.x

Kellermanns, F. W., Eddleston, K. A., Sarathy, R., & Murphy, F. (2012). Innovativeness in family firms: A family influence perspective. *Small Business Economics, 38*(1), 85–101. doi:10.100711187-010-9268-5

Kellermanns, F. W., & Floyd, S. (2005). Strategic consensus and constructive confrontation: Unifying forces in the resource accumulation process. In S. Floyd, J. Ross, C. Jacobs, & F. W. Kellermanns (Eds.), *Innovating strategy process* (pp. 149–162). Oxford, UK: Blackwell Publishing.

Kepes, S., & Delery, J. E. (2007). HRM systems and the problem of internal fit. In P. Boxall, J. Purcell, & P. Wright (Eds.), *The Oxford University Press Handbook of Human Resource Management* (pp. 385–404). Oxford, UK: Oxford University.

Khan, M. A. (2010). Effects of human resource management practices on organizational performance – an empirical study of oil and gas industry in Pakistan. *European Journal of Economics, Finance and Administrative Sciences, 24*(6), 157–174.

Kidwell, R. E., & Fish, A. J. (2007). High-performance human resource practices in Australian family businesses: Preliminary evidence from the wine industry. *The International Entrepreneurship and Management Journal, 3*(1), 1–14. doi:10.100711365-006-0020-1

Kirst-Ashman, K., & Hull, G. (2015). *Generalist Practice with Organizations and Communities* (6th ed.). Independence, KY: Cengage Learning.

Klein, S. B., Astrachan, J. H., & Smyrnios, K. X. (2005). The F-PEC scale of family influence: Construction, validation, and further implications for theory. *Entrepreneurship Theory and Practice, 29*(3), 321–339. doi:10.1111/j.1540-6520.2005.00086.x

Lai, Y., & Saridakis, G. (2013). Employee attitudes, HR practices and organisational performance: what's the evidence? In G. Saridakis & C. L. Cooper (Eds.), *How can HR drive growth?* (pp. 170–214). Cheltenham, UK: Edward Elgar Publishing Ltd. doi:10.4337/9781781002261.00015

Lawler, J. J., Chen, S. J., Wu, P. C., Bae, J., & Bai, B. (2011). High-performance work systems in foreign subsidiaries of American multinationals: An institutional model. *Journal of International Business Studies, 42*(2), 202–220. doi:10.1057/jibs.2010.42

Le Breton-Miller, I., & Miller, D. (2014). Temporal considerations in the study of family firms: Reflections on "the study of organizational behavior in family business". *European Journal of Work and Organizational Psychology, 23*(5), 669–673. doi:10.1080/1359432X.2014.907276

Le Breton-Miller, I., Miller, D., & Steier, L. P. (2004). Toward an integrative model of effective FOB succession. *Entrepreneurship Theory and Practice, 24*(4), 305–328. doi:10.1111/j.1540-6520.2004.00047.x

Lepak, D. P., Liao, H., Chung, Y., & Harden, E. E. (2006). A conceptual review of human resource management systems in strategic human resource management research. *Research in Personnel and Human Resources Management, 25,* 217–271.

Lepak, D. P., & Shaw, J. D. (2008). Strategic HRM in North America: Looking to the future. *International Journal of Human Resource Management, 19*(8), 1486–1499. doi:10.1080/09585190802200272

Levie, J., & Lerner, M. (2009). Resource Mobilization and Performance in Family and Nonfamily Businesses in the United Kingdom. *Family Business Review, 22*(1), 25–38. doi:10.1177/0894486508328812

Lumpkin, G. T., & Dess, G. G. (1996). Clarifying the entrepreneurial orientation construct and linking it to performance. *Academy of Management Review, 21*(1), 135–172. doi:10.5465/amr.1996.9602161568

Mani, D., Srikanth, K., & Bharadwaj, A. (2014). Efficacy of R&D Work in Offshore Captive Centers: An Empirical Study of Task Characteristics, Coordination Mechanisms, and Performance. *Information Systems Research, 25*(4), 846–864. doi:10.1287/isre.2014.0552

Marks, M. A., Mathieu, J. E., & Zaccaro, S. J. (2001). A temporally based framework and taxonomy of team processes. *Academy of Management Review, 26*(3), 356–376. doi:10.5465/amr.2001.4845785

Marler, J. H., & Fisher, S. L. (2013). An evidence-based review of e-HRM and strategic human resource management. *Human Resource Management Review, 23*(1), 18–36. doi:10.1016/j.hrmr.2012.06.002

Marlow, S., & Patton, D. (2002). Minding the gap between employers and employees. The challenge for owner-managers of smaller manufacturing firms. *Employee Relations, 24*(5), 523–539. doi:10.1108/01425450210443294

Martín-Alcázar, F., Romero-Fernandez, P. M., & Sanchez-Gardey, G. (2005). Strategic human resource management: Integrating the universalistic, contingent, configurational and contextual perspectives. *International Journal of Human Resource Management, 16*(5), 633–659. doi:10.1080/09585190500082519

Mathis, R. L., & Jackson, J. H. (2004). *Human resource management.* Singapore: Thomson Asia Pte. Ltd.

Meuer, J. (2016). Exploring the Complementarities within High-Performance Work Systems: A Set-Theoretic Analysis of UK Firms. *Human Resource Management, 56*(4), 651–672. doi:10.1002/hrm.21793

Mezirow, J. (1985). Concept and action in adult education. *Adult Education Quarterly, 35*(3), 142–152. doi:10.1177/0001848185035003003

Miles, R. E., & Snow, C. C. (1994). *Fit, Failure and the Hall of Fame.* New York, NY: Macmillan.

Miller, D., & Le Breton-Miller, I. (2005). *Managing for the long run: Lessons in competitive advantage from great family businesses.* Boston: Harvard Business School Press.

Miller, D., & Le Breton-Miller, I. (2006). Priorities, practices and strategies in successful and failing family businesses: An elaboration and test of the configuration perspective. *Strategic Organization, 4*(4), 379–407. doi:10.1177/1476127006069575

Moores, K., & Mula, J. (2000). The salience of market, bureaucratic, and clan controls in the management of family firm transitions: Some tentative Australian evidence. *Family Business Review, 13*(2), 91–106. doi:10.1111/j.1741-6248.2000.00091.x

Morgeson, F. P., & Humphrey, S. E. (2006). The work design questionnaire (WDQ): Developing and validating a comprehensive measure for assessing job design and the nature of work. *The Journal of Applied Psychology, 91*(6), 1321–1339. doi:10.1037/0021-9010.91.6.1321 PMID:17100487

Morgeson, F. P., Lindoerfer, D., & Loring, D. J. (2010). Developing team leadership capability. In E. V. Velsor, C. D. McCauley, & M. N. Ruderman (Eds.), *The Center for Creative Leadership Handbook of Leadership Development* (pp. 285–312). New York: Jossey-Bass.

Moshavi, D., & Koch, M. J. (2005). The adoption of family-friendly practices in family-owned firms. Paragon or paradox? *Community Work & Family, 8*(3), 237–249. doi:10.1080/13668800500142210

Murphy, D. L. (2005). Understanding the complexities of private family firms: An empirical investigation. *Family Business Review, 18*(2), 123–133. doi:10.1111/j.1741-6248.2005.00036.x

Mustakallio, M., Autio, E., & Zahra, S. A. (2002). Relational and contractual governance in family firms: Effects on strategic decision-making. *Family Business Review, 15*(3), 205–222. doi:10.1111/j.1741-6248.2002.00205.x

Nahapiet, J., & Ghoshal, S. (1998). Social capital, intellectual capital, and the organizational advantage. *Academy of Management Review, 23*(2), 242–266. doi:10.5465/amr.1998.533225

Naz, F., Aftab, J., & Awais, M. (2016). Impact of Human Resource Management Practices (HRM) on Performance of SMEs in Multan, Pakistan. *International Journal of Management, Accounting and Economics, 3*(11), 699–708.

Newman, K. (2000). Organizational transformation during institutional upheaval. *Academy of Management Review, 25*(3), 602–619. doi:10.5465/amr.2000.3363525

Nóbrega, G. J., & Hoffmann, V. E. (2014). Family businesses and the creation of entrepreneurship through their internal resources. *Revista Pensamento Contemporâneo en Administração, 8*(2), 92. doi:10.12712/rpca.v8i2.464

Noe, R. A., Hollenbeck, J. R., Gerhart, B., & Wright, P. M. (2010). *Human resource Management: Gaining a competitive Advantage* (7th ed.). New York: McGraw-Hill/Irwin.

Nordqvist, M., Sharma, P., & Chirico, F. (2014). Family Firm Heterogeneity and Governance: A Configuration Approach. *Journal of Small Business Management, 52*(2), 192–209. doi:10.1111/jsbm.12096

Ogunyomi, P., & Bruning, N. S. (2015). Human resource management and organizational performance of small and medium enterprises (SMEs) in Nigeria. *International Journal of Human Resource Management, 6*, 612–634.

Okhuysen, G. A., & Bechky, B. A. (2009). Coordination in Organizations: An Integrative Perspective. *The Academy of Management Annals, 3*(1), 463–502. doi:10.5465/19416520903047533

Oladipo, J. A., & Abdulkadir, D. S. (2011). Strategic human resource management and organizational performance in the Nigerian manufacturing sector: An empirical investigation. *International Journal of Business and Management, 6*(9), 46–56.

Osman, I., Ho, T. C. F., & Galang, M. C. (2011). The relationship between human resource practices and firm performance: An empirical assessment of firms in Malaysia. *Business Strategy Series, 12*(1), 41–48. doi:10.1108/17515631111100412

Othman, A. E. A. (2009). Strategic HRM practices: Perspectives of Malaysian and Japanese owned companies in Malaysia. *Global Business and Management Research, 1*(1), 1–22.

Parsons, T. (1951). *The social system.* New York: Free Press.

Perry-Smith, J. E., & Blum, T. C. (2000). Work-family human resource bundles and perceived organizational performance. *Academy of Management Journal, 43*, 1107–1117.

Phan, P., Chan, E., & Lee, S. H. (2005). The impact of HR configuration on firm performance in Singapore: A resource-based explanation. *International Journal of Human Resource Management, 16*(9), 1740–1758. doi:10.1080/09585190500239465

Ployhart, R. E., Weekley, J. A., & Baughman, K. (2006). The structure and function of human capital emergence: A multilevel examination of the attraction-selection-attrition model. *Academy of Management Journal, 49*(4), 661–677. doi:10.5465/amj.2006.22083023

Podsakoff, P. M., MacKenzie, S. B., Paine, J. B., & Bachrach, D. G. (2000). Organizational citizenship behaviors: A critical review of the theoretical and empirical literature and suggestions for future research. *Journal of Management, 26*(3), 513–563. doi:10.1177/014920630002600307

Porter, M. E. (1985). *Competitive Advantage.* New York: The Free Press.

Poza, E. J., Hanlon, S., & Kishida, R. (2004). Does the Family Business Interaction Factor Represent a Resource or a Cost? *Family Business Review, 17*(2), 99–118. doi:10.1111/j.1741-6248.2004.00007.x

Prahalad, C. K. (1983). Developing strategic capability: An agenda for top management. *Human Resource Management, 22*(3), 237–254. doi:10.1002/hrm.3930220304

Rabl, T., Jayasinghe, M., Gerhart, B., & Kühlmann, T. M. (2014). A meta-analysis of country differences in the high-performance work system - business performance relationship: The roles of national culture and managerial discretion. *The Journal of Applied Psychology, 99*(6), 1011–1041. doi:10.1037/a0037712 PMID:25222523

Randall, D. M., Fedor, D. B., & Longenecker, C. O. (1990). The Behavioral Expression of Organizational Commitment. *Journal of Vocational Behavior, 36*(2), 210–224. doi:10.1016/0001-8791(90)90028-Z

Reid, R. S., & Adams, J. S. (2001). Human resource management-A survey of practices within family and non-family firms. *Journal of European Industrial Training, 25*(6), 310–320. doi:10.1108/03090590110401782

Reid, R. S., Morrow, T., Kelly, B., & McCartan, P. (2002). People Management in SMEs: An Analysis of Human Resource Strategies in Family and Non-Family Businesses. *Journal of Small Business and Enterprise Development, 9*(3), 245–259. doi:10.1108/14626000210438571

Rhoades, L., & Eisenberger, R. (2002). Perceived organizational support: A review of the literature. *The Journal of Applied Psychology, 87*(4), 698–714. doi:10.1037/0021-9010.87.4.698 PMID:12184574

Riketta, M. (2002). Attitudinal organizational commitment and job performance: A meta-analysis. *Journal of Organizational Behavior*, *23*(3), 257–266. doi:10.1002/job.141

Robbins, S. P. (2000). *Essentials of organizational behavior* (6th ed.). Upper Saddle River, NJ: Prentice-Hall.

Roca-Puig, V., Beltrán-Martín, I., Escrig-Tena, A. B., & Bou-Llusar, J. C. (2005). Strategic flexibility as a moderator of the relationship between commitment to employees and performance in service firms. *International Journal of Human Resource Management*, *16*(11), 2075–2093. doi:10.1080/09585190500315026

Salvato, C. (2004). Predictors of entrepreneurship in family firms. *Journal of Private Equity*, *7*(3), 68–76. doi:10.3905/jpe.2004.412339

Saridakis, G., Lai, Y., & Cooper, C. L. (2017). Exploring the relationship between HRM and firm performance: A meta-analysis of longitudinal studies. *Human Resource Management Review*, *27*(1), 87–96. doi:10.1016/j.hrmr.2016.09.005

Schein, E. H. (1996). Culture: The missing concept in organizational studies. *Administrative Science Quarterly*, *41*(2), 229–240. doi:10.2307/2393715

Schmidt, J. A., Willness, C. R., Jones, D. A., & Bourdage, J. S. (2016). Human resource management practices and voluntary turnover: A study of internal workforce and external labor market contingencies. *International Journal of Human Resource Management*, 1–24.

Schon, D. A. (1987). *Educating the reflective practitioner*. San Francisco: Jossey-Bass.

Schuler, R. S., & Jackson, S. E. (1987). Organizational Strategy and Organizational Level as Determinants of Human Resource Management Practices. *Human Resource Planning*, *10*, 125–141.

Schulze, W. S., Lubatkin, M. H., & Dino, R. N. (2003). Toward a theory of agency and altruism in family firms. *Journal of Business Venturing*, *18*(4), 473–490. doi:10.1016/S0883-9026(03)00054-5

Schwandt, D. R., & Marquardt, M. J. (2000). *Organizational learning: From world-class theories to global best practices*. New York: St. Lucie Press.

Seth, A. K., Dienes, Z., Cleeremans, A., Overgaard, M., & Pessoa, L. (2008). Measuring consciousness: Relating behavioral and neurophysiological approaches. *Trends in Cognitive Sciences*, *12*(8), 314–321. doi:10.1016/j.tics.2008.04.008 PMID:18606562

Sharma, P., & Irving, G. (2005). Four bases of family business successor commitment: Antecedents and consequences. *Entrepreneurship Theory and Practice*, *29*(1), 13–33. doi:10.1111/j.1540-6520.2005.00067.x

Sharma, P., & Manikutty, S. (2005). Strategic divestments in family firms: Role of family structure and community culture. *Entrepreneurship Theory and Practice*, *29*(3), 293–311. doi:10.1111/j.1540-6520.2005.00084.x

Shaw, J. D., Park, T., & Kim, E. (2013). A resource-based perspective on human capital losses, HRM investments, and organizational performance. *Strategic Management Journal*, *34*(5), 572–589. doi:10.1002mj.2025

Sheehan, M. (2014). Human resource management and performance: Evidence from small and medium-sized firms. *International Small Business Journal, 32*(5), 545–570. doi:10.1177/0266242612465454

Sherif, K., Zmud, R., & Browne, G. (2006). Managing peer-to-peer conflicts in disruptive information technology innovations: The case of software reuse. *Management Information Systems Quarterly, 30*(2), 339–356. doi:10.2307/25148734

Shockley-Zalabak, P. S. (2006). *Foundation of Organizational Communication: Knowledge, Sensitivity, Skills, Values* (6th ed.). Boston, MA: Pearson Education.

Simon, H. A. (1957). *Administrative Behavior* (2nd ed.). The Free Press.

Sirmon, D. G., & Hitt, M. A. (2003). Managing resources: Linking unique resources, management, and wealth creation in family firms. *Entrepreneurship Theory and Practice, 27*(4), 339–358. doi:10.1111/1540-8520.t01-1-00013

Sitt, J. D., King, J. R., El Karoui, I., Rohaut, B., Faugeras, F., Gramfort, A., ... Naccache, L. (2014). Large-scale screening of neural signatures of consciousness in patients in a vegetative or minimally conscious state). *Brain, 137*(8), 2258–2270. doi:10.1093/brain/awu141 PMID:24919971

Stavrou, E. T., & Brewster, C. (2005). The Configurational Approach to Linking Strategic Human Resource Management Bundles with Business Performance: Myth or Reality?'. *Management Review, 16*(2), 186–201.

Stewart, A., & Hitt, M. A. (2012). Why Can't a Family Business Be More Like a Nonfamily Business? Modes of Professionalization in Family Firms. *Family Business Review, 25*(1), 58–86. doi:10.1177/0894486511421665

Sun, L., Aryee, S., & Law, K. S. (2007). High performance human resource practices, citizenship behavior, and organizational performance: A relational perspective. *Academy of Management Journal, 50*(3), 558–577. doi:10.5465/amj.2007.25525821

Thomas, J. B., Clark, S. M., & Gioia, D. A. (1993). Strategic sensemaking and organizational performance: Linkages among scanning, interpretation, action, and outcomes. *Academy of Management Journal, 36*(2), 239–270. PMID:10125120

Thompson, J. (1967). *Organizations in Action.* McGraw-Hill.

Timmermans, B., & Cleeremans, A. (2015). How can we measure awareness? An overview of current methods. In M. Overgaard (Ed.), *Behavioural Methods in Consciousness Research* (pp. 21–46). Oxford, UK: Oxford University Press. doi:10.1093/acprof:oso/9780199688890.003.0003

Toh, S. M., Morgeson, F. P., & Campion, M. A. (2008). Human resource configurations: Investigating fit with the organizational context. *The Journal of Applied Psychology, 93*(4), 864–882. doi:10.1037/0021-9010.93.4.864 PMID:18642989

Tolbert, P. S., & Hall, R. (2009). *Organizations: Structures, Processes and Outcomes* (10th ed.). Boston, MA: Pearson Education.

Tsai, W. H., Chien, S. W., Hsu, P. Y., & Leu, J. D. (2005). Identification of critical failure factors in the implementation of enterprise resource planning (ERP) system in Taiwan's industries. *International Journal of Management and Enterprise Development*, *2*(2), 219–239. doi:10.1504/IJMED.2005.006312

Tsao, C. W., Chen, S. J., Lin, C. S., & Hyde, W. (2009). Founding-family ownership and firm performance: The role of high-performance work systems. *Family Business Review*, *22*(4), 319–332. doi:10.1177/0894486509339322

Tsui, A. S., Pearce, J. L., Porter, L. W., & Hite, J. P. (1995). Choice of employee-organization relationship: Influence of external and internal organizational factors. *Research in Personnel and Human Resources Management*, *13*, 117–151.

Ulrich, D., Younger, J., Brockbank, W., & Ulrich, M. D. (2013). The state of the HR profession. *Human Resource Management*, *52*(3), 457–471. doi:10.1002/hrm.21536

Upton, N., Teal, E. J., & Felan, J. T. (2001). Strategic and business planning practices of fast-growing family firms. *Journal of Small Business Management*, *39*(4), 60–72. doi:10.1111/0447-2778.00006

West, M. A., & Altink, W. M. M. (1996). Innovation at Work: Individual, Group, Organizational and Social Historical Perspectives. *European Journal of Work and Organizational Psychology*, *5*(1), 3–11. doi:10.1080/13594329608414834

Wheeler, A. R., Harries, K. J., & Harvey, P. (2010). Moderating and mediating the HRM effectiveness—intent to turnover relationship: The roles of supervisors & job embeddedness. *Journal of Managerial Issues*, *22*(2), 182–196.

Wiesner, R., & Innes, P. (2010). Bleak house or bright prospect?: HRM in Australian SMEs over1998-2008. *Asia Pacific Journal of Human Resources*, *48*(2), 151–184. doi:10.1177/1038411110368465

Wiklund, J., & Shepherd, D. (2003). Knowledge-based resources, entrepreneurial orientation and the performance of small and medium-sized businesses. *Strategic Management Journal*, *24*(13), 1307–1314. doi:10.1002mj.360

Willem, A., Buelens, M., & Scarbrougb, H. (2006). The role of inter-unit coordination mechanisms in knowledge sharing: A case study of a British MNC. *Journal of Information Science*, *32*(6), 539–561. doi:10.1177/0165551506067128

Williams, J. G., & Mohamed, R. B. (2010). A comparative study of the effects of "best practice" HRM on worker outcomes in Malaysia and England local government. *International Journal of Human Resource Management*, *21*(5), 653–675. doi:10.1080/09585191003658821

Williamson, I., & Cable, D. (2003). Organization hiring patterns, inter-firm network ties, and inter-organizational imitation. *Academy of Management Journal*, *46*(3), 349–359.

Wolfgang, K. (1947). *Gestalt Psychology*. New York: Liveright.

Woodall, J. (2000). Corporate support for work-based management development. *Human Resource Management Journal*, *10*(1), 18–32. doi:10.1111/j.1748-8583.2000.tb00011.x

Wright, P. M., Dunford, B. B., & Snell, S. A. (2001). Human resources and the resource-based view of the firm. *Journal of Management, 27*(6), 701–721. doi:10.1177/014920630102700607

Wright, P. M., Gardner, T. M., Moynihan, L. M., & Allen, M. R. (2005). The relationship between HR practices and firm performance: Examining causal order. *Personnel Psychology, 58*(2), 409–446. doi:10.1111/j.1744-6570.2005.00487.x

Xianga, D., Worthington, A. C., & Higgs, H. (2014). Family Ownership, Altruism and Agency Costs in Australian Small- and Medium-Sized Enterprises. *Applied Economics, 46*(32), 3907–3921. doi:10.1080/00036846.2014.946183

Yukl, G. (2006). Leadership in Organizations (2nd ed.). Upper Saddle River, NJ: Prentice-Hall.

Zahra, S., Hayton, J., & Salvato, C. (2004). Entrepreneurship in family vs. nonfamily firms: A resource-based analysis of the effect of organizational culture. *Entrepreneurship Theory and Practice, 28*(4), 363–381. doi:10.1111/j.1540-6520.2004.00051.x

Zahra, S. A. (2005). A theory of international new ventures: A decade of research. *Journal of International Business Studies, 36*(1), 20–28. doi:10.1057/palgrave.jibs.8400118

Zajac, E. J., Kraatz, M. S., & Bresser, R. K. F. (2000). Modeling the dynamics of strategic fit: A normative approach to strategic change. *Strategic Management Journal, 2*(4), 429–453. doi:10.1002/(SICI)1097-0266(200004)21:4<429::AID-SMJ81>3.0.CO;2-#

Zakaria, N. (2011). Investigating the role of human resource management practices on the performance of SME: A conceptual framework. *Journal of Global Management, 3*(1), 74–92.

Zellweger, T. (2013). Toward a paradox perspective of family firms: The moderating role of collective mindfulness of controlling families. In L. Melin, M. Nordqvist, & P. Sharma (Eds.), *The SAGE handbook of family business* (pp. 648–655). Thousand Oaks, CA: SAGE Publications.

Zellweger, T., & Sieger, P. (2012). Entrepreneurial orientation in long-lived family firms. *Small Business Economics, 38*(1), 67–84. doi:10.100711187-010-9267-6

Zhang, B., & Morris, J. L. (2014). High-performance work systems and organizational performance: Testing the mediation role of employee outcomes using evidence from PR China. *International Journal of Human Resource Management, 25*(1), 68–90. doi:10.1080/09585192.2013.781524

Zheng, C., O'Neill, G., & Morrison, M. (2009). Enhancing Chinese SME performance through innovative HR practices. *Personnel Review, 38*(2), 175–194. doi:10.1108/00483480910931334

KEY TERMS AND DEFINITIONS

Awareness: Represents the building and sharing of knowledge as a cognitive learning process and experience development.

Configurational Approaches to HRM: Identify a system of practices, differently combined to achieve consistent internal configurations with the environmental and the organizational variables.

Configurational models present nonlinear relationships with organizational performances, since the interdependence multiply (or divide) the combined effect. HRM practices can be analyzed only as a complex and interactive system.

Family Firms: Organizations dominantly controlled by a family with the vision to sustain family control across generations potentially.

Human Resources Management Practices: Represent a bundle of policies within a Human resources management system that influences competencies, behaviors, and performances of employees.

Needs for Coordination: The requirements for efficient management of interdependencies among tasks, resources, and people.

Needs for Explicit Coordination Mechanisms: Ground on task and communication coordination mechanisms when the routine aspects of a task present more predictable interdependencies and more addressable with a programmed approach.

Needs for Implicit Coordination Mechanisms: Coordination activities not pre-defined by routinized processes but driven by emerging characteristics of the environment and defined by the actor(s) involved.

Organizational Variables: The organizational structure, the coordination mechanisms, and power dynamics.

This research was previously published in the Handbook of Research on Entrepreneurial Leadership and Competitive Strategy in Family Business; pages 295-331, copyright year 2019 by Business Science Reference (an imprint of IGI Global).

Chapter 19
Transformational Human Resource Management:
Crafting Organizational Efficiency

Ikramul Hasan
Independent University, Bangladesh

MD. Nazmul Islam
iD https://orcid.org/0000-0002-6778-508X
University of Malaya, Malaysia

Mohammad Ashraful Ferdous Chowdhury
iD https://orcid.org/0000-0001-8540-1353
Shahjalal University of Science and Technology, Bangladesh

ABSTRACT

Human Resource Management plays an essential role for attaining organizational goals. Nowadays, practitioners, researchers, and academicians around the world are emphasizing to transform and re-shape the practice of human resource. However, very few research works have been done in the area of Transformational Human Resource Management (T-HRM). Hence, the aim of this chapter is to propose an integrated framework of T-HRM and organizational efficiency. In light of that, this study has proposed potential factors of the T-HRM. Secondly, this study presented positive effect of the factors of T-HRM on organizational efficiency management. Concept of knowledge management has introduced as a potential mediator, and ICT and organizational alignment has presented as a potential moderator of this study. Finally, knowledge of this study will provide better insights on T-HRM for ensuring organizational efficiency.

DOI: 10.4018/978-1-6684-3873-2.ch019

INTRODUCTION

Transformational human resource management (T-HRM) is currently a new concept in the area of human resource management. Now-a-days academicians, researchers and practitioners around the world in the area of organization behavior, management and human resource management are highlighting the importance of transformational human resource management. Alike transformational leadership (Shih & Orochena, 2016), T-HRM also considers employee as a partner in the organizational innovation and improvement. T-HRM is an outcome of cross-functional activities, which results impact on achieving organizational objective. T-HRM has potential impact on employee efficiency development. Being a modern HRM practices, T-HRM also confirms potency to develop employee through the effective knowledge management (Edvardsson, 2008; Oltra, 2005) training (Seeck & Diehl, 2017), leadership (Mehmood & Arif, 2011) talent management (Iles et al., 2010), information technology usage (Bourke & Crowley, 2015; Steijn & Tijdens, 2005) innovation and change (Santangelo & Pini, 2011; Lin & Sanders, 2017), social responsible human resource management (Barrena-Martínez et al., 2017; Milfelner et al., 2015) and organizational alignment (Shih & Chiang, 2005). However, due to the current changes in business industry and more importantly rate of failures or unsuccessful organizational changes or transformations in contemporary business era (Lewis, 2019; Habersang et al., 2019), reducing the rate of employee retention (Silva et al., 2019), job dissatisfaction (Moussa & Somjai, 2019; De Clercq et al., 2019), lack of trust (Mooijman et al., 2019), lack of commitment (Souza et al., 2019), disengagement (Wolff, 2019) and improper alignment (Davidson & Butcher, 2019) between individual employee skills, job attributes, organizational strategy as well as diversify workforce (Karim et al, 2019), global competition (Gershon, 2019) have provoked the notion of T-HRM. In order to attain organizational efficiency in highly competitive changing business environment and to ensure sustainable competitive advantage in organization, T-HRM has become one of the important factor for the organization. Transactional HR activities expressing employees are more likely clerical mundane work whereas Transformational HR activities are strategic.

In contemporary business world, involvement of HR division of an organization not only limited to the transactional functions but also align HR activities with organizational objective. Moreover, T-HRM is more involved with the activities that are strategic, forward thinking, proactive and comprehensive with more technology based to aid HR processes to make them effective, support organizational change and improvement (Manzoor et al., 2019). Hence, T-HRM is concerned with complete revamping and constant pruning of HR processes in order to make them best in class maximize efficiency as well as to ensure sustainable competitive advantage for the organization. However, very limited research work has been done in the area of T-HRM. With this background, formulation of this research is to identify factors of T-HRM and its impact of organizational effectiveness as well as to propose model for integrating factors of T-HRM and organizational efficiency management. Hence, this study will address the following questions:

- What are the important factors of transformational human resource management (T-HRM)?
- Are different factors of T-HRM influences organizational effectiveness?

In order to address the following questions, comprehensive literature review will be conducted to link potential relationships. This study also exhibits association to bring the key factors involved in T-HRM (knowledge management, training and development, organizational leadership, talent management, information technology, innovation and change, socially responsible human resource management and organizational alignment) in order to understand organizational efficiency management. Presenting the relationship among the constructs this study will postulate a number of effective relationships, which confirms the impact or influence on organizational efficiency management. Finally, this study will propose a conceptual framework. This study will contribute to HRM literature and will give new insights to the researchers and practitioners by adding the notion of T-HRM and its factors as an antecedent of employee development as well as organizational efficiency management.

This paper will be organized in four steps. First, this study will propose different factors of T-HRM. Secondly, this study will present the impact of the factors of T-HRM on organizational effectiveness. Then this study will present a conceptual model by connecting different factors of T-HRM as an independent, mediator and moderating variable (leadership, T&D, talent management, innovation and change, SR-HRM as independent variable, knowledge management as a mediator, ICT and organizational alignment as a moderator). Finally, this study will propose implications, future research and conclusion based on the discussion of the paper this study.

METHODOLOGY

The chapter aims to attain dual objectives of creating academic knowledge and develop assumption through the conceptual model in order to address and identify potential problems. In order to capture as many studies as possible and to limit biases caused by the study-identification process, the procedure was followed as proposed by Rosenbusch et al., (2011); Islam et al., (2018) and Hasan et al., (2018). A computerized keyword searches in the databases (e.g., Web of Science (ISI), Scopus, Web of Knowledge, ABI, Google Scholar) was conducted to explore the highly pertinent studies on HRM. In addition, most relevant journals in T-HRM elements, knowledge management, and organizational efficiency management, ICT (e.g., *The Leadership Quarterly, Management Information Systems Quarterly, Organizational Behavior and Human Decision Processes, Strategic Organization*) were searched manually. As a third step, the reference sections of the relevant articles are searched. Three keywords "antecedences of transformational human resource management to confer efficiency management" were used in the literature search.

LITERATURE REVIEW

Transformational Human Resource Management (T-HRM)

T-HRM is one of the contemporary areas in the field of human resource management. Due to the globalization, high level of competition, innovation and continuous change and up gradation in the technology or shift in market are the main forces for the transformation of human resource management (Beer, 1997). Moreover, being a key engine for the organization HR has drawn a considerable attention for ensuring organizational efficiency, effectiveness, success and sustainability, which drives HR to go for transformation. T-HRM addresses and fulfills the requirements and demands of internal and external stakeholders of the organization (Ulrich et al., 2009). Transformational Human Resource Management is more strategic, practical, flatter, faster, forward linking, less bureaucratic, more prompt and remove hierarchical barriers (Beer, 1997) than the traditional/conventional HR in order to achieve competitive advantages as well as ensures organizational efficiency and effectiveness. Moreover, T-HRM ensures alignment among the different departments in the organization, ensures commitment to continuous employee development, enhances competitiveness in organizational leadership and management level, ensures organizational innovativeness, and develops an environment for knowledge sharing and smooth communication in the organization (Beer, 1997).

Organizational Efficiency

Maintaining organizational efficiency is an important assignment for every organization. Efficiency measures how your organization transforms their input into output, moreover organizational efficiency can be realized by measuring the difference between input and output (Low, 2000). While discussing about the efficiency in their research Pinprayong and Siengthai (2012) presented two different types of efficiency such as business efficiency and organizational efficiency. In addition, authors highlighted the difference between two types of efficiency. Business efficiency represents the ratio of the input – output performance of the business, whereas organizational efficiency represents the enhancement of organizational internal process such as organizational culture, structure and community. Kumar and Gulati (2010) describe efficiency as allocating different resources of the organization for various uses. Similarly, Bartuševičienė and Šakalytė (2013) stated that organizational excellent performance is not known as efficiency whereas organizational excellence in operation is a more related to efficiency. Organizations are emphasizing to manage the efficiency level of the organization in order to optimize the organizational resource as well as to achieve organizational goals. Efficient organizations are more capable of competing with the other players or opponents and ensure organizational sustainability. Karlaftis (2004) stated that inefficient organization has no clear vision as well as inefficiency in an organization causes high employee turnover and costly organizational failure.

Conceptual Model for Integrating Factors of T-HRM and Organizational Efficiency

HR transformation is assumed as an integrated, aligned, innovative, and business focused approach that defines how HR is working within the organization so that it could fulfill the objectives of the customers, investors, and other stakeholders. While HR transformation, organization needs to consider factors related to both the internal and external environment of the organization. Ulrichet et al. (2009) have highlighted that organization need to transform HR in order to enhance organizational efficiency and it can be achieved not only by focusing on organizational profit maximizing but also identifying and fulfilling the needs of stakeholders of the organization. Transformational HRM will support organization to transform their activities in order to achieve organizational objective by identifying key stakeholders (shareholder, customer, supplier, competitors, employee, regulator and community) and their needs and expectations as well as by aligning HRM activities such as recruiting, training, motivating and rewarding etc., with the organizational objectives and stakeholder's expectation.

However, different factors may consider important for human resource transformation but in line with the previous literature related to the transformation, this study will consider knowledge management, organizational leadership, information and communication technology infrastructure, talent management, training, innovation and change management, SR-HRM and organizational alignment as important factors for managing human resource transformation. Notable, in capability aspects of the organization, Gold and his colleagues theorized knowledge management capabilities as multidimensional concepts and incorporate an infrastructural perspective as an important capability. They present it as knowledge infrastructure capabilities, which actually work as KM enablers too; Alavi and Leidner (2001); Lee and Choi (2003) also support these facts. In considering knowledge infrastructural capability, they comprise technology, organizational culture, and organizational structure as multiple composed dimensions (Gold et al., 2001). Handzic (2011) developed a socio-technical knowledge management model where she claimed that as a knowledge enabler various social and technical initiatives could facilitate the KM process and foster the development of organizational knowledge by emphasizing factors. Hence, this study propose mediating effect of knowledge management between the proposed factors of T-HRM and organizational efficiency. Consequently, leadership of the organization also refers to the process of influencing others to achieve some desired goals in which knowledge sharing occurs, as well as creating the incentives for doing so (Handzic, 2011; de Jong & Hartog, 2007; Kerr & Clegg, 2007). Also, modern day HR practices is concern about the importance of talent management (Ashton & Morton, 2005) for retaining and attracting talented and potential employee in organization (Deery, 2008; Christensen & Rog, 2008). Besides, contemporary training and development opportunity provided by the HRD in an organization improves the knowledge level and capacity of the employee of the organization. Similarly, T-HRM emphasizes on organizational innovation because HRM is also considered another antecedents of organizational innovation (Shipton et al., 2006). Hence, T-HRM integrates innovation and HR strategy in order to ensure organization competitiveness, effectiveness and sustainability (De Leede & Looise, 2005). Moreover, T-HRM underlines the importance of internal and external stakeholders of the organization, hence, socially responsible human resource management (SR-HRM) is another essential factor for T-HR for achieving organizational efficiency, goal and success (Nie et al., 2018; Milfelner et al., 2015). Because, organizational efficiency management determines the goals of the organization. Most of the literature also supports these facts and suggest IT as a strong influencer in today's organizational practice. In this study, the researchers follow the transformational side of the HR literature. Sharing among the employees is a social exchange process; social exchange theory supports this fact (Cabrera & Cabrera, 2005). Information technology is considered an important factor in transformation literature and confirm the flows in the areas of smooth's knowledge repositories, data mining, and decision support systems (Hahn & Subramani, 2000) by providing a platform for communication and sharing. Therefore, heading towards communication aspects as a facilitator, this study proposes the ICT infrastructure of the organization as a moderator between T-HRM and efficiency management. Furthermore, different studies also have presented the moderating effects of organizational alignment (Bezrukova et al., 2012; Byrd et al., 2006). Because organizational alignment connects organizational strategy, different departments and employee of the organization for achieving organizational objective and transforming organization (Henderson & Venkatraman, 1999). Hence, this study also considers organizational alignment as an important factor of T-HRM and propose a moderating effect of organizational alignment between knowledge management and organizational efficiency.

Figure 1 depicts the components of T-HRM developed in this study to analyze the influences on organizational efficiency management.

Figure 1. Components of T-HRM

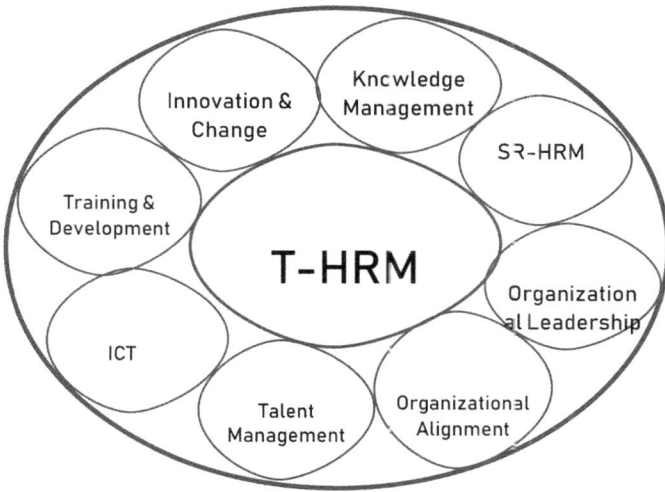

Knowledge Management

Knowledge is a valuable resource for business organizations. According to Grant (1996b) knowledge is considered as the firm's most important and precious asset to sustain its competitive advantage (Davenport & Prusak, 1998; Suppiah & Sandhu, 2011). Davenport and his colleagues found knowledge management as the improvement process of knowledge exercise for the organizations to achieve its organizational objectives (Davenport et al., 1998). Knowledge entails iteration and interaction between individuals in the workplace (Howell & Annansingh, 2013). A number of activities was recognized from the knowledge management literature to manage knowledge for the organizations. Heiseg (2009) explored 166 different terms in his study that are used to describe KM activities after analyzing 117 KM frameworks. Nevertheless, based on further classification, from the literature, knowledge management can be explored as the process of (1) knowledge acquisition (i.e., collecting and identifying useful information), (2) organizing knowledge (i.e., enabling employees to retrieve organizational knowledge), (3) knowledge leverage (i.e., exploiting and usefully applying knowledge), (4) knowledge sharing (i.e., disseminating knowledge through the whole organization), and (5) organizational memory (i.e., storing the knowledge in the repository; Kim & Lee, 2013; Nonaka & Takeuchi, 1995; Rowley, 2000). Nonetheless, Wang and Noe (2010) found the success of KM initiative in knowledge sharing because sharing the information to the right person on time to continue the action in ways that foster organizational performance. Consequently, knowledge sharing also is important in the area of innovation, organizational learning, the development of new skills and capabilities of the employee, increasing productivity, and maintaining a competitive advantage for organizations (Kim & Lee, 2012; Senge, 2006). Hence, knowledge management gains central attention in the area of HR management transformation to utilize employee efficiencies in generating new ideas and competencies to produce competitive advantage.

Organizational Leadership

Organizational leadership refers to the process of influencing others towards achieving some desired goals (de Jong & Hartog, 2007). Durcker (1996) has defined "a leader is someone who has followers." According to Packard (2009), in organizations, leadership connects organizational goal, aligns an employee with the vision, develop strategies, and motivates staff. Organizational and management literature also support this fact and studies report that leadership is a crucial element for organizational efficiency enhancement (Benson & Blackman, 2011; Carson, Tesluk, & Marrone, 2007). Considering effective leadership, Ozcelik et al. (2008) give more emphasis on cognitive tasks (e.g., planning, coordinating, organizing, and decision-making) since the practices aimed by the leaders to capitalize on the employees' emotional resources is a differentiating factor for organizational-level performance. Emphasizing leader-follower (employee) relationships, Epitropaki and Martin (2013) also place more importance on interpersonal influence, as it is thought to be a cornerstone factor for organizations. Contractor et al. (2012) also claimed in their study that the behavior of the leaders has a rigorous influence on collectives, including teams and units.

Information and Communication Technology Infrastructure

Technology comprises a crucial element for the organization in creating new knowledge. Using information and communication technology, an organization can integrate its previously stored information and knowledge (Gold et al., 2001). Consequently, apart from storing and retrieving data, it can improve the access of knowledge and eliminate temporal and spatial barriers between knowledge workers. Information and communication technology (ICT) can enhance knowledge sharing among the employees in different levels (Tohidinia & Mosakhani, 2010). The organizations invest in comprehensive IT infrastructure it can facilitates in rapid collection, storage, and exchange of knowledge among the employees (Lee & Choi, 2003). Representing ICT in an organizational perspective, Dalkir (2011) represented communication and collaboration technology. Though these technologies are invariably intertwined, communication technologies include the telephone, fax, video conferencing, teleconferencing, chatrooms, instant messaging, phone text messaging (SMS), Internet telephone (voice over IP or VOIP), e-mail, and discussion forums (Dalkir, 2011). Alternatively, groupware and collaboration technology represent a system that enhance the groups communication among colleagues (work groups) and involved them to a communication network (e.g., LAN) to organize their activities e.g. scheduling meetings and allocating resources, e-mail, password protection for documents, telephone utilities, electronic newsletters, and file distribution. Therefore, the ICT are usually integrated with some form of collaboration and work as a dissemination tool for knowledge sharing.

Talent Management

"The terms "talent management", "talent strategy", "succession management", and "human resource planning" are often used interchangeably" (Lewis & Heckman, 2006). Talent management deals with the talent "supply", "demand" and "flow" in the organization (Pascal, 2004). Transformation, technological up gradation and change in the current business world, organization are seriously struggling to develop perfect workforce for the organization (Panayiotou et al., 2019). In order to meet expectation of the modern era organizations are facing problem because of the growing number of skill or talent gap

(Hora, 2019). Now a day because of the slowdown of the employee turnover, it has become challenging for any business organization for attracting, and retaining talented employee. Traditional style of the HRD of the organization are not suitable to meet the challenge to overcome the issue related with the talent management. T-HRM as a modern approach of HRM with the help of the emotional intelligence, considers talent management as an essential element to achieve organizational efficiency (Laborde et al., 2019). T-HRM creates engine room for developing internal talent in an organization as well as ensures talent retention and external talent attracting strategy by developing proper organizational environment. Moreover, by offering competitive compensation and benefit for the both internal and external talented employee for managing organizational talent as well as ensuring organizational efficiency.

Training and Development

Training and Development (T&D) is considered as one of the important components of HR (Dhamodharan et al., 2010). Training and development involves with the gaining knowledge through improving skills of the employee for achieving organizational objective. Likewise, T-HRM also considers T&D as an important factor to achieve organizational goal and efficiency. Because, T&D not only improves employee knowledge level by providing training and coaching to their employee to achieve organizational objective but also enhances employee commitment (Brown & Sitzmann, 2011). Hence, in order to compete with the different competitors, also to ensure organizational transformation and innovation T&D will play very crucial role in the domain of T-HRM. Love and Singh (2011) in their research study have pointed out that T&D is one of eight aspects of HRD success. Because through T&D employee gets up-to-date and gain saleable knowledge which add value to their qualification and career progress and works as a strong motivating factor which results lower turnover in organization. Moreover, Kim and Ployhart (2014) stated that T&D not only motivates and develops employee competences but also improves organizational performance and competitiveness. Mainly, T-HRM will ensure accurate connection between organizational goal, employee skill gap and required training of the employee for achieving organizational efficiency. Alongside, training and development works as a predictor of employee and organizational performance. Training and development helps employee to enhance knowledge in their specialized area as well as enhance employee commitment and effort to achieve organizational goal and ensure organizational efficiency (Brown & Sitzmann, 2011).

Innovation and Change

Innovation and change is a modern-day topic, which focuses on importance and process of organizational change (Nilakant & Ramnarayan, 2006). In this modern and competitive business environment, it is difficult for any business organization to survive and out compete the rivalry organizations. Therefore, organization has to constantly looking forward to bring innovation and change in organization in order to ensure their sustainability. However, bring innovation and change in organization is a difficult process. Organization has to face numerous obstacles to bring innovation and change in organization (Sune & Gibb, 2015; Pascale et al., 1997). Most importantly, employee behavior during organizational change is another concerning issue for organizational dealing with change and transformation. Because, success and failure of the organization depends on the employee attitudes towards change, employee cynicism and employee readiness towards change (Choi, 2011; Bommer et al., 2005; Herscovitch & Mayer, 2002). Many business organizations are struggling in dealing with employee attitude and behavior during organizational change and innovation. Therefore, T-HRM will play important role for shaping employee attitude and behavior (Wood & De Menezed, 1998) through transformational HR practice and helps organization to innovate, change and transform. Moreover, T-HRM supports organization to become innovative, transformative and managing change successfully in order to ensure organizational effectiveness and efficiency (Linnenluecke & Griffiths, 2010; Lines, 2004).

Social Responsible Human Resource Management (SR-HRM)

SR-HRM is a combination of corporate social responsibility (CSR) and human resource management (HRM). The notion of SR-HRM involves with improving work-file quality of the employee in the viewpoint of the principles of CSR.SR-HRM focuses on organizational fairness, objectivity, employee empowerment and non-discrimination. Shen and Zhu (2011) classified SR-HRM in three sections, such as employee oriented human resource management (EO-HRM). EO-HRM focuses on employee empowerment, workplace democracy as well as employee personal development and employee family needs. Another section is known as legal compliance human resource management (LC-HRM), which works with the labor law and international standards such as ILO to ensure employee workplace safety and compliance, rules and regulation of employee wage etc. Similarly, general facilitation human resource management (GF-HRM) emphasizes on welfare of both employees and other stakeholders of the organization. SR-HR helps organization to achieve competitive advantage. Similarly, number of research studies have highlighted the importance of SR-HRM for improving employee behavior and organizational performance. Hence, T-HRM also considered SR-HRM as an important factor for achieving organizational goal and efficiency. Shen and Benson (2016) stated that SR-HRM ensures organizational short-term effectiveness and long-term sustainability. Therefore, T-HRM emphasizes SR-HRM for transforming HR of the organization in order to achieve organizational efficiency, effectiveness and sustainability (Shen & Zhu, 2011).

Organizational Alignment

Alignment is known as the fit and linkage between different departments or units of the organization. Organizational alignment is one of the contemporary areas in the field of strategic management (Tan and Tan, 2005). Moreover, alignment units' organizational culture, organizational strategy and structure for ensuring organizational efficiency. Organizational alignment works as a linkage between organizational strategy, culture and its structure. Porter (1996) describes organizational alignment as a common understanding of the objectives and goals of the organization between the managers of different levels and ladders of the organization. In order to achieve organizational competitiveness organization must align its instruments and resources. Nadler and Tushman (1988) in their studies also highlighted the importance of organizational alignment because appropriate alignment directs organization in right path for achieving organizational effectiveness and efficiency. Therefore, HR department of the organization also emphasizes aligning activities of the organization with the organizational goals and objectives for transforming human resources. Different scholars pointed that although it import for every organization to ensure alignment in order to achieve its organizational goal and efficiency but it is not an easy task to ensure organizational alignment (Hinings et al., 1996), hence transactional or traditional HR will not be suitable to achieve proper organizational alignment. Henceforth, T-HRM will transform HRD activities and link with organizational goal and plan strategy accordingly to ensure proper organizational alignment. Through proper alignment, T-HRM of the organization can ensure organizational effectiveness.

Figure 2. Proposed model

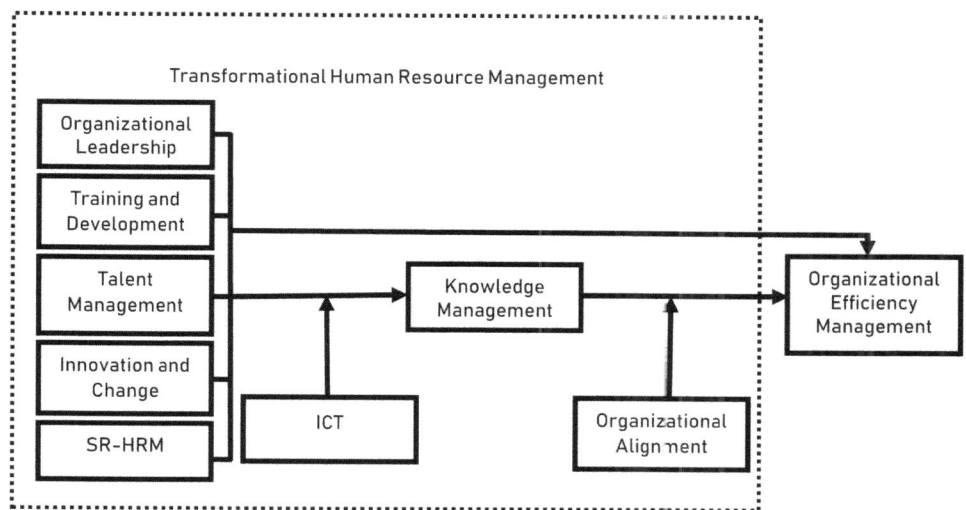

DISCUSSION

Limited research work has exhibited the factors of T-HRM and its effects on organizational efficiency management. This paper proposes a model to suggest the relationship between factors of T-HRM and organizational effectiveness. In this study, training and development, organizational leadership, talent management, change and innovation and social responsible human resource management serve as dependent variables, knowledge management serves as a mediating variable, both ICT and organizational alignment serve as moderating variables and organizational efficiency management serves as a dependent variable. The proposed model will help to link the factors of T-HRM, ICT, knowledge management and organizational alignment to ensure organizational efficiency management. The paper contributes the literature of T-HRM and organizational efficiency management theory and practices in numerous ways, which will provide new insights for both researchers and practitioners.

THEORETICAL AND PRACTICAL IMPLICATIONS

Proposed model of this study will contribute in the literature of T-HRM and organizational efficiency management in several ways. First, this study has identified a gap in the literature. Secondly, this study has satisfied the gap by suggesting several factors of T-HRM and integrating those factors of the T-HRM with organizational efficiency in order to see the effects of T-HRM on organizational efficiency management. Notably, to the best of the authors' knowledge such effects of T-HRM on organizational efficiency management not yet presented in the literature before.

In the practical point of view, the proposed conceptual model (Figure-2) could be useful for the organization for achieving organizational efficiency. This study sheds light on T-HRM, which is an essential and contemporary area in the field of HRM, which will provide proper guideline for organization as well as help leaders and managers of the organization to achieve competitive advantage, improve organizational performance, ensure efficiency and achieve organizational goal.

CONCLUSION

This paper proposed a number of influential factors of T-HRM, which have strong association with organizational efficiency management and open a space for further empirical investigation. Eventually, existing literature supports that proposed factors of T-HRM in this study, enhances organizational efficiency to achieve goals and objectives of the organization. Therefore, an empirical research on T-HRM and influence of its different factors as independent variable, mediating variable and moderating variable on organizational efficiency in an integrated model would offer new knowledge. However, proposed framework concluded that in order to achieve organizational efficiency, factors of T-HRM plays a vital role. Therefore, insights of this study will provide new scope for the researchers and practitioners around the world in the area of HRM and organizational study. Moreover, empirical rationalization of this proposed model will validate the strength of the model as well as will open a new area of further investigation.

REFERENCES

Alavi, M., & Leidner, D. (2001). Knowledge management and knowledge management systems: Conceptual foundations and research issues. *Management Information Systems Quarterly*, *25*(1), 107–136. doi:10.2307/3250961

Amburgey, T. L., Kelly, D., & Barnett, W. P. (1990, August). Resetting the clock: The dynamics of organizational change and failure. In Academy of Management Proceedings (Vol. 1990, No. 1, pp. 160-164). Briarcliff Manor, NY 10510: Academy of Management.

Ashton, C., & Morton, L. (2005). Managing talent for competitive advantage: Taking a systemic approach to talent management. *Strategic HR review, 4*(5), 28-31.

Barrena-Martínez, J., López-Fernández, M., & Romero-Fernández, P. M. (2017). Towards a configuration of socially responsible human resource management policies and practices: Findings from an academic consensus. *International Journal of Human Resource Management*, 1–37. doi:10.1080/0958 5192.2017.1332669

Bartuševičienė, I., & Šakalytė, E. (2013). Organizational assessment: Effectiveness vs. efficiency. *Social Transformations in Contemporary Society*, *1*(1), 45–53.

Beer, M. (1997). The transformation of the human resource function: Resolving the tension between a traditional administrative and a new strategic role. *Human Resource Management: Published in Cooperation with the School of Business Administration, The University of Michigan and in alliance with the Society of Human Resources Management, 36*(1), 49-56.

Benson, A. M., & Blackman, D. (2011). To distribute leadership or not? A lesson from the islands. *Tourism Management*, *32*(5), 1141–1149. doi:10.1016/j.tourman.2010.10.002

Bezrukova, K., Thatcher, S., Jehn, K. A., & Spell, C. S. (2012). The effects of alignments: Examining group faultlines, organizational cultures, and performance. *The Journal of Applied Psychology*, *97*(1), 77–92. doi:10.1037/a0023684 PMID:21744943

Bommer, W. H., Rich, G. A., & Rubin, R. S. (2005). Changing attitudes about change: Longitudinal effects of transformational leader behavior on employee cynicism about organizational change. *Journal of Organizational Behavior: The International Journal of Industrial, Occupational and Organizational Psychology and Behavior*, *26*(7), 733–753. doi:10.1002/job.342

Bourke, J., & Crowley, F. (2015). The role of HRM and ICT complementarities in firm innovation: Evidence from transition economies. *International Journal of Innovation Management*, *19*(05). doi:10.1142/S1363919615500541

Brown, K. G., & Sitzmann, T. (2011). Training and employee development for improved performance.

Byrd, T. A., Lewis, B. R., & Bryan, R. W. (2006). The leveraging influence of strategic alignment on IT investment: An empirical examination. *Information & Management*, *43*(3), 308–321. doi:10.1016/j.im.2005.07.002

Cabrera, E. F., & Cabrera, A. (2005). Fostering knowledge sharing through people management practices. *International Journal of Human Resource Management*, *16*(5), 720–735. doi:10.1080/09585190500083020

Carson, J. B., Tesluk, P. E., & Marrone, J. A. (2007). Shared leadership in Tams: An investigation of antecedent conditions and performance. *Academy of Management Journal*, *50*(5), 1217–1234.

Choi, M. (2011). Employees' attitudes toward organizational change: A literature review. *Human Resource Management*, *50*(4), 479–500. doi:10.1002/hrm.20434

Christensen Hughes, J., & Rog, E. (2008). Talent management: A strategy for improving employee recruitment, retention and engagement within hospitality organizations. *International Journal of Contemporary Hospitality Management*, *20*(7), 743–757. doi:10.1108/09596110810899086

Contractor, N. S., DeChurch, L. A., Carson, J., Carter, D. R., & Keegan, B. (2012). The topology of collective leadership. *The Leadership Quarterly*, *23*(6), 994–1011. doi:10.1016/j.leaqua.2012.10.010

Dalkir, K. (2011). Knowledge Management in Theory and Practice (2nded.). Cambridge, MA: The MIT Press.

Davenport, T. H., & Prusak, L. (1998). *Working Knowledge*. Boston, MA: Harvard Business School Press.

Davidson, S. L., & Butcher, J. (2019). Rural Superintendents' Experiences with Empowerment and Alignment to Vision in the Application of Principle-Centered Leadership. *Rural Educator*, *40*(1).

De Clercq, D., Haq, I. U., Azeem, M. U., & Ahmad, H. N. (2019). The relationship between workplace incivility and helping behavior: Roles of job dissatisfaction and political skill. *The Journal of Psychology*, 1–21. PMID:30696391

De Jong, J. P., & Hartog, D. N. D. (2007). How leaders influence employees' innovative behaviour. *European Journal of Innovation Management*, *10*(1), 41–64. doi:10.1108/14601060710720546

Deery, M. (2008). Talent management, work-life balance and retention strategies. *International Journal of Contemporary Hospitality Management*, *20*(7), 792–806. doi:10.1108/09596110810897619

deLeede, J., & Looise, J. K. (2005). Innovation and HRM: Towards an integrated framework. *Creativity and Innovation Management*, *14*(2), 108–117. doi:10.1111/j.1467-8691.2005.00331.x

Dhamodharan, V., Daniel, B. J. C., & Ambuli, T. V. (2010). An empirical study on assessing trainees' expectations and their perceptions. *International Business Research*, *3*(2), 174. doi:10.5539/ibr.v3n2p174

Drucker, P. F. (1996). Your leadership is unique. *Leadership*, *17*(4), 54.

Edvardsson, I. R. (2008). HRM and knowledge management. *Employee Relations*, *30*(5), 553–561. doi:10.1108/01425450810888303

Epitropaki, O., & Martin, R. (2013). Transformational–transactional leadership and upward influence: The role of Relative Leader–Member Exchanges (RLMX) and Perceived Organizational Support (POS). *The Leadership Quarterly*, *24*(2), 299–315. doi:10.1016/j.leaqua.2012.11.007

Gershon, R. A. (2019). Transnational Media and the Economics of Global Competition. *Global Communication. Multicultural Perspectives*, 37.

Gold, H. A., Malhotra, A., & Segars, H. A. (2001). Knowledge Management: An organizational Capabilities Perspective. *Journal of Management Information Systems*, *18*(1), 185–214. doi:10.1080/07421222.2001.11045669

Grant, R. M. (1996b). Toward a knowledge-based theory of the firm. *Strategic Management Journal*, *17*(S2), 109–111. doi:10.1002mj.4250171110

Habersang, S., Küberling-Jost, J., Reihlen, M., & Seckler, C. (2019). A Process Perspective on Organizational Failure: A Qualitative Meta-Analysis. *Journal of Management Studies*, *56*(1), 19–56. doi:10.1111/joms.12341

Hahn, J., & Subramani, M. R. (2000). A framework of knowledge management systems: issues and challenges for theory and practice. *Proceedings of the International Conference on Information Systems, ICIS'2000*, 302-12.

Handzic, M. (2011). Integrated socio-technical knowledge management model: An empirical evaluation. *Journal of Knowledge Management*, *15*(2), 198–211. doi:10.1108/13673271111119655

Hasan, I., Khan, A. N. M. S., Karim, M. A., Khan, S. R., Alam, S., & Sanjana, B. (2018). Health and safety compliance in the readymade garment sector of Bangladesh: Practices and Observations. *Independent Business Review*, *11*(1-2), 25–32.

Heisig, P. (2009). Harmonisation of knowledge management–comparing 160 KM frameworks around the globe. *Journal of Knowledge Management*, *13*(4), 4–31. doi:10.1108/13673270910971798

Heisig, P. (2009). Harmonisation of knowledge management – comparing 160 Km frameworks around the globe. *Journal of Knowledge Management*, *13*(4), 4–31. doi:10.1108/13673270910971798

Henderson, J. C., & Venkatraman, H. (1999). Strategic alignment Leveraging information technology for transforming organizations. *IBM systems journal, 38*(2.3), 472-484.

Herscovitch, L., & Meyer, J. P. (2002). Commitment to organizational change: Extension of a three-component model. *The Journal of Applied Psychology, 87*(3), 474–487. doi:10.1037/0021-9010.87.3.474 PMID:12090605

Hinings, C. R., Thibault, L., Slack, T., & Kikulis, L. M. (1996). Values and organizational structure. *Human Relations, 47*(7), 885–916. doi:10.1177/001872679604900702

Hora, M. T. (2019). *Beyond the skills gap: Preparing college students for life and work*. Cambridge, MA: Harvard Education Press.

Howell, K. E., & Annansingh, F. (2013). Knowledge generation and sharing in UK universities: A tale of two cultures? *International Journal of Information Management, 33*(1), 32–39. doi:10.1016/j.ijinfomgt.2012.05.003

Iles, P., Chuai, X., & Preece, D. (2010). Talent management and HRM in multinational companies in Beijing: Definitions, differences and drivers. *Journal of World Business, 45*(2), 179–189. doi:10.1016/j.jwb.2009.09.014

Islam, M. Z., Jasimuddin, S. M., & Hasan, I. (2018). Determinants that influence knowledge sharing: An integrated literature review. *International Journal of Knowledge Management Studies, 9*(4), 363–380. doi:10.1504/IJKMS.2018.096318

Karaa, D., Uysalb, M., Sirgyc, M. J., & Leed, G. (2013). The effects of leadership style on employee well-being in hospitality. *International Journal of Hospitality Management, 34*, 9–18. doi:10.1016/j.ijhm.2013.02.001

Karim, A. S., Zaki, A. R., & Mubeen, M. H. (2019). Managing Workforce Diversity in Multicultural Organizations. *Journal of European Studies, 35*(1), 79–91.

Karlaftis, M. G. (2004). A DEA approach for evaluating the efficiency and effectiveness of urban transit systems. *European Journal of Operational Research, 152*(2), 354–364. doi:10.1016/S0377-2217(03)00029-8

Kerr, M., & Clegg, C. (2007). Sharing knowledge: Contextualizing socio–technical thinking and practice. *The Learning Organization, 14*(5), 423–435. doi:10.1108/09696470710762646

Kim, T., & Lee, G. (2012). A modified and extended Triandis model for the enablers–process–outcomes relationship in hotel employees' knowledge sharing. *Service Industries Journal, 32*(13), 2059–2090. doi:10.1080/02642069.2011.574276

Kim, T. T., & Lee, G. (2013). Hospitality employee knowledge-sharing behaviors in the relationship between goal orientations and service innovative behavior. *International Journal of Hospitality Management, 34*, 324–337. doi:10.1016/j.ijhm.2013.04.009

Kim, Y., & Ployhart, R. E. (2014). The effects of staffing and training on firm productivity and profit growth before, during, and after the Great Recession. *The Journal of Applied Psychology, 99*(3), 361–389. doi:10.1037/a0035408 PMID:24377393

Kumar, S., & Gulati, R. (2010). Assessing the Effect of Ownership on the Efficiency of Indian Domestic Banks. *IUP Journal of Bank Management, 9*(3).

Laborde, Z. B., Burbano, K. B., Reinoso, V. G., Bangeppagari, M., Mulla, S. I., & Selvanayagam, M. (2019). Emotional Intelligence Models as Generators of Business Management Change in the Human Talent Area. *Journal of Artificial Intelligence, 12*(1), 1–10. doi:10.3923/jai.2019.1.10

Laborde, Z. B., Burbano, K. B., Reinoso, V. G., Bangeppagari, M., Mulla, S. I., & Selvanayagam, M. (2019). Emotional Intelligence Models as Generators of Business Management Change in the Human Talent Area. *Journal of Artificial Intelligence, 12*(1), 1–10. doi:10.3923/jai.2019.1.10

Lee, H., & Choi, B. (2003). Knowledge management enablers, process, and organizational performance: An integrative view and empirical examination. *Journal of Management Information Systems, 20*(1), 179–228. doi:10.1080/07421222.2003.11045756

Lewis, L. (2019). *Organizational change: Creating change through strategic communication.* Hoboken, NJ: Wiley-Blackwell. doi:10.1002/9781119431503

Lewis, R. E., & Heckman, R. J. (2006). Talent management: A critical review. *Human Resource Management Review, 16*(2), 139–154. doi:10.1016/j.hrmr.2006.03.001

Lin, C. H., & Sanders, K. (2017). HRM and innovation: A multi-level organisational learning perspective. *Human Resource Management Journal, 27*(2), 300–317. doi:10.1111/1748-8583.12127

Lines, R. (2004). Influence of participation in strategic change: Resistance, organizational commitment and change goal achievement. *Journal of Change Management, 4*(3), 193–215. doi:10.1080/1469701042000221696

Linnenluecke, M., & Griffiths, A. (2010). Beyond adaptation: Resilience for business in light of climate change and weather extremes. *Business & Society, 49*(3), 477–511. doi:10.1177/0007650310368814

Love, L. F., & Singh, P. (2011). Workplace branding: Leveraging human resources management practices for competitive advantage through "Best Employer" surveys. *Journal of Business and Psychology, 26*(2), 175–181. doi:10.100710869-011-9226-5

Low, J. (2000). The value creation index. *Journal of Intellectual Capital, 1*(3), 252–262. doi:10.1108/14691930010377919

Manzoor, F., Wei, L., Bányai, T., Nurunnabi, M., & Subhan, Q. A. (2019). An Examination of Sustainable HRM Practices on Job Performance: An Application of Training as a Moderator. *Sustainability, 11*(8), 2263. doi:10.3390u11082263

Mehmood, Z. U. I., & Arif, M. I. (2011). Leadership and HRM: Evaluating new leadership styles for effective human resource management. *International Journal of Business and Social Science, 2*(15).

Milfelner, B., Potočnik, A., & Žižek, S. Š. (2015). Social responsibility, human resource management and organizational performance. *Systems Research and Behavioral Science, 32*(2), 221–229. doi:10.1002res.2263

Mooijman, M., van Dijk, W. W., van Dijk, E., & Ellemers, N. (2019). Leader power, power stability, and interpersonal trust. *Organizational Behavior and Human Decision Processes*, *152*, 1–10. doi:10.1016/j.obhdp.2019.03.009

Moussa, M., & Somjai, K. (2019). *Job dissatisfaction and employee turnover: A qualitative case study in Thailand*. Sage Publications: Sage Business Cases Originals.

Nadler, D. A., & Tushman, M. L. (1988). Organizational frame bending: Principles for managing reorientation. *The Academy of Management Perspectives*, *3*(3), 194–204. doi:10.5465/ame.1989.4274738

Nie, D., Lämsä, A. M., & Pučėtaitė, R. (2018). Effects of responsible human resource management practices on female employees' turnover intentions. *Business Ethics (Oxford, England)*, *27*(1), 29–41. doi:10.1111/beer.12165

Nilakant, V., & Ramnarayan, S. (2006). *Change management: Altering mindsets in a global context*. Sage Publications India.

Nonaka, I., & Takeuchi, H. (1995). *The Knowledge Creation Company: How Japanese Companies Create the Dynamics of Innovation*. New York, NY: Oxford University Press.

Oltra, V. (2005). Knowledge management effectiveness factors: The role of HRM. *Journal of Knowledge Management*, *9*(4), 70–86. doi:10.1108/13673270510610341

Ozcelik, H., Langton, N., & Aldrich, H. (2008). Doing well and doing good: The relationship between leadership practices that facilitate a positive emotional climate and organizational performance. *Journal of Managerial Psychology*, *23*(2), 186–203. doi:10.1108/02683940810850817

Packard, T. (2009). Leadership and performance in human services organizations. Chapter 7 in The handbook of human services management, Sag5e, 143-164.

Panayiotou, A., Putnam, L. L., & Kassinis, G. (2019). Generating tensions: A multilevel, process analysis of organizational change. *Strategic Organization*, *17*(1), 8–37. doi:10.1177/1476127017734446

Pascale, R., Millemann, M., & Gioja, L. (1997). Changing the way we change. *Harvard Business Review*, *75*(6), 126. PMID:10174794

Pinprayong, B., & Siengtai, S. (2012). Restructuring for organizational efficiency in the banking sector in Thailand: A case study of Siam Commercial Bank. *Far East Journal of Psychology and Business*, *8*(2), 29–42.

Porter, M. E. (1996). What is strategy? *Harvard Business Review*, *74*(6), 61–78. PMID:10158474

Rehman, S., Zahid, M., Rahman, H. U., & Habib, M. N. (2019). A Partial Least Squares Approach to the Leadership Styles, Organizational Culture, and Employees' Productivity: A Case of Pakistan Banking Industry. *International Journal of Asian Business and Information Management*, *10*(1), 55–64. doi:10.4018/IJABIM.2019010104

Rosenbusch, N., Brinckmann, J., & Bausch, A. (2011). Is innovation always beneficial? A meta-analysis of the relationship between innovation and performance in SMEs. *Journal of Business Venturing*, *26*(4), 441–457. doi:10.1016/j.jbusvent.2009.12.002

Rowley, J. (2000). From learning organisation to knowledge entrepreneur. *Journal of Knowledge Management*, 4(1), 7–15. doi:10.1108/13673270010315362

Santangelo, G. D., & Pini, P. (2011). New HRM practices and exploitative innovation: A shopfloor level analysis. *Industry and Innovation*, 18(6), 611–630. doi:10.1080/13662716.2011.591977

Schweyer, A. (2010). *Talent management systems: Best practices in technology solutions for recruitment, retention and workforce planning*. Hoboken, NJ: John Wiley & Sons.

Seeck, H., & Diehl, M. R. (2017). A literature review on HRM and innovation–taking stock and future directions. *International Journal of Human Resource Management*, 28(6), 913–944. doi:10.1080/0958 5192.2016.1143862

Senge, P. M. (2006). The Fifth Discipline: The Art and Practice of the Learning Organization. Currency, New York, NY.

Shen, J., & Benson, J. (2016). When CSR is a social norm: How socially responsible human resource management affects employee work behavior. *Journal of Management*, *42*(6), 1723–1746. doi:10.1177/0149206314522300

Shen, J., & Jiuhua Zhu, C. (2011). Effects of socially responsible human resource management on employee organizational commitment. *International Journal of Human Resource Management*, 22(15), 3020–3035. doi:10.1080/09585192.2011.599951

Shih, C. P., & Orochena, O. D. C. P. (2016). Analyzing the Effect of Transformational Leadership on Innovation and Organizational Performance. *International Journal of Productivity Management and Assessment Technologies*, 4(2), 11–27. doi:10.4018/IJPMAT.2016070102

Shih, H. A., & Chiang, Y. H. (2005). Strategy alignment between HRM, KM, and corporate development. *International Journal of Manpower*, 26(6), 582–603. doi:10.1108/01437720510625476

Shipton, H., West, M. A., Dawson, J., Birdi, K., & Patterson, M. (2006). HRM as a predictor of innovation. *Human Resource Management Journal*, 16(1), 3–27. doi:10.1111/j.1748-8583.2006.00002.x

Silva, M. R. A., de Amorim, J. C., & Dias, A. L. (2019). Determinants of Employee Retention: A Study of Reality in Brazil. In Strategy and Superior Performance of Micro and Small Businesses in Volatile Economies (pp. 44–56). Hershey, PA: IGI Global. doi:10.4018/978-1-5225-7888-8.ch004

Souza, J. G. S., Lages, V. A., Sampaio, A. A., Souza, T. C. S., & Martins, A. M. E. D. B. (2019). The absence of functional dentition is associated with the lack of commitment to oral functions among Brazilian adults. *Ciencia & Saude Coletiva*, 24(1), 253–260. doi:10.1590/1413-81232018241.30432016 PMID:30698258

Steijn, B., & Tijdens, K. (2005). Workers and Their Willingness to Learn: Will ICT-Implementation Strategies and HRM Practices Contribute to Innovation? *Creativity and Innovation Management*, 14(2), 151–159. doi:10.1111/j.1476-8691.2005.00335.x

Steijn, B., & Tijdens, K. (2005). Workers and Their Willingness to Learn: Will ICT-Implementation Strategies and HRM Practices Contribute to Innovation? *Creativity and Innovation Management*, 14(2), 151–159. doi:10.1111/j.1476-8691.2005.00335.x

Sune, A., & Gibb, J. (2015). Dynamic capabilities as patterns of organizational change: An empirical study on transforming a firm's resource base. *Journal of Organizational Change Management, 28*(2), 213–231. doi:10.1108/JOCM-01-2015-0019

Suppiah, V., & Sandhu, M. S. (2011). Organisational culture's influence on tacit knowledge-sharing behaviour. *Journal of Knowledge Management, 15*(3), 462–477. doi:10.1108/13673271111137439

Tan, J., & Tan, D. (2005). Environment–strategy co-evolution and co-alignment: A staged model of Chinese SOEs under transition. *Strategic Management Journal, 26*(2), 141–157. doi:10.1002mj.437

Tohidinia, Z., & Mosakhani, M. (2010). Knowledge sharing behavior and its predictors. *Industrial Management & Data Systems, 110*(4), 611–631. doi:10.1108/02635571011039052

Ulrich, D., Allen, J., Brockbank, W., Younger, J., & Nyman, M. (2009). HR Transformation Building Human Resources from the Outside In. New York, NY: McGraw-Hill.

Wang, S., & Noe, R. A. (2010). Knowledge sharing: A review and directions for future research. *Human Resource Management Review, 20*(2), 115–131. doi:10.1016/j.hrmr.2009.10.001

Wolff, B. (2019). The Truth About Employee Disengagement. *Professional Safety, 64*(2), 24–24.

Wood, S., & De Menezes, L. (1998). High commitment management in the UK: Evidence from the workplace industrial relations survey, and employers' manpower and skills practices survey. *Human Relations, 51*(4), 485–515. doi:10.1177/001872679805100403

This research was previously published in the Handbook of Research on Managerial Practices and Disruptive Innovation in Asia; pages 264-281, copyright year 2020 by Business Science Reference (an imprint of IGI Global).

Chapter 20
An Integration of Human Resources and Supply Chain Management for a Sustainable Competitive Advantage:
A Resource-Based View

Çağlar Doğru

https://orcid.org/0000-0002-4215-8979

Ufuk University, Turkey

ABSTRACT

In this chapter, a multi-disciplinary approach for creating sustainable competitive advantage is examined. This is the integration of human resources management and supply chain management. The primary aim is to come up with a solution to the research question of 'how do organizations create sustainable competitive advantage by integrating human resources and supply chain management?' In order to put forth the solutions, the resource-based approach is employed. A detailed literature review is given on the integration of two business functions to create sustainable competitive advantage. This chapter contributes to the literature, first by laying out the importance of resource-based view in both human resources and supply chain management, second by examining how do these two functions unite in order to obtain sustainable competitive advantage, and lastly, by enriching the limited number of studies so far on the integration of human resources and supply chain management with the help of a literature review.

INTRODUCTION

One of the eye-catching topics in strategic management which is the resource-based view has roots in the early study of Penrose (1959) named as *The Theory of the Growth of the Firm*. On the contrary to Rugman and Verbeke (2002), Penrose added much to the strategic management literature by fostering the concept of competitive advantage and the circumstances for sustaining this advantage by interacting

DOI: 10.4018/978-1-6684-3873-2.ch020

with economic parties (Kor and Mahoney, 2003). And even after Wernerfelt (1984) generated the basis of modern resource-based view, the concept could not attract enough attention until 90s. But since 90s, there is a huge interest in resource-based approach. Along with this approach in strategic management another concept that is competitive advantage has been at the heart of business management. Early works of Ansoff (1965) and Porter (1980), concentrated on the internal strengths and weaknesses as well as opportunities and threats in the environment. These internal strengths and weaknesses have been built upon the resource-based view in strategic management.

Human resources management is unquestionably a factor that enhances both internal strength and competitive advantage for organizations. So far many researchers have underlined that effective human resources practices lead an organization to attain its goals and to have advantages over other organizations (i.e. Amarakoon et al., 2018; Chadwick and Dabu, 2009; Mayfield et al., 2016; Wright et al., 1994). Naturally, it is because of the importance of human resources as a valuable and unique asset for an organization since human resources are widely accepted as crucial sources by resource-based approach (Omondi-Ochieng, 2019; Wright et al, 2001).

Like human resources management, supply chain management is a vital function of a business since it includes management of raw materials, transportation, manufacturing, distribution and retailing activities (Hugos, 2018). With the help of globalization and improvements in information technologies, today supply chain management requires bringing separate organizations together which are responsible for every single chains of supply. This enables organizations to operate effectively and to interact with other organizations in their supply chains. To be successful in these operations, organizations need to develop capabilities for supply chain management so as to gain competitive advantage. This will also enhance them to possess unique resources from the perspective of resource-based approach.

In this chapter, it is aimed to integrate two vital functions of business management which are human resources management and supply chain management within the perspective of resource-based approach so as to gain sustainable competitive advantage. This will be achieved by carefully providing a literature review, and taking the supply chain management capabilities of human resources as a valuable resource for organizations. In previous research it was noted that human resources management played a key-role for supply chain management (e.g. Bendoly, 2006; Santos, 2000). Up to now, only limited studies have attempted to integrate these two main functions and they concentrate mostly on sustainability (e.g. Gowen and Tallon, 2003; Jabbour and de Sousa Jabbour, 2016). Nowadays, the whole world is facing a pandemic and it reshapes the whole manufacturing, distributing and retailing activities around the globe. This underlines the importance of supply chain management. It is obvious that only the organizations investing on effective supply chain management will survive. This can be attained by the organizational resources and one of the crucial factor is human resources. In this respect, after giving a brief background that provides definitions of sustainable competitive advantage and resource-based view, firstly human resources management for sustainable competitive advantage will be given. Following this section, human resources management will be taken from the perspective of resource-based view. In addition to this, supply chain management activities will be examined from the same perspectives. After discussing these concepts in two main sections, an effective integration of them will be provided. At last; contributions to the theory, future research directions, and conclusion sections will be given.

BACKGROUND

Sustainable Competitive Advantage

In the strategic management literature the concept of competitive advantage has attracted attention from many scholars (e.g. Albrecht et al., 2015; Powell, 2001; Tallman et al., 2004). In addition to this, a further improvement has been achieved by defining the circumstances for sustaining the competitive advantage of firms in a long range of time. With the help of this attempt, the concept of sustainable competitive advantage has gained more importance lately. This is achieved based on the early contributions of Porter (1985) and Barney (1991). According to Barney (1995), an organization is supposed to have sustainable competitive advantage only when it has rare and valuable capabilities, skills and assets.

Organizations with sustainable competitive advantages seem to possess rare and inimitable capacities, capabilities, assets or wealth which make rival organizations unable to use same resources. Organizations generally try to get sustainable competitive advantages by generating knowledge (Mahdi et al., 2019), making innovations (Chatzoglou and Chatzoudes, 2018), hiring and motivating high-skilled employees (Barney and Wright, 1998), generating or using latest technologies, machines and equipment (Powell and Dent-Micallef, 1997) and having effective production, marketing or management capabilities (Aaker, 1989). From this point of view sustainable competitive advantage is widely used in resource-based view.

Resource-Based View

Built upon the competitive advantage literature, resource-based view is an approach that defines and examines the factors which enhance sustainable competitive advantages (Peteraf, 1993). Up to now, numerous researchers have contributed to the resource-based view to gain importance in strategic management literature (e.g. Alexy et al., 2018; Conner, 1991; Mahoney 2001). According to Barney (1991), the core proposition of resource-based view is an organization's need for acquiring and using rare, valuable, inimitable and non-substitutable resources, capabilities, assets and capital so as to possess sustainable competitive advantage. Serving for the proposition of resource-based view, some previous researches were also assessed the approaches: distinctive competences (Bryson et al., 2007; Coates and Mcdermott, 2002), dynamic capabilities (Eisenhardt, and Martin, 2000; Kim et al., 2015), knowledge-based approach (Cabrera-Suárez et al., 2001).

With the contributions of resource-based view to strategic management literature, organizations generate strategies to acquire and hold valuable and inimitable resources. In the literature, some factors were found to be related to resource-based view in order to get sustainable competitive advantage. Among them there exist; corporate environmental strategy (Aragón-Correa and Sharma, 2003), technology (Dubey et al., 2019), human resources management (Colbert, 2004), social responsibility (Sodhi, 2015), operations management (Bromiley and Rau, 2016), supply chain management (Shibin et al., 2020).Since the aim of this chapter is to examine the human resources and supply chain management to have sustainable competitive advantage, in the following section these two functions are analyzed.

MAIN FOCUS OF THE CHAPTER

Human Resources Management from the perspective of Resource-Based View

Human resources management consists of activities related to the members or employees of an organization. It concentrates on the human side of organizations which is a vital factor for reaching organizational goals and objectives. Among the basic human resources management practices there exist; analyzing and designing jobs, human resources planning, recruiting, selecting, placing, and orienting employees, conducting training and development programs, managing compensation, motivating human resources, evaluating performance and managing talents and careers (Armstrong and Taylor, 2020; DeCenzo et al., 2016; Noe et al., 2018). Besides the basic practices, human resources management includes leadership and organizational behavior. Moreover, with the latest development in digitalization era, human resources management has built close relationships with knowledge management and artificial intelligence applications.

In the resource-based view literature, in order to provide sustainable competitive advantage, organizational resources, assets or capabilities must be valuable, rare, non-substitutable and inimitable (Barney, 1991). Moreover according to the resource-based view, an organization uses human resources management to generate competencies, which are specific to the organization. These competencies and capabilities are tangible or intangible specific approaches based on knowledge generated within and organization (Amit and Belcourt, 1999). It also gains the capability of generating tacit knowledge (Aït Razouk et al., 2009) and building social and organizational networks among members (Collins and Clark, 2003). In this respect, human resources management plays an active role in creating and using new knowledge as a way of gaining power for adaptation to the environment. This process is called as organizational learning (Snell et al., 1996). Furthermore, human resources management helps the organization build a shared climate for organizational success, and provide effective leadership for employees. Also gaining these types of capabilities, innovation and creative work behavior will be enhanced. And with the help of these capabilities, organizations will generate specific and valuable resources.

Human Resources as a Sustainable Competitive Advantage

The organization-specific, tangible and intangible resources, capabilities and competencies that ease an organization to have competitive advantage are called as 'strategic assets' (Amit and Shoemaker, 1993). In this respect lately in the literature, strategy and human resources management are combined as strategic human resources management. At this point, human resources are absolutely the most strategic and valuable assets of an organization to achieve sustainable competitive advantage. This is because, an organization can hire high-skilled employees, create knowledge, manage talent, build social relationships, demonstrate effective leadership, increase individual and group performance, enhance organizational commitment, organizational citizenship behavior and job satisfaction of employees by the help of human resources. These resources are inimitable, valuable and incompatible for an organization which in turn provide competitive advantage. Other organizations may easily imitate strategies but they won't probably hire the same high-skilled and motivated employees.

As also previously discussed by Dunford et al. (2001), there is a debate on whether human resources itself or human resources management practices provide basis for sustainable competitive advantage. According to Lado and Wilson (1994), it was the human resources practices that enhance organizations to have sustainable competitive advantages. They have proposed that, unless there are effective human resources systems applied for recruitment, selection, training development, performance appraisal, pay and promotion; members or employees of the organizations can't be taken as a primary source of competitive advantage on their own. Because they claim that, unless there are effective human resources systems, the human capital is not capable of a sustainable competitive advantage for an organization. And these human resources systems should utilize managerial and transformational competencies and should also enhance the development of human capital in an organization (Lado and Wilson, 1994). On the contrary Wright et al. (1994), claimed that human resources could be imitated by other organizations, so competitive advantage was held if only human resources are high skilled and highly motivated. This understanding underlines the importance of human capital instead of human resources practices and systems. So which party is right? Obviously in today's unstable and uncertain business environment, organizations should both set effective human resources systems and should attract high skilled and highly motivated members so as to have sustainable competitive advantage. This approach is demonstrated on Figure 1.

Figure 1. Human resources as a sustainable competitive advantage

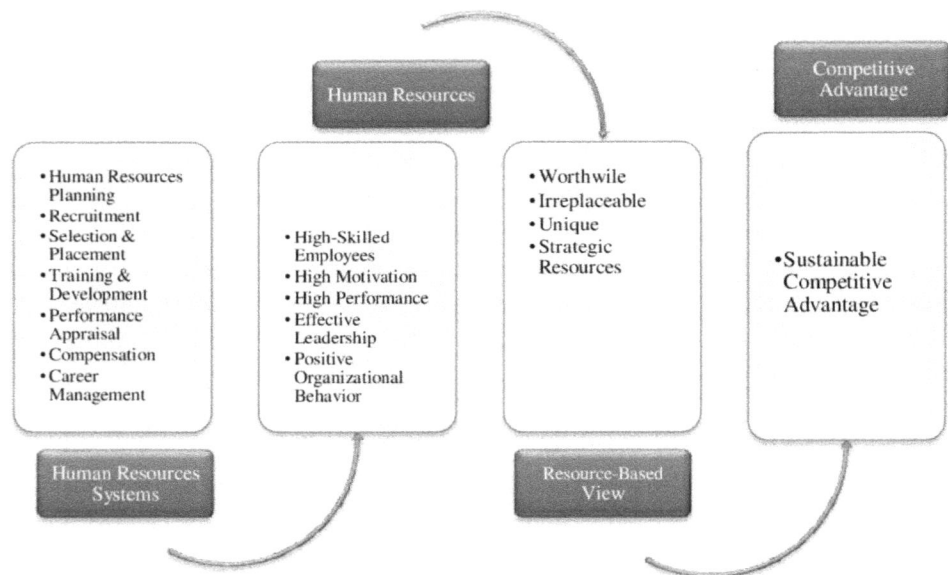

Supply Chain Management and Resource-Based View

Based on the needs of complex and uncertain business environment, supply chain management concept has gained importance since 1990s. Among the principal reasons of gaining more and more importance, there exist, (1) the rise of globalization (Koberg and Longoni, 2019) and its forcing managers to rethink the effectiveness of flow of materials in and out of their firm (Mentzer et al., 2001), (2) tendency of building close relationship with suppliers (Wu and Choi, 2005), (3) the need for meeting quality standards of goods and services (Flynn and Flynn, 2005), (4) customer expectances of timely and accurate deliveries

(Garg et al., 2006) (5) companies' need of generating competitive advantage by effective supply chain management (Barney, 2012; Markley and Davis, 2007).

In general, supply chain management is built upon logistics which is a one-time plan for achieving the flow of materials or goods and services. Supply chain management is a broad concept which focuses on the link, cooperation and coordination among the members of the chain (e.g. suppliers, distributors, customers) and also processes (Christopher, 2016). Among the main functions in supply chain management, there exist; supplying raw materials or other inputs, procurement activities, operations management, distributing products and reaching out to customers by achieving supply base management, strategic orientation, cross-functional groups and process driven approach (Monczka et al., 2015).

Establishing supply network and building mutually beneficial relationships with supply chain members enable organizations to have vital resources. These resources can also be accepted as valuable, unique and inimitable assets from the perspective of resource-based view. This is because members of a supply chain integrate information systems and share knowledge or create new knowledge. Moreover, they exert cooperative efforts in a wide variety of activities including i.e. product development, product design, marketing research, pricing, placing and promotion (Cooper et al. 1997). The cooperation, coordination and value sharing capabilities are valuable resources for organizations which will lead them achieve effective supply chain management.

Supply Chain Management for Sustainable Competitive Advantage

Since the supply chain management capabilities serve as valuable and specific resources of organizations, they are also accepted as the assets for sustainable competitive advantage over competitor firms. The reason is that, in the supply chains, companies are fully cooperative and they share knowledge with each other as evident in the literature (e.g. Marra et al., 2012; Shih et al., 2012). These close relationships foster innovation and new knowledge generation that enhance cost reductions and quality improvements in products. Moreover, supply chains provides more productivity and effectiveness in every step of value creating. All of these results provide sustainable competitive advantage for the firms in the supply chain over their rival firms in the market.

Every effort for increasing the quality of supply chain network and strengthening the relationships between member organizations in the network is beneficial for the sustainable competitive advantage. These efforts are likely to be generating open communication channels, knowledge sharing, supporting suppliers contributions for improving quality, cost and performance, developing management and technical capabilities (Lawson et al., 2015; Monczka et al., 2015; Prajogo et al., 2012). A typical supply chain for generating sustainable competitive advantage is shown on Figure 2.

Integration of Human Resources Management and Supply Chain Management

Latest developments in supply chain management necessitate a more holistic and multidisciplinary approach so as to sustain advantages obtained in the supply chain network. There are studies in the literature proposing more multidisciplinary perspectives for supply chain management (e.g. Hirsch-Hadorn et al., 2006; Pagell and Shevchenko, 2014). Hence, one of the most important perspectives for enriching the supply chain management is absolutely the human resources. This is because human resources are vital for customer and supplier partnerships (Jick, 1990), operations management (Boudreau, et al., 2003; Palšaitis et al., 2017), retailing (Rosenthal et al., 1997), storage and distribution (Kasonde and Steele,

2017), knowledge generation and sharing (Cabrera and Cabrera, 2005), leadership and innovation (Chen and Huang, 2009).

Figure 2. Supply chain as a sustainable competitive advantage

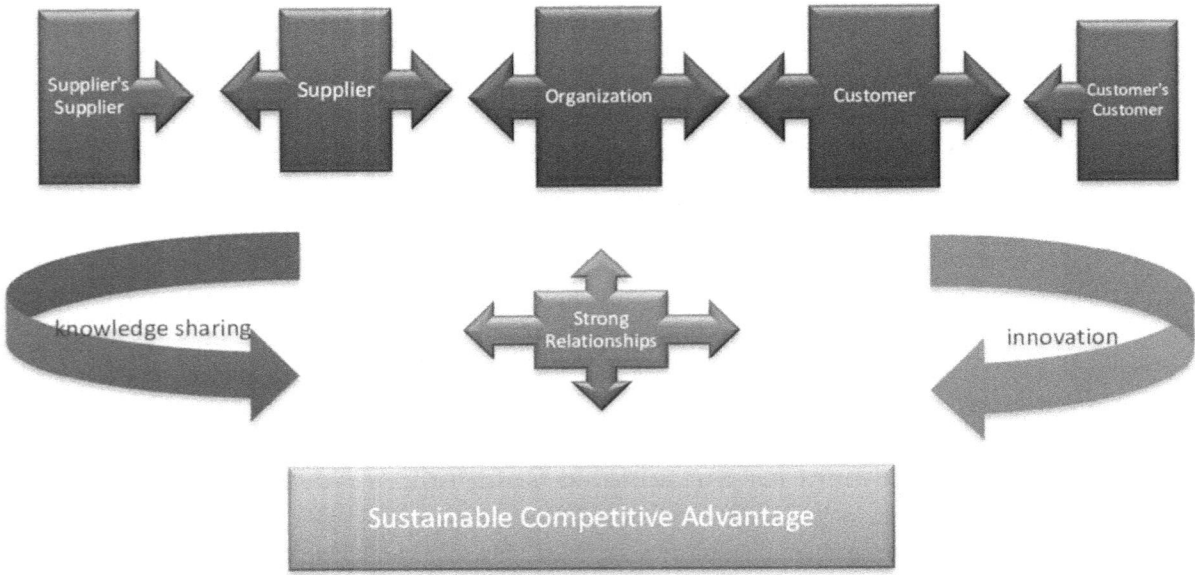

Although human resources management and supply chain management were treated as unrelated structures in the past, now there are enough evidences that their union is beneficial for organizations (e.g. Lengnick-Hall et al., 2013; Scarbrough, 2000). Specifically, in the literature there are studies revealing the causal relationship between human resources and supply chain management both in causal (e.g. Vanichchinchai and Igel, 2011) and empirical research (e.g. Gómez-Cedeño et al., 2015).

Human resources strengthen the capacity of supply chain management and for this reason the integration of them provides effectiveness and efficiency in organizations and ease them to have competitive advantage in the market. This is due to several reasons:

1. Human resources practices and systems reinforce the effectiveness of supply chain practices and help supply chain employees develop new skills and competencies (Ellinger and Ellinger, 2014),
2. Human resources management increases the likelihood of supply chain management success, since it develops training and development programs for supply chain employees, evaluates their performance and gives feedback to them and also rewards and motivates them for high performance (Gowen and Tallon, 2003),
3. Recruiting and selecting high-skilled and highly motivated employees helps improve supply chain management performance,
4. A multi-functional approach to supply chain management reinforces the competitiveness of supply chains since they are already compromised of several business functions like, human resources management, financial management, marketing management, operations management, etc.

5. Human resources management provides basis for positive attributions towards the supply chain by creating a suitable climate which in turn enhances employees to demonstrate favorable behaviors,
6. Human resources management helps employees build effective communication channels not only in their own organizations but also in the supply chain. This process fosters knowledge sharing and improves creativity in the supply chain.

The integration of human resources management and supply chain management for sustainable competitive advantage is reinforced by some additional factors which are illustrated on Figure 3.

Figure 3. The integration of human resources management and supply chain management

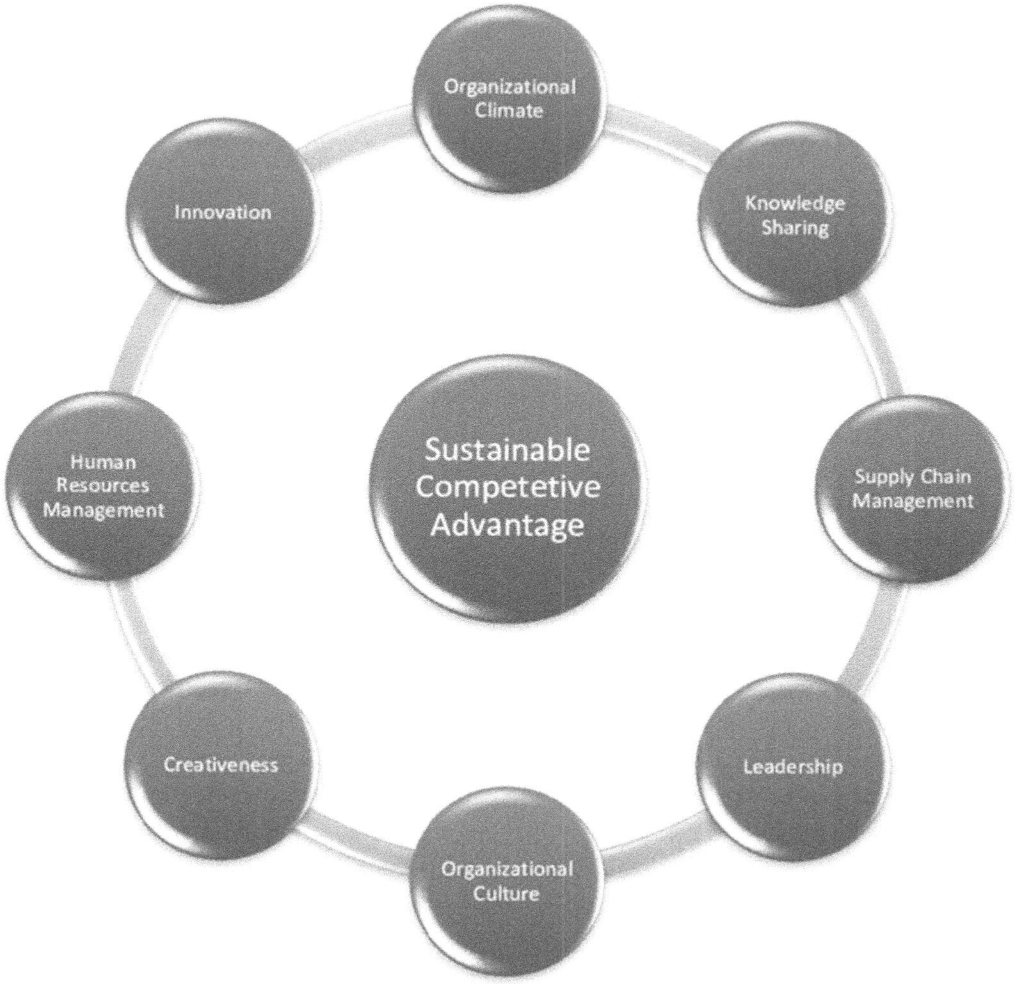

FUTURE RESEARCH DIRECTIONS

As noted in this chapter that there are limited studies revealing the advantage of the integration of human resources management and supply chain management. So, it is obvious that there is a strong need for future research. Future research should examine the role of each human resource practices on reinforcing the supply chain management. Moreover, examining which activities should be conducted by human resources managers to provide supportive and creative climate for supply chain practices would be beneficial for the literature. Also, empowering employees should be investigated so as to reveal its advantages on supply chain management.

Another underemphasized point in the literature is leadership. The subject of which types of leadership foster the linkage between human resources management and supply chain management would be expected to be beneficial. Although there are more studies concentrated on the link between green human resources and green supply chain management, there is still need for more research on these topics. Specifically the effects of talent management on supply chain management capabilities should also be observed. Lastly, it is vital to note here that, in the future researchers should test the effects of this linkage between human resources and supply chain by conducting empirical research including qualitative, quantitative or mixed methods.

CONCLUSION

In business life no organizations can survive without generating adaptation strategies and capabilities to changing demands and conditions. To achieve this, organizations look for ways to acquire strategic and valuable resources. Furthermore, in such a competitive market, organizations do not only need to survive, but they also need to have resources, capabilities and capacities which others do not possess. This is because, with such resources and assets, organizations will have competitive advantages. Resource-based view suggests that organizations will have competitive advantage when their resources are valuable, exceptional and unique.

In this chapter, human resources management and supply chain management functions are examined for providing sustainable competitive advantage from the perspective of resource-based view. Based on a conceptual framework with the help of previous studies it was understood that, human resources management functions and systems enhance supply chain management efficiency. The integration of these two business functions enhances sustainable competitive advantage for several ways. When employees are trained, developed and motivated for gaining competencies for effective supply chain practices, organizations gain advantage by building strong relationships with other organizations in the supply network, especially with the suppliers. Furthermore, with the help of human resources management, organizational support for creativeness and knowledge sharing becomes apparent. This is a vital factor for effectiveness in supply chain. Moreover, human resources practices and systems make it possible to manage talents of employees, empower them and demonstrate high performance in supply chain activities.

Consequently, when human resources of an organization are high-skilled, highly motivated and committed to knowledge creation and sharing, also with the help of human resources management systems, the flow of materials, knowledge and assets in the supply chain occurs perfectly. When materials are acquired, produced and distributed on right time, right quantity and at right quality, organizations gain competitive advantage. Additionally when these organizations share knowledge and enhance innovation, they attain sustainable competitive advantage.

REFERENCES

Aaker, D. A. (1989). Managing assets and skills: The key to a sustainable competitive advantage. *California Management Review*, *31*(2), 91–106. doi:10.2307/41166561

Aït Razouk, A., Bayad, M., & Wannenmacher, D. (2009). Strategic human resource management and tacit knowledge transfer: A case study. *Human Systems Management*, *28*(1-2), 77–82. doi:10.3233/HSM-2009-0694

Albrecht, S. L., Bakker, A. B., Gruman, J. A., Macey, W. H., & Saks, A. M. (2015). Employee engagement, human resource management practices and competitive advantage: An integrated aproach. *Journal of Organizational Effectiveness: People and Performance.*, *2*(1), 7–35. doi:10.1108/JOEPP-08-2014-0042

Alexy, O., West, J., Klapper, H., & Reitzig, M. (2018). Surrendering control to gain advantage: Reconciling openness and the resource-based view of the firm. *Strategic Management Journal*, *39*(6), 1704–1727. doi:10.1002mj.2706

Amarakoon, U., Weerawardena, J., & Verreynne, M. L. (2018). Learning capabilities, human resource management innovation and competitive advantage. *International Journal of Human Resource Management*, *29*(10), 1736–1766. doi:10.1080/09585192.2016.1209228

Amit, R., & Belcourt, M. (1999). Human resources management processes: A value-creating source of competitive advantage. *European Management Journal*, *17*(2), 174–181. doi:10.1016/S0263-2373(98)00076-0

Amit, R., & Schoemaker, P. J. (1993). Strategic assets and organizational rent. *Strategic Management Journal*, *14*(1), 33–46. doi:10.1002mj.4250140105

Ansoff, H. I. (1965). *Corporate strategy: An analytic approach to business policy for growth and expansion*. McGraw-Hill.

Aragón-Correa, J. A., & Sharma, S. (2003). A contingent resource-based view of proactive corporate environmental strategy. *Academy of Management Review*, *28*(1), 71–88. doi:10.5465/amr.2003.8925233

Armstrong, M., & Taylor, S. (2020). *Armstrong's handbook of human resource management practice*. Kogan Page Publishers.

Barney, J. (1991). Firm resources and sustained competitive advantage. *Journal of Management*, *17*(1), 99–120. doi:10.1177/014920639101700108

Barney, J. B. (2012). Purchasing, supply chain management and sustained competitive advantage: The relevance of resource-based theory. *The Journal of Supply Chain Management*, *48*(2), 3–6. doi:10.1111/j.1745-493X.2012.03265.x

Barney, J. B., & Wright, P. M. (1998). On becoming a strategic partner: The role of human resources in gaining competitive advantage. *Human Resource Management*, *37*(1), 31–46. doi:10.1002/(SICI)1099-050X(199821)37:1<31::AID-HRM4>3.0.CO;2-W

Bendoly, E. (2006). Editorial-Incorporating behavioral theory in OM empirical models. *Journal of Operations Management*, *24*(6), 735–736. doi:10.1016/j.jom.2006.09.003

Boudreau, J., Hopp, W., McClain, J. O., & Thomas, L. J. (2003). On the interface between operations and human resources management. *Manufacturing & Service Operations Management*, *5*(3), 179–202. doi:10.1287/msom.5.3.179.16032

Bromiley, P., & Rau, D. (2016). Operations management and the resource based view: Another view. *Journal of Operations Management*, *41*(1), 95–106. doi:10.1016/j.jom.2015.11.003

Bryson, J. M., Ackermann, F., & Eden, C. (2007). Putting the resource-based view of strategy and distinctive competencies to work in public organizations. *Public Administration Review*, *67*(4), 702–717. doi:10.1111/j.1540-6210.2007.00754.x

Cabrera, E. F., & Cabrera, A. (2005). Fostering knowledge sharing through people management practices. *International Journal of Human Resource Management*, *16*(5), 720–735. doi:10.1080/09585190500083020

Cabrera-Suárez, K., De Saá-Pérez, P., & García-Almeida, D. (2001). The succession process from a resource-and knowledge-based view of the family firm. *Family Business Review*, *14*(1), 37–48. doi:10.1111/j.1741-6248.2001.00037.x

Chadwick, C., & Dabu, A. (2009). Human resources, human resource management, and the competitive advantage of firms: Toward a more comprehensive model of causal linkages. *Organization Science*, *20*(1), 253–272. doi:10.1287/orsc.1080.0375

Chatzoglou, P., & Chatzoudes, D. (2018). The role of innovation in building competitive advantages: An empirical investigation. *European Journal of Innovation Management*, *21*(1), 44–69. doi:10.1108/EJIM-02-2017-0015

Chen, C. J., & Huang, J. W. (2009). Strategic human resource practices and innovation performance—The mediating role of knowledge management capacity. *Journal of Business Research*, *62*(1), 104–114. doi:10.1016/j.jbusres.2007.11.016

Christopher, M. (2016). *Logistics & Supply Chain Management*. Pearson.

Coates, T. T., & McDermott, C. M. (2002). An exploratory analysis of new competencies: A resource based view perspective. *Journal of Operations Management*, *20*(5), 435–450. doi:10.1016/S0272-6963(02)00023-2

Colbert, B. A. (2004). The complex resource-based view: Implications for theory and practice in strategic human resource management. *Academy of Management Review*, *29*(3), 341–358. doi:10.5465/amr.2004.13670987

Collins, C. J., & Clark, K. D. (2003). Strategic human resource practices, top management team social networks, and firm performance: The role of human resource practices in creating organizational competitive advantage. *Academy of Management Journal*, *46*(6), 740–751.

Conner, K. R. (1991). A historical comparison of resource-based theory and five schools of thought within industrial organization economics: Do we have a new theory of the firm? *Journal of Management, 17*(1), 121–154. doi:10.1177/014920639101700109

Cooper, M. C., Lambert, D. M., & Pagh, J. D. (1997). Supply chain management: More than a new name for logistics. *International Journal of Logistics Management, 8*(1), 1–14. doi:10.1108/09574099710805556

DeCenzo, D. A., Robbins, S. P., & Verhulst, S. L. (2016). *Fundamentals of human resource management*. John Wiley & Sons.

Dubey, R., Gunasekaran, A., Childe, S. J., Blome, C., & Papadopoulos, T. (2019). Big data and predictive analytics and manufacturing performance: Integrating institutional theory, resource-based view and big data culture. *British Journal of Management, 30*(2), 341–361. doi:10.1111/1467-8551.12355

Dunford, B. B., Snell, S. A., & Wright, P. M. (2001). *Human resources and the resource based view of the firm* (CAHRS Working Paper# 01-03). Ithaca, NY: Cornell University.

Eisenhardt, K. M., & Martin, J. A. (2000). Dynamic capabilities: What are they? *Strategic Management Journal, 21*(10-11), 1105–1121. doi:10.1002/1097-0266(200010/11)21:10/11<1105::AID-SMJ133>3.0.CO;2-E

Ellinger, A. E., & Ellinger, A. D. (2014). Leveraging human resource development expertise to improve supply chain managers' skills and competencies. *European Journal of Training and Development, 38*(1/2), 118–135. doi:10.1108/EJTD-09-2013-0093

Flynn, B. B., & Flynn, E. J. (2005). Synergies between supply chain management and quality management: Emerging implications. *International Journal of Production Research, 43*(16), 3421–3436. doi:10.1080/00207540500118076

Garg, D., Narahari, Y., & Viswanadham, N. (2006). Achieving sharp deliveries in supply chains through variance pool allocation. *European Journal of Operational Research, 171*(1), 227–254. doi:10.1016/j.ejor.2004.08.033

Gómez-Cedeño, M., Castán-Farrero, J. M., Guitart-Tarrés, L., & Matute-Vallejo, J. (2015). Impact of human resources on supply chain management and performance. *Industrial Management & Data Systems, 115*(1), 129–157. doi:10.1108/IMDS-09-2014-0246

Gowen, C. R. III, & Tallon, W. J. (2003). Enhancing supply chain practices through human resource management. *Journal of Management Development, 22*(1), 32–44. doi:10.1108/02621710310454842

Hadorn, G. H., Bradley, D., Pohl, C., Rist, S., & Wiesmann, U. (2006). Implications of transdisciplinarity for sustainability research. *Ecological Economics, 60*(1), 119–128. doi:10.1016/j.ecolecon.2005.12.002

Hugos, M. H. (2018). *Essentials of supply chain management*. John Wiley & Sons. doi:10.1002/9781119464495

Jabbour, C. J. C., & de Sousa Jabbour, A. B. L. (2016). Green human resource management and green supply chain management: Linking two emerging agendas. *Journal of Cleaner Production, 112*, 1824–1833. doi:10.1016/j.jclepro.2015.01.052

Jick, T. D. (1990). Customer–supplier partnerships: Human resources as bridge builders. *Human Resource Management, 29*(4), 435–454. doi:10.1002/hrm.3930290408

Kasonde, M., & Steele, P. (2017). The people factor: An analysis of the human resources landscape for immunization supply chain management. *Vaccine, 35*(17), 2134–2140. doi:10.1016/j.vaccine.2017.01.084 PMID:28364921

Kim, M., Song, J., & Triche, J. (2015). Toward an integrated framework for innovation in service: A resource-based view and dynamic capabilities approach. *Information Systems Frontiers, 17*(3), 533–546. doi:10.100710796-014-9505-6

Koberg, E., & Longoni, A. (2019). A systematic review of sustainable supply chain management in global supply chains. *Journal of Cleaner Production, 207*, 1084–1098. doi:10.1016/j.jclepro.2018.10.033

Kor, Y. Y., & Mahoney, J. T. (2004). Edith Penrose's (1959) contributions to the resource-based view of strategic management. *Journal of Management Studies, 41*(1), 183–191. doi:10.1111/j.1467-6486.2004.00427.x

Lado, A. A., & Wilson, M. C. (1994). Human resource systems and sustained competitive advantage: A competency-based perspective. *Academy of Management Review, 19*(4), 699–727. doi:10.5465/amr.1994.9412190216

Lawson, B., Krause, D., & Potter, A. (2015). Improving supplier new product development performance: The role of supplier development. *Journal of Product Innovation Management, 32*(5), 777–792. doi:10.1111/jpim.12231

Lengnick-Hall, M. L., Lengnick-Hall, C. A., & Rigsbee, C. M. (2013). Strategic human resource management and supply chain orientation. *Human Resource Management Review, 23*(4), 366–377. doi:10.1016/j.hrmr.2012.07.002

Mahdi, O. R., Nassar, I. A., & Almsafir, M. K. (2019). Knowledge management processes and sustainable competitive advantage: An empirical examination in private universities. *Journal of Business Research, 94*, 320–334. doi:10.1016/j.jbusres.2018.02.013

Mahoney, J. T. (2001). A resource-based theory of sustainable rents. *Journal of Management, 27*(6), 651–660. doi:10.1177/014920630102700603

Markley, M. J., & Davis, L. (2007). Exploring future competitive advantage through sustainable supply chains. *International Journal of Physical Distribution & Logistics Management, 37*(9), 763–774. doi:10.1108/09600030710840859

Marra, M., Ho, W., & Edwards, J. S. (2012). Supply chain knowledge management: A literature review. *Expert Systems with Applications, 39*(5), 6103–6110. doi:10.1016/j.eswa.2011.11.035

Mayfield, M., Mayfield, J., & Wheeler, C. (2016). Talent development for top leaders: Three HR initiatives for competitive advantage. *Human Resource Management International Digest, 24*(6), 4–7. doi:10.1108/HRMID-07-2015-0120

Mentzer, J. T., DeWitt, W., Keebler, J. S., Min, S., Nix, N. W., Smith, C. D., & Zacharia, Z. G. (2001). Defining supply chain management. *Journal of Business Logistics, 22*(2), 1–25. doi:10.1002/j.2158-1592.2001.tb00001.x

Monczka, R. M., Handfield, R. B., Giunipero, L. C., & Patterson, J. L. (2015). *Purchasing and supply chain management*. South-Western Cengage Learning.

Noe, R. A., Hollenbeck, J. R., Gerhart, B., & Wright, P. M. (2013). *Fundamentals of human resource management*. McGraw-Hill.

Omondi-Ochieng, P. (2019). Resource-based theory of college football team competitiveness. *The International Journal of Organizational Analysis, 27*(4), 834–856. doi:10.1108/IJOA-04-2018-1403

Pagell, M., & Shevchenko, A. (2014). Why research in sustainable supply chain management should have no future. *The Journal of Supply Chain Management, 50*(1), 44–55. doi:10.1111/jscm.12037

Palšaitis, R., Čižiūnienė, K., & Vaičiūtė, K. (2017). Improvement of warehouse operations management by considering competencies of human resources. *Procedia Engineering, 187*, 604–613. doi:10.1016/j.proeng.2017.04.420

Penrose, E. T. (1959). *The theory of the growth of the firm*. John Wiley and Sons.

Peteraf, M. A. (1993). The cornerstones of competitive advantage: A resource-based view. *Strategic Management Journal, 14*(3), 179–191. doi:10.1002mj.4250140303

Porter, M. E. (1980). *Competitive strategy: Techniques for analyzing industries and competitors*. Free Press.

Porter, M. E. (1985). *Competitive advantage: Creating and sustaining superior performance*. Free Press.

Powell, T. C. (2001). Competitive advantage: Logical and philosophical considerations. *Strategic Management Journal, 22*(9), 875–888. doi:10.1002mj.173

Powell, T. C., & Dent-Micallef, A. (1997). Information technology as competitive advantage: The role of human, business, and technology resources. *Strategic Management Journal, 18*(5), 375–405. doi:10.1002/(SICI)1097-0266(199705)18:5<375::AID-SMJ876>3.0.CO;2-7

Prajogo, D., Chowdhury, M., Yeung, A. C., & Cheng, T. C. E. (2012). The relationship between supplier management and firm's operational performance: A multi-dimensional perspective. *International Journal of Production Economics, 136*(1), 123–130. doi:10.1016/j.ijpe.2011.09.022

Rosenthal, P., Hill, S., & Peccei, R. (1997). Checking out service: Evaluating excellence, HRM and TQM in retailing. *Work, Employment and Society, 11*(3), 481–503. doi:10.1177/0950017097113005

Rugman, A. M., & Verbeke, A. (2002). Edith Penrose's contribution to the resource-based view of strategic management. *Strategic Management Journal, 23*(8), 769–780. doi:10.1002mj.240

Santos, F. C. (2000). Integration of human resource management and competitive priorities of manufacturing strategy. *International Journal of Operations & Production Management, 20*(5), 610–628. doi:10.1108/01443570010318986

Scarbrough, H. (2000). The HR implications of supply chain relationships. *Human Resource Management Journal*, *10*(1), 5–17. doi:10.1111/j.1748-8583.2000.tb00010.x

Shibin, K. T., Dubey, R., Gunasekaran, A., Hazen, B., Roubaud, D., Gupta, S., & Foropon, C. (2020). Examining sustainable supply chain management of SMEs using resource based view and institutional theory. *Annals of Operations Research*, *290*(1), 301–326. doi:10.100710479-017-2706-x

Shih, S. C., Hsu, S. H., Zhu, Z., & Balasubramanian, S. K. (2012). Knowledge sharing—A key role in the downstream supply chain. *Information & Management*, *49*(2), 70–80. doi:10.1016/j.im.2012.01.001

Snell, S. A., Youndt, M. A., & Wright, M. (1996). Establishing a framework for research in strategic human resource management: Merging resource theory and organizational learning. *Research in Personnel and Human Resources Management*, *14*, 61–90.

Sodhi, M. S. (2015). Conceptualizing social responsibility in operations via stakeholder resource-based view. *Production and Operations Management*, *24*(9), 1375–1389. doi:10.1111/poms.12393

Tallman, S., Jenkins, M., Henry, N., & Pinch, S. (2004). Knowledge, clusters, and competitive advantage. *Academy of Management Review*, *29*(2), 258–271. doi:10.5465/amr.2004.12736089

Vanichchinchai, A., & Igel, B. (2011). The impact of total quality management on supply chain management and firm's supply performance. *International Journal of Production Research*, *49*(11), 3405–3424. doi:10.1080/00207543.2010.492805

Wernerfelt, B. (1984). A resource-based view of the firm. *Strategic Management Journal*, *5*(2), 171–180. doi:10.1002mj.4250050207

Wright, P. M., Dunford, B. B., & Snell, S. A. (2001). Human resources and the resource based view of the firm. *Journal of Management*, *27*(6), 701–721. doi:10.1177/014920630102700607

Wright, P. M., McMahan, G. C., & McWilliams, A. (1994). Human resources and sustained competitive advantage: A resource-based perspective. *International Journal of Human Resource Management*, *5*(2), 301–326. doi:10.1080/09585199400000020

Wu, Z., & Choi, T. Y. (2005). Supplier–supplier relationships in the buyer–supplier triad: Building theories from eight case studies. *Journal of Operations Management*, *24*(1), 27–52. doi:10.1016/j.jom.2005.02.001

ADDITIONAL READING

Farndale, E., Paauwe, J., & Boselie, P. (2010). An exploratory study of governance in the intra-firm human resources supply chain. *Human Resource Management*, *49*(5), 849–868. doi:10.1002/hrm.20387

Hohenstein, N. O., Feisel, E., & Hartmann, E. (2014). Human resource management issues in supply chain management research: A systematic literature review from 1998 to 2014. *International Journal of Physical Distribution & Logistics Management*, *44*(6), 434–463. doi:10.1108/IJPDLM-06-2013-0175

Hunt, S. D., & Davis, D. F. (2008). Grounding supply chain management in resource-advantage theory. *The Journal of Supply Chain Management*, *44*(1), 10–21. doi:10.1111/j.1745-493X.2008.00042.x

Hunt, S. D., & Davis, D. F. (2012). Grounding supply chain management in resource-advantage theory: In defense of a resource-based view of the firm. *The Journal of Supply Chain Management, 48*(2), 14–20. doi:10.1111/j.1745-493X.2012.03266.x

Li, S., Ragu-Nathan, B., Ragu-Nathan, T. S., & Rao, S. S. (2006). The impact of supply chain management practices on competitive advantage and organizational performance. *Omega, 34*(2), 107–124. doi:10.1016/j.omega.2004.08.002 PMID:17876965

Pablos, P. O. D., & Lytras, M. D. (2008). Competencies and human resource management: Implications for organizational competitive advantage. *Journal of Knowledge Management, 12*(6), 48–55. doi:10.1108/13673270810913612

Progoulaki, M., & Theotokas, I. (2010). Human resource management and competitive advantage: An application of resource-based view in the shipping industry. *Marine Policy, 34*(3), 575–582. doi:10.1016/j.marpol.2009.11.004

Schuler, R. S., & MacMillan, I. C. (1984). Gaining competitive advantage through human resource management practices. *Human Resource Management, 23*(3), 241–255. doi:10.1002/hrm.3930230304

Singh, R., Sandhu, H. S., Metri, B. A., & Kaur, R. (2010). Relating organised retail supply chain management practices, competitive advantage and organisational performance. *Vision (Basel), 14*(3), 173–190. doi:10.1177/097226291001400303

Stevens, G. C. (1990). Successful supply-chain management. *Management Decision, 28*(8), 25–30. doi:10.1108/00251749010140790

Zaid, A. A., Jaaron, A. A., & Bon, A. T. (2018). The impact of green human resource management and green supply chain management practices on sustainable performance: An empirical study. *Journal of Cleaner Production, 204*, 965–979. doi:10.1016/j.jclepro.2018.09.062

KEY TERMS AND DEFINITIONS

Human Resources: All of the resources related to the human side of organizations including the capabilities, skills, educational background, personality and behaviors of employees.

Human Resources Management: The organizational function in which employees are recruited, selected, placed, trained, developed, evaluated, and compensated.

Resource-Based View: A strategic and managerial concept generated for determining the most valuable, rare, and strategic resources to attain sustainable competitive advantage.

Supply Chain: A network in which organizations build strong relationships with suppliers and distributors to provide goods and services.

Supply Chain Management: An integrated system of flow of materials, money and knowledge so as to provide goods and services to customers effectively and efficiently.

Sustainable Competitive Advantage: Organizational abilities, assets and capacity which are valuable and inimitable by other organizations.

This research was previously published in the Handbook of Research on Recent Perspectives on Management, International Trade, and Logistics; pages 69-84, copyright year 2021 by Business Science Reference (an imprint of IGI Global).

Chapter 21
A Critical Assessment and Enhancement of Metrics for the Management of Scarce Human Resources

Olaf Radant
https://orcid.org/0000-0002-0646-1268
Ginkgo Management Consulting, Germany

Vladimir Stantchev
https://orcid.org/0000-0002-1551-419X
SRH Hochschule-Berlin, Germany

ABSTRACT

The effect of digitalization and its transformative power in all aspects of corporate strategies and organizations are visible everywhere. As leaders try to make sense of the "digital tornado" and prepare, try out, and set courses in new business directions, the authors propose to take a step back and focus on what is still at the core of corporate change – the people of your organization. In this chapter, the authors reflect on the forces and challenges that employees are facing in times of rapid and digitally driven change. They also mirror this, considering structural, sociological, and demographic change in the workforce, especially with regards to younger employees. They provide a set of fundamental metrics that can quantify the human resource strategy of an organization to derive measures which can be controlled via a DMAIC cycle. This contribution is an extended version of and includes an enhanced set of metrics to address challenges of digitalization and agile work environments. Further, approaches to possible solutions and first steps for an implementation in companies are presented.

DOI: 10.4018/978-1-6684-3873-2.ch021

INTRODUCTION

Keywords like agile or fluid organizations are on everyone's mind right now and rightfully so. In a permanently changing business environment, companies and especially their HR strategies and departments must adapt to changes in the market to be more agile and customer oriented than ever before. To succeed, the productivity of employees is the key solution to changing business environments. Therefore, the allocation and retention of these scarce resources in the best possible way is even more important.

One of the main challenges for companies is to improve the enterprise not only on the side of the organizational and process level but to develop new strategies and approaches in human resource management (Painter-Morland, Kirk, Deslandes, & Tansley, 2019). Only a symbiosis of the discipline's information technology, organization, psychology and management will enable relevant and indispensable employees to promote loyalty to the company (Adeinat & Kassim, 2019). Loyal employees are happy employees which ultimately fosters the productivity of employees.

In this fast pace environment, it is simply not enough to just implement organizational changes like building squads, tribes or chapters. There are several other layers to that topic that a company must consider if it wants to be more responsive (Dhir, 2019; Thorgren & Caiman, 2019). The usage of big data, state of the art technology and new ways of working are building a triangle to enable a company to manage and lead their personnel in the best way possible and to derive measures for further development.

Companies need to put their people first. In times of automation, robotics and artificial intelligence, innovations by a company's own employees will be the lifeblood and key to success in the future. A loss of talent should not be tolerated in any circumstances and companies need to take the appropriate measures to counteract such possibly harmful developments (Singh, 2019).

This paper is a critical examination and an enhancement of the results of the research of the authors from 2016 in the area of agile organizations and leadership. Also, findings and experiences of the implementation of this framework from several projects with different companies are included.

DERIVATION OF METRICS FOR A FRAMEWORK TO MANAGE SCARCE RESOURCES – THE RESULTS OF 2016

The results from the initial structured literature review are still as important as they were in 2016. Therefore, we haven´t change the finding that are presented in the following section.

Search Strategy

The research strategy follows the model of the structured literature review. It includes search terms, literature resources and search process, which are detailed one by one as follows:

The search string has to be defined based on the population under study, and the keywords and their synonyms. Therefore, the study population includes the relevant keywords from all five layers of the proposed framework.

With this population the list of keywords and their synonyms, used to generate the search string was:

- employee wages: employee salary
- education of employees: education of personnel, untapped potential in organizations

- psychological development of employees: psychological changes of employees
- workplace environment: workplace optimization, workplace development
- Work life balance

To generate the search string a Boolean language with AND and OR, and quotation marks for exact text were used. The string format is recognized by all sources of information used, as well as many others. So finally the search string used is as follows: ("employee wages" OR "employee salary") AND ("education of employees" OR "education of personnel" OR "untapped potential in organizations") AND ("psychological development of employees" OR "psychological changes of employees ") AND ("workplace environment " OR "workplace optimization" OR "workplace development") AND ("work life balance"). Given the variety of sources to be consulted electronically via the web, five electronic databases of established literature resources were used for the present SLR. This systematic review considers the following list of sources:

- IEEE Digital Library (http://ieeexplore.ieee.org),
- ACM Digital Library (http://portal.acm.org),
- SpringerLink (http://link.springer.com),
- IDEAS Digital Library (http://ideas.repec.org/) and
- ScienceDirect (http://www.sciencedirect.com/)

The SLR was conducted in the following way: at first, the named digital libraries were searched according to the defined search items for relevant publications. Second, the publications found were reviewed by title and abstract in order to estimate their relevance for the topic. After that, a full text review was conducted which leads to a set of primary studies. Fourth, the primary studies were reviewed whether there are references to other publications with other relevant papers to this topic.

Figure 1. Search process metrics

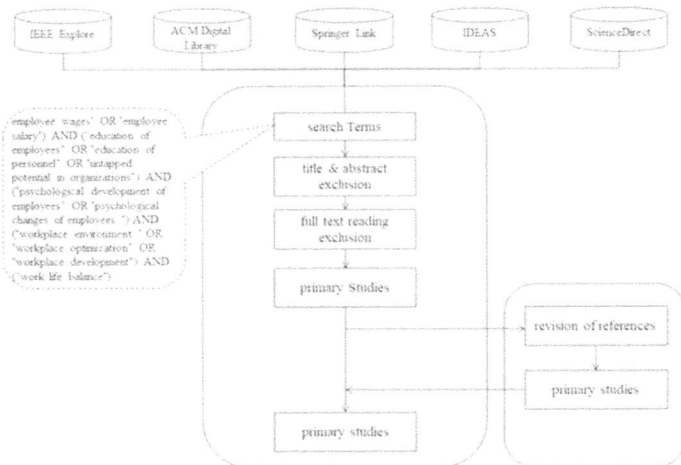

The data extracted from each paper was documented and kept in a reference manager. After identification of the papers, the following data was extracted:

- source (journal or conference),
- title,
- authors,
- publication year,
- classification,
- summary of the research, including which questions were solved.

The goal of this SLR is to identify which preliminary papers and other scientific materials are published about corresponding metrics up to this date (August 2015). For this reason, it is mandatory to develop a set of research questions to search, identify and extract the significant publications. The questions this work proposes are the following:

RQ1: What are metrics for the identified factors for fundamental wages for high skilled employees in IT-departments?

RQ2: What are metrics for the identified factors for measures to optimize and educate the employee pool with reference to untapped potential within an organization?

RQ3: What are metrics for the identified factors for measures to support the psychological healthiness of the employees?

RQ4: What are metrics for the identified factors for measures to optimize the work environment of the employees?

RQ5: What are metrics for the identified factors for measures to support the work-life balance of the employees?

The search strategy, search terms, literature resources and search process will be the same as before. The specific approach can be read in the previous chapter.

The data extracted from each paper was documented and kept in a reference manager. After identification of the papers, the following data was extracted:

- source (journal or conference),
- title,
- authors,
- publication year,
- classification,
- summary of the research, including which questions were solved.

Based on the criteria for classifying papers, all the papers were reviewed, and the corresponding data was extracted. With the information collected in that form, it was possible to obtain qualitative and quantitative information to answer the planned research questions. In particular, the following information was collected:

- metrics for fundamental wages for high skilled employees in IT-departments,
- metrics for measures to optimize and educate the employee pool,
- metrics for measures to support the psychological healthiness,
- metrics for measures to optimize the work environment,
- metrics for measures to support the work-life balance.

For a better understanding and organization of the researched publications, a classification was conducted. For this purpose, the publications were divided into five areas. These areas are defined according to the search terms.

Included and excluded studies are presented in stages following the search process described above. Because of the length of some of the list of references, they have been hosted online and can be downloaded at any time.

Once initial search results were retrieved, an exclusion/inclusion review procedure was applied with the following inclusion and exclusion criteria:

- Inclusion criteria:
  - publications that match one of the search items,
  - publications, that are related to an allocation of resources in scarce resource situations,
  - publications, that are related to Information Technology departments,
  - publications, that are related to more than five EU-Countries,
  - publications, that are related to a highly qualified workforce,
  - publications, that are related to the research questions.
- Exclusion criteria:
  - publications that not match one of the search items,
  - publications that are published before or on the 31.12.2004.

Primary studies obtained in the first phase

The first search was conducted in August 2015, returning 300 papers in total. Irrelevant and duplicate papers were removed and a set of 296 unique papers remained. The result is shown in the following table.

Table 1. First phase results without filtering

IEE Explore	43
ACM Digital Library	51
ScienceDirect	81
Springer Link	55
IDEAS	69
Total	300
Total (without duplication)	**296**

Of the 191 searched papers, 4 were duplicated. Table 2 shows the distribution of the searched papers and its source with reference to the search items.

Table 2. First phase results – distribution without duplication

	IEEE	ACM	Science Direct	Springer Link	IDEAS	Sum
Employee wages	9	4	22	10	13	58
Education of employees	14	23	10	8	12	67
Psychological development of employees	5	5	20	22	16	68
Workplace environment	5	9	9	5	9	37
Work life balance	8	10	20	9	19	66
Sum	41	51	81	54	69	**296**

Of these remaining 296 results, 43 were discarded for being incomplete or not related to the research questions. Of the 253 remaining, 124 were excluded after reading the title and abstract, which left 129 results to be filtered by full-text reading using the inclusion and exclusion criteria. If there was doubt about the relevance of a publication, it was included in the relevant group, leaving the possibility of discarding the paper during the next phase when the full texts of the papers were studied.
Primary studies obtained from the second phase

Table 3. First phase results

Excluded	124
Included	**129**
Total	253

The reference lists from the primary studies obtained from the first phase were retrieved and the same filters previously used were applied to them. A total of 129 references were obtained by reading the title and abstract. From these references, 71 were finally selected using the criteria of inclusion and exclusion.

Table 4. Second phase results

Excluded	58
Included	**71**
Total	129

Findings

In this section, the final papers will be matched to the research questions. Furthermore, the research questions are tried to answer with the help of these papers. The findings of the SLR are shown in the following chapter in which the five research questions are answered.

RQ1: What are metrics for fundamental wages for high skilled employees in IT-departments?

1. Earnings per employee /timeframe after tax
   This metric represents the earnings of an employee after payment of taxes, social insurance and other indirect labour costs (Eurostat, 2013). Labour Costs are the total expenditure spend by employers for the purpose of employing staff. The following table contains data on average hourly labour costs which are defined as total labour costs divided by the corresponding number of hours worked by the yearly average number of employees, expressed in full-time units. Labour costs cover wages and salaries and non-wage costs, employers social contributions plus taxes less subsidies (Eurostat, 2014a).

Recommended Assessment Method: Labour costs in € per timeframe.

2. Earnings per employee /timeframe after tax/ incl. incentives
   This metric represents the earnings of an employee after payment of taxes, social insurance and other indirect labour costs inclusive possible incentives like bonus or car services (Weiguo & Yanchun, 2010).

Recommended Assessment Method: Earnings per employee per timeframe

3. Labour costs per unit or price/unit labour cost ratio pre-tax
   Given that software development is highly intensive in human capital, the key factor for industry is personnel (Devarakonda, Gupta, & Tang, 2013). Therefore it is important to compare the costs of a produced unit or the provision of a service with the needed labour costs to achieve the result (Diao, Keller, Parekh, & Marinov, 2007; Gabrisch, 2008).

Recommended Assessment Method:

$$Labour\ costs\ per\ unit = \frac{labour\ costs}{price\ per\ unit}$$

4. Future growth of labour costs pre-taxes
   Since labour costs one of the important factors for the competitiveness of an IT-Company it is therefore essential to project the future growth of labour costs. This can be achieved through a consideration of different variables for example the raise of employee compensation in average (including wages, salaries in cash and in kind, employers' social security contributions), vocational

training costs, other expenditure such as recruitment costs, spending on working clothes and employment taxes regarded as labour costs minus any subsidies received (Eurostat, 2014a).

Recommended Assessment Method: Projection via statistical extrapolation

5. Comparison of indirect labour costs in European Union
    This metric evaluates the differences of indirect labour costs in different countries and in this case for the EU, but it can easily be extended to other counties or continents.

Recommended Assessment Method: For similar currencies, like in the Euro Area, the statistics of the EU can be used. For countries with different currencies the calculation is the following.

$$Comparison\ of\ labour\ costs\ in\ non\ \ countries = \frac{labour\ costs\ country\ A}{labour\ costs\ country\ B}$$

Country A represents the basis value and country B the reference value of the calculation. Via this calculation, an index is created which allows a company to calculate the value of every spend Euro of labour costs in comparison to other countries.

Gender Pay Gap

The gender pay gap, which represents the imbalances in wages between men and women. It is defined as the difference between the average gross hourly earnings of men and women expressed as a percentage of the average gross hourly earnings of men (Eurostat, 2015). The following table represents the unadjusted gender pay gap in Enterprises employing 10 or more employees which compares the hourly earnings of men and women in general (Peruzzi, 2015).

Due to the high number of variables, the gender pay gap needs to be adjusted. The general aim of adjusting the gender pay gap is to include a range of personal characteristics which may differ, and which may therefore explain some of the difference in average pay between men and women. Reasons for the difference can be the chosen profession, the level of experience, negotiating skills etc. For example, the adjusted gender pay gap in Germany in the year 2010 was 7% (Destatis, 2014).

Recommended Assessment Method: Comparison of the average salary of men to the average salary of women, if necessary, per department.

6. Earnings per IT-employee in average to other departments after tax and earnings per IT-employee in average to other (IT-) companies after tax
    Since wages are not the, but one of the important reasons for employees to stay in a company it is necessary for a firm to pay satisfying wages (Institute for opinion survey Allensbach, 2014). Since every employee defines the term satisfying on their own, a company should orientate their wage policy on the average payments of the market.

Recommended Assessment Method: Comparison of the average salary of department one to the average salary of department two.

RQ2: What are metrics for measures to optimize and educate the employee pool with reference to untapped potential within an organization?

1. Real output (gross value added) divided by the total number of persons employed
    The essential aim of a company is to produce goods and sell them on the market to make profit. The performance of employees is a substantial factor to achieve this goal. Gross value added (GVA) measures the contribution to an economy of an individual producer, industry, sector or region (Financial Times Lexicon, 2013). It provides a financial value for the amount of goods and services that have been produced, less the cost of all inputs and raw materials that are directly attributable to that production. This metric can serve as an orientation and major benchmark for the success of implemented measures in a company.

Recommended Assessment Method:

$$\text{Gross value added} = \frac{Real\,output\,in\quad per\,timeframe}{Number\,of\,employees}.$$

2. Evaluation of throughput time and lead time
    For any company, productivity is one of the major ratios. The evaluation of throughput time and lead time offers a deeper insight in this complex issue. Throughput time is the period required for a material, part, or subassembly to pass through the manufacturing process and lead time is the number of minutes, hours, or days that must be allowed for the completion of an opetion or process, or must elapse before a desired action takes place (van den Bos, Kemper, & de Waal, 2014).

Recommended Assessment Method: Throughput time and lead time in timeframe.

3. Expenditure for education of a company or department
    It is assumed, that higher economic value added transmits to higher human capital correlated with higher level of education and thus higher expenditure of education (Verner, 2011). This metric analyses the investments in training of employees and is calculated by dividing the total costs of training and the number of employees of the whole company or a specific department.

Recommended Assessment Method: Sum per timeframe per company or department.

4. Number of employees in training per year
    This metric simply states the number of employees in training measures per year. It can easily be extended to gain further information by dividing the number of employees in training per year and the total number of employees in a company and putting these figures in a relation.

Recommended Assessment Method:

$$\frac{Number\ of\ employees\ in\ training}{Total\ number\ of\ employees} \times 100$$

5. Employee requirements analysis
    A company has to be aware of the development of their employees and the needed profiles to gain a growth in productivity and revenues in future (Dainty, Raidén, & Neale, 2009). Therefore, an analysis to answer the following questions is needed:

    *   Which profiles does the company need to fulfil my strategic goals?
    *   How many employees does the company need to achieve my strategic goals?
    *   How many new hires does the company have to recruit per year?

    This analysis should be a recurrent process every year. Also, the underlying assumptions and goals need to be audited as well to determine necessary changes. A possible qualitative method to gain the needed information could be a survey conducted with the different heads of departments. To conduct a quantitative measurement, basic elements for an employee requirements analysis are needed:

    *   the current employee capacity,
    *   estimations for the workload in a timeframe per employee or workstation,
    *   an evaluation of the proposed changes with a consideration of the impact on the required staffing and
    *   a plausibility check against references.

    After the collection of the data, possible seasonal peaks need to be added to estimate the utilization of the employees over a timeframe of a year.

    Recommended Assessment Method: Statistics of current utilization of employees in comparison to needed utilization to fulfil requirements of the market.

6. Employee potential analysis
    The identification and development of high potential employees (commonly referred to as talent management) has been pinpointed by both management scholars and practitioners as one of the major challenges faced by the twenty-first century human resource function (Dries, 2012). So as important as the information which profiles, I need in the future is the information what kind of potential and potentials does the company have in their organization. With a tool like an employee survey in connection with employee work appraisals it is possible to derive employees which for example want to work in other departments, want to develop themselves in a certain way or are feasible candidates for executive careers. Further, the identification of those "hidden gems" in an organization is crucial (Pollitt, 2005).

Recommended Assessment Method: Survey with middle management executives to filter possible candidates.

7. Age distribution analysis
   The complex of the best age distribution of a company, in contrast to the size distribution, is rarely discussed in the literature (Cirillo, 2010; Coad, 2010). For the conduction of an age distribution analysis, only few data are needed:

   - date of birth
   - date of entering the company
   - department
   - organizational status
   - contract status (temporary employment, permanent contract)

Recommended Assessment Method: Analysis via age statistics of departments and hierarchical structure of company.

8. Employee performance management system (goal setting, monitoring and evaluation)
   The employee performance management system is an organized assessment process for employees in a company or department of a company. It is used to ensure that employee's activities and outcomes are aligned with the organisation's objectives and strategy (Becker, Antuar, & Everett, 2011). Employees that achieve the organisational goals are rewarded with favourable reviews and bonuses in line with their performance and contribution to the organisation. Tools of an employee performance management system are e.g. goal-setting (planning), monitoring (feedback) and evaluation (appraising) (Decramer, Smolders, & Vanderstraeten, 2013).

Recommended Assessment Method: Existence of employee performance management system and corresponding policies to foster a satisfying usage.

9. IT vacancies in company
   This metric represents the vacant positions of an IT-department. According to BITKOM, the information technology union in Germany, there are 41.000 job vacancies for IT experts in Germany in 2013 (Pfisterer, 2013). Almost three-quarters (71%) of ICT companies are looking for software developers, especially with skills on cloud computing (53%) and big data (44%), followed by knowledge in social media (34%), programming of classical web properties (28%) and mobile websites or apps (26%). Similar numbers can be found in mostly all countries in Europe (Empirica, 2013, 2014).

Recommended Assessment Method: Investigation of current utilization and possible utilization if all market requirements are met.

10. Female integration and leadership programs
    It is necessary to encourage cultural changes to make IT departments more attractive to women. However, there are high hurdles, as expectations diverge greatly from those of men (Ahuja, 2002) and interpersonal skills are a much more important factor (Cappelli, 2000). Female students and

employees attach above average importance to a profession that can be arranged well with family and private life, in which they can help other people and promises them a good working environment (Institute for opinion survey Allensbach, 2014).

Recommended Assessment Method: Existence of diversity programs and corresponding policies to foster a satisfying usage. Yearly evaluation of the success of these programs via survey and statistical analysis. The programs should be aligned to actual needs of women, which should be compiled via survey.

Retention Rate

The retention rate is a figure which represents a comparison the number of employees which are employed by the beginning and the end of a year or timeframe. This number is an important indicator for a company because it displays the number of employees which needed to be recruited only compensate the losses of workforce of the year and remain on the same headcount (Allen, Armstrong, Reid, & Riemenschneider, 2009).

Recommended Assessment Method:

$$Retention\ rate = \frac{number\ of\ employees\ t_1}{number\ of\ employees\ t_2}$$

11. Gap analysis between existing and targeted skills of employees
    The company's strategy sets the target for the development of the organization and its employees. It defines the necessary skills that are needed to fulfil the goals of the strategy. A gap analysis between existing and targeted skills of employee's reveals missing skills and capabilities of the workforce in comparison to the strategy of the company. If a company conduct this analysis, they will be able to allocate and promote them in the best possible way. Often the actual employment is not equal to the actual skills of the employees (Colomo-Palacios, Casado-Lumbreras, Soto-Acosta, García-Peñalvo, & Tovar-Caro, 2013).

Recommended Assessment Method: Survey with middle management executives and derivation of an action plan to close identified gaps.

12. Educational strategy and lifelong learning programs
    Due to a highly changing IT-environment, lifelong learning is a must for every employee and company to stay competitive. Companies that support a culture of lifelong learning will have a competitive edge on the market. These programs are an essential part of the educational strategy of a company and should be audited at least every year to include necessary changes and review the success of the learning measures. As many observers have noted, programmers can easily become obsolete when the programming languages that they know fall out of favour (Cappelli, 2000). A constant development of the knowledge of the employees is thus fundamentally.

Recommended Assessment Method: Existence, development and yearly evaluation of educational strategies and corresponding policies.

13. Knowledge management/ transfer initiative/ system

    KM is fundamentally the management of the corporate knowledge and intelligent assets that can improve a range of organizational performance characteristics and add value by enabling an enterprise to act more intelligently (Bose, 2004). In a globalized world, it has become crucial for global organisations to have the ability to convert all precious data to useful knowledge (Hasan & Zhou, 2015). The challenge for companies is the motivation of the employees to share their knowledge with other people, which will be even more important with a scarcity of resources and a reduction of available employees with needed knowledge. Especially for IT-departments it is necessary to implement knowledge management initiatives because often head monopolies are generated due to a needed high degree of specialization (Corbin, Dunbar, & Zhu, 2007).

Recommended Assessment Method: Existence of a knowledge management system and corresponding policies to foster the usage and data quality.

RQ3: What are metrics for measures to support the psychological healthiness of the employees?

1. Company culture

   The company culture defines the acting, work ethic and behaviour of employees on nearly every level of a company. According to Ken Favaro, Senior Manager of the consulting company Strategy& the culture often tops the strategy of a company (Favaro, 2014): "Strategy is on paper whereas culture determines how things get done. Anyone can come up with a fancy strategy, but it's much harder to build a winning culture. Moreover, a brilliant strategy without a great culture is 'all hat and no cattle,' while a company with a winning culture can succeed even if its strategy is mediocre. Plus, it's much easier to change strategy than culture." Strategy and culture need to foster themselves and mature together to achieve the desired results (Dickmann, 2006).

Recommended Assessment Method: Figure determined via employee survey aligned with the company's vision, values, norms.

2. Hierarchical structure and organizational permeability

   The structure of a company and its permeability is one of the important factors for young graduates (Institute for opinion survey Allensbach, 2014). This generation of possible employees is unlike other generations, a segment of employees which is considered to be in need of focused attention and with unique and challenging expectations like participation in companies decision making (Shatat, El-Baz, & Hariga, 2010). Therefore, a company needs to foster and promote employee participation especially through the middle management of the company. Also, a fair amount of decent career opportunities is necessary, to provide a sufficient permeability of the organization which meet the expectations of younger employees.

Recommended Assessment Method: Degrees of freedom of management level in given timeframe and existence of employee participation programs.

3.   Employee expectations
      Organizations need to make sure that not only the performance and the learning agility of their employees is high, but also their commitment. In order to achieve high commitment, organizations need to establish an employment relationship with them based on mutual benefit (Dries, 2013). Demands and expectations of employees are based on the job they perform, the possibilities of progress, the ways of controlling their work, as well as compensation. Also, the expectations of highly educated workforce, and their satisfaction with the workplace and the assignments they fulfil is a very important factor of the success of the organisation. (Jaksic & Jaksic, 2013).

Recommended Assessment Method: Expectations gathered with employee survey.

4.   Existence of employee wellbeing programs
      Employee wellbeing programs are not initiatives to pamper employees, they are helping an organization to reduce illness and therefore a loss of workforce (Dunning, 2015). Organizations health and wellness offerings have expanded beyond traditional programs, which formerly focused on physical health, to integrated well-being programs are now including mental and emotional health, financial health, work life effectiveness, and workplace environment and stress (Spears, 2012).

Recommended Assessment Method: Existence of policies and programs developed with employee representatives or work councils.

5.   Psychological induced Sick days of employees
      IT employees facing high job demands (Zeng, Zheng, & Shi, 2010). The stress factor with the highest influence on the working people is emotional exhaustion. In consideration of this, it does not surprise that the impact of the demographic change on IT personnel is relatively high compared to other departments. (Zeng et al., 2010). The outcome of this situation is a high rate of mental or physiological illnesses, like boreout and burnout (Christensen & Knardahl, 2012) and a lower level of quality and productiveness of the department and the employees.

Recommended Assessment Method: Psychological induced Sick days of employees in a given timeframe:

$$\frac{psychological\ induced\ sick\ day\ of\ company\ or\ department\ in\ timeframe}{number\ of\ workdays\ in\ timeframe}$$

6.   Rate of change in used technology/ timeframe and time of adoption
      Additionally, to the factors mentioned above, Lee et al. pointed out that technologically induced stress is a crucial multiplier. This is caused due strong technological transformation of an organization (Lee, Foo, & Cunningham, 1995).

Recommended Assessment Method: The assessment method depends on the type of the organization. The measurements could be releases per year, major patches and updates or the number of new applications or programs which are launched in a given timeframe.

7. Job complexity
   The complexity of a working field is still one of the main reasons for psychological diseases like depression or burnout. Complexity is a term which will define every employee for himself. However, the stress report of the German governmental organization BAUA conducted a survey which researched the main stressors for a complex work environment. These stressors are e.g. different tasks at the same time, pressure from deadlines or interruptions in the workplace (Kliner, Rennert, & Richter, 2015).

Recommended Assessment Method: Variety of working fields per employee and number of waiting tasks. Distractions, interruptions and necessary task-switching in the workplace identified via process analysis or employee survey

8. IT misuse and security policy breaches in the workplace
   With the commonly known positive effects of Information Technology, several downsides came along with this development. Several studies explored the implications of IT-induced technology stress, technology addiction and IT misuse in the workplace. (Monideepa Tarafdar, John D'Arcy, Ofir Turel, & Ashish Gupta, 2014).

Recommended Assessment Method: Number of reported incidents.

9. Reported incidents of workplace violence, mobbing and bullying
   The definition of workplace violence, mobbing and bullying refers to situations where a person repeatedly and over a period of time is exposed to negative acts (i.e. constant abuse, offensive remarks or teasing, ridicule or social exclusion) on the part of co-workers, supervisors, or subordinates (Branch, Ramsay, & Barker, 2013; Einarsen, 1999). These issues have obviously large consequences for individuals, including higher body-mass, chronic diseases and illnesses, certified and uncertified absence which results in unproductive employee behaviour (Boddy, 2014; Devonish, 2013).

Recommended Assessment Method: Number of reported incidents.

10. Job (in)security: status of used employment contracts in an organization
    The definition of job insecurity is regarded as an overall concern about the continuous existence of the workplace in the future (Chambel & Fontinha, 2009). Besides the economic development of a company, research has proven that the contract status of employees has both, positive and negative influence of the well-being of an employee (Bernhard-Oettel, Sverke, & De Witte, 2005; Martin Olsthoorn, 2014).

Recommended Assessment Method:

$$\frac{number\ of\ part\ time\ comtracts}{number\ of\ all\ employee\ contracts}$$

11. Work environment and office design which supports employee networking determined via employee survey

    Human beings need interaction and company in their personal and professional life for their well-being in order to perform on a high level and be productive. From a psychological standpoint, an office should have several characteristics to support this issue like social density, view quality and type or light quality (Aries, Veitch, & Newsham, 2010).

Recommended Assessment Method: Existence of an office plan which includes latest scientific research and has not only the best utilization of workstations as its goal.

RQ4: What are metrics for measures to optimize the work environment of the employees?

1. Implementation of proper security policies like EU directive 89/391, DIN 4543

   The objective of Directives like 89/391/EEC or DIN 4543 is to foster and improve the protection of workers through measures regarding the prevention of work-related risks, the protection of safety and health, the elimination of risk and accident factors and also the informing, consultation, balanced participation and physiological training of workers (Niskanen, Naumanen, & Hirvonen, 2012). These directives implemented responsibilities and obligations of employers in form of risk assessments, creation of protection, prevention services and the duties of (Martínez Aires, Rubio Gámez, & Gibb, 2010).

Recommended Assessment Method: Existence of workplace design plans and implemented policies which supports psychological healthiness.

2. High level of flexibility in the work organization and allocation of employees via job rotation, job enlargement, job enrichment

   A flexible organization supports various positive developments for a company and its employees. Besides the mentioned benefits for the knowledge transfer within the organization, learning, development and a higher satisfaction of the employees (Bennett, 2003), different environments and movements support a greater psychological health and reduce ergonomic risks (Otto & Scholl, 2012).

Recommended Assessment Method: Existence of policies that support a high level of flexibility in the organization.

RQ5: What are metrics for measures to support the work-life balance of the employees?

1. Work-life/ family policies

   The goal of work-life or families in companies is to generate greater productivity of employees due to a higher satisfaction. These policies assisting employees to simultaneously fulfil their responsibilities both at work and at home (McDonald, Guthrie, Bradley, & Shakespeare-Finch, 2005). These policies cannot just include regulations and rules for part-time employment or paid leave. They also have to support career opportunities especially for women, because despite women and mothers increased involvement in paid work, little change has taken place in the organization and provision of unpaid domestic and care work (Baxter & Chesters, 2011).

Recommended Assessment Method: Existence of Work-life/ family policies, which are constantly reviewed via employee and management surveys to provide the best balance between

2. Financial costs/ benefits of company in the context of Work-life Balance
    Work-life initiatives are often a reason for discussion within the management of companies because they don't provide instant improvement of productivity or an increase of revenue (Todd & Binns, 2013). Of course, the installed initiatives need to be controlled and questioned if they provide the anticipated results. A controlling of the implemented policies requires an inclusion of different variables and an evaluation via a business case. Obvious variables are the productivity of the individual, the number of sick days due to child illness, annual spending in work-life initiatives or the number of employees which use these opportunities. Also, further variables like turnover intention, retention rate have to take into consideration as well. This case should be a long-term examination of the retrieved figures and statistics.

Recommended Assessment Method: Calculation of a business case which considers the relevant productivity measures of the company or department and the employee. This Business Case should be controlled in certain timeframes.

3. Innovative working (time) models
    There are several different working models which can be offered to employees. The most common models are trust-based working time (Singe & Croucher, 2003), flexible work schedule (Coenen & Kok, 2014), annualised and variable working hours (Corominas & Pastor, 2010), job-sharing (Crampton & Mishra, 2005), part-time employment (Rose, Hewitt, & Baxter, 2013), home office (Răvaş, 2013), telework (Coenen & Kok, 2014) and working-time accounts (Lusa & Pastor, 2011).

Recommended Assessment Method: Calculation of a business case which considers the relevant productivity measures of the company or department and the employee. The variables of this business case should be controlled in certain timeframes.

4. Availability of employees
    The common business day for employees has a nine to five schedule and is limited to workdays. In reality, these agreements are shifting to overtime duties and a permanent availability via e-mail or other communication channels (McMenamin, 2007). As described in earlier chapters, permanent availability has negative effects on employees and could result in a decline of productivity. Several companies like BMW, Volkswagen and Mercedes block the devices of their employees after certain working hours to limit communication and allow the employees to recover from the workday (Kaufmann, 2014).

Recommended Assessment Method: Communication (traffic) in leisure time of employees.

5. Working time per week per timeframe
    The working time per employee in a given timeframe has important effects on employees. It defines in the most part its productivity, rates of error or the well-being in of the individual in general. For

a society and also a company in a whole it provides advantages regarding social equity through redistribution of working hours and raises voluntary social engagement (Buhl & Acosta, 2015).

Recommended Assessment Method: Evaluation of the working hours of employee or department per timeframe.

NOVEL RESEARCH CONTRIBUTIONS SINCE CONDUCTING THE ORIGINAL RESEARCH

The results of 2016 have not lost their actuality but are more important than ever. Since a large number of companies are trying to transfer their rigid hierarchies in agile and fluid organizations, the results of 2016 have to be extended by one area, which is called *organizational conditions and leadership*. Consequently, a sixth research question was built.

RQ6: What are metrics for measures to support organizational change and leadership for agile organizations?

The answering of this question follows the same presented approach of 2016 supplemented with the search term organisational conditions and leadership. The new search string as Boolean language with AND and OR, and quotation marks for exact text is the following. The search string is used as follows: ("employee wages" OR "employee salary") AND ("education of employees" OR "education of personnel" OR "untapped potential in organizations") AND ("psychological development of employees" OR "psychological changes of employees ") AND ("workplace environment " OR "workplace optimization" OR "workplace development") AND ("work life balance") AND ("organizational conditions" OR "organizational change" OR "leadership"). The following metrics present the enhancement of the framework researched and developed in 2016.

1. Methodological competence of employees and leadership
   The transformation of a hierarchical to an agile organisation is a huge step for companies. The basis for the transformation is a deep understanding of agile frameworks and methods. Starting from the top of the organization, leaders as role models, have to understand the opportunities, challenges and risks that are associated with these changes. Employees on the other hand need the methodological competence to execute the changes on the operational level (Niemi & Laine, 2016). A change like this can only be successful if both parties comply to an agile organization (Poston & PATEL, 2016).

Recommended Assessment Method: Training investments devoted to methodological development of employees

2. Speed of decision making
   Due to the high rate of usage of agile methods in projects and organizations, the speed of decision making has to adapt to that circumstance as well (Feng et al., 2018). This is a huge task, especially if companies are in the change from traditional, hierarchical decision-making to shared decision-

making (Moe, Aurum, & Dybå, 2012) processes. But, to overcome the challenge of fast changing markets and environments, this is a necessity (Radant, Colomo-Palacios, & Stantchev, 2016b).

Recommended Assessment Method: Needed time for selected decisions in organizations

3. Distribution of responsibilities
   As mentioned, companies must adapt to the fast-changing environments of the economic world. One part of this adoption is the right distribution of responsibilities. If the goal of the company is an agile environment, leaders must let traditional views of responsibilities go and trust their employees that they make the right decisions (Malgorzata Ali, 2016). These circumstances have to be formalized in job descriptions of the employees to empower them to make these decisions without having to fear consequences.

Recommended Assessment Method: Content of job specifications and job descriptions

4. Innovative power of an organization
   To gain and generate business value, companies must understand and quickly respond to a number of market forces and innovations are the key to success (Paz, 2017). Due to the increasingly rapid pace of change in technology, organizations need to foster innovative thinking within their employees and departments (Chesbrough & Brunswicker, 2013). The basis are processes that support innovations and an environment that allows employees to share and discuss thoughts and ideas.

Recommended Assessment Method: Number of innovations in a timeframe; patent utilization ration, funding of innovation processes; Success rate of projects which are based on innovation; number of innovative ideas by employees in a timeframe

5. Servant leadership
   (Front-line) managers are critical to an organization's performance as their ability to motivate and direct staff is fundamental. But several studies have shown that they are often too focused on their operative work (Holtzhausen & de Klerk, 2018; Pathak, Parker, & Holesgrove, 2015). Therefore, they are not able to concentrate on the development and management of their staff. The results are e.g. underperforming employees and less innovation. Furthermore, the actual corporate environments are mostly not helpful to counteract these problems. Because of the short-term focus and the figure-driven orientation of the companies, long-term investments in employees and a change of the way of work are often seen as "lost money". But in the current labour environment with less loyal employees and scarcity of resources, this is a harmful strategy in the long run.

Recommended Assessment Method: Results gathered with employee survey or distribution of working hours of (front) line managers

6. Agility of the organization
   Since the process of the change to an agile organization is tough and time intense, it is reasonable to measure the progress of the transformation regularly. This will allow the employees to see the

success on a quantified level and it allows leadership to identify possible weak spots to derive measures for optimization (Horlach, Drews, Schirmer, & Boehmann, 2017).

Recommended Assessment Method: Organizational model; Flexibilization of teams and work

After the inclusion of a sixth area, the distribution of metrics is the following

Table 5. Distribution of metrics after including a sixth area

Area	Metrics
Employee wages	8
Education of employees and untapped potential in organizations	14
Psychological development of employees	11
Workplace environment	2
Work life balance	5
Organizational conditions and leadership	6
Sum	**46**

These metrics provide companies with a toolset to assess themselves and quantify their actual state regarding labour in general and their human resource policies in particular. Especially regarding the expectations of generation Y. The identified metrics answer the question "how" human resources in times of scarcity of talent should be measured. The presented metrics enable organizations and their respective executives to assess their already implemented measures derive potential threats as well as potential new measures to complement the existing strategies.

The presented findings are subject to the usual limitations of a literature review. The results completely rely on previously published research, the availability of these studies using the method outlined in the search methodology and the appropriateness of these studies with the criteria of the selection/exclusion procedure. However, the results provide a strong fundament for further research activities.

APPROACHES TO SOLUTIONS FOR COMPANIES

There are no "silver bullet" solutions and rarely best practices to tackle these kind of personnel related challenges. On the one hand because of the inherent differences in every organization and on the other hand due to the pace of the economic, sociological and technology changes. The best example for the fundamental impact of e.g. a technological change is the introduction of the iPhone eleven years ago and how it changed our ways of working, thinking and living.

Every generation has different perceptions and opinions how something should be done. Statistics show that the generation of the baby-boomers will retire in the next five to seven years (Eurostat, 2014b). This means, that companies have exactly this timeframe to incorporate changes in their organizations to meet the changed expectations of the workforce. These new expectations refer mostly to the management of their respective superiors and the way how a workday is organized. For employees of the generation

Y and Z, flexibility is one of the most important factors. The basis for that is the management with goals and objectives.

This mind-set requires to challenge the actual processes and helps to include levels of flexibility in the work environment which will have profound effects on the productivity of the employees. The developments of the fourth industrial revolution are showing a lot of possible methods and tools which would benefit the employees as well as the companies. Apart from that, quantitative surveys showed that the salary is still an important factor for the workforce, but it is far away from being the most important one as it was in earlier years and decades. A study has shown, that 36% of employees would give up $5,000 a year in salary to be happier at work (Rebecca Henderson, 2018). Employee compensation is a short-term solution which satisfies short-term needs, when not raised significantly periodically.

The overall aim of HR departments should be to provide companies with insights to better understand possible long-term needs of the staff and how they can align them with e.g. organizational optimization of the company. With the goal of identifying all pain points and value drivers of their employees, companies need a holistic and transparent view on their employees which allows them to identify threats, derive measures and evaluate their success (Radant, 2014). The first step is a common understanding regarding the way of working, the company culture and the way in which employees should be managed. This leads to an understanding of how the organization should be built. Any discussion about tools and technology should follow this step and incorporate chosen strategic and organizational concepts.

Changes regarding organization, personnel and culture are critical endeavours which should be implemented with caution and enough time(Radant, Colomo-Palacios, & Stantchev, 2014). Initiatives in this area mostly aren't failing because of budget or time constraints but because of the impatience of management. As mentioned earlier, there is no simple pattern for employee management in the future. Nevertheless, every manager can gain loyalty of employees with the following nine steps to improve productivity.

1. Measure employee engagement – Start measuring employees' passion about work and the work environment.
2. Identify what employees like – By gathering praise in addition to concerns, your company can find out if its engagement efforts make a meaningful, lasting contribution to employees.
3. Help employees see the big picture – Employees want to contribute and make a difference. Help them to see the big picture and how they contribute to a functioning whole. This will also empower employees to make decisions, which raises commitment.
4. Use training to increase confidence – Employees need training to do their job confidently and to facilitate career advancement.
5. Promote team building – Encourage team building activities among employee groups to create trust and acceptance. Strong, loyal teams provide acceptance, and teamwork between departments provides positive communication and work atmosphere.
6. Build a supportive environment – Often, dissatisfaction with wages and benefits masks problems that relate back to acceptance by a team or manager. Encourage employees to be outspoken.
7. Don't be afraid to tell the truth – Respect your employees through degrees of transparency. Give your employees information to understand shifts in corporate policy.
8. Recognize employee contributions – Recognition from a supervisor of at least two ranks above an employee makes a meaningful, engaging difference in employee morale.

9.   Controlling of measures – Use DMAIC cycles to control the effects and benefits of the implemented measures. Use this method also to assess yourself and your actions.

Besides the daily use of these nine steps, if a company wants to take on this journey, transparency is key and therefore data is key (Joh & White, 2018). Regular employee surveys can be a first step for companies but normally they will deliver the same old results and insights. It is therefore recommended to build small interdisciplinary teams, depending on the size of the organization, that deliver their results and messages anonymously. With this method, management can identify possible weak spots and find room for improvement. The basis for productivity is always leadership that reflects the needs of the employees and a state-of-the-art technology that fits the current and future business needs (Eom, 2015). If that foundation is in place, companies should concentrate their activities on measures that foster productivity, happiness and loyalty. Unfortunately, there are no interchangeable measure that will work in every company and every department, every time.

The leadership of a company has to understand how the way we work is already changing and will change in the upcoming years (Bellou, Xanthopoulou, Gkorezis, Xanthopoulou, & Gkorezis, 2018). To be in the hunt for high profile employees, they must adapt to that circumstance. The following figure is specifying the actual situation and compares the current working culture with the working life of employees in the future.

It is therefore important, that leadership and employees work together to find solutions that benefits the organization and the personnel at the same time with the common goal to achieve higher productivity, more innovation and higher retention (Radant et al., 2016b). An important side effect is that management shows to the employees, that they are taking the needs of the employees seriously and that they are an integral part of the company. If detailed measures are identified, the company should not be hesitant to pilot them in a department or small area in the organization and if they are working, spread them out to other departments.

FIRST STEPS OF AN IMPLEMENTATION IN ORGANIZATIONS

As stated, employees are the most important asset for a company, especially in times of digitalization and scarcity of talent. Therefore, the most important information for management is what kind of employees does the company need in the future. Based on extensive research and different customer engagements in several industries, the authors recommend the following steps to tackle this issue in a sustainable manner.

Besides the already mentioned need for transparency, the first step is to create the awareness that change is required. Key questions are:

1.   What is the strategic situation of the company and which employees are needed in the future to achieve the strategic goals?
2.   How good is my retention rate in comparison to my competitors and what are the reasons for the results?
3.   What is the cultural situation in the organization? Is there a gap between expectations of employees and management and if yes, why is that the case?

The main output from this phase is the case for change, which outlines the necessity for a transformation. This case states the current situation of the company with regards to human resources and the organization as well as actual challenges and emerging threats. These examples could be, for instance, a high retention rate or a high average age of employees. It is important that the management team acknowledges that the organization needs to change, recognizes potential and significant benefits and has engaged employees to conduct further analysis (Radant, Colomo-Palacios, & Stantchev, 2016a). Possible further results are age analyses or demographic outlooks for the company and the market, possible references from other companies currently facing similar problems.

The second step is the combination of the results of the key questions with the company's strategy to identify gaps between the long-term goals of the organization and the current state. The outcomes will lead to a better understanding of the situation and are necessary to derive measures going forward, weather they are cultural, technical or strategy based. To measure the success of the initiative, 46 metrics to quantify the success are presented in this publication.

The journey to put your people first, is a journey that the whole organization has to go together. Organizations are responsible for the development and healthiness of their employees. This was already the case before, but now it is a much more needed prerequisite than ever for a company to be successful. This challenge can't be solved by HR departments alone and is a task for every manager, every day of the week.

REFERENCES

Ahuja, M. K. (2002). Women in the information technology profession: A literature review, synthesis and research agenda. *European Journal of Information Systems*, *11*(1), 20–34. doi:10.1057/palgrave.ejis.3000417

Allen, M. W., Armstrong, D. J., Reid, M. F., & Riemenschneider, C. K. (2009). IT Employee Retention: Employee Expectations and Workplace Environments. *Proceedings of the Special Interest Group on Management Information System's 47th Annual Conference on Computer Personnel Research*, 95–100. 10.1145/1542130.1542148

Aries, M. B. C., Veitch, J. A., & Newsham, G. R. (2010). Windows, view, and office characteristics predict physical and psychological discomfort. *Journal of Environmental Psychology*, *30*(4), 533–541. doi:10.1016/j.jenvp.2009.12.004

Baxter, J., & Chesters, J. (2011). Perceptions of Work-Family Balance: How Effective are Family-Friendly Policies? *Australian Journal of Labour Economics*, *14*(2), 139–151.

Becker, K., Antuar, N., & Everett, C. (2011). Implementing an employee performance management system in a nonprofit organization. *Nonprofit Management & Leadership*, *21*(3), 255–271. doi:10.1002/nml.20024

Bellou, V., Xanthopoulou, D., Gkorezis, P., Xanthopoulou, D., & Gkorezis, P. (2018, April 27). *Organizational change and employee functioning : Investigating boundary conditions*. doi:10.4324/9781315386102-2

Bennett, B. (2003). Job rotation. *Training Strategies for Tomorrow*, *17*(4), 7.

Bernhard-Oettel, C., Sverke, M., & De Witte, H. (2005). Comparing three alternative types of employment with permanent full-time work: How do employment contract and perceived job conditions relate to health complaints? *Work and Stress, 19*(4), 301–318. doi:10.1030/02678370500408723

Boddy, C. R. (2014). Corporate Psychopaths, Conflict, Employee Affective Well-Being and Counterproductive Work Behaviour. *Journal of Business Ethics, 121*(1), 107–121. doi:10.100710551-013-1688-0

Bose, R. (2004). Knowledge management metrics. *Industrial Management & Data Systems, 104*(5/6), 457–468. doi:10.1108/02635570410543771

Branch, S., Ramsay, S., & Barker, M. (2013). Workplace Bullying, Mobbing and General Harassment: A Review. *International Journal of Management Reviews, 15*(3), 280–299. doi:10.1111/j.1468-2370.2012.00339.x

Buhl, J., & Acosta, J. (2015). Work less, do less? *Sustainability Science*, 1–16. doi:10.100711625-015-0322-8

Cappelli, P. (2000). Is there a shortage of information technology workers. *A Report to McKinsey and Company*. Retrieved from http://knowledge.wharton.upenn.edu/papers/979.pdf

Chambel, M. J., & Fontinha, R. (2009). Contingencies of Contingent Employment: Psychological Contract, Job Insecurity and Employability of Contracted Workers. *Revista de Psicología del Trabajo y de las Organizaciones, 25*(3), 207–217. doi:10.43211576-59622009000300002

Chesbrough, H., & Brunswicker, S. (2013). *Managing Open Innovation in Large Firms*. Academic Press.

Christensen, J. O., & Knardahl, S. (2012). Work and headache: A prospective study of psychological, social, and mechanical predictors of headache severity. *Pain, 153*(10), 2119–2132. doi:10.1016/j.pain.2012.07.009 PMID:22906887

Cirillo, P. (2010). An analysis of the size distribution of Italian firms by age. *Physica A, 389*(3), 459–466. doi:10.1016/j.physa.2009.09.049

Coad, A. (2010). Investigating the Exponential Age Distribution of Firms. *Economics, 4*(17), 1–30A.

Coenen, M., & Kok, R. A. W. (2014). Workplace flexibility and new product development performance: The role of telework and flexible work schedules. *European Management Journal, 32*(4), 564–576. doi:10.1016/j.emj.2013.12.003

Colomo-Palacios, R., Casado-Lumbreras, C., Soto-Acosta, P., García-Peñalvo, F. J., & Tovar-Caro, E. (2013). Competence gaps in software personnel: A multi-organizational study. *Computers in Human Behavior, 29*(2), 456–461. doi:10.1016/j.chb.2012.04.021

Corbin, R. D., Dunbar, C. B., & Zhu, Q. (2007). A three-tier knowledge management scheme for software engineering support and innovation. *Journal of Systems and Software, 80*(9), 1494–1505. doi:10.1016/j.jss.2007.01.013

Corominas, A., & Pastor, R. (2010). Replanning working time under annualised working hours. *International Journal of Production Research, 48*(5), 1493–1515. doi:10.1080/00207540802582227

Crampton, S. M., & Mishra, J. M. (2005). Job Sharing: A Viable Work Alternative for the New Millennium. *The Journal of Applied Management and Entrepreneurship*, *10*(2), 13–34.

Dainty, A. R. J., Raidén, A. B., & Neale, R. H. (2009). Incorporating employee resourcing requirements into deployment decision making. *Project Management Journal*, *40*(2), 7–18. doi:10.1002/pmj.20119

Decramer, A., Smolders, C., & Vanderstraeten, A. (2013). Employee performance management culture and system features in higher education: Relationship with employee performance management satisfaction. *International Journal of Human Resource Management*, *24*(2), 352–371. doi:10.1080/095851 92.2012.680602

Destatis. (2014). *Pressemitteilungen - Verdienstunterschied zwischen Frauen und Männern in Deutschland weiterhin bei 22% - Statistisches Bundesamt (Destatis)*. Retrieved August 29, 2015, from https://www. destatis.de/DE/PresseService/Presse/Pressemitteilungen/2015/03/PD15_099_621.html

Devarakonda, M., Gupta, P., & Tang, C. (2013). Labor Cost Reduction with Cloud: An End-to-End View. *2013 IEEE Sixth International Conference on Cloud Computing (CLOUD)*, 534–540. 10.1109/CLOUD.2013.90

Devonish, D. (2013). Workplace bullying, employee performance and behaviors: The mediating role of psychological well-being. *Employee Relations*, *35*(6), 630–647. doi:10.1108/ER-01-2013-0004

Diao, Y., Keller, A., Parekh, S., & Marinov, V. V. (2007). Predicting Labor Cost through IT Management Complexity Metrics. *10th IFIP/IEEE International Symposium on Integrated Network Management, 2007. IM '07*, 274–283. 10.1109/INM.2007.374792

Dickmann, F. J. (2006). Ensuring "Strategy" Isn't On 'Culture's Breakfast Plate. *Credit Union Journal*, *10*(45), 4–4.

Dries, N. (2012). *The role of learning agility and career variety in the identification and development of high potential employees*. Retrieved September 6, 2015, from http://www.emeraldinsight.com.strauss. uc3m.es:8080/doi/pdfplus/10.1108/00483481211212977

Dries, N. (2013). Adding value with learning agility: How to identify and develop high-potential employees. *Development and Learning in Organizations*, *27*(5), 24–26. doi:10.1108/dlo-07-2013-0043

Dunning, M. (2015). Employers look beyond wellness: Many companies have modified their benefits programs to include incentives aimed at improving their employees' overall well-being. *Business Insurance*, *49*(13). Retrieved from http://search.proquest.com.strauss.uc3m.es:8080/docview/1691108317/citation

Einarsen, S. (1999). The nature and causes of bullying at work. *International Journal of Manpower*, *20*(1/2), 16–27. doi:10.1108/01437729910268588

Empirica. (2013). *E-Skills for jobs in europe: measuring progress and moving ahead*. Retrieved from Prepared for the European Commission website: http://eskills-monitor2013.eu/fileadmin/monitor2013/documents/MONITOR_Final_Report.pdf

Empirica. (2014). *e-Skills in Europe - Countryreport Spain*. European Commission.

Eom, M. T. (2015). How Can Organization Retain IT Personnel? Impact of IT Manager's Leadership on IT Personnel's Intention to Stay. *Information Systems Management, 32*(4), 316–330. doi:10.1080/1 0580530.2015.1080001

Eurostat. (2013, January). *Labour costs per hour in euro, whole economy.* Retrieved August 29, 2015, from http://ec.europa.eu/eurostat/statistics-explained/index.php/Earnings_statistics

Eurostat. (2014a). *Hourly labour costs - Statistics Explained.* Retrieved August 29, 2015, from http:// ec.europa.eu/eurostat/statistics-explained/index.php/Hourly_labour_costs

Eurostat. (2014b). *Population and population change statistics.* Retrieved from http://epp.eurostat. ec.europa.eu/statistics_explained/index.php/Population_and_population_change_statistics#

Eurostat. (2015, February 1). *Gender pay gap statistics - Statistics Explained.* Retrieved August 29, 2015, from http://ec.europa.eu/eurostat/statistics-explained/index.php/Gender_pay_gap_statistics

Favaro, K. (2014, May 22). *Strategy or Culture: Which Is More Important?* Retrieved October 17, 2015, from strategy+business website: http://www.strategy-business.com/blog/Strategy-or-Culture-Which-Is-More-Important?gko=26c64

Feng, Y., Huang, H., Cheng, G., Chen, C., Huang, J., Liu, Z., & Huang, K. (2018). An Optimization Model to Evaluate Dynamic Assignment Capability of Agile Organization. *2018 4th International Conference on Big Data and Information Analytics (BigDIA),* 1–6. 10.1109/BigDIA.2018.8632798

Financial Times Lexicon. (2013). *Gross Value Added definition.* Retrieved September 5, 2015, from http://lexicon.ft.com/Term?term=gross%20value%20added%20GVA

Gabrisch, H. (2008). *Institutional deficits in the euro area: the problem of divergent labour costs.* Retrieved August 29, 2015, from http://search.proquest.com.strauss.uc3m.es:8080/docview/209551006?pq-origsite=summon

Hasan, M., & Zhou, S. N. (2015). Knowledge Management in Global Organisations. *International Business Research, 8*(6), 165–173. doi:10.5539/ibr.v8n6p165

Henderson, R. (2018). *2018 Randstad Talent Trends Report.* Retrieved from https://www.randstad.it/hrsolutions/talent-trends-report-2018.pdf

Holtzhausen, N., & de Klerk, J. J. (2018). Servant leadership and the Scrum team's effectiveness. *Leadership and Organization Development Journal, 39*(7), 873–882. doi:10.1108/LODJ-05-2018-0193

Horlach, B., Drews, P., Schirmer, I., & Boehmann, T. (2017, January 4). *Increasing the Agility of IT Delivery: Five Types of Bimodal IT Organization.* doi:10.24251/HICSS.2017.656

Institute for opinion survey Allensbach. (2014). *Study conditions in 2014 - Study finance, foreign travel, and living situation.* Retrieved from http://www.sts-kd.de/reemtsma/Studie-Lang-Allensbach-2014h.pdf

Jaksic, M., & Jaksic, M. (2013). Performance Management and Employee Satisfaction. *Montenegrin Journal of Economics, 9*(1), 85–92.

Joh, E., & White, W. (2018). How We Can Apply AI, and Deep Learning to our HR Functional Transformation and Core Talent Processes? *Student Works*. Retrieved from https://digitalcommons.ilr.cornell.edu/student/200

Kaufmann, M. (2014, February 17). Erreichbarkeit nach Dienstschluss Deutsche Konzerne kämpfen gegen den Handy-Wahn. *Spiegel Online*. Retrieved from http://www.spiegel.de/karriere/berufsleben/erreichbar-nach-dienstschluss-massnahmen-der-konzerne-a-954029.html

Kliner, K., Rennert, D., & Richter, M. (2015, July). *BKK Gesundheitsatlas*. Retrieved October 17, 2015, from http://www.bkk-dachverband.de/fileadmin/publikationen/gesundheitsatlas/BKK_Gesundheitsatlas_2015.pdf

Lee, T. S., Foo, C. T., & Cunningham, B. (1995). Role of organizational demographics in managing technology-induced stress. *Engineering Management Conference, 1995. Global Engineering Management: Emerging Trends in the Asia Pacific., Proceedings of 1995 IEEE Annual International*, 38–43. 10.1109/IEMC.1995.523906

Lusa, A., & Pastor, R. (2011). Planning working time accounts under demand uncertainty. *Computers & Operations Research*, *38*(2), 517–524. doi:10.1016/j.cor.2010.07.012

Malgorzata Ali, I. (2016). Doing the Organizational Tango: Symbiotic Relationship between Formal and Informal Organizational Structures for an Agile Organization. *Interdisciplinary Journal of Information, Knowledge, and Management, 11*, 55–72. doi:10.28945/3439

Martínez Aires, M. D., Rubio Gámez, M. C., & Gibb, A. (2010). Prevention through design: The effect of European Directives on construction workplace accidents. *Safety Science*, *48*(2), 248–258. doi:10.1016/j.ssci.2009.09.004

McDonald, P., Guthrie, D., Bradley, L., & Shakespeare-Finch, J. (2005). Investigating work-family policy aims and employee experiences. *Employee Relations*, *27*(4/5), 478–494. doi:10.1108/01425450510612013

McMenamin, T. M. (2007). A time to work: Recent trends in shift work and flexible schedules. *Monthly Labor Review*, *130*(12), 3–15.

Moe, N. B., Aurum, A., & Dybå, T. (2012). Challenges of shared decision-making: A multiple case study of agile software development. *Information and Software Technology*, *54*(8), 853–865. doi:10.1016/j.infsof.2011.11.006

Niemi, E., & Laine, S. (2016). Competence Management System Design Principles: Action Design Research. *ICIS 2016 Proceedings*. Retrieved from https://aisel.aisnet.org/icis2016/ISDesign/Presentations/4

Niskanen, T., Naumanen, P., & Hirvonen, M. L. (2012). An evaluation of EU legislation concerning risk assessment and preventive measures in occupational safety and health. *Applied Ergonomics*, *43*(5), 829–842. doi:10.1016/j.apergo.2011.12.003 PMID:22233692

Olsthoorn, M. (2014). Measuring Precarious Employment: A Proposal for Two Indicators of Precarious Employment Based on Set-Theory and Tested with Dutch Labor Market-Data - Springer. *Social Indicators Research*, *119*(1), 421–441. doi:10.100711205-013-0480-y

Otto, A., & Scholl, A. (2012). Reducing ergonomic risks by job rotation scheduling. *OR-Spektrum, 35*(3), 711–733. doi:10.100700291-012-0291-6

Pathak, R., Parker, D. W., & Holesgrove, M. (2015). Improving productivity with self-organised teams and agile leadership. *International Journal of Productivity and Performance Management, 64*(1), 112–128. doi:10.1108/IJPPM-10-2013-0178

Peruzzi, M. (2015). Contradictions and misalignments in the EU approach towards the gender pay gap. *Cambridge Journal of Economics, 39*(2), 441–465. doi:10.1093/cje/bev007

Pfisterer, D. S. (2013, October 29). *39.000 job vacancies for IT experts*. Retrieved October 31, 2014, from http://www.bitkom.org/de/themen/54633_77765.aspx

Pollitt, D. (2005). Leadership succession planning "affects commercial success.". *Human Resource Management International Digest, 13*(1), 36–38. doi:10.1108/09670730510576419

Poston, R., & Patel, J. (2016). Making Sense of Resistance to Agile Adoption in Waterfall Organizations: Social Intelligence and Leadership. *AMCIS 2016 Proceedings*. Retrieved from https://aisel.aisnet.org/amcis2016/ITProj/Presentations/34

Radant, O. (2014). Demographic Change: The Reasons, Implications and Consequences for IT Departments. *International Journal of Human Capital and Information Technology Professionals, 5*(1), 41–54. doi:10.4018/ijhcitp.2014010104

Radant, O., Colomo-Palacios, R., & Stantchev, V. (2014). Analysis of Reasons, Implications and Consequences of Demographic Change for IT Departments in Times of Scarcity of Talent: A Systematic Review. *International Journal of Knowledge Management, 10*(4), 1–15. doi:10.4018/ijkm.2014100101

Radant, O., Colomo-Palacios, R., & Stantchev, V. (2016a). Assessment of Continuing Educational Measures in Software Engineering: A View from the Industry. *Trends in Software Engineering for Engineering Education, 32*(2), 905–914.

Radant, O., Colomo-Palacios, R., & Stantchev, V. (2016b). Factors for the Management of Scarce Human Resources and Highly Skilled Employees in IT-Departments: A Systematic Review. *Journal of Information Technology Research, 9*(1), 65–82. doi:10.4018/JITR.2016010105

Radant, O., & Stantchev, V. (2018). Metrics for the Management of IT Personnel: A Systematic Literature Review. *International Journal of Human Capital and Information Technology Professionals, 9*(2), 32–51. doi:10.4018/IJHCITP.2018040103

Răvaş, O.-C. (2013). Homeworking Contract and Teleworking - Importance and Role in the Economy. *Annals of the University of Petrosani. Economics, 13*(2), 221–230.

Rose, J., Hewitt, B., & Baxter, J. (2013). Women and part-time employment Easing or squeezing time pressure? *Journal of Sociology (Melbourne, Vic.), 49*(1), 41–59. doi:10.1177/1440783311419907

Shatat, A., El-Baz, H., & Hariga, M. (2010). Employee expectations: Perception of Generation-Y engineers in the UAE. *2010 Second International Conference on Engineering Systems Management and Its Applications (ICESMA)*, 1–6.

Singe, I., & Croucher, R. (2003). The management of trust-based working time in Germany. *Personnel Review, 32*(4), 492–509. doi:10.1108/00483480310477551

Spears, V. P. (2012). Employee Wellness Programs Expand to Well-Being. *Employee Benefit Plan Review, 66*(11), 30.

Tarafdar, M., D'Arcy, J., Turel, O., & Gupta, A. (2014, December 16). *The Dark Side of Information Technology*. Retrieved September 26, 2015, from MIT Sloan Management Review website: http://sloanreview.mit.edu/article/the-dark-side-of-information-technology/

Todd, P., & Binns, J. (2013). Work-life Balance: Is it Now a Problem for Management? *Gender, Work and Organization, 20*(3), 219–231. doi:10.1111/j.1468-0432.2011.00564.x

van den Bos, A., Kemper, B., & de Waal, V. (2014). A study on how to improve the throughput time of Lean Six Sigma projects in a construction company. *International Journal of Lean Six Sigma, 5*(2), 226–212. doi:10.1108/IJLSS-10-2013-0055

Verner, T. (2011). National Competitiveness and Expenditure on Education, Research and Development. *Journal of Competitiveness, 3*(2). Retrieved from http://search.proquest.com.strauss.uc3m.es:8080/docview/1315218679/abstract

Weiguo, C., & Yanchun, L. (2010). Research on Motivation System of Employees-Analysis of Human Resources Management from a Psychological Perspective. *2010 International Conference on Management and Service Science (MASS)*, 1–4. 10.1109/ICMSS.2010.5578035

Zeng, C., Zheng, S., & Shi, K. (2010). Relationship between job demands-resources and job burnout of IT employees. *2010 IEEE 2nd Symposium on Web Society (SWS)*, 548–553. 10.1109/SWS.2010.5607390

Chapter 22
Greening the Compensation Design and Management of the Human Resource Function

Tinuke Fapohunda
Lagos State University, Nigeria

ABSTRACT

There is a rising necessity for the incorporation of environmental management into human resource management (HRM) practices. This attempt is recognized as the Green HRM initiative. An organization's human resource function can be powerful in aiding an all-inclusive approach to building a culture of sustainability. The strategy entails executing transformations to the diverse functions of HR like determining employee compensation. Gaps continue to exist in the literature on the green aspects of compensation and reward systems. This chapter considers the environmental management features of the compensation and reward system and factors a mould of the procedures entailed in green compensation and reward system. it cores on examining green reward management systems practices from the standpoint of subsisting research in the area and proposes inventive process moulds in green reward management systems. The green reward management system is presented as a smart and superior method of reward management systems.

INTRODUCTION

Green HRM (GHRM) is a materializing theme in contemporary circumstances. It is developing into a trendy subject in the contemporary world for several motivations such as surplus consumption of natural resources and raw materials by diverse commercial organizations and industries. At the moment, problems like carbon credits, global warming, and pollution ensuing from high profile industrial accidents and the transformations in the climate are talked about with elevated significance. The problems could consequence in earthquakes, recurrent floods and extinction of definite species and animals. Shaikh (2010) contends that the misuse of natural resources worldwide has resulted in concerns like global

DOI: 10.4018/978-1-6684-3873-2.ch022

warming, depletion of ozone layers and augmentation of CFC and C02 in the environment. Misuse of natural resources has in addition impinged on the flora and fauna, consequences in decrease in forest animals, disturbances to the food chains and the ecosystems. Therefore, world environmentalists have been talking about ecological concerns worldwide.

In the management field, there is rising research literature on green management in general but, in contrast, research on green human resource management (GHRM) is comparatively varied and little by little. Studies contend that workers must be motivated, empowered, and environmentally conscious of green initiatives to exhibit expected workplace green behaviour (Atiku, 2019; Fields & Atiku, 2017; Mandip 2012; Mathapati, 2013; Prasad, 2013). An organization's human resource function can be powerful in aiding an all-inclusive approach to building a culture of sustainability. The strategy entails executing transformations to the diverse functions of HR like recruitment, induction, training and development, carrying outing performance appraisal, and determining employee compensation. Wekesa and Nyaroo (2013) affirms that green HRM entails two fundamental constituents: environment-friendly HRM practices and conservation of knowledge capital. Reine (2015) contends that proper management of people by organisations especially in a tumultuous environment is fundamental to the achievement of sustainable competitive advantage and accomplishment of organisational goals. Gaps continue to exist in literature on the - Green aspects of Human Resource Management especially as it concerns an informative guide on the evolving literature, its scale and coverage, in addition to a procedural form in the area. This chapter considers the environmental management features of the compensation and reward system and factors a mould of the procedures entailed in Green compensation and reward system. The chapter cores on examining the practices from the standpoint of subsisting research in the area. It reviews and documents green Reward Management Systems practices based on subsisting literature and utilizes a new and combined examination of literature in Green Reward Management Systems. It charts the field in the turf, and proposes inventive process moulds and research outlines in Green Reward Management Systems. It further presents the conception of green Reward Management Systems as a smart and superior method of Reward Management Systems.

Background

Human Resource Management

Key elements in the factors of production include capital, natural and human resources. While Capital and natural resources are passive agents of development, only human beings constitute the active agents since they alone are equipped to accumulate capital, exploit natural resources and build political and social organizations. Fapohunda (2003) suggests that human resources are the energies, skills, talents and knowledge of people that are, or have the prospect of being applied to the production of goods and the rendering of services. Thus, of all the resources an organization or nation needs, human resources are the most imperative. Human beings make things happen and efficient human beings make things happen efficiently. The importance of human resources to an organization whether it is private or public cannot be over-emphasized. Efficiency of other factors of production is largely dependent on the quality and quantity of the available manpower/human resources. Moreover, human resources are themselves the most dynamic, complex and unpredictable.

Hence managing human resources effectively is principal to the realization of organizational goals and visions. Cole (2012) and Prasad (2013) affirm that managing human resources involves the organization of staff resources in order to allow people to make flexible, multi-skilled inputs to the general aims of the organization whether it is a business or in the public sector. Effective human resource management has become vital to organizations today. Porter and Kramer (2011), Peattie (2012) and Opatha (2013) indicate that more prominently, contemporary organizations do not only seek for sufficient human resources but also devise objective programmes intended to augment the quality of their work force. The intensified altitude of global competition, necessity for tactics to eliminate competitors, the volatility of the labour market and the advancement in technological knowhow, most particularly in the area of information technology has alerted all organizations to the truth that all their resources must be of best functionality and must be employed better than ever before. Fapohunda (2013) asserts that Human Resources Management refers to the management of people at work in an organization. It is concerned with the development and effective utilization of human resources to achieve organizational goals and objectives. HRM is the management function through which managers recruit, select, train, and develop organization members. French (2018) distinguishes HRM as entailing the philosophies, policies, procedures and practices related to the management of people within an organization. It is that element of management, which is concerned with the management of people at work and their affiliations within an enterprise. It concerns not only industry and commerce but also all areas of employment. HRM involves the design and execution of policies and all the practices that can aid the promotion of proficient employment of human resources.

French (2018) further depicts HRM in the process-systems terms. Here, a process is a particular course of correlated incidents moving towards identical goals, outcome or conclusion e.g. the staffing process, which is a flow of correlated incidents that results in the constant filling of positions within an organization. Such incidents comprise actions like recruiting candidates, taking hiring decisions and managing career changes such as transfers and promotions. A system is a group of processes and mechanisms assigned to administer a process in an expected way. This notion of system indicates a mutually supporting connection of constituents e.g. the staffing structure of an organization could comprise such mechanisms and practices as application blanks, interviews, reference checks, a six-month probation period, a procedure for applying for transfers. Consequently, the expression process implies an amalgamation of events that produce some result and the term "systems" recognizes particular modus operandi and mechanisms employed to direct those events. According to the process-systems view, HRM constitutes the methodical planning, development and control of a system of correlated processes influencing and entailing members of an organization. To successfully manage these processes, HR schemes are planned, developed and executed utilizing the merged efforts of all managers and HR specialists in an organization. In all, the schemes are projected to add to the accomplishment of significant organizational results, such as efficiency, competence, enlargement and member satisfaction. The excellence of the design and administration of the systems employed to direct and manipulate HR processes is straightforwardly associated with an organization's general efficacy. Systems in HRM must be devised to advance, not encumber, the achievement of organizational goals. In some organizations, the system employed in HRM can be so burdensome that its own officialdom stifles the organization.

Green Human Resource Management

Pillai and Sivathanu (2014) asserts that Green Human Resource Management (HRM) entails the integration of environmental management into Human Resource Management (HRM) research and practice and the obligation for it is rising. Cole (2012), and Milliman and Clair (2016) suggest that in current times, numerous organizations in the worldwide setting seem to be practicing green human resource management. Dessler (2005), Daily, Bishop and Steiner (2007), and Bird (2011) indicate that considering and combining such green HRM practices either already in practice or designated for practice by organizations adds significantly both academically and fundamentally to the HRM territory. Green HRM represents an evolving area of research in contemporary organisational studies. To aid scholars, researchers and practitioners, a concise cataloguing, indicating ample existing research to direct the moulding is obligatory in the area. Green human resource management (GHRM) refers to a set of HRM practices that organizations adopt to improve employee workplace green performance.

Waddock, Bodwell, and Graves (2002) affirm that for some time now, the corollaries of business activities on the environment have been strictly examined by diverse stakeholder groups. Consequently, business organizations face enhanced demands to execute green schemes, which constitute a vital piece of corporate social responsibility. As Porter and Kramer (2011) observe, effective commitment to green initiatives has consequently; developed into an organizational responsibility and a vital source of organizational competitive advantage. Guest (2011), and Kehoe and Wright (2013) add that successfully managing an organization's human resources (HR) plays a significant role in the successful accomplishment of organizational strategies through developing positive employee workplace attitudes and behaviours. Organizations have to assume effective green human resource management (GHRM) to encourage and educe employee green behaviour with the aim of achieving organizational green goals. Jackson and Seo (2010) define Green HRM as a set of HRM practices adopted to achieve organizational green goals that are a part of perceived CSR initiatives. Studies like Benz and Frey (2013), Ayesha, Amna, Tahleel, and Hina (2015) and Arulrajah, Opatha and Nawaratne (2016) observe that green HRM practices may comprise thinking about a candidate's green values during the recruitment and selection process, carrying out green awareness and skills training, thinking about an employee's green behaviour during periods of promotions, compensation, and performance appraisals. Moreover, according to Berrone and Gomez-Mejia (2009) and Bird (2011), Green HRM facilitates the development of employee green skills and awareness, and inspires employees to share in organizational green initiatives and activities. Green HRM is therefore a vital organizational device used to execute green initiatives.

HRM practices are the tangible human resource programmes, processes and techniques that are actually implemented in an organisation. Similarly, Dessler (2005) observes that green HRM practices comprise the tangible green HRM programmes, processes and techniques that in actuality are utilized in organisations with the intention of trimming down destructive or enhancing cooperative environmental effects of the organisations. Firdaus and Udin (2014) elucidates that the vital objective of green HRM practices is to brighten organisation sustainable environmental performance. Jackson, Renwick, Jabbour and Muller-Camen (2011) emphasize that, surrounded by the environmental management structure; human resources are required to attain environmental management plans suitably. Consequently, as argued by Guest (2011) and Garg (2014) this resulted in the management of employees 'greenly', utilizing the green human resource management (GHRM) structure. In a nutshell, green HRM should be distinguished as employing and retaining employees that are environmentally careful. Wekesa and Nyaroo (2013) notes that, to many professionals and scholars in human resource management (HRM), worldwide and particularly within the African context, the initiative of green human resource management (GHRM) is a comparatively novel one. Opatha (2013) asserts that green HRM is associated with every practice obligatory for the formation, handling and constant preservation of a system that is instituted with the intention of making the delegates of a company green. Phillips (2011), and Wekesa and Nyaroo (2013) explicate that it comprises the components of human resource management engaged with adapting everyday delegates into green delegates with the intention of realizing the environmental objectives of the company, and finally making a pledge to being sustainable. It is connected to the approaches, actions and structures that adjust the employees of the organization into the green association for the advantage of the individual, society, natural environment and the business. This exhibits the underlying principle why green HRM practices are basic to the management of businesses sustainably in a turbulent environment.

The United Nations General Assembly (1987) observes that the idea of sustainable development is cored on cultivating economic development and growth, while simultaneously preserving the quality of the environment. It establishes a scheme for the integration of environmental policies and strategies for development. Renwick, Redman and Maguire (2013) insist that the incorporation of environmental management into HRM is termed green HRM.

Lado and Wilson (1994) defines HRM system as a set of separate but interconnected activities, functions, and process aimed at attracting, developing, and maintaining an organization's human resource. Organizations commonly arrange HR practices into systems that are consistent with their culture and business strategy. Waddock, Bodwell and Graves (2002) propose that Green initiatives incorporated into HRM proposals constitute an element of corporate social responsibility in the long run. Nowadays, organizations are executing and assimilating green initiatives in their plans with the assistance of their human resource. Managers certify that their HR is making use of the green human resource practices in suitable ways. In the same vein, Shane (2003) argues that it is imperative to encourage many technical and management skills among all workers of the organization with the aim of executing a successful corporate green management system in organizations. Organizations across the globe are integrating and aiming at employing GHRM practices to achieve competitive advantages in the business world. Furthermore, Roa (2011) contends that while totally embracing and incorporating GHRM in business may be unattainable, it necessitates a transformed method pertaining to the subsisting HR practices by both the management in addition to workers at the same time. A principal task for HR environmental executives could be to direct line managers regarding gaining complete workforce co-operation as it pertains to putting into action environmental policies which connotes HR requirements to care for supporters and generate systems of problem-solvers prepared to do something to alter the existing status quo. Various concerns associated with GHRM that must be considered by the HR department prior to executing green initiatives.

Compensation and Reward Management Systems

One of the most vital human resource management functions able of augment the productivity and growth of an organization is the Compensation and Reward Management Systems. Organisations utilize and administer a team of individuals that allow them to execute their purposes and aspire to attain the stated goals for which they are instituted. Compensation is a contractual occurrence. It is a dual input and output exchange between a worker and an employer. The input of efforts and the output of remunerations to workers are time-honoured. According to Wekesa and Nyaroo (2013), Compensation and reward management also called wages and salaries administration is one of the most important features of HRM and it includes economic remuneration such as wages, salaries and other forms of economic payments known as fringe benefits, indirect compensation or supplementary pay. Cole (2012) adds that it includes everything that a worker receives in return for his labour i.e. basic pay and other financial and non-financial rewards all of which define how well the worker lives in the society.

The Roles of Compensation and Reward Management Systems

Firdaus and Udin (2014) demonstrate that compensation is important since it offers income to workers and institutes a significant cost item to the employer. It is the largest single cost item for many organizations. For the workers it provides the means of satisfying their wants and needs. Again, as Dessler (2005) indicates, compensation involves the various devices that provoke the loyalty, cooperation and efforts of individuals. The consistency and recognized objectivity of pay by workers institutes a dire element in compensation management. Studies like Fapohunda (2013), Daily, Bishop and Steiner (2007) as well as Fapohunda and Azeez (2017) illustrate that the bulk of employee satisfaction or dissatisfaction and work performance is founded on pay. Garg (2014) corroborates that differences in pay (whether internal or external) can completely pressure employee-employer rapport and jeopardize industrial peace. Employee compensation is commonly not disturbed by levels of aspirations and pay history. Holt, (1993) posits that, to individual employees, compensation plays economic, social and psychological roles in their lives and all of them are contemplations for the importance of pay. Ayesha, Amna, Tahlee and Hina (2015) affirm that it is routinely recognized that employees are people who ascertain important sources of competitive edge for organizations. Therefore, employees are the priceless resources of any organization. To maintain competitive and productive edge the employees require sufficient compensation.

Roa (2011) emphasizes that compensation is what employees are given in exchange for their input to the organization. Employees typically proffer their services for three types of rewards which are base pay, pay incentives and benefits. Wekesa and Nyaroo (2013) affirms that Benardin and Russel (1993) observes that compensation has an enormous control on workers' recruitment, motivation, productivity and turnover. Organisations employ and administer a group of individuals that facilitate them to execute their functions and aim to accomplish the affirmed goals for which they are instituted. The core tactic for attaining organisational goals is by having competent and efficient workers. Holt (1993) contends that compensation includes the yield and the benefit that workers obtain by way of pay, wages and also some rewards like monetary exchange for the employees to increase the performance. Dessler (2005) adds that it is all types of payments or rewards given to workers which emanate from employment. It constitutes one of the fundamental motivations for workers to seek employment. Workers are reimbursed for their services and endeavours on their work. Harrison and Liska, (2008) established that reward is the focal point of the employment contract since; it is the foremost rationale for working.

Ivancevich (2004) observes that reward system is a human resource management function that is concerned with all types of reward individuals obtain in return for executing organizational duties, with a preferred upshot of an employee who is attracted to the work, satisfied, and motivated to do a good job for the employer. The consistency and perceived objectivity of pay by workers constitute a serious issue in compensation management. Yet again, disparities in pay (whether internal or external) can extremely pressure employee /employer relationship and endanger industrial peace. In addition, employee compensation is frequently unaffected by levels of ambitions and pay history. Pay is a means of acquitting necessities, luxuries and needs. It is the worth or price of one's labour.

Moreover, Fapohunda (2012) advises that pay is a mark of social status and defines social ranking in the society. Acceptability in the society is regulated by the extent of a person's financial assets. Furthermore, Mandip (2012) found that pay and higher financial standing provides one access and the use of power and influence which consecutively puts the individual on greater financial footing. Social status and the political role of compensation reinforce one another. Similarly, Margaretha and Saragih (2013) assert that growth and maturity within an organization is habitually revealed in a worker's pay. It designates age, performance and capability in the organization. In the same vein, pay works as a mechanism for encouraging desired behaviour. Kehoe and Wright (2013) note that it stimulates and chastises and also moderates anxiety. The necessity for financial compensation conditions a person's behaviour. Arising from these roles and the contribution of compensation, efficient packages that will meet the expected desires of workers and fulfil organization productivity and development objectives need to be formulated.

Objectives of a Good Compensation and Reward System

The major objectives of a good compensation and reward system are numerous. These include the attraction, motivation and retaining of workers. As Lado and Wilson (1994) puts it, an organization's level of pay is a foremost enticing dynamic to prospective workers or newcomers. Next, as corroborated by Mandip (2012), management regulates wages and salaries and labour costs through sensibly packaged compensation schemes with job evaluation etc. Furthermore, Margaretha and Saragih (2013) and Masters (2014) observe that worker loyalty and commitment to the employer as well as increased job satisfaction, reduced (turnover, absenteeism, complaints and grievances) which could arise with non-competitive and inadequate pay levels can be built. Moreover, pay is perceived as a motivator to increase employee morale and subsequently expand productivity. Fapohunda (2014) submits that wages are anticipated to have maximum positive influence on performance when workers: perceive a perfect correlation between their performances and their wages; pecuniary intentions are strong; the pre-existing stimulus to perform their jobs successfully from non-economic motives is feeble; workers' ability to perform their jobs is high and special pressure to increase output is not created. Financial reward is a foremost factor in attracting individuals to an organization, persuading them to remain and inducing them to contribute possibility to the achievement of corporate goals.

Green Reward Management Systems

Green compensation and reward management seek to distinguish the inputs of workers in the construction of a more sustainable organization. It is the consequence of the achievement of workers in their ecological performance assessment and the evidence that an organization's tactical sustainability objectives are being emulated and achieved (at any rate up to a particular level) from the top to the bottom. There are three diverse kinds of rewards. First are monetary-based rewards- by way of salary increase, cash incentives, and bonuses. Second involves non-monetary rewards like sabbaticals, special leaves, discounts or gifts to workers. Third, involves recognition-based rewards which entail emphasizing the green involvements of workers through wide publicity, public praise and gratitude for sustainability endeavours by the top management.

It is imperative nevertheless, to take into account that such a structure with efficient monetary motivations could be testing to grow since is it tough to correctly and reasonably assess environmental behaviours and performances all over the organization. Rewards and compensation constitute the foremost

HRM functions for rewarding workers for their performance. Rewards and compensation functions are the most commanding techniques that connect a person's interest to that of the organization. Ramus (2002) contends that incentives and rewards are capable of manipulating workers' interest to the utmost at work and inspire them to put forth greatest attempts on their part to accomplish organizational goals. Within the agenda of Green HRM, rewards and compensation can be understood as prospective tools for maintaining environmental activities in organizations. Contemporary organizations are growing reward schemes to promote eco-friendly programmes brought on board by their employees. Phillips (2011) affirms that a CIPD/KPMG survey carried out in the United Kingdom approximated that 8% of UK firms were remunerating green behaviours with diverse kinds of awards or financial incentives. Ramus (2002) states that these practices can be valuable in stimulating workers to create eco-initiatives. In the same vein, Forman and Jorgensen (2001) in a study on the significance of worker's participation in environmental programmes detected that worker's commitment to environment management programmes was enhanced by the offer of compensation to assume responsibilities associated with environmental accountability. Berrone and Gomez-Mejia (2009) in a study conducted on 469 United States organizations working in high-polluting industries asserts the usefulness of green rewards and compensation. The study reports that organizations boasting eco-friendly performance remunerated their CEOs more than non-eco-friendly organizations. They concluded that long-term business outcomes in agreement to pay were connected with better pollution prevention accomplishment.

Renwick et al, (2013) asserts that green compensation and rewards initiate the utmost degree of job satisfaction which considerably augments environmental performance. Green rewards and compensation boast a considerable impact on employee satisfaction for eco-initiatives. The employment of rewards and recognition founded on environmental sustainability puts an affirmative effect on employees' motivation to try out green initiatives.

Compensations and rewards constitute reinforcement to motivation and obligate workers to be environmentally accountable. Daily and Huang (2001) emphasize that a reward system can be employed methodically to inspire workers to execute craved behaviours with the intention that the organization and its workers can obtain gains from the plan. Compensation and reward management should distinguish assistance in green management.

Compensation schemes are supposed to be tailored to reward the attainment and successes of green skills by employees. For green achievements of workers, monetary- based, non-monetary based and recognition- based rewards can be employed. Prasad (2013) affirms that monetary-based remunerations for inputs in environment management can be billed through salary increase, cash inducements and bonuses whereas non-monetary compensations may comprise sabbaticals, special leaves and gifts to workers as well as their family members. For the recognition-based awards, the CEO or top management executives could emphasize green inputs of workers by way of extensive publicity and public eulogies and positive reception of green endeavours.

The Importance of Green Reward Management Systems

Embracing green HRM helps the organization to realize its green goals. Renwick et al (2013) suggest that by implementing green HRM practices, the organization transmits an obvious message to employees that it is dedicated to the social green cause ahead of any financial gains. Owing to their self-enhancement motives, employees are predisposed to respond positively to perceived green HRM practices. Rangarajan and Rahm (2011) reports that the adoption of GHRM practices by organizations, indicate to both current and prospective workers that they boast a well-built corporate social programme and value the environment and social priorities. They suggest that these messages encourage external reputation, and the organizations have a higher propensity to become more "attractive" to workers. Besides, implementing GHRM practices (like offering green training and recognizing and rewarding green behaviour) persuades and affords workers with chances to partake and connect with green activities.

Green reward management systems entail assuming environment-friendly schemes to support sustainable practices and enhance worker commitments and corporate sustainability. It entails reducing expenditures and augmenting worker engagement and retention which, consequently, assists organizations to decrease workers' carbon trails.

As part of reward management systems, organizations can proffer green rewards to employees such as a nature-friendly workplace and lifestyle advantages. Consequently, this could incorporate carbon credit offsets, free bicycles and pollution-free vehicles for commuting to and from the workplace in order to engage people in the green plan. Additionally, talented employees seek self-actualization in their jobs to facilitate staying committed to their organizations. Green reward management systems can facilitate the formation of this by following green values and practices. Other green activities can incorporate the least use of paper and printed materials in reward management systems. To boot, green business can incorporate amplified recycling, reusable grocery and lunch bags, and proscribing the use of bottled water and plastic and Styrofoam cups in the workplace. Work stations can include fluorescent light bulbs and other energy saving and green appliances.

Also to underscore the significance of green reward management systems, organizations can initiate their workers to modify their travel and transportation inclinations by restricting official car trips, employing public transport for business travel and carpooling, offering interest-free loans to acquire hybrid cars, and cycling or walking to work. Business meetings and conferences can be carried out through the internet with the aim of reducing business travel. Greening is vital to circumventing or curtailing global warming; evading or reducing natural disasters, health diseases arising from pollution, injury to animals and other natural creatures guarantee balance in affiliations between life and environment and making certain of survival of humans and business organizations.

Effectiveness generated by Green Reward Management Systems can reduce operational expenditures and make it possible for industry professionals to achieve their corporate social responsibilities in a better way. Green Reward Management Systems consist of all the activities, practices, and policies that are concerned with the growth, accomplishment, and continuing upholding of a system that is intended at turning workers of an organization green. It is the side of GHRM that aspires to accomplish the environmental goals of the organization and at last to make a considerable input to environmental sustainability.

Several organizations are employing a greener approach in their operations. They reflect on two vital components: environmentally friendly HR practices and the protection of knowledge capital. Besides, they are indenting affirmative and pleasant consequences on the models of reward management systems in the organization. This also has a positive power on the attitude of workers because they think that aside from their practical involvement on the job, they have an imperative duty in conserving the environment. Therefore, as Shrivastava (1994) observes the environmentally negative nature of organizational activities and results has added to the present environmental concerns worldwide. Rugman and Verbeke (1998) assert that environmental concerns are a few of the mainly intricate and important managerial tests of the twenty-first century. They comprise climate change, resources reduction and decline of biodiversity, and ecosystem integrity. Organizations are liable for the environmental deprivation. Governments and organizations are employing natural resources generously for the creation of diverse goods and services required by people who desire to augment their living standards.

Providentially, a few governments, organizations, and individuals, as well as environmentalists and nature lovers, are presently and progressively paying solemn attention to conserve and protect the environment and decrease environmental pollution. Consequently, amplified awareness was created among policy makers, leaders, and owners of the organizations, managerial employees, customers, and scholars concerning environmental sustainability.

Green Reward Management Systems actions assist companies locate alternate ways to reduce outlays exclusive of losing their talent in green economy. Organizations boast remarkable growth prospects by going green and constructing a new environmental DNA which can result in enormous operational savings by trimming down their carbon trail. As part of reward management systems, organizations can proffer green rewards to employees such as a nature-friendly workplace and lifestyle advantages. Consequently, as mentioned earlier, this could incorporate carbon credit offsets, free bicycles and pollution-free vehicles for commuting to and from the workplace in order to engage people in the green plan. Green reward management systems can facilitate in the formation of self-actualization in their jobs by following green values and practices. To boot, green business can incorporate amplified recycling, reusable grocery and lunch bags in the workplace. Greening is vital to circumvent or curtail global warming; evade or reduce natural disasters, health diseases arising from pollution, injury to animals and other natural creatures guarantee balance in affiliations between life and environment and make certain of the survival of humans and business organizations. Employees can also be presented chances to "tele work" or work from home. With the internet and intranet organizations can now commune with workers via emails thus decreasing the necessity for printing and of paper. Moreover, to emphasize physical fitness, good nutrition, and healthy life-style, wellness programmes for workers, their family members, and the general public can be arranged.

Greening the Reward Management Systems

To the extent that the Rewards Management function is concerned, work organisations are appropriately distinguished to profit from establishing a reward management scheme for group developed waste reduction practices. Because they are differentiated as central elements in enduring performance, compensation schemes are correlated to the achievement of particular skills and proficiencies rather than just performance only. As Peattie (2012) delineates, occurrences of severe accidents or proscribed discharges could be forestalled by a comprehension of environmental laws or composition. Masters (2014) avows that in the United States, several organizations have Environmental Respect rewards schemes that discern employee environmental achievements, while others offer rewards for schemes created by individual employees to relieve the environment and boost organizational prosperity. Generally, such organisations are perceived to oblige the development of compensation schemes that engender required behaviours in environmental management, and this obliges proficient use of both incentives and disincentives. Conceivably as designated by the U.S. episode, negative reinforcements (for example suspensions, reprimands and warnings) are mandatory to get employees to attain environmental improvements. Peattie (2012) nevertheless proposes that as an alternative, organisations could assume offering workers positive inducements like oral responses from managers, that could aid workers drive to environmental upgrading. Again, economic-based environmental compensation systems have been developed, particularly with performance upshots in environmental management determining considerable ratios of monthly managerial bonuses. Reiner

(2015) observes that some organisations initiate their executive compensation and bonus plans in part on environmental stewardship exercises and integrate environmental performance goals as a standard constituent of the bonus system. The managers are permitted to allot compensations to motivate workers. Bird (2011) adds that some organizations now integrate environmental management issues into their performance associated payment plans, either as a supplementary performance gauge or standard to be attained to be entitled to performance related payment. Furthermore, Firdaus and Udin (2014) establish that in diverse organisations in the United States, there are recognition-based compensations for supervisors though the calculated swell of such compensation schemes to all workers is attributable to the fact that the majority of organisations have relatively new environmental evaluation plans. Some of the issues here include: novel compensations obligatory to inspire more youthful individuals, and how compensations such as promotion can be linked to workers' environmental performances. Margaretha and Saragih (2013) designate that there are several methods of offering encouragements in an environmentally pleasing method together with expanding car mileage for corporation vehicles to bicycle rides. Furthermore, employees could be offered economic substitutes for car allowances besides encouraging carpooling and sharing provisions. Monetary carrots can as well be included into compensation plans, as tax incentives and eliminations encouraging bicycle lending and less contaminating car convoys too. It could in addition involve offering financial inducements to workers for their good green performance of job and non-financial compensations like praise and recognition to employees for their greening. Green reward and compensation must be integrated in organization HRM policies and practices. Mandip (2012) indicates that reward systems have the capability to develop the organization's efforts to executing sustainable practices and they include more than just financial recompense. Schedule flexibility, profit-sharing, benefits and incentives, recognition, paid time off and holidays, favoured parking and gift certificates are also forms of rewards. Integrating green reward and compensation practice in HRM policies and practices can be done by compensating environmental champions with bonuses. It could be by way of employee recognition where the environmental stars are given public praise. Furthermore, green reward and compensation can be integrated through the incidence of a policy on green reward in the organization.

In the framework of Green HRM, rewards and compensation can be presumed as prospective tools for sustaining environmental activities in organizations. Garg (2014) in a study exploring the involvement of workers in environmental work programmes indicates that rewards and compensation can be employed to make workers take on accountability of partaking in environmental endeavours. Organization management could tailor their reward package to reveal their environmental objectives. There could be offering of gifts to staff members deemed environmental champions to emphasize positive environmental behaviours and certificating remuneration policies and computerization of reward processes. Other forms of reward include schedule flexibility and organization shared profits as a form of appreciation. In addition, workers who champion environmental issues can be given paid time off. Reward perks up organization attempt to execute sustainable practices. Employees' recognition can be utilized as a type of reward in the organization. Green reward and compensation practices can manipulate environmental sustainability to a reasonable level.

Impact of Greening the Reward Management Systems

With Green Human Resource plans organizations receive assistance in discovering replacement options to slash expenditure. It entails the involvement of people management procedures and actions towards this more extensive programme. It is a significant concern for Human Resource since it is as well very imperative for all workers, in addition to customers and other stakeholders. Moreover, greening the Reward Management Systems certifies that Human Resource can boast an immense effect devoid of originating a great deal of overheads. Furthermore, by offering financial support for green benefits to keep staff occupied, excellent environmental management can perk up sales and decrease expenditures. If greened, the conventional reward management systems function will facilitate organisation(s) attainment of sustainable development in addition to assisting in appropriate management of people in tumultuous environment(s).

Arulrajah, Opatha and Nawaratne (2016) suggest that Green Reward Management Systems practices are charts, processes and techniques implemented in the organisations aimed at shrinking negative environmental upshots or advancing positive environmental influences of the organisations. Thus, the decisive rationale of green reward management systems practices is to augment organisations' sustainable environmental performance especially in turbulent environment(s), where managing people effectively is desirous. Milliman and Clair (1996) affirms that greening the reward management systems presents environmentally affable items for consumptions and procedures to administer corporate environmental agendas effectively, and to surmount execution challenges of corporate environmental agendas.

As Ayesha, Amna, Tahleel, and Hina (2015) stipulates, organizations that are capable of lining up compensation and rewards practices with intents of environmental management can be victorious in the corporate environmental management journey. The reality that the most advanced attributes of environmental management of the ISO 14001 certified organizations are inclined to be connected with just about all of the practical and cutthroat elements of human resource management was established by a 2010 study conducted by Jabbour and Santos. In sum, some central effects of Green rewards management include: achieving insight, reputation and benevolence. It also brings about cost efficiency and smarter performance converted into less expensive products. Moreover, it results in improved power function. In addition, it is cost-effectively functional, consequently having undeviating effects on earnings while also augmenting the return on outlays.

Rewards and compensation are the foremost HRM processes through which workers are rewarded for their performance. It is the HR practice that serves as the most potent technique which connects an individual's concern to that of the organization. Motivations and rewards can sway workers' consideration to the utmost at work and stimulate them to apply greatest effort on their part to realize organizational goals.

In the perspective of Green HRM, rewards and compensation are potential tools for supporting environmental activities in organizations. Benz and Frey (2007), (2011) and (2013) also show that inducements persuade executives to employ accounting and other works to attain short-term outcomes and improve themselves. Increased prominence should be provided on studies that establish efficient techniques that will aid creating and executing green compensation practices and possibly initiate the accomplishment of corporate environmental goals.

Milliman and Clair (1996) suggest that green compensation and rewards develops into an obligation so as to present environmentally friendly products and operations to manage corporate environmental programmes productively, and to surmount accomplishment challenges of corporate environmental programmes. Jabbour (2011) affirms that organizations with the capability to array compensation and rewards practices with goals of environmental management can be successful in the corporate environmental management expedition. Jabbour and Santos (2010) confirm that the most developed features of environmental management of the ISO 14001 certified organizations have a tendency to be connected with nearly all of the functional and competitive elements of compensation and rewards. Green HR compensation and rewards strategies assist organizations in locating substitutes to slash expenditures. It alludes to the input of people management policies and activities towards the wider plan. It is a vital subject for HR since it is as well extremely essential for all workers, customers and other stakeholders. Besides, it is a subject where HR can have a huge effect devoid of originating many expenses. Furthermore, good environmental management can advance sales and decrease expenditures by offering funding for green gains to keep staff occupied. In recent times, across many organizations, to facilitate counselling of employers on "green" consciousness in the workplace, various practice groups are being initiated with the intention of the groups executing best practices that will develop the work environment through decreasing, reprocessing, and recovering some materials. Moreover, the practice groups counsel employers on educating their employees on how their activities both in the office and at home influence the environment. Organizations should adjust to transforming lifestyles and altering workforces. Benz and Frey (2011), indicate that an ample number of employees in organizations that assumed the agenda made considerable transformations in their everyday activities, comprising augmented recycling, reduced printing, eradication or decrease in the utilization of bottled water, plastic and Styrofoam cups, employing re-serviceable grocery and lunch bags, changing to compact fluorescent light bulbs and other energy saving and green products, and modifying transportation traditions. Therefore, a few significant effects of green compensation and rewards include: achieving insight, reputation and good will; cost efficiency; more elegant performance converting into more economical products; improved power function and reasonably helpful and consequently undeviating effect on profit as well as improved returns on investments.

An increased attention is now created among stakeholders with respect to environmental sustainability. Improved employee morale, stronger public image, increased consumer/ customer confidence, employee loyalty and brand recognition, position as an employer of choice, increased workforce productivity, efficiency, and motivation and employee retention are few of the many advantages and benefits an organization can have by committing to green compensation and rewards.

Challenges to Greening the Reward Management Systems

The use of green reward and compensation persuades environmental sustainability of the organizations. Fernandez, et. al. (2003) however observe that while green compensation and rewards increase green initiatives in organizations, it is by no means absolutely free from a few mismanagements. Developing effective monetary incentives can be challenging by reason of the complexity of correctly and reasonably assessing environmental behaviours and performances. Again, including green rewards in the human resource policies does not necessarily influence environmental sustainability at any rate. While some studies like Shane (2003) indicate that it involves the organization recognizing diverse reward strategies which may possibly be monetary and non-monetary gains offered to workers in return for their environmental contributions. Other studies like Daily and Huang (2001) designate that rewards are reinforcements to inspiration and entrust workers to be environmentally accountable. A reward system can be utilized methodically to stimulate workers to execute required behaviours so that both the organization and its employees can obtain gains from the programme. These gains incorporate bonuses, special leaves, gift vouchers, flexible schedules, paid holidays, profit sharing schemes, and paid time off and they improve workers' execution of required behaviours, which consecutively makes certain that organizations sustainable practices are enhanced. Where such rewards are established, it constitutes a sign that non-monetary incentives are significant and workers value them but it is not designed to lure them to work towards developing the environment. Compensation and reward management must distinguish inputs in green management. Prasad (2013) contends that for green attainments of workers, monetary- based, non-monetary based and recognition- based rewards can be employed. Monetary-based remunerations for involvements in environment management can be assigned through salary increments, cash inducements and bonuses while non-monetary rewards could embrace sabbaticals, special leave and gifts to workers and members of their families.

Aligning green rewards and compensation schemes to the HRM process, motivates a green culture in organizations and integrating components of green management in the compensation programme, allows managers to encourage the green behaviours among the workers. Additionally, managers can request workers to convey precise green proposals relating to their personal jobs which can by way of joint decisions be incorporated into the goals to accomplish in the approaching year. Accomplishing the goals would constitute the foundation of obtaining incentives. Employee compensation plans can be adjusted to offer bonuses founded partly on the worker's assessment ratings on the behavioural and technical capabilities and workers may possibly be given bonuses for their exceptional work on unique schemes. Pillai and Sivathanu (2014) observes that green compensation and rewards could embrace the utilization of workplace and lifestyle gains, varying from carbon credit compensations to free bicycles, involving people in the green plan and persisting in identifying their input.

Worldwide, modern environmental concerns have further compounded the environmentally pessimistic character of organizational acts and outcomes. Environmental concerns constitute some of the mostly complicated and significant managerial tests of the twenty-first century. They comprise reduction in climate change resources and decrease in biodiversity, and ecosystem uprightness. Alshuwaikhat and Abubakar (2008) and Haden, Oyler and Humphreys (2009) contend that organizations are liable for the environmental deprivation. Governments and organizations are employing natural resources generously for the production of diverse goods and services considered necessary by people who desire to improve their living standards. Providentially, a few governments, organizations, and individuals, comprising environmentalists and lovers of nature, are presently and more progressively giving solemn consideration to conserve (to shield) and protect (to keep) the environment and curtail environmental pollution.

RECOMMENDATIONS

It is important to employ green rewards to promote worker's behaviour towards realizing environmental goals. Compensation schemes have to be tailored to remunerate the possession and attainment of green skills by workers. Rewards and compensation constitute the principal HRM process through which workers are rewarded for their efforts. These HR practices are the most powerful methods which links together an individual's interest to that of the organization. Therefore, organizations are required to design reward programmes that can be inspirational to all workers in order to enhance environmental sustainability. As earlier mentioned, a few of the recommended green reward and compensation practices consist of gifting workers who are campaigners of green practices, receiving bonuses and directives for positive behaviours. Green reward can be exercised through computerization of reward processes, granting of exceptional leaves and sabbaticals to employees. To offer financial incentives and non-financial rewards to workers for their good green job performance, the HR Department can create Green/EM (Environmental Management) job descriptions for workers with higher-level executives taking superior responsibility for green schemes. Besides, green objectives must be incorporated into managerial job descriptions.

Organizations are required to devise energy-competent products and procedures, and develop motivations to speed up their reception. Sustainability is becoming a principal focus for several organizations. Going further than environmental sustainability, the idea incorporates all kinds of social and environmental effects that demonstrate why employers are obligated to build up a novel scheme of doing business. Beyond centring on financial profits, sustainable organizations must also reflect on social and environmental effects in taking business decisions. The HR functions have a vital responsibility in environmental sustainability. The green work-life interface to green compensation and rewards has revealed that it can be valuable to go ahead of "greening workers" and to think about the whole human being together with their private life and consumer behaviour. Such an idea builds on the grave appreciation of environmental concerns in an organization's management. The greening support of workers as human beings only becomes successful if environmental features are reflected on in all central business procedures and practices. More organizations build on the grave appreciation of environmental concerns in an organization's management.

CONCLUSION

More organizations now appreciate the significance of sustainability which is offered in incorporating green customs as a foundation which human resources has on their competitiveness, repute, and capability to attract and retain strong talent. Sustainable organizations now look for contributions from a wide and varied set of stakeholders-both in-house and outside-in forming their business tactics and operations being watchful of their economic, societal, and environmental effects. The HR function generally has a vital role to play. HRM can facilitate the creation and implementation of sustainable business strategy all over the organization employing the HR skills in organizational procedures, change management and culture stewardship. This could necessitate the development of innovative HR proficiencies. HR must therefore, in addition to becoming proficient at using Green HRM tools to entrench the sustainability strategy and mission in the organization, also gain knowledge of shaping the structure itself so that its effects on workers, districts, and other stakeholders support the sustainability dream of the organization. Organizations are encouraged to create committees on environmental and sustainability awareness which are multidisciplinary and have activities in diverse units. For most organizations in today's economic ambience, the resources are already drawn out to the utmost where they can attain the height of going green.

REFERENCES

Alshuwaikhat, H. M., & Abubakar, I. (2008). An integrated approach to achieving campus sustainability: Assessment of the current campus environmental management practices. *Journal of Cleaner Production*, *16*(16), 1777–1785. doi:10.1016/j.jclepro.2007.12.002

Arulrajah, A. A., Opatha, H. H. D. N. P., & Nawaratne, N. N. J. (2016). Green human resource management practices: A review. *Sri Lankan Journal of Human Resource Management*, 5(1), 1–16. doi:10.4038ljhrm.v5i1.5624

Atiku, S. O. (2018). Institutionalizing Social Responsibility through Workplace Green Behaviour. In *Contemporary Multicultural Orientations and Practices for Global Leadership* (pp. 183–199). IGI Global.

Ayesha, A., Amna, G., Tahleel, T., & Hina, M. (2015). Impact of compensation and reward system on the performance of an organization: An empirical study on banking sectorof Pakistan. *European Journal of Business and Social Sciences*, *4*(8), 319–325.

Benz, M., & Frey, B. S. (2007). Corporate governance: What can we learn from public governance? *Academy of Management Review*, *32*(1), 92–104. doi:10.5465/amr.2007.23463860

Benz, M., & Frey, B. S. (2011). M.A. Promoting employee's proenvironmentalbehavior throughgreen human resource management practices. *Corporate Social Responsibility and Environmental Management*, *2011*(26), 424–438.

Benz, M., & Frey, B. S. (2013). Corporate greening through prosocial extrarole behaviours—A conceptualframework for employee motivation. *Business Strategy and the Environment*, *2013*(16), 554–570.

Berrone, P., & Gomez-Mejia, L. R. (2009). Environmental performance and executive compensation: An integrated agency-institutional perspective. *Academy of Management Journal*, *52*(1), 103–126. doi:10.5465/amj.2009.36461950

Bird, A. (2011). Training for Environmental Improvement. Academic Press.

Cole, G. A. (2012). *Management Theory and Practice*. DP Publications.

Daily, B., & Huang, S. (2001). Achieving sustainability through attention to human resource factors in environmental management. *International Journal of Operations & Production Management*, *21*(12), 1539–1552. doi:10.1108/01443570110410892

Daily, B. F., Bishop, J., & Steiner, R. (2007). The mediating role of EMS teamwork as it pertains to HR factors and perceived environmental performance. *Journal of Applied Business Research*, *23*, 95–109.

Dessler, G. (2005). *Human resources management* (10th ed.). Prentice-Hall.

Fapohunda, T. M. (2012). Pay Disparity and Pay Satisfaction In Public And Private Universities in Nigeria. *European Scientific Journal*, *8*(28), 120–135.

Fapohunda, T. M. (2013). Comparative Analysis of Wage Determination in Unionized and Non-Unionized Organizations In Nigeria. *Educational Research*, *3*(1), 72–79.

Fapohunda, T. M. (2014). Increasing Organizational Effectiveness Through Better Talent Management. *The Journal of Human Resources*, *2*(4), 1–14.

Fapohunda, T. M., & Azeez, R. O. (2017) Managing People in a Turbulent Environment: Is 'GREEN HRM' the Light and Salvation? In *Conference Proceedings, Department of Business Administration 2017 Annual Conference*. Lagos State University.

Fernández, E., Junquera, B., & Ordiz, M. (2003). Organizational culture and human resources in the environmental issue: A review of the literature. *International Journal of Human Resource Management*, *14*(4), 634–656. doi:10.1080/0958519032000057628

Fields, Z., & Atiku, S. O. (2016). Collective Green Creativity and Eco-Innovation as key drivers of Sustainable Business Solutions in Organisations. In *Collective Creativity for Responsible and Sustainable Business Practice* (pp. 1–25). IGI Global.

Firdaus, M., & Udin, Z. M. (2014). Green human resource management (HRM) towards SMES: A conceptual view. *The 4th International Conference on Technology and Operations Management*, 135–140.

Forman, M., & Jorgensen, S. (2001). The social shaping of participation of employees in environmental work within enterprises—Experiences from a Danish context. *Technology Analysis and Strategic Management*, *13*, 71–90. doi:10.1080/09537320120040455

Garg, Y. Y. (2014). *Pay for performance raises performance*. Springer.

Guest, V. P. (2011). Agency cost of free cash flow: Corporate finance and takeovers. *The American Economic Review*, *76*(May), 323–329.

Haden, S. S. P., Oyler, J. D., & Humphrey, J. H. (2009). Historical, practical, and theoretical perspectives on green management. *An Exploratory Analysis Management Decision*, *47*, 1041–1055.

Harrison, D. A., & Liska, Z. (2008). Promoting regular exercise in occupational fitness programme. *Journal of Personnel Psychology*, *5*(5), 27–45.

Holt, D. H. (1993). *Management: concept and practices*. Prentice Hall, Englewood Cliffs.

Ivancevich, J. M. (2004). *Human resource management*. McGraw-Hill/Irwin.

Jabbour, C. J., Jabbour, L. S., Govindan, K., Teixeira, A. A., & Freitas, W. R. (2011). Environmental management and operational performance in automotive companies in Brazil: The role of human resource management and lean manufacturing. *Journal of Cleaner Production*, *47*, 129–140. doi:10.1016/j.jclepro.2012.07.010

Jabbour, C. J. C., Santos, F. C. A., & Nagano, M. S. (2010). Contributions of HRM throughout the stages of environmental management: Methodological triangulation applied to companies in Brazil. *International Journal of Human Resource Management*, *21*(7), 1049–1089. doi:10.1080/09585191003783512

Jackson, J., Currie, K., Graham, C., & Robb, Y. (2010). The effectiveness of interventions to reduce undernutrtion and promote eating in older adults with dementia: A systematic review. *JBI Library of Systematic Reviews*, *9*(37), 1509–1550. doi:10.11124/jbisrir-2011-119 PMID:27819926

Jackson, S. E., Renwick, D. W., Jabbour, C. J., & Muller-Camen, M. (2011). State-of-the-art and future directions for green human resource management: Introduction to the special issue. *German Journal of Human Resource Management*, *25*(2), 99–116. doi:10.1177/239700221102500203

Kehoe, M. N., & Wright, P. R. (2013). Lean and green: Exploring the spillovers from lean production to environmental performance. *Production and Operations Management*, *10*(3), 1–13.

Lado, A. A., & Wilson, M. C. (1994). Human resource systems and sustained competitive advantage: A competency based perspective. *Academy of Management Review*, *19*(4), 699–727. doi:10.5465/amr.1994.9412190216

Mandip, G. (2012). Green HRM: People management commitment to environmental sustainability. *Research Journal of Recent Sciences*, *1*, 244–252.

Margaretha, M., & Saragih, S. (2013). Developing new corporate culture through green human resource practice. In *International Conference on Business, Economics, and Accounting* (pp. 1-10). Academic Press.

Masters, J. P. (2014). Greening of human resources: Environmental awareness and training interests within the workforce. *Industrial Management & Data Systems, 101*(2), 57–63.

Milliman, J., & Clair, J. (2016). Best Environmental HRM Practices in the US. Academic Press.

Opatha, H. H. D. N. P. (2013). *Green Human Resource Management: A Simplified Introduction, HR Dialogue*. Department of HRM, Faculty of Management Studies and Commerce, University of Sri Jayewardenepura.

Peattie, K. (2012). *Green Marketing*. Pitman.

Phillips, L. (2007). Go green to gain the edge over rivals. *People Management, 13*, 9.

Phillips, L. (2011). Motivating employees for environmental improvement. *Industrial Management & Data Systems, 104*, 364–372.

Pillai, R., & Sivathanu, B. (2014). Green Human Resource Management. *Zenith International Journal of Multidisciplinary Research, 4*, 72–82. Retrieved 5 November, 2019 from www.zenithresearch.org.in

Porter, F. Y., & Kramer, M. R. (2011). The role for the personnel practitioner in facilitating environmental responsibility in work organisations. In W. Wehrmeyer (Ed.), *Greening people: Human resources and environmental management* (pp. 185–198). Greenleaf.

Prasad, R. P. (2013). Best environmental HRM practices in the USA. In W. Wehrmeyer (Ed.), *Greening people – Human resources and environmental management* (pp. 49–73). Greenleaf Publishing.

Ramus, C. A. (2002). Encouraging innovative environmental actions: What companies and managers must do. *Journal of World Business, 37*(2), 151–164. doi:10.1016/S1090-9516(02)00074-3

Rangarajan, R. P., & Rahm, H. Y. (2011). The roles of supervisory support behaviors and environmental policy in employee "ecoinitiatives" at leading-edge European companies. *Academy of Management Journal, 43*(4), 605–626.

Reiner, G. (2015). The Greening of European Management Education. Academic Press.

Renwick, D. W., Redman, T., & Maguire, S. (2013). Green human resource management: A review and research agenda. *International Journal of Management Reviews, 15*(1), 1–14. doi:10.1111/j.1468-2370.2011.00328.x

Roa, V. S. P. (2011). *Human resource management: Texts and cases*. Excel Books.

Rugman, A., & Verbeke, A. (1998). Corporate strategy and international environmental policy. *Journal of International Business Studies, 29*(4), 819–833. doi:10.1057/palgrave.jibs.8490053

Shane, D. O. (2003) *Using corporate social responsibility to attract, motivate and retain human resources: Two case studies D* (Master's Thesis). Lulea University of Technology Sweden. Retrieved from http://www.epubl.Luth.se/1402 1552/2009/007/index.html

Shrivastava, P. (1994). Technological and organizational roots of industrial crises: Lessons from Exxon Valdez and Bhopal. *Technological Forecasting and Social Change, 45*(3), 237–253. doi:10.1016/0040-1625(94)90048-5

United Nations General Assembly. (1987). *Report of the world commission on environment and development: Our common future*. United Nations General Assembly.

Waddock, L. A., Bodwell, W. D., & Graves, T. O. (2002). Environmental pro-activity and business performance: An empirical analysis Omega. *International Journal of Management Sciences, 33*, 1–15.

Wekesa, J. N., & Nyaroo, S. (2013). Effect of compensation on performance of public secondary school teachers in Eldoret municipality Kenya. *International Journal of Scientific and Research Publications, 3*(6), 1–18.

Chapter 23
The Wasta Model:
Impact on Human Resource Practices and HRM Within Lebanese Universities

Elizabeth Kassab Sfeir

(iD) https://orcid.org/0000-0002-6913-781X

Université Antonine, Lebanon

ABSTRACT

This article explores the concept of Wasta, an interpersonal influence. It is defined by Mohamed and Mohamed as involvement of a third-party person to attain a favour. This research examines the impact that Wasta has on human resources practices in Lebanon. A mixed methods approach, being questionnaires and interviews, was used in order to obtain data. Implications of Wasta in a new model are illustrated showing the effect on employees when recruited through knowing someone. It subsequently shows the influences on other HR practices of training and development, compensation, and career development. This paper is the first of its kind illustrating the impact of Wasta on employee engagement. It is a pillar for future research, giving added value to the minimal studies available on HR practices in Lebanon and the Middle East.

INTRODUCTION

The continued sustainability of organizations depends on the quality of their human capital. In a world that has become ever more global, diverse and multicultural, the development of human resources is imperative. Kipkebut (2010) states, "various studies have stressed the benefits to organizations of a loyal and committed workforce." Business practices must recognize that HRM practices are now an international phenomenon (Robbins and Judge, 2015) important to any multinational company. In order to focus on internal systems to gain a competitive advantage in the local and international marketplace, businesses must now ensure that they conform to globally adapted HR practices (Morris et al. 2009), recognizing that organizational culture plays a significant role in their HR practices.

DOI: 10.4018/978-1-6684-3873-2.ch023

In the aftermath of the global financial crisis, the Middle East is at a new stage regarding international relationships with international partners: there is a realization of the imperative to break away from the legacy of the long Ottoman reign – namely, a 'Byzantinian' lack of transparency and top-heavy bureaucratic management – in order to achieve competitiveness and become part of the global economy (Leigh, 2009). One central aspect of this legacy is the Middle Eastern cultural phenomenon known as *Wasta,* which refers to the 'intervention of a patron in favor of a client in an attempt to obtain privileges or resources through a third party (Mohamed and Mohamed, 2011, p.412); in the Middle East, the term *Wasta* is synonymous with 'social networks or connections'. This research explores the extent to which this phenomenon continues to influence HR practices within the context of Lebanon's higher education sector – namely universities. Notwithstanding that Lebanon is emerging from a civil war, with its attendant continuous political instability, the Middle East, and particularly Lebanon is, according to Budhwar and Mellahi (2006), currently in the process of making changes and improvements in strategies and in the implementation of practices and procedures. Thus, it is timely for close scrutiny to be directed at the intersection of the pervasive *Wasta* system of preferment and HRM practices within a Middle Eastern organizational culture.

For the purposes of this research, HRM practices are seen to include the following: recruitment and selection; training and development; compensation and benefits; performance appraisals; and, career development. The aims of this research is to prove that *Wasta* has an impact on HR practices within the organization. In doing so, this paper will contribute to attesting to *Wasta* and its effects providing much-needed data to corroborate this phenomenon.

BACKGROUND

HRM has gone through various changes over the years. Cohen (2015) discusses the evolution of HRM and states that it was formally recognized in the early 1800s. HRM goes back to when all levels of business organizations – employers and employees, skilled tradesmen and apprentices, supervisors and managers, companies and the people who work for them – were first recognized; this was a time when the "welfare secretary" started to appear. These 'secretaries' oversaw the hiring, paying, disciplining and developing of the employees. Hence, Cohen shows that the HR process actually began when the first person agreed to be paid for work completed. This author further explains that 'personnel', which was the term previously used before 'HR', began in the Industrial Revolution and in the era of scientific management.

Thus, the long-standing recognition in the literature of the importance of HRM in western business institutions creates a pathway for turning the focus on this aspect of employment and business management in the Middle East. The literature issuing from the Middle East is more anecdotal (Zahra, 2011) and case-study based. Budhwar & Mellahi (2007) give some interesting insights about HR in the Middle East, however they are still only 'insights'. These insights are the changes in the level of ownership in several Middle Eastern countries due to privatization; identifying key differences in HRM practices between large and small firms in public and private sectors; the change in the role of the government towards HRM policies; GCC countries investing in HR however they are finding difficulties in meeting the demands of the labour market and the employment of locals (Emiratization etc.) Afiouni et al (2013) note that most of the HR research being conducted in the Middle East increased in 2007 and the quality also improved.

Currently, Afiouni et al (2013) note that HR practices are being looked at in terms of the differences between practices across various countries. The writers note that the observed differences are largely related to cultural factors and employment policies. The research that is found in the western counterpart is far more extensive in terms of developed HR strategies and management. The transformation of HR has gone from the administrative function to being viewed as a core business function that contributes to organizational effectiveness (Ulrich & Dulebohn, 2015). The authors illustrate that HRM has transformed through four different waves, HR administrative wave (traditional administrative functions), HR practices (hiring, training, career management), HR strategy (HR practices being aligned with the business strategy) and the HR and context (HR working for individuals, organizational and leadership) that is the HR investments or specifically where the resources need to be targeted (Ulrich &Dulebohn, 2015).

Although there is a growing body of research on various aspects of Lebanese culture and society, limited research exists on the intersections of HR practices and culture in the country. The literature that is available on HR development in this region (Dirani, 2006; Dirani, 2009; Afiouni 2007; Tlaiss, 2013) focuses merely on the existence of basic personnel practices, culture, work values, and the lack of real HR development practices. Thus, understanding in what way and to what extent *Wasta* is an important aspect in HRM in the higher education sector in Lebanon, adds a central strand of information and forms the core of this study.

Tlaiss and Kauser (2011) further support the notion, that gaining a systematic understanding of *Wasta* in the Arab world is a worthwhile objective, given that *Wasta* is an important component of Middle Eastern culture and is reflected strongly in the influence of social and family connections – an influence that carries over to the workplace (p.468).

The dynamic of *Wasta* appears to be very much alive in the Middle East, as witnessed by the welter of items appearing on social media and in reputable business publications, such as the Wall Street Journal (2010). Feghali (2014) views *Wasta* as having transformed over time from its corruption, nepotism and cronyism:

While Wasta may have a positive side whereby it humanises bureaucracy ... it also hampers economic development and impacts business by providing unfair advantage, yielding decisions based on connections instead of merit and reducing productivity (p.1).

However, the literature, including empirical research and case studies, relating to HRM in the Middle Eastern region, and HR practices in Lebanon in particular, evidences a dearth of information, inviting closer and more extensive investigation (Dirani, 2006). In order to achieve organizational and personal success in the Middle East (ME), one must understand the foundations of the culture that individuals live and work in (Mohamed and Singh, 2010).

Research into particular areas of HRM practice as they operate in Lebanese universities is scant; while literature relating to the influence of *Wasta* on HRM practices within Lebanese universities is even less forthcoming. The literature relating generally to the HRM practices chosen for investigation provides a context for studying the influence of *Wasta* against a set of accepted norms and standards; more specific Lebanese-centric literature allows us to view current Lebanese recruitment practices and their effects on other HR practices, serving to contextualize the investigation as to what extent and in what manner *Wasta* plays a part in HRM in the university sector.

Recruitment and Selection Process

Recruitment and selection is an important HR practice – that is, hiring the right person for the job (Robbins & Judge, 2015). As the authors state, with continuing unemployment issues, there are numerous candidates that apply for open jobs. Organizations are turning to their own HR professionals in order to recruit the right people. Dessler and Al Ariss (2013) state that the recruitment process starts with employee planning. Mathis and Jackson (2010) state that as labor markets are shifting recruiting is becoming more important. The cost of unfilled jobs is also costly to the organization. Hence the recruitment process is a central process to the organizations success. In simple terms the recruiting function's mission is to employ talented people in order contribute to the organization's strategies so they can achieve or sustain a competitive advantage (Phillips & Gully, 2015).

The recruitment process is an empirical process, which requires fairness (Phillips & Gully, 2015). The concept of fairness is vital in business practices and is also linked to the individual's psychological contract formed during the actual recruitment process. Iles et al. (2012) state that, even though it may promote positive working conditions, *Wasta* also denies equal opportunity, and influences recruitment, selection, compensation and promotion in the public sector within the ME. However, they do not state 'how' this is affected.

Selection is another HR practice that needs to follow clear procedures as choosing the right person with the correct qualification indicates proper accountability and transparency. When an employee is selected through a *Wasta* and does not have the appropriate qualifications, the effects on other employees needs to be examined.

Stone et al (2007) describe the idea that cultural influences also affect the selection process in that applicants often vary due to their skills, knowledge and abilities. These types of differences also affect their job performance. Hence it is important to understand that various cultures use different selection techniques. In the Middle East, it would seem to this researcher to be advantageous to adopt certain western practices in order to standardize and create quality procedures in selection.

Training and Development

Training, development and retraining are vital HR processes within organizations. Competition forces business to change and adapt in order to sustain a competitive advantage. Training and development is defined as the process "whereby people acquire capabilities to perform jobs" (Mathis & Jackson, 2010, p. 250). How this process is managed in a system underpinned by *Wasta* is not clear in the current literature.

The purpose of training and development is to ensure that the new employee is given valid information and is given the right tools in order to complete their jobs. The first step is orienting the new employee. Orientation programs provide them with basic information that is required for the job. These days, orientation sessions explain the mission and vision of the company and the employees' roles in the mission of the organization (Schwind et al, 2013). Information regarding policies and rules as well as procedures is very important in orienting the new employee. Without the basics the employee will not understand how the organization works and on what basis (Dessler, 2013). Orientation can range between 10 minutes to a weeklong program. This is where policies and printed information are given to them as well as orientation around the organization's website for any need to know information.

Performance Management

Dessler and Al Ariss (2013) define performance management as "a process that unites goal setting, performance appraisal (PA), and development into a single, common system whose aim is to ensure that the employee's performance is supporting the company's strategic aims" (p.223). Hence, performance management involves creating a PA system (PAS), goal setting, and ensuring that these goals meet the strategic aims of the organization.

Performance management plays a significant role in impacting salaries, feedback, promotions, training, development and understanding of an individual's strengths and weaknesses. It is not hard to surmise that, due its lack of fairness and transparency, *Wasta* impacts on the performance of the individual. Giangreco et al. (2010) explain that, in the Middle East, there is a need for control in terms of performance appraisals. Hofstede (cited in Giangreco et al. 2010) maintains that organizations in this region have more of a bureaucratic approach. In Western organizations, there is a focus on individual performance, in contrast to a focus on collective performance in the Middle East.

Giangreco et al. also infer that there are issues and limitations when applying a PAS in the Middle East. These limitations are primarily a result of cultural differences, contextual constraints and lack of financing. They attest that the PAS should be adapted accordingly in order to be effective; thus, customizing the system to suit the current environmental forces that affect the institution is necessary. Abu Doleh and Weir (2007) also confirm that much work needs to be completed in this area in the Middle East.

Dirani (2006) also infers that in efforts to delineate HR development in Lebanon, the author recommends that individuals must consider contradictions between eastern and western culture; that is, spiritual, material, ritual and modern aspects of both sides of the world should be taken into account. One particular concern is, when implementing HR models and practices, organizations experience the pressure of paternalistic relationships that take over to a greater or their performance.

Career Development

Mathis and Jackson (2010) discuss the perspectives that organizations need to make a more concerted effort in career training and development in order to keep their talent. Armstrong (2009) also states that career development also leads to a positive psychological contract. Baruch (2003) infers that the employee can be seen as the only stakeholder in their career development, asserting that careers are still, to a certain extent, the responsibility of the organization and ideally managed by the HRM system of the company. Normally organizations provide a wide set of career practices – for example, career management techniques, activities, programs and associated practices within HRM. The author also states that these types of areas are powerful management tools with regard to people's careers. However, these tools need to be refined and brought up to a twenty-first century standard. Baruch notes that it is important, for example, to examine how these organizations can utilize these practices for the future. These activities should not just be provided as stand-alone activities, but as part of an integrative career system. However, it is not very clear how these practices relate to each other and what makes them different. Certain models should replicate the difficultness and multi-dimensional nature of career systems, and they need to also be adapted to this global and dynamic environment. Research question two examines the affects of *Wasta* on career development, being able to provide distinct data regarding the position of the individual within the organization. This information is pivotal in understanding the individual employee's point of view, perceptions and motivations towards their work. Afiouni (2007) offers the example of various banks in Lebanon where there is a lack of coherence in the HRM practices that are applied, including no human resource planning, and no career paths for employees, even though there are performance appraisals conducted, but not taken seriously, by the line managers. The literature thus evinces a dearth of study, particularly anywhere outside the Western academy, into HR practices and how they are affected by cultural phenomena such as *Wasta*.

METHODOLOGY

As *Wasta* in HR practices is a relatively new research area, both qualitative and quantitative methods have been used to gather the data that is needed. The data being sought after comprises information from employees of universities in Lebanon. Using both methods allows the definition of the problem of the research– the effects of *Wasta* – in such a way as to reflect an external validity that is going to be situational and cultural.

The mixed methods approach was used for this research project. Quantitative methods alone only examine the data that is received and then analyzed. Kiessling and Harvey (2005) state that the qualitative component completes the quantitative method by allowing the researcher to immediately respond to context-specific difficulties. As the *Wasta* phenomena is a concept within Middle Eastern culture that is not really spoken about, and due to the collectivist nature of the Middle Eastern culture, qualitative measures were imperative. The interview approach used here allowed the researcher to delve deeper into the underlying issues that are not observable in the quantitative data yielded by the survey questionnaire.

An investigation was conducted via a questionnaire and interviews in order to determine the possible influences of *Wasta* on HR practices within the Lebanese university sector. Three hypotheses were developed to test a regression analysis of the statistics obtained through the questionnaire:

H_0 *Wasta* and training have no relationship
H_1 *Wasta* and training have a relationship
H_0 *Wasta* and compensation have no relationship
H_1 *Wasta* and compensation have a relationship
H_0 *Wasta* and career development have no relationship
H_1 *Wasta* and career development have a relationship

Recruitment and selection, one of the HR practices being investigated, was examined through one question in the survey, that being "How were you employed". This direct question provided the answer that was used as the independent variable against the other variables of training; compensation and career development – the latter being the HR practices that are examined within this research.

The Survey (Appendix A)

The survey determined the following areas:

- the employee's individual profile – age, marital status etc.
- educational background – level of education achieved and details of where educated
- recruitment and selection – how they applied to the university and the process that was taken

- training and development – training that was achieved or not achieved and future developments
- compensation and benefits – details of compensation, packages and promotions
- performance appraisal – how staff are appraised for work done organizational strategies – university strategies

The number of surveys distributed amongst staff of universities amounted to a total of 466. Of this number, 349 surveys were returned and used for this research. This created a response rate of 75%. In Table 1 are the number of universities and the surveys returned to the researcher. The universities are labelled A, B, C and D, where University A, with three campuses, had a total of 119 surveys received. University C and D had two campuses where 60 and 70 surveys were obtained. This leaves only University B which has only one campus, where 100 surveys were obtained.

Table 1. Number of university campuses participating and number of surveys returned

University	No of campuses	Total No of Surveys received
University A	3	119
University B	1	100
University C	2	60
University D	2	70
N=		349

The survey was developed in English. The participating universities provided distribution lists, which included emails as to where to send the questionnaire. Any employee of the university was able to fill in the anonymous and voluntary questionnaire. The participants were able to return the questionnaire survey by pre-paid postage envelopes. The front page of the questionnaire contained a participation request and provided a clarification of the contents and purpose of the survey. Therefore, respondents who answered the questionnaire thereby indicated that they consented and agreed to participate. Completed questionnaires were mailed back anonymously.

The Interview (Appendix B)

The semi-structured interview (Appendix 1) was chosen over other forms of qualitative methods, as it was able to cover both the factual and interpretative level with the participant in a meeting format. Qu and Dumay (2011) state that semi-structured interviews are created to guide the questioning using set themes. They allow the researcher to reach the story behind the participant's experiences and gather in-depth information. Wadsworth (2012) states, 'Many people prefer to stay with what they know, even if they have to live with feelings of unease.' *Wasta* is a complex issue and the semi-structured interviews played a pivotal role in understanding its impacts on employees, allowing them to express their true feelings, knowing that there were no expectations. For reasons of reticence resulting from cultural expectations, this style of interview was well suited to the purposes of the research.

RESULTS

Survey Results

Figure 1 illustrates respondents answers to who the primary wage earner is in the household, whether the female or male. It shows that female respondents, although greater in number, are not the primary wage earner. This conforms to the norm in Lebanese society, a patriarchal society, which sees the male as the primary wage earner. The fourteen percent (14%) of males that stated they were not the primary wage earners would be explained by the fact that they are single and not married.

Figure 1. Number of respondents Male/Female according to primary wage earner status

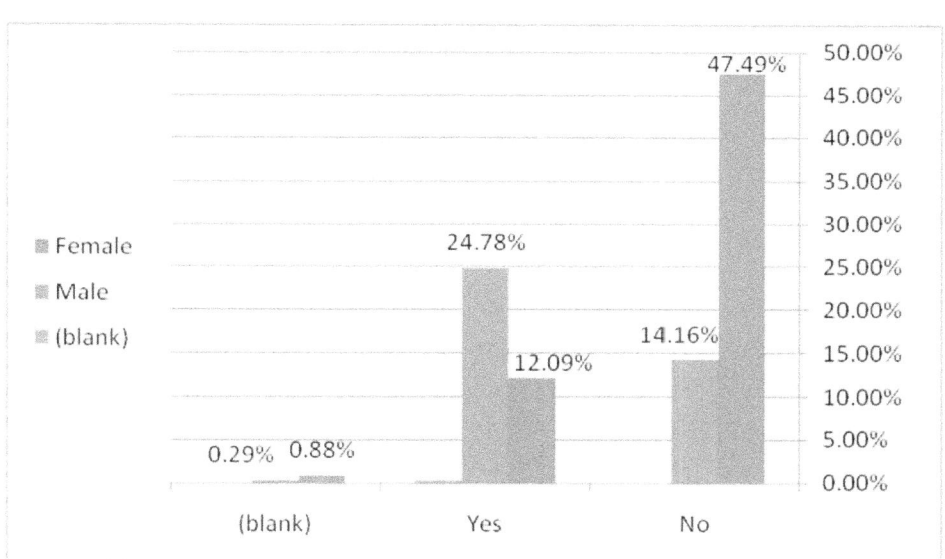

Table 2 provides the respondents educational background of those working within the Lebanese university sector. The totals show 30.38% of female respondent obtaining a master's degree in comparison to 17.99% of male respondents. At the bachelor's level, the data reveals 14.75% of females and 10.91% of males with bachelor's degree. The data here supports the concept even further that private higher education graduates a higher level of bachelor's, masters and doctoral students.

Table 3 shows by cross analysis that more participants came from private sector than public sector universities; it also shows which position they hold. The greater number of respondents, 41.30%, work in a private university in administration section, and 27.43% work in the academic section. In the public universities, 13.57% work in the administration section and 5.60% work in the public section.

Table 2. Highest level of education attained according to gender

Count of respondents	I am		
My highest education level	Female	Male	Total
Bachelors	14.75%	10.91%	25.66%
Brevet (gr.9)	0.29%	0.00%	0.29%
Doctoral	5.90%	7.37%	13.27%
Masters	30.38%	17.99%	48.67%
Technical Certificate (TAFE)	0.88%	0.29%	1.18%
Terminal (gr.12)	5.90%	1.77%	7.67%
(blank)	2.36%	0.88%	3.24%
Total	60.47%	39.23%	100.00%

Table 3. Position and sector

Count of respondents?	Public private		
I currently hold a position in	Private	Public	Total
Academic	27.43%	5.60%	33.04%
Administration	41.30%	13.57%	55.16%
Both	7.08%	1.77%	8.85%
(blank)	2.65%	0.29%	2.95%
Total	78.47%	21.24%	100.00%

Table 4 demonstrates the different types of benefits received by respondents. Compensation and benefits in Lebanon are based on a base salary, national social security fund (NSSF) or insurance and retirement fund. The results show that 83.22% of the respondents earn the basic early and only 56.38% are actually registered in the NSSF fund. Only 17.11% of the respondents will actually receive a retirement fund.

The research shows quite explicitly the lower levels of benefits that are being given and the lack of benefits that are also not given in this sector. It is unfortunate that in no area of benefits were respondents receiving the compensation that they deserved. As well, most of the respondents receive one type of package – salary and the social security.

Survey question 14 asks: 'How did you apply to the university?' The responses to this question are in Figure 2, where 47.91% got their job through knowing someone, or *Wasta*.

Word-of-mouth is also a way of 'knowing someone' and the amount of respondents that received their job through this channel is over 10.91%. That makes a total of over 58%, a significant percentage, of respondents who got their jobs through *Wasta*. The first research question asks, 'How does *Wasta* influence HR practices of the university?' This question tests the recruitment and selection procedures of the university. As the percentage is significant, it shows a relationship between *Wasta* and recruitment and selection.

Table 4. Percentage of respondents receiving benefits

Answer Choices	Responses	
Basic Salary	83.22%	248
Social Security	56.38%	168
Insurance	31.21%	93
Retirement	17.11%	51
Bonuses	5.70%	17
Overtime	11.07%	33
Total Respondents: 298		

Figure 2. Application process of respondents to the university

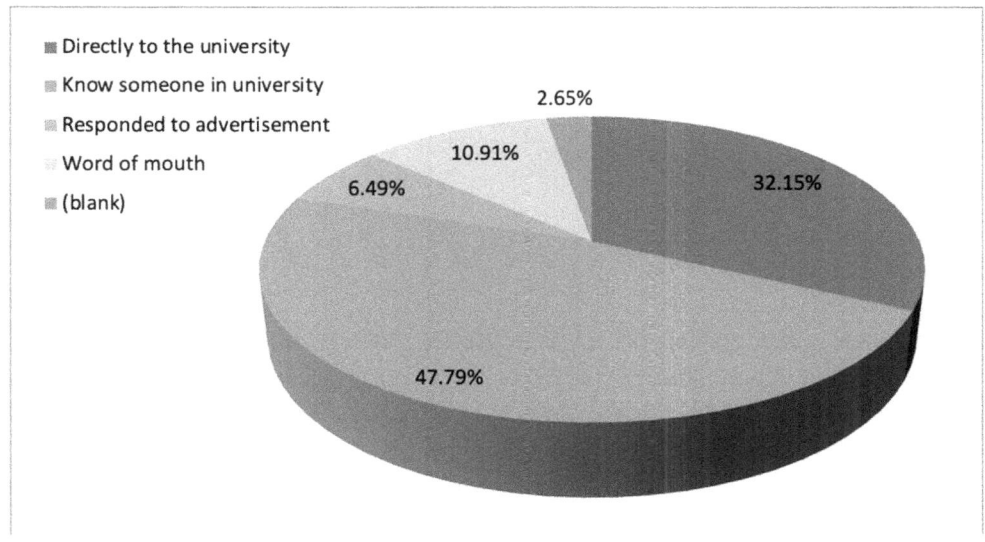

Figure 2 clearly shows the significance of this research and displays important statistics to be published. It illustrates the total percentages of how the respondents applied for a job at the university. It clearly shows that "knowing someone and word of mouth" take a large share of the recruitment style of

Lebanese universities. Over 50% of the respondents got their position through knowing someone within the organization and/or having been told by someone.

Regression Analysis

The regression analysis in Table 5 has tested the impact of Wasta on three HR practices. Below are the question numbers in the survey that was distributed. The total added results of the responses to selected questions were used for the regression analysis (please see the appendix for survey).

- Question 14 as the dependent variable
- Question 17 (for performance)
- Question 23 (for compensation)
- Question 28 (for training)

The first model examines the influence of Wasta on compensation.

Table 5. ANOVA Table – Compensation

ANOVA^b

Model		Sum of Squares	df	Mean Square	F	Sig.
1	Regression	14.185	1	14.185	23.889	.000^a
	Residual	206.039	347	.594		
	Total	220.223	348			

a. Predictors: (Constant), *Wasta*

b. Dependent variable: *compensation*

The ANOVA table is the analysis of variance (Kothari, 2004). In Table 5 the important figure to concentrate on is the Sig. which indicates the exact significance level of ANOVA. If the numbers here are less than the critical value of alpha, then it is said to be significant (Kothari, 2004). This value is normally set at 0.5. Should the value in the Sig. column be less than that, then it is said to be significant. Note that even though the Sig. is noted at .000 it is not really zero, however the number is too small to show up in the number of decimals. Being significant denotes that the 'means' differ more than what is expected by chance alone.

Regarding the influence of Wasta on compensation, there is a positive relationship and the correlation coefficient is 0.25. Based on the regression equation and the t-test results, there is a significant relationship between Wasta and compensation at a 95% confidence level. However, it appears from the ANOVA table that R^2 is limited and equal to 6.4%. So, the variation of the independent variable explains only 6.4% of the variation of the dependent variable; this can be explained by the fact that other factors than Wasta contribute in the explanation regarding compensation.

Regarding the influence of Wasta on training (Table 6), there is also a positive relationship but the correlation coefficient is 0.15. Apparently, training and Wasta have a weaker correlation than the one that exists between compensation and Wasta. Again, it appears from the ANOVA table that R^2 is limited and equal to 2.3%. So the variation of the independent variable explains only 2.3% of the variation of the dependent variable; this can be explained by the fact that other factors than Wasta contribute in the explanation of the training. However, we can say that there is a positive relationship, which is shown by the confidence level of 95%. Hence, H1 Wasta and training have a relationship The ANOVA for training in table 6above shows a Sig. of .005, which is still below the 0.5. This makes it significant.

Table 6. ANOVA and training

ANOVA[b]

Model		Sum of Squares	df	Mean Square	F	Sig.
1	Regression	5.492	1	5.492	8.138	.005[a]
	Residual	231.505	343	.675		
	Total	236.997	344			

a. Predictors: (Constant), *Wasta*

b. Dependent variable: *training*

In Table 7 the important figure to concentrate on is the Sig. which indicates the exact significance level of ANOVA. If the numbers here are less than the critical value of alpha, then it is said to be significant (Kothari, 2004). This value is normally set at 0.5. Should the value in the Sig. column be less than that, then it is said to be significant. Note that even though the Sig. is noted at .000 it is not really zero, however the number is too small to show up in the number of decimals. Being significant denotes that the 'means' differ more than what is expected by chance alone. The significance in the ANOVA table in table 9 shows a figure of .001 which is also still below the .005. This indicates that it is significant. In the third model, the results are similar to the first two models. There is a positive relationship between Wasta and career, and the correlation between these two variables is 0.17. The relationship is significant at a 95% confidence level, but the explanatory power of the model given by R^2 is limited to 3.1%. These results suggest that Wasta has a significant influence on the different variables considered, but it is not the only factor. As the relationship shows a confidence level of 95%, it can be deduced that H1 Wasta and career have a relationship.

Table 7. ANOVA and career

ANOVA[b]

Model		Sum of Squares	df	Mean Square	F	Sig.
1	Regression	7.688	1	7.688	10.894	.001[a]
	Residual	242.752	344	.706		
	Total	250.439	345			

a. Predictors: (Constant), *Wasta*

b. Dependent variable: *career*

The three regression models above explain the following: that *Wasta* is related to training, compensation and career development. Each one alone is not strong in correlation. It seems that there are different factors that are also involved, which opens further avenues for more specific research into each area. Moreover, these three models have been able to prove a positive relationship between three HR practices and *Wasta* that have not been tested before.

Interview Results

Hofstede's cultural values for Lebanon discuss the prominence of obedience to authority and control. It also discusses the view of importance of family life, where people give up their independence (Dirani, 2006; Kabasakal, 2012). When it comes to personal questions, Lebanese fear disappointing the hierarchy, so it is believed that not all the questions were filled in. Noting this, 69 surveys were not completed properly. According to Hofsetede as well, Lebanese loyalty is quite prominent (Dirani, 2006) and this is also another factor in the data having a weaker correlation. Consequently, as this research is exploratory, it is imperative that qualitative data are obtained in order to validate the information collected, and provide an even clearer picture of *Wasta*.

The frequency of the words used within the interviews shows the importance of this aspect within HR practices. When a person uses words or phrases such as '*Wasta*', 'know someone', 'someone I know', 'a friend', 'family friend' and 'personal friend who introduced me', it shows the degree of frequency of the presence of *Wasta* and the extent of its influence in people's daily lives.

Table 8, which collates responses to the interview questions, demonstrates the presence of *Wasta* within HRM practices in the Lebanese university sector.

Table 8. Collated responses to interview questions

Interview question	Collated Reponses
How did you hear about the job?	*a friend I know; someone I know; knowing someone* (17/20)
Was there an interview for the selection process?	*Sometimes yes/sometimes no; no real recruitment process*
Are jobs advertised?	*They do not advertise; there is nothing on the website; they ask around to see if there is someone suiting who they want; mostly 'word-of-mouth*
Did it help in getting the job if you knew someone in the institution?	*provides more leverage; different if you know someone; your qualifications don't really matter* (20/20)
How does *Wasta* affect the workplace?	*without Wasta, you can be pushed around/transferred/unable to speak up ; receive higher salary; receive special treatment covertly; better promotions; gives more confidence; can be used to intimidate;*
How do people advance in their career?	*it's who you know, not what you know that counts (14/20); you need merit (4/20) you need merit and Wasta; you cannot advance unless you have a Wasta;*
Is there performance appraisal system (PAS) in place?	*No performance appraisal (5/20); some places have a PAS*

DISCUSSION AND CONTRIBUTION

Wasta is an interpersonal process of influence operating in the Middle East that needs to be better understood, particularly as it relates to human resource management. There is limited information regarding HR practices in Lebanon and the Middle East and a dearth of empirical studies of the effects of *Wasta* in a business context. However, it is important to reiterate here that this is the first time *Wasta* has been tested with other variables in order to measure its impact. There is no previous literature that examines the impact or influence of *Wasta* on HR practices (Tlaiss & Kauser, 2011).

Thus, this research has defined *Wasta* within HR practices and duly within HRM. Through the data analysis, including the regression analyses and the provision of qualitative data, this project has been able to prove that *Wasta* does have an effect on HR practices and HRM. It has been able to examine the effects of *Wasta* on employees, including on motivation. Through surveys and interviews, this research has captured individual's thoughts, experiences and feelings with regards to *Wasta*. The response rate to the survey was high and provided this research with important data to prove that there is a significant relationship between *Wasta* and HR practices. This research has defined the effects of *Wasta* on HR practices and created a Model as a foundation for future research – the Wasta Model.

In summary, the research concludes that *Wasta* influences recruitment, selection, compensation and promotion in the Lebanese university sector, as follows:

1. Significantly, 58.6% of participants reported attaining their job through 'knowing someone'. Thus, it is concluded that *Wasta* is one of the most important ways of recruiting and selecting employees in Lebanese universities.
2. A positive correlation was established between *Wasta* and training. This constitutes a major issue for HRM in the institutions studied. It is unfortunate that over 46% of respondents disagree that they are able to access information, workshops and training to better themselves and complete necessary HRP. Additionally, given that similar cultural mores and value systems exist across the Middle East region, it can be extrapolated that training in Middle Eastern universities requires urgent attention to ensure that correct HRM procedures are being followed. Institutions disregarding the rights of its employees can expect to encounter serious issues regarding HRM issues.
3. *Wasta* and compensation were shown to have a positive relationship, but there were also other factors involved. Survey results showed that a majority of employees in the Lebanese university sector are being given benefits below their entitlement. It is unfortunate that none of the sections were fully receiving the compensation that they deserve. The resulting insecurity and feelings of being undervalued in their workplace is of real concern for a majority of the respondents studied in the interviews. The incentive to perform to their full potential was found to be lacking across the study sites and this has important implications for organisations in terms of their HRM.
4. The effects of *Wasta* on career development were established, with a correlation of 0.17. Data gleaned from the interviews demonstrates the role that a large number of the respondents (70%) feel *Wasta* plays in advancing their careers; it is also acknowledged that factors other than *Wasta* are also in play. The literature indicates that it is when employees have the chance of being a part of a system that they are encouraged to develop their own interests and paths (Schwind et al, 2013). It is demonstrated that *Wasta* excludes many employees from this process.

Thus, *Wasta* has a significant impact on central HR practices and prevents HR practices within the university sector in Lebanon to be carried out effectively. To counter this adverse influence, the *Wasta* Model has been developed to assist in identifying problems stemming from this indirect and corrosive means of influencing one's position within the university.

The *Wasta* Model

Rationale

The *Wasta* Model has been created as a product of the research undertaken for this project, and the resulting data analysis performed. It is the first Model of its kind and is an original contribution to knowledge. It can now be understood how *Wasta* affects each HR practice and the pernicious tracks that it creates are able to be followed. This has not been known before and as a result of this research, the effects of *Wasta* are now understood.

This model provides individuals, managers, strategic planners, employees, students and researchers with a benchmark to build on and improve HR practices within an organisation. In addition, a model is needed in order for western business practices to fathom the variables that are in play and of concern when dealing with Middle East business partners. This model is based on the data that was received through the three hypotheses that were tested, where it was found that:

- H₁*Wasta* and training have a relationship
- H₁*Wasta* and compensation have a relationship
- H₁*Wasta* and career development have a relationship

The model thus explicates the whole *Wasta* picture allowing the weak points in the HRPs of an organization to be mapped, and managers to determine issues or difficulties in recruiting strategies. The resulting improvement in the strength of the HRM structure of an organization will also strengthen the human capital and thereby promote the sustainability of an organization.

Theoretical Basis for the Wasta Model

Budhwar & Mellahi (2006) and Iles et al. (2012) state that the micro and macro environment play a vital role in the careers of individuals – culturally, socially and legally. Also, Hofstede's dimensions denote that culture plays a significant role. In Figure 3 below, the outer frame of the *Wasta* Model includes the economic, social, cultural and political environments that constantly influence the organizational culture of an institution.

The political environment plays an integral role in the Middle East (Hasrouny, 2012; UNDP report, 2013; Dessler, 2003). Lebanon is an under-developed country and has continuously been going through political instability for the last 40 years. It is currently still undergoing political strife due to the surrounding politics, both external and internal to the country. The social factors include the society at large, social values and family factors, as well as the socioeconomic status and educational background of the individuals (Dessler, 2003, Dutch, 2013; Afiouni et al, 2013).

The economic factors, which include currency fluctuations, import and export businesses, international trade and foreign policies and investments, also play a role, (Dessler, 2003; UNDP, 2013). These factors of course play a role for any organization in understanding and trying to sustain itself in any economic crisis within Lebanon.

Culture is another important factor within the model as it contains issues like cultural differences between countries (between neighboring countries) as well as religious and ethnic issues. Also sub-cultures within regional areas and within organizations. As researchers have pointed out like Dirani, 2006; Iles et al, 2012, Jamali et al, 2010, that the family plays a pivotal role and its effects on the employees are very important to understand for any Lebanese organization. The effects on employees are imperative for any manager to understand in order to be help in the motivation and development of employees as well as employee retention.

Figure 3. Wasta Model developed for this research

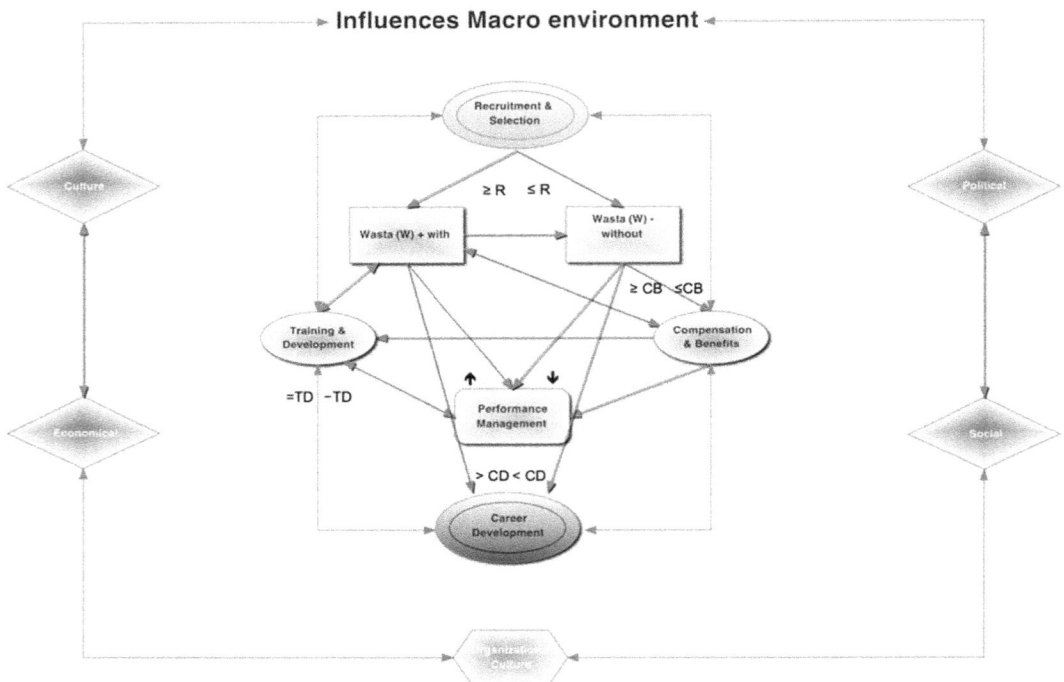

Within the middle of the model are the HR practices that affect each individual from within the organization. To reiterate, the features of these HR practices are as follows: Recruitment and Selection is the procedure by which one applies to an organization with the view to selection for employment (Mathis & Jackson, 2010). Training and Development is the process of being given orientation and training sessions in order to have the skills to get the job done (Armstrong, 2009). Compensation and Benefits is the package that a person receives, including base salary plus any other benefits like insurance, retirement and so on, in exchange for work completed (Schwind et el, 2013), and Performance Management is the process of getting appraised through evaluations by setting goals and objectives and getting feedback.

Finally, Career Development is the opportunity to enhance oneself and get promoted to another position due to hard work or promotion (Dessler, 2013).

Table 9 introduces the abbreviations for the *Wasta* model to be used as a legend when discussing the model.

Table 9. Wasta model- legend of abbreviations

+W	With the use of a *Wasta*
−W	Without the use of a *Wasta*
R>	Greater chance of recruitment/or positively recruited
R<	Less chance of recruitment/not recruited
T=	Received training & development
T-	No training received
CB>	Improved compensation & Benefits
CB<	Declining Compensation & Benefits
CD>	Promotion in career development
CD<	No further/minimal career development

Structure of the Wasta Model

As can be seen in the model, there are arrows that connect that macro-environment showing that each factor is also affected by the other. The macro environment certainly impacts the organization and its success within the organization and within society. In the middle of the model are the HRPs labeled denoting the HRPs of any organization. Within the model, the reader will see the word *Wasta* designated by the letter (W) and (+), meaning 'with *Wasta*', on the left side of the model and (-) meaning 'without *Wasta*' on the right side of the model.

The model begins at the top with recruitment and selection. As in any organization this is the first step in entering a company. Most recruitment, according to Robbins & Judge (2015), Phillips & Gully (2015), Dessler (2013), is done through various channels where applicants apply for advertised positions. Hence, the recruitment process begins objectively through accepting applications and then selecting according to selection procedures. As stated above, the data from this research project has shown that applicants did not apply through the normal means of responding to an advertisement. They received a job through *Wasta*. Hence, should an individual get a job through *Wasta*, they are in the 'with *Wasta* (W+)' section of the model. According to the research data, over 58% of individuals got their job through knowing someone. This supports the fact that there are individuals who have begun their job with *Wasta* and the latter's pernicious influence continues through subsequent HRPs. The interviews also indicated this. Once a person enters via *Wasta* ('W+'), the *Wasta* follows them throughout the other HRPs. This means that with a *Wasta* 'W+' a person gets training at the organization (=TD). This follows through compensation, which means that with 'W+', the person gets better compensation and benefits. This is denoted by the symbol $\geq$ CB. The person with *Wasta* also gets an actual performance appraisal or a better performance appraisal, this denoted by the symbol $\uparrow$ within the *Wasta* chain, when a person has a *Wasta*, they also have better chances of further advancing their career, denoted by the following symbol >CD. The regression analysis, although it showed a weak correlation, indicated that there was a relationship between the HRPs and *Wasta*. The interviews in section 5.7 also indicated strongly that once an individual had a *Wasta* within the organization, it made things much easier when completing the employment cycle.

The concept is that should a person have *Wasta* (W+), then the HR practices to follow shall have a greater chance of being affected. Should the person not have *Wasta* (W-), the HR practices to follow will have a lesser chance of being affected by *Wasta*.

If a person is recruited without a *Wasta* (W) –, then they are recruited as $\leq$R, so then, when it comes to training and development, they do not always get any training (–TD). They also do not have a chance of getting better compensation ($\leq$ CB) hence they get less compensation than the others. Without *Wasta* also means that the individual does not get a performance appraisal, which is denoted by the symbol $\downarrow$ in the *Wasta* model. The individual also has less chance of getting a better career or being promoted to another job is denoted by the symbol <CD.

It was also found through both the survey and interviews that;

- *Wasta* and recruitment have a relationship
- *Wasta* and performance management have a relationship.

This model has shown that *Wasta* has an impact on the HRPs of the organization and it has a domino effect on all the HRPs. When a person enters the organization via *Wasta*, they are seen to be strong and confident. They are a 'force'' to be reckoned with, in that they have someone supporting them throughout their career. They will always have this *Wasta*, this relationship that they need to support and be supported by. A person that does not have *Wasta* and by chance gets recruited by the organisation, enters without support and finds the situation difficult within the organization. That is, they do not have the support of *Wasta* and find that whatever needs to get done, gets done in a difficult manner, as there is no support.

Through the interviews that were conducted, the researcher was able to support the concept of a *Wasta* model with specific details of difficulties encountered by employees and their opinions on that topic. Various individuals discussed within their interviews their frustrations with the fact that they did not have *Wasta* and/or did not know someone within the organization and that this made their job dissatisfying due to the difficulties in getting proper employment. It also led to the fact that if an individual did not have *Wasta*, it made it more difficult to get employed. This is transcribed to less chance of recruitment (<R), without *Wasta*; it also means in terms of compensation that the individual who does not have *Wasta* will not receive the right compensation or equitable compensation (<C). Many individuals stated that as they did not know anyone within the organization it was difficult to obtain the wages that they deemed fair and equitable for their position. Others indicated that, for the same position across the university, different people were on different wage levels and it was not dependent on their educational qualification. One person even indicated that there were those individuals that did not have

the appropriate educational qualifications, but were earning much more than the individuals who had the proper qualifications. The arrows within the model indicate the interchangeable effects that each HR practice has on the other or following HR practice. Thus, the *Wasta* model elucidates the concept, " the weak get weaker and the strong get stronger".

RECOMMENDATIONS

A number of recommendations are suggested in order to decrease the use of Wasta and implement appropriate HRPs within Educational Institutions. The recommendations listed below are three-fold, beginning with recommendations for the Higher Education Institution, Ministry of Higher Education and the Ministry of Labour in Lebanon.

It is recommended that Higher Education institutions conduct both an internal and external audit of their organizations HR policies and procedures. In doing so they will need to create job descriptions and specifications based on each level within the organization. In order to reflect transparency, higher education institutions need to create standardized recruitment and selection procedures, including job fit and testing. In doing so, they would have to ensure appropriate training and development programs that allow for introductory orientation and continual training needs depending on the employee's knowledge, skills and abilities.

It is responsibility of the Ministry of Higher Education to enact guidelines and pass national laws to control recruitment, selection, compensation and benefit laws. This would create standards for which both the only public and private universities would benefit from. Hence creating the driving force in order to monitor transparency and equal employment issues within the higher education sector.

The Ministry of Labour has equal responsibilities in updated its labour law from 1943 and institute higher education reforms, supporting the creation of new standards and objectives for Higher Education institutions.

CONCLUSION

This research is considered important because it provides an insight into the impact of *Wasta* on HRM practices in the Middle East and other regions. However, the research on *Wasta* and its effects on HR and HRM has only just begun. The impact of *Wasta* on individuals is greater than what has been illustrated or displayed in this research. Thus, the importance of *Wasta* within a culture like Lebanon must be discussed further and extended to all areas where *Wasta* negatively impacts on employees and organisations.

This research thus undertook to elucidate this area of study into HR practices, focusing on the higher education sector in Lebanon. In doing so, it has set the groundwork for future researchers to continue important research into an area of HRM. This continuing scrutiny has the potential to positively affect the lives of personnel employed by organizations and institutions in the Middle East by assisting in the process of organizational reform. This research has set a pillar in order to continue the path of uncovering the effects of Wasta in other industries in Lebanon.

Wasta is a pervasive and pernicious feature of the culture of the Middle East and its effect on performance and standards within organizations in the region is unfortunate. Though it may never be totally eliminated, being so endemic to the culture, it presents a challenge to future researchers to find ways to counter and negotiate it, while introducing new and healthier HR practices. It is hoped the *Wasta* model will ensure optimum performance in workplaces across the region, particularly in the university sector in Lebanon, from which the future leaders of this troubled country will emerge.

The *Wasta* Model marks the beginning in understanding how *Wasta* plays a role in the HR practices within any organization. It is imperative that this beginning has been made in order to open doors for future research. The *Wasta* Model is the first of its kind and it is the hope of the researcher that it is the beginning of finding a solution to the negative effects that *Wasta* has on employee motivation and organizational behavior.

This research has defined Wasta within the HR practices and duly within HRM. Through the data analysis, including the regression analysis and the provision of qualitative data, this project has been able to prove that Wasta does have an effect on HR practices and HRM. This research has examined the effects of HR practices within four universities based on the responses of 349 employees in universities in Lebanon. The response rate was high and provided this research with important data to prove that there is a significant relationship between Wasta and HR practices. This research has defined the effects of Wasta on HR practices and created a framework as a foundation for future research.

REFERENCES

Abu-Doleh, J., & Weir, D. (2007). Dimensions of performance appraisal systems in Jordanian private and public organizations. *International Journal of Human Resource Management, 18*(1), 75–84. doi:10.1080/09585190601068334

Afiouni, F. (2007). Human Resource Management and strategy in the Lebanese Banking sector: Is there a fit? *Journal of American Academy of Business, 12*(1), 63-69. Retrieved from: https://www.academia.edu/200418/Human_Resource_Management_and_Strategy_in_the_Lebanese_Banking_sector_Is_there_a_fit

Afiouni, F., Karam, C. M., & El-Hajj, H. (2013). The HR value proposition model in the Arab Middle East: Identifying the contours of an Arab Middle Eastern HR model. *International Journal of Human Resource Management, 24*(10), 1895–1932. doi:10.1080/09585192.2012.722559

Armstrong, M. (2009). *Armstrong's Handbook of Human Resource Management Practices.* Kogan Page.

Baruch, Y. (2003). Career systems in transition. *Personnel Review, 32*(2), 231–251. doi:10.1108/00483480310460234

Budhwar, P. S., & Mellahi, K. (2006). *Managing Human Resources in the Middle East.* Routledge Taylor & Francis Group. Retrieved from: www.eBookstore.tandf.co.uk

Cohen, D. J. (2015). HR Past, present & future: A call for consistent practices and a focus on competencies. *Human Resource Management Review, 25*(2), 205–215. doi:10.1016/j.hrmr.2015.01.006

Dessler, G. (2003). *Human Resource Management* (9th ed.). Prentice Hall.

Dessler, G. (2013). *Human Resource Management* (13th ed.). Pearson Education.

Dessler, G., & Al Ariss, A. (2013). *Human Resource Management* (Global Edition). Pearson Education.

Dirani, K. (2006). Exploring Socio-Cultural Factors that Influence HRD Practices in Lebanon. *Human Resource Development International*, 9(1), 85–98. doi:10.1080/13678860500523270

Dirani, K. (2009). Measuring the learning organization culture, organizational commitment and job satisfaction in the Lebanese banking sector. *Human Resource Development International*, 12(2), 189–208. doi:10.1080/13678860902764118

Dutch, M. (2013, Mar.). A Symbiotic Framework of Human Resources, Organizational Strategy and Culture. *Amity Global Business Review*, 9-14. Retrieved from: http://eds.a.ebscohost.com.ezproxy.cqu.edu.au/eds/pdfviewer/pdfviewer?vid=36&sid=1cf1e33d-d010-44d7-80fd-db87f99a276a%40sessionmgr4004&hid=4202

Feghali, R. (2014). Wasta: Connections or Corruption in the Arab World. *The Global Investigator*. Retrieved at: http://www.nardelloandco.com/wastaconnections-corruption-arab-world

Giangreco, A., Carugati, A., Pilati, M., & Sebastiano, A. (2010). Performance appraisal systems in the Middle East: Moving beyond Western logics. *European Management Review*, 7(3), 155–168. doi:10.1057/emr.2010.13

Hasrouny, A. (2012). Lebanon: Higher Education at risk without reform. *University World News*, 155. Retrieved from: https://www.universityworldnews.com/article.php?story=20110122084153924

Iles, P., Almhedie, A., & Baruch, Y. (2012). Managing HR in the Middle East: Challenges in the Public Sector. *Public Personnel Management*, 41(3), 465–492. doi:10.1177/009102601204100305

Jamali, D., Abdallah, H., & Hmaidan, S. (2010). The challenge of moving beyond rhetoric. *Equality, Diversity and Inclusion*, 29(2), 167–185. doi:10.1108/02610151011024484

Kabasakal, H., Dastmalchian, A., Karacay, G., & Bayraktar, S. (2012). Leadership and culture in the MENA region: An analysis of the GLOBE project. *Journal of World Business*, 47(4), 519–529. Advance online publication. doi:10.1016/j.jwb.2012.01.005

Kiessling, T., & Harvey, M. (2005). Strategic global human resource management research in the twenty-first century: an endorsement of the mixed methods research methodology. *International Journal of Human Resource Management*, 16(1), 22-45. doi:10.1080/0958519042000295939

Kipkebut, D. (2010). Human Resource Management Practices and Organizational Commitment in Higher Educational Institutions: A Kenyan Case. *The IUP Journal of Organizational Behavior*, 9(1 & 2), 45-70.

Kothari, C. R. (2004). Research Methodology, Methods and Techniques. New Delhi: New Age International (P) Ltd.

Leigh, L. (2009). Breaking down corporate secrecy in the Middle East: Lessons learned from a successful "infomediary". *European Business Review*, 23(2), 154–166. doi:10.1108/09555341111111183

Mathis, R. L., & Jackson, J. H. (2010). *Human Resource Management*. South-Western Cengage Learning.

Mohamed, A., & Mohamed, S. (2011). The effect of Wasta on perceived competence and morality in Egypt. *Cross Cultural Management*, 18(4), 412–425. doi:10.1108/13527601111179492

Mohamed, F., & Singh, S. (2010). HRM Practices in local and multinational companies: Survey and Conceptual Model, Proceedings of the European Conference on Management. *Leadership & Governance*, 241-248. Retrieved from: http://eds.a.ebscohost.com.ezproxy.cqu.edu.au/eds/pdfviewer/pdfviewer?sid=3a3

Morris, S., Wright, P., Trevor, J., Stiles, P., Stahl, G., Snell, S., Paauwe, J., & Farndale E. (2009). Global Challenges to Replicating HR: The Role of People, Processes and systems. *Human Resource Management*, *48*(6), 973-995. doi:10.1002/hrm.20325

Phillips, J. M., & Gully, S. M. (2015). *Strategic Staffing*. Pearson.

Qu, S., & Dumay, J. (2011). The qualitative research interview. *Qualitative Research in Accounting & Management*, *8*(3), 238–264. doi:10.1108/11766091111162070

Robbins, S. P., & Judge, T. A. (2015). *Organizational Behavior*. Pearson.

Schwind, H., Das, H., Wagar, T., Fassina, N., & Bulmash, J. (2013). *Canadian Human Resource Management: A Strategic Approach*. McGraw Hill Ryerson.

Stone, D. L., Stone-Romero, E. F., & Lukaszewski, K. M. (2007). The impact of cultural values on the acceptance and effectiveness of human resource management policies and practices. *Human Resource Management Review*, *17*(2), 152–165. doi:10.1016/j.hrmr.2007.04.003

Tlaiss, H. (2013). Determinants of job satisfaction in the banking sector: The case of Lebanese Managers. *Employee Relations*, *35*(4), 377–395. doi:10.1108/ER-10-2011-0064

Tlaiss, H., & Kauser, S. (2011). The importance of Wasta in the career success of Middle Eastern managers. *Journal of European Industrial Training*, *35*(5), 467–486. doi:10.1108/03090591111138026

Ulrich, D., & Dulebohn, J. H. (2015). Are we there yet? What's next for HR? *Human Resource Management Review*, *25*(2), 188–204. doi:10.1016/j.hrmr.2015.01.004

United Nations Development Program. (2013). *The Lebanon We Want: Post-2015 National Consultations in Lebanon*. Retrieved from: www.undp.org/lb

Wadsworth, Y. (2012). How to make (more) common sense: Inquiry cycles as a meta-epistemology of multiple methods, methodologies, perspectives and approaches. *International Journal of Multiple Research Approaches, 6*(1), 88-96. Retrieved from https://search-informit-com-au.ezproxy.cqu.edu.au/documentSummary;dn=738656488356913;res=IELHSS

Wall Street Journal. (2010). *Abu Dhabi's 'Wasta' could save BP*. Retrieved from https://blogs.wsj.com/source/2010/07/07/abu-dhabis-wasta-could-save-bp/

Yahchouchi, G., & Bouloukian, N. (2014). Empowerment, job insecurity and quality of job performance of faculty members: An empirical analysis. *European Journal of Education Sciences*, *1*(2), 283–296. http://ejes.eu/wpcontent/uploads/2016/01/1-2-21.pdf

Zahra, S. (2011). Doing research in the (New) Middle East: Sailing the wind. *The Academy of Management Perspectives*, *25*(November), 6–21. doi:10.5465/amp.2011.0128

This research was previously published in the International Journal of Applied Management Sciences and Engineering (IJAMSE), 7(2); pages 20-42, copyright year 2020 by IGI Publishing (an imprint of IGI Global).

APPENDIX A. QUESTIONNAIRE

Questionnaire _____

This questionnaire is intended solely for research, it aims to analyze the relationship between employees in universities and Human resource management strategies. All information collected will remain anonymous and will provide data for the objective in the development of research on the Difficulties in implementing HR strategies in Lebanese universities. Attached you will find a detailed information sheet for your perusal. Should you wish to participate in the research study, kindly fill in this questionnaire. This will be deemed as consent in participating. So thank you for kindly responding honestly to these questions.

EMPLOYEE PROFILE

1. I am:	☐ Female	☐ Male			
2. I live in:	☐ Beirut City	☐ Mount Leb.	☐ North Leb.	☐ South Leb.	☐ Bekaa
	Please specify:				
3. My age is (in years):	☐ 16-29	☐ 30-39	☐ 40-49	☐ 50-59	☐ +60
4. I am the primary wage earner in the household:	☐ Yes	☐ No			
5. What is your marital status?	☐ Married	☐ Single	☐ Divorced	☐ Widowed	

EDUCATION PROFILE

6. I graduated from a:	☐ Public School ☐ Private School	Please name which school?_____
	☐ Public University ☐ Private University	Please name which university?_____
7. My highest education level:	☐ Brevet (Gr.9) ☐ Terminal (Gr.12)	☐ Bachelors ☐ Masters ☐ Doctoral
	Other:_____	
8. My area of Specialization is:	☐ Business ☐ Science ☐ Literature ☐ Engineering ☐ Law	
	☐ Human Sciences Other:_____	

WORK EXPERIENCE

9. I hold the position of:	☐ Administration ☐ Academic	Please specify:_____		

10. List of positions held during professional experience (you can choose more than one):

Position				
Administrative assistant	☐ <2	☐ 3-5	☐ 6-10	☐ >10
Assistant to the dean	☐ <2	☐ 3-5	☐ 6-10	☐ >10
Student adviser	☐ <2	☐ 3-5	☐ 6-10	☐ >10
Head of department	☐ <2	☐ 3-5	☐ 6-10	☐ >10
Dean	☐ <2	☐ 3-5	☐ 6-10	☐ >10
Others:_____	☐ <2	☐ 3-5	☐ 6-10	☐ >10

11. Type of contract:	☐ Yearly contract	☐ Tenure contract	☐ Part-time job	☐ Full-time job
12. Hours per week employed:	☐ <20	☐ 20-39	☐ >40	
13. Years of service with this organization:	☐ <2	☐ 3-5	☐ 6-10	☐ >10
14. I applied to the university:	☐ Responded to advertisement	☐ Know someone in university	☐ Directly to the university	☐ Word of mouth
15. I signed a contract for my job that details all the duties that I must perform			☐ Yes	☐ No
16. I received a promotion during the last two years			☐ Yes	☐ No
If yes, please specify: _____				
17. Performance appraisal programs are implemented in your organization			☐ Yes	☐ No
If yes, how often:	☐ Once per 6 months		☐ Once per 12 months	
18. Who completes the performance appraisal? (you can choose more than one)	☐ External Organization	☐ HR department	☐ Supervisor	☐ Employee
	Others:_____			
19. I am in the following salary range (USD):	☐ <650	☐ 650-1200	☐ 1200-2300	☐ >2300
20. The remuneration package includes: ☐ Basic salary ☐ Overtime	☐ Social Security	☐ Insurance	☐ Retirement	☐ Bonuses
	Other:_____			
21. The employee can be promoted on basis of (you can choose more than one):	☐ Vacant position to be filled	☐ Evaluation by supervisor	☐ External evaluation	Other:_____
22. The employee gets a raise on basis of (you can choose more than one):	☐ Seniority	☐ New laws	☐ Performance appraisal	
	Others:_____			
23. I received an increase in wages during the last two years			☐ Yes	☐ No
24. I have been on the same wage since I began working for the organization			☐ Yes	☐ No
25. I plan to be working for this organization in two years			☐ Yes	☐ No

Please tick the number	1: Strongly agree	2: Agree	3: Neutral	4: Disagree	5: Strongly disagree		
26. I received all the relevant information about my job before I was employed	□1	□2	□3	□4	□5		
27. It takes too long to hire someone when a position becomes vacant	□1	□2	□3	□4	□5		
28. When I first began my job I received proper training	□1	□2	□3	□4	□5		
29. I was told all the duties that I was to perform in the beginning of my job	□1	□2	□3	□4	□5		
30. The duties that I perform actually match the duties indicated in the job description	□1	□2	□3	□4	□5		
31. I was told about the policies and procedures of the institution:	□1	□2	□3	□4	□5		
32. I feel I am being paid a fair amount for the work I do	□1	□2	□3	□4	□5		
33. Salaries are competitive with similar jobs in the community	□1	□2	□3	□4	□5		
34. Benefits are comparable to those offered in other jobs	□1	□2	□3	□4	□5		
35. People get ahead as fast here as they do in other places	□1	□2	□3	□4	□5		
36. I am satisfied with my chances for promotion	□1	□2	□3	□4	□5		
37. There are benefits we do not have which we should have	□1	□2	□3	□4	□5		
38. I am satisfied with my sick leave	□1	□2	□3	□4	□5		
39. I am satisfied with my vacation	□1	□2	□3	□4	□5		
40. I am satisfied with my retirement	□1	□2	□3	□4	□5		
41. I meet with my supervisor to discuss my performance during the last phase at work	□1	□2	□3	□4	□5		
42. My performance is evaluated fairly	□1	□2	□3	□4	□5		
43. I receive constructive criticism from my supervisor	□1	□2	□3	□4	□5		
44. My supervisor is consistent when administering policies concerning employees	□1	□2	□3	□4	□5		
45. Alternative work schedules (flex-time, compressed work weeks, job sharing, telecommuting) are offered to employees	□1	□2	□3	□4	□5		
46. I like doing the things I do at work	□1	□2	□3	□4	□5		
47. The benefit package we have is equitable	□1	□2	□3	□4	□5		
48. I got the training I need to do my job well.	□1	□2	□3	□4	□5		
49. Training is made available to us for personal growth and development	□1	□2	□3	□4	□5		
50. Training is made available to us so that we can do our jobs better	□1	□2	□3	□4	□5		
51. We have access to information about job opportunities, conferences, workshops, & training	□1	□2	□3	□4	□5		
52. Our team is well matched	□1	□2	□3	□4	□5		
53. I sometimes feel my job is routine	□1	□2	□3	□4	□5		
54. Every employee is valued	□1	□2	□3	□4	□5		
55. The right information gets to the right people at the right time	□1	□2	□3	□4	□5		
56. The work atmosphere encourages open and honest communication	□1	□2	□3	□4	□5		
57. There is a basic trust among employees and supervisors	□1	□2	□3	□4	□5		
58. The amount of work I am asked to do is reasonable	□1	□2	□3	□4	□5		
59. There is a real feeling of teamwork	□1	□2	□3	□4	□5		
60. The environment supports a balance between work and personal life	□1	□2	□3	□4	□5		
61. My job meets my expectations	□1	□2	□3	□4	□5		
62. We balance our focus on both long range and short term goals	□1	□2	□3	□4	□5		
63. People who challenge the status quo are valued	□1	□2	□3	□4	□5		
64. Work groups are actively involved in making work processes more effective	□1	□2	□3	□4	□5		
65. The people I work with treat each other with respect	□1	□2	□3	□4	□5		
66. Our employees are generally ethical in the workplace	□1	□2	□3	□4	□5		
67. We work well with other organizations	□1	□2	□3	□4	□5		
68. We feel a sense of pride when we tell people that we work for this organization	□1	□2	□3	□4	□5		
69. Would you recommend others to work in your organization?	□1	□2	□3	□4	□5		

70.   What are the reasons you would/wouldn't recommend others to work for your organization?

APPENDIX B – INTERVIEW QUESTIONS

This interview is for research purposes only. The thesis covers HR practices in Lebanese universities and your input would be invaluable. Your thoughts and opinions as well as any observations that you may have are important to this project. I guarantee that all information is confidential and names will not be given.

1. How long have you been in your current position?
2. How did you come to know about the job that you currently hold?
3. Do you know someone within the organization?
4. If yes do you feel that it helped somehow? How did it help?
5. Was there an interview process?
6. Can you describe the interview situation? Individual or panel interview?
7. Did anyone support your position?
8. When you accepted your job, were you given a contract to sign? Job description?
9. Did the compensation and benefits package that was offered to you meet your expectations?
10. Would it be different if you knew someone within? Can you share any examples?
11. When you got the job were you given any training or participated in an orientation session?
12. What type of training were you provided with?
13. Can you describe your experience?
14. Does the organization provide any further training and development?
15. Do you believe that staff requires further training and development? Do they receive further training dependent on knowing someone within?
16. How does the recruitment & selection process take place in your university?
17. Does it make a difference if you know someone in the organization or not?
18. How does it make a difference?
19. How do people advance in their career? Is it based on merit? Or who you know?
20. How do you feel about your job? Are you motivated? Why or why not? Are you affected by others around you?

Chapter 24

Identifying HRM Practices for Improving Information Security Performance:
An Importance–Performance Map Analysis

Peace Kumah

Ghana Education Service, Accra, Ghana

Winfred Yaokumah

(iD) https://orcid.org/0000-0001-7756-1832

Department of Information Technology, Pentecost University College, Accra, Ghana

Charles Buabeng-Andoh

(iD) https://orcid.org/0000-0003-3781-684X

Pentecost University College, Ghana

ABSTRACT

This article focuses on identifying key human resource management (HRM) practices necessary for improving information security performance from the perspective of IT professionals. The Importance-Performance Map Analysis (IPMA) via SmartPLS 3.0 was employed and 232 samples were collected from information technology (IT) professionals in 43 organizations. The analysis identified information security training, background checks and monitoring as very important HRM practices that could improve the performance of organizational information security. In particular, the study found training on mobile devices security and malware; background checks and monitoring of potential, current and former employees as of high importance but with low performance. Thus, these key areas need to be improved with top priority. Conversely, the study found accountability and employee relations as being overly emphasized by the organisations. The findings raised some useful implications and information for HR and IT leaders to consider in future information security strategy.

DOI: 10.4018/978-1-6684-3873-2.ch024

INTRODUCTION

Securing sensitive and critical information is a global concern (Ikenwe, Igbinovia, & Elogie, 2016; White, Hewitt, & Kruck, 2013). It involves protection of information assets from unauthorized access, accidental loss, destruction, disclosure, modification, or misuse (Tassabehji, 2005). Information security is a multi-disciplinary area involving professional activity of developing and implementing technical, organisational, human-oriented security mechanisms in order to keep information systems free from threats (Cherdantseva & Hilton, 2013). As a result of increasing dependency on information technology (IT) systems and emerging security threats and vulnerabilities relating to privacy, identity theft, and cybercrime, the role of IT professionals become crucial for maintaining security of information resources (Khao, Harris, & Hartman, 2010). Information security breaches may result in loss of sensitive information and productivity which may lead to huge financial liabilities, adversely affecting the reputation of the organisation (Abawajy, 2014). Information technology professionals are facing challenging tasks analysing, designing, and deploying solutions to protect information resources. Notwithstanding, previous studies acknowledge that human factors are the major sources of many security failures (Abawajy, 2014; Driscoll & McKee, 2007; Furnell & Thomson, 2009; Komatsu, Takagi, & Takemura, 2013). Human beings are vulnerable to a wide range of security attacks, which range from deliberate violation of security policy to circumvention of physical and technical security controls (Stewart, Tittel, & Chapple, 2005). Moreover, people underestimate the likelihood of the occurrence of security breaches (Herath & Rao, 2009).

A key area in information security research is discovering ways to motivate employee to engage in more secure behaviors (Boss et al., 2015). Human resource management (HRM) practices can address the problem of the human-oriented factors. Human resource management practices of employee recruitment and selection, training and development, performance monitoring and appraisals are very important to improve organisational performance (Naz, Aftab, & Awais, 2016). Investing in training and development can motivate staff and support the growth of the organisation (Leidner & Smith, 2013). IT security and data privacy training can serve as critical controls for safeguarding organisation's information resources (Baxter, Holderness, & Wood, 2016). However, to achieve the best results, security training and awareness programs should be regularly evaluated so that corrective actions can be taken (Rantos, Fysarakis & Manifavas, 2012). In addition, employee relations are seen by employers as critical in achieving job performance through employee involvement, commitment and engagement (Radhakrishna & Raju, 2015). Moreover, employee monitoring is a significant component of employers' efforts to maintain employee productivity (Ford et al., 2015). Employee background checks are important to ascertain criminal records, character, and fitness of the employee (Sarode & Deore, 2017). Furthermore, employee's accountability can improve information security (Vance, Lowry, & Eggett, 2013). However, accountability can have both positive and negative effect on work behavior (Ossege, 2012).

Improving information security by focusing on human resource management practices has not received much attention by researchers. From the perspective of IT professionals, this current study focuses on identifying key HRM practices that can improve information security performance using Importance-Performance Map Analysis (IPMA) (Ringle & Sarstedt, 2016). Specifically, the study identifies the HRM practices that IT professionals perceive as important and whose performance is necessary to improve information security in organisations. The study answers the following research questions:

1. What are the important HRM practices (factors) that can improve the performance of organisational information security?
2. What are the important indicators for enhancing the performance of organisational information security?

Reviewing studies on the use of partial least squares structured equation modelling (PLS-SEM) (Hair et al., 2012; Ringle et al., 2012; Sarstedt et al., 2014) reveals that information security researchers basically rely on the standard PLS path model analysis, ignoring the Importance-Performance Map Analysis (IPMA). IPMA provides guidance for the prioritization of managerial activities of high importance but require performance improvements (Ringle & Sarstedt, 2016). It is particularly useful for generating additional findings and conclusions from the standard PLS-SEM. Thus, in this study IPMA is used to evaluate the level of importance organisations attach to each of the HRM factors and indicators, which can improve information security performance.

BACKGROUND

Concept of Importance-Performance Map Analysis

The study first explains the principles underlying and procedures involved in using IPMA. The first step in creating an importance-performance map (IPM) requires selecting the target construct of interest in the PLS path model (Ringle & Sarstedt, 2016). Consider the PLS path model in Figure 1 with five constructs (C_1 to C_5). In PLS path model in Figure 1, C_5 represents the key target construct. C_5 is directly predicted by C_1 to C_4. Also, C_1 has indirect effect on C_5 via C_2, C_3, and C_4. To perform Importance-Performance Map Analysis, the PLS path model in Figure 1 will be transformed into IPMA grid as shown in Figure 2 with two dimensions – importance and performance dimensions. The addition of the predecessor constructs' (C_1 to C_4) direct and indirect effects yields their total effects on C_5. This represents the importance dimension in the IPMA (Ringle & Sarstedt, 2016). On the other hand, the constructs' average latent variable scores represent the performance dimension in IPMA. The higher values indicate a greater performance and vice versa (Ringle & Sarstedt, 2016). Also, in Figure 1, x_{ij} (for example x_{11}, x_{22}, x_{42}) represents the indicators of the constructs C_i and p_i (p_1 to p_9) represents the path coefficients.

Now, the two dimensions can be plotted graphically by placing the total effects (Importance dimension) on the x-axis and the rescaled latent variable scores (re-scaled on a range from 0 to 100), representing the Performance dimension on the y-axis. This results in an Important-Performance Map in Figure 2. Moreover, the two dimensional IPMA model is further divided into four quadrants. To achieve this, two lines are drawn on the Importance-Performance Map. The vertical line is the mean importance value and the horizontal line is the mean performance value of the constructs. Thus, these two lines divide the Importance-Performance Map into four areas with importance and performance values below and above the average (Figure 2). Generally, when analyzing the Importance-Performance Map, constructs appearing in the lower right area (i.e. Quadrant I) are of the highest interest to achieving improvement in the target construct (C_5), followed by the higher right (i.e. Quadrant II), lower left (i.e. Quadrant III) and, finally, the higher left areas (i.e. Quadrant IV) (Ringle & Sarstedt, 2016).

Figure 1. Concept of path model of IPMA

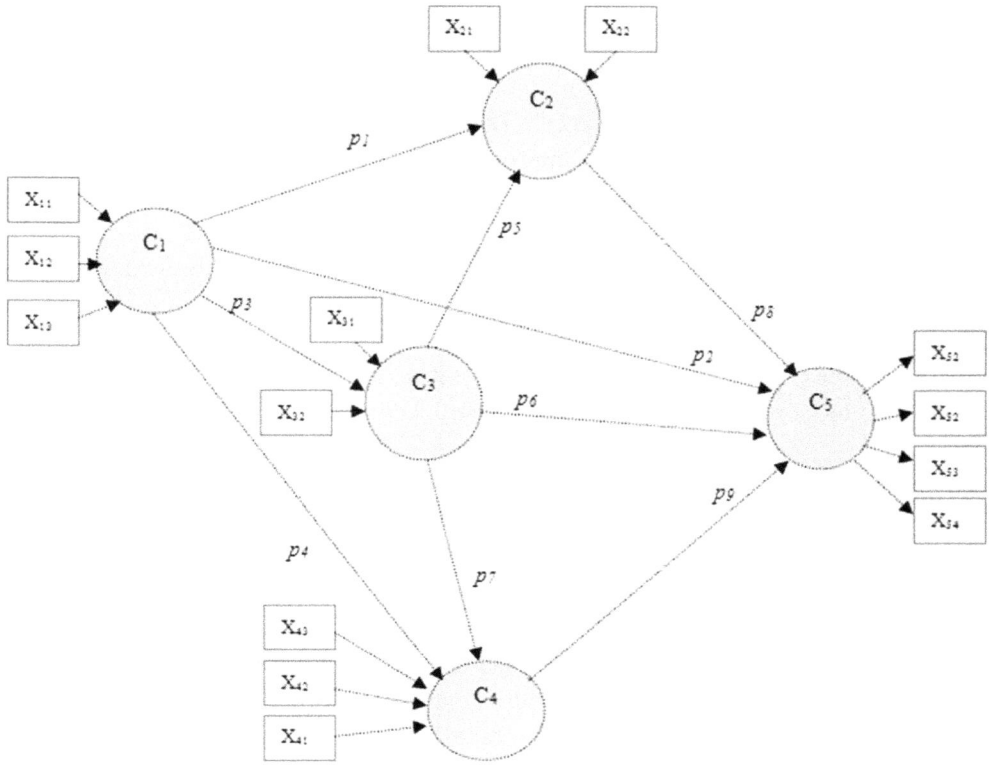

Figure 2. Relative importance-performance regions

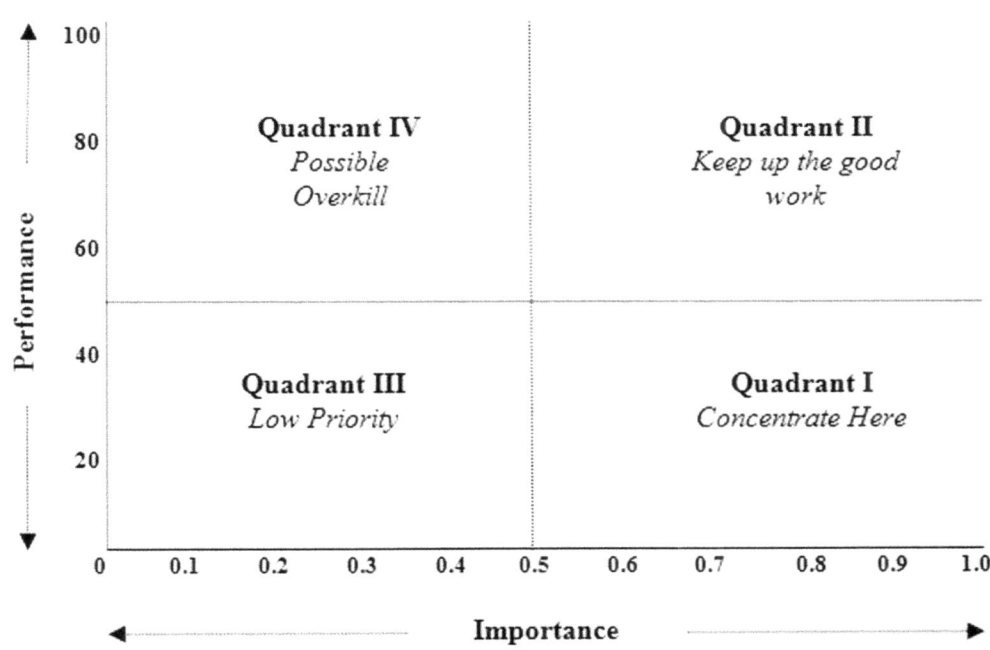

The four quadrants (Figure 2) are generally referred to as *concentrate here (Quadrant I), keep up the good work (Quadrant II) low priority (Quadrant III)*, and *possible overkill (Quadrant IV)*. The constructs and indicators that fall within the quadrants can be interpreted as below (Ringle & Sarstedt, 2016).

Quadrant I (High Importance/Low Performance). The constructs or indicators that fall within this quadrant represent key areas that need to be improved with top priority.

Quadrant II (High Importance/High Performance). All constructs or indicators that fall within this quadrant are the strength of the organisations.

Quadrant III (Low Importance/Low Performance). Any of the constructs or indicators that falls within this quadrant is not important to the organisations.

Quadrant IV (Low Importance/High Performance). This denotes constructs or indicators that are overly emphasized by the organisations. Organisations, instead of continuing to focus in this quadrant, should allocate more resources to deal with constructs or indicators that fall within *Quadrant I*.

In particular, to further explain the concept, Figure 3 and Figure 4 demonstrate IPM for both constructs and indicators respectively. In Figure 3, C_1 is particularly important to improve the performance of the target construct C_5, as it falls within the *Quadrant I* (High Importance/Low Performance). More precisely, a one-unit point increase in C_1's performance increases the performance of C_5 by the value of C_1's total effect on C_5. Thus, in Figure 3, the performance of C_1 is relatively low; there is therefore substantial room for improvement, making this construct particularly relevant for managerial actions. Moreover, to generate IPM for indicators, individual data points in the Importance-Performance Map are derived from indicator mean values and their total effect on a particular target construct, C_5. As can be observed in Figure 4, x_{11}, x_{23} have the highest importance but low performance values (Quadrant I). Thus, these indicators will require management attention to improve their performance in order to enhance the performance of the target construct, C_5.

Figure 3. Constructs - IPMA on the target construct, C_5

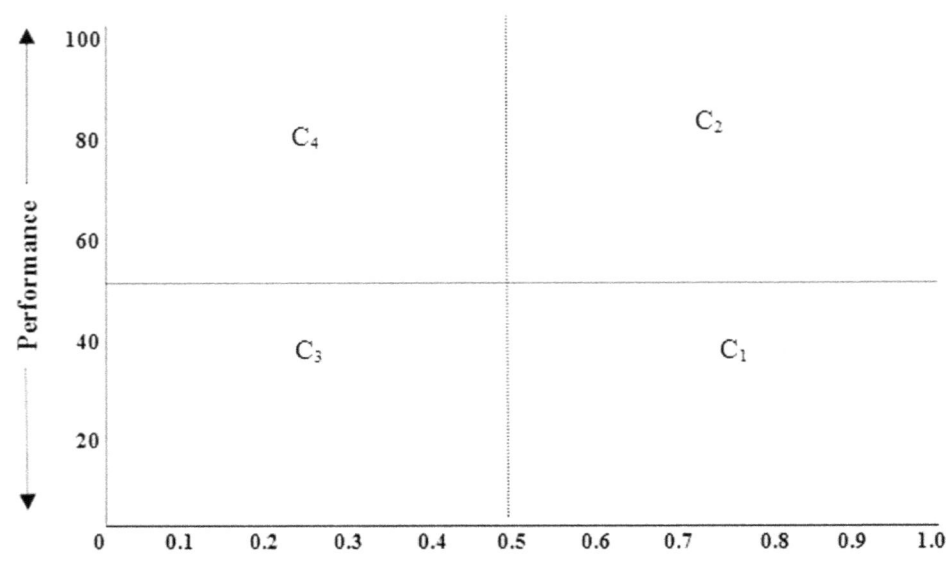

Figure 4. Indicators - IPMA on the Target Construct, C_5

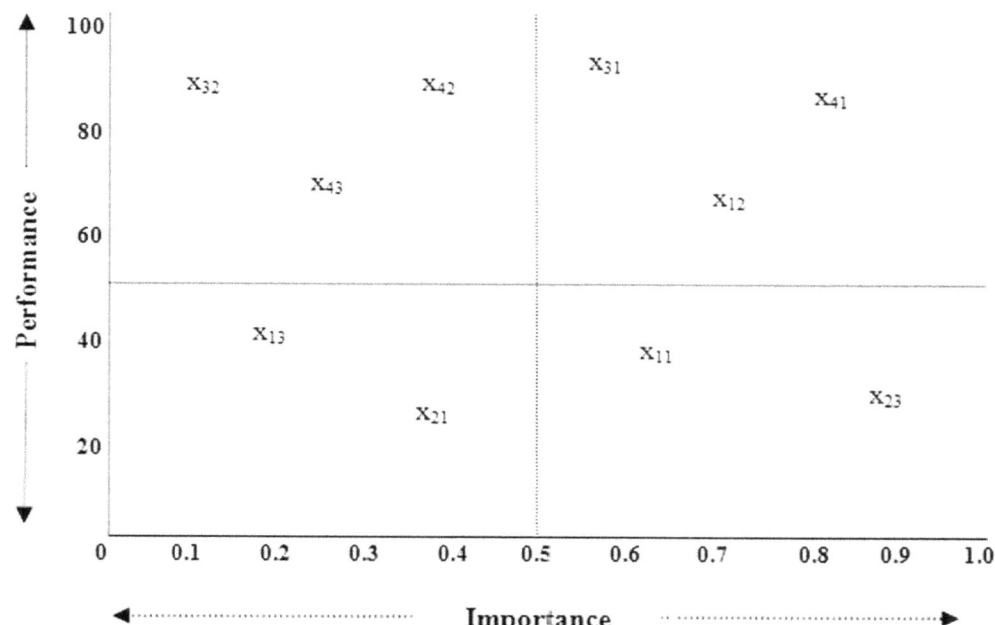

Empirical Background

Information Security

Information security involves managing risks related to the use, processing, storage, transmission of information or data and the systems and processes used for those purposes (Yalman & Yesilyurt, 2013). One of the key challenges in information security management is to understand how human factors affect the outcomes of information security in an organisation (Hu et al., 2012). Organisations are taking measures to ensure the security of information (Yalman & Yesilyurt, 2013). However, organisations invest inefficiently in information technology security measures (Zhao, Xue, & Whinston, 2013), while human attitude was identified as having significant impact on compliance with security policy (Zhang, Reithel, & Li, 2009). Thus, technological security solutions alone are ineffective at reducing security breaches. Accordingly to Angst, Block, D'Arcy and Kelley (2017), information technology (IT) security investments are effective at reducing the incidence of data security breaches when they are balanced with institutional factors. According to Herath and Rao (2009), organisational commitment, social influence, and threat perceptions about the severity of breaches affect employees' attitudes toward policy compliance. Burns et al. (2017) established the relationship between organisational insiders' psychological capital with information security threat and coping appraisals. Self-control is a major factor influencing individual behaviour's towards information security (Hu, West, & Smarandescu, 2015).

Organisations should measure their information security performance in order to make the right decisions (Bernik & Prislan, 2016) and channel resources to areas of high importance that will lead to high security performance. A recent study showed that a high level of information security performance is mostly dependent on measures aimed at managing employees (Bernik & Prislan, 2016). Managing employees' security behaviors for better information security performance will require security training and development programs, creating employee relations, background checks and monitoring, and accountability.

Security Training and Development

Investing in training and development can motivate staff and support the growth of the organisations (Leidner & Smith, 2013). While lack of security training often lies behind many contemporary breaches (Lacey, 2010), security education enables skilled professionals and ensures adequate security awareness among end users (Kaspersky & Furnell, 2014). Abawajy (2014) evaluated the effects of various information security awareness delivery methods that could improve end-user information security awareness and behavior. By conducting experiments on information security awareness using three different methods: text-based, game-based and video-based, the study suggested that combined delivery methods of improving end-users' information security awareness and behaviour are better than individual security awareness delivery method (Abawajy, 2014). A related study determined the impact of cyber threat education and awareness intervention on changes in user security behaviour (McCrohan, Engel, & Harvey, 2010). The study was based on protection motivation theory and an experimental was performed by using undergraduate business school students. McCrohan, Engel and Harvey (2010) found that when users are educated of the threats to e-commerce and trained about proper security practices, their behavior could be changed to enhance information security. Hence, security and assurance should be a core component of the curriculum for all information security and business students (White, Hewitt, & Kruck, 2013).

Moreover, a survey conducted on 196 undergraduate students in a business college to investigate students' understanding and attitudes toward information security suggested that when universities provide easily accessible security training programs to students, information security improves (Kim, 2014). In a related study, Da Veiga (2016) determined the influence information security policy had on the information security culture by comparing the security behavior of employees who read the policy to those who did not. An empirical study was conducted at four intervals over eight years across 12 countries using a validated information security culture assessment (ISCA) questionnaire. The overall information security culture was significantly more positive for employees who had read the information security policy compared with employees who had not. Employees' information security training can improve adherence to security policies when employees are shown the reasons behind the written policies (Ramakrishna & Figueroa, 2017). Accordingly, organisational security education, training and awareness efforts influence employees' threat and coping appraisals (Posey, Roberts, & Lowry, 2015).

Employer-Employee Relationship

Employee relations are seen by employers as critical in achieving job performance through a focus on employee involvement, commitment and engagement. The emphasis of employee relations is now focussed on relationship with individual employees (Radhakrishna & Raju, 2015). Organisational commitment is a means by which information security threats become personally relevant to employees (Posey, Roberts, & Lowry, 2015). A previous study revealed that IT employees were treated with only moderate fairness/justice by the organisations, however, their commitment to their organisation was fairly high (Patrick, 2012). It was found that organisational justice significantly influenced organisational commitment of IT employees. The results of this study provided considerable insight into the IT employees' perceptions of fairness could promote commitment (Patrick, 2012). Also, D'Arcy and Greene (2014) examined the influence of security-related and employment relationship factors on employees' security compliance decisions. Data were collected using two online surveys that were administered at separate points in time. The study found that security culture is a driver for employees' security compliance in the workplace and that employee's feeling of job satisfaction influences security compliance intention (D'Arcy & Greene, 2014).

Background Checks and Monitoring

Background checks of potential employee have become essential task for HR personnel so that the organisation could avoid recruiting the wrong persons (Sarode & Deore, 2017). Hughes, Keller, & Hertz (2010) discussed issues of higher education institutions' policies and procedures with regard to background checks for students, staff, and faculty in light of homeland security concerns. Brody and Cox (2015) emphasized the need for thoroughness and accuracy of background checks and security clearance investigations. Brody (2010) explored the various methods available when conducting a pre-employment screening investigation in attempt to hire honest employees, those less likely to commit fraud against their organisation. Using interviews with experts in the area of background investigation services, the study recommended that organisations should consider performing other screening techniques before hiring an employee. Brody (2010) cautioned that merely relying on the most basic background check may lead to the hiring of the wrong employee, one likely to commit fraud. Besides, employees are increasingly monitored concerning their behaviors and actions. The use of monitoring systems has been advocated for improved performance, increased productivity, and reduced costs (Holt, Lang, & Sutton, 2017). Without effective monitoring disgruntled employees can expose valuable business trade secrets or engage in corporate espionage or sabotage (Ford et al., 2015). They may render the organisation to several risky situations (Rigon et al., 2014).

Security Responsibility and Accountability

Employees should be accountable to and be responsibility for preventing security breaches. According to Styles and Tryfonas (2009), employees are duty-bound to consider the security of the computing and information resources they interact with. Accountability makes employees answerable for accomplishing a goal or assignment (U.S. Office of Personnel Management, n.d.). It often connotes punishment or negative consequences of punishing employees, creating fear and anxiety in the work environment. But accountability can produce positive and valuable results. When used constructively, it can improve employee performance, enhance participation and involvement, increase feelings of competency, enhance commitment to the work, improve creativity and innovation, and produce higher employee morale and satisfaction with the work (U.S. Office of Personnel Management, n.d.). Accountability should focus not only on punishment but also reward. Parker (2008) remarked that without security rewards and sanctions in all employee job performance appraisals, any attempt to secure information assets in an organisation is purely cosmetics. Thus, those who control security, those who are constrained by it, and those who use and possess the assets must be sufficiently motivated to make it work (Parker, 2008).

In a recent study, Zaman and Saif (2016) found that perceived accountability has a significant positive relationship with job performance. Thomson and van Niekerk (2012) showed how employee apathy towards information security can be addressed through the use of existing theory in social sciences. Based on goal-setting theory, the study suggested that employees' performance of their roles and responsibilities can contribute towards organisational culture of information security (Thomson & van Niekerk, 2012). To understand security behaviour by developing a security behaviour typology based on the concepts of discipline and agility, Harnesk and Lindström (2011) undertook a case study to analyze security behaviors. The study found that security behaviour can be shaped by discipline and agility and that both can exist collectively if organisations consider the constitutional and existential aspects of information security (IS) management. Vance, Lowry, and Eggett (2013) presented a new approach for reducing access policy violations. Drawing from the theory of accountability, the study identified four system mechanisms that heighten an individual's perception of accountability: identifiability, awareness of logging, awareness of audit, and electronic presence (Vance, Lowry, & Eggett, 2013).

METHODOLOGY

A structured survey questionnaire was used to collect data from IT professionals (Information Security Officers, Chief Information Officers, IT Managers, IT Specialists, other IT staff) in forty three organisations within five main industry sectors (government public service institutions, public utility companies - water, electricity, and telecommunication, financial institutions, educational institutions, healthcare institutions, and others - manufacturing, oil and gas, IT) in Ghana. The human aspects of US-CCU (United States Cyber Consequences Unit) Cyber-security Questionnaire (Bumgarner & Borg, 2007) were adapted. The questionnaire was developed to be used to assess an organisation's personnel security management. The items on the questionnaire were modified to address the context of the study. In general, the awareness of cyber related crimes among employees in Ghanaian organisations is below the minimum cyber security threshold and most businesses and government organisations lagged behind in the implementation of information security measures to mitigate security threats and vulnerabilities (Cybercrime Unit, 2016). Overseas Security Advisory Council (OSAC, 2011) of the U.S. Department of State reported that there are increasing numbers of people who become victims to credit card fraud in Ghana.

Some items on the questionnaire were slightly altered as a result a field test conducted, with comments received from experts (two information security practitioners, two HR practitioners, and one senior academic faculty) to establish the validity of the instrument. The questionnaires were administered to the respondents through post and by email. The first part of the questionnaire was designed to reflect the profile of the respondents. The second part contained questions that reflect the four independent constructs and one dependent target construct. The questionnaire comprised of measurement items relating to information security training (11-items), employee relations (5-items), background checks and monitoring (4-items), accountability (11-items), and information security (9-items). Ratings were done on a Likert scale of 1 (strongly disagree) to 5 (strongly agree). Respondents were asked to rate the extent to which each variable could improve the performance of information security in their organisations. Out of the five hundred questionnaires sent to the respondents, 232 were completed and used in the data analysis. This represents a response rate of 46.4 percent.

Importance-Performance Map Analysis within the context of partial least squares structural equation modeling (PLS SEM) via SmartPLS 3.0 was used to identify the key determinants (factors and indicators) for improving the performance information security. Instrument reliability and validity were tested via Cronbach's alpha and outer loadings. According to Hair et al. (2017), items with outer loading less than zero should be removed from further analysis. Consequently, items whose outer loadings were less than zero were removed from the study (see Table 1). Moreover, the Cronbach's alpha shows the reliability coefficients of the measures: Security Training and Awareness (.778), Employer-Employee Relationship (.849), Background Checks and Monitoring (.811), Responsibility and Accountability (.696), and Information Security (.790) (see Table 1). Apart from Responsibility and Accountability, all the measures were all found to be far above the threshold of 0.7 (or higher) and were considered acceptable according to Nunally's (1978) guidelines.

DATA ANALYSIS

The data analysis follows the procedure recommended by Ringle and Sarstedt (2016). These are 1) requirements checking, 2) computation of the performance values, 3) computation of the importance values, 4) Importance-Performance Map creation, and 5) ascertaining the factors and indicators on the Importance-Performance Map. These will be done under two sections: a) assessment of the measurement model and b) evaluation of the importance-performance map analysis.

Assessment of the Measurement Model

When using IPMA, three requirements must be met (Ringle & Sarstedt, 2016). Firstly, the latent variable scores should be re-scaled on a range of 0 and 100, thus requiring that all indicators in the PLS path model should use a metric or quasi-metric scale (Sarstedt & Mooi, 2014). Secondly, all the indicator coding must have the same scale direction. The minimum value of an indicator must represent the worst outcome and the maximum value must represent the best outcome of the indicator (for instance 1 represents strongly disagree and 5 strongly agree). Otherwise, conclusion cannot be drawn that the higher latent variable scores represent better performance. Accordingly, the current study used a metric with 5 likert scale which can be scaled between 0 and 100. Thirdly, regardless of the measurement model being formatively or reflectively, the outer weights estimates must be positive. Negative outer weights might be a result of high indicator collinearity and these indicators should be removed from the analysis (Hair et al., 2017). To meet this requirement, all the items whose outer weights were negative have been removed (see Table 1).

Furthermore, the blindfolding and bootstrapping techniques were used. The blindfolding procedure was used in assessing the predictive relevance (Stone-Geisser's Q^2 value) of the structural model (Geisser, 1974; Stone, 1974). According to Hair et al. (2014), a Q^2 value larger than zero for the reflective endogenous latent variable indicates the path model's predictive relevance. Table 2 showed the structural model's predictive relevance. Also, bootstrapping was performed. It is a nonparametric procedure that allows testing the statistical significance of various PLS-SEM results, such as path coefficients, Cronbach's alpha, and R^2 values (Hair et al., 2017). The results from bootstrapping with 5,000 samples using the no sign change option and the 95 percent confidence intervals showed that all the path coefficients were statistically significant (Table 3). More specifically, TRAINING, MONITORING, ACCOUNTABILITY, and RELATIONSHIP each has significant and positive effects on INFORMATION SECURITY. Thus, the bootstrapping results demonstrated that all total effects on the target construct, INFORMATION SECURITY, were significant.

Table 1. Validity, reliability and descriptive statistics

Constructs	Indicators	Outer Weight > 0	Mean	SD	Cronbach Alpha
SECURITY TRAINING AND AWARENESS					
ST01	Employees are given periodic training on security policies.	0.272	3.95	.997	
ST02	Employees are trained to keep mobile devices secured.	0.362	3.53	.925	
ST06	Employees are trained to be suspicious of any software that arrives in the mail, even though it may appear to be packaged and sent by trusted persons or vendors.	0.290	3.25	.984	.778
ST10	Employees have been made aware of the fact that mass produced and mass distributed software could still contain targeted malware.	0.361	3.40	.954	
EMPLOYER-EMPLOYEE RELATIONSHIP					
ER01	The organisation makes fairness and good faith in the treatment of employees a priority.	0.732	3.87	.803	
ER02	The organisation provides adequate mechanisms for employees to express their grievances without penalty and for them to see those grievances being conscientiously addressed.	0.017	3.60	.755	
ER03	The organisation handles re-deployment/down-sizing in a manner that minimizes hostile feelings on the part of former employees.	0.117	3.64	.774	.849
ER04	The organisation offers a procedure which allows employees to report attempts by outsiders to extort their organisation in circumventing security.	0.251	3.72	.718	
ER05	If an employee is going through a period of great difficulties in his or her personal life, there is a policy for temporarily reducing that employee's responsibilities for critical systems and access to critical systems.	0.053	3.73	.815	
BACKGROUND CHECKS AND MONITORING					
BC02	If an employee is promoted to a considerably higher level of responsibility and access, a new background check is carried out.	0.477	3..35	.973	
BC03	Background screening is carried out for of potential and third parties.	0.359	3.18	.845	.811
BC04	An effort is made to track the current whereabouts of former employees who were deeply acquainted with critical systems and procedures.	0.333	3.25	1.045	
RESPONSIBILITY AND ACCOUNTABILITY					
SA02	All employees are required to sign confidentiality and intellectual property agreements.	0.291	3.34	.862	
SA06	Information security policies defined the proper use of e-mail, internet access, and instant messaging by employees.	0.689	3.53	1.058	.696
SA11	Employees are given adequate incentives to report security breaches and bad security practices.	0.237	3.51	.817	
INFORMATION SECURITY					
BEC06	Information is generally disseminated throughout the organisation on a need-to-know basis.	0.298	3.75	.692	
BEC07	Areas of responsibility are distributed among employees in such a way that a single employee cannot carry out a critical operation without the knowledge of other employees.	0.329	3.47	.768	
BEC08	The employee's physical and electronic access logs are periodically reviewed to identify access patterns that are not motivated by normal work responsibilities.	0.301	3.73	.725	.790
BEC09	Employees are required to take periodic vacations, so that ongoing activities they might otherwise be able to conceal would be noticed by their temporary replacements.	0.346	3.70	.808	

As has been observed in Table 1, Table 2, and Table 3, the requirements of the measurement model assessment have been met. The outer weights were above zero. Those items below zero were removed from further analysis. The instrument validity and reliability requirements were fulfilled. The predictive relevance via blindfolding technique was also fulfilled. Through the bootstrapping results, the structural model also showed that all the constructs had significant effect on the target construct. Based on these, the study proceeded to create Importance-Performance Map.

Table 2. Stone-Geisser's Q² values

Constructs	SSO	SSE	Q² (=1-SSE/SSO)
ACCOUNTABILITY	954	672.471	0.295
INFORMATION SECURITY	1,272	920.981	0.276
MONITORING	954	742.136	0.222
RELATIONSHIP	1,590	1,352.801	0.149
TRAINING	1,272	1,272.000	-

Table 3. Path coefficients and statistical significance

Constructs	Sample Mean	Standard Deviation	Path Coefficients	T Statistics	p-values
ACCOUNTABILITY -> INFORMATION SECURITY	0.180	0.077	2.333	2.333	0.020
MONITORING -> ACCOUNTABILITY	0.334	0.059	5.713	5.713	0.000
MONITORING -> INFORMATION SECURITY	0.242	0.064	3.804	3.804	0.000
MONITORING -> RELATIONSHIP	0.383	0.067	5.691	5.691	0.000
RELATIONSHIP -> INFORMATION SECURITY	0.290	0.054	5.280	5.280	0.000
TRAINING -> ACCOUNTABILITY	0.485	0.056	8.718	8.718	0.000
TRAINING -> INFORMATION SECURITY	0.135	0.054	2.501	2.501	0.012
TRAINING -> MONITORING	0.576	0.035	16.461	16.461	0.000
TRAINING -> RELATIONSHIP	0.247	0.062	3.856	3.856	0.000

Table 4. Performance / index values and path coefficients

Constructs	LV Index Values	Performances	ACCOUNTABILITY	INFORMATION SECURITY	MONITORING	RELATIONSHIP
ACCOUNTABILITY	3.477	61.933		0.134		
INFORMATION SECURITY	3.660	66.499				
MONITORING	3.261	56.537	0.323	0.178		0.313
RELATIONSHIP	3.801	70.015		0.252		
TRAINING	3.516	62.904	0.507	0.106	0.616	0.214

LV – Latent Variable

HRM Factors for Improving Information Security Performance

The IPMA technique produced the structural model and Important-Performance Map (Figure 5) to identify the important HRM practices that can improve the performance of organisational information security. Table 4 and Figure 5 show the path coefficients and the performance values of the constructs. Table 5 shows the direct, indirect, and the total effects (the Importance dimension) together with the Performance values (re-scaled between 0 and 100). These values were used to create the graphical representation of the Importance-Performance Map (Figure 6). The Important-Performance Map utilises unstandardized total effects for the importance-dimension (x-axis) and the re-scaled performance values of the latent and manifest variables on the performance dimension (y-axis).

Figure 5. Structural model of importance-performance analysis

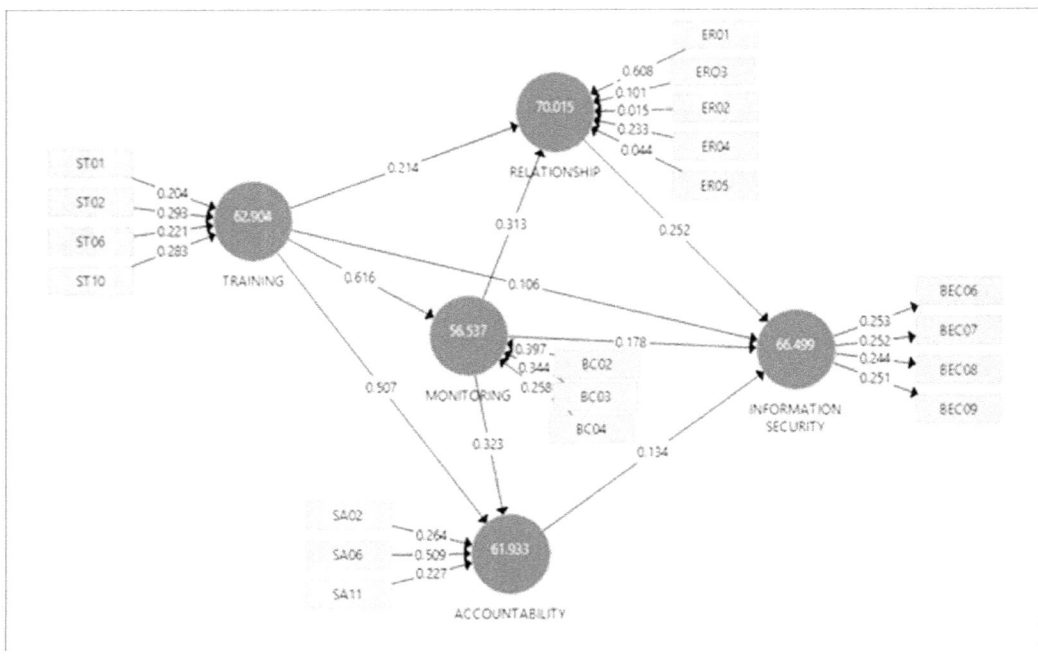

Table 5. Direct, indirect, and total effects of importance-performance construct values

Predecessor Construct	Direct Effect on Security	Indirect Effect on Security	Total effect on Security/ Importance	Performance
ACCOUNTABILITY	0.134	-	0.134	61.933
MONITORING	0.131	0.169	0.300	56.537
RELATIONSHIP	0.252	-	0.252	70.015
TRAINING	0.023	0.390	0.413	62.904
Average			0.275	62.847

Notes: All effects denote unstandardized effects.

Figure 6 reveals that two direct predecessors of INFORMATION SECURITY, MONITORING and TRAINING, have a particularly high importance but relatively low performance (Quadrant I). Observably, TRAINING construct has considerably higher importance than the MONITORING construct. Managerial actions should therefore prioritize improving the performance of security TRAINING. Moreover, the importance of MONITORING was relatively high but its performance was relatively low. Attention also needs to be paid on improving the performance of MONITORING, which can be achieved by focusing on the predecessor construct of MONITORING, which is TRAINING. On the other side, the result showed that too much attention has been paid to RELATIONSHIP (Quadrant IV). This denoted that RELATIONSHIP constructs was overly emphasized by the organisations. Instead of continuing to focus on RELATIONSHIP, organisations should allocate more resources to increase the performance of TRAINING and MONITORING. Surprisingly, ACCOUNTABILITY fell within Quadrant III, indicating low importance and performance.

Figure 6. IPM Constructs on Information Security

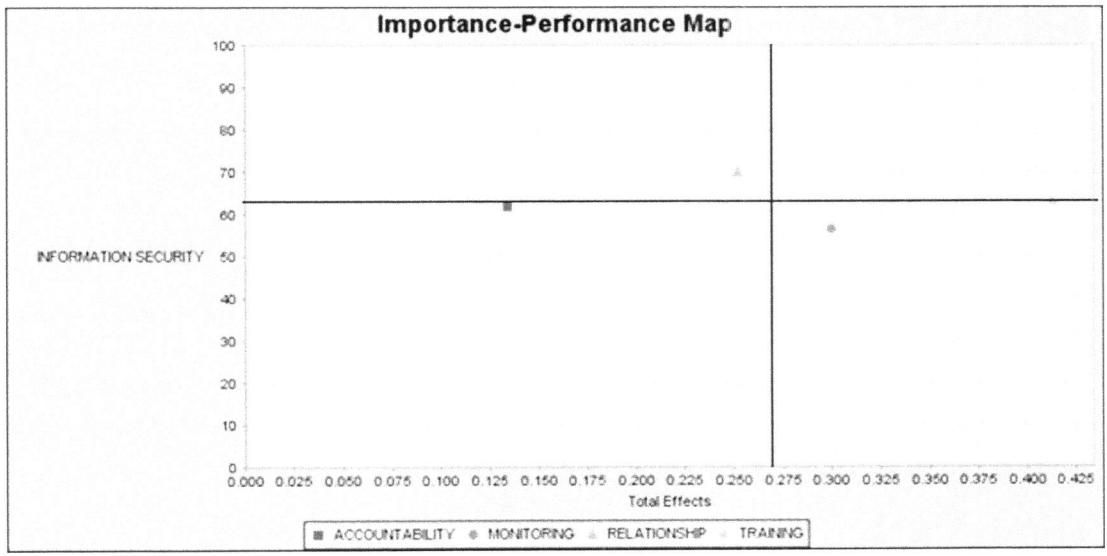

Key Indicators for Improving Information Security Performance

In the previous section, TRAINING and MONITORING were identified as very important for improving information security performance. However, to gain more specific information as to which key training and monitoring indicators will increase the performance of organisational information security, the indicator level Importance-Performance Map Analysis was performed. Table 6 shows the total effects (Importance dimension) and the information security (performance dimension) values at the indicator level. These values were used to create the indicator level Importance-Performance Map, as shown in Figure 7. The four quadrants on the IPM is made possible using the mean level of importance of 0.073 and the mean level of performance of 63.051, indicated by the vertical and the horizontal lines on the map.

In Quadrant I, *Concentrate Here*, the respondents perceived the attributes within this region as highly important, but their performance was very low. From the map (Figure 7), six key indicators/attributes were found that could improve information security performance. These are classified under the two constructs:

Security Training

- ST02: Employees are trained to keep mobile devices secured.
- ST06: Employees are trained to be suspicious of any software that arrives in the mail, even though it may appear to be packaged and sent by trusted persons or vendors.
- ST10: Employees have been made aware that mass distributed software could contain targeted malware.

Monitoring

- BC02: If an employee is promoted to a considerably higher level of responsibility and access, a new background check is carried out.
- BC03: Background screening is carried out for potential and third parties (suppliers, contractors, building maintenance personnel).
- BC04: An effort is made to track the current whereabouts of former employees who were deeply acquainted with critical systems and procedures.

Moreover, the following two indicators fell within Quadrant II (High Importance/High Performance). These indicators are the strength of the organisations. The indicated that the organisation must "keep up good works" in these areas to maintain security performance.

- ST01: Employees are given periodic training on security policies.
- ER01: The organisation makes fairness and good faith in the treatment of employees a priority.

Conversely, seven indicators of EMPLOYEE RELATIONS and EMPLOYEE ACCOUNTABILITY constructs were categorised as low importance but high performance, as they fell within Quadrant III and Quadrant IV respectively. The indicators are listed below.

Employee Relations

- ER02: The organisation provides adequate mechanisms for employees to express their grievances without penalty and for them to see those grievances being conscientiously addressed.
- ER05: If an employee is going through a period of great difficulties in his or her personal life, there is a policy for temporarily reducing that employee's responsibilities for critical systems and access to critical systems.
- ER03: The organisation handles re-deployment and down-sizing in a manner that minimizes hostile feelings on the part of former employees.
- ER04: The organisation offers a procedure which would allow employees to report attempts by outsiders to extort their organisation in circumventing security.

Accountability

- SA02: All employees are required to sign confidentiality and intellectual property agreements.
- SA06: Information security policies defined the proper use of e-mail, internet access, and instant messaging by employees.
- SA11: Employees are given adequate incentives to report security breaches and bad security practices.

Table 6. Importance-performance indicator values

Indicators	Total Effect (Importance)	Information Security (Performance)
BC02	0.119	58.648
BC03	0.103	54.403
BC04	0.077	56.132
ER01	0.153	71.698
ER02	0.004	64.937
ER03	0.025	65.881
ER04	0.059	68.082
ER05	0.011	68.239
SA02	0.035	58.491
SA06	0.068	63.365
SA11	0.030	62.736
ST01	0.084	73.742
ST02	0.121	63.208
ST06	0.091	56.132
ST10	0.117	60.063
Average	0.073	63.051

Figure 7. IPM indicators on information security

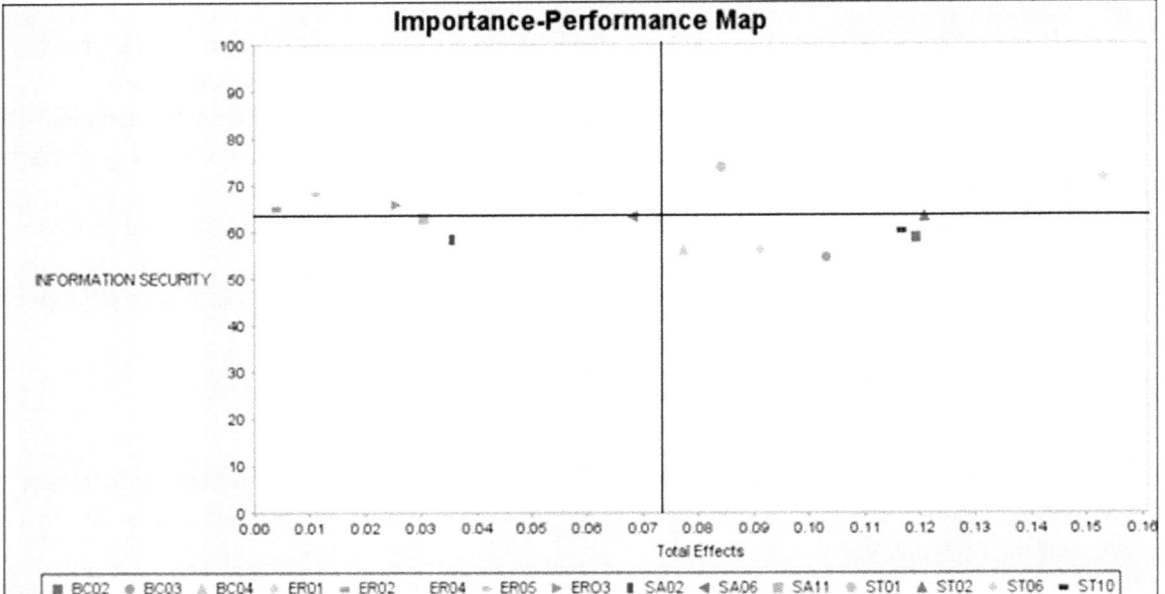

DISCUSSION

The study identified security training, background checks and monitoring as the major HRM practices that can improve the performance of information security in organisations. Managerial actions should therefore prioritize improving training, background checks and monitoring. While lack of security training often lie behind many contemporary breaches (Lacey, 2010), investing in training and development can motivate staff and support the growth of the organisation (Leidner & Smith, 2013). HRM practices on security policy compliance found training for career development as positively associated with employees' behavioral intent to comply with security policy (Youngkeun Choi, 2017). Hence, information security training effectively reduces employees' non-compliance (Hwang et al., 2017). Security training, at the indicator level, ST02 ("Employees are trained to keep mobile devices secured") has a relatively high importance when focusing on information security but required some room for performance improvement. Hence, performance improvements can focus on offering high-quality security trainings to provide users with the skills and knowledge they need to protect the mobile devices (Yaokumah, 2016). Similarly, other indicators, ST06 and ST10, focused on employee training on malware. This should be given particular attention regarding improving the information security performance.

Moreover, the background checks and monitoring of the current employees, third parties, and former employees were found as important HRM practices that can improve the performance of organisational information security. A thorough and accurate background checks and security clearance investigations (Brody & Cox, 2015) can help an organisation to hire honest employees, those less likely to commit fraud against the organisation (Brody, 2010). Likewise, employee monitoring systems can improve performance, increase productivity, and reduce costs (Holt, Lang, & Sutton, 2017). In particular, at the indicator level, BC02 ("If an employee is promoted to a considerably higher level of responsibility and access, a new background check is carried out") has a relatively high importance but required performance improvement. Similarly, the BC03 ("Background screening is carried out for potential employees and third parties - suppliers, contractors, building maintenance personnel") and BC04 ("An effort is made to track the current whereabouts of former employees who were deeply acquainted with critical systems and procedures") required performance improvement. Thus, further improvement efforts should be concentrated on mobile devices security, malware, monitoring and background screening of current and former employees, including third party contractors.

Two indicators were found to be the strength of the organisations as they have attained the highest importance and performance levels in the organisations. These are ST01 ("Employees are given periodic training on security policies") and ER01 ("The organisation makes fairness and good faith in the treatment of employees a priority"). Accordingly, the organisations should continue to provide regular security training on security policies to the employees. Employees' information security training enhances adherence to security policies (Ramakrishna & Figueroa, 2017) and influences employees' threat and coping appraisals (Posey, Roberts, & Lowry, 2015). Besides, fairness in treating employees positively influences information security behaviour. Employees' perceptions of fairness promote commitment (Patrick, 2012).

On the contrary, two HRM practices, Employee Relations and Accountability were found to be of low importance but with high performance. This signified that these two constructs were overly emphasized by the organisations. Thus, accountability might not have remarkable impact on employees' security compliance behavior (Abed & Roland, 2016). Rather, instead of continuing to focus in employee relations and accountability, organisations should allocate more resources for security training programs, background checks and employee monitoring.

CONCLUSION

In this study, the IPMA technique was discussed and applied to measure HRM practices from the perspective of IT professionals to identify priority areas for the allocation of resources to improve the performance of organisational information security. A survey was conducted on the IT professionals' perceptions to identify areas of importance and performance of HRM practices. Using IPMA technique, the study identified security training, background checks and monitoring as highly important that needed to be improved in order to enhance organisational information security performance. Two indicators (periodic training in adherence to security policy and fairness in treating employees) were found to have attained the highest importance and performance levels in the organisations. In terms of key indicators for specific management actions, attention needed to be paid to: (a) training to keep mobile devices secured, b) training on malware, (c) tracking of the whereabouts of former employees who were deeply acquainted with critical systems and procedures, and d) background checks on employee promoted to a considerably higher level of responsibility and system access. Organisations need to consider allocating resources to training, background check and monitoring.

Practically, the significance importance of security training, background checks and monitoring on improving information security offer an important opportunity for information security management practices. Organisations can improve information security by channelling resources from less important activities and invest them in security training, background checks and monitoring. Besides, before applying IPMA, this study demonstrated the concept and the use of importance-performance map analysis. By combining the analysis of the importance and performance dimensions of the IPMA, the study allowed the IT and HR leaders to identify and prioritize HRM practices and indicators that were most important for improving the performance of the organisations' information security. The study also provided guidance for the formulation of information security strategy that could accurately allocate resources to maximise a high return on security investment.

Theoretically, the findings extended information security research literature by showing how HRM practices (training, background checks and monitoring) can play a major role in improving information security. Our results provided one of the few empirical validations of information security to be recognized as a multi-disciplinary issue as conceptualized through HRM practices. In addition, the study extended information security research by considering the role of employee relations and accountability from the HRM literature. However, some HRM practices were not included in the current study. For example, including remuneration and rewards might further enhance information security literature. Moreover, because HRM practices may differ among the organisations, future research using a multi-group analysis that allows for contrasting group results might produce an insightful finding.

REFERENCES

Abawajy, J. (2014). User preference of cyber security awareness delivery methods. *Behaviour & Information Technology*, *33*(3), 237–248. doi:10.1080/0144929X.2012.708787

Abed, J., & Roland, W. H. (2016). Understanding deterrence theory in security compliance behavior: A quantitative meta-analysis approach. In *SAIS 2016 Proceedings*. Retrieved from http://aisel.aisnet.org/sais2016/28

Angst, C. M., Block, E. S., D'Arcy, J., & Kelley, K. (2017). When do IT security investments matter? Accounting for the influence of institutional factors in the context of healthcare data breaches. *Management Information Systems Quarterly*, *41*(3), 893–916. doi:10.25300/MISQ/2017/41.3.10

Baxter, R. J., Holderness, D. K. Jr, & Wood, D. A. (2016). Applying basic gamification techniques to it compliance training: Evidence from the lab and field. *Journal of Information Systems*, *30*(3), 119–133. doi:10.2308/isys-51341

Bernik, I., & Prislan, K. (2016). Measuring Information Security Performance with 10 by 10 model for holistic state evaluation. *PLoS One*, *11*(9), 1–33. doi:10.1371/journal.pone.0163050 PMID:27655001

Boss, S. R., Galletta, D. F., Lowry, P. B., Moody, G. D., & Polak, P. (2015). What do systems users have to fear? Using fear appeals to engender threats and fear that motivate protective security behaviors. *Management Information Systems Quarterly*, *39*(4), 837–864. doi:10.25300/MISQ/2015/39.4.5

Brody, R. G. (2010). Beyond the basic background check: Hiring the "right" employees. *Management Research Review*, *33*(3), 210–223. doi:10.1108/01409171011030372

Brody, R. G., & Cox, V. L. (2015). Background investigations a comparative analysis of background checks and federal security clearance investigations. *Business Studies Journal*, *7*(1), 84–94.

Bumgarner, J., & Borg, S. (2007). US-CCU Cyber-Security Questionnaire. US-CCU (Cyber Consequences Unit) Cyber-Security Check. Retrieved from www.usccu.us

Burns, A. J., Posey, C., Roberts, T. L., & Lowry, P. B. (2017). Examining the relationship of organisational insiders' psychological capital with information security threat and coping appraisals. *Computers in Human Behavior*, *68*, 190–209. doi:10.1016/j.chb.2016.11.018

Cherdantseva, Y., & Hilton, J. (2013). Information security and information assurance. The discussion about the meaning, scope and goals. In F. Almeida & I. Portela (Eds.), *Organisational, Legal, and Technological Dimensions of Information System Administrator*. IGI Global.

Choi, Y. (2017). Human resource management and security policy compliance. *International Journal of Human Capital and Information Technology Professionals*, *8*(3), 14. doi:10.4018/IJHCITP.2017070105

Cybercrime Unit. (2016). Government will fight Cyber Crime. Retrieved from http://cybercrime.gov. gh/?p=313

D'Arcy, J., & Greene, G. (2014). Security culture and the employment relationship as drivers of employees' security compliance. *Information Management & Computer Security*, *22*(5), 474–489. doi:10.1108/IMCS-08-2013-0057

Da Veiga, A. (2016). Comparing the information security culture of employees who had read the information security policy and those who had not: Illustrated through an empirical study. *Information & Computer Security*, *24*(2), 139–151. doi:10.1108/ICS-12-2015-0048

Driscoll, C., & McKee, M. (2007). Restorying a culture of ethical and spiritual values: A role for leader storytelling. *Journal of Business Ethics*, *73*(2), 205–217. doi:10.00710551-006-9191-5

Ford, J., Willey, L., White, B. J., & Domagalski, T. (2015). New concerns in electronic employee monitoring: Have you checked your policies lately? *Journal of Legal. Ethical & Regulatory Issues*, *18*(1), 51–70.

Furnell, S., & Thomson, K. L. (2009). From culture to disobedience: Recognizing the varying user acceptance of IT security. *Computer Fraud & Security*, *2*(2), 5–10. doi:10.1016/S1361-3723(09)70019-3

Geisser, S. (1974). A Predictive Approach to the Random Effects Model. *Biometrika*, *61*(1), 101–107. doi:10.1093/biomet/61.1.101

Hair, J. F., Hult, G. T. M., Ringle, C. M., & Sarstedt, M. (2014). *A primer on partial least squares structural equation modeling (PLS-SEM)*. Thousand Oaks, CA: Sage.

Hair, J. F., Hult, G. T. M., Ringle, C. M., & Sarstedt, M. (2017). *A primer on partial least squares structural equation modeling (PLS-SEM)*. Thousand Oaks, CA: Sage.

Hair, J. F., Sarstedt, M., Ringle, C., & Mena, J. A. (2012). An assessment of the use of partial least squares structural equation modeling in marketing research. *Journal of the Academy of Marketing Science*, *40*(3), 414–433. doi:10.100711747-011-0261-6

Herath, T., & Rao, H. R. (2009). Protection motivation and deterrence: A framework for security policy compliance in organisations. *European Journal of Information Systems*, *18*(2), 106–125. doi:10.1057/ejis.2009.6

Holt, M., Lang, B., & Sutton, S. G. (2017). Potential employees' ethical perceptions of active monitoring: The dark side of data analytics. *Journal of Information Systems*, *31*(2), 107–124. doi:10.2308/isys-51580

Hu, Q., Dinev, T., Hart, P., & Cooke, D. (2012). Managing employee compliance with information security policies: The critical role of top management and organisational culture. *Decision Sciences Journal, 43*(4), 615–659. doi:10.1111/j.1540-5915.2012.00361.x

Hu, Q., West, R., & Smarandescu, L. (2015). The Role of Self-Control in Information Security Violations: Insights from a Cognitive Neuroscience Perspective. *Journal of Management Information Systems, 31*(4), 6–48. doi:10.1080/07421222.2014.1001255

Hughes, S., Keller, E. W., & Hertz, G. T. (2010). Homeland security initiatives and background checks in higher education. *New Directions for Institutional Research, 2010*(146), 51–62. doi:10.1002/ir.342

Hwang, I., Kim, D., Kim, T., & Kim, S. (2017). Why not comply with information security? An empirical approach for the causes of non-compliance. *Online Information Review, 41*(1), 2–18. doi:10.1108/OIR-11-2015-0358

Ikenwe, I. J., Igbinovia, O. M., & Elogie, A. A. (2016). Information Security in the Digital Age: The Case of Developing Countries. *Chinese Librarianship, 42*, 16–24.

Javad, A., & Weistroffer, H. R. (2016). Understanding Deterrence Theory in Security Compliance Behavior: A Quantitative Meta-Analysis Approach. In *SAIS 2016 Proceedings*. Retrieved from http://aisel.aisnet.org/sais2016/28

Karlsson, F., Åström, J., & Karlsson, M. (2015). Information security culture – state-of-the-art review between 2000 and 2013. *Information & Computer Security, 23*(3), 246–285. doi:10.1108/ICS-05-2014-0033

Kaspersky, E., & Furnell, S. (2014). A security education Q&A. *Information Management & Computer Security, 22*(2), 130–133. doi:10.1108/IMCS-01-2014-0006

Khao, B., Harris, P., & Hartman, S. (2010). Information security governance of enterprise information systems: An approach to legislative compliant. *International Journal of Management and Information Systems, 14*(3), 49–55.

Kim, E. B. (2014). Recommendations for information security awareness training for college students. *Information Management & Computer Security, 22*(1), 115–126. doi:10.1108/IMCS-01-2013-0005

Komatsu, A., Takagi, D., & Takemura, T. (2013). Human aspects of information security: An empirical study of intentional versus actual behavior. *Information Management & Computer Security, 21*(1), 5–15. doi:10.1108/09685221311314383

Lacey, D. (2010). Understanding and transforming organisational security culture. *Information Management & Computer Security, 18*(1), 4–13. doi:10.1108/09685221011035223

Leidner, S., & Smith, S. M. (2013). Keeping potential job-hoppers' feet on the ground. *Human Resource Management International Digest, 21*(1), 31–33. doi:10.1108/09670731311296492

McCrohan, K. F., Engel, K., & Harvey, J. W. (2010). Influence of awareness and training on cyber security. *Journal of Internet Commerce, 9*(1), 23–41. doi:10.1080/15332861.2010.487415

Naz, F., Aftab, J., & Awais, M. (2016). Impact of Human Resource Management Practices (HRM) on Performance of SMEs in Multan, Pakistan. *International Journal of Management. Accounting & Economics*, *3*(11), 699–708.

Nunnally, J. C. (1978). *Psychometric theory* (2nd ed.). New York, NY: McGraw-Hill.

Ossege, C. (2012). Accountability – are we better off without it? *Public Management Review*, *14*(5), 585–607. doi:10.1080/14719037.2011.642567

Overseas Security Advisory Council (OSAC). (2012). Ghana 2012 OSAC crime and safety report. Retrieve from https://www.osac.gov

Parker, D. B. (2008). Security accountability in job performance. *Information Systems Security*, *3*(4), 16–20. doi:10.1080/10658989509342474

Patrick, H. A. (2012). Commitment of information technology employees in relation to perceived organisational justice. *IUP Journal of Organisational Behavior*, *11*(3), 23–40.

Posey, C., Roberts, T. L., & Lowry, P. B. (2015). The impact of organisational commitment on insiders' motivation to protect organisational information assets. *Journal of Management Information Systems*, *32*(4), 179–214. doi:10.1080/07421222.2015.1138374

Radhakrishna, A., & Raju, S. R. (2015). A study on the effect of human resource development on employment relations. *IUP Journal of Management Research*, *14*(3). 28–42.

Ramakrishna, A., & Figueroa, N. (2017). Is seeing believing? Training users on information security: Evidence from Java Applets. *Journal of Information Systems Education*, *28*(2), 115–122.

Rantos, K., Fysarakis, K., & Manifavas, C.(2012). How effective is your security awareness program? An evaluation methodology. *Information Security Journal: A Global Perspective*, *21*(6), 328-345.

Rigon, E. A., Westphall, C. M., dos Santos, D. R., & Westphall, C. B. (2014). A cyclical evaluation model of information security maturity. *Information Management & Computer Security*, *22*(3), 265–278. doi:10.1108/IMCS-04-2013-0025

Ringle, C. M., & Sarstedt, M. (2016). Gain more insight from your PLS-SEM results: The importance-performance map analysis. *Industrial Management & Data Systems*, *116*(9), 1865–1886. doi:10.1108/IMDS-10-2015-0449

Sarode, A. P., & Deore, S. S. (2017). Role of third party employee verification and background checks in HR management: An overview. *Journal of Commerce & Management Thought*, *8*(1), 86–96. doi:10.5958/0976-478X.2017.00005.2

Stewart, J. M., Tittel, E., & Chapple, M. (2005). *Certified Information Systems Security Professional (Study Guide)* (3rd ed.). San Francisco: Sybex.

Stone, M. (1974). Cross-Validatory Choice and Assessment of Statistical Predictions. *Journal of the Royal Statistical Society. Series A (General)*, *36*(2), 111–147.

Styles, M., & Tryfonas, T. (2009). Using penetration testing feedback to cultivate proactive security amongst end-users. *Information Management & Computer Security*, *17*(1), 44–52. doi:10.1108/09685220910944759

Tassabehji, R. (2005). Information security threats: From evolution to prominence. In *Encyclopedia of Multimedia Technology and Networking*. Hershey, PA: IGI Global. Retrieved from http://encyclopedia. jrank.org doi:10.4018/978-1-59140-561-0.ch058

Thomson, K., & van Niekerk, J. (2012). Combating information security apathy by encouraging prosocial organisational behaviour. *Information Management & Computer Security*, *20*(1), 39–46. doi:10.1108/09685221211219191

U.S. Office of Personnel Management. (n.d.). Retrieved from https://www.opm.gov

Vance, A., Lowry, P. B., & Eggett, D. (2013). Using accountability to reduce access policy violations in information systems. *Journal of Management Information Systems*, *29*(4), 263–290. doi:10.2753/ MIS0742-1222290410

White, G. L., Hewitt, B., & Kruck, S. E. (2013). Incorporating global information security and assurance in I.S. education. *Journal of Information Systems Education*, *24*(1), 11–16.

Yalman, Y., & Yesilyurt, M. (2013). Information Security Threats and Information Assurance. *TEM Journal*, *2*(3), 247–252.

Yaokumah, W. (2016). The influence of students' characteristics on mobile device security measures. *International Journal of Information Systems and Social Change*, *7*(3), 44–66. doi:10.4018/IJISSC.2016070104

Zaman, U., & Saif, M. I. (2016). Perceived accountability and conflict management styles as predictors of job performance of public officials in Pakistan. *Gomal University Journal of Research*, *32*(2), 24–35.

Zhang, L., & McDowell, W. C. (2009). Am I really at risk? Determinants of online users' intentions to use strong passwords. *Journal of Internet Commerce*, *8*(3–4), 180–197. doi:10.1080/15332860903467508

Zhao, X., Xue, L., & Whinston, A. B. (2013). Managing interdependent information security risks: Cyberinsurance, managed security services, and risk pooling arrangements. *Journal of Management Information Systems*, *30*(1), 123–152. doi:10.2753/MIS0742-1222300104

This research was previously published in the International Journal of Human Capital and Information Technology Professionals (IJHCITP), 9(4); pages 23-43, copyright year 2018 by IGI Publishing (an imprint of IGI Global).

Chapter 25
Unlocking Drivers for Employee Engagement Through Human Resource Analytics

Kanupriya Misra Bakhru

Jaypee Institute of Information Technology, India

Alka Sharma

Jaypee Institute of Information Technology, India

ABSTRACT

The authors have discussed in detail the meaning of employee engagement and its relevance for the organizations in the present scenario. The authors also highlighted the various factors that predict the employee engagement of the employees in the varied organizations. The authors have emphasized on the role that HR analytics can play to identify the reasons for low level of engagement among employees and suggesting ways to improve the same using predictive analytics. The authors have also advocated the benefits that organizations can reap by making use of HR analytics in measuring the engagement levels of the employees and improving the engagement levels of diverse workforce in the existing organizations. The authors have also proposed the future perspectives of the proposed study that help the organizations and officials from the top management to tap the benefits of analytics in the function of human resource management and to address the upcoming issues related to employee behavior.

INTRODUCTION

In increasing competitive world which is undergoing a rapid transformation organizations need talented employees, but the biggest challenge is to retain them. Talented employees have many opportunities available as everything is transparent and easily traceable in this digital world. What makes them stay back is productive, engaging and most importantly enjoyable work experience. Having engaged employees is one of the key objectives to which Human Resource (HR) functions are expected to strive. Employee engagement is a condition where employees are passionate about their work and feel proud

DOI: 10.4018/978-1-6684-3873-2.ch025

to be associated with the organization thus contributing to its success. According to recent report by Deloitte engagement remains one of the top priorities for organizations in 2017, it was reported that only 22 percent people feel that their organizations are able to build differentiated employee experience (Deloitte, 2017). Another study conducted by Global Human Capital Trends revealed that there is a drop of 14 percent in the organization's ability to address engagement issues as compared to last year.

Employee engagement is highly desirable because an engaged employee has high level of creativity (Gawke et al., 2017; Orth and Volmer, 2017), organizational citizenship behavior and exhibits better in-role task performance (Christian et al., 2011) leading to client satisfaction (Bakker et al., 2014) and better financial results (Xanthopoulou et al., 2009). Also engaged workers are more inclined to help their colleagues, engagement creates a ripple effect in teams (Bakker et al., 2006; Gutermann et al., 2017; Van Mierlo and Bakker, 2018). Engaged employees are found to be brisk and ardent about their tasks, and are wholly engrossed in their vocation (May et al., 2004; Macey and Schneider, 2008a; Schaufeli et al., 2008). Employee engagement is of much interest to practitioners as it leads to higher performance (Harter et al., 2002; Rich et al, 2010), profitability, productivity, quality, customer satisfaction which results in higher shareholder returns (Wellins et al. (2005); Macey et al., 2009). On employee front engagement leads to lower absenteeism and turnover (Harter et al., 2002; Schaufeli and Bakker, 2004; Bakker et al., 2005; Saks, 2006). Since employee engagement is an affective-motivational construct, employees experiencing it have positive job attitude (Harter at al., 2002; Schaufeli et al., 2008) and get a sense of fulfilment in discharging their duties and responsibilities (Xanthopoulou et al., 2009).

Research on employee engagement have been surging since past few years, though highlighted by practitioners (Bennett and Bell, 2004; Baumruk et.al 2006, Gallup Management Journal 2006, Parsley 2006, Woodruffe 2005), it is still largely undermined in academic literature (Robinson et al., 2004). It is an area where rigorous academic research is required (Macey and Schneider 2008b). This book chapter is an attempt to bridge this gap. With recent advent of big data, predictive analytics and artificial intelligence, there is an inevitable need to focus on practical application of analytics on work engagement. A study done by King et al. (2015) proposed application of big data analytics on employee social media activity by capturing managers' and employees' brief unconscious "microexpression" data, which might be used to provide indications of employee engagement. Similar studies can be done which may be of vital use to executives and practitioners wanting to better understand and predict employee experience leading to better performance and well-being (Schaufeli and Salanova, 2010; Guest, 2014; Power, 2017).

DEFINITIONS OF EMPLOYEE ENGAGEMENT

Employee engagement has been defined by many researchers, to explain in simple words it is emotional and intellectual commitment of an individual (Baumruk, 2004; Shaw, 2005; Richman, 2006). It can also be defined as "discretionary effort" exhibited by people in their jobs (Frank et al., 2004). It focuses on "psychological availability, safety, and meaningfulness" in discharging formal role requirements (Kahn, 1990; May et al., 2004; Saks, 2006; Bhatnagar, 2007; Bhatnagar, 2009). W. A. Kahn in 1990 first conceptualized work engagement as ''the harnessing of organization members' selves to their work roles; in engagement, people employ and express themselves physically, cognitively, and emotionally during role performances''. Another researcher Csikszentmihalyi (1990) defined it as "flow", flow is a more complex concept that involves momentary peak experiences that can occur outside of work. Leiter and Maslach (1998) viewed engagement as the opposite pole of burnout defining it as "an energetic experience of involvement with personally fulfilling activities that enhance a staff member's sense of professional efficacy".

According to another popular description of engagement by Buckingham and Coffman (1999) "the right people in the right roles with the right managers drive employee engagement". In 2001 yet another definitions of employee engagement emerged. Rothbard (2001) defined engagement as "psychological presence" but the definition went further to state that it involved two critical components: "attention and absorption". According to Maslach et al. (2001), engagement is characterized by energy, involvement, and efficacy. Schaufeli et al. (2002) defined engagement "as a positive, fulfilling, work-related state of mind that is characterized by vigor, dedication, and absorption." According to them engagement is not a momentary and specific state, but rather, it is "a more persistent and pervasive affective-cognitive state that is not focused on any particular object, event, individual, or behavior". Harter et al. (2002) defined employee engagement as "the individual's involvement and satisfaction with as well as enthusiasm for work".

According to Towers Perrin, Employee Engagement Workforce Study (2003) engagement is defined as "employees' willingness and ability to help their company succeed, largely by providing discretionary effort on a sustainable basis". Since 2003, employee engagement was defined more completely, for instance Nelson and Simmons (2003) defined as feeling positive towards work, finding it meaningful and manageable and having hope about the future. Engagement has also been viewed as feeling responsible for and committed to superior job performance (Britt, 1999). A very refined definition emerged in 2004, where May et al. (2004) defined engagement as "flow". This study was conducted to create a measurement tool in this area. The definition includes three-dimensional concept of work engagement which are as follows: emotional component, physical component, and cognitive component. Robinson et al. (2004) defined employee engagement as "a positive attitude held by the employee towards the organization and its value. An engaged employee is aware of business context, and works with colleagues to improve performance within the job for the benefit of the organization. The organization must work to develop and nurture engagement, which requires a two-way relationship between employer and employee."

Hewitt Associates LLC (2004) defined employee engagement as "the state in which individuals are emotionally and intellectually committed to the organisation or group, as measured by three primary behaviours: Say, stay and strive". Schaufeli and Salanova (2007) defined engagement as being fully absorbed in a role. Fleming and Asplund (2007) went a step further by adding a spiritual element and presented employee engagement as "the ability to capture the heads, hearts, and souls of your employees to instil an intrinsic desire and passion for excellence". Macey and Schneider (2008b) described engagement as a construct consisting of "state, trait, and behavioural" forms that signify a blend of affective energy and discretionary effort directed to one's work and organization. Schaufeli and Bakker (2010) defined work engagement as "the psychological state that accompanies the behavioural investment of personal energy".

Predictors of Employee Engagement

In order to develop a conceptual framework for employee engagement analytics, it is important to explore the measures of employee engagement and its predictors in the past literature. The 17-item Utrecht Work Engagement Scale (UWES) is a popular tool used in past literature that measures three areas of engagement representing behavioral, emotional, and cognitive dimensions (Schaufeli et al., 2006). These three dimensions correspond to worker engagement themes of vigor, dedication, and absorption, respectively, in one's work. Another important model that has been used in research for enhancing employee engagement is Job Demands–Resources (JD-R) model. According to the JD-R model, the work environment can be divided into demands and resources. Job demands refer to features of a job that require sustained physical and/or psychological effort. Job resources refer features of a job that are functional in that they help achieve work goals, reduce job demands, and stimulate personal growth, learning, and development (Bakker and Demerouti, 2007). The predictors of employee engagement identified in literature have been discussed in the following segment.

Job Characteristics

According to Kahn (1990, 1992) psychological meaningfulness involves a sense of return and can be achieved from task characteristics that provide challenging work, allow the use of different skills, personal discretion, and the opportunity to make important contributions. It is based on Hackman and Oldham's (1980) job characteristics model and in particular, the five core job characteristics (i.e. skill variety, task identity, task significance, autonomy, and feedback). Maslach et al. (2001) model also suggested the importance of job characteristics for engagement. May et al. (2004) found that job enrichment was positively related to meaningfulness and meaningfulness mediated the relationship between job enrichment and engagement. In order to measure Job Characteristic six items scale from Hackman and Oldham (1980) can be used, in which each item corresponds to a core job characteristic (autonomy, task identity, skill variety, task significance, feedback from others, and feedback from the job). Another aspect of job is job redesign; specific elements of job can be redesigned to match the employees' abilities with their job leading to better person–environment fit (Barling et al., 2005; Alfes et al., 2013; Holman and Axtell, 2016).

Rewards and Recognition

Returns can come in form of external rewards and recognition in addition to meaningful work. According to Kahn (1990) people can have different perception of the benefits they receive from a role and accordingly their engagement will also vary. Maslach et al. (2001) also suggested that appropriate rewards and recognitions are important for increasing engagement level of employees. According to a study conducted by Saks and Rotman in 2006, recognition emerged as a significant antecedent of employee engagement. Irrespective of the quantity or type of reward, it is the employee's perception of the same that determines his/her content and thereby one's engagement in the job. It can involve both financial and non-financial rewards; financial rewards can be in form of pay, bonuses, and other financial rewards. Non-financial rewards can be like voucher schemes and extra holiday.

Perceived Organizational Support and Perceived Supervisor Support

Perceived organizational support (POS) is defined as the belief that an individual possesses that their organization cares about them and their well-being (Pati and Kumar, 2010; Rhoades and Eisenberger, 2002). It predicts organizational commitment, citizenship behaviour, engagement and finally retention (Saks, 2006; Pati and Kumar, 2010). There is a direct effect of POS on employee engagement (Biswas and Bhatnagar, 2013). According to Gillet et al. (2013) employees who feel supported by organization through reward and recognition, display higher motivation and engagement. Supportive relationships and supportive management promotes psychological safety of an individual (Kahn, 1990). Hence POS leads to psychological safety which results in higher employee engagement. It is thus obvious that organizations that ensure POS are expected to have a higher competitive advantage than those that do not foster support to their workers (Alvi et al., 2014). POS is generally measured using the eight-item version of the survey of perceived organizational support (SPOS) (Eisenberger et al., 1986). Participants can rate these items using a seven-point Likert-type scale ranging from 1 ("strongly disagree") to 7 ("strongly agree").

Perceived supervisor support (PSS) in defined as an employee's "general views concerning the degree to which supervisors value their contributions and care about their well-being" (Eisenberger et al., 2002). According to Sparrowe and Liden (2005) quality of the supervisor-subordinate relationship has some influence on engagement. Furthermore, Brunetto et al. (2013) concluded that supervisor-subordinate relationship promotes teamwork which has a positive impact on engagement. May et al. (2004) also found that a supportive supervisor relation was positively related to psychological safety, which in turn leads to higher employee engagement. Perceived supervisor support (PSS) can be measured with 4-item scale used by Bouckenooghe et al. (2009).

Team and Co-Worker Relationship

Teamwork is an important aspect involving employees supporting and assisting one another that leads to employee engagement (Rasmussen and Jeppesen, 2006). According to Kahn (1990) supportive team and interpersonal relationships promote employee engagement. May et al. (2004) found that workplace relationship has a significant impact on meaningfulness, which is one of the components of engagement. Similarly according to Locke and Taylor (1990) individuals having positive interpersonal interactions with their co-workers experience greater meaning in life leading to higher engagement. Rasmussen and Jeppesen (2006) concluded that teamwork is linked with better organizational commitment. Kindermann (1993) found that continuity in the motivational structure of peer groups increased the engagement level of each individual. Schaufeli and Bakker (2004) found that support from colleagues predicted engagement.

Distributive and Procedural Justice

Distributive justice pertains to one's perception of the fairness of decision outcomes; procedural justice refers to the perceived fairness of the means and processes used to determine the amount and distribution of resources (Colquitt, 2001; Rhoades et al., 2001). For organizations it is important to be consistent and predictable in terms of the distribution of rewards as well as the procedures used to allocate them. Justice perception is related to organizational outcomes such as job satisfaction, organizational commitment, organizational citizenship behavior, withdrawal, and performance (Colquitt et al., 2001). Procedural justice can be measured by seven-item scale, while distributive justice can be measured by four-item scale. Both scales have been developed by Colquitt in 2001. Participants can respond using a five-point Likert-type scale with anchors (1) to a small extent to (5) a large extent.

Leadership

One of the most important predictor found in literature is leadership. An increasing number of studies suggests that leaders play an important role in employee work engagement, for example, by showing transformational leadership, thereby influencing employee personal and job resources (Tims et al., 2011; Tuckey et al., 2012; Ghadi et al., 2013; Breevaart et al., 2014). Leadership style and support is crucial for encouraging employee engagement. Years of occupational health psychology research have revealed that a "transformational leadership" style is effective for this task (Barling, 2007). According to Schaufeli & Salanova (2008) leaders who are high in task and support behaviour are effective at promoting engagement. According to Zhu et al. (2009) managers' perceptions of the transformational leadership qualities of their executive leaders were found to be positively associated with the managers' own engagement. Seijts and Crim (2006) found that leadership behaviour can have positive impact as employees become more engaged. Lockwood (2007) also inferred that engagement can be influenced by effective communication between leader and their employees. Engagement occurs naturally when leaders are inspiring (Wallace and Trinka, 2009). Authentic and supportive leadership can impact engagement as it increases their involvement, satisfaction and enthusiasm for work (Schneider et al., 2009). Thus it is concluded that leadership plays an important role for enhancement of employee engagement, be it transformational, authentic or supportive leadership.

Training, Coaching and Feedback

It has been seen that training improves accuracy and thereby impacts employee performance and engagement (Paradise, 2008). Training and development not only increases knowledge and confidence of employees but also motivates them to be more engaged in their job. According to Alderfer (1972) if an organization offers employee a chance to grow it is equivalent to rewarding people. He emphasised that "satisfaction of growth needs depend on a person finding the opportunity to be what he or she is most fully and become what he or she can". The opportunities given to the employees for growth and development will increase the level of engagement. Another important predictor related to training is coaching. Coaching can help people with planning, highlighting difficulties, offering advice and emotional support, which in turn fosters engagement (Schaufeli and Salanova, 2007). Effective training and coaching is finally related to feedback for better performance. Positive feedback is also likely to promote engagement and performance. Xanthopoulou et al. (2009b) found that feedback is positively associated with engagement.

Other factors that can also be explored are the personal resources of an individual such as self-efficacy, optimism, resilience, Big Five personality characteristics, positive affect and attitudes. Employees high in work engagement have higher levels of personal resources, including self-efficacy, optimism, and resilience (Mäkikangas et al., 2013). Employees displaying positive affect and attitudes are more involved and attached with their job and their organization (Biswas and Bhatnagar, 2013). Studies show that personality characteristics impact engagement (Liao et al., 2013). A study by Mäkikangas et al. (2013) concluded that the Big Five factors such as: extraversion, emotional stability, and conscientiousness were able to predict variance in work engagement. Future research could usefully be devoted to systematically understanding what influences engagement in specific demographic groups, across specific industry sectors and in differing occupations.

HUMAN RESOURCE ANALYTICS

What Is Human Resource Analytics?

"Big Data" has made its entry into the business world, where data is defined as large in volume, diverse in variety, high in velocity, relational in nature, flexible in nature, fine-grained in resolution but still exhaustive in scope (Kitchin, 2014; Strong, 2015). Big data has been defined as something which ranges from 'a few dozen terabytes to multiple petabytes' that is too large for a typical database to be able to capture, store, manage and analyze (Manyika, et al., 2011). Explosion in self-reporting on social media has led to datafication of emotions, sentiments and relationships which has led our lives becoming 'datafied' (Strong, 2015). Analytics play an important role here; it helps us in analyzing and interpreting the big data. Analytics is an interdisciplinary term that has developed at the intersection of engineering, computer science, statistics and decision-making which helps us to organise, analyse and make decisions from the big data being generated by contemporary societies (Mortensen et al., 2015). Analytics, in general, refers to "the use of analysis, data and systematic reasoning to make decisions" (Davenport et al., 2010). Analytics has been described as a 'must-have' capability for HR profession as it helps in creating value from data collected from people thus broadening the strategic influence of the HR function (CIPD, 2013). Adding HR component to analytics implies that data analysis and interpretation is related to human resources of the organization (Heuvel and Bondarouk, 2017). There have been many success stories of organizations generating million dollars in saving, improving engagement and retaining their key talent, due to these stories HR analytics is fast becoming mainstream and an indispensable HR tool (Boston Consulting Group, 2014, Fecheyr-Lippens et al., 2015). Even though being much talked about the capabilities required in HR analytics are not well developed (Wolfe et al., 2006, Carlson and Kavanagh, 2012). According to Deloitte report (2015) HR and people analytics is one of the major capability gaps in today's HR practice. Deloitte report adds that only 35 percent of the respondents indicated that HR analytics was under active development. Even in academia empirical research on HR analytics is virtually non-existent (Boudreau and Ramstad, 2005).

HR analytics moves one step beyond HRIS (human resource information system), it helps to analyze and interpret the data available through projects, absenteeism records and performance appraisals. Scholarly literature available lacks explicit definition of HR Analytics. The term has been explained using various keywords. According to Lawler et al. (2004) HR analytics uses "statistical techniques and experimental approaches" to test the causal relationship between HR practices or policies and performance outcomes. Furthermore, according to KPMG (2013) HR analytics gives "decision making support to the management of people in organizations". While other researchers defined it is "first a mental framework, a logistical progression, and second a set of statistical operations" (Fitz-enz and Mattox II, 2014), it is a tool that includes "rigorously tracking HR investments and outcomes" (Ulrich and Dulebohn, 2015).

Organizations have started using HR analytics to improve their business outcome. Rasmussen and Ulrich (2015) have cited two such examples of HR analytics projects. In first example HR analytics was used to determine the relationship between leadership quality and turnover data, the outcome resulted into higher customer satisfaction. In the second example effectiveness of company's graduate training program was assessed, it resulted into getting higher benefits for the business. Similarly Sparrow et al. (2015) has cited other examples like how Tesla applied analytics to understand its workforce and its customers. McDonalds applied analytics to optimise restaurant performance by identifying staff demographics, management behaviour and employee attitude. We all are aware Google was the first company to set a benchmark by applying analytics in its human resource (Sullivan J, 2013). Although many organisations have started applying HR analytics, there is little evidence of its strategic use (Parry and Tyson, 2011; Rasmussen and Ulrich, 2015). Customization is the key that Coolen (2015) foresee is the next big thing, organizations will need "business user friendly self-service analytical software".

Application of Human Resource Analytics in Organizations

Although Human Resource Analytics is in huge demand these days, most organizations are still struggling to move from operational reporting to analytics. However some organizations have successfully applied it in their operations. Leading companies like Google, Proctor & Gamble, BestBuy, and Sysco have applied human resource analytics to get the most value from their talent. Similarly, a business analytics solution provider organization named BRIDGEi2i helps global business service organizations to identify and act on levers for improving satisfaction and engagement levels of their large, diversified employee base. Leading organizations are increasingly adopting analytics to analyze their employee data for increasing their competitive advantage. Some of the leading examples that have been given in Harvard Business Review article have been summarized in Figure 1 given below.

Figure 1. Application of talent analytics at best places to work
Source: Davenport et al. (2010)

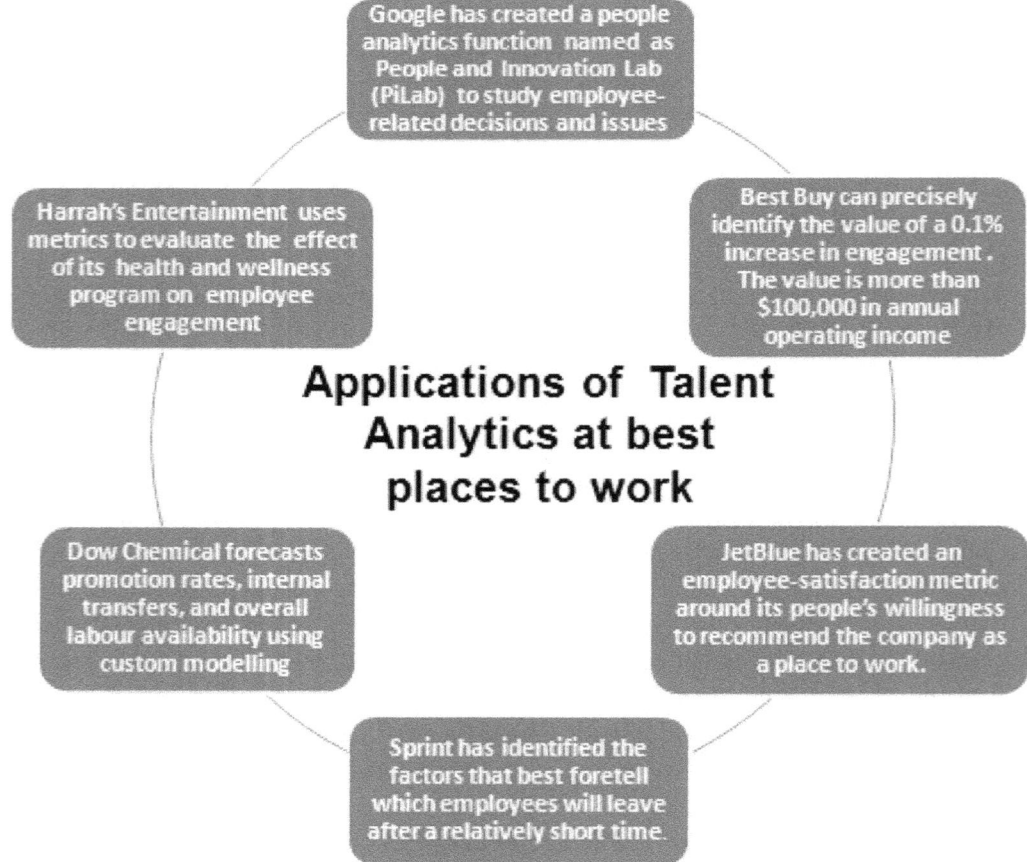

Application of Human Resource Analytics in India

According to a report published by LinkedIn in 2018 there has been a 70 percent increase in analytics professionals in HR across the Asia-Pacific region whereas India has shown a higher growth at 77 percent (Business Standard, 2018). The focus areas for use of analytics in HR in the Asia-Pacific region are namely talent acquisition, talent development and Compensation and benefits. HR practitioners in India are currently prioritizing on three areas that are: compensation and benefits, talent acquisition, productivity and performance. The top three industries to adopt talent analytics in India are financial services and insurance, technology-software, and professional services. As in the west, financial service sector is leading the way. Financial institutions and banks in India are using data mining and analytics for better business outcomes. Credit card companies use analytics to predict customer risk profile, similarly insurance providers also use analytics for risk estimation (Vohra, 2017). Retail sectors in India are also using analytics by analyzing the sale data and thus determining the marketing strategies. Telecom is another fast-growing sector that uses analytics for improving customer profitability and minimizing churn. Other sectors that use analytics are Pharmaceuticals, e-commerce and the airlines industry. Several Indian organizations have started using an assessment tool called Predictive Index (PI), which creates behavioural profiles of people (Singh, 2016). Amway for example used PI tool for selecting a candidate during internal job posting as the behavioural indices of the person fitted well with the desired profile. WithMe a fashion social network was facing problem in getting the right candidate, PI gave interesting outputs on the behavioural characteristics of the individuals which provided useful insights in selecting the candidate. HCL Technologies applies analytical tool which uses intelligent neural network engine using natural language processing and semantic analysis. This tool analyzes employee records and provides recruiters predictive intelligence to hire right candidate. This tool also helps in predicting employee retention, talent fulfilment as well as profiling talent to enhance performance. With the help of demographic analysis they are able to predict ROI ((return on investment) of programmes, policies and practices with higher accuracy. Few of the Indian companies that are using analytics in different fields are as follows: ICICI, IDBI, Axis Bank (Banks), Bajaj Allianz, ICICI Lombard (Insurance), Bharti, Tata Indicom (Telecom), Shopper's Stop, Arvind mills, Tanishq, Planet M, Gitanjali group (Retail), Naukri, Bharat matrimony, Time of India (online) (E-commerce), Jet Airways, Kingfisher (Travel), Ranbaxy, Pfizer, GlaxoSmithKline (Pharma).

CONCEPTUAL FRAMEWORK FOR EMPLOYEE ENGAGEMENT ANALYTICS

HR Analytics can prove to be an excellent tool for giving insight into employee engagement. This can be done by converting HR problem into a mathematical problem using DCOVA problem solving framework using discrete steps define, collect, organize, visualize, and analyze.

Define

First and foremost we should define the problem and understand what it is in the organization that drives their employees and can these drivers lead to superior performance. These drivers can be related to work, organization, manager, team, personal life and other similar factors. Through literature review many predictors of employee engagement have been identified these are as follows: Job Characteristics,

Rewards and recognition, Perceived organizational support, Perceived supervisor support, Team and co-worker relationship, Distributive justice, Procedural justice, Leadership, Training, Coaching and Feedback. Other drivers that can also be included are self-efficacy, optimism, resilience, Big Five personality characteristics, positive affect and attitudes.

Figure 2. Conceptual framework of employee engagement analytics

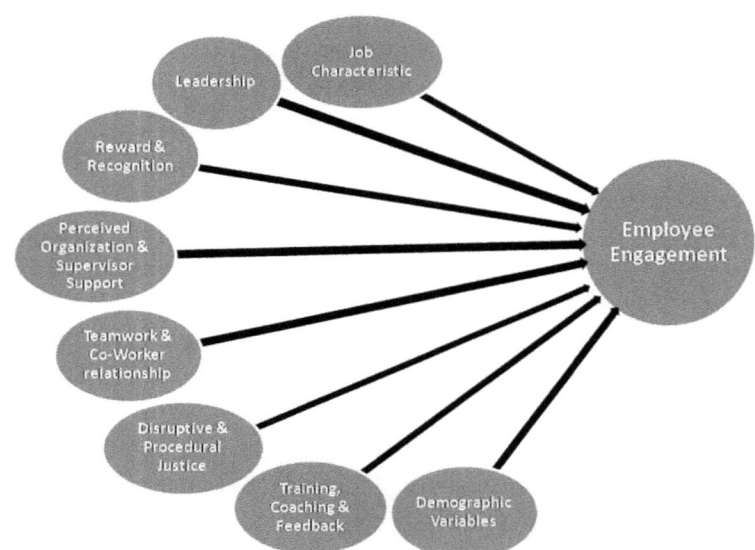

Collect

Then data should be collected, in order to unlock the value of engagement data, also it is necessary to combine engagement data collected with other information such as data from performance management system and business outcome data. Data can be collected from employees using standardized measuring scales available in academic literature. The 17-item Utrecht Work Engagement Scale (UWES) a popular tool used in literature can be used to measures three areas of engagement representing behavioral, emotional, and cognitive dimensions (Schaufeli et al., 2006). In order to measure Job Characteristic six items scale from Hackman and Oldham (1980) can be used, in which each item corresponds to a core job characteristic (autonomy, task identity, skill variety, task significance, feedback from others, and feedback from the job). In order to measure POS using the eight-item version of the survey of perceived organizational support (SPOS; Eisenberger et al., 1986). Perceived supervisor support (PSS) can be measured with 4-item scale used by Bouckenooghe (2009). Procedural justice can be measured by seven-item scale, while distributive justice can be measured by four-item scale (Colquitt, 2001). Other predictors can be similarly measured using standardized scales. Demographic details can be collected for comparison of engagement data across teams, gender, age groups etc.

Organize

The collected data should be organized and cleaned such that it can be used for analysis. Associative and descriptive statistics can be used to identify the key variables. Questions not adding value to the analysis can be dropped. In order to organize and identify the appropriate analysis technique Table 1 will be useful. The dependent variable in this case is Employee engagement and the drivers are independent variables.

Table 1.

Dependent Variable (DV)	Independent Variable (IV)	Analysis Test
Categorical DV (Binary, Nominal, or Ordinal)	• Categorical and only one IV • Continuous or together continuous and categorical	• Chi-Square • Logistic Regression

Continuous DV (Interval or Ratio-and sometimes Ordinal)	• Categorical –Binary IV
	  Group A Group B
	• 2 Category –Time Based Binary IV
	  Group A at Time 1 versus
	  Group A at Time 2
		• Independent samples t-test
		• Paired samples t-test

Continuous DV (Interval or Ratio-and sometimes Ordinal)	• Categorical IV with three or more groups, Group A versus Group B versus Group C • Category–Time Based IV with three or more time points (eg Group A at Time 1 versus Group A at Time 2 versus Group A at Time 3) • Continuous (assumed) DV and only one other continuous IV • Time-based categorical IV with two or more time points- Time 1 versus Time 2 (etc) in combination with one or more categorical IVs (eg Gender)	• One-way independent ANOVA • One-way repeated measures ANOVA • Pearsons's correlation or Simple linear regression • Repeated measures ANOVA
Continuous DV (Interval or Ratio-and sometimes Ordinal)	• Two or more continuous IVs • Both categorical and continuous IVs	• Multiple Regression (linear) • Multiple Regression (linear)

Source: Edwards and Edwards (2016)

Visualize and Analyze

Data can then be visualized and analyzed using appropriate statistical technique. Overall engagement scores can be mapped against individual engagement scores. It can be seen here that if we are taking standardized scale for employee engagement measurement like 17-item Utrecht Work Engagement Scale (UWES), the dependent variable is then continuous as the scale is Interval or Ratio-and or sometimes Ordinal. Similarly the predictors (i.e. independent variables) like Job Characteristics, Rewards and recognition, Perceived organizational support, Perceived supervisor support, Team and co-worker relationship, Distributive justice, Procedural justice, Leadership, Training, Coaching and Feedback are also continuous. Only demographic variables are categorical. Thus the appropriate technique that can be used for employee engagement analytics is regression. Multiple regression can be used as independent variables are both categorical and continuous and the dependent variable is continuous. In order to understand what influences engagement in specific demographic groups (e.g. people with disabilities; millennials; older workers) t-test and ANOVA can be used.

The process does not stop at analysis; the most important step after analysis is interpretation. The result obtained should be interpreted by relating it to the bigger picture, for instance identifying the key drivers for employee engagement, finding their impact on individual performance as well as organization's performance and identifying how demographic variables impact employee engagement. This step will help managers making informed decisions that can be backed up with verifiable data.

CONCLUSION

People are key to success for any organization. In a race to survive and sustain in the cutthroat market it's imperative for the organisation to put their best talent to work. The first challenge before every organization is to attract and retain the best. Second challenge is to ensure that those who are retained are engaged. Nowadays, employee engagement is widely talked about due its recognition as a tool which holds your best employees in your organization. The rising demand of the employees of the meaningful work and fulfilling workplace demands the organisations to create environment and culture which increases positive attitudes and behaviours and drive improved business performance. Engaged employees are one who are emotionally committed to their organisations and its goals and display discretionary efforts which results in engagement-profit chain. The employees become more caring, productive, gives better advice and stay in the jobs for longer periods. This ultimately leads to happy and satisfied customers, who purchase and refer more, which drives higher sales and profits for the firms and appreciation in stock prices.

The leading organizations can improve the overall employee experience and increase their engagement level with the support of Human resource analytics. This can be done by adopting tools like pulse feedback, designing wellness and fitness apps and developing self-service technologies that can help improve employee engagement. The HR department with the help of analytics driven tools and analysis can have better understanding of the employees' experience. The new age concepts like sentiment analysis, journey maps, design thinking and many more tools gives leverage to HR to measure employees behavioral traits and psyche and taking corrective strategies.

The analytics is providing opportunity to the firms to analyse the voluminous data they have gathered over the years from information systems and internal social platforms and get cues on how to manage the available resources effectively and remove the barriers by deep diving into the data and having investigative ideas about company's wellbeing from employees' perspective. In such circumstances, predictive analytics can propose a talent value model which can help in addressing vital questions like "What makes employees stay with our company?" what are the liking and disliking of the employees and likewise which can help in creating analytical models to study, understand and predict employees behavior. This will help the managers to assess the their strategies against that of competitors and deep dive into the HR issues ranging from matching recruitment offer, planning personalised performance inducements or deciding right time to make important announcement related to increments and promotions. The analytics is tried and tested and has proved its utility and relevance in the present times. The predictive analytics can be boon and can act as wonderful tool for the organisations due to its innate capability of providing valuable insights and forecasting for the future.

The chapter has made an attempt to highlight the utility of analytics in predicting the behavioural aspects of the employees in the organization. The study substantiated the claim with the help of the suitable examples and available literature from the past studies. Employee engagement is a burning issue in front of the organisation demanding immediate attention to attract and sustain best talent. This issue needs to be relooked from different perspective for which it's required to be measured accurately by applying suitable tools and techniques to draw meaningful inferences and taking preventive measures. The future researchers can study the impact of predictive analytics on the employees' behavior and organizational efficiency and performance. This will help in better evaluation of the contribution made by analytics in the field of human behaviour and management of the organizations.

REFERENCES

Alderfer, C. P. (1972). *Human Needs in Organisational Settings.* New York, NY: Free Press of Glencoe.

Alfes, K., Shantz, A. D., Truss, C., & Soane, E. C. (2013). The link between perceived human resource management practices, engagement and employee behavior: A moderated mediation model. *International Journal of Human Resource Management*, 24(2), 330–351. doi:10.1080/09585192.2012.679950

Alvi, K., Abbasi, S., & Haider, R. (2014). Relationship of perceived organisational support and employee engagement. *Science International*, 26(2), 949–952.

Bakker, A. B., & Demerouti, E. (2007). The job demands–resources model: State of the art. *Journal of Managerial Psychology*, 22(3), 309–328. doi:10.1108/02683940710733115

Bakker, A. B., Demerouti, E., & Sanz-Vergel, A. I. (2014). Burnout and work engagement: The JD-R approach. *Annual Review of Organizational Psychology and Organizational Behavior*, 1(1), 389–411. doi:10.1146/annurev-orgpsych-031413-091235

Bakker, A. B., Demerouti, E., & Schaufeli, W. B. (2005). The crossover of burnout and work engagement among working couples. *Human Relations*, 58(5), 661–689. doi:10.1177/0018726705055967

Bakker, A. B., Van Emmerik, I. J. H., & Euwema, M. C. (2006). Crossover of burnout and engagement in work teams. *Work and Occupations*, 33(4), 464–489. doi:10.1177/0730888406291310

Barling, J. (2007). *Ten key factors in building a psychologically healthy workplace.* Paper presented at the 2nd Canadian Congress on Research on Mental Health and Addiction in the Workplace, Vancouver, BC, Canada.

Barling, J., Kelloway, E. K., & Frone, M. R. (Eds.). (2005). *The handbook of work stress.* Newbury Park, CA: Sage.

Baumruk, R. (2004). The missing link: The role of employee engagement in business success. *Workspan*, 47, 48–52.

Baumruk, R. Gorman, B., Jr., Gorman, R. E., & Ingham, J. (2006). Why Managers Are Crucial to Increasing Engagement. *Strategic HR Review, 5*(2), 24-27.

Bennet, M., & Bell, A. (2004). *Leadership and Talent in Asia.* Singapore: Pte Ltd.

Bhatnagar, J. (2007). Talent management strategy of employee engagement of Indian ITES employees: Key to retention. *Employee Relations*, 29(6), 640–663. doi:10.1108/01425450710826122

Bhatnagar, J. (2009). Exploring psychological contract and employee engagement In India. In The changing face of people management in India. London: Routledge: Taylor and Francis.

Biswas, S., & Bhatnagar, J. (2013). Mediator analysis of employee engagement: Role of perceived organizational support, P-O fit, organizational commitment and job satisfaction. *Vikalpa, 38*(1), 27–40.

Boston Consulting Group. (2014). *Creating people advantage 2014-2015*. Boston, MA: The Boston Consulting Group, Inc.

Bouckenooghe, D., Devos, G., & Broeck, H. V. D. (2009). Organizational Climate Questionnaire-Climate of Change, Processes, and Readiness: Development of a New Instrument. *The Journal of Psychology, 143*(6), 559–599. doi:10.1080/00223980903218216 PMID:19957876

Boudreau, J. W., & Ramstad, P. M. (2005). Talentship, talent segmentation, and sustainability: A new HR decision science paradigm for a new strategy definition. *Human Resource Management, 44*(2), 129–136. doi:10.1002/hrm.20054

Breevaart, K., Bakker, A. B., Hetland, J., Demerouti, E., Olsen, O. K., & Espevik, R. (2014). Daily transactional and transformational leadership and daily employee engagement. *Journal of Occupational and Organizational Psychology, 87*(1), 138–157. doi:10.1111/joop.12041

Britt, T. W. (1999). Engaging the self in the field: Testing the triangle model of responsibility. *Personality and Social Psychology Bulletin, 25*(6), 696–706. doi:10.1177/0146167299025006005

Brunetto, Y., Xerri, M., Shriberg, A., Farr-Wharton, R., Shacklock, K., Newman, S., & Dienger, J. (2013). The impact of workplace relationships on engagement, well-being, commitment and turnover for nurses in Australia and the USA. *Journal of Advanced Nursing, 69*(12), 2786–2799. doi:10.1111/jan.12165 PMID:23651183

Buckingham, M., & Coffman, C. (1999). *First, Break All the Rules: What the World's Greatest Managers Do Differently*. New York, NY: The Gallup Organization, Simon and Schuster.

Carlson, K. D., & Kavanagh, M. (2012). HR metrics and workforce analytics. In M. J. Kavanagh, M. Thite, & R. D. Johnson (Eds.), *Human Resource Information Systems: Basics applications and future directions* (2nd ed.; pp. 150–174). Thousand Oaks, CA: Sage.

Christian, M. S., Garza, A. S., & Slaughter, J. E. (2011). Work engagement: A quantitative review a test of its relations with task and contextual performance. *Personnel Psychology, 64*(1), 89–136. doi:10.1111/j.1744-6570.2010.01203.x

CIPD. (2013). *Talent Analytics and Big Data – The Challenge for HR*. London: Chartered Institute for Personnel and Development.

Colquitt, J. (2001). On the dimensionality of organizational justice: A construct validation of a measure. *The Journal of Applied Psychology, 86*(3), 386–400. doi:10.1037/0021-9010.86.3.386 PMID:11419799

Coolen, P. (2015). *The next big thing in HR analytics*. Available at: https://www.linkedin.com/pulse/next-big-thing-hr-analytics-patrick-coolen

Csikszentmihalyi, M. (1990). *Flow: The psychology of optimal experience*. New York: Harper & Row.

Davenport, T. H., Harris, J., & Shapiro, J. (2010). Competing on Talent Analytics. *Harvard Business Review*, 2–6. PMID:20929194

Davenport, T. H., Harris, J. G., & Morison, R. (2010). *Analytics at Work: Smarter Decisions, Better Results*. Boston, MA: Harvard Business School Press.

Deloitte. (2015). *Global Human Capital Trends 2015, leading in the new world of work*. Deloitte University Press.

Deloitte University Press (2017). *Rewriting the rules for the digital age*. 2017 Deloitte Global Human Capital Trends Report.

Edwards, M. R., & Edwards, K. A. (2016). *Predictive HR analytics: Mastering the HR metric*. London: Kogan Page.

Eisenberger, R., Huntington, R., Hutchison, S., & Sowa, D. (1986). Perceived organisational support. *The Journal of Applied Psychology*, *71*(3), 500–507. doi:10.1037/0021-9010.71.3.500

Eisenberger, R., Stinglhamber, F., Vandenberghe, C., Sucharski, I. L., & Rhoades, L. (2002). Perceived supervisor support: Contributions to perceived organizational support and employee retention. *The Journal of Applied Psychology*, *87*(3), 565–573. doi:10.1037/0021-9010.87.3.565 PMID:12090614

Fecheyr-Lippens, B., Schaninger, B., & Tanner, K. (2015). Power to the new people analytics. *The McKinsey Quarterly*, *51*(1), 61–63.

Fitz-enz, J., & Mattox, J. R. II. (2014). *Predictive Analytics for Human Resources*. Hoboken, NJ: John Wiley & Sons, Inc. doi:10.1002/9781118915042

Fleming, J. H., & Asplund, J. (2007). *Human sigma*. New York, NY: Gallup Press.

Frank, F. D., Finnegan, R. P., & Taylor, C. R. (2004). The race for talent: Retaining and engaging workers in the 21st century. *Human Resource Planning*, *27*(3), 12–25.

Gallup Management Journal. (2006). Retrieved from http://gmj.gallup.com

Gawke, J. C. L., Gorgievski, M. J., & Bakker, A. B. (2017). Employee intrapreneurship and work engagement: A latent change score approach. *Journal of Vocational Behavior*, *100*, 88–100. doi:10.1016/j.jvb.2017.03.002

Ghadi, M. Y., Fernando, M., & Caputi, P. (2013). Transformational leadership and work engagement: The mediating effect of meaning in work. *Leadership and Organization Development Journal*, *34*(6), 1–34.

Gillet, N., Huart, I., Colombat, P., & Fouquereau, E. (2013). Perceived organizational support, motivation, and engagement among police officers. *Professional Psychology, Research and Practice*, *44*(1), 46–55. doi:10.1037/a0030066

Guest, D. E. (2014). Employee engagement: fashionable fad or long-term fixture? In C. Truss, R. Delbridge, K. Alfes, A. Shantz, & E. Soane (Eds.), *Employee Engagement in Theory and Practice* (pp. 221–235). Oxon, UK: Routledge.

Gutermann, D., Lehmann-Willenbrock, N., Boer, D., Born, M., & Voelpel, S. C. (2017). How leaders affect followers' work engagement and performance: Integrating leader-member exchange and crossover theory. *British Journal of Management, 28*(2), 299–314. doi:10.1111/1467-8551.12214

Hackman, J. R., & Oldham, G. R. (1980). *Work Redesign*. Reading, MA: Addison-Wesley.

Harter, J. K., Schmidt, F. L., & Hayes, T. L. (2002). Business-unit-level relationship between employee satisfaction, employee engagement, and business outcomes: A meta-analysis. *The Journal of Applied Psychology, 87*(2), 268–279. doi:10.1037/0021-9010.87.2.268 PMID:12002955

Heuvel, S. V. D., & Bondarouk, T. (2017). The rise (and fall?) of HR analytics: A study into the future application, value, structure, and system support. *Journal of Organizational Effectiveness: People and Performance, 4*(2), 157–178. doi:10.1108/JOEPP-03-2017-0022

Hewitt Associates LLC. (2004). *Research brief: employee engagement higher at double-digit growth companies*. Available at: www.hewitt.com

Holman, D., & Axtell, C. (2016). Can job redesign interventions influence a broad range of employee outcomes by changing multiple job characteristics? A quasi-experimental study. *Journal of Occupational Health Psychology, 21*(3), 284–295. doi:10.1037/a0039962 PMID:26641482

Kahn, W. A. (1990). Psychological conditions of personal engagement and disengagement at work. *Academy of Management Journal, 33*, 692–724.

Kahn, W. A. (1992). To be full there: Psychological presence at work. *Human Relations, 45*(4), 321–349. doi:10.1177/001872679204500402

Kindermann, A. (1993). Natural peer groups as contexts for individual development: The case of children's motivation in school. *Developmental Psychology, 29*(6), 970–977. doi:10.1037/0012-1649.29.6.970

King, E. B., Tonidandel, S., Cortina, J. M., & Fink, A. A. (2015). Building understanding of the data science revolution and I-O psychology. In S. Tonidandel, E. B. King, & J. M. Cortina (Eds.), *Big Data at Work: The Data Science Revolution and Organizational Psychology* (pp. 1–15). New York, NY: Routledge.

Kitchin, R. (2014). *The Data Revolution: Big data, open data, data infrastructures and their consequences*. SAGE Publications Ltd.

KPMG. (2013). *People are the real numbers: HR analytics has come of age*. A report by KPMG International Cooperative.

Lawler, E. E., Levenson, A., & Boudreau, J. (2004). HR Metrics and Analytics Uses and Impacts. *Human Resource Planning, 27*(4), 27–35.

Leiter, M. P., & Maslach, C. (1998). Burnout. In H. S. Friedman (Ed.), *Encyclopedia of mental health, 1*. New York: Academic Press.

Liao, F., Yang, L., Wang, M., Drown, D., & Shi, J. (2013). Team-member exchange and work engagement: Does personality make a difference? *Journal of Business and Psychology, 28*(1), 63–77. doi:10.100710869-012-9266-5

Locke, E. A., & Taylor, M. S. (1990). Stress, coping, and the meaning of work. In A. Brief & W. R. Nord (Eds.), *Meanings of Occupational Work* (pp. 135–170). Lexington: Lexington Books.

Lockwood, R. (2007). Leveraging employee engagement for competitive advantage: HR's strategic role. *HRMagazine*, *52*(3), 1–11.

Macey, W. H., & Schneider, B. (2008a). Engaged in engagement: We are delighted we did it. *Industrial and Organizational Psychology: Perspectives on Science and Practice*, *1*(1), 76–83. doi:10.1111/j.1754-9434.2007.00016.x

Macey, W. H., & Schneider, B. (2008b). The meaning of employee engagement. *Industrial and Organizational Psychology: Perspectives on Science and Practice*, *1*(01), 3–30. doi:10.1111/j.1754-9434.2007.0002.x

Macey, W. H., Schneider, B., Barbera, K. M., & Young, S. A. (2009). *Employee Engagement: Tools for Analysis, Practice, and Competitive Advantage*. Wiley-Blackwell.

Mäkikangas, A., Feldt, T., Kinnunen, U., & Mauno, S. (2013). Does personality matter? Research on individual differences in occupational well-being. In A. B. Bakker (Ed.), *Advances in Positive Organizational Psychology, 1* (pp. 107–143). Bingley, UK: Emerald. doi:10.1108/S2046-410X(2013)0000001008

Manyika, J., Chui, M., Brown, B., Bughin, J., Dobbs, R., Roxburgh, C., & Byers, A. (2011). *Big data: the next frontier for innovation, competition and productivity*. McKinsey & Company.

Maslach, C., Schaufelli, W. B., & Leiter, M. P. (2001). Job burnout. *Annual Review of Psychology*, *52*(1), 397–422. doi:10.1146/annurev.psych.52.1.397 PMID:11148311

May, D. R., Gilson, R. L., & Harter, L. M. (2004). The psychological conditions of meaningfulness, safety and availability and the engagement of the human spirit at work. *Journal of Occupational and Organizational Psychology*, *77*(1), 11–37. doi:10.1348/096317904322915892

Mone, E. M., & London, M. (2010). *Employee Engagement Through Effective Performance Management: A Practical Guide for Managers*. New York, NY: Routledge.

Mortensen, M., Doherty, N., & Robinson, S. (2015). Operational research from taylorism to terabytes: A research agenda for the analytics age. *European Journal of Operational Research*, *241*(3), 583–595. doi:10.1016/j.ejor.2014.08.029

Nelson, D. L., & Simmons, B. L. (2003). Health psychology and work stress: A more positive approach. In J. C. Quick & L. E. Tetrick (Eds.), Handbook of occupational health psychology (97–119). Washington, DC: American Psychological Association.

Orth, M., & Volmer, J. (2017). Daily within-person effects of job autonomy and work engagement on innovative behaviour: The cross-level moderating role of creative self-efficacy. *European Journal of Work and Organizational Psychology*, *26*(4), 601–612. doi:10.1080/1359432X.2017.1332042

Paradise, A. (2008). Influences engagement. ASTD. *Training & Development*, *62*(1), 54–59.

Parry, E., & Tyson, S. (2011). Desired goals and actual outcomes of e-HRM. *Human Resource Management Journal*, *21*(3), 335–354. doi:10.1111/j.1748-8583.2010.00149.x

Parsley, A. (2006). Road Map for Employee Engagement. *Management Services*, *50*(l), 10–11.

Pati, P., & Kumar, P. (2010). Employee engagement: Role of self-efficacy, organizational support and supervisor support. *Indian Journal of Industrial Relations*, *46*(1), 126–137.

Perrin, T. (2003). *Working Today: Understanding What Drives Employee Engagement.* The 2003 Towers Perrin Talent Report U.S Report. Available: http://www.towersperrin.com/tp/getwebcachedoc? Webc = HRS/USA/2003/200309/Talent_2003.pdf

Power, H. (2017). How Harley-Davidson used artificial intelligence to increase New York sales leads by 2,930%. *Harvard Business Review.* Available at: https://hbr.org/2017/05/how-harley-davidsonused-predictive-analytics-to-increase-new-york-sales-leads-by-2930

Rasmussen, T., & Jeppesen, H. (2006). Teamwork and associated psychological factors: A review. *Work and Stress*, *20*(2), 105–128. doi:10.1080/02678370600920262

Rasmussen, T., & Ulrich, D. (2015). Learning from practice: How HR analytics avoids becoming a fad. *Organizational Dynamics*, *44*(3), 236–242. doi:10.1016/j.orgdyn.2015.05.008

Rhoades, L., & Eisenberger, R. (2002). Perceived organizational support: A review of the literature. *The Journal of Applied Psychology*, *87*(4), 698–714. doi:10.1037/0021-9010.87.4.698 PMID:12184574

Rhoades, L., Eisenberger, R., & Armeli, S. (2001). Affective commitment to the organization: The contribution of perceived organizational support. *The Journal of Applied Psychology*, *86*(5), 825–836. doi:10.1037/0021-9010.86.5.825 PMID:11596800

Rich, B. L., Lepine, J. A., & Crawford, E. R. (2010). Job engagement: Antecedents and effects on job performance. *Academy of Management Journal*, *53*(3), 617–635. doi:10.5465/amj.2010.51468988

Robbins, P., & Judge, A. (Eds.). (2012). *Organizational Behavior* (14th ed.). Upper Saddle River, NJ: Prentice Hall.

Robinson, D., Perryman, S., & Hayday, S. (2004). *The Drivers of Employee Engagement.* Brighton, UK: Institute for Employment Studies.

Rothbard, N. P. (2001). Enriching or depleting? The dynamics of engagement in work and family roles. *Administrative Science Quarterly*, *46*(4), 655–684. doi:10.2307/3094827

Saks, A. M. (2006). Antecedents and consequences of employee engagement. *Journal of Managerial Psychology*, *21*(7), 600–619. doi:10.1108/02683940610690169

Saks, A. M., & Rotman, J. L. (2006). Antecedents and consequences of employee engagement. *Journal of Managerial Psychology*, *21*(7), 600–619. doi:10.1108/02683940610690169

Schaufeli, W., & Salanova, M. (2007). Work engagement: An emerging psychological concept and its implications for organizations. In S. W. Gilliland, D. D. Steiner, & D. P. Skarlicki (Eds.), *Managing social and ethical issues in organizations* (pp. 135–177). Greenwich, CT: Information Age Publishing.

Schaufeli, W. B., & Bakker, A. B. (2004). Job demands, job resources, and their relationship with burnout and engagement: A multi-sample study. *Journal of Organizational Behavior*, *25*(3), 293–315. doi:10.1002/job.248

Schaufeli, W. B., & Bakker, A. B. (2010). Defining and measuring work engagement: bringing clarity to the concept. In A. B. Bakker & M. P. Leiter (Eds.), *Work Engagement: A Handbook of Essential Theory and Research* (pp. 10–24). Hove, NY: Psychology Press.

Schaufeli, W. B., Bakker, A. B., & Salanova, M. (2006). The measurement of work engagement of with a short questionnaire: A cross-national study. *Educational and Psychological Measurement*, 66(4), 701–716. doi:10.1177/0013164405282471

Schaufeli, W. B., & Salanova, M. (2008). Enhancing work engagement through the management of human resources. In K. Näswall, J. Hellgren, & M. Sverke (Eds.), *The individual in the changing working life* (pp. 380–402). New York: Cambridge University Press. doi:10.1017/CBO9780511490064.018

Schaufeli, W. B., & Salanova, M. (2010). How to improve work engagement? In S. L. Albrecht (Ed.), *Handbook of Employee Engagement: Perspectives, Issues, Research and Practice* (pp. 399–415). Cheltenham, UK: Edward Elgar. doi:10.4337/9781849806374.00044

Schaufeli, W. B., Salanova, M., Gonzalez-Roma, V., & Bakker, A. B. (2002). The measurement of engagement and burnout: A two sample confirmatory factor analytic approach. *Journal of Happiness Studies*, 3(1), 71–92. doi:10.1023/A:1015630930326

Schaufeli, W. B., Taris, T. W., & van Rhenen, W. (2008). Workaholism, burnout, and work engagement: Three of a kind or three different kinds of employee wellbeing? *Applied Psychology*, 57(2), 173–203. doi:10.1111/j.1464-0597.2007.00285.x

Schneider, B., Macey, W. H., & Barbera, K. M. (2009). Driving customer satisfaction and financial success through employee engagement. *People and Strategy*, 32(2), 23–27.

Schwartz, J., Collins, L., Stockton, H., Wagner, D., & Walsh, B. (2017). *Rewriting the rules for the digital age.* 2017 Deloitte Global Human Capital Trends.

Seijts, G., & Crim, D. (2006). What engages employees the most, or the ten Cs of employee engagement. *Ivey Business Journal*, 70(4), 1–5.

Shaw, K. (2005). An engagement strategy process for communicators. *Strategic Communication Management*, 9(3), 26–29.

Singh, N. (2016). India companies use analytics tools to spot talent and trouble. *The Times of India.* Available at https://timesofindia.indiatimes.com/trend-tracking/India-companies-use-analytics-tools-to-spot-talent-and-trouble/articleshow/54790024.cms

Sparrow, P., Hird, M., & Cooper, C. (2015). *Do We Need HR? Repositioning People Management for Success.* Basingstoke, UK: Palgrave Macmillan. doi:10.1057/9781137313775

Sparrowe, T., & Liden, C. (2005). Two routes to influence: Integrating leader-member exchange and social network perspectives. *Administrative Science Quarterly*, 50(4), 505–535. doi:10.2189/asqu.50.4.505

Standard, B. (2018). *India sees 77% growth in HR analytics professionals in 5 years, says report.* Available at: https://www.business-standard.com/article/companies/india-sees-77-growth-in-hr-analytics-professionals-in-5-years-says-report-118052100040_1.html

Strong, C. (2015). *Humanizing Big Data: Marketing at the Meeting of Data, Social Science and Consumer Insight.* Kogan Page Ltd.

Sullivan, J. (2013). *How Google is using People Analytics to Completely Reinvent HR.* Available at: https://www.tlnt.com/how-google-is-using-people-analytics-to-completely-reinvent-hr/

Tims, M., Bakker, A. B., & Xanthopoulou, D. (2011). Do transformational leaders enhance their followers' daily work engagement? *The Leadership Quarterly, 22*(1), 121–131. doi:10.1016/j.leaqua.2010.12.011

Towers, P. T. R. (2003). *Working today: understanding what drives employee engagement.* Available at: www.towersperrin.com/hrservices/webcache/towers/United_States/publications/Reports/Talent_Report_2003/Talent_2003.pdf

Tuckey, M. R., Bakker, A. B., & Dollard, M. F. (2012). Empowering leaders optimize working conditions for engagement: A multilevel study. *Journal of Occupational Health Psychology, 17*(1), 15–27. doi:10.1037/a0025942 PMID:22409390

Ulrich, D., & Dulebohn, J. H. (2015). Are we there yet? What's next for HR? *Human Resource Management Review, 25*(2), 188–204. doi:10.1016/j.hrmr.2015.01.004

Van Mierlo, H., & Bakker, A. B. (2018). Crossover of engagement in groups. *Career Development International, 23*(1), 106–118. doi:10.1108/CDI-03-2017-0060

Vohra, G. (2017). *Indian Companies Using Analytics.* Available at: https://analyticstraining.com/indian-companies-using-analytics/

Wallace, L., & Trinka, J. (2009). Leadership and employee engagement. *Public Management, 91*(5), 10–13.

Wellins, R. S., Bernthal, P., & Phelps, M. (2005). Employee Engagement: The Key to Realizing Competitive Advantage. Retrieved from http://www.ddiworld.com/ddi/media/monographs/employeeengagement_mg_ddi.pdf?ext=.pdf

Wolfe, R., Wright, P., & Smart, D. (2006). Radical HRM innovation and competitive advantage: The Moneyball story. *Human Resource Management, 45*(1), 111–126. doi:10.1002/hrm.20100

Woodruffe, C. (2005). Employee engagement: The real secret of winning a crucial edge over your rivals. Manager. *British Journal of Administrative Management, 50*(1), 28–29.

Xanthopoulou, B., Bakker, A. B., Demerouti, E., & Schaufeli, W. B. (2009). Work engagement and financial returns: A diary study on the role of job and personal resources. *Journal of Occupational and Organizational Psychology, 82*(1), 183–200. doi:10.1348/096317908X285633

Xanthopoulou, D., Bakker, A. B., Demerouti, E., & Schaufeli, W. B. (2009b). Reciprocal relationships between job resources, personal resources, and work engagement. *Journal of Vocational Behavior, 74*(3), 235–244. doi:10.1016/j.jvb.2008.11.003

Zhu, W., Avolio, B. J., & Walumbwa, F. O. (2009). Moderating role of follower characteristics with transformational leadership and follower work engagement. *Group & Organization Management, 34*(5), 590–619. doi:10.1177/1059601108331242

Chapter 26
Human Resource Information System Use, Satisfaction, and Success

Sonalee Srivastava

(iD) https://orcid.org/0000-0002-8092-9658
Jaypee Institute of Information Technology, India

Santosh Dev
Jaypee Institute of Information Technology, India

Badri Bajaj
Jaypee Institute of Information Technology, India

ABSTRACT

With the advent of technology in the workplace, the applicability of the human resource information system (HRIS) within organizations has gained momentum widely. Indeed, employees' perceptions towards human resource information system has changed gradually. Human resource information system is influencing employees' work activities to such an extent that it has become imperative precedence for organizations' to maintain HRIS quality. Keeping this in the background, the study aims to examine the relationship of HRIS system quality, HRIS information quality, HRIS service quality, and HRIS perceived usefulness in determining HRIS system use and its users' satisfaction. Further, the study also aims to analyze the relationship of HRIS system use and HRIS users' satisfaction in determining HRIS success in Indian organizations. A sample of 116 HR staffs and managers working in IT-enabled service sector from National Capital Region (India) has been taken for step-wise regression analyses. The findings of the study revealed that HRIS service quality and perceived usefulness showed a significant positive relationship with HRIS system use. The results also revealed that HRIS system quality and perceived usefulness showed a significant positive relationship with users' satisfaction. Further, the findings also revealed that HRIS system use and HRIS users' satisfaction has a significant relationship with HRIS success.

DOI: 10.4018/978-1-6684-3873-2.ch026

1. INTRODUCTION

In this modern era, with the initiation of technology, human resource management gets its makeover both in its effectiveness and competence (Al Shibly, 2011; Marhraoui M.A., El Manouar A. 2020). The movement of Human Resource Information System(HRIS) from administrative to strategic business decision making role has been examined by many scholars (Bali, 2020; Broderick & Bounreau, 1992; Ernst Kossek, Willard Young, 1994; Masum, A.K., 2018; Ngai & Wat, 2006). Prior to the onset of HRIS, HR had to dissipate lots of time in managing task and in generating reports which required cumbersome retrieval of data (Singh, Jindal, & Samim, 2011).

In the current competitive and challenging business environment; organizational growth and development depends on the effective functioning of its human resources, which could be effectively managed by HRIS. DeSanctis (1986) defined HRIS as a "systematic procedure for collecting, storing, maintaining, retrieving, and validating data needed by an organization about its human resources, personnel activities, and organizational unit characteristics". Further Tannenbaum (1990) has defined HRIS as a "technological system that is used to acquire, store, manipulate, analyze, retrieve & distribute pertinent information regarding an organizational human resource". Additionally, Kavanagh et al, (2012) has defined "HRIS as a system used to acquire, store, manipulate, analyze, retrieve, and distribute information regarding an organization's human resources to support HRM & managerial decisions". Recently Rietsema, (2016) defined HRIS as "a suite of software, databases & cloud computing which provide an all- encompassing solution for managing every aspect of a workforce". Thus the movement of HRIS could be seen from these definitions; initially it started with managing employees' data then it started assistance in HRM activities further it encompasses solutions to every aspects of workforce. Thus automation of HR functions plays an important strategic tool in the hands of HR and helps in managing and taking effective decision for organization and for its employees (Fenech, R., Baguant, P., & Ivanov, D. 2019 ; Nagendra & Deshpande, 2014).

Researchers have acclaimed the benefits and usage of HRIS from time to time as it enhances the accuracy and speed of the employees' work (Hosnavi and Ramezan 2010); ease in the information access and helps in strategic decision making (Lengnick-Hall and Steve 2003; Nejib Ben Moussaa, Rakia El Arbi,2020; Rangriz,Mehrabi & Azadegan 2011). Further, HRIS improves HR quality (A Davarpanah & N Mohamed, 2020; Reddick, 2009) and employee productivity which leads to the overall fulfillment of individual and organizational objectives (H Begum et al., 2020; Lengnick-Hall & Steve, 2003; M. I. R. Imron, 2020; Rand H. Al-Dmour, 2020). HRIS supports all the HR and management practices within an organization (Aizhan Tursunbayeva et al, 2020; Irum, A. & Yadav, R.S. 2019; Tursunbayeva et al., 2016). Therefore implementation of HRIS initiates innovation in HR activities within an organization (Túlio Gomes Mauro & Jairo Eduardo Borges-Andrade, 2019).

Nowadays, organizations spend heavily on information system for enhancing the strategic role of Human Resource Management (Aswanth Kumar & Brijball Parumasur, 2013; Bayraktaroglu et al., 2019; Brandon-Jones & Kauppi, 2018; P Goktas & Y Akgul, 2019; Sanjeev R., Natrajan N.S. 2020). Organizations have taken utmost consideration while managing information effectiveness that supports the business functioning of any organization (Bal, Bozkurt, & Ertemsir, 2012; L. Syafiraliany, M. Lubis & R. W. Witjaksono, 2019). For facilitating a strategic value to an organization, HRIS is becoming a prominent tool in the hands of an organization which improves its information processing via lowering HR cost along with leveraging productivity (Boateng, 2007; Dery, Grant, & Wiblen, 2007; Rand H. Al-Dmour, 2020).

HRIS helps not only in storing employees' information in its database but also helps in managing almost all HR functions (Bayraktaroglu et al., 2019) within an organization. Technology digitally saves the large amount of data and thus it is cost effective and helps in enhancing work speed and employees efficiency (Bayraktaroglu et al., 2019; Bondarouk, Parry, & Furtmueller, 2017). Though organization has been started implementing HRIS for their HR in particular and employees in general, but still it is lacking to its full utilization and so less return of investment for organizations have been mentioned by various researchers (Al-Dmour, Love, & Al-Debei, 2016; Sablok, Stanton, Bartram, Burgess, & Boyle, 2017).

2. THEORETICAL BACKGROUND AND RESEARCH MODEL DEVELOPMENT

HRIS basically facilitates HR department and marks its presence by providing number of benefits to all levels of management (Bondarouk, Parry, & Furtmueller, 2017; Ruël, Bondarouk, & Looise, 2004). Al Shibly, (2011 & 2014) has established a relationship between system quality and information quality with HRIS users satisfaction and with HRIS success. But they missed out one major construct of HRIS success model i.e., service quality, which equally plays a significant role in determining HRIS success within an organization (Muturi, Kiflemariam, & Acosta, 2018; Al Shibly, 2011; AlShibly, 2014). The literature also reveals that there has been no study measuring Human Resource Information System success model along with perceived usefulness and its relations to HRIS system use and users' satisfaction. Further, there is a paucity of research in determining the predictors of HRIS success in Indian organizations from employees' perspectives. The study has attempted to analyze employees' perception towards service quality of HRIS along with other dimensions of Delone and Mclean Model. Literature has suggested that Information System (IS) success model and Technological Acceptance Model (TAM), separately could not justify the full meaning of HRIS success or its effectiveness (Al Shibly, 2011). So for the purpose of the study we have incorporated HRIS perceived usefulness along with Delone and Mclean model of information system (IS).

Prior researched theories & models have been proposed to analyze the acceptance of Information Technology among employees or potential system users. Technological acceptance model (TAM) provides empirical evidence that employees' perception towards information system represents their system usage intention, which accordingly influence their actual usage behavior (Daghfous, Belkhodja, & Ahmad, 2018; Davis, 1989; Venkatesh & Davis, 2000; Wu & Chen, 2017). Researchers accepted and used TAM as a theoretical technology model for their studies (Razmak & Bélanger, 2018; Ukpabi & Karjaluoto, 2017). When an organization implements HRIS, each employee evaluates the new introduction differently in terms of its usefulness and ease (Davis, 1989; Maier, 2012, Shahreki, 2019a, 2019b).

Prior studies states that the TAM factors (perceived usefulness and ease of use) have a noteworthy effect on system use and users' satisfaction (Al-Khowaiter, W., Dwivedi, Y., Willams, 2014, Fawad Ahmed et al., 2019). For the study purpose as we have integrated IS Success model with TAM, we have not taken ease of use as factors in the study as system quality variable measures the ease of use employees gets from HRIS system (William DeLone,2004). Information System success model claims that satisfaction is a key element to measure HRIS systems (Alzahrani et al., 2019; DeLone & McLean, 2003; Nguyen et al., 2015). In the similar line, Haines & Petit evaluated the success of HRIS with two determinants i.e., users' satisfaction and HRIS system use (F.A.Noutsa et al., 2017; Haines & Petit, 1997). According to Pitt et al. service quality is one of the most important variables while measuring the effectiveness of Information System. It is associated with smooth functioning of HRIS and consequently is significant for measuring overall success of HRIS (DeLone & McLean, 2003; Pitt, 1995). Drawing from the above discussion, we propose the objectives of the study.

2.1. Objectives of the Study

1. To study the relationship between Human Resource Information System- system quality, information quality, service quality and perceived usefulness with HRIS system use.
2. To study the relation between Human Resource Information System- system quality, information quality, service quality and perceived usefulness with HRIS satisfaction.
3. To analyze the relationship between HRIS system use and its users' satisfaction with HRIS success.
4. To investigate the relationship between HRIS system use and HRIS users' satisfaction.

On the basis of the previous studies and objectives, the variables which will be studied and empirical analyzed in this study are: HRIS System Quality, HRIS Information Quality, HRIS Service Quality and HRIS System Use; HRIS Perceived Usefulness; HRIS Users' Satisfaction and HRIS Success. Thus, we propose the research model of the study in Figure 1.

Figure 1. Theoretical research model

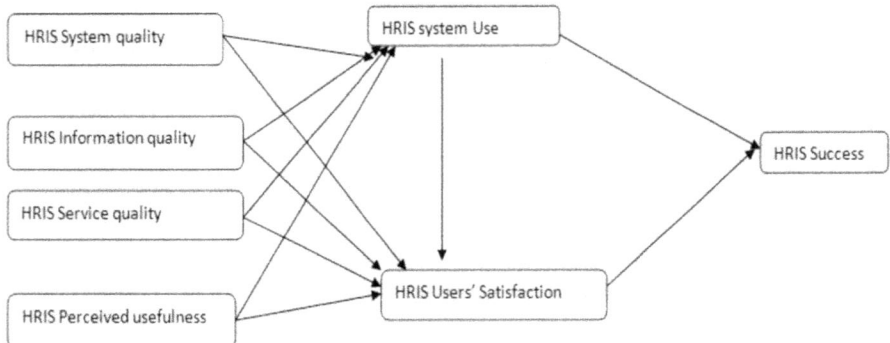

2.2. Hypotheses Development

2.2.1. System Quality

It focuses on distinctiveness of the system performance (William DeLone, 1992). Several authors have quoted data accuracy, reliability, response time, system flexibility, ease of use and completeness as important measurements of HRIS system quality (Al Shibly, 2011; Aletaibi, 2016; AlShibly, 2014; P. Nguyen, Chi, & City, 2018; William DeLone, 1992). In terms of system quality, the HRIS application is required to be simple, well organized and free from efforts. Higher HRIS system quality is expected to be used more by their end users and thereby lead to higher users' satisfaction which positively impacts organizational productivity and HRIS success (Ozlem Efiloglu Kurt, 2019; Seddon, Kiew, & Patry,

1994). System quality is considered to be a critical success factor that influences HRIS system use and HRIS users' satisfaction (DeLone & McLean, 2003). Thus, we assume:

H1a: There exist a positive relationship between HRIS perceived system quality and HRIS system use.
H1b: There exist a positive relationship between HRIS perceived system quality and users' satisfaction.

2.2.2. Information Quality

Information quality is defined as the completeness, accuracy, format and exchange of information produced by HRIS (William DeLone, 1992). It is a measure of the system quality of output which produces the information in forms of reports & on-screen (Gable, 2008). It focuses on the output that system produces and the information usefulness that users acquire from the system and it is one of the major components explaining user satisfaction (Kala Kamdjoug, J.R., Bawack, R.E. and Tayou, A.E.T. (2020); Ozlem Efiloglu Kurt, 2019; Al Shibly, 2011; William DeLone, 1992). Hence, we assume:

H2a: There exist a positive relationship between HRIS perceived information quality and HRIS system use.
H2b: There exist a positive relationship between HRIS perceived information quality and users' satisfaction.

2.2.3. Service Quality

While performing HR functions the hands-on experience which the employees have could be a determinant of HRIS services quality (Kala Kamdjoug, J.R., Bawack, R.E. and Tayou, A.E.T. (2020); N. B. M. Urbach, 2011). When employees perceive that quality assistance concerning HRIS is available, they start using the system and extend their support towards it which formulates their satisfaction level for the system. Prior studies also supported that HRIS users' satisfaction and its system use have been influenced by service quality (Aletaibi, 2016). Thus, we assume:

H3a: There exist a positive relationship between HRIS perceived service quality and HRIS system use.
H3b: There exist a positive relationship between HRIS perceived service quality and users' satisfaction.

2.2.4. Perceived Usefulness

This variable refers to the degree to which an employee perceives that their performance could be significantly enhanced by using the HRIS system (Davis, 1989; F.A.Noutsa et al., 2017). Prior studies state that employees perception towards HRIS system use is directly related to HRIS satisfaction (Zviran, Pliskin, & Levin, 2005). When people perceive that HRIS is useful for their work they start using the system and like the experience which determines their satisfaction level towards HRIS. So, we assume:

H4a: There exist a positive relationship between HRIS perceived usefulness and HRIS system use.
H4b: There exist a positive relationship between HRIS perceived usefulness and users' satisfaction.

2.2.5. HRIS Success

It is the achievement of employees and organizational goals by the application and usability of HRIS. It is the actual benefits received by the adopters while maintaining the internal efficiency through cost reduction. Prior studies have taken two determinants i.e., users' satisfaction and system use as a means to evaluate HRIS impact on individual and organizational effectiveness (Haines & Petit, 1997; Noutsa Aime Fobang, 2017, 2019). Organization spends lots of money in acquiring these HRIS tools for enhancing their employees' and organizational productivity and efficiency. Thus it became imperative to check the success level of these HRIS tools. In order to fulfill its implementation goal, HRIS must be in aligning with its users and organizational goals (Noor & Razali, 2011). HRIS success would be considered successful only when users' are motivated about the technology and willingly start using it more often (V.Venkatesh, 2003).

H5a: There exist a positive relationship between HRIS system use and HRIS success.
H5b: There exist a positive relationship between HRIS users' satisfaction and HRIS success.

2.2.6. HRIS System Use

It defines the degree to which users utilize and use the function of the system for accomplishing their daily professional work activities (Davarpanah & Mohamed, 2013; F.A.Noutsa et al., 2017). Thus, it measures the amount, frequency and purpose of HRIS use. More usage indicates more inclination towards HRIS which in-turn may lead to user satisfaction (Freeze, R et al., 2010). Additionally, employees may find HRIS successful, when it leads to maximize their perceived level of system use, satisfaction and productivity (Mueller, Strohmeier, & Gasper, 2010). So, we assume:

H6: There exist a positive relationship between HRIS system use and HRIS users' satisfaction.

2.2.7. HRIS Users' Satisfaction

It is both an evaluative judgment and affective attitude of the employees who interact directly or indirectly with HRIS (William DeLone, 1992). Various scholars have admitted that the HRIS users' acceptance mainly depends on the extent of their satisfaction with it, which further determine HRIS success levels (Bailey & Pearson, 1983; Freeze, R et al., 2010; F.A.Noutsa et al., 2017). The previous studies have also shown that the system quality, information quality and usefulness explains 72% measures of users satisfaction (F.A.Noutsa et al., 2017; Seddon et al., 1994; William DeLone, 1992).

3. RESEARCH METHODOLOGY

In order to achieve our research objectives, data have been collected, using a structured questionnaire. The study population comprised IT enabled service sector from National Capital region, India obtained from the industries listed in NASSCOM. The unit of analysis was the service sector organization of National Capital Region whereas the unit of inquire was the HR staffs and functional Managers in these organization. Indian service sector represents 61.5% of the total GDP. Two hundred questionnaires were distributed to the HR staff and manager; only 116 useable (58%) questionnaires were taken further for analysis. Standardized items were taken for the study which was previously validated by various authors in different contexts of their studies:

- For measuring system quality construct, a six-item scale was used from the studies of Al Shibly, (2011); Wixom & Todd, (2005).
- Further, Information quality construct has been measured by a six-item scale which was validated by various researchers like Aletaibi, (2016); N. Urbach, Smolnik, & Riempp, (2010).
- A four-item scale of service quality was taken for the study based on previous research of Nils Urbach (2010).
- For studying perceived usefulness, a six- item scale was adopted based on the studies of Al Shibly, (2011); Sun & Zhang, (2006).
- A seven-item scale of system use was used from the study based on Aletaibi, 2016; N. Urbach et al., 2010 studies.
- A five-item scale was adopted for measuring HRIS users' satisfaction based on the prior studies of Aletaibi, 2016; Seddon et al., 1994; N. Urbach et al., 2010.
- Finally, six-item scale of HRIS success were based on the study of Al-Shibly (2011).

3.1. Data Analysis and Findings

3.1.1. Demographic Information

The respondent of this study were asked to give information about their gender, age, education level and experience. The final sample accounted for 116 unit managers (male respondent (67.2%) and the female ones (32.8%)). The participant average age was between 26 and 40 (82.7%). Considering educational background most of the respondents are holding graduate (51.7%) and post graduate (47.4%) degrees. The respondents are mostly at the experience of 1-14 yrs, so it becomes imperative to check the employees' system use and satisfaction level towards HRIS.

3.2. Reliability Testing (Cronbach Alpha)

In order to check the scale reliability Cronbach alpha coefficient were evaluated. Indeed, the alpha ranges from 0.759 to 0.844, which exceed the prescribed threshold limits of 0.70. Thus it indicates a good internal consistency among the items(Cortina, 1993). The Cronbach alpha coefficients have been tabulated in Table 1.

3.3. Hypothesis Testing

Before testing the hypothesis, a correlation Matrix was computed between the variables. A value of 0.75 and above indicates high correlation among the variables (Obeidat, 2012; Sekaran, 2010). The results in the Table 2 shows all are below 0.75. All the variables (Table 2) system quality, information quality, service quality & perceived usefulness show a significant positive relationship with HRIS system use, HRIS users' satisfaction and with HRIS success.

Table 1. Cronbach Alpha Coefficients

Variables	Cronbach Alpha
HRIS System Quality	.812
HRIS Information Quality	.763
HRIS Service Quality	.819
HRIS Perceived Usefulness	.761
HRIS System Use	.814
HRIS Users' Satisfaction	.777
HRIS Success	.833

Table 2. Correlation among variables

	Variables	Correlations						
		1	2	3	4	5	6	7
1	HRIS System Quality	1						
2	HRIS Information Quality	.573**	1					
3	HRIS Service Quality	.566**	.533**	1				
4	HRIS Perceived Usefulness	.226*	.254**	.210*	1			
5	HRIS System Use	.341**	.303**	.349**	.421**	1		
6	HRIS User Satisfaction	.382**	.265**	.187*	.634**	.406**	1	
7	HRIS Success	.696**	.504**	.597**	.287**	.420**	.417**	1

**. Correlation is significant at the 0.01 level (2-tailed).
*. Correlation is significant at the 0.05 level (2-tailed).
Note: N=116, ** $p<0.01$ *$p<0.05$

In order to test the objectives and hypotheses, multiple regression analysis was used. Regression analysis has been done in four phases, in the first phase we have examined the influence of HRIS system quality, HRIS information quality, HRIS service quality and HRIS perceived usefulness with HRIS system use. In the second phase, the influence of HRIS system quality, HRIS information quality, HRIS service quality and HRIS perceived usefulness on HRIS satisfaction have been examined. In the third level, the relationship between HRIS system use and HRIS users' satisfaction with HRIS success variable has been established. Finally, the impact of HRIS system use on users' satisfaction has been examined.

3.4. Impact of System Quality, Information Quality, Service Quality and Perceived Usefulness on Human Resource Information System Use

The first objective was to study the relationship between HRIS system quality, HRIS information quality, HRIS service quality and HRIS perceived usefulness with HRIS system use. The determinants of HRIS system use are found out using stepwise regression. Here the dependent variable is HRIS system use and Independent variables are system quality, information quality, service quality and perceived usefulness.

3.4.1. HRIS System Use

A stepwise regression analysis was done in order to find the determinants of HRIS system use. Only those variables are taken further for analysis that contributes to a model while the non-contributing variables are discarded. The results have been shown in Figure 2.

The regression results show that perceived usefulness is one of the significant predictors of HRIS system use (β=0.36**, p£ 0.01). The impact of perceived usefulness on HRIS system use was recognized by previous researchers (Aletaibi, 2016; Noutsa Aime Fobang, 2017, 2019; V.Venkatesh, 2003). It might be because people perceive the usefulness of HRIS in their work and if they perceived its usability they start using the system often. The results also show that service quality is also significant predictor of HRIS system use (β=0.27**, p£.01). The value R square is 0.248 as shown in Table 3. It states that 24.8% of HRIS system use can be explained by these factors. The finding is congruent to the previous studies of HRIS system use (Al-Khowaiter, W., Dwivedi, Y., Willams, 2014; Al Shibly, 2011; Aletaibi, 2016; F.A.Noutsa et al., 2017; Targowski & Deshpande, 2001; Yi-ShunWanga & Yi-WenLiao, 2006). Therefore, the study's first objective has been achieved which incicate that the service quality and perceived usefulness has a positive significant relationship with HRIS system use.

Table 3. HRIS system use

Dependent Variable: HRIS System Use			
Independent Variables	**Beta**	**Simple r**	**t-value**
Service Quality	0.27**	0.349**	3.282
Perceived Usefulness	0.36**	0.226**	4.326
R Square= 0.248			

Notes: **Significant at 0.01 level.

Figure 2. Relationship between HRIS System Quality, HRIS Information Quality, HRIS Service Quality and HRIS Perceived Usefulness with HRIS System Use

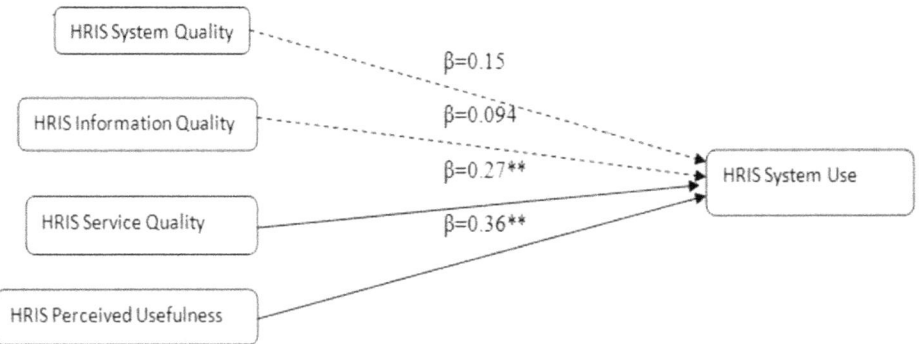

3.5. Impact of System Quality, Information Quality, Service Quality and Perceived Usefulness on Human Resource Information Users' Satisfaction

3.5.1. Human Resource Information System Users' Satisfaction

The second objective was to study the relationship between HRIS system quality, information quality, service quality and perceived usefulness with HRIS users' satisfaction. The determinants of HRIS satisfaction are found out using stepwise regression. Here the dependent variable is HRIS users' satisfaction and Independent variables are system quality, information quality, service quality and perceived usefulness. Only those variables are taken further for analysis that contributes to a model while the non-contributing variables are discarded. The results have been shown in Figure 3.

The regression results is tabulated in Table 4 reveal that that HRIS perceived usefulness is a significant predictors of HRIS users' satisfaction ($\beta = 0.57**$, p£0.01). Further the results also state that HRIS system quality is a significant predictor of HRIS users' satisfaction ($\beta = 0.25**$, p£.01). The value of R square is 0.46 as shown in Table 4. It states that 46% of HRIS users' satisfaction with HRIS system quality and HRIS perceived usefulness can be explained by these factors. The finding is congruent to the previous studies of HRIS system use (Al-Khowaiter, W., Dwivedi, Y., Willams, 2014; Al Shibly, 2011; Aletaibi, 2016; F.A.Noutsa et al., 2017; Targowski & Deshpande, 2001; Yi-ShunWanga & Yi-WenLiao, 2006). Thus, the paper's second objective achieved which shows that HRIS system quality and HRIS perceived usefulness has a positive significant relationship with HRIS users' satisfaction.

Table 4. HRIS users' satisfaction

Dependent Variable: HRIS User's Satisfaction			
Independent Variables	**Beta**	**Simple r**	**t-value**
HRIS System Quality	0.251	0.382**	3.548
HRIS Perceived Usefulness	0.577	0.634**	8.145
R Square= 0.46			

Notes: **Significant at 0.01 level.

Figure 3. Relationship between HRIS System Quality, HRIS Information Quality, HRIS Service Quality and HRIS Perceived Usefulness with HRIS Users' Satisfaction

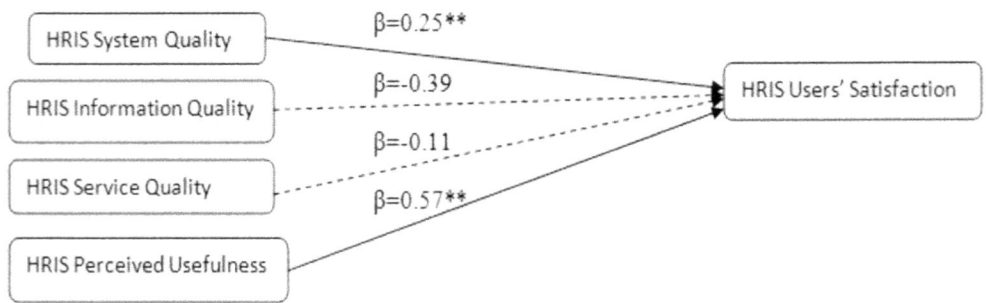

3.6. Human Resource Information System Success

The third objective was to study the relationship of HRIS system use and HRIS users' satisfaction with HRIS success. The determinants of HRIS success are found out using stepwise regression. Here the dependent variable is HRIS Success and the Independent variables are HRIS system use and HRIS users' satisfaction. The results have been shown in Figure 4.

Table 5. HRIS success

Dependent Variable: HRIS Success			
Independent Variables	**Beta**	**Simple r**	**t-value**
HRIS System Use	.30**	.420**	3.361
HRIS Users' Satisfaction	.29**	.417**	3.305
R Square= 0.249			

Notes: **Significant at 0.01 level

Figure 4. Determinants of HRIS success

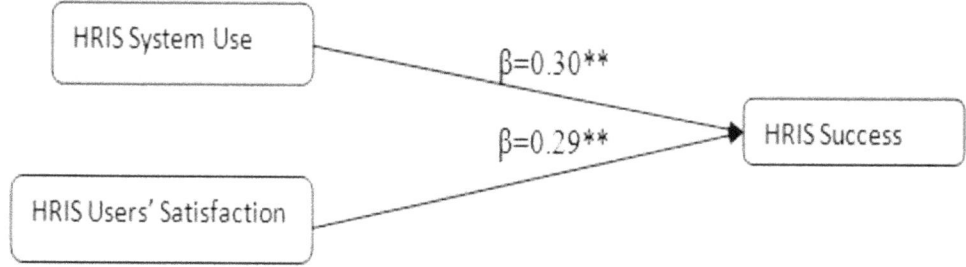

The regression analysis shows the effect of HRIS system use and HRIS users' satisfaction on HRIS success. The regression results shown in Table 5 reveal that HRIS system use and HRIS users' satisfaction have been significantly correlated with HRIS success (r=0.420, p£0.01 and r=0.417**, p£0.01 respectively). The regression results show that HRIS system use and HRIS users' satisfaction are significant predictors of HRIS success in Indian organization (β=0.30**, p£0.01 and β=0.29**, p£0.01 respectively) and the value of R square is 0.249. It states that 24.9% of the HRIS success variable can be explained by HRIS system use and HRIS users' satisfaction. Therefore, the third objective of the study has been achieved, as it is evident from the analysis that both HRIS system use and HRIS satisfaction are the predictors of HRIS success.

3.7. HRIS System Use and Users' Satisfaction

The last objective was to study the impact of HRIS system use on HRIS users' satisfaction. The results have been shown in Figure 5.

Figure 5. Relationship between HRIS system use and users' satisfaction

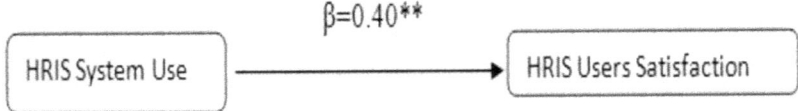

$$\beta=0.40**$$

Table 6. Relationship between HRIS system use and HRIS Users' satisfaction

Dependent Variable: HRIS Users' Satisfaction			
Independent Variables	Beta	Simple r	t-value
System Use	.40**	.406**	4.744
R Square= 0.165			

Notes: ** Significant at 0.01 level

The regression results shown in Table 6 reveal that HRIS system use is significantly correlated with HRIS users' satisfaction (r=0.406, p£0.01). The regression results show that HRIS system use is a significant predictor of HRIS users' satisfaction (β=0.40**, p£0.01) and the value of R square is 0.165. It states that 16.5% of the HRIS satisfaction can be explained by HRIS System Use. Thus the analysis is in sync with the previous studies while determining HRIS users' satisfaction (Aletaibi, 2016; F.A. Noutsa et al., 2017) and thus it satisfy paper's last objective.

4. DISCUSSION

Based on the outcome of the analysis, many interesting findings have come to light. As shown in the correlation matrix that all the dimensions of HRIS have a significant positive relationship with HRIS system use and HRIS users' satisfaction. Further both the system use and HRIS users' satisfaction have shown a significant positive relationship and have an impact on HRIS success.

4.1. HRIS System Use

HRIS perceived system quality was hypothesized to have a significant relationship with HRIS system use. The result of this study found that this hypothesis (H1a) was not supported. The finding does not agree that HRIS system quality plays a significant role in determining system use. The findings of the study agree with the prior studies that demonstrate that perceived system quality and perceived information quality are not significant predictors of HRIS system use (Iivari, 2005). Further it was hypothesized to have a significant relationship of information quality with HRIS system use (H2a), which is not supported. However the result was in congruence with the prior studies, which states that there is a week association between information quality and HRIS system use (McGill, 2003; Livaris 2005). HRIS service quality was hypothesized to have a significant relationship with HRIS System use (H3a). The findings of this study supported the stated hypothesis. A strong association of HRIS service quality with HRIS system use was found in various prior studies (Al-Khowaiter, W., Dwivedi, Y., Willams, 2014, 2015; AlShibly,

2014; Wang & Hsieh, 2006). When employee perceived that HRIS assistance and the knowledgeable HR personnel are available they would start using the system. Furthermore, it was hypothesized that HRIS perceived usefulness has a significant relationship with HRIS system use. The results of this study support the above hypothesis (H4a) which is in congruence with the findings of Aletaibi, (2016); Noutsa Aime Fobang, (2017, 2019); V.Venkatesh, (2003). Davis (1989) defined perceived usefulness as the "degree to which a person believes that using a particular system would enhance his or her job performance". As employees perceive the usefulness of HRIS beneficial for their performance they start using it more. Thus, it is also one of the determinants of HRIS system use. Therefore, the hypotheses H3a, H4a are supported and hypotheses H1a and H2a have been rejected.

4.2. HRIS Users' Satisfaction

HRIS perceived system quality was hypothesized to have a significant relationship with HRIS users' satisfaction. The results of this study find that this hypothesis (H1b) was supported. The results agree with the fact that system quality of HRIS plays an important role in determining users' satisfaction. Prior studies also support the findings of this study and state that one of the prominent factors for HRIS users' satisfaction is system quality (Aletaibi, 2016; F.A.Noutsa et al., 2017). Previous studies investigated HRIS success model and found that system quality had a significant relationship with users' satisfaction (Almutairi & Subramanian, 2005; Iivari, 2005; Petter, Delone, & McLean, 2013). It was also hypothesized that information quality and service quality have a significant relationship with HRIS satisfaction (H2b and H3b) are not in sync with the previous studies (Aletaibi, 2016; Igbaria & Baroudi, 1993). Though the information quality and service quality has positively correlated with HRIS users' satisfaction but they were not the prominent influencer of HRIS users' satisfaction. The reason might be due to the fact that sense of satisfaction could be created among employees after using the system, i.e., it is a long run evaluation that leads to satisfaction (Parasuraman et al 1988) Furthermore, it was hypothesized that perceived usefulness has a significant relationship on HRIS users' satisfaction (H4b). The findings is in line with the prior studies finding Al Shibly, 2011; V.Venkatesh, 2003. The satisfied employees engaged more in work activities which are beneficial for attaining individual and organizational goals. Therefore, hypotheses H1b and H4b are supported and rest i.e., H2b, H3b are rejected.

4.3. HRIS Success

Additionally, our findings reveal that both HRIS system use and HRIS user's satisfaction have a good potential value to influence HRIS success which is similar to one of the findings of Al Shibly (2011), who claims that HRIS users' satisfaction is significantly explained by HRIS success. The orientation of employees shows that HRIS system uses and the satisfaction that they incorporate through HRIS in their daily professional activities could be a predictive factor for HRIS success. When users are satisfied, they easily accept the system and utilize the system in their daily work activities that might impact their work related consequences like their performance. Thus, both the hypotheses, H5a and H5b are supported.

4.4. Relationship Between HRIS System Use and Users' Satisfaction

Further, our results show that there exists a relationship between HRIS system use and HRIS users' satisfaction. The results also show that HRIS users' satisfaction has been significantly influenced by HRIS system use. The results are again supported by prior findings of Aletaibi, R. G. (2016), F.A. Noutsa et al. (2017). Prior studies have taken HRIS system use and HRIS users' satisfaction as a substitute for HRIS success (AlShibly, 2014; Bailey & Pearson, 1983; Doll & Torkzadeh, 1988). Further, HRIS users' satisfaction has been considered as an important pillar for HRIS success (Davarpanah & Mohamed, 2013). Therefore, hypothesis H6 is supported.Final model has been shown in Figure 6.

The hypotheses H1b and H4b showed a positive relationship between HRIS system quality, HRIS perceived usefulness with HRIS users' satisfaction. In the similar way, hypotheses H3a and H4a showed a positive relationship between HRIS service quality, HRIS perceived usefulness with HRIS system use. Furthermore, both the hypotheses H5a and H5b have a positive relationship with HRIS success. In addition to this, there also exist a positive relationship between HRIS system use and HRIS users' satisfaction (H6).

Figure 6. Final model

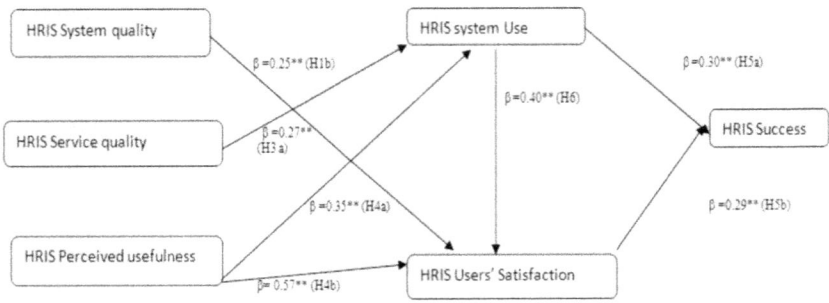

5. LIMITATION AND FUTURE SCOPE

The findings of this study may affect generalization as the study is limited to the National Capital Region/ Delhi, Indian. Further the sample size (N=116) somewhat limiting the results to be generalized. Therefore, we believe that results can be analyzed further with large sample size from different environmental settings. The scope lies in the fact that, future researchers can include work- related consequences like job satisfaction, productivity for measuring the success level of HRIS. Moreover HRIS success could be seen from both individual and organizational level consequences. Though the researchers have identified and empirically tested the predictive variables from the literature but still many more variable combinations can be made and relationship could be established among these variables like ease of use, impact of HRIS on individual and organization performance, so as to get more prominent predictors of HRIS system use, its satisfaction and HRIS success. Further, mediating or moderating variables like training, employee involvement, management supports and moderator variables like age, number of HRIS experience could be checked in relations to HRIS system use, satisfaction and success.

6. IMPLICATIONS

The findings of the study indicate that by ensuring proper employees' HRIS system use organization could enhance employees' HRIS satisfaction. By automating tasks and analyzing reports, companies can use HRIS system to its greatest potential. We live in a dynamic era were new technology and up-gradation of the existing one is a continuous phenomenon. Thus, it requires HR managers and organizational leaders to be cognizant about these changes. With the help of the findings of this study HR Manager and organization at large would know the prominent focus area of important. Thus by enhancing the HRIS system quality, HRIS service quality and HRIS perceived usefulness, organization might get an overall benefit of HRIS implementation. By implementing systems that can help to automate processes, such as Human Resources Information Systems, companies may actually change the fundamental structure of the workplace and the way daily tasks are performed.

7. CONCLUSION

By applying Delone and McLean Information System success model along with perceived usefulness construct this research certainly adds new knowledge to the existing literature. One theoretical contribution done by the study is that it empirically tested the HRIS service quality and HRIS perceived usefulness variables in relation to HRIS system use and user's satisfaction; this was not previously analyzed, as per researcher knowledge. Prior research of Al Shibly (2011), Al-Khowaiter et al., (2014); Aletaibi, R. G.(2016), F.A. Noutsa et al.(2017) are in congruence with some of the findings of this research (Al-Khowaiter, W., Dwivedi, Y., Willams, 2014; Al Shibly, 2011; Aletaibi, 2016; F.A.Noutsa et al., 2017). Human Resource Information System is the important element that not only activates Human Resource Department but each and every functioning of an organization. And unless and until end users' would be satisfied and use the system to its full capacity, the success level of HRIS within an organizations could not be justified. This research has extended the understanding of HRIS system use and satisfaction along with HRIS success by testing the phenomenon from the perspective of employees in Indian organizations. It is obvious that organization can benefit from HRIS only when the system is extensively used and accepted by its end users. The far-reaching implications of the study could be seen as it gives new insights towards HRIS; aid HR managers in establishing better strategic decision regarding HRIS implementation in their organization. Additional, the practical implication of the findings could be seen from the point of HR leaders, as they have to focus on employees' HRIS system quality, HRIS service quality and HRIS perceived usefulness so as to enhance the usability and satisfaction level of HRIS.

REFERENCES

Tursunbayeva, A., Bunduchi, R., & Pagliari, C. (2020). "Planned Benefits" Can Be Misleading in Digital transformation Projects: Insights From a Case Study of Human Resource Information Systems Implementation in Healthcare. *SAGE Open*, *10*(2). Advance online publication. doi:10.1177/2158244020933881

Al-Dmour, R. H., Love, S., & Al-Debei, M. M. (2016). Factors influencing the organizational adoption of human resource information systems: A conceptual model. *International Journal of Business Innovation and Research*, *11*(2), 161–207. doi:10.1504/IJBIR.2016.077986

Al-Khowaiter, W., Dwivedi, Y., & Willams, M. (2014). Examining the Adoption of Human Resource Information System in the Context of Saudi Arabia. *Association for Information System S*, 1–21.

Al Shibly, H. (2011). Human Resources Information System Success Assessment: An Integrative Model. *Australian Journal of Basic and Applied Sciences*, *5*, 157–169.

Aletaibi, R. G. (2016). *An analysis of the adoption and use of HRIS in the public Universities in Saudi Arabia*. Retrieved from https://core.ac.uk/download/pdf/78653029.pdf

Almutairi, H., & Subramanian, G. H. (2005). An empirical application of Delone and Mclean model the Kuwaiti private sector. *Journal of Computer Information Systems*, *4*(3), 113–122. doi:10.1080/088 74417.2005.11645849

AlShibly, H. H. (2014). the Effects of Characteristics of Electronic Document Management Systems on Their Acceptance: An Empirical Study in Jordan. *International Journal of Information, Business and Management*, *6*(4), 126–145. https://search.proquest.com/docview/1552838308?accountid=45394

Alzahrani, A. I., Mahmud, I., Ramayah, T., Alfarraj, O., & Alalwan, N. (2019). Modelling digital library success using the DeLone and McLean information system success model. *Journal of Librarianship and Information Science*, *51*(2), 291–306. doi:10.1177/0961000617726123

Bali, A. S. (2019). An analytical study of applications of human resource information system in modern human resources management. *International Journal of Sustainable Agricultural Management and Informatics*, *5*(4), 216. Advance online publication. doi:10.1504/IJSAMI.2019.104617

Davarpanah & Mohamed. (2020). Human Resource Information Systems Implementation and Influences in Higher Education: Evidence From Malaysia. *International Journal of Asian Business and Information Management, 11*(3), 65-84.

Aswanth Kumar, N., & Brijball Parumasur, S. (2013). Managerial Perceptions of the Impact of HRIS on Organizational Efficiency Nikhal. *Journal of Economics and Behavioral Studies*, *5*(12), 861–875. doi:10.22610/jebs.v5i12.459

Bailey, J. E., & Pearson, S. W. (1983). Development of a Tool for Measuring and Analyzing Computer User Satisfaction. *Management Science*, *29*(5), 530–545. doi:10.1287/mnsc.29.5.530

Bal, Y., Bozkurt, S., & Ertemsir, E. (2012). The Importance of Using Human Resources Information Systems(HRIS) and a Research on Determining the Success of HRIS. *Management Knowledge and Learning International Conference*, 53–62.

Bayraktaroglu, Kahya, V., Atay, E., & Ilhan, H. (2019). Application of Expanded Technology Acceptance Model for Enhancing the HRIS Usage in SMEs. *International Journal of Applied Management and Technology*, *18*(1), 48–66. doi:10.5590/IJAMT.2019.18.1.04

Boateng, A. A. (2007). *The Role of Human Resource Information Systems (HRIS) in Strategic Human Resource Management (SHRM)*. HANKEN-Swedish School of Economics and Business Administration.

Bondarouk, T., Parry, E., & Furtmueller, E. (2017). Electronic HRM: Four decades of research on adoption and consequences. *International Journal of Human Resource Management, 28*(1), 98–131. doi:10.1080/09585192.2016.1245672

Brandon-Jones, A., & Kauppi, K. (2018). Examining the antecedents of the technology acceptance model within e-procurement. *International Journal of Operations & Production Management, 38*(1), 22–42. doi:10.1108/IJOPM-06-2015-0346

Broderick, R., & Bounreau, J. W. (1992). Human resource management, information technology, and the competitive edge. *CAHRS Working Paper Series, 6*(351), 7–17. doi:10.5465/ame.1992.4274391

Cortina, J. M. (1993). What Is Coefficient Alpha? An Examination of Theory and Applications. *The Journal of Applied Psychology, 78*(1), 98–104. doi:10.1037/0021-9010.78.1.98

Daghfous, A., Belkhodja, O., & Ahmad, N. (2018). Understanding and managing knowledge transfer for customers in IT adoption. *Information Technology & People, 31*(2), 428–454. doi:10.1108/ITP-10-2016-0222

Davarpanah, A., & Mohamed, N. (2013). Human Resource Information Systems (HRIS) success factors in a public higher education institution context. *International Conference on Research and Innovation in Information Systems, ICRIIS, 2013*, 79–84. 10.1109/ICRIIS.2013.6716689

Davis, F. D. (1989). Perceived Usefulness, Perceived Ease of Use, and User Acceptance of Information Technology. *Management Information Systems Quarterly, 13*(3), 319–340. doi:10.2307/249008

DeLone, W. H., & McLean, E. R. (2003). The DeLone and McLean model of information systems success: A ten-year update. *Journal of Management Information Systems, 19*(4), 9–30. doi:10.1080/07421222.2003.11045748

Dery, K., Grant, D., & Wiblen, S. (2007). Human Resource Information Systems (HRIS): Replacing or Enhancing HRM. Work and Organisational Studies: The University of Sydney.

Doll, W. J., & Torkzadeh, G. (1988). The measurement of end-user computing satisfaction. *MIS Quarterly: Management Information Systems, 12*(2), 259–273. doi:10.2307/248851

Efiloglu Kurt, O. (2019). Examining an e-learning system through the lens of the information systems success model: Empirical evidence from Italy. *Education and Information Technologies, 24*(2), 1173–1184. doi:10.100710639-018-9821-4

Kossek, E., & Young, W. D. C. G. (1994). Waiting for Innovation in the Human Resouces Department: Godot Implements a Human Resource Information System. Academic Press.

Noutsa, F. A., Kala Kamdjoug, J. R., & Fosso Wamba, S. (2017). Acceptance and Use of HRIS and Influence on Organizational Performance of SMEs in a Developing Economy: The case of Cameroon. *Recent Advances in Information Systems and Technologies, 571*(March), 563–580. Advance online publication. doi:10.1007/978-3-319-56535-4_57

Ahmed, F., Yuan, J. Q., & Martínez, L. (2019). Sustainable Change Management through Employee Readiness: Decision Support System Adoption in Technology-Intensive British E-Businesses. *Sustainability, 11*(11), 2998. doi:10.3390u11112998

Fenech, R., Baguant, P., & Ivanov, D. (2019). The Changing Role Of Human Resource Management In An Era Of Digital Transformation. *Journal of Management Information and Decision Sciences, 22*(2), 1–10.

Freeze, R., Alshare, K., Lane, P., & Wen, J. (2010). IS Success Model in E-Learning context based on student's perceptions. *Journal of Information Systems Education,* 21.

Gable, G., Sedera, D., & Chan, T. (2008). Re-conceptualizing information system success: The IS-impact measurement model. *Journal of the Association for Information Systems, 9*(7), 377–408. doi:10.17705/1jais.00164

Goktas, P., & Akgul, Y. (2019). The Investigation of Employer Adoption of Human Resource Information Systems at University Using TAM. In *Structural Equation Modeling Approaches to E-Service Adoption.* IGI Global. doi:10.4018/978-1-5225-8015-7.CH001

Begum, H., Bhuiyan, F., Alam, A. S. A. F., Awang, A. H., Masud, M. M., & Akhtar, R. (2020). Cost reduction and productivity improvement through HRIS. *International Journal of Innovation and Sustainable Development, 14*(2), 185. doi:10.1504/IJISD.2020.106235

Haines, V. Y., & Petit, A. (1997). Conditions for successful human resource information systems. *Human Resource Management, 36*(2), 261–275. doi:10.1002/(SICI)1099-050X(199722)36:2<261::AID-HRM7>3.0.CO;2-V

Hosnavi, R., & Ramezan, M. (2010). Measuring the effectiveness of a human resource information system in National Iranian Oil Company an empirical assessment. *Education, Business and Society, 3*(1), 28–39. doi:10.1108/17537981011022797

Igbaria, M., & Baroudi, J. J. (1993). A short-form measure of career orientations: A psychometric evaluation. *Journal of Management Information Systems, 10*(2), 131–154. doi:10.1080/07421222.1993.11518003

Iivari, J. (2005). An Empirical Test of the DeLone-McLean Model of Information System Success. *The Data Base for Advances in Information Systems, 36*(2), 8–27. doi:10.1145/1066149.1066152

Irum, A., & Yadav, R. S. (2019). Human resource information systems: A strategic contribution to HRM. *Strategic Direction, 35*(10), 4–6. doi:10.1108/SD-02-2019-0043

Kala Kamdjoug, J.R., Bawack, R.E. & Tayou, A.E.T. (2020). An ERP success model based on agency theory and IS success model: The case of a banking institution in Africa. *Business Process Management Journal.* ahead-of-print. doi:10.1108/BPMJ-04-2018-0113

Lengnick-Hall, M. L., & Steve, M. (2003). The impact of e-HR on the human resource management function. *Journal of Labor Research, 24*(3), 365–379. doi:10.100712122-003-1001-6

Syafiraliany, L., Lubis, M., & Witjaksono, R. W. (2019). Analysis of Critical Success Factors from ERP System Implementation in Pharmaceutical Fields by Information System Success Model. *2019 Fourth International Conference on Informatics and Computing (ICIC),* 1-5. 10.1109/ICIC47613.2019.8985678

Imron, M. I. R., Hidayanto, A. N., Fitriani, W. R., Nugroho, W. S., & Inan, D. I. (2019).Analysis of Cloud-Based Human Resource Information System Adoption Factors Prioritization in Micro, Small, and Medium Enterprises. *2019 International Conference on Advanced Computer Science and information Systems (ICACSIS)*, 295-300, 10.1109/ICACSIS47736.2019.8979937

Maier, C., Laumer, S., Eckhardt, A., & Weitzel, T. (2012). Analyzing the impact of HRIS implementations on HR personnel's job satisfaction and turnover intention. *The Journal of Strategic Information Systems*, 22(3), 193–207. doi:10.1016/j.jsis.2012.09.001

Marhraoui, M. A., & El Manouar, A. (2020). Organizational Agility and the Complementary Enabling Role of IT and Human Resources: Proposition of a New Framework. In Y. Baghdadi, A. Harfouche, & M. Musso (Eds.), *ICT for an Inclusive World. Lecture Notes in Information Systems and Organisation, 35.* Springer. doi:10.1007/978-3-030-34269-2_4

Masum, A. K., Beh, L. S., Azad, A. K., & Hoque, K. (2018). Intelligent Human Resource Information System (i-HRIS): A Holistic Decision Support Framework for HR Excellence. *The International Arab Journal of Information Technology*, 15, 121–130.

Mueller, D., Strohmeier, S., & Gasper, C. (2010). HRIS design characteristics: Towards a general research frame-work. *CEUR Workshop Proceedings*, 570, 250–267.

Muturi, B., Kiflemariam, A., & Acosta, F. (2018). Towards a Robust Human Resource Information System's Success Measurement Model. *International Journal of Academic Research in Business and Social Sciences*, 8(3), 1–14. doi:10.6007/IJARBSS/v8-i3/3895

Nagendra, A., & Deshpande, M. (2014). Human Resource Information Systems (HRIS) in HR planning and development in mid to large sized organizations. *Procedia: Social and Behavioral Sciences*, 133, 61–67. doi:10.1016/j.sbspro.2014.04.169

Ngai, E. W. T., & Wat, F. K. T. (2006). Human resource information systems: A review and empirical analysis. *Personnel Review*, 35(3), 297–314. doi:10.1108/00483480610656702

Nguyen, T. D. (2015). Information Systems Success : A literature Review. Lecture Notes in Computer Science, 9446, 242–256. doi:10.1007/978-3-319-26135-5

Nguyen, P., Chi, H., & City, M. (2018). Repurchase Intention : The Effect of Service Quality, System Quality, Information Quality, and Customer Satisfaction as Mediating Role : A PLS Approach of M-Commerce Ride Hailing Service in Vietnam. *Marketing and Branding Research*, 5(January), 78–91.

Noe, R. A., Hollenbeck, J. R., Gerhart, B., & Wright, P. M. (2017). *Human resource management: Gaining a competitive advantage.* McGraw-Hill Education New York.

Fobang, N. A. (2017). Exploring Factors Affecting the Adoption of HRIS in SMEs in a Developing Country: Evidence from Cameroon. *Lecture Notes in Information Systems and Organisation*, 30(March), 281–295. doi:10.1007/978-3-030-10737-6_18

Noutsa Fobang, A., Fosso Wamba, S., & Kala Kamdjoug, J. R. (2019). Exploring Factors Affecting the Adoption of HRIS in SMEs in a Developing Country: Evidence from Cameroon. In Y. Baghdadi & A. Harfouche (Eds.), *ICT for a Better Life and a Better World. Lecture Notes in Information Systems and Organisation* (Vol. 30). Springer. doi:10.1007/978-3-030-10737-6_18

Obeidat, B. Y. (2012). The Relationship between Human Resource Information System (HRIS) Functions and Human Resource Management (HRM) Functionalities. *Journal of Management Research, 4*(4). Advance online publication. doi:10.5296/jmr.v4i4.2262

Petter, S., Delone, W., & McLean, E. R. (2013). Information systems success: The quest for the independent variables. *Journal of Management Information Systems, 29*(4), 7–61. doi:10.2753/MIS0742-1222290401

Pitt, L., Watson, R. T., & Kavan, C. B. (1995). Service quality : A measure of information systems effectiveness. *Management Information Systems Quarterly, 19*(2), 173. doi:10.2307/249687

Al-Dmour, R. H. (2020). The Influence of HRIS Usage on Employee Performance and Mediating Effects of Employee Engagement in Five Stars Hotels in Jordan. *International Journal of Information Systems in the Service Sector, 12*(3), 1–18. Advance online publication. doi:10.4018/IJISSS.2020070101

Rangriz, H., Mehrabi, J., & Azadegan, A. (2011). The impact of human resource information system on strategic decisions in Iran. *Computer and Information Science, 4*(2), 81–87. doi:10.5539/cis.v4n2p81

Razmak, J., & Belanger, C. (2018). Using the Technology acceptance model to predict patient attitude towards personal health records in regional communities. *Information Technology & People, 31*. doi:10.1108/ITP-07-2016-0160

Reddick, C. (2009). Human resources information systems in Texas City govern-ments: Scope and perception of its effectiveness. *Public Personnel Management, 38*(4), 19–34. doi:10.1177/009102600903800402

Ruël, H., Bondarouk, T., & Looise, J. K. (2004). E-HRM: Innovation or Irritation. An Explorative Empirical Study in Five Large Companies on Web-based HRM. *Management Review, 15*(3), 364–380. doi:10.5771/0935-9915-2004-3-364

Sablok, G., Stanton, P., Bartram, T., Burgess, J., & Boyle, B. (2017). Human resource development practices, managers and multinational enterprises in Australia: Thinking globally, acting locally. *Education + Training, 59*(5), 483–501. doi:10.1108/ET-02-2016-0023

Sanjeev, R., & Natrajan, N. S. (2020). An Empirical Research on the Role of Cloud-Based HRIS & HRM Functions in Organizational Performance. In P. Kapur, G. Singh, Y. Klochkov, & U. Kumar (Eds.), *Decision Analytics Applications in Industry. Asset Analytics (Performance and Safety Management)*. Springer. doi:10.1007/978-981-15-3643-4_3

Seddon, P. B., Kiew, M.-Y., & Patry, M. (1994). A Partial Test and Development of the DeLone and McLean Model of IS Success. *ICIS 1994 Proceedings*.

Sekaran, U. (2010). *Research and Markets: Research Methods for Business - A Skill Building Approach*. John Wiley & Sons.

Shahreki, J. (2019a). Electronic Human Resource Management and Employee Efficiency: Test of the Mediating Role of Impersonal Trust. *Journal of Soft Computing and Decision Support Systems, 6*(4), 20–29.

Shahreki, J., Ganesan, J., Raman, K., Chin, A.L.L. & Chin, T.S. (2019b). The effect of human resource information system application on employee satisfaction and turnover intention. *Entrepreneurship and Sustainability Issues, 7*(3), 1462-1479. doi:10.9770/jesi.2019.7.2(47)

Singh, H. P., Jindal, S., & Samim, S. A. (2011). Role of Human Resource Information System in Banking Industry of Developing Countries. *The First International Conference on Interdisciplinary Research and Development*, 1–4. Retrieved from http://ijcim.com/SpecialEditions/v19nSP1/02_44_19C_Harman Preet Singh_[4].pdf

Sun, H., & Zhang, P. (2006). The role of moderating factors in user technology acceptance. *International Journal of Human-Computer Studies, 64*(2), 53–78. doi:10.1016/j.ijhcs.2005.04.013

Targowski, A. S., & Deshpande, S. P. (2001). The utility and selection of an HRIS. *Advances in Competitiveness Research, 9*(1), 42–56.

Mauro, T. G., & Borges-Andrade, J. E. (2020). Human resource system as innovation for organisations. *Innovation & Management Review, 17*(2), 197–214. doi:10.1108/INMR-03-2019-0037

Tursunbayeva, A., Bunduchi, R., Franco, M., & Pagliari, C. (2016) Human resource information systems in health care: A systematic evidence review. *Journal of the American Medical Informatics Association*, 633–654. doi:10.1093/jamia/ocw141 PMID:27707821

Ukpabi, D. C., & Karjaluoto, H. (2017). Consumers' acceptance of information and communications technology in tourism: A review. *Telematics and Informatics, 34*(5), 618–644. doi:10.1016/j.tele.2016.12.002

Urbach, N. B. M. (2011). Information systems theory. *Information Systems, 2*(4), 207–219. doi:10.1016/0306-4379(77)90009-6

Urbach, N., Smolnik, S., & Riempp, G. (2010). An empirical investigation of employee portal success. *The Journal of Strategic Information Systems, 19*(3), 184–206. doi:10.1016/j.jsis.2010.06.002

Venkatesh, V., Morris, Davis, & Davis. (2003). User Acceptance Of Information Technology : Towards A Unified View. *Management Information Systems Quarterly, 27*(3), 425–478. doi:10.2307/30036540

Venkatesh, V., & Davis, F. D. (2000). A theoretical extension of the technology acceptance model: Four longitudinal field studies. *Management Science, 46*(2), 186–204. doi:10.1287/mnsc.46.2.186.11926

Wang, W., & Hsieh, P.-A. (2006). Beyond Routine: Symbolic Adoption, Extended Use, and Emergent Use of Complex Information Systems in the Mandatory Organizational Context. *ICIS 2006 Proceedings*. https://aisel.aisnet.org/icis2006/48

Al-Khowaiter, W. A. A., Dwivedi, Y. K., & Williams, M. D. (2015). Examining the Role of Social Influence, Usefulness and Ease of Use for Determining the Mandatory Use of a Human Resource Information System in the Context of Saudi Ministries. *International Journal of Electronic Government Research, 11*(3), 24–42. Advance online publication. doi:10.4018/IJEGR.2015070102

DeLone, W. H., & McLean, E. R. (2004). Measuring e-Commerce Success: Applying the DeLone & McLean Information Systems Success Model. *International Journal of Electronic Commerce*, *9*(1), 31–47. doi:10.1080/10864415.2004.11044317

William DeLone, E. M. (1992). Information Systems Success:The Quest for the Dependent Variable. *Information Systems Research*, *3*(1), 60–95. doi:10.1287/isre.3.1.60

Wixom, B. H., & Todd, P. A. (2005). A theoretical integration of user satisfaction and technology acceptance. *Information Systems Research*, *16*(1), 85–102. doi:10.1287/isre.1050.0042

Wu, B., & Chen, X. (2017). Continuance intention to use MOOCs: Integrating the technology acceptance model (TAM) and task technology fit (TTF) model. *Computers in Human Behavior*, *67*, 221–232. doi:10.1016/j.chb.2016.10.028

Wanga, & Liao. (2006). Assessing eGovernment systems success: A validation of the DeLone and McLean model of information systems success. *Government Information Quarterly*, *25*(4), 717–733.

Zviran, M., Pliskin, N., & Levin, R. (2005). Measuring user satisfaction and perceived usefulness in the ERP context. *Journal of Computer Information Systems*, *45*(3), 43–52. doi:10.1080/08874417.200 5.11645842

This research was previously published in the International Journal of Enterprise Information Systems (IJEIS), 17(1); pages 106-124, copyright year 2021 by IGI Publishing (an imprint of IGI Global).

Chapter 27
Research on Human Resource Allocation Model Based on SOM Neural Network

Jing Xu

Department of Economics Management, Shanxi Institute of Technology, Xi'an, China

Bo Wang

Department of Electrical Engineering, Shanxi Institute of Technology, Xi'an, China

Gihong Min

Department of Game Engineering, Paichai University, Daejeon, South Korea

ABSTRACT

With the fierce competition of the enterprise market, the human resource allocation of enterprises will face multiple risks. This article takes the connotation of human resource configuration management as the research object and establishes the human resource configuration model through SOM neural network. And the model is trained, learned, and tested. What's more, it is applied to human resources management to adjust the allocation of human resources for the enterprise in a timely manner. It provides a detailed basis for proposing coping strategies and has a great application value.

1. INTRODUCTION

Since the 1990s, with the global competition and the in-depth development of the market economy, the competition among enterprises has become increasingly fierce, and human resource management has also become an important factor in the success of enterprises. In the actual operation of an enterprise, the reliance on human resources gradually increases, which in turn causes human resources management to face multiple forms of risk.

DOI: 10.4018/978-1-6684-3873-2.ch027

The risk of human resources management is caused because the employing organization does not use the relevant human resources rationally, resulting in tangible or intangible wastage of human resources, and even the emergence of risks (Gherman et al., 2016). The scope of this risk will involve the key links, such as recruitment, training, performance appraisal, and remuneration of human resources. If these important risks are handled improperly, it will cause incalculable losses, or even cause the decline of the enterprise. Therefore, companies or related organizations should establish daily human resources management to monitor early human resource management risks, so that enterprises can make effective analysis, judgments, and take relevant measures as soon as possible. This has played an important role for enterprises to gain advantages in the highly competitive market economy environment (Xie, 2017; Li & Zhu, 2018)

No matter from the historical development process, or from the current development needs of enterprises, the allocation of human resources is a core issue in the development of enterprises. Because of this, the problem of enterprise human resource allocation has always been of common concern to both theoretical researchers and management practitioners. However, whether it is for the western developed countries (Marshall & Treuren, 2016; Lin, 2016), or for economically underdeveloped developing countries, people have not come up with the best strategies for human resource allocation.

Since the beginning of the new century, China's economic development has been accompanied by challenges. The situation in the development of enterprises is constantly changing, and the increasing mobility of the company's employees has brought great challenges to human resources management. It can be said that how to achieve "Optimize the allocation of human resources in enterprises to improve their productivity and competitiveness, and to achieve maximum economic benefits under limited human and material conditions" has become a topic of focus. This paper discusses the optimal matching of dynamic allocation of human resources in the enterprise.

Li et al constructs the best human resource management model based on the law of diminishing marginal utility of economics (Yang & Wang, 2016). The model can solve the optimal investment quota of each index under any given total utility level or cost input, and obtain the optimal cost investment plan, so as to realize the optimal allocation of human resource investment in human resource management. Based on the analysis of traditional human resource management methods, Xu et al uses the three-dimensional fuzzy model to construct a new human resource management model of three-dimensional fuzzy mode (Jing & Wang, 2014).

This paper proposes a human resource allocation model based on SOM neural network. Both SOM neural network and human resource management are global. Therefore, the SOM neural network system is used to establish the human resource allocation model, the training function, weight adjustment function and performance function are applied to the model training, learning and testing. The experiment shows that the proposed method can adjust the human resource allocation for the enterprise in time and provides a detailed basis for the different competition strategies of the enterprise.

2. RELATED CONCEPT ANALYSIS

2.1. Enterprise Human Resources Allocation

The so-called "corporate human resources allocation" means that the enterprise scientifically and reasonably arranges various types of talents to suitable jobs through assessment, selection, recruitment, training, etc. Make it better integrate with other economic resources and produce a realistic economic movement to achieve the best results for people and their best use. In other words, the purpose of the allocation of human resources in the enterprise is to maximize the productivity of human resources and improve the overall effectiveness of the organization, which made companies to create more social and economic benefits (Liu, Fu & Deng, 2013; Liu, Fu & Zhao, 2013. Lassi, Musavi & Maliqi, 2016).

In the allocation of corporate human resources, the two most important variables are talents and positions. Among them, talent has two characteristics. One is that there are differences among talents, and different people have different levels of energy development. The second is that different talents are deployed in different ways. Technical talents are deployed vertically based on job requirements, while management talents are mainly based on horizontal deployment. In the same company, the level and type of post are different, and their position and energy level are also different (Yali, 2017; Liu, Liu & Fu, 2015).

2.2. Dynamic Configuration of Human Resources in Enterprises

In theory, the allocation of enterprise human resources is to enable all employees of the company to achieve individual energy levels that correspond to job levels and types. However, in the process of enterprise development, especially in the application of new technologies and changes in the external market environment, the original energy matching model of enterprises cannot gradually meet the business needs of enterprises. We must rebuild the new energy matching model. Therefore, the allocation of human resources in the company presents a dynamic and changing process, namely the dynamic configuration of enterprise human resources (Yang & Liu, 2014; Lopez-Torres & Prior, 2016). In this dynamic process, the mobility of people is an important indicator. Affected by organizational decisions, managers within an enterprise need to start from the talents themselves and through the flow of talents to maximize their job satisfaction and work efficiency. This is what we call the best match.

The flow of talent can be expressed as a cost-return model. We mainly consider the total output value and economic efficiency as two main indicators for measuring the development of the enterprise. For enterprises, talents need to flow needs to see that the difference in utility between the target job position and the current job if it can offset the direct costs generated by the flow of talent. In addition, the economic benefits of companies are the cumulative utility of different jobs. If the utility generated by the current job is considered as the talent flow opportunity cost, the cost-benefit formula for the flow of talent are follows.

"Talent flow" is VEE-VBE-TCO>0.
"Talent does not flow" is VEE-VBE-TCO<0.

Among them, VEE is the utility provided by the transfer of talents, VBE is the utility provided by the current post structure, and TCO is the total cost of talent flow. Therefore, when the flow income is greater than the flow cost (including opportunity cost and total cost), VEE-VBE-TCO>0, talents will make flow decisions. When the flow income is less than the flow costs (including opportunity cost and total cost), VEE-VBE-TCO<0, the talent will make a non-flow decision. From the macro perspective of the company, in order to maximize the economic efficiency of the company, the company's talents must flow on the job and achieve an overall optimum.

3. THE THEORETICAL BASIS OF HUMAN RESOURCE MANAGEMENT MODEL

Considering the comparability and rationality of the research results, this study selected the engineering construction projects in the electronic bidding and tendering as the main research object. Take the ratio of the bid control price and the bid price as the explained variable. The explanatory variables include the quantity of engineering, cost of construction materials, number of bidders, scale of successful bidder, ability to build successful bidders, business environment, etc. Using year and industry as control variables. Among them, the amount of engineering and engineering material costs examine the impact of internal factors on the allocation of resources. The number of bidders, the size of the successful bidder, and the ability of the successful bidder to build a bid, etc., are an examination of the impact of bidders' competition on the allocation of resources. The business environment is an examination of the impact of the market environment and the legal environment on the allocation of resources (Zheng, Ming & Li, 2017).

In order to ensure the accuracy of the research results, this study used the bidding project data from the trading platforms of Beijing, Guangdong and Shanghai in 2015 to 2017 as the original data. All data comes from project bidding announcements and project audit reports. Remove the following sample:(1) The original data is incomplete. (2) Projects that have not been completed or have been placed on hold. (3) Bidding for special engineering projects, eventually obtaining 189 research samples.

3.1. Meaning of Human Resource Management Risk

There are three main risks in human resource management. The first point is the lack or excess of human resources, the irrational structure, and the imperfect development mechanism, which may make the development strategy of the enterprise difficult to achieve; The second point is that the human resources incentive and restraint system is unreasonable, and the management of key positions is imperfect, which may lead to brain drain, economic inefficiency or leakage of key technologies, trade secrets and state secrets; The third point is that the human resources withdrawal mechanism is improper, which may lead to legal proceedings or corporate reputation damage. Under the current market economy, human resource management risks are mainly concentrated on the neglect of human resources management in the production process, which has caused the company to be disconnected from related conditions such as job creation, employee recruitment process, and employee training. This has caused unpredictable losses to the company's production, and hindered the company's development.

3.2. Meaning of SOM Neural Network

SOM (Self-organizing feature Map) neural network is a self-organizing neural network. It is an unsupervised learning neural network. It can capture the attributes and rules in the sample by itself, which similar to the sensory channel of the human brain. When a large number of sensory units are close to human sensory organs, the relevant specific neurons of the brain begin to excite and approach the output. Finally, a unique network structure is formed. This process is the learning process [16-17]. The input layer in the SOM neural network collects external relevant information and passes the input information to the competition layer. This layer reclassifies and combines this information to find the rules and sort them in order. Among them, the minimum transmission distance between neurons can be expressed by Equation (1).

$$P_a = \left| \hat{E} - \hat{F}_a \right| = \sqrt{ \sum_{a=1}^{b} \left[E - \hat{F}_a \right]^2 } \tag{1}$$

Among them, a and b are two neurons, E is the weight between neurons a and b. F_a is the output value of neuron a. The smaller P_a, the closer the distance between E and F_a, the more similar the two are [4]. The SOM neural network carries out the transmission of relevant information through a supervisory training model. The training process can be expressed by Equation (2).

$$E_{ab}(h+1) = E_{ab}(h) + \delta(G_b - F_b)S_a(h) \tag{2}$$

Among them, E_{ab} represents the weight value of neuron a to neuron b, h is the interval, G_b is the expected output value of the neuron, F_b is the actual output value of the neuron, and S_a is the state of neuron a at h. If neuron a is active, then S_a is represented by 1. If neuron a is in dormant state, S_a is represented by 0. δ is the speed constant during the training.

3.3. Feasibility Study of Human Resource Management Risk Based on SOM Neural Network

SOM neural network has strong self-adaptive ability and fast running speed (Pan, Liu & Fu, n.d.; Sena et al., 2013). It is suitable for non-linear mapping of input information and output information, so that it can learn relevant parameters through adaptive capacity in the fastest time, and the early warning time is more advanced. At the same time, the SOM neural network has global characteristics. Human resource management is a linear structure. Any kinds of linear risk will possibly cause incalculable losses. It can be seen that human resource management also has a global structure, which has the same attributes as SOM neural networks. Therefore, the research of human resource management model was developed using SOM neural network system.

4. RESEARCH MODEL CONSTRUCTION PRINCIPLE

This article applies linear regression analysis to build a human resource allocation analysis model, as follows.

$$\begin{aligned} BCP/BP = {}& \alpha_0 + \alpha_1 EP + \alpha_2 \ln EMC \\ & + \alpha_3 NB + \alpha_4 \ln BS \\ & + \alpha_5 BCC + \alpha_6 BE \\ & + \alpha_7 Year + \alpha_8 IND + \phi \end{aligned} \tag{3}$$

In the above formula, BCP/BP is the ratio of bid control price and bid price of human resources. EP is the quantity variable. EMC is the engineering material cost variable. NB is the bidder quantity variable. BS is the successful bidder scale variable. BCC is the successful bidder's construction capacity variable. *BE* is the business environment variable. The control variables are the year variable *Year* and the industry variable *IND*.

4.1. Human Resource Management Model Based on SOM Neural Network

The construction of human resource management model based on SOM neural network is shown in Figure 1.

Figure 1. Human resource management model based on SOM neural network

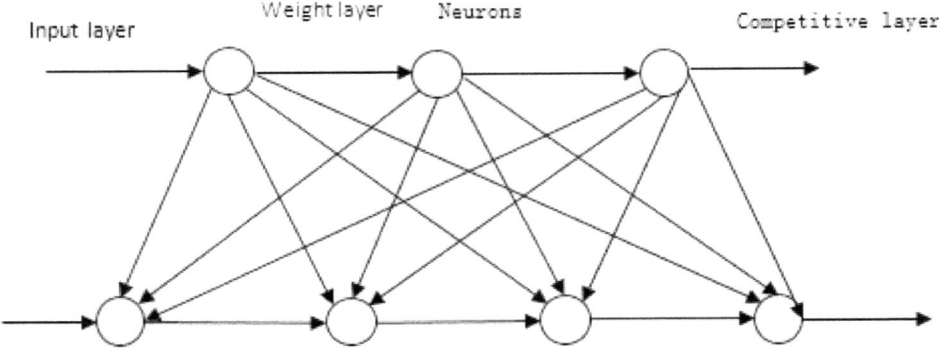

The construction of this model mainly uses the following steps.

1. Determine the set of risk factors for data analysis

Enterprises can choose to meet the actual human resource risk factors of the unit, such as recruitment risk, training risk, performance assessment risk, and compensation risk, etc. are used as risk assessment standards, as shown in Equation (4).

$$W_{mn} = \exp\left\{-\frac{\left|W_m - W_n\right|^2}{2\delta^2}\right\} (m = 1, 2, \cdots, n) \tag{4}$$

Among them, W_{mn} is the risk assessment standard function. δ is the speed constant during a train. Wm is the initial value of the risk element set, and Wn is the final value of the risk element set.

2. Select the input information point of the SOM neural network

When using this risk early warning model, the timeliness and accuracy of its prediction will depend on the selection of input information points. When human resource management risk is used as an early warning object, it will use the previously determined set of risk factors, as well as automatically convert into a closed interval with a range of values [0, 1]. Using the normalization process to deal with risk warning results may have vague issues (Jing & Wang, 2014). Its normalized function is shown in Equation (5).

$$P_{mn} = \frac{W_{mn} - W_m}{W_{mn} - W_N} \tag{5}$$

Among them, $W_m = \min(W_{nm})$, $W_n = \max(W_{nm})$. $P_{nm}\hat{I}[0,1]$ is the result of the normalized function.

3.   Select the hidden information points of the SOM neural network

In the use of this risk early warning model, the improvement of its training efficiency mainly depends on the correctness of the selection of hidden information points. The selection of hidden information points is too small, the effective information obtained by SOM neural network will be reduced, and the accuracy of network capture will be reduced. If too few hidden information points are selected, the effective information obtained by the SOM neural network will be too much, increasing the training time. Equation (6) can be used to get the best number of hidden information points.

$$Q = \sqrt{\frac{\sum_{n=1}^{m}(W_m - W_n)}{P - 1}} \tag{6}$$

Among them, Q is the best hidden information point number, P is a random constant. Through the calculation can obtain the best training time, its efficiency. The accuracy will be the best.

4.   Select the output information point of the SOM neural network

The final output of the system directly determines the outcome of the risk warning. Different risks determine different levels of risk. Generally, the risk level can be divided into five levels from high to low. They are Level 1 (most secure), Level 2 (safe), Level 3 (basic), Level 4 (danger), and Level 5 (most dangerous). It can be shown by equation (7).

$$H = \begin{vmatrix} j_{01} & j_{02} & \cdots & j_{0t} \\ j_{11} & j_{12} & \cdots & j_{1t} \\ \cdots & \cdots & \cdots & \cdots \\ j_{i1} & j_{i2} & \cdots & j_{it} \end{vmatrix} = \sum_{t=1}(j_i - j_t)L(j_i, j_t) \tag{7}$$

Among them, H is the number of output information points, j is the proportion of risk elements, and L is the system constant to adjust the speed of output results.

4.2. Training and Results of Human Resource Management Model

SOM neural network-based human resource configuration model is designed in this paper to train import relevant parameters, start to create a network, and start the training mode. There are three main parameters used, where the first parameter is the *TRAINLM* training function which is used to solve the problem of the number of training samples; the second parameter is the *LEARNGDM* weight adjustment function which is used to control the training time and improve the training efficiency; the third is *MSC* performance function which is used to adjust the error value of the input information point and the output information point. According to relevant parameters, the training curve of human resources deployment warning model shown in Figure 2 is obtained.

Figure 2. Human resource deployment risk early warning model training curve based on SOM neural network

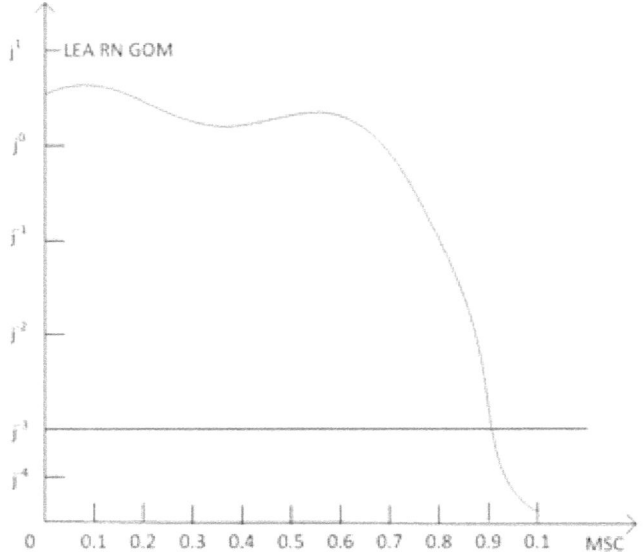

5. EXPERIMENTAL RESULTS AND ANALYSIS

In order to ensure the accuracy of the research results, this study used the bidding project data on the trading platforms of Beijing, Guangdong and Shanghai from 2015 to 2017 are as the original data, all data are from the project bidding announcement and project audit report. Then, we remove the following samples: (1) the original data is incomplete; (2) the project that has not completed the bidding or the project that is put on hold; (3) the bidding of the special project. Finally, 189 research samples are obtained.

1.   **Descriptive Statistics:** As can be seen from Table 1, the data selected in this study meets the three major data information criteria and can be applied to data analysis. The average value of the explanatory variables is 1.1293, which means the ratio of the bid control price to the bid price of human resources is 1.1293. It is in line with the estimation range of experts and scholars such as

Zhang Shuibo (2016) and Shen Wenxin (2017). The maximum value of the explained variable is 1.2482, and the minimum value is 1.0098. This shows that the overall resource allocation of the selected sample is within a reasonable range.

2. **Regression Analysis Results:** From Table 2, it can be seen that regardless of whether the industry and the year are controlled, the cost of construction materials, the size of bidders, and the construction capacity are all important factors influencing the allocation of bidding resources. Specifically, the higher the cost of engineering materials, the lower the project's resource allocation than the bid control price. The main reason is that during the construction of the project, the price of material procurement is the easiest to reduce, and the higher the total cost of materials, the greater the space for compressible costs. Therefore, the total material cost of the bidding project will affect the bid price.

Table 1. Descriptive statistics

Mean dependent var	1.1293	Max dependent var	1.2482
S.D. dependent var	36.0458	Min dependent var	1.0098
S.E. of regression	5.7670	Akaike info criterion	4.4148
Sum squared resid	34.2801	Schwarz criterion	7.1294
Log likelihood	-13.7641	Hannan-Quinn criter.	5.2741
Avg. log likelihood	-1.4133		

Table 2. Regression analysis results

	Uncontrolled industry variables	Uncontrolled year variable	Control industry variables	Control year variable
c	-32.6467	-34.0827	-32.3203	-33.7419
EP	1.8301**	1.6886	1.8018**	1.6617*
EMC	4.6930***	4.4584**	4.6461**	4.5476**
NB	2.5536*	2.4760**	2.5381	2.4612
BS	-7.1906**	-6.8311*	-7.1187*	-6.9677*
BCC	4.0989	3.8940**	4.0579**	3.9719
BE	-1.9245	-1.8282*	-1.9052*	-2.0957**

Note: *, **, *** indicate significant levels of 10%, 5%, and 1%, respectively.

Secondly, the larger the successful bidder, the closer the bidding price is to the bid control price. The main reason may be that there is a relationship between the successful management of the successful bidder and the formalized management. The larger the scale of the successful bidder and the more standardized the operation, and the stricter the project quality control, the closer its resource allocation to the bid control price.

In addition, the stronger the ability of the successful bidder to build and the lower the resource allocation. The main reason is that the more the number of successful urban construction projects for the successful bidder, the more likely it is to obtain raw material prices from their suppliers. Compared with bidders with a small number of construction projects, successful bidders are more likely to use cost advantages to reduce resource allocation and obtain project construction contracts.

It is worth noting that the higher the cost of engineering materials, the lower the project's resource allocation than the bid control price. This cannot rule out the possibility of bidders intending to cut corners. In addition, the number of bidders participating in human resources has a certain degree of influence on the allocation of resources, but compared with the traditional open tender period, the impact of the number of bidders has weakened. The main reason is that during the electronic bidding process, the information asymmetry problem has been improved, and bidders cannot accurately obtain the information of potential bidders. They can only pay more attention to the project itself and focus on the project construction plan, budget, and profit management.

From the empirical results, we can see that the implementation of the SOM neural network controls the total cost of the project. At the time of electronic tendering and bidding, the cost of project materials, the size of bidders and the capacity of construction are the most important factors affecting resource allocation. Therefore, this article proposes to strengthen the management of e-bidding projects from the following three aspects.

First of all, further improve the public bidding and public service platform. In the data collection process, this paper finds that the current electronic bidding and tendering service platform is still in the stage of rapid construction. There are too many entrances on the service platform, and the process of querying information and downloading data is cumbersome. There is a lack of unified models for portals of government departments in various regions. Although the "Electronic Bidding and Bidding Procedures" stipulates a unified platform data interaction interface technology and standards, for cross-regional bidding companies, it still takes a lot of time and manpower to understand the bidding process and the local policy rules in advance. This raises the threshold for cross-regional bidding and reduces the efficiency of bidding applications. Therefore, this paper proposes to introduce a more effective and clear project bidding process introduction and link on the current bidding service platform, so as to help prospective bidders to reasonably confirm the resource allocation and complete the bid successfully.

Second, strengthen project quality and project material procurement supervision. From the data statistics and analysis results, there is a negative correlation between the cost of engineering materials and the allocation of project resources, that is, it may be that the bidders plan to cut corners. For example, in the cable incident of the Xi'an Metro project that was recently exposed, the cable material fee of the subway project accounted for a relatively high proportion. The higher the illegally obtained proceeds, the more competitive the bid was, and the successful bidder provided the unqualified cable. Therefore, the bidding unit must focus on supervising the project quality. The audit on raw material procurement must be more stringent. Not only must the raw materials be purchased according to technical requirements, but also the raw materials for sampling inspection should be sent to relevant inspection departments for quality inspection in order to ensure project quality.

Finally, increasing the punishment, to avoid string and dark box operation. Electronic bidding has improved the information asymmetry, conspiracy of bids, and promotion of bid prices in the traditional bidding mode to a certain extent. However, there is still the possibility of string bidding and black box operations. In particular, China's Internet security awareness is relatively weak, and stakeholders may employ network hackers to attack trading platforms, steal information from bidders, and distort competitors' bids. On the one hand, bidders, government departments, and related institutions need to strengthen cyber security awareness, protect the account information and password of the bidding website, and also review bid progress in time. On the other hand, electronic bidding and trading platforms, service platforms, and related portals also need to strengthen security protection, promptly patch system vulnerabilities, and increase network monitoring efforts. Once illegal bidders or related stakeholders are found, they must increase penalties, and minimize the possibility of conspiracy to bid and black-box operations. At the same time, they need to increase their illegal costs, and build a healthy, orderly and fair human resource competition environment.

6. CONCLUSION

The implementation of the SOM neural network controls the total cost of the project. In the electronic bidding, the project material cost, bidder size and construction capacity are the most important factors affecting resource allocation. Therefore, this paper strengthens the management of electronic bidding projects from the following three aspects.

First, further improve the electronic service platform for electronic bidding. This paper finds current electronic bidding service platform in the stage of rapid construction. Besides, it still takes a lot of time and a lot of manpower to understand the bidding process and local policy requirements in advance. Therefore, this paper proposes to introduce more effective and clear project bidding process to help potential bidders to reasonably confirm the resource allocation.

Second, there is a negative correlation between the cost of engineering materials and the allocation of project resources. The higher the gains that can be illegally obtained, the more competitive the bidding at the time. Therefore, it is necessary not only to check whether the raw materials are purchased according to the technical requirements, but also to send the raw materials for inspection to the relevant inspection departments.

Finally, it is needed to increase penalties and avoid stringing and black-box operations. On the one hand, bidders, government departments, and related institutions need to strengthen their network security awareness, as well as protect the account information and passwords of bidding websites. On the other hand, electronic bidding trading, service platforms and related portals also need to strengthen security and increase network monitoring efforts.

Generally, modern enterprises in fierce market competition, human resources management has risen to an extremely important position. It is a problem to be resolved that enterprise managers timely obtain optimal allocation of enterprise human resources and resolve the risk of enterprise human resources deployment. This paper establishes a human resource management model based on SOM neural network so that it can provide effective protection for the benign operation of human resource management from multiple aspects and provide power for the rapid development of the enterprise.

REFERENCES

Gherman, R., Adamescu, B., Brad, I., & Dincu, A. M. (2016). Efficiency of human resources at national and multinational companies. *Journal of Biotechnology*, *23*(1), 88. doi:10.1016/j.jbiotec.2016.05.314

Jia, B., Liu, S., & Yang, Y. (2014). Fractal Cross-layer Service with Integration and Interaction in Internet of Things. *International Journal of Distributed Sensor Networks*, *10*(3), 760248. doi:10.1155/2014/760248

Lassi, Z. S., Musavi, N. B., Maliqi, B., Mansoor, N., de Francisco, A., Toure, K., & Bhutta, Z. A. (2016). Systematic review on human resources for health interventions to improve maternal health outcomes: Evidence from low- and middle-income countries. *Human Resources for Health, 14*(1), 10. doi:10.118612960-016-0106-y PMID:26971317

Li, X., & Zhu, D. (2018). An Adaptive SOM Neural Network Method to Distributed Formation Control of a Group of AUVs. *IEEE Transactions on Industrial Electronics, 5*, 1–1.

Li & Wang. (2016), Marginal utility function based optimal human resource management model. *Systems Engineering —Theory & Practice, 36*(1), 106-112.

Lin, W. (2016). Human Resources Management of Track and Field Web Course in College Physical Education. *International Journal of Emerging Technologies in Learning, 11*(4), 95. doi:10.3991/ijet.v11i04.5463

Liu, M., & Liu, S. (2015). Distributional Escape Time Algorithm based on Generalized Fractal Sets in Cloud Environment. *Chinese Journal of Electronics, 24*(1), 124–127. doi:10.1049/cje.2015.01.020

Liu, S., Fu, W., & Deng, H. (2013). Distributional Fractal Creating Algorithm in Parallel Environment. *International Journal of Distributed Sensor Networks*. doi:10.1155/2013/281707

Liu, S., Fu, W., & Zhao, W. (2013). A Novel Fusion Method by Static and Moving Facial Capture. *Mathematical Problems in Engineering*. doi:10.1155/2013/503924

López-Torres, L., & Prior, D. (2016). Centralized allocation of human resources. An application to public schools. *Computers & Operations Research, 73*(C), 104–114. doi:10.1016/j.cor.2016.04.001

Marshall, L., & Treuren, G. (2016). Dimensions and determinants of declining employment opportunities for mature aged male practitioners within the human resources profession: Occupational change, age and gender. *Research in Nursing & Health, 18*(2), 85–95.

Pan, Z., Liu, S., & Fu, W. (2017, August). A review of visual moving target tracking. *Multimedia Tools and Applications, 76*(16), 16989–17018. doi:10.100711042-016-3647-0

Sena, P., Attianese, P., Pappalardo, M., & Villecco, F. (2013). FIDELITY: Fuzzy inferential diagnostic engine for on-line support to physicians. In *IFMBE Proceedings*. Springer. 10.1007/978-3-642-32183-2_95

Sena, P., D'Amore, M., Pappalardo, M., Pellegrino, A., Fiorentino, A., & Villecco, F. (2013). Studying the influence of cognitive load on driver's performances by a fuzzy analysis of lane keeping in a drive simulation. *IFAC Proceedings, 46*(21), 151-156.

Wu, J., Jiang, Y., & Zhu, J. (2016). Human Resource Allocation Combined with Team Formation. *International Conference on Computational Intelligence and Applications*, 67-71. 10.1109/ICCIA.2016.20

Xie, S. (2017). Sensing of mobile device threat status based on big data and SOM neural network. Boletin Tecnico/ technical. *Bulletin, 55*(7), 332–340.

Xu & Wang. (2014). Research on the Management Model of Human Resource Based on 3D Fuzzy Pattern. *Journal of Shandong Agricultural University (Natural Science Edition)*, (5), 785-788.

Yali, W. (2017). Human resource allocation and performance analysis based on DEA model. *Agro Food Industry Hi-Tech, 28*(1), 754–758.

Yang, G., & Liu, S. (2014). Distributed Cooperative Algorithm for k-M Set with Negative Integer k by Fractal Symmetrical Property. *International Journal of Distributed Sensor Networks, 398583.* doi:10.1155/ 2014

Zheng, M., Ming, X., & Li, G. (2017). Dynamic Optimization for IPS2 Resource Allocation Based on Improved Fuzzy Multiple Linear Regression. *Mathematical Problems in Engineering, 17*(6), 1–10.

This research was previously published in the International Journal of Mobile Computing and Multimedia Communications (IJMCMC), 10(1); pages 65-76, copyright year 2019 by IGI Publishing (an imprint of IGI Global).

Chapter 28
Theory of Constraints and Human Resource Management Applications

Brian J. Galli

(iD) https://orcid.org/0000-0001-9392-244X

Assistant Professor and Graduate Program Director, Master of Science in Engineering Management Industrial Engineering, Hofstra University, USA

ABSTRACT

This purpose of this article is to assess constraints and suggest a theory that can improve Human Resource Management Systems (HRMS's). It investigates the relationship between Theory of Constraints (TOC) and operation management, which is based on the Critical Chain PMs book entitled The Goal. In 1984, the author, Goldratt, introduced an entire management philosophy about the TOC. The mental process and improvement theory tools discussed in his book mainly focus on manufacturing environments. However, the practice and examples in the book helped many organizations succeed, even in the private sectors. This study offers definitions of throughput, operating expense, and inventory measurements, and uses the principle of TOC to identify bottlenecks and constraints in every business process. By using these analyses, the study remodels the system to increase performance measurements of HRMS.

1. INTRODUCTION

"If you can't measure it, you can't manage it." (The W. Edwards Deming Institute Blog)

The author of *The Goal* visited the Human Resources (HR) Departments (HRD) of many organizations and asked if they implemented process management. Many HR representatives responded, that they have not done so because it is a difficult task to measure the HR process, which contributes to overall the business outcome. Process management is used as a tool for HR to outline the process for tasks. The new age of HRD requirements is to hire a highly qualified line manager who's actively involved in managing

DOI: 10.4018/978-1-6684-3873-2.ch028

people and then filtering the highly trained workers. Employing this process promises to deliver, to the organization, productive employees to reduce company stakes (Anderson et al., 2006; Andersen, 2014).

The typical set of high-level HR process consists of: (Process Management)

- Plan people requirements
- Provide people
- Develop people
- Manage people performance
- Reward and recognize people
- Lead people exists

In 1984, Dr. Eliyahu M. Goldratt introduced his philosophy on Theory of Constraints (TOC) to help organizations continually achieve their goals. The book titled *The Goal* (Goldratt, 1984) highlights a dispute to the factor of constraints for not achieving the goals. The book provides a comprehensive range of examples of a manageable system with limited numbers of constraints. This research paper focuses on employee evaluation processes, based on the below factors from the book *The Goal:*

1. The role of the HRD needs to identify:
   a. Who customers are?
   b. What are their requirements?
2. Based on the above Fundamentals, HR needs to:
   a. Plan a process.
   b. Check the procedure with:
      i. Line Managers
      ii. Financial Department
3. Timeline for Vacancy Filling
4. Employee Training Plan
5. Cost Process for Measurements

2. RESEARCH PURPOSE

The research application of this paper arises from the need turn functionally managed organizations into more process-managed entities. It is important for any organization to be clear about its goals before determining processes. The business process management discussed in Chapter 3 of *The Goal* (Goldratt, 1984), is one example of a common constraint.

Alex, the manufacturing manager, was given one year to improve the division. If improvements were not made, the entire division would be eliminated. At the end of the meeting, he was given a handout with new targets for the upcoming years (Ward & Daniel, 2012). Management was unaware of the intricacies of the factory environment or the workflow within the organization. All management knew was that the plant was losing money due to late orders, high cost, low efficiencies and 20% cutbacks. Providing new goals without any process control measurements can result in the biggest failure (HR Manager Toolkit). Therefore, the role of HR is to establish performance focus before providing any goals. The next step is to deliver ongoing training aligned with the performance plan. In addition to the business process management, an HRM should focus on enhancing the process by workflow to better manage the company (Atkinson, 1999 Bakker, 2010; & Bazeley, 2007). Such concepts are discussed in this research.

3. MAIN FINDINGS

3.1 Business Process Management

Business Process Management has an abundance of methodologies. In *Business Process Management: a boundary-less approach to modern competitiveness*, researcher and author Zairi outlines the process as a method to convert inputs into outputs (Zairi, 1997). By applying this approach, an organization can achieve its goals, since this is the most reliable, repeatable, and consistent way to use resources. Chapters 8 and 10 in *The Goal* (Goldratt, 1984) demonstrate how Alex and his team discussed the meaning of throughput. The way in which the Human Resource Management (HRM) understood the process is depicted below in the diagram (Figure 1):

Figure 1. Process

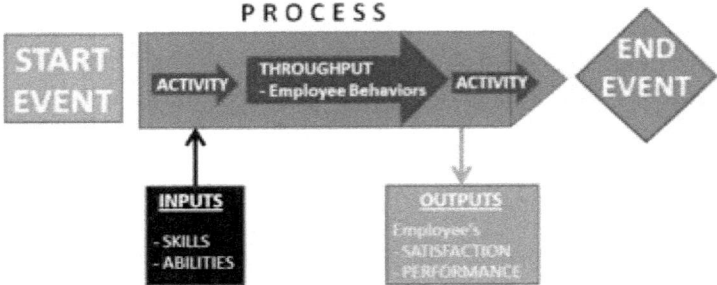

Figure 1 demonstrates the process discussed between Alex and his college professor Jonah in Chapter 8. As per Jonah, the system produces money over sales, which is considered the Throughput Rate. Inventory is the total amount of money, which is invested in purchasing items for future sale. Operation expense, money spent, is what is used to turn inventory into throughput (Webster & Watson, 2002; Winter et al., 2006a; Galli, 2017). Jonah advises Alex about critical primary measurements to achieve the goal, which is demonstrated in the equations below:

Throughput = Sales – Total Variable Cost

Net Profit = Throughput – Operating Expense

This approach is very statistical and close to reality. Alex discovered that the plant has two phenomena (Webster & Watson, 2002; Winter et al., 2006a; Galli, 2016):

1. Dependent Actions, where raw materials move from A to B to C. C cannot achieve more than B provides it. B cannot work until it obtains parts from A. A cannot do the job until it receives Raw Material.

2. Statistical Fluctuations. In chapter 10, Alex reviewed the definition of performance with his team members (Bob, the production manager, Lou, the accountant, and Stacey, the plant manager). Lou explained that the money comes in via Throughput and the Inventory contains money that is currently in the system. So, to generate Throughput, the organization must incorporate operation expenses.

3.2 Critical Chain

The advantages of expanding the critical chain theory in project management are numerous and diverse. As per the book, the key factor for higher budget costs for any project is the process of generating estimates with respect to time. This also leads to a situation in which projects are not completed on time (Bradley, 2010). The primary achievement of any project should always be requested, since this will provide great benefit. Furthermore, the assigned resources for a project should place an emphasis on responsibilities at hand and not on numerous tasks and projects (Critical Chain Book).

For improved project management, the technique of schedule generation should be employed. In this technique, all responsibilities have a realistic timeframe for accomplishment estimation. This also secures the safety of the entire project, not just individual responsibilities. An additional take away, which can be functional in project management, is in the situation of multiple projects. It is a known fact that projects use shared resources (Breese, 2012; Bryman, 2008). The idea described in the book will help HR achieve and pursue similar projects by emerging and formulating ranking arrangement as a benefit in defining the precise order in which the responsibilities are accomplished (Critical Chain PM).

Regarding disadvantages that HR sees in consuming these theories, the resource practice is not very secure because they are implied and often involved in the project network. Still, they require documentation, so resource necessities must be observed (Kohli & Grover, 2008; Galli, 2017). The author, Goldratt inquires about the current constraint which can be the base of other constraints. Furthermore, he recommends reinforcing the existing constraint based on quality. He prioritizes the constraint via three steps (Critical Chain):

*   Identify the constraint
*   Treat it as the highest priority to remove the objectionable consequences
*   Avoid future recurrence of the constraint

This leads us to the theory of constraints (TOC).

3.3 Theory of Constraints

The author defines five steps of the theory of constraints (TOC). They are defined as follows:

1. **Identify** the constraint (Six Sigma). It is the backbone of the entire practice. It identifies limiting elements in the system. Some constraints may rise, and they may rank according to total impact on the company's goal.

2. **Exploit** it by scheduling arrangement of work to make sure the restriction (or bottleneck process) is running fulltime (Six Sigma). In simple terms, it calls for seeking methods to get the best out of the quantified constraints without spending much money.

3. **Subordinate** all other processes, provided that a buffer is needed to keep the constraint operating at maximum capacity (Six Sigma). It also requires matching the entire system, specifically the non-constraints.

4. **Elevate** the constraint by surging its volume. Add resources in ways that abbreviate the delicate chain and increase processes along with it (Six Sigma). That means trying alternate ways to enhance the output of bottlenecks after the internal misuses and relegations are approved.

5. **Repeat**, because if you're positive, a new constraint will occur. This is the occasion for continuous improvement (Six Sigma).

In the first step, Identify, the constraint is internal or external, tangible or intangible. The second step, Exploit, reduces wastage of resources to perfect efficiency of the workflow. The third step, Subordinate, is challenges the inadequacy of performance exertion, when there is a constraint permitting the entire system to work on minimal instead of optimal performance (Lycett et al. 2004). The fourth step, Elevate, looks at the system as a whole. To achieve the potential of the complete system, there might be a necessity for obtaining new equipment or a surge of staff. The fifth step, Repeat, debates the condition of existing constraint elimination and new constraint formation. Enhancing processes allows the TOC to offer a continuous process in which the constraint is removed and creates different constraint advent (Melville et al., 2004). HR influence is crucial in any organization where the department is unable to deliver loyal and quality staff organization management, and HR should employ its leadership to this particular unit. Otherwise, the organization would still be camouflaging the high employee turnover and permanent profit losses (Zwikael & Smyrk, 2012; Galli, 2016).

3.4 Bottleneck

The theory of constraints (TOC) is a significant tool for cultivating procedures. The inferences of the theory are, by far, an accomplishment regarding understanding bottlenecks and better handling these bottlenecks to generate an efficient method flow (Reducing bottleneck). The the TOC is a valuable tool for operations managers to accomplish bottlenecks and improve development flows (Bottleneck Conundrum).

According to the Theory of Constraints by Jaideep Motwani, time quality management "...philosophies are solidly rooted in the concept that any improvement, anywhere in the process, improves the performance of the whole organization..." (Jaideep Motwani). However, the TOC relies on development efforts, which should only emphasize the weakest links of a system. So, it can be the main resolution of the TOC to ease the burden on bottlenecks that exclude a company from reaching its goals. Now, these bottlenecks do not primarily include physical constraints, such as inadequacy of raw materials and machines, absence of plant space, or lack of workers (Money, 2006; Row, 2012; Galli, 2017). The strategies of an organization may well be similarly critical constraints that are named "bottlenecks."

The book, *The Goal* (Goldratt, 1984), claims that most obstacles in an organization are about operating processes and policy constraints that are embedded in the foundation of the organization. TOC attempts to create an ongoing development, since, whenever the volume of bottlenecks increase, it jumps to achieve simultaneously with additional components in the system. The additional constraints will ultimately rise in another part of the system, so they must be constantly watched (Zwikael & Smyrk,

2012). According to Goldratt, further constraints or bottlenecks may rise in the system after references are executed and the system is assured to be a focus to at least one constraint. Therefore, the system is obligated to pursue the Five Steps of concentrating on recognizing new constraints (Zwikael & Smyrk, 2012). Time should be spent on finding solutions to achieve and elevate the constraints. This is part of the cycle of ongoing improvement (Rowe, 2014).

3.4.1 Herbie

In the book, *The Goal,* the author demonstrates his point with the story of a Scout troop on a hike. The protagonist, Alex, had to bring the troop to the campground in a reasonable timeframe, while also keeping the group close together to maintain observation (Herbie And A Beginner's Mind). The constraint was known as Herbie, the slowest moving "overweight kid" in the Scout troop. He was recognized because of the line of scouts behind him and the growing space between Herbie and the scouts in front of him (Zwikael & Smyrk, 2012; Galli, 2017). Due to this, Herbie became the constraint (Schryen, 2012). The term "constraint," as used in this paper, is the source within a system that disrupts the system output from accomplishing a goal. Following is the constraint which was identified by the queue. It is known for starving the resources:

Constraint = Whatever limits a system's productivity

Constraint = Borderline situation

Constraint = Cause of a restrictive source

Alex made numerous attempts to create the best out of Herbie's abilities by boosting him. Unfortunately, Alex constantly failed. His work was not enough to meet the end goal. The Scout troop got frustrated by Herbie's walking speed, which determined the group's pace. However, Herbie's speed was not sufficient to reach the target. Alex tried cause-and-effect investigation to stimulate the constraint (Schryen, 2012; Galli, 2017). He indicated the cause to be the heavy backpack, and resolved this issue by allocating Herbie's materials among the faster Scouts. Alex was attentive to appraise the Scouts for taking on this new constraint. Fortunately, although Herbie continued to be the constraint, this activity increased volume to meet the goal. By off-loading Herbie's backpack, his throughput was improved. As a direct result, the entire troop's throughput also improved (Schryen, 2012).

3.4.2 Drum-Buffer-Rope Mechanism

The Theory of Constraints (TOC) introduces another set of intelligent ideologies that becomes a planning and development tool at the manufacturing level. It is called the "Drum-Buffer-Rope" approach. To recognize the philosophy behind the Drum-Buffer-Rope, the illustrations below (Figures 2 – 4 below) demonstrate the practices.

Alex learned about statistical fluctuations and dependent events. The extreme deviation of an above process will become the starting point for the following action (Schryen, 2012). However, Alex's slowest source was not in front of the line, so he had to take the approach depicted below (Figure 5).

Figure 2. Scouts losing speed

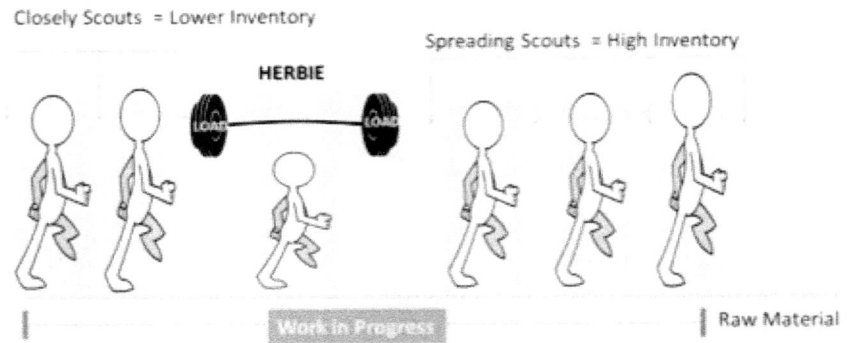

Figure 3. Herbie in lead

Figure 4. Divide the load

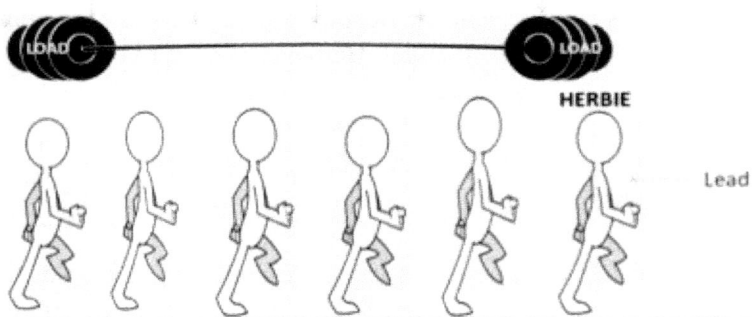

Figure 5. Drum-buffer-rope approach at Unico

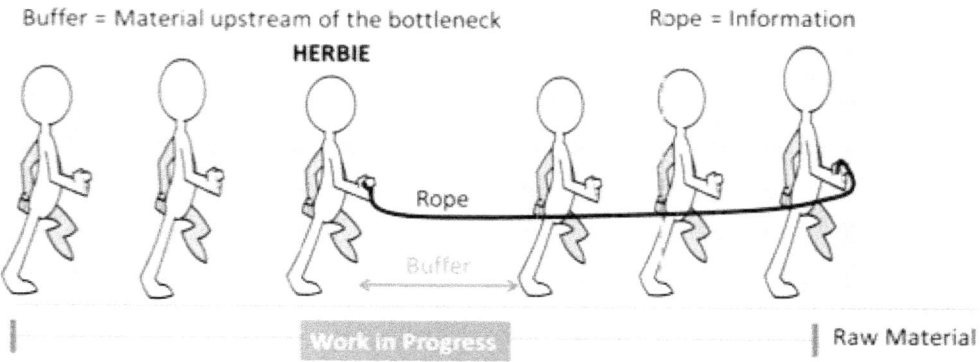

The above illustration demonstrates "Herbie" as the bottleneck and the buffer as the material in front of him. The rope represented the information (Schryen, 2012). If Herbie processes parts, then the buffer moves onward. The rope also works as a signal, alerted when the material is out to provide information to refill another part at the beginning of the process. Alex then tried the "Drum and Rope" approach at UniCo, where the first task was constraining operation or restricting the distance among them by limiting the work-in-progress. During this process, Alex changed certain policies by exploiting the use of Herbie (Schryen, 2012).

3.4.3 Bottleneck Impact

The "Rope and Drum" approach helped UniCo's HR department identify the capacity as a limiting resource constraint in the plant. The company realized why it needed to spend more time observing and discovering where the bottleneck was and how to stop it (Shenhar & Levy, 1997; Rowe, 2014). Once the bottleneck was identified, HR found the capacity for the bottleneck and did not move them so they had enough capacity to meet the demand. The two bottlenecks were an NCX-10 machine and the Heat Treat. HR moved QC in the front of bottlenecks and made a list of all late jobs and components that flow through bottleneck machines. However, the scheduling system failed because the new job elements were not showing in front of bottleneck machines (Shenhar & Levy, 1997; Rowe, 2014; Galli, 2016).

Then, HR created a list of due date orders and instructed bottleneck operators to work only on red tagged/high priority jobs in that order. By creating red and green tags, the jobs with red tags arrived at the machine as a priority (Shenhar & Levy, 1997; Rowe, 2014). Any green tagged jobs were stopped until the red tags were completed. HRM took the following steps to offload from the bottleneck (Zwikael & Smyrk, 2012):

- Attached gold tags with the parts that traveled through the bottlenecks to watch for damage
- Dedicated a person at NCX-10 and heat-treated machines to ensure they were not idle
- Sent out heat-treated machine parts to vendor
- Found old equipment that was more cost-efficient and ran equivalent to the NCX-10
- Fully loaded mixed batches when possible
- Reduced set-up time for gears

- Alternated the routes where heat-treating wasn't obligatory

The altered process pace resulted in a new monthly shipping record. UniCo went from 2 million to 3 million shipments, and 26 new customers placed orders compared to the existing 31 customers. Finally, work-in-progress inventories reduced by 12%. As new bottlenecks began to appear, HR reduced the time for non-bottlenecks (Zwikael & Smyrk, 2012). As per Jonah, "a system of local optimums is not an optimum system at all; it is a very inefficient system." (Goldratt, 1984). To fix the problem, HR kept current bottleneck machines working at the same rate as the bottleneck, just like the "Rope and Drum" approach. The Rope is the bottleneck machine to the front of the assembly line, and the length of the rope signifies the inventory. The Drum represents communication between the assembly line and bottleneck (Zwikael & Smyrk, 2012).

To improve, HR also cut batch sizes for non-bottleneck parts in half. This significantly decreased the time that parts spent on the plant. This helped the organization by increasing marketing sales by 15% and reducing the lead time to complete orders (Shenhar & Levy, 1997; Rowe, 2014). The bottleneck had moved to customer demand, and quick response on promised due dates was translated into a modest advantage (Zwikael & Smyrk, 2012; Galli, 2017). HR Managment assumed that parts cost was increasing. However, it was actually going down, as demonstrated with the formulas below:

Cost per part = Direct Labor + Raw Material + Burden Cost

Burden cost is all the cost of the indirect labor

Burden =Burden Factor x Direct labor

Cost per part rose since there was more setups occur in the small batch sizes. This increased the number of configurations, without increasing the cost. Performance measures reflected well on HR when inventory was calculated as an asset in the balance sheet. The employees worked hard to reduce the inventory to progress the throughput of the entire system (Shenhar & Levy, 1997; Rowe, 2014). HR was able to make the plant a successful one because it changed the company's focus from "COST" to "THROUGHPUT" (see Figure 6 below).

Figure 6. Change in focus

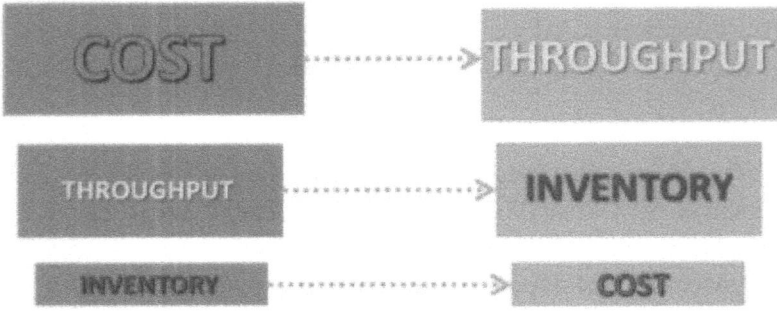

3.4.4 Union

The Goal defines a situation where management avoids unions in the beginning and later seeks a partnership approach with them. Unions are a challenging facet for any organization. Companies desire to have its working atmosphere union free. However, in most cases, it is rare not to find unions in large companies (Shenhar & Levy, 1997; Rowe, 2014).

Workers will not form a union if they are pleased with the organizational policies, rules, and guidelines. Workers unionize for fundamental reasons including better pay, better working conditions, and advocating against employer unfairness (Smyrk & Zwikael, 2011). Furthermore, readily established union power is important for employeesi, if they want to form a union. The central demand that the workers raise pertains to job security (Zwikael & Smyrk, 2012). In this competitive world, job stability is critical. Workers require the same security for their jobs. So, an organization must make them feel confident about their respective jobs (Smyrk & Zwikael, 2011; Galli, 2017).

Today, it is obligatory for workers to be able to negotiate with the workers' union. It is the task of HR and leadership to distinguish the varying titles of workers. It is not the workers' responsibility to figure this out. Workers should not feel threatened if they want to join a union. There should be no rule prohibiting them in exercising their rights in the organization, compelling them starting labor unions, inducing them to soften union movements, and observing carefully their movements (Zwikael & Smyrk, 2012). An organization cannot prohibit workers from having a bargaining process with the union leaders. Likewise, there are systematized standards for union laborers, so that, for example, unions cannot restrict workers from exercising their rights and responsibilities (Smyrk & Zwikael, 2011).

The Union cannot force a worker to arrange or release their union members in any case. It also cannot decline bargains in good faith nor be involved in asking the company to compensate for the services the union did not achieve (Zwikael & Smyrk, 2012). The organization has the right to speak against the union in public (Smyrk & Zwikael, 2011). And finally, any bargaining between unions and laborers will require following several steps, such as writing an initial contact, obtaining authorization cards, holding a hearing, complaining, and then an election (Smyrk & Zwikael, 2011; Galli, 2017).

3.5 Training

HR can have the ultimate impact on any organization. Below are some suggestions and strategies that can be applied by HR to positively improve the organization (Smyrk & Zwikael, 2011):

- Every person should take a formal training program. Formal training will help develop professional approaches towards the job's responsibility.
- A performance metric should be prepared and monitored to measure performance. A performance metric will help the employer identify areas in which an employee needs help.
- Have a Q&A session and give rewards on performance appraisals. One-on-one sessions will contribute to creating a transparent procedure and endorse communications.
- Continue assessment of each employee for skills measurements. Assessment will help with future predictions of change.
- Evaluation process should be made to identify each employee's capabilities, qualifications, and special interests. Further evaluation should be performed to train these employees to improve their skills.

- Prepare a defined career path for each employee that will enhance motivation. Then, the employee will take proactive steps to fulfill their responsibilities.
- Monitor employee performance to help employer make ethical decisions for promotions.
- The most productive employees can be sent to different branch locations to learn best practices. They should also be brought to new locations as new positions open.
- Every culture has different hospitality so, by exposing employees to a versatile culture, they will learn universal cultural values. This is helpful when an employee brings in knowledge from a different aspect of the world and applies it to other locations. This will increase career opportunities for everyone.

3.6 HR Business Process Management Approach

A new organization believes in a process-centered methodology that leads to large developments in performance and organizational compliance. So, HRM applies the improved process performance, which provides the chance for cheaper variation (Zwikael & Smyrk, 2012). Thus, it delivers the basics of business strategy. This is a part of the business process that management fears. The business approach is a structured method to appraise and continually progress any business activities. As this research paper focuses on the human resource factor, activities such as valuation and collection process, engagement, training, assessment, maintaining, and promotion are debated. Figure 7 shows the process of separation being stopped from the corporate strategy (Harmon & Wolf).

Figure 7. Business process management approach Source: Harmon, Paul (2014) - The State of Business Process Management, p.47

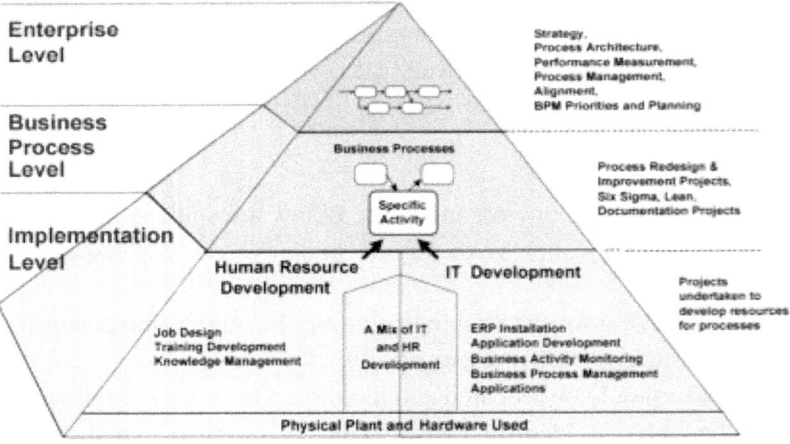

3.6.1 Human Resource and Technology

As figure 7 shows, HR and technology form the base of the pyramid. If the Pyramid is built on Physical Plant and Hardware, the fundamentals for any organization, then how is Technology involved? (Smyrk & Zwikael, 2011) The new era is the age of Internet, smartphones, and nanotechnology, which are meant to communicate with other people. The industry is changing with the rapid pace of technological growth. Even though it was not designed for HR, the new challenges sparked innovation within HR for organizations and social media, such as "LinkedIn," to evaluate and use these channels to recruit employees (Zwikael & Smyrk, 2012). After all, it was indicated that "92% of recruitment use social media to find high-quality candidates" (Morrison).

Another example of applicable technology is machine-learning applications that are developed for HR to mainly focus on an employee's predictive analytics and discover new talent to grow the organization. Organizations are also adopting cloud computing to solve the inefficiency of workforce productivity (Smyrk & Zwikael, 2011). The tools provide training and focus on engagement challenges that increase productivity and align humans on the path to meet business goals (Zwikael & Smyrk, 2012).

3.7 Process Improvement

HRM can apply variability of policies and tools for process enhancement, such as Six Sigma, Total Quality Management (TQM), Kaizen, and Lean Management. Some of these are explained in the proceeding sections (Soderlund, 2011; Soderlund & Bakker, 2014).

3.7.1 Six Sigma

Six Sigma is a "method that provides organizations tools to improve the capability of their business processes. This increase in performance and decrease in process variation lead to defect reduction and improvement in profits, employee morale, and quality of products or services. Six Sigma quality is a term used to indicate a process is well controlled" (ASQ.org).

Six Sigma tools are applicable to management. Those specific tools are listed below:

- **Process Map:** A visual map which shows processes and steps
- **DMAIC:** Project Management tool
  - **D**efine opportunities
  - **M**easure the action
  - **A**nalyze connection between in input and outputs
  - **I**mprove strategy
  - **C**ontrol and improve
- **Ishikawa Fishbone Diagram:** Used to define the possible cause of imperfection and solve these issues (Fishbone Diagram) (see Figure 8 below).
- **Lean:** Famous for its attitude about loss and waste elimination
- **Kaizen:** Well-known strategy of small improvements at all managerial levels.

3.7.2 Human Resource Strategies

Below are the most important HR strategies to apply for continued improvement (Soderlund, 2011; Soderlund & Bakker, 2014)

- **Strategic Objectives:** Define what is supposed to be achieved.
- **Plan of Action:** How objectives should be met.

- **Performance Management:** Strategic aim towards productivity, customer satisfaction improvement, quality increase, and profit advantages.
- **Commitment Management:** Teamwork and information sharing with team members to solve problems.
- **Involvement Management:** Increase involvement with employees and give opportunities to evaluate performance.
- **Learning Organization:** Adjust and acknowledge changes around the environment.
- **Behavioral Competencies:** Required to see results in teamwork, leadership, communication, and decision-making.
- **Technical Competencies:** Hire knowledgeable and skilled employees
- **Leanness:** HR should be actively involved in decision-making.
- **Career Opportunities:** Search more promising technology and knowledge about the economy.
- **Employee Engagement:** Develop an atmosphere where employees are willing to go extra miles for the organization.

Figure 8. Ishikawa fishbone diagram Source: Dutch Renaissance retrieved from http://www.timvandevall. com/templates/fishbone-diagram-template/

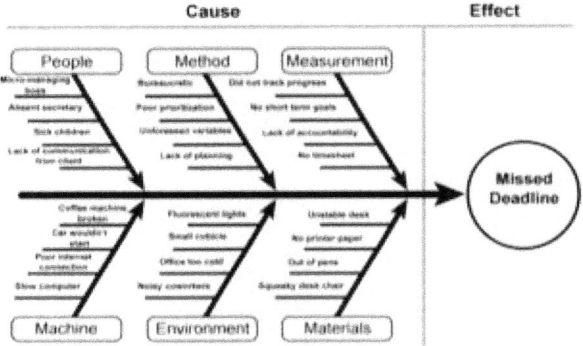

4. CONCLUSION

4.1 Relevance and Implications for Management and Project Environments

Based on the acquired skills and management strategies from the research, there is a need to make use of human resources in conducting business projects and project management. This can be achieved by ensuring well-functioning human resources that make use of the distinct skills to create a team that understands the company or projects ultimate goals. In this case, there is a need to invest substantially in human resources before thinking of the mode of technology to use in the project or management. The findings from this research study of *The Goal* help to identify several managerial implications. More specifically, these results highlight the importance of a top-down and bottom-up approach to leadership and strategic planning, especially with regards to elements of operations management and process improvement. The results of this study highlight the criticality of integrating human resource principles into the leadership styles and tools leaders use to manage their human resources.

The findings from this study also highlight the importance of human resources throughout all aspects of an organization; obviously HRM is one element in an organization's business model, but this study shows that the human resource element directly impacts many other elements of an organization. Management and leadership of any organization need to have the training and skill sets to, not only manage their human resources, but to manage it effectively. This study has shown that many of the current-state issues seen within the factory of *The Goal* stemmed from the leadership's lack of effectively leading and managing their employees. If the leadership has the tools and knowledge to effectively manage their human resources instead of focusing on the bottom line (i.e. profits and costs), then the performance of an organization will improve and, as a result, the profits and costs will also improve. A major highlight of this study is that business leaders tend to mainly focus on the financial elements of their business, while ignoring or minimizing the human resource element; this might work in the short-term, but the factory in *The Goal* shows that it is not a good long-term strategy. Over the long-term, leadership must have a multi-faceted approach where they manage operations, human resources, financials, performance, and strategy from one overarching understanding that all of these elements are critical and they are all related. By understanding this view, a business leader will be better equipped to lead a successful company in both the short- and long-term.

4.2 Limitations

The study and results are somewhat restricted due to a few research limitations that should be discussed. The main limitation was the fact that the study had a limited sample size (i.e. one book) and it only studied key factors from this limited sample. The limitation of sample size introduces some potential bias and validity behind the findings and conclusions identified in the study, all of which could be alleviated by executing the study with a larger sample. Another limitation was that this study only examined the key factors and their relationship in terms of a project environment; therefore, the conclusions and analysis are specific to project environments and the findings cannot necessarily be extrapolated to other arenas such as supply chain management, operations management, or strategic management. This is a limitation since the conclusions and analysis are specific and makes it difficult to argue that the findings from this study could be deployed and used in other industries or managerial settings.

4.3 Future Research

Future research should explore a few different arenas. For example, future research could investigate these factors and the relationship, but in the context of other industries and managerial settings. In these settings or contexts, it would be interesting to study the strength of these variables and their relationship as well as the factors that impact these variables and their relationship. Another avenue of research could be to explore these variables and their relationship, but from different perspectives, such as from an organizational, strategic, or cultural point of view. This would shed further light into the how this relationship is perceived across many different views and further understand the degree of impact that factors such as culture, strategy, human resources, operations have on the key variables and their relationship.

4.4 Conclusion and Originality

In this paper, the philosophies and actions of the Theory of Constraints were applied to the Human Resource Managment. The goal is to obtain understanding about business process management and process improvement through Human Resources Departments (Svejvig & Anderson; Thorgren et al., 2010). This results in process optimization for any organization. Due to innovative technology, the HR recruitment process highly depends on assessing the qualified and skilled employees for the organization. The technology is a required part to compare two employees in order to determine the best candidate. For the employees of an HR Department, implementation of process management is the best solution, where they can also apply Six Sigma methodologies to optimize the system and provide training according to that workflow (Tranfield et al, 2003; Vom Brocke et al., 2009).

The primary challenge in applying TOC is the adoption and understanding of Throughput, Inventory, Operating systems, and not allowing inertia to become the system's constraint (Zwikael & Smyrk, 2012). Below are the five steps which HRM applied at UniCo. These five steps can be applied to any organization seeking continuous improvement, which is the main take away of this paper (Zwikael & Smyrk, 2012).

Figure 9. Five steps

1. IDENTIFY the system's constraints ⟵ - - - - - - - - - - - - - ⟶
2. Decide how to EXPLOIT the system's constraints
3. SUBORDINATE the whole thing for the above decision making
4. ELEVATE the system's constraint
5. If the previous steps has a constraint, GO BACK TO STEP 1.

The important benefit of this paper is for educational purposes that combine the analysis process for HR practices. Many organizations do not see the necessity of process management implementation in daily HR operations. Therefore, this research assists organizations by offering several guidelines for the organization and employees concerning HRM. Good management should be based on the fact that, for a company to achieve the ultimate goal of profit maximization, there is a need for well-established coordination that ensures both the human capital and technology are adequately used. There is a need to nurture human capital foster delivery in the most appropriate and optimal levels. There is also the need to ensure the company produces the product that will create and maintain customer loyalty. In this case, the quality of the product must be taken into consideration throughout all processes and decision-making. This quality can only be ensured through standards set by the human resource and proper planning on the step-by-step strategies to be employed. The book, therefore, demonstrates the management techniques that engage the human resource in achieving the goals of a company.

Review of the literature showed that there is limited research that explored the concepts and their relationships. Therefore, this study sought to further analyze these concepts and the relationships between them in general. In an effort to fill a void in the research identified earlier on this study and alleviate previously preconceived risks and uncertainty.

The results of this research study contribute to several different fields of research and topics, including: human resource management, theory of constraints, project management, and process improvement. By performing this study, the results help to enhance and evolve these fields of research and topics since this study not only built on existing research, but attempted to expand and fill a gap in the research that was identified earlier on this study. By more thoroughly understanding these concepts and their relationships, we can understand the advantages and disadvantages, which in turn should help improve their effectiveness.

This study also contributes since it introduces new ideas and avenues for future research in each of these fields of research and topics. Not only did this study seek to explore different variables and their relationships, but it also sought to understand the relationships and identify new ways of thinking about the variables under study. The results of this study were also valuable, from a practitioner perspective, since the understanding of these variables and relationships helped to introduce ideas and strategies that a practitioner can deploy to be more effective in their profession. The results from this study help a practitioner to understand the relationships and variables but also the implications related to these variables and relationships.

REFERENCES

Andersen, E. S., Birchall, D., Jessen, S. A., & Money, A. H. (2006). Exploring project success. *Baltic Journal of Management*, *1*(2), 127–147. doi:10.1108/17465260610663854

Andersen, E. S. (2014). Value creation using the mission breakdown structure. *International Journal of Project Management*, *32*(5), 885–892. doi:10.1016/j.ijproman.2013.11.003

ASQ.org. (n.d.). Overview. Retrieved from http://asq.org/learn-about-quality/six-sigma/overview/overview.html

Atkinson, R. (1999). Project management: Cost, time and quality, two best guesses and a phenomenon, it's time to accept other success criteria. *International Journal of Project Management*, *17*(6), 337–342. doi:10.1016/S0263-7863(98)00069-6

Bakker, R. M. (2010). Taking stock of temporary organizational forms: A systematic review and research agenda. *International Journal of Management Reviews*, *12*(4), 466–486. doi:10.1111/j.1468-2370.2010.00281.x

Bazeley, P. (2007). *Qualitative Data Analysis with NVivo*. London: Sage Publications Ltd.

Bottleneck Conundrum. (n.d.). Retrieved from http://0-search.proquest.com.liucat.lib.liu.edu/abicomplete/docview/847137677/DDE10C80F5CD4E97PQ/1?accountid=12142

Bradley, G. (2010). *Benefit Realisation Management: A Practical Guide to Achieving Benefits through Change* (2nd ed.). Farnham: Gower.

Breese, R. (2012). Benefits realisation management: Panacea or false dawn? *International Journal of Project Management*, *30*(3), 341–351. doi:10.1016/j.ijproman.2011.08.007

Bryman, A. (2008). *Social Research Methods* (3rd ed.). Oxford: Oxford University Press.

Communication Plan. (n.d.). Retrieved from https://pma.doit.wisc.edu/DoIT%20Templates_Examples/Stage%203%20-%20Plan/Stage%2...

Baggerud, E. (2002). Book report on Critical Chain by Eliyahu M. Goldratt. Retrieved from http://www.byggai.se/pl/att/refCriticalChain.pdf

Critical Chain Book Review. (2007). Retrieved from http://fortboise.org/useful/critical_chain.html

Aitken, C. (2012). Critical Chain Project Management: An Overview. Retrieved from https://baylor-ir.tdl.org/baylor-ir/bitstream/handle/2104/8352/Critical%20Chain%20Project%20Management.pdf?sequence=1

Tim's Printables. (n.d.). Fishbone Diagram. Retrieved from http://www.timvandevall.com/templates/fishbone-diagram-template/

Galli, B. (2017). How To Truly Win in Business With Leadership – A Case Study Report. *Middle Eastern Journal of Management*, *4*(3), 235–245. doi:10.1504/MEJM.2017.086426

Galli, B. (2017). The Effective Approach of Managing Risk in New Product Development (NPD). *International Journal of Applied Management Sciences and Engineering*, *4*(2), 27–40. doi:10.4018/IJAMSE.2017070103

Galli, B. (2017). Applying Strategic Analysis to Quantify Investor Risk: Case Study of Pfizer. *International Journal of Risk and Contingency Management*, *6*(3), 1–13. doi:10.4018/IJRCM.2017070101

Galli, B. (2016). A shared leadership approach to transformational leadership theory: Analysis of research methods and philosophies. *International Journal of Strategic Decision Sciences*, *7*(3), 1–42. doi:10.4018/IJSDS.2016070101

Goldratt, E. M. (1984). *The Goal*. Great Barrington, MA: The North River Press Publishing Corporation.

Gupta, M., & Boyd, L. (2008). Theory of constraints: A theory for operations management. *International Journal of Operations & Production Management*, *28*(10), 991-1012. Retrieved from http://www.emeraldinsight.com/doi/abs/10.1108/01443570810903122

Harmon, P., & Wolf, C. (2014). The State of Business Process. *BP Trends*. Retrieved from http://www.bptrends.com/bpt/wp-content/uploads/BPTrends-State-of-BPM-Survey-Report.pdf

Herbie And A Beginner's Mind. (2009). Retrieved from http://www.thebusinessofbeingcreative.com/2009/12/16/herbie-and-a-beginners-mind/

HR Manager Toolkit. (n.d.). Retrieved from http://hr.columbia.edu/helpful-tools/hr-manager-toolkit/managing-staff/goal-setting-managing-performance/guide-performance

Management Study Guide. (n.d.). HRM in Leadership Development. Retrieved from http://www.managementstudyguide.com/role-of-hrm-in-leadership-development.htm

Jaideep Motwani, D. K. (n.d.). *Theory of Constraints.* Retrieved from http://togarsim.tripod.com/toc/motwani1.pdf

Kohli, R., & Grover, V. (2008). Business value of it: An essay on expanding research directions to keep up with the times. *Journal of the Association for Information Systems, 9*(1), 23–28, 30–34, 36–39. doi:10.17705/1jais.00147

Lycett, M., Rassau, A., & Danson, J. (2004). Programme management: A critical review. *International Journal of Project Management, 22*(4), 289–299. doi:10.1016/j.ijproman.2003.06.001

Melville, N., Kraemer, K., & Gurbaxani, V. (2004). Information technology and organizational performance: An integrative model of IT business value. *Management Information Systems Quarterly, 28*(2), 283–322. doi:10.2307/25148636

Money, A. H. (2006). Exploring project success. *Baltic Journal of Management, 1*(2), 127–147. doi:10.1108/17465260610663854

Morrison, K. (2015). Survey: 92% of recruiters use social media to find high-quality candidates. *AD-WEEK.* Retrieved from http://www.adweek.com/digital/survey-96-of-recruiters-use-social-media-to-find-high-quality-candidates/

Improvement skills Consulting LTD. (2009). Process Management in human resources. Retrieved from https://ianjseath.files.wordpress.com/2009/05/process-management-in-hr.pdf

LIU. (n.d.). Reducing bottleneck. Retrieved from http://0-search.proquest.com.liucat.lib.liu.edu/abicomplete/docview/1494641094/DDE10C80F5CD4E97PQ/7?accountid=12142

Rowe, F. (2012). Toward a richer diversity of genres in information systems research: New categorization and guidelines. *European Journal of Information Systems, 21*(5), 469–478. doi:10.1057/ejis.2012.38

Rowe, F. (2014). What literature review is not: Diversity, boundaries and recommendations. *European Journal of Information Systems, 23*(3), 241–255. doi:10.1057/ejis.2014.7

Schryen, G. (2012). Revisiting IS business value research: What we already know, what we still need to know, and how we can get there. *European Journal of Information Systems, 22*(2), 139–169. doi:10.1057/ejis.2012.45

Shenhar, A. J., & Levy, O. (1997). Mapping the dimensions of project success. *Project Management Journal, 28*, 5–13.

Kahmra Khan. (n.d.). Applying Theory of Constraints to Manage Bottlenecks. *Six Sigma.* Retrieved from https://www.isixsigma.com/methodology/theory-of-constraints/applying-theory-constraints-manage-bottlenecks/

Smyrk, J., & Zwikael, O. (2011). *Project Management for the Creation of Organisational Value.* Springer.

Söderlund, J. (2011). Pluralism in project management: Navigating the crossroads of specialization and fragmentation. *International Journal of Management Reviews, 13*(2), 153–176. doi:10.1111/j.1468-2370.2010.00290.x

Söderlund, J., & Bakker, R. M. (2014). The case for good reviewing. *International Journal of Project Management, 32*(1), 1–6. doi:10.1016/j.ijproman.2012.11.007

Svejvig, P., & Andersen, P. (2015). Rethinking project management: A structured literature review with a critical look at the brave new world. *International Journal of Project Management, 33*(2), 278–290. doi:10.1016/j.ijproman.2014.06.004

John Hunter. (2015). Myth: If You Can't Measure It, You Can't Manage It [Blog post]. *The W. Edwards Deming Institute Blog.* Retrieved from https://blog.deming.org/2015/08/myth-if-you-cant-measure-it-you-cant-manage-it/

Thorgren, S., Wincent, J., & Anokhin, S. (2010). The importance of compensating strategic network board members for network performance: A contingency approach. *British Journal of Management, 21*(1), 131–151. doi:10.1111/j.1467-8551.2009.00674.x

Tranfield, D., Denyer, D., & Smart, P. (2003). Towards a methodology for developing evidence-informed management knowledge by means of systematic review. *British Journal of Management, 14*(3), 207–222. doi:10.1111/1467-8551.00375

Vom Brocke, J., Simons, A., Niehaves, B., Riemer, K., Plattfaut, R., & Cleven, A. (2009). Reconstructing the giant: On the importance of rigour in documenting the literature search process. *ECIS 2009 Proceedings, 161*, 1–13.

Angry Animator. (n.d.). tutorial-2: walk cycle [blog post]. Retrieved from http://www.angryanimator.com/word/2010/11/26/tutorial-2-walk-cycle/

Ward, J., & Daniel, E. (2012). *Benefits Management: How to Increase the Business Value of Your IT Projects.* West Sussex, UK: Wiley. doi:10.1002/9781119208242

Webster, J., & Watson, R. T. (2002). Analyzing the past to prepare for the future: Writing a literature review. *Management Information Systems Quarterly, 26*, xiii–xxiii.

Winter, M., Andersen, E. S., Elvin, R., & Levene, R. (2006a). Focusing on business projects as an area for future research: An exploratory discussion of four different perspectives. *International Journal of Project Management, 24*(8), 699–709. doi:10.1016/j.ijproman.2006.08.005

Zairi, M. (1997). Business process management: a boundaryless approach to modern competitiveness. *Business Process Management, 3*(1), 64-80. Retrieved from https://pdfs.semanticscholar.org/8f71/37a45e07186331bf4b785bf5d4a3723aa780.pdf

Zwikael, O., & Smyrk, J. (2012). A general framework for gauging the performance of initiatives to enhance organizational value. *British Journal of Management, 23*, S6–S22. doi:10.1111/j.1467-8551.2012.00823.x

This research was previously published in the International Journal of Strategic Engineering (IJoSE), 2(1); pages 61-77, copyright year 2019 by IGI Publishing (an imprint of IGI Global).

Index

A

Accountability 45, 56-57, 62-63, 189, 235, 284, 286, 410, 413, 425, 448-449, 454-457, 461-463, 465-466, 469-470, 574, 633-634, 637, 659, 661-663, 670, 674-675, 678-679, 818, 1061, 1091, 1251-1252, 1254, 1256-1257, 1262-1263, 1265, 1267, 1269, 1275, 1277, 1378, 1447, 1524, 1526, 1532, 1540, 1544, 1611, 1627, 1636, 1642, 2092-2093, 2095-2099, 2154

active ageing 1843, 1847, 1850-1851, 1853, 1861, 1863, 1866-1867

Administrative Decentralization 660, 678

administrative reform 659-662, 678

Adoption 9-10, 18-21, 26, 31, 74, 93-94, 96-99, 106-113, 167, 175, 196, 198, 204-205, 210-212, 214, 216-218, 229, 243, 276, 288, 292, 296, 310, 314, 319, 322, 333, 387, 392, 401, 410, 506-511, 540, 570, 585, 589-590, 597-598, 600-604, 626, 639, 654, 660, 662, 671, 696, 713, 725, 727-728, 730, 732, 738, 756, 758, 780, 783, 793, 913-916, 960, 990, 1038, 1044, 1049, 1086-1087, 1090, 1094-1096, 1104-1106, 1114, 1116, 1120-1121, 1130-1145, 1148, 1150-1151, 1185, 1187, 1201, 1289, 1291, 1317, 1329-1334, 1339, 1371, 1373, 1385, 1418, 1483, 1562, 1567, 1582, 1584, 1586, 1591, 1597, 1618, 1660, 1712-1713, 1720, 1817, 1829, 1847, 1878, 1896, 1911-1912, 1919, 1921-1922, 1925, 1929, 1990-1996, 2009, 2011, 2013-2014, 2017-2020, 2022-2026, 2029, 2031-2033, 2035-2040, 2043-2047, 2049-2051, 2053, 2056, 2060, 2063, 2065, 2084, 2119, 2123, 2158

Advanced Manufacturing Technology (AMT) 760-761, 779-785, 787-788, 790, 2051

Advertising 797-798, 898, 1303, 1339, 1492, 1495, 1695, 1841, 2071, 2132, 2134, 2155, 2159, 2161-2163, 2166-2167, 2169-2171, 2173-2174, 2176, 2178

advertising industry 2163, 2169-2170, 2174, 2178

Age Management at Workplace 1867

Agile HR 1549, 1560, 1565-1566, 1577

Agile Management 640, 1884, 1892, 1894, 1898

Agility 201, 387, 392, 398-399, 456, 509, 592, 713, 732-733, 753, 1161, 1257, 1560, 1601-1622, 1885, 1897, 1911, 2018, 2039, 2046, 2096-2097, 2100

Agribusiness 939-940, 943-961, 1145

Airlines 73-74, 78, 82, 84, 87, 479, 1360, 1370, 1386, 1645, 2033

Algorithm 251-252, 255-257, 266, 268-273, 524-525, 695-696, 700-705, 782, 816, 829-830, 839, 846, 1109-1110, 1784, 1789, 1791, 1798

Amazon 1492, 1549-1551, 1553, 1555, 1560-1562, 1564-1565, 1569-1576, 1669, 2108

AMO model 1230, 1232, 1237-1238, 1240, 1243-1244, 1250

AMOS 1015, 1477, 1714, 1717, 1727

AMT benefits 760, 762-765, 772, 775-776, 778-779

Anti-Red Tape Act 9485 249

Arab World Higher Education 1074

Array List 273

Artificial Intelligence 220, 243, 246-247, 249, 255, 271-273, 288, 295, 354, 361, 375, 471-472, 488, 593, 599-600, 602-604, 609, 611, 616, 713, 719, 727, 733, 754, 911-915, 918-919, 1134, 1158, 1275, 1395, 1404, 1554, 1572, 1628, 1653, 1756, 1784, 1791, 1797, 1926, 2009, 2040, 2046

audience and consumer demand 2164, 2166-2167, 2169, 2173, 2178

augmented workforce 1549, 1569

AUTh 1491, 1503-1507, 1509-1517, 1521, 1523

Automation 94, 109, 185, 202, 213, 220, 223, 230-231, 252-253, 375, 492, 600, 611, 685, 737, 741, 784, 911-920, 1096, 1131, 1150, 1212, 1394, 1396-1397, 1404, 1469, 1554, 1574, 1653, 1691-1692, 1776, 1910, 1919, 2011, 2023, 2029, 2034, 2128-2129

Automation Technology 220, 685

Awareness 19-20, 31, 48, 133, 136, 176, 238, 293, 298,

300, 303-305, 307-308, 310-319, 321-323, 336, 338, 395, 406, 412, 417, 420, 449, 454, 456-457, 466, 468-469, 522-523, 590, 596, 605, 622, 630, 646, 654, 662, 688, 697-698, 700, 706, 793, 880, 988-990, 993, 999, 1044, 1089-1090, 1124, 1171, 1195, 1198-1199, 1204, 1252, 1254-1255, 1257, 1262, 1270, 1274-1275, 1281, 1284, 1287, 1337, 1339, 1342, 1345, 1377-1378, 1382-1384, 1399-1400, 1405-1406, 1412, 1415-1419, 1421, 1423, 1425, 1427, 1512, 1581, 1603, 1606, 1608-1609, 1612, 1614-1616, 1668, 1719, 1761, 1797, 1817, 1820, 1828, 1851, 1853, 1859, 1937, 1939, 2011, 2058, 2096, 2103-2110, 2114, 2116, 2122, 2124, 2156, 2160, 2163, 2174, 2181-2182, 2204

B

Baby Boomer Generation 1626, 1641
Background Checks 448-449, 454-457, 464-466, 468-469, 792, 1251-1252, 1254, 1256, 1262, 1268-1271, 1273, 1276, 1919
Business Analytics 478, 865-866, 1001, 1007, 1016, 1019, 1628, 2038, 2047
Business Ethics 301, 355, 397, 467, 996, 1145, 1272, 1387, 1412-1416, 1421, 1425, 1427, 1429-1435, 1456, 1821, 1844, 1864, 1906, 2043, 2118, 2136, 2153-2154

C

C# 273
Capital Disclosures 629-632, 2086
Carbon Footprint 21, 997, 1291, 1337-1340, 1343
Career Counseling 1170, 1892-1893, 1898
Career Development 57, 62-63, 66, 88, 91, 118, 156, 190-191, 234, 276-277, 283, 285, 422-423, 426-427, 434, 436-437, 439, 464, 490, 630, 660, 668, 679, 707, 729, 799, 819, 931-932, 947, 1025, 1033, 1080, 1098-1099, 1174, 1242, 1268, 1298, 1377, 1447, 1473, 1535-1536, 1547, 1703, 1814, 1853, 1862, 1865, 1883, 1886, 1888-1890, 1892-1897, 1899, 1901-1904, 1923, 1939, 1980, 1986, 2092, 2096, 2098, 2142, 2152, 2198
Career Management 8, 144, 190, 197, 200, 204, 208, 211, 424, 426, 640, 899, 928, 931-932, 947, 1080, 1162, 1355, 1524, 1526, 1531, 1535, 1539, 1541, 1547, 1712, 1821, 1889-1890, 1899, 1905, 1910, 1972-1974, 1980, 1983-1984
career mentoring 1892-1893, 1898-1899, 1906
career resilience 1884-1895, 1897-1899, 1901, 1903, 1905-1907

career shocks 1884, 1887-1888, 1891, 1898-1899, 1907
Career Shocks and Stressors 1884
Career Stressors 1888, 1907
Civil Service Commission 233-234, 237, 243-247, 249
Cloud Computing 217, 384, 398, 492, 537, 599, 603, 613, 739, 742-743, 756, 759, 1038, 1275, 1316, 1333, 1564, 1692, 1990-1991, 2000, 2017-2018, 2021, 2023, 2026, 2029-2030, 2040, 2042-2043, 2045-2049, 2051-2052
Cloud-Based Environment 735, 1990, 1995, 2013
cloud-based HR solutions 735
Clustering 269, 272-273, 1244
Coaching 3, 6, 210, 213, 276, 280, 282, 284-285, 288-289, 311, 347, 476, 480-481, 576, 809-810, 812, 871, 931, 947, 1224, 1730, 1732, 1861, 1893, 1901, 1905, 2097
Commercial benefits 760, 762-766, 772, 775-779, 785
comparative HRM 141, 143
Compensation And Benefits 135, 197, 209, 318, 423, 428, 430, 438, 440, 447, 479, 574, 748, 873, 940, 944, 946-947, 950-951, 954, 961, 1097, 1566-1567, 1902, 1904-1905, 2006, 2031
Compensation Management 408, 612, 614, 945, 960, 1098-1099, 1538-1539, 1547
Competency-Based Recruitment and Qualification Standards 244, 249
Competitive Advantage 3-4, 6, 8-9, 13, 16, 55, 65, 67, 111, 165-166, 179, 193-194, 199, 204, 212, 218-219, 224-225, 228, 230-231, 277, 284, 286, 304-305, 308, 318, 322, 324-325, 327, 332-334, 341, 345, 348, 350, 354, 358-368, 370-373, 404, 406, 419, 422, 425, 475, 478, 487, 490, 509, 581, 607, 621, 633-634, 638, 640, 693-694, 697, 707-708, 712, 714, 716-717, 732-734, 761, 763, 868, 901, 907, 925, 934-936, 940, 943, 957-958, 960-961, 966, 982, 988, 997, 1022-1023, 1025, 1035, 1038, 1063, 1068, 1072, 1074, 1077, 1079, 1089-1090, 1115, 1122-1124, 1129-1130, 1132, 1144, 1146, 1161, 1164-1165, 1185, 1197, 1209, 1212, 1228, 1230-1231, 1249-1250, 1254, 1280, 1283-1284, 1293, 1298-1299, 1342, 1344, 1379, 1388, 1413, 1434, 1469, 1524, 1526, 1532, 1539, 1548-1550, 1571, 1580-1581, 1595, 1598, 1602-1603, 1605, 1609-1610, 1612-1615, 1618, 1623-1624, 1628, 1636-1637, 1642, 1645-1646, 1649, 1651-1653, 1660, 1662, 1677, 1710, 1719, 1722, 1725-1726, 1747, 1756, 1785, 1788, 1790-1791, 1796, 1801, 1803-1804, 1818, 1845, 1848, 1852, 1873, 1886, 1890-1892, 1894, 1911-1913, 1929-1933, 1938-1941, 1945-1946, 1961, 1989, 1992, 2032, 2049, 2052, 2061, 2068, 2070-2071, 2076-2079, 2082-

2083, 2085, 2089, 2117, 2138-2139, 2142, 2145, 2149, 2153, 2195, 2206, 2208, 2219

complex systems theory 1782

configuration management 513

Configurational Approaches to HRM 338

configurational model 303, 307, 320-322

configurational perspective 11, 16, 316, 322

Contact Center Ng Bayan 235, 239, 241, 249

Contextual Analysis 1132, 1139

Contextual Perspective 11, 16

Contingency Approach 11, 14, 127, 307, 324, 544, 1234, 1250, 1708, 1710, 1719

Contingency Perspective 10, 16, 311, 1244, 1862, 1985

Core Competencies 48, 814, 1214, 1604, 1642, 1652, 1808, 2159, 2204

Corporate Culture 222, 230, 419, 578, 580, 612, 634, 681, 823, 1052-1053, 1168, 1170, 1565, 1762, 1770-1771, 1780, 1782, 1817, 2071

Corporate Social Responsibility 16, 18, 20, 24, 231, 348, 406-407, 418, 420, 922, 993, 996-997, 1040, 1042, 1044, 1048, 1175, 1184, 1271, 1285, 1293, 1413, 1428-1429, 1432-1433, 1485, 1630, 1680, 1817, 1821, 1852, 1864, 2107, 2113, 2119, 2127, 2133, 2137-2143, 2145, 2147, 2149-2154

corporate sustainability and responsibility 1158

Cranet 939-940, 946, 948-954, 958-959

criminal tendencies 695, 697

crisp set 814, 826

Critical Chain 526, 529, 542

Critical To Quality 867, 876, 880, 889

cross cultural contexts 1868

Cross-Cultural Management 141-143, 564, 1188, 1679, 1902

Cross-Culture 161, 1177, 1191, 1666, 1680

CSR 24, 348, 356, 406, 922, 993, 995, 1040, 1048, 1158, 1167-1169, 1173, 1293, 1339, 1428-1430, 1676, 2083, 2119, 2137-2152, 2154

CSV 255-257, 260, 263-264, 266-267, 273

Customer Relationship Management (CRM) 1063, 1072

cybernation 911-918

D

Data Analysis 125, 187, 266, 436-437, 442, 456-457, 477, 497, 518, 520, 541, 547, 689, 781, 847, 849, 873, 927, 936, 998, 1000, 1072, 1107, 1117, 1138-1139, 1145, 1323, 1360, 1371, 1485, 1577, 1744, 1748, 1751-1752, 2035, 2083

data structure 259, 261, 273

Decision Support System (DSS) 1098, 1120

Decision Tree 269, 272-273

Defects Per Million Opportunities (DPMO) 680, 686

Delphi technique 2211, 2224

Demographic Development in Europe 374

Descriptive Statistical Techniques 847

Design Thinking 482, 636-637, 640-645, 648-649, 652-658

Digital HR 602, 736-738, 752, 956, 1549, 1569, 1995, 2030, 2037, 2045, 2047, 2051

Digital HRTransformation 2022

Digital Media 600, 1492, 1522, 2159, 2163, 2170, 2172-2174, 2178

Digital Transformation 200, 505, 508, 711-714, 725, 727, 731, 733-734, 744, 914, 956-957, 1403, 1628, 1926, 1990-1992, 1994, 2023

DMAIC 374, 395, 537, 688, 867, 871, 878, 880, 888-889

Dollar Shave Club 1549, 1555-1557, 1569, 1571-1572, 1575

Downsizing 71, 1164, 1434, 1627, 1900, 2123, 2204, 2213, 2218, 2220-2224

Duterte Administration 233-234, 236, 245, 249

Dynamic Capability 178, 781, 1642

E

E-Application 1926

Ease of Doing Business and Efficient Government Service Delivery 236, 249

e-career management 190, 200, 208-209, 211, 213

E-Compensation 195, 200, 209, 215, 218, 718, 733, 1355, 2041

economic sustainability 1278, 1281-1282, 1289, 1292

Efficient Consumer Response (ECR) 1063, 1072

Ego-Evaluation Energy (EEE) 1770-1771, 1782

E-HRM Operational Effectiveness 733

E-HRM Outcomes 180, 718, 753, 2039

E-HRM Relational Effectiveness 733

E-HRM Strategic Effectiveness 734

E-HRM Types 184, 711, 715, 717

Electronic Data Processing (EDP) 1098, 1120

Electronic Human Resource Management (E-HRM) 14, 182, 193-194, 196-198, 215, 217, 511, 657, 711, 732, 737, 753-754, 957, 1116, 1352-1357, 1359, 1371-1373, 1692, 1703, 1909, 1923-1924, 2015, 2017, 2019, 2039, 2042, 2045, 2049

Electronic Recruitment Systems 198

Electronic remuneration (E-remuneration) 198

Electronic Theft Hacking 695

e-mentoring 191, 202, 207-208, 216, 218

emotional engagement 2179, 2187-2189, 2191

emotional labor 73-74, 76-78, 81-82, 84-91

Emotional labour strategies 73

Employability 157, 301-302, 397, 925, 928-932, 1172, 1254, 1274, 1281, 1621, 1854-1856, 1889-1890, 1893, 1899-1901, 1906-1907

Employee advocacy 683

employee cost 2058, 2062

Employee Engagement 26, 84, 114, 167, 178, 297, 367, 394, 422, 471-476, 479-490, 510, 538, 566, 591, 593, 595, 608, 614, 616, 793, 851, 868, 876, 925, 957, 1049, 1081, 1091-1093, 1162-1163, 1172-1173, 1276, 1285, 1297, 1299, 1313, 1338, 1436-1438, 1441-1443, 1446-1471, 1473-1474, 1478-1482, 1484-1489, 1575, 1609, 1618, 1721, 1848, 1857, 1864, 2144, 2153, 2179-2182, 2184-2187, 2192-2201

Employee Experience 287, 472, 482, 636, 648, 650, 652, 740, 911, 918, 1557, 1559, 1569

Employee Performance 26-27, 52, 61, 65, 175, 194, 248, 384, 396, 398, 455, 476, 510, 536, 608, 641, 670, 682, 727, 848, 851, 857, 917, 919, 993, 1123, 1147, 1162, 1228, 1234, 1237, 1247, 1250, 1252, 1254, 1256-1257, 1274, 1276, 1285, 1321, 1340, 1382, 1441-1442, 1446, 1463, 1468, 1470, 1472-1474, 1478-1484, 1486, 1488, 1569, 1700-1701, 1785, 1787-1788, 1947, 1960, 2103, 2111, 2119, 2180, 2193, 2196, 2207, 2214, 2219, 2221-2222

Employee Productivity 95, 119, 203, 213, 374, 449, 492, 592, 1081, 1161, 1252, 1436

Employee Relations 18, 119, 179, 197, 217, 227, 300, 332, 352, 398, 400, 444, 448-449, 454, 456, 462-463, 465-466, 483, 574, 584, 605, 730, 753, 757-758, 800, 819, 918, 922, 936, 946, 958, 988-989, 991, 1037-1038, 1097, 1251-1252, 1254-1255, 1267, 1269, 1373, 1393, 1452, 1458, 1463, 1605, 1703, 1705, 1721, 1841, 1852, 1863, 1925, 1942, 2015-2016, 2019-2020, 2038, 2041, 2048, 2050, 2103, 2106, 2112, 2116, 2221

Employee Retention 293, 341, 356, 396, 415, 438, 479, 485, 609, 614, 757, 900-901, 903, 1380, 1543, 1761, 1892, 1943, 2018, 2046, 2138-2142, 2144-2152

Employee Selection 18, 276-278, 598-599, 602, 705, 922, 925, 1170, 1270, 1496, 1926

Employee Self Service (ESS) 199

employees in the public sector 659, 667-671, 674, 678-679

employer-employee relations 1251

Engagement Drivers 1092, 1436, 1442, 1448

Enterprise Management 93, 1762, 1906

Entrepreneurial Resources Planning Systems (ERPS) 1063, 1073

entropy 1762, 1764, 1766, 1769-1771, 1774, 1776, 1779, 1781-1782

Environment Management 297, 300, 410, 416, 1288, 1337, 1341

Environmental Degradation 300, 990, 997, 1000, 1287, 1290, 1377, 1385, 2103-2106, 2115-2116, 2120

environmental dynamism 1743-1744, 1747, 1749, 1751-1752, 1754-1756, 1758-1759, 1761

Environmental Sustainability 22-24, 32, 410-413, 415-417, 419, 987-989, 991, 998-1000, 1049, 1130, 1280-1282, 1285, 1290-1292, 1294, 1343, 1375-1376, 1378, 1381, 1384-1385, 1387, 1389, 1403, 2103-2108, 2115-2116, 2118, 2120, 2124-2125, 2132, 2135-2136

Environmentally-friendly 1278

E-Performance Appraisal 210, 213, 218, 1352, 1354-1356, 1358-1359, 1361, 1363-1370

E-Performance Management 188-189, 200, 718, 734, 1355, 1594

E-Recruitment 186-187, 194-195, 198, 200, 202, 205-206, 213, 216-218, 601-602, 718, 733-734, 753, 791, 793-794, 799-801, 954, 956, 1352, 1354-1356, 1358-1361, 1363-1367, 1370, 1696, 1706, 1908, 1910, 1914-1917, 1919-1926, 2015-2016, 2038, 2041-2042

E-Recruitment and E-Selection 734

E-Training 189-190, 200, 206-208, 213, 215-216, 218, 718, 732, 734, 1352, 1354-1356, 1358-1361, 1363-1368, 1370

E-Training And Development 189-190, 734, 1355

Event Management 1688, 1694-1696, 1702, 1704-1706

Expatriates 141-142, 144, 148, 150-154, 156-160, 577, 897, 900, 1181, 1215, 1228, 1676, 1684, 1871-1876, 1878-1879, 1881

explicit coordination 314-321, 339

extra role behavior 1250, 1449

F

Family Business 131, 304-305, 309-310, 322-325, 327-329, 331-339, 368, 589, 598-599, 603-604, 939, 948, 956, 1148, 1189, 1195-1196, 1201, 1203-1204, 1206-1210, 1247, 1413, 1415, 1427-1435, 1578, 1580, 1582-1584, 1586-1591, 1593-1595, 1597-1598, 1928, 1930-1933, 1935-1943

Family Firms 303-325, 327-328, 330-331, 333, 335-339, 588, 590-591, 598, 1193-1210, 1247, 1412-1417, 1419, 1421-1435, 1578-1584, 1588, 1591-1598, 1928-1935, 1937-1943, 2087

family management 1200

family owned firms 588-598

Family-Owned Company 961, 1433
financial market 619-622, 624, 628-632
Financial Statements 619-620, 622-623, 625-626, 628-629, 634, 2055, 2060, 2155, 2160, 2172
Firm Performance 5, 167, 179, 304, 326-327, 334-335, 337-338, 368, 566, 585, 782, 936, 938, 958, 1035, 1068, 1129, 1161, 1174, 1206-1207, 1210, 1244-1245, 1247, 1312, 1373, 1431, 1434, 1543, 1594-1595, 1597, 1599, 1618, 1621-1622, 1640, 1684, 1726, 1743-1744, 1747-1748, 1750-1756, 1759, 1761, 1858, 1862, 1900, 1929, 1943, 1988, 2066, 2077, 2117-2118, 2180, 2196
First-Generation Rights 1392, 1398-1399, 1410
Four Elements 1438, 2080
Four Generation of Rights 1390
Fourth Industrial Revolution 17-18, 31, 33, 394, 1158, 1392-1394, 1403-1405, 2127-2128, 2130-2131, 2133, 2137, 2224
fourth-generation rights 1391-1392, 1397, 1399-1400, 1410
fuzzy logic 814, 816, 827-829, 843

G

Gamification 466, 595, 598-599, 601-604, 1271, 1785
Gas gas emission 1278
Generation X 1566, 1626, 1638, 1642, 1777, 2180
Generation Z 1566, 1777, 1884-1886, 1888-1898, 1900-1906
generational diversity 1638, 2179, 2182, 2195
generational succession 1193-1195, 1197, 1199, 1201-1205
generational transition 1578
Generic Model 1132-1133, 1137, 1140, 1143
GHRM 18-21, 23, 25, 30, 403-404, 406-407, 410-411, 1279-1293, 1343, 1379-1380, 1382, 1384-1385, 2104-2107, 2109, 2111-2112, 2116-2120
Gig Economy 711, 713, 719-721, 723-726, 730, 734, 1569
Gig Work Management (GWM) 711-712, 727
gig workers 711-712, 714, 719-721, 724-727, 734
Good Dominant Logic 803
Green Compensation 403-404, 409-410, 414-417, 987-988, 990-991, 1000, 1286-1288, 1292, 2111
Green Compensation Practices 414, 987, 2111
Green Employee Relation 1000
Green Gas Emission 1295
Green Goals 297-298, 406, 410, 1337, 1340-1343, 2125
green healthcare 17
Green HRM 292-293, 295, 299-301, 403-404, 406-407, 410, 413-414, 417-419, 960, 994, 1123-1124,

1128, 1130-1131, 1294-1295, 1337-1339, 1341-1343, 1376, 1381, 1383, 1386-1388, 2106-2107, 2117-2120, 2125-2127, 2134, 2136
Green Human Resource Management 18, 33-34, 300-301, 369, 373, 404, 406-407, 417, 419-420, 995-1000, 1131, 1278-1279, 1284, 1286, 1289, 1293-1296, 1340, 1343, 1375, 1379-1382, 1385-1388, 2103-2104, 2106, 2136-2137
green human resource practice 291, 419
Green Human Resources 17, 25, 31, 366, 987, 989, 992, 999-1000, 1040, 1042, 1044, 1049, 1378, 1380, 1382, 2117-2118, 2122
Green Initiatives 20, 31, 298-299, 404, 406-407, 410, 415, 990, 1044, 1278, 1281, 1285, 1288, 1292, 1337-1342, 2105, 2107, 2110-2113
Green Job Design 988, 1000
Green Management 302, 404, 407, 410, 416, 419, 998, 1285, 1287, 1289, 1292, 1294, 1379-1380, 1389, 2104, 2109, 2111-2112, 2114, 2119-2120
green organizational cultures 1040, 1042
Green Recruitment 300, 987-989, 993-994, 1000, 1284-1286, 1292, 2105-2108, 2112, 2118-2119
Green Recruitment Practices 300, 987, 989, 994, 1286, 1292
green sustainability 25-27, 34
Green Training And Development 20, 987-988, 990, 994, 1000, 1044, 1285-1287, 1292, 2104-2105, 2108-2109
Green Training And Development Practices 987, 994, 1287, 2109
Grounded Theory 937, 1132, 1137-1139, 1145, 1149

H

hard HRP 2202
Health Administration 2092
health organizations 1202-1203
Healthcare human resources 2092
healthcare sustainability 17
High Commitment Work Practices 188, 322, 1230, 1240, 1242
Higher Education 37, 67, 216, 227, 247, 398, 423-424, 429, 441, 443, 455, 468, 506-507, 545, 547, 550, 554-556, 558-560, 562-563, 620, 671, 707, 732-733, 962, 965, 973, 976-978, 981, 986, 998, 1074, 1094-1095, 1100, 1106, 1114, 1119-1120, 1186, 1245, 1256, 1273, 1298, 1300, 1305, 1314-1315, 1320-1321, 1323, 1326-1328, 1330, 1332-1333, 1433, 1483, 1510, 1616, 1628, 1900
High-Performance Work Systems 165, 322, 331-332, 337-338, 564-566, 582-585, 934, 1035, 1244-

1245, 1484, 1488, 1618

Hiring Cycle 867, 873, 876, 878, 880-881, 886, 1916

Hofstede dimensions 576

Holistic Approach 28, 181, 601, 981, 1045, 1106, 1119, 1375, 1503, 1776, 1782, 1992, 2002

Holonic Enterprise Model (HEM) 1061, 1073

Hospital Management 1347, 1351, 2092

Hospitality 73-74, 76-77, 81-84, 86-92, 228, 351-353, 536, 800, 1036, 1125, 1148, 1150, 1315, 1333, 1376, 1385, 1455-1456, 1463, 1467, 1469-1470, 1486-1487, 1619, 1623, 1628-1629, 1635, 1639, 1706, 1827-1828, 1863, 1901, 1937, 1947-1948, 1953, 1957, 1960-1962, 2042, 2117, 2152

Host-country national 141

HPWS 564-570, 572-573, 578-581, 1124, 1183

HR Accounting 868, 890, 2053-2054, 2056-2058, 2060-2064

HR adaptation 141

HR Analytics 471, 477-479, 484-486, 488-489, 595, 599, 602, 609, 847-849, 851, 864-865, 914, 1576-1577, 1993-1994, 2013-2014, 2017-2018, 2020, 2022, 2024, 2026, 2028, 2031, 2035, 2037, 2045, 2050

HR Effectiveness 682, 1129, 1197

HR KPI 2022

HR Management 143, 204, 222, 244, 345, 469, 588-590, 592, 597-598, 605, 640, 693, 757, 1023, 1086, 1091, 1183, 1210, 1234, 1276, 1327, 1380, 1435, 1469, 1574, 1600, 1618, 1774-1775, 1782, 1796, 1935, 1943, 1946, 1995, 2011, 2026, 2035, 2203

HR Metrics 484, 486, 847-848, 853, 864-865, 890, 1576, 1990, 1993-1994, 1996-1997, 2001, 2006, 2011-2012, 2014-2015, 2017, 2035, 2040, 2044, 2202

HR Policies 5, 8, 136, 138, 145-146, 225, 441, 573, 589, 591, 597, 617, 713, 988-989, 1024-1025, 1030, 1034, 1122-1125, 1128, 1186, 1212, 1231, 1341, 1353, 1380, 1442, 1447, 1532, 1556, 1609-1610, 2094, 2116

HR Practices 10, 20, 73, 85, 95, 139, 141-147, 162-163, 165-166, 174-175, 179, 182, 212-213, 230, 244-245, 292, 304-307, 316, 325, 331, 338, 344, 407, 411, 416, 422-424, 427, 431-432, 434, 436-438, 440-442, 447, 477, 540, 566, 574, 579-581, 584, 589, 591, 593, 618, 637, 648, 682, 848, 865, 892, 902, 938, 941, 946, 948, 956, 987-990, 993-999, 1032, 1034, 1036, 1044, 1122-1125, 1128-1129, 1178, 1185, 1194, 1196-1197, 1205, 1210, 1212, 1229, 1231, 1235, 1238-1240, 1243, 1247, 1250, 1285, 1294, 1297-1300, 1308, 1310-1311, 1337-1338, 1343, 1346, 1350, 1353, 1434, 1459,

1469, 1473, 1526, 1531, 1539, 1541, 1599, 1610, 1612, 1614, 1616, 1619, 1708, 1710, 1712-1714, 1716-1717, 1719-1722, 1783, 1786, 1803, 1882, 1934-1935, 1937-1938, 1943, 1995, 2061, 2063, 2095, 2107, 2109, 2111, 2117, 2136

HR Scaffolding 162-163, 169, 174

HR Transformation 343, 357, 692, 735-737, 740-742, 751-752, 1990, 1995, 1997, 2026, 2029, 2037

HRADP 2053, 2057

HRCloud 2022

HRIS Applications 110, 1329, 1469-1470, 1473-1475, 1477, 1481-1483

HRM Global Practices 564

HRM Practices 10, 52, 146, 163-167, 173-177, 180, 182, 188, 193, 216, 222, 244, 293-294, 299-307, 316, 319, 323-324, 327, 334, 339, 341, 354, 356, 404, 406-407, 410, 420, 422-424, 427, 434, 441, 444, 448-450, 460, 464-466, 565-566, 568-569, 571-573, 683, 712-714, 718, 732-733, 892-893, 895-897, 899, 902-905, 907, 921-922, 924-928, 932-933, 943-945, 947, 956, 1022-1026, 1031, 1034, 1036, 1038, 1071, 1092, 1122, 1124-1126, 1128-1129, 1131, 1185-1187, 1190, 1194, 1196-1197, 1206-1207, 1211, 1213-1216, 1218, 1222, 1226-1229, 1231-1232, 1234-1236, 1238, 1241-1245, 1251-1252, 1256, 1263, 1268-1270, 1284-1286, 1290, 1299, 1311-1312, 1338, 1341, 1343, 1350, 1379-1380, 1429, 1432, 1525, 1529-1530, 1532, 1537, 1541, 1549-1550, 1555, 1559-1560, 1562, 1568, 1570, 1605, 1607, 1609-1610, 1612, 1721-1723, 1863, 1871-1882, 1891, 1948, 1961, 1964-1965, 1972-1974, 1976, 1978-1979, 1983-1984, 2020, 2040, 2044, 2117, 2119, 2125-2126, 2134, 2221

HRM Project 751, 940, 1990

HRM Roles 180, 1345, 1494, 2096

HRMP configurations 304, 320-321, 323

Human Capital 6, 8, 11, 17-22, 31, 74, 92, 113, 124, 134, 157, 164-166, 178, 295, 306, 326, 334-335, 362, 380, 382, 401, 422, 437, 467, 470-472, 485, 489, 540, 585, 609, 617, 619-635, 656, 694, 709, 729, 741, 757, 783, 785, 793, 851, 864-865, 868, 893, 895-896, 898, 905, 907, 921-929, 931-937, 939-940, 943-945, 959-960, 986, 1018, 1022, 1035, 1059, 1075, 1077-1079, 1084, 1088-1092, 1158-1161, 1163-1165, 1167, 1170, 1172-1175, 1194, 1196, 1200, 1212-1213, 1231, 1233, 1246-1247, 1252, 1271-1272, 1274, 1276, 1279, 1281-1282, 1289, 1291, 1294, 1312, 1314-1315, 1338, 1380, 1462, 1465, 1496, 1532, 1569, 1573, 1599, 1605, 1610, 1615, 1625, 1628, 1637-1643, 1649, 1678,

1684, 1710, 1725, 1742, 1783-1786, 1788-1789,
1795, 1798-1800, 1803, 1807, 1809, 1816, 1821,
1851-1852, 1886, 1891, 1898, 1928, 1930-1933,
1938-1939, 1941, 1945, 1948, 1961, 1992, 2016,
2030, 2040-2041, 2044, 2047-2048, 2052, 2054,
2056, 2068-2071, 2075-2080, 2082-2090, 2095-
2096, 2098, 2100, 2106, 2136, 2206, 2213, 2224
Human Capital Development 17, 20, 22, 898, 907,
1158, 1161, 1167, 1174, 1615, 1639, 1784, 1803
Human Capital Performance 1161, 1314, 1783-1785
Human Capital Resources 925-926, 1158, 1164, 1174,
1605, 2069
Human Resource (HR) Strategy 6, 1622
Human Resource Analytics 471, 477-479, 482, 609,
2014, 2038, 2044
Human Resource Development (HRD) 545-546, 563,
638, 1683
Human Resource Function 94, 278, 292, 350, 383, 403-
404, 608, 694, 868, 1077-1078, 1314, 1852, 2015
Human Resource Information System Success 491,
493, 501
Human Resource Information Systems (HRMS) 93-94,
110-113, 182, 226, 477, 491-493, 498, 500-501,
505-511, 917, 1094-1095, 1105-1106, 1119-1120,
1132-1134, 1145-1148, 1329, 1331-1333, 1468,
1484, 1486-1487, 2014, 2038, 2040, 2042, 2044,
2050-2051
Human Resource Management (HRM) 1-22, 33-35,
51-52, 60, 66-69, 71, 73, 77, 85-86, 88-89,
91-94, 111-115, 125-126, 129-130, 134-139,
141-143, 159-161, 177-180, 182-183, 192-198,
205, 215-217, 220, 222, 227-231, 233-234,
236-237, 242, 244-249, 276-277, 282, 291-295,
297-298, 300-303, 323-338, 340-342, 344, 348-
351, 354-357, 367-373, 375, 398, 401, 403-408,
414, 417-421, 436, 442-444, 448-449, 467-469,
471, 483-484, 487, 490, 492, 506-511, 513-514,
516-518, 520, 523-524, 526, 528, 541, 564-565,
570, 581-586, 588, 600-609, 611, 614-618, 655,
657-658, 661, 666, 670, 674-675, 680-684,
693-694, 708, 711, 727-729, 732, 737, 753-758,
783, 792-793, 799-800, 803, 810, 818-819, 845,
847, 851, 864-865, 867, 869, 892-893, 904-907,
909-910, 912, 921-922, 934-940, 943, 946,
956-961, 968, 983, 986, 995-1000, 1021-1024,
1034-1039, 1049, 1061, 1067-1072, 1074-1078,
1084-1085, 1087, 1089-1092, 1095, 1097-1100,
1116-1118, 1120, 1123, 1128-1131, 1134-1135,
1145-1148, 1166-1167, 1174, 1184, 1189,
1191, 1193-1196, 1200, 1204-1205, 1207-1210,
1212, 1214, 1227-1230, 1232-1233, 1243-1252,

1254, 1256, 1270-1272, 1274-1280, 1284, 1286,
1289-1290, 1293-1297, 1311-1313, 1331, 1333,
1340, 1343-1346, 1348, 1352-1357, 1359, 1371-
1375, 1378-1382, 1384-1389, 1393-1394, 1396,
1412-1419, 1421, 1424-1435, 1444, 1452-1453,
1455, 1457, 1459, 1462-1464, 1466-1467, 1471,
1484-1489, 1491, 1494, 1496, 1531, 1542-1547,
1549-1550, 1552, 1555, 1571-1572, 1575, 1578,
1594-1599, 1601-1607, 1609-1610, 1612-1613,
1616, 1618-1622, 1637, 1641, 1655, 1660, 1663,
1666, 1668, 1677, 1679-1680, 1683-1684, 1686,
1689-1692, 1696, 1700, 1703-1706, 1708-1709,
1720-1726, 1737, 1741-1742, 1757-1758, 1780,
1782-1785, 1798, 1802, 1804-1805, 1818-1819,
1821, 1823, 1839-1840, 1843, 1845, 1847, 1852,
1861-1863, 1865-1866, 1868, 1870, 1881-1886,
1889-1890, 1892, 1894, 1897-1900, 1902-1903,
1906, 1908-1909, 1923-1925, 1928-1934, 1938,
1940-1943, 1945-1948, 1955, 1957, 1960-1963,
1972, 1983-1984, 1986-1989, 2014-2020, 2023,
2038-2043, 2045-2046, 2048-2049, 2051-2052,
2055, 2063-2065, 2075-2076, 2080, 2082, 2084-
2085, 2089, 2092, 2094-2095, 2098, 2101-2106,
2114-2120, 2124, 2134-2140, 2144, 2153-2154,
2184, 2197-2202, 2205, 2220-2224
Human Resource Management Practices 3, 10, 19,
33-34, 66-67, 77, 139, 159, 178, 192-193, 229,
292, 300, 323, 326, 329-331, 333, 335, 338, 355,
367, 373, 417-418, 421, 442-443, 449, 469, 483,
584, 755, 867, 905-906, 909, 935, 957-958, 986,
995, 997-998, 1000, 1021-1022, 1024, 1037-1038,
1071, 1076, 1128, 1147, 1189, 1195, 1204-1205,
1207-1209, 1230, 1245, 1247, 1249-1250, 1252,
1254, 1270, 1274-1276, 1278-1279, 1284, 1286,
1289, 1293, 1295-1296, 1311, 1333, 1357, 1372,
1379, 1381, 1385, 1412-1419, 1421, 1424-1427,
1429, 1431-1434, 1444, 1452, 1484, 1487, 1595-
1598, 1613, 1618-1619, 1722, 1724-1725, 1784,
1861, 1882, 1885-1886, 1890, 1892, 1897-1898,
1928, 1932-1933, 1938, 1940, 1948, 1960, 1987-
1989, 2043, 2064, 2076, 2080, 2085, 2101, 2106,
2120, 2137, 2220
Human Resource Management Reforms 233, 249
Human Resource Practices 78, 141-142, 230, 247,
277, 291-296, 300, 325-327, 330-331, 334, 336,
366, 368, 407, 422, 588, 591, 605, 608, 654,
892, 896, 958, 998, 1023-1025, 1033-1035,
1037, 1039, 1070, 1128, 1130, 1182, 1196, 1206,
1209, 1212, 1229, 1235, 1238, 1245, 1247-1248,
1276, 1285, 1290, 1344, 1371, 1428, 1432-1434,
1594-1595, 1707, 1721, 1723-1724, 1756, 1783,

1868, 1928-1931, 1933, 1935, 1938-1941, 1985, 1989, 2060, 2105

Human Resources 1-2, 4-6, 9-11, 13, 15-20, 22, 25-31, 35-36, 51-52, 90, 94, 110-111, 114-116, 120, 122-124, 130, 134, 136-137, 139, 148, 177-189, 191-198, 200-205, 209, 211-220, 222, 224-225, 227, 229-230, 251, 254-255, 277-278, 280, 284, 286-287, 291, 293, 296, 301-305, 309, 317, 319, 322, 327-328, 332, 337-339, 348, 350, 354, 357-374, 393, 396, 401-402, 404-406, 417-418, 420, 422, 442-443, 477, 485, 489, 492, 505-506, 509-510, 513-517, 520, 522-524, 526, 538-540, 543, 560-563, 566-567, 571-574, 582, 585, 589, 598-599, 601, 603-607, 609, 616, 618-619, 621, 623, 626, 628, 630-632, 635-639, 647-648, 654-655, 657-662, 665-666, 668, 672, 674, 679-684, 693, 695, 697-700, 702-703, 705, 707, 709, 711, 724, 727, 730-732, 736-737, 754-758, 760-763, 765, 768, 772, 775-779, 785, 793, 798-799, 814, 816, 819, 848, 863-864, 866-868, 872-873, 877, 890, 899, 905-907, 909, 911-915, 918-924, 926, 931-932, 934-935, 939-944, 946, 958-960, 962-965, 967-970, 981, 985-987, 989, 992, 998-1002, 1015, 1022, 1025, 1032, 1034, 1036, 1038, 1040-1049, 1052-1056, 1058-1060, 1062-1068, 1070-1072, 1074-1077, 1079, 1081-1082, 1085-1097, 1099-1100, 1106, 1114-1115, 1129-1131, 1134-1136, 1142, 1146, 1170, 1172, 1174, 1189-1190, 1193-1194, 1201, 1205, 1207-1209, 1211-1212, 1229, 1231, 1233-1235, 1244, 1247-1250, 1252, 1270-1271, 1284, 1287, 1295, 1298, 1311-1315, 1317, 1329, 1331, 1333-1334, 1344-1348, 1350-1351, 1353-1354, 1356-1358, 1370-1373, 1375-1376, 1378-1382, 1384, 1387, 1389-1397, 1401-1406, 1410, 1412-1419, 1421-1422, 1424-1428, 1435, 1455-1457, 1468-1469, 1483-1484, 1487-1489, 1494-1496, 1508, 1524-1532, 1537, 1539, 1542, 1545-1551, 1557, 1561, 1568, 1571, 1574, 1594-1595, 1598-1599, 1602-1605, 1607, 1609-1611, 1613-1618, 1621-1622, 1623, 1625, 1633-1636, 1639-1640, 1642, 1644-1646, 1650, 1652-1657, 1659-1660, 1663, 1666-1667, 1672, 1677, 1679-1681, 1683, 1685, 1688-1694, 1696-1699, 1701-1706, 1710, 1720-1722, 1725-1726, 1762, 1771, 1780-1781, 1792, 1798, 1800-1802, 1804, 1806, 1809-1811, 1813-1814, 1816-1817, 1819, 1821, 1823-1825, 1827-1828, 1839-1840, 1847, 1849, 1852, 1860-1861, 1869, 1882, 1886, 1899, 1903-1904, 1906, 1908-1919, 1921, 1925-1926, 1928-1933, 1935-1937, 1939-1941, 1944-1951, 1953, 1955-1957, 1959-1963, 1965-1966, 1986,

1991-1992, 2016-2018, 2020, 2022-2023, 2026, 2029, 2035, 2039, 2041, 2043-2044, 2047, 2049-2051, 2053-2067, 2069, 2075-2076, 2087, 2092-2095, 2101, 2105, 2107, 2109, 2114, 2117-2118, 2120, 2122, 2130, 2139, 2160, 2164, 2178, 2203, 2205-2206, 2210, 2222, 2224

Human Resources Department 20, 94, 111, 182-183, 192, 213-214, 637, 648, 654-655, 680-681, 1077, 1095-1096, 1379, 1392, 1394, 1396, 1402, 1410, 1529, 1688, 1690-1692, 1814, 1912, 1935, 1939

Human Resources Management 6, 13, 19, 31, 35, 51-52, 115, 177, 180-182, 184-185, 187, 193-195, 197-198, 201-202, 204, 209, 211-212, 214-215, 222, 229-230, 301, 303-304, 327, 332, 337, 339, 350, 354, 358-361, 363-368, 372-373, 402, 405, 418, 506, 513-514, 516, 523-524, 582, 585, 599, 604, 606, 613, 637-638, 659-660, 697-698, 711, 736, 754-755, 793, 799, 866, 890, 906, 935, 939-941, 946, 959, 963, 965, 967-969, 985, 992, 998-999, 1049, 1052-1056, 1058-1060, 1062-1066, 1068, 1070, 1072, 1074-1077, 1085-1094, 1096-1097, 1190, 1207-1208, 1212, 1231, 1233, 1244, 1247, 1331, 1344, 1346, 1350, 1354, 1358, 1370, 1372-1373, 1375-1376, 1379-1382, 1384, 1391, 1394-1395, 1397, 1421, 1457, 1483, 1494, 1524-1526, 1528, 1545, 1547-1548, 1594-1595, 1602, 1605, 1611, 1616, 1654, 1666-1667, 1672, 1677, 1688-1594, 1696, 1698-1699, 1701, 1703-1704, 1706, 1721, 1725, 1762, 1780-1781, 1792, 1798, 1800-1802, 1811, 1816-1817, 1821, 1823, 1847, 1849, 1852, 1860, 1904, 1908-1909, 1911, 1917, 1925-1926, 1932, 1944-1949, 1957, 1959-1963, 1965-1966, 1991-1992, 2016-2017, 2041, 2043, 2092, 2101, 2114, 2117-2118, 2122

Human Resources Management Practices 193, 211, 303, 339, 354, 361, 1089, 1091, 1381, 1526, 1528, 1667, 1691, 1694, 1932, 2118

Human Rights 46-47, 1390-1393, 1397-1406, 1408-1410, 1417, 1435, 2141

I

IBM Corporation 921-922, 926, 932-933

ICT 111-112, 170-171, 222, 340, 342, 344, 346, 349, 351, 384, 509-510, 659, 713, 903, 927, 1283-1284, 1372, 1508, 1628, 1688, 1986, 2089

Impediments 28, 1045, 1986

Implementation 5-7, 11-13, 18-19, 24, 32, 55, 93-94, 98-99, 106-112, 114-115, 117, 119, 122-124, 152, 165-166, 172, 175, 181-182, 188, 193, 207, 222, 227-228, 233-239, 241-245, 249, 251, 255-256,

266, 269, 290, 298, 300, 302, 318, 337, 374-375, 389, 395, 417, 423, 456, 492, 496, 505-506, 508, 522-523, 540, 548, 564-572, 578, 581, 584, 591, 596, 614-615, 622, 642-645, 659-660, 662, 666, 671, 673, 681, 683, 689, 697, 700, 712-713, 716, 727-728, 730-731, 735, 737-738, 741, 743-753, 756, 760, 762-766, 768-772, 776-784, 787, 790, 800, 816, 819-821, 839, 843, 846, 869-873, 887-888, 928, 936, 939-940, 944, 965, 993, 996, 999, 1023, 1031, 1033, 1043, 1048, 1052, 1056, 1065, 1071, 1077-1078, 1095-1096, 1100-1101, 1105, 1118, 1131, 1134-1135, 1139-1141, 1146, 1168, 1170, 1172, 1194, 1196, 1199, 1212, 1230-1231, 1234, 1236, 1241-1242, 1248, 1256, 1280, 1284, 1294, 1311, 1314-1320, 1326, 1328-1329, 1331, 1333, 1337-1339, 1343, 1353, 1370, 1377, 1379, 1402, 1405, 1425, 1427, 1429, 1446, 1470, 1483, 1485, 1505, 1509-1511, 1514, 1548, 1597, 1608, 1610, 1613, 1641, 1649-1650, 1652-1656, 1660, 1663, 1673, 1682, 1687, 1703, 1708, 1721, 1724, 1776, 1788, 1792-1793, 1800, 1816, 1820, 1827, 1847, 1852, 1909, 1914, 1935, 1939, 1945, 1966, 1991-1995, 1997, 2001-2005, 2008, 2011, 2013, 2015-2016, 2022-2024, 2028-2029, 2031-2033, 2035-2036, 2038, 2041-2043, 2045-2046, 2051, 2061, 2063, 2078, 2093, 2107, 2110-2111, 2113, 2115, 2117, 2121-2122, 2128-2129, 2133, 2193, 2196, 2203

implicit coordination 303, 314-318, 321, 339

Importance-Performance Map Analysis 448-450, 456-457, 462, 465, 469, 1111, 1113, 1119, 1251-1252, 1257, 1259, 1266, 1269, 1276, 2044

Incentives 8, 26, 29, 118, 135, 145, 235, 238, 245, 249, 306, 344, 380, 398, 408-410, 412-413, 415-416, 463, 566, 593, 612, 620, 639, 674, 819-820, 899, 902, 991, 1047, 1062, 1067, 1070-1071, 1090, 1160, 1189, 1218, 1239, 1267, 1287-1288, 1299, 1341, 1347, 1525, 1537, 1707, 1712-1714, 1717-1720, 1782, 1802, 1878, 1896, 1904, 1933, 1972-1974, 1982-1984, 2082-2084, 2088-2089, 2096, 2111, 2125, 2143, 2207, 2219

Inclusive Organization 1577

industrial company 1800-1801, 1811, 1816, 1822

Industry 4.0 601, 604, 734, 911, 1392, 1394-1395, 1397, 1403-1406, 1411, 1894, 2121-2122, 2127-2130, 2133, 2135-2136

Industry Trends 2155

Information Quality 491, 493-500, 502-503, 509, 1002, 1115, 1314, 1316, 1318-1319, 1322-1323, 1325-1328, 1331-1332, 1335, 1472

Information Security 448-450, 453-457, 460-470, 600, 605, 695, 697-698, 700, 705-706, 709, 741, 757-758, 1251-1255, 1257, 1260, 1262-1263, 1265-1277, 2044, 2052

Information Security Training 448, 454, 456, 464-465, 1255, 1268-1269

Information System 93-94, 110-113, 182, 184, 187, 198, 226, 396, 467, 477, 491-493, 498, 500-501, 505-511, 668, 674, 917, 1017, 1063, 1094-1096, 1098, 1103, 1105-1106, 1114-1115, 1119-1120, 1132-1134, 1142, 1145-1148, 1272, 1315-1317, 1327, 1329-1333, 1468, 1483-1484, 1486-1488, 1509, 1812-1813, 2014, 2026, 2038, 2040, 2042, 2044, 2050-2051

Information Systems Security 469, 707, 1251-1253, 1260, 1263, 1265, 1275-1276

Information Systems Success 507, 509-510, 512, 727, 756, 1001, 1016, 1018, 1105, 1115, 1119, 1148, 1314, 1316, 1318, 1330, 1332-1333, 1483, 2046

Information Technology 21, 93, 111, 113, 126, 181-182, 184, 194-195, 197-198, 217-218, 220, 228, 276, 289, 336, 341-342, 344, 353, 371, 374-375, 378, 384, 388, 396-397, 401-402, 405, 448-449, 453, 466-467, 469-471, 491, 493, 507, 509-511, 543, 592, 596, 598, 600, 603, 605, 610, 657, 660-662, 707-708, 710-711, 728-729, 731, 737, 753-754, 756-757, 799-800, 911, 973, 1019, 1041-1044, 1047, 1051, 1072, 1095-1096, 1101, 1118, 1120, 1133, 1135-1136, 1187, 1217, 1252-1254, 1256, 1270-1272, 1274-1276, 1315, 1329, 1334, 1337, 1353-1355, 1373, 1395, 1462, 1465, 1469, 1483-1484, 1486, 1488-1489, 1491-1492, 1503, 1505-1506, 1618, 1620, 1682, 1688, 1691, 1693, 1703-1704, 1742, 1759, 1865, 1908, 2015-2017, 2019, 2023, 2029, 2038, 2040-2041, 2044-2046, 2048-2049, 2052, 2083, 2122

inheritance law 1578, 1580-1581, 1591

Innovative Behavior 353, 635, 982, 1236, 1238, 1240-1241, 1245, 1248-1249, 1727, 1729, 1733-1736, 1740-1741

innovative work behavior 1230, 1232-1244, 1246, 1248

instructional design 545-550, 552-563

instructional design model 545, 558-559, 563

instrumental theory 987, 992

Intangible Assets 166, 621-622, 624-626, 640, 868, 1079, 1625, 1642, 1787, 1796, 1799, 2056, 2071, 2075-2076, 2078-2079, 2083, 2085-2086, 2089, 2112

Internal Corporate Social Responsibility 2138, 2140, 2143, 2147, 2149-2152

Internationalization 141-142, 144, 148, 154, 893, 939, 1037, 1177-1180, 1186-1188, 1191, 1519, 1521,

1602, 1748, 1756, 1883

Internet Of Things 243, 246, 249, 523, 605, 611, 708-709, 1411, 1628, 2128

Internet Protocol Television 1497, 1522

Interpersonal Relationship 804, 1177, 1180, 1182, 1191, 1535, 1851

Intervention and Innovation Model for Organization Management (IIMOM) 1063, 1067, 1073

Intranet 181, 183, 189-190, 199, 206, 209-210, 412, 712, 1096, 1115, 1118, 1135, 1217, 1224, 1833, 1835, 2109

Intrapreneurship 485, 1067, 1070-1071, 1124, 1129-1130, 1892, 1895, 1898, 1904

IPCA 1623-1624, 1628, 1635

IPP 1623-1624, 1628

ISO 12207 251-252, 254, 273

IT Professionals 93, 448-449, 456, 465, 719, 1130, 1253, 1256, 1270, 1746, 2034

IT TV 1491-1492

J

j48 algorithm 251, 266, 269, 272-273

Japanese Management 846, 1868-1872, 1874, 1877-1880, 1882

Java 251-252, 254-256, 258, 266-267, 269-270, 273, 469, 928, 1275

JD.com 1560, 1564-1568, 1570, 1573-1574

Jframe 256, 273

Job Analysis 36, 38-44, 46, 48, 51-52, 114, 120, 123, 298, 819, 941, 1286, 1394, 1470, 1690, 1697-1698, 1701, 1706, 1823-1824, 2202, 2205, 2211, 2219

Job Design 15, 18, 40, 84-85, 300, 304, 317, 333, 988, 1000, 1196, 1237-1238, 1240, 1246, 1317, 1457, 1464, 1469, 1581, 1698, 1844, 1853, 1866, 1972, 1974, 1979-1980, 1983, 2193, 2195, 2200, 2214, 2224

Job Enlargement 389, 684, 2214, 2224

Job Performance 55, 60, 63-64, 66, 69, 71, 91, 287, 335, 354, 416, 425, 444, 449, 454-455, 469-470, 473, 488, 503, 591, 594-595, 709, 819, 1001-1002, 1004-1006, 1009-1010, 1013-1014, 1017-1019, 1161, 1247-1248, 1252, 1255, 1257, 1275, 1277, 1319, 1372, 1442, 1456, 1462-1463, 1466, 1484-1486, 1488, 1527, 1618, 1622, 1730, 1807, 1851, 1864, 1920, 1975, 2153, 2199-2200

Job Rotation 167, 285, 389, 396, 401, 568, 574, 928, 931-932, 947, 1240, 1933, 2109, 2214, 2224

Job Satisfaction 52, 55, 60-62, 66, 69, 71, 76-78, 84, 86-87, 89-90, 189, 302, 361, 409-410, 443-444, 455, 475, 484, 504, 509, 515, 582, 584, 589,

604, 615, 706, 756, 944, 1035-1036, 1038, 1080, 1124, 1161-1162, 1255, 1276, 1298, 1308, 1394, 1396, 1436-1437, 1440-1442, 1444, 1446, 1448, 1451-1454, 1456-1457, 1461, 1464-1465, 1470, 1472, 1474, 1487-1488, 1534, 1607, 1626, 1636, 1724-1725, 1730-1731, 1788, 1817, 1844, 1856, 1858, 1863, 1865-1866, 1892, 1894, 1899, 1981, 1992, 2017, 2045, 2062, 2096, 2141-2142, 2144, 2153, 2182, 2214

Job Sharing 398, 1291, 2217, 2220-2221, 2224

K

key partners 2079-2080

knowledge brokerage 1743-1748, 1750-1756, 1758-1759, 1761

Knowledge Management 20, 27-34, 67, 112, 140, 167, 207, 340-345, 349-357, 361, 368, 370, 373, 386, 397, 399, 401, 591, 600, 602, 620, 632, 634, 659, 675, 678, 684, 691, 708-709, 713, 715, 800, 922, 925, 936, 995, 1040-1042, 1044-1050, 1069-1070, 1092-1093, 1098, 1115, 1117, 1130, 1187-1188, 1212-1214, 1224, 1228-1229, 1271, 1284, 1293-1295, 1313, 1331-1332, 1356, 1358, 1371-1374, 1455, 1482-1483, 1616, 1621, 1744, 1746, 1756-1757, 1759-1760, 1801, 1818, 1820-1821, 1852, 1924, 1974, 1979, 1981-1983, 1985-1986, 1988-1989, 2016, 2050, 2085, 2095, 2097, 2116

knowledge repository 1352-1354, 1356-1359, 1361, 1363-1370

Knowledge Sharing 20, 315, 337, 343-346, 351, 353, 357, 363, 365-366, 368, 372, 1043-1044, 1130, 1213-1217, 1223-1229, 1333, 1567, 1609, 1669, 1965-1966, 1969-1986, 1989, 2036

Knowledge Society 633, 1616, 1780, 1800

Knowledge Transfer 20, 28, 153, 367, 389, 507, 746, 750, 895, 899, 901, 907, 1042, 1044-1045, 1181, 1194, 1211, 1213-1214, 1216-1218, 1221-1222, 1224-1225, 1227-1229, 1373, 1617, 1678, 1682, 1757, 1986

knowledge-driven growth 1601

Kwara State University 987

L

Labour Demand Forecasting 2210, 2224

Labour Supply Forecasting 2224

Learning Content 190, 545, 556-557, 559, 563

Learning Mindset 289

Learning Organizations 560, 637-638, 654, 1625, 1635, 1642

Learning Transfer 545, 557-559, 561, 563, 1329
Legal Framework 233, 663, 1400, 2034
Levels of Abstraction 1183, 1192
Line Manager 36, 48, 51, 179, 196, 210, 212, 216, 324, 526, 928, 930, 1241, 1823, 1914, 1984
Linkedin 479, 484, 537, 589, 591, 601, 605, 611-612, 615, 757, 791-794, 797, 799-800, 949, 952, 954, 1007, 1560, 1817, 1904, 1910, 1918, 1923, 2163
Literature Review 19, 33, 61, 94, 110, 115, 127, 236, 293, 341-342, 351, 353, 356, 358-359, 370, 372, 375, 393, 396, 401, 479, 509, 543-544, 548, 600, 602, 637, 678, 696, 706, 714, 752, 758, 765, 787-788, 790, 793, 804, 808, 903, 912, 921-923, 926, 1023, 1074-1076, 1125, 1134, 1207, 1213, 1241, 1245, 1249, 1308, 1354, 1386, 1428, 1436, 1451, 1460, 1470, 1474, 1483, 1619, 1625, 1628, 1640, 1646, 1667, 1678, 1729, 1738, 1745, 1813, 1820, 1844-1845, 1862, 1930, 1944, 1948, 1960-1961, 1988, 1995, 2020, 2022-2024, 2026, 2028-2029, 2036-2037, 2042, 2050-2051, 2054, 2063, 2066, 2094, 2106, 2108, 2117, 2141, 2150, 2164, 2203, 2220
literature survey 1865, 1944, 1949, 2141
Loop 259, 273, 311-312, 724

M

Machine Learning 220, 251-253, 255, 266, 268, 272-274, 611, 1564, 1570, 1628, 1798-1799
Macroergonomics 251-252, 274
Macroergonomy 273
Management Control 323, 634, 1447, 1627, 1636, 1640, 1642, 1968
management information system (MIS) 1098, 1120
management of older employees 1843-1844, 1847, 1849, 1859-1860
managerial ambidexterity 1743-1745, 1748, 1750-1756, 1761
Manpower Planning 129, 134, 137, 1347, 1828, 2205, 2208-2209, 2213, 2220
market participants 619-622, 624, 628-632
Material Requirement Planning (MRP) 1063, 1073
media business 2155-2156, 2160-2164, 2166-2168, 2171-2175, 2178
media business literacy 2155-2156, 2160, 2164, 2168, 2172, 2174-2175, 2178
Mentoring 3, 86, 161, 204, 207-208, 216, 555, 600, 803-813, 871, 928, 930-932, 947, 950, 952, 955, 957, 1162, 1170, 1174, 1239, 1284, 1405, 1559, 1730, 1732, 1861, 1892-1893, 1898-1899, 1901, 1904-1906, 2102

Microfinance Institutions 129-132, 134-135, 137-139
Middle East 139, 422-426, 436-437, 441-444, 571, 1074, 1091, 1297-1298, 1300, 1311-1312, 1834
Middle Managers 177, 779, 1018, 1021, 1352, 1655, 1707-1714, 1716-1725, 1745, 1759, 1895
Millennials 26, 481, 913-914, 918, 1535, 1623-1624, 1626-1627, 1629-1634, 1636-1639, 1642, 1778, 1885, 1900, 1902, 1905, 2108, 2179-2181, 2184-2185, 2187-2193, 2195, 2197-2198, 2200
Mobility of Employees 670, 678
Model Study 231, 513, 2149
Modernization 679, 913, 970, 1052, 1067, 1070, 1073, 1075, 1370, 1640
Modernization Model for Organizations Management (MMOM) 1073
Monitoring 24, 47, 173-174, 191, 201, 224, 384, 448-449, 454-457, 461-462, 464-467, 523, 602, 614, 616, 624, 719, 817, 825, 849, 867, 869, 888-890, 961, 989, 1074, 1251-1252, 1254, 1256, 1262, 1265-1270, 1272-1274, 1286, 1320, 1355, 1393, 1488, 1509, 1539, 1558, 1628, 1700, 2177, 2209
Multinational Companies 353, 444, 523, 565, 570, 905-906, 1189, 1228, 1312, 1379, 1733, 1819, 1881, 1883, 2023, 2108, 2121-2122
Multinational Corporation 161, 1177, 1192, 1386, 1803, 1882, 2032

N

needs for coordination 316, 321, 339
Needs for Explicit Coordination Mechanisms 339
Needs for Implicit Coordination Mechanisms 339
New Paradigm 798, 864, 1613, 1615, 1637, 1686, 1762, 1780, 2065

O

Object-Oriented Programming 273-274, 695-696
Older Employees 956, 1843-1861, 1865-1867, 2185, 2194
Onboarding 223, 297, 915-916, 920, 1577, 2193
Operational Efficiency 18, 235, 620, 687, 1609, 1947
organisational citizenship behaviour 1293, 1436, 1474
Organisational Efficiency 1436, 1469, 2119, 2218
Organisational Performance 229, 331, 373, 449, 959, 1022-1023, 1031, 1035-1036, 1166, 1252, 1276, 1708-1710, 1720, 1722-1724, 1726, 1848, 1994, 2101, 2106, 2112, 2120, 2202, 2208, 2216-2217, 2219
Organisational Sustainability 1278-1284, 1286-1292, 1294-1296, 2136

Organization Strategy 867

Organizational Agility (OA) 509, 732, 1601-1620, 1622, 1910

Organizational Alignment 340-344, 348-349, 1426

Organizational Capital 1213, 1528, 1625, 1643, 1675, 2083, 2088

Organizational change in healthcare 2092

Organizational Choices 303-304, 308-309, 312, 1579

Organizational Citizenship Behavior 60, 63-64, 66-67, 69-71, 196, 302, 361, 472, 475, 1091, 1248, 1250, 1449, 1453, 1457, 1460-1463, 1467, 1577, 1729, 2153

Organizational Commitment 3, 19-20, 55, 62-63, 66-72, 76, 78, 86, 211, 329, 334-335, 354, 356, 361, 443, 474-475, 484, 589, 709, 728, 899, 909, 1091, 1125, 1128, 1131, 1232, 1234-1235, 1239-1240, 1244, 1250, 1254, 1298-1299, 1312, 1351, 1412, 1438, 1444, 1446, 1448, 1453-1454, 1626, 1678, 1727-1737, 1740-1741, 1857-1858, 1866, 1889, 1899, 1902, 1905, 1914, 1992, 2136, 2141-2142, 2153-2154, 2184

Organizational Components 1052-1053, 1057, 1059-1060, 1064-1065, 1070-1071, 1651

Organizational Culture 8, 15, 18, 22, 26, 85, 150, 192, 223, 229, 281-283, 301, 338, 343-344, 348, 355, 418, 422-423, 437, 565, 569, 574, 579-582, 584, 604, 656, 682, 754, 944, 997-998, 1041-1043, 1048, 1050, 1053, 1056-1060, 1062, 1065-1066, 1068, 1070-1071, 1092, 1135-1136, 1171, 1188, 1213, 1297-1299, 1308-1312, 1358, 1379-1380, 1383, 1485, 1536, 1558, 1627, 1630, 1643, 1677, 1683, 1685, 1745, 1852, 1858, 1863, 1866, 1967, 1972, 1976-1977, 1984-1985, 1987, 1995, 2093-2094

Organizational Development 18, 152, 202, 234, 244, 819, 872-873, 1041, 1048, 1070, 1078, 1082, 1115, 1358, 1372, 1442, 1538, 1605, 1608, 1610, 1614-1616, 1622, 1649, 1699, 1801, 1818, 2095, 2221

Organizational Efficiency 110, 340-344, 346-350, 355, 483, 506, 714, 1013, 1147, 1436, 1486-1487, 1529, 1602, 1612, 1817

Organizational ethics 1412

Organizational Innovation 341, 344, 585, 641, 657, 1115, 1129, 1231-1232, 1235, 1352-1359, 1361, 1363-1372, 1728, 1739, 1977, 1986-1987, 1989, 2017, 2033, 2045

Organizational Learning 202, 214-215, 310-311, 324, 327, 335, 345, 361, 372, 580, 620, 1000, 1071, 1091, 1093, 1212-1213, 1249, 1464, 1487, 1537, 1603-1606, 1608, 1610, 1612-1614, 1620-1622, 1625, 1642, 1649, 1737, 1745, 1758, 1857, 1977,

1979-1980, 1985-1987, 2087

Organizational Performance 5, 9-11, 13, 16, 70, 126, 138, 162-165, 167, 172-177, 180, 189, 222, 247, 274, 305, 327, 330-331, 333-336, 338, 345, 347-348, 350, 354-356, 373, 386, 507, 510, 543, 564-566, 582, 584, 604, 851, 905, 935, 1035, 1069-1070, 1079-1082, 1091-1092, 1094-1095, 1115, 1123-1124, 1128, 1147, 1207, 1213, 1228, 1232, 1238, 1244-1245, 1250, 1254, 1256, 1270, 1274-1276, 1298, 1407, 1436-1437, 1443-1444, 1461, 1486, 1488, 1492, 1528, 1538, 1542, 1594-1595, 1601-1620, 1622, 1637, 1747, 1757, 1799, 1858, 1893, 1896, 1923, 1945, 1961, 1969, 1979, 1982, 1986, 1992-1993, 2055, 2064-2066, 2093-2094, 2220, 2222

Organizational Resilience 311, 1427, 1884, 1911

Organizational Variables 83, 307-310, 313, 319, 338-339, 1530

OTRS 1491, 1512, 1514

Overgas 1153, 1167-1173

P

People Analytics 477, 485, 490, 600, 602, 865, 1549, 1569, 1577, 1788, 2015, 2020, 2051

People Management 51, 92, 141, 159, 317, 334, 351, 368, 413, 415, 419-420, 484, 489, 570, 572, 585, 639, 683, 693, 717, 801, 908, 925, 989, 998, 1130, 1189, 1207, 1210, 1214, 1227, 1229, 1279, 1294, 1344, 1378-1379, 1387, 1412, 1527, 1598, 1628, 1643, 1671, 1783-1784, 1788, 1792, 1796, 1804, 1945, 2047, 2116

Perceived Ease Of Use 507, 752, 754, 1003, 1017, 1094-1095, 1101-1102, 1105-1107, 1111-1112, 1114, 1120, 1992, 2015, 2033, 2041

Perceived Usefulness 491, 493-495, 497-500, 503-505, 507, 512, 752, 754, 1003, 1020, 1094-1095, 1101-1102, 1105-1107, 1111-1112, 1114-1115, 1121, 1992, 2015, 2041

Performance Appraisal 2, 6, 85, 119, 124, 142-144, 202, 204, 210, 218, 288, 304, 306, 316, 318, 320, 362, 404, 426, 428, 440, 442-443, 514, 580, 613-614, 655, 733, 747-748, 819, 899, 929, 940, 944-947, 950-951, 953, 955, 957, 961, 1022, 1032, 1056, 1064, 1097, 1100, 1200, 1211, 1215, 1218, 1225-1226, 1234, 1251, 1285, 1349, 1354-1355, 1359, 1366, 1391, 1393-1395, 1444-1445, 1447-1448, 1450, 1456, 1458, 1470, 1529, 1538-1539, 1543, 1553, 1556, 1565-1566, 1581, 1712, 1876, 1879, 1895, 1929, 1972-1974, 1981-1984, 2104-2105

Performance Evaluation 3, 18, 188-189, 210, 280, 284-

285, 298, 566, 640, 650, 678, 784, 1091, 1125, 1170, 1194, 1196, 1217, 1240, 1256, 1355, 1382, 1494, 1539, 1559, 1632, 1656, 1690, 1700-1702, 1706, 1876, 1879, 2098

Performance Management 3, 6, 40, 70, 119, 122-123, 136, 156, 163-164, 185, 188-189, 198, 200, 204, 210, 213, 234, 237, 244, 248, 276-277, 280-281, 283-286, 290, 295-296, 384, 396, 398-399, 401, 426, 438, 440, 480, 487, 538, 595, 607-608, 611-612, 614, 616, 718-719, 732, 757, 783, 876, 916-917, 920, 925, 945, 1024-1025, 1035, 1079-1080, 1090-1091, 1098-1099, 1142, 1146, 1150, 1185, 1238-1239, 1284-1286, 1292, 1314, 1320-1321, 1331, 1340, 1355, 1379, 1382, 1429, 1456, 1473, 1484-1485, 1489, 1524, 1530-1531, 1538-1541, 1546, 1548, 1565, 1569, 1609, 1616, 1619, 1688, 1690, 1692-1693, 1700-1701, 1703, 1722, 1724, 1785, 1809, 1821, 1833, 1876, 1879, 1883, 1909-1910, 1982, 1984, 2018, 2030, 2040, 2042, 2046, 2098, 2192-2198, 2207, 2209, 2219

Performance Measurement 159, 190, 675, 1280, 1429, 1474, 1537-1540, 1544, 1680, 1707, 2020, 2035, 2042, 2050

Person-Group Fit 278-279, 286, 290, 1450

Person-Job Fit 290, 1450

Personnel Management 2, 4, 13, 94, 111, 125, 181, 198, 443, 455, 470, 510, 608, 640, 662, 680-682, 693, 730, 819, 901, 941, 958, 961, 968-969, 1019, 1093, 1095, 1100, 1147, 1256-1257, 1277, 1312, 1350, 1494-1495, 1686, 1909, 2044, 2222

Person-Organization Fit 732, 799, 1450, 1459, 1577, 1917, 1921, 1925, 2096, 2198

Philippine Development Plan 2017-2022 243-245, 249

Portal for Employees in the Public Sector 659, 667-668, 679

Practice-Based Training 1783

Predictive Analytics 369, 471-472, 482-483, 485, 537, 855, 864-866, 1007, 1014

process capability 867, 882

Process Improvement 20, 114, 123, 125, 526, 537-538, 540-541, 681, 869, 873, 877-879, 1044, 1212, 1605, 2011

Process Theories 162-164, 166

Production Process 117, 121-122, 516, 607, 619-620, 622-623, 760-765, 772, 775-779, 786, 969, 1066, 1159, 1391, 1395, 2053

productive activity 2068-2069, 2071, 2079-2080

productive organisations 2069, 2071, 2215

Productivity 7, 9, 18, 25, 33, 37, 70, 82, 94-95, 116, 118-120, 122-123, 134-135, 139, 154, 165-168, 174, 178, 187, 190, 192, 203, 213, 224, 247, 252,

255, 326, 330, 345, 353, 355-356, 363, 374-375, 382-383, 389-390, 394-395, 401, 407-409, 415, 424, 449, 455, 464, 472, 479, 487, 492, 494, 496, 504, 508, 514-515, 531, 537-538, 546, 563, 566, 583-584, 592-593, 595, 607, 609, 611-614, 618, 620, 623, 632, 642, 644, 672, 689, 725, 762, 765, 783, 818, 894, 899, 910, 940-942, 945, 958, 960, 965, 969, 981, 1004, 1018, 1022, 1032-1033, 1054-1055, 1060, 1062-1063, 1067, 1074, 1079-1081, 1094-1095, 1097, 1100-1101, 1123-1124, 1128-1129, 1140, 1146, 1159-1161, 1172, 1186, 1189, 1208, 1212, 1246-1247, 1252-1253, 1256, 1268, 1297, 1299, 1314-1315, 1317, 1326-1329, 1331, 1336, 1345, 1348, 1391, 1393-1394, 1436-1442, 1444, 1447, 1453, 1455-1456, 1471-1473, 1484, 1489, 1492, 1509, 1527-1528, 1536-1537, 1568-1569, 1596, 1603, 1605, 1611, 1655, 1667, 1680, 1698, 1710, 1719, 1721-1722, 1724, 1728, 1745, 1774, 1783, 1785, 1790, 1799, 1811, 1832, 1836-1838, 1841, 1847-1849, 1853, 1855, 1859-1861, 1865, 1887, 1896, 1911, 1930, 1946, 1949, 1952, 1979, 2042-2043, 2055, 2058-2059, 2064, 2070, 2073, 2075, 2081, 2083, 2088, 2095, 2103, 2107, 2109, 2112, 2115, 2123, 2126, 2129, 2134, 2143, 2180-2181, 2184, 2196, 2202, 2208, 2210, 2214-2215, 2217-2218, 2221, 2223

Professional Practices 588, 864, 2134

Project Management 112, 114, 123, 125-128, 288-289, 328, 398, 402, 529, 537-538, 541-544, 640, 689, 693, 736, 742, 752-753, 814-818, 820-823, 825-826, 843-846, 887, 889, 931, 1050, 1277, 1373, 1678, 1681, 1683-1684, 1744, 1756-1757, 2023, 2028, 2032, 2038, 2041-2043, 2046, 2049, 2051

Psychological Contract 55-72, 167, 397, 425-426, 484, 1240, 1250, 1255, 1271, 1452, 1455, 1527, 1638, 1831, 1886, 1890, 1899, 1905, 1982

Public Service Delivery Audit 235, 237, 250

public television 1522

python 267, 269-270, 274

Q

Qualitative Approach 570, 648, 744, 922, 926, 1991, 2204

qualitative forecasting 2202

Qualitative Research 177, 444, 581-582, 585, 744, 755, 808, 926, 937, 997, 1132, 1137, 1145, 1147, 1628, 1639, 1739, 1928, 1997, 2016, 2025, 2137

quality of working life 1784-1790, 1792, 1795, 1797-1798, 1849, 1861

Quantifiability 680, 1776

quantitative forecasting methods 2202

R

RECOGNITION AND REWARD 682
Recruitment And Selection 2, 6, 39, 49, 52, 129, 142-
144, 162, 204, 304, 306, 316, 406, 423, 425, 427,
431, 438-439, 441, 449, 574, 657, 754, 792, 798,
801, 940, 944, 946-949, 952, 968, 1022, 1097,
1125, 1213, 1215, 1217-1218, 1222, 1225-1227,
1251-1252, 1276, 1285-1286, 1303, 1333, 1340,
1470, 1529, 1531, 1560, 1581, 1676, 1688, 1692,
1706, 1724, 1814, 1828, 1833-1834, 1852, 1910,
1913, 1915, 1918, 1920, 1923-1925, 1929, 1931,
1933, 1972, 1978, 1983, 2042, 2105, 2202, 2205,
2209, 2219, 2222-2223
Regression Techniques 847, 855
Relational Psychological Contract 57, 72
repatriates 155-158, 161
replacement table 1193, 1195, 1200-1201, 1205
residual rights 2069, 2080
Resource-Based View 67, 179, 325-326, 338, 358-363,
366-373, 925, 1161, 1454, 1610, 1886, 1890,
1897, 1930-1933, 1943, 1961, 1963, 2069, 2083,
2086-2087, 2089
Responsibility And Accountability 235, 455, 457,
1251, 1256, 1263
Reward And Compensation 413, 415-416, 990, 1000,
1211, 1223, 1226
Role of Families 1928
Ruby 267, 270, 274, 1004, 1019

S

Scarce Resources 22, 375, 818, 1994, 2165
Scientific HR 1549, 1553, 1577
Second-Generation Rights 1398-1399, 1411
security breach 696, 700
Selection And Recruitment 52, 218, 227, 598-599,
602, 1096, 1211, 1217, 1223, 1690, 1914, 1938
self-esteem factor 1784
Service Behavior 1021-1022, 1038, 1964
Service Dominant Logic 803-804, 808, 810, 812
Service Quality 74, 81-82, 491, 493-495, 497-500,
502-505, 509-510, 567, 1002, 1025, 1036, 1038,
1105, 1115, 1129, 1289, 1291, 1316, 1318-1320,
1322, 1326, 1334-1335, 1347, 1406, 1446, 1464,
1503, 1525, 1607, 1639, 1948, 1960, 1964, 1995
Service System 233-234, 237, 803, 808-810, 812
Sexual Orientation and Gender Identity and Expression
Equality Bill 244, 250

Shortage 131, 137, 397, 659, 666, 901, 1004, 1074-
1075, 1344, 1439, 1802, 1813, 1816, 1859, 1869,
1874, 1879, 2197, 2203, 2206, 2208, 2213-2215,
2219
Skill Development 318, 595, 684, 892-893, 897, 899,
901, 979, 1470, 1889, 1894, 2110, 2204
Slovakia 944, 959, 1762, 1800-1801, 1811, 1813-1820
Small And Medium Enterprises (SME) 326, 329,
333, 744, 948, 1021, 1023-1024, 1026, 1032,
1036-1038, 1052, 1055, 1067, 1072-1073, 1091,
1187-1188, 1201, 1208, 1315, 1331, 1412, 1414,
1417, 1615, 1653-1654, 1711, 1760, 1805, 1837,
1924, 1992, 2051, 2064, 2223
social enterprise 1524-1525, 1527-1530, 1532-1538,
1541-1543, 1545-1548
Social Media 171, 184, 200-201, 384, 424, 472, 477,
537, 543, 591-592, 598-603, 605, 611, 616, 731,
791-794, 797-801, 947, 949, 952, 954, 958, 1091,
1130, 1373, 1572, 1654, 1692, 1817, 1889, 1896,
1910, 1915, 1917-1922, 1924-1925, 2155, 2162-
2163, 2169, 2173-2174, 2176-2177
Social Network 479, 489, 555, 591, 598, 602, 604, 611-
612, 621, 794, 800, 990, 1019, 1297-1298, 1300,
1305-1307, 1312-1313, 1563, 1743-1744, 1747,
1749-1752, 1754-1756, 1761, 1922-1924, 1926
Social System 334, 1762, 1771, 1773-1774, 1776, 1782
soft HRP 2202
SOM neural network 513-514, 516-520, 522-524
Spiral Management 1762, 1764, 1766-1777, 1779-1782
Staffing 2, 19, 22, 141-142, 148, 159-160, 224, 353,
383, 405, 444, 674, 718, 818-819, 893, 899-900,
904, 906, 909, 939, 941, 946, 1004, 1164, 1182,
1215, 1225, 1345, 1468, 1526-1527, 1557, 1814,
1829, 1841, 1876, 1879, 1925, 1965, 1972-1974,
1979, 1983, 2094, 2206-2207, 2210-2212, 2222
Stakeholders 17-19, 21-22, 24-25, 29-30, 114-115,
120, 185, 204-205, 210-211, 222, 243-245, 280-
281, 284, 291-292, 307, 342-344, 348, 414-415,
417, 522-523, 546, 588, 592, 622, 631, 636, 645,
655, 667, 686, 697, 747, 752, 818, 825, 845, 871,
880, 987-988, 1033, 1036, 1046, 1049, 1172,
1185, 1278, 1283-1284, 1289, 1291-1292, 1341,
1343-1344, 1378, 1383, 1426, 1437, 1444, 1500,
1507, 1527, 1540, 1606, 1619, 1643, 1649, 1655,
1675, 1694-1695, 1807, 1911-1912, 1945, 1976,
1994-1995, 2007, 2034, 2056, 2058, 2092, 2095,
2097, 2100, 2113, 2132, 2139, 2141-2142, 2145,
2150, 2155, 2160, 2193
standars 251
Statistics 37, 191, 239, 381, 383-384, 390, 393, 399, 427,
431, 458, 477, 481, 520-522, 597, 604-605, 682,

686, 719, 722, 847-849, 851, 853, 973-976, 978, 983, 995-996, 1009, 1011, 1014, 1023, 1054, 1069, 1117, 1222, 1261, 1308, 1323, 1334, 1417, 1419, 1421, 1475, 1485, 1510, 1523, 1575, 1647, 1712, 1831, 1932, 1995, 2020, 2129, 2137, 2140, 2197

Strategic Alignment 351, 353, 615, 746, 848, 1192, 1330, 1427, 1609

Strategic Human Resource Management (SHRM) 1, 3-16, 111, 138, 180, 194, 196, 222, 228, 294, 297, 302, 326, 330, 332-333, 336, 367-368, 370, 372, 506, 564, 585, 658, 756, 934-938, 1021-1022, 1024, 1035, 1037, 1039, 1067, 1072, 1075-1078, 1089, 1092, 1130, 1232-1233, 1244, 1246-1249, 1275, 1284, 1372, 1374, 1379-1380, 1387, 1543, 1550, 1597, 1599, 1601-1607, 1613, 1618-1622, 1655, 1663, 1704, 1723, 1737, 1821, 1845, 1847, 1852, 1861-1863, 1865, 1897-1898, 1903, 1948, 1961, 1963, 2017, 2045, 2063-2064, 2082, 2222

Strategic Management 4-7, 14-15, 114-115, 124, 152, 160, 177-178, 193, 215, 304, 323, 326, 329-330, 335, 337-338, 348, 352, 357-360, 367, 369-372, 419, 539, 565, 585, 616, 635, 640, 662, 681, 709, 800, 925-926, 936-937, 957, 982, 1024, 1041, 1056, 1060, 1066-1069, 1071, 1074, 1077, 1173, 1189-1190, 1210, 1234, 1249, 1347, 1376, 1379, 1388, 1472, 1494, 1610-1611, 1619, 1637-1638, 1644-1646, 1649-1650, 1652-1653, 1656-1657, 1660, 1708-1709, 1719-1721, 1723, 1726, 1757, 1781, 1804, 1853, 1882, 1923, 1931, 1961, 1963, 1986, 1988, 2011, 2031, 2075, 2081, 2083-2087, 2089, 2099, 2153, 2177

Strategic Planning 94, 123, 328, 538, 685, 713, 718, 733, 780, 944, 985, 988, 1056, 1074, 1077, 1134, 1231, 1234, 1252, 1506, 1539, 1607, 1610, 1614, 1650, 1652-1653, 1721, 1725, 1828, 2100-2102, 2209, 2221

Strategic Roles 181, 1328, 1707-1714, 1716-1720, 1724

streaming 1492, 1498, 1500, 1502-1503, 1519, 1522

Structural Equation Modelling (SEM) 456, 467, 508, 760, 762, 767, 774, 780-783, 1009, 1015, 1017, 1037, 1105, 1115-1118, 1120-1121, 1129, 1219, 1273, 1485, 1714, 1721, 1724-1725, 1734, 1739, 1757

Succession 217, 225-226, 295, 306, 318, 331, 346, 368, 401, 568, 725, 727, 739, 748, 863, 947, 1142, 1148, 1163, 1174, 1193-1210, 1428, 1470, 1539, 1578-1583, 1589-1593, 1595-1598, 1600, 1805, 1818, 1831, 1930, 2009, 2031, 2092, 2095, 2097-2098, 2100-2101, 2129, 2185, 2205, 2212-2213

Succession Planning 225-226, 295, 306, 318, 401, 568, 727, 739, 748, 1142, 1174, 1193-1205, 1208,

1210, 1539, 1582, 1818, 1831, 2009, 2031, 2100-2101, 2212-2213

Supply Chain 124, 289, 324, 358-360, 362-373, 539, 768, 781-783, 958, 962-967, 971, 980-982, 984, 986, 1071, 1073, 1178, 1180, 1295, 1386, 1401, 1546, 1618, 1621, 1680, 1873, 1878, 2015, 2113, 2118

Supply Chain Management 124, 324, 358-360, 362-373, 539, 783, 962, 965-967, 971, 980-982, 984, 986, 1295, 1386, 2118

Survey Research 730, 1733

Sustainability In Healthcare 17, 1388, 2118

Sustainability management 1065

Sustainable Business Solutions 32, 418, 987-988, 990-994, 996, 1000, 1294, 2117

Sustainable Competitive Advantage 284, 286, 304-305, 341, 358-367, 370, 373, 404, 621, 638, 640, 707, 936, 940, 943, 966, 1022, 1122-1124, 1129, 1165, 1280, 1283, 1293, 1610, 1612, 1614, 1649, 1660, 1818, 1891, 1930, 2085, 2117, 2206, 2219

Sustainable Development 242, 244, 246, 295, 407, 414, 508, 717, 903, 967-968, 982, 985, 989, 995, 997, 999, 1080, 1130, 1169-1170, 1173, 1279-1281, 1286, 1289-1292, 1294-1295, 1337-1338, 1340-1341, 1343, 1375, 1377-1379, 1383-1385, 1389-1390, 1399-1400, 1403, 1406, 1744, 1754, 1780, 1948, 1961, 2066, 2105-2106, 2115, 2117-2118, 2132-2133, 2141-2142

System Quality 491, 493-500, 502-505, 509, 1002, 1106, 1114-1115, 1316, 1318-1320, 1322-1323, 1325-1326, 1332, 1335, 1472-1473

System Use 491, 493-505, 1002, 1006, 1016, 1019, 1105, 1316

T

Talent Acquisition 165, 225, 276-277, 290, 295-296, 299-300, 479, 615-616, 810, 873, 1525, 1542, 1569, 1802, 1817-1818

Talent Management 20, 52, 190, 202, 204, 226, 287, 341-344, 346-347, 349-354, 356, 366, 383, 418, 483, 614, 727, 738-740, 745, 748, 756, 800, 851, 868, 903, 917, 920, 925, 934-935, 937, 945, 960, 968, 1037, 1044, 1053, 1068, 1075, 1078, 1080-1081, 1084, 1089-1093, 1163, 1182, 1191, 1395, 1557, 1627, 1638, 1673, 1679-1680, 1693, 1721-1722, 1800-1806, 1808-1822, 1852, 1885, 1913, 1991, 2004, 2009, 2011-2012, 2019, 2026, 2030-2031, 2036, 2051

Team 9, 13, 26, 36, 40, 51, 108-109, 116-123, 130, 158, 168, 170, 172, 188, 193, 209, 223, 227, 252,

254-255, 276-287, 295-297, 327, 332-333, 368, 371, 394, 396, 399, 407, 475, 479-481, 524, 528-529, 538, 546, 576-577, 580, 583-584, 590, 595, 607-610, 612-615, 620, 636, 638, 642-644, 654, 688, 705, 713, 722, 726, 746, 749-752, 793, 814-818, 820-826, 831-837, 839, 843-846, 869-871, 873, 877-878, 880, 882, 885, 887-889, 896, 899, 947, 1035, 1045, 1049, 1054, 1077-1078, 1144, 1182-1183, 1215-1217, 1225, 1228, 1240, 1310, 1339-1343, 1417-1418, 1429, 1439, 1450, 1473, 1511, 1532-1533, 1539, 1550, 1555, 1557-1560, 1564-1565, 1571, 1574, 1595, 1626, 1630, 1632-1633, 1636, 1651, 1660, 1669-1672, 1678, 1680, 1686, 1694, 1696, 1707, 1712-1714, 1717-1720, 1722, 1724, 1728, 1732, 1744, 1756-1757, 1784, 1788-1790, 1792, 1795-1797, 1809, 1812, 1818, 1823, 1830, 1854, 1858, 1874, 1895, 1918, 1968, 1977, 1981-1984, 1987-1988, 2070, 2099, 2139, 2208-2209, 2213

Teamwork 3, 60, 118, 124, 306, 394, 418, 475, 488, 538, 573, 636-637, 640-641, 648, 654, 752, 805, 810, 817-818, 826, 947, 950, 952, 955, 957, 997, 1034, 1161, 1170, 1172, 1218, 1227, 1528, 1559, 1565, 1626, 1669, 1671, 1683, 1698, 1868, 1872, 1874, 1877, 1889, 1972-1974, 1976, 1980-1981, 1983-1984, 2093-2094, 2110, 2117, 2159

Technological Advancements 24, 246, 588, 1122, 1124, 1317, 1896, 2039

Technology Acceptance Model (TAM) 512, 1094-1095, 1101, 1114, 1121, 2033

Technology Adoption 31, 601, 780, 1095, 1104-1106, 1120, 1317, 1618, 1922, 1925, 1992, 2022, 2084

technology manufacturing firms 1743-1744, 1748, 1754-1755

theories of justice 1448

Theory Of Constraints 114-116, 124-127, 526-527, 529-531, 540-543, 690-691, 694

Third Country National 149, 900

Third-Generation Rights 1392, 1399-1400, 1411

Tour operators 73, 82, 84

Tourism Businesses 1390, 1624, 1645

Training And Development 2, 6, 18, 20, 26, 40-41, 134-136, 181, 185, 189-190, 200, 202, 204, 217, 222, 228, 297, 304, 306, 316, 322, 341, 344, 347, 349, 361, 364, 369, 404, 422-423, 425-426, 428, 438, 440-441, 447, 449, 454, 464, 476, 546, 550-551, 562, 566, 574, 580, 608, 610, 614-617, 670, 683, 718, 803, 808, 820, 870, 901-903, 906, 939-941, 944-948, 950, 952-953, 961, 987-990, 994, 1000, 1022, 1044, 1097, 1123-1125, 1141-1142, 1150-1151, 1161, 1170, 1211, 1213, 1215,

1217-1218, 1222-1223, 1225-1227, 1240, 1251-1252, 1254, 1268, 1270, 1276, 1279, 1285-1287, 1289, 1291-1292, 1341, 1355, 1379, 1382, 1444, 1452-1453, 1456, 1470-1471, 1529-1530, 1539, 1562, 1564, 1581, 1621, 1629, 1649, 1656, 1681, 1683, 1685-1686, 1688, 1698, 1706, 1712, 1831, 1834, 1841, 1891, 1899, 1929, 1931, 1933, 1936, 1938-1939, 1942, 2057, 2096, 2099, 2103-2105, 2108-2110, 2115, 2192, 2202, 2212, 2215-2216, 2219, 2221-2222

Transactional Psychological Contract 57, 63, 72

transfer of practice 1868, 1873, 1879

Transformational Human Resource Management 340-342, 1692

Transformational Leadership 67, 126, 341, 356, 475-476, 484-485, 490, 542, 583, 690, 1069, 1092, 1224, 1382, 1483, 1485, 1619-1620, 1727-1728, 1730-1731, 1733, 1735-1741, 1977, 1985-1986

Turnover 8, 19, 22, 26, 31, 55, 60, 62, 65-67, 70, 72, 76-77, 84, 86, 89-91, 117, 134-135, 161, 167, 178, 186, 243, 283, 321, 330, 335, 337, 343, 347, 355, 390, 403-409, 472, 477, 484, 509, 511, 530, 566-568, 574, 583-584, 589, 594, 599, 609, 616-618, 626, 682, 756, 848-849, 851, 863, 868, 876, 921, 969, 997, 1015, 1035, 1075, 1093, 1161-1162, 1177, 1187, 1189, 1200, 1208, 1245-1247, 1344, 1406, 1442, 1444, 1455, 1469-1470, 1472, 1474, 1484, 1487-1488, 1530, 1534, 1596, 1605, 1611, 1626, 1666, 1697, 1719, 1721, 1724, 1728, 1730, 1786-1788, 1830-1831, 1837-1839, 1858, 1860, 1863, 1866, 1884, 1887-1889, 1892, 1897-1898, 1900, 1902, 1904, 1907, 1912-1913, 1992-1993, 2017, 2035, 2042-2043, 2045, 2071, 2084, 2095, 2108, 2123, 2140-2141, 2143, 2145, 2149, 2181, 2184-2185, 2195, 2199-2200, 2203, 2212, 2217

Turnover Intentions 55, 60, 65-66, 72, 76-77, 91, 161, 248, 355, 599, 1035, 1730, 1858, 1863, 1866, 2181, 2184, 2195

U

Universalistic 1, 10-11, 13-16, 306, 332, 1035, 1232-1233, 1244, 1246, 1250, 1543, 1737

Universalistic Perspective 10-11, 16, 1233, 1250, 1737

V

Valuation of Employees 2053

VOC 867, 876-877

vocational high schools 962, 965, 971, 973, 986

Vocational Schools of Higher Education 962, 976-

978, 986

Vocational Training 380, 667-668, 671-672, 679, 811, 898, 901, 970-971, 973-974, 981

Volunteers 719, 1516, 1526-1530, 1532-1533, 1535-1536, 1539, 1543-1544, 1696-1699, 1702, 1706

W

Warby Parker 1549, 1558-1559, 1565, 1571, 1574-1575

Wasta 422-428, 430-434, 436-444, 1297-1305, 1308-1313

WEKA 252, 266, 274

Work Engagement 472-473, 475-476, 480-481, 483-490, 728, 941, 982, 1453, 1455-1457, 1460, 1463-1464, 1466, 1468, 1471, 1473-1475, 1481-1488, 1622, 1843-1845, 1848-1849, 1858, 1861-1863, 1865, 1867, 1969, 1980, 2185-2186, 2193, 2196-2197, 2199

work flow 1355

Workforce Planning 35, 38, 195, 304, 316, 356, 739, 745, 848, 1273, 1347, 1581, 1835, 1839, 1852, 2004, 2009, 2030-2031, 2036, 2202-2209, 2213, 2218-2223

Workplace 6, 16, 26, 31, 34, 55, 59-61, 66, 69, 72, 78, 86-87, 91, 162-164, 168-169, 173-175, 177, 192, 225-228, 230, 252, 272-273, 293, 295-297, 313, 321, 345, 348, 351, 354, 357, 376, 387-389, 391, 396-398, 400, 404, 406, 411-412, 415-417, 424, 436, 455, 475, 482-484, 491, 505, 563, 588-590, 592-593, 595-596, 598, 601, 604-606, 608, 611, 614-615, 620, 635, 639, 672, 713, 725-727, 730, 758, 804, 806, 811-812, 819, 897, 913-914, 917-918, 924, 973, 990, 995, 1001-1002, 1004, 1035, 1043, 1072, 1093, 1124, 1129, 1132-1133, 1149, 1161, 1163, 1172, 1180, 1184, 1248-1250, 1255-1256, 1274, 1281, 1288-1293, 1296, 1299, 1303, 1308, 1311-1312, 1331, 1353, 1378, 1382, 1396, 1412, 1415, 1417-1419, 1427, 1434, 1436-1439, 1442, 1445-1446, 1449, 1451-1460, 1462-1464, 1466-1467, 1469, 1471, 1485-1487, 1544, 1550, 1554-1555, 1566, 1569, 1573-1574, 1577, 1594, 1623-1624, 1626, 1629-1630, 1632-1633, 1637-1639, 1641, 1681, 1685-1686, 1699, 1740-1741, 1761, 1784, 1788-1790, 1792, 1794-1795, 1797, 1824-1825, 1827, 1843-1844, 1846, 1848-1849, 1853-1856, 1859, 1862-1865, 1867, 1874, 1884-1885, 1887-1888, 1890-1893, 1895, 1900-1903, 1905-1906, 1914, 1923, 1926, 1974-1975, 1983, 1987, 1989, 2039, 2076, 2095, 2104-2105, 2109-2117, 2120-2121, 2124-2126, 2129, 2132-2134, 2144-2145, 2157, 2159, 2180-2183, 2185-2186, 2194-2198, 2200-2201, 2204, 2222

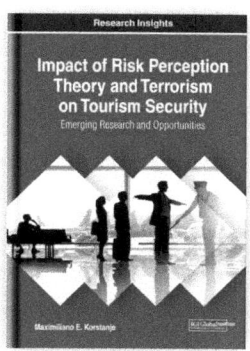

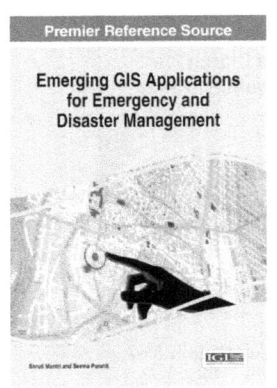
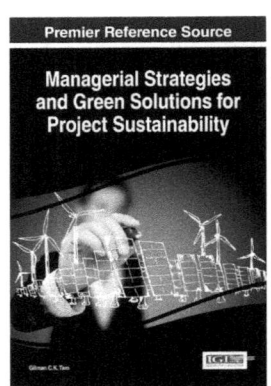

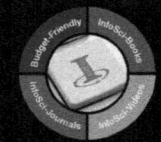

IGI Global
PUBLISHER of TIMELY KNOWLEDGE
www.igi-global.com

Publisher of Peer-Reviewed, Timely, and
Innovative Academic Research Since 1988

IGI Global's Transformative Open Access (OA) Model:
How to Turn Your University Library's Database Acquisitions Into a Source of OA Funding

Well in advance of Plan S, IGI Global unveiled their OA Fee Waiver (Read & Publish) Initiative. Under this initiative, librarians who invest in IGI Global's InfoSci-Books and/or InfoSci-Journals databases will be able to subsidize their patrons' OA article processing charges (APCs) when their work is submitted and accepted (after the peer review process) into an IGI Global journal.

How Does it Work?

Step 1: **Library Invests in the InfoSci-Databases:** A library perpetually purchases or subscribes to the InfoSci-Books, InfoSci-Journals, or discipline/subject databases.

Step 2: **IGI Global Matches the Library Investment with OA Subsidies Fund:** IGI Global provides a fund to go towards subsidizing the OA APCs for the library's patrons.

Step 3: **Patron of the Library is Accepted into IGI Global Journal (After Peer Review):** When a patron's paper is accepted into an IGI Global journal, they option to have their paper published under a traditional publishing model or as OA.

Step 4: **IGI Global Will Deduct APC Cost from OA Subsidies Fund:** If the author decides to publish under OA, the OA APC fee will be deducted from the OA subsidies fund.

Step 5: **Author's Work Becomes Freely Available:** The patron's work will be freely available under CC BY copyright license, enabling them to share it freely with the academic community.

Note: This fund will be offered on an annual basis and will renew as the subscription is renewed for each year thereafter. IGI Global will manage the fund and award the APC waivers unless the librarian has a preference as to how the funds should be managed.

Hear From the Experts on This Initiative:

"I'm very happy to have been able to make one of my recent research contributions *freely available* along with having access to the *valuable resources* found within IGI Global's InfoSci-Journals database."

– Prof. Stuart Palmer,
Deakin University, Australia

"Receiving the support from IGI Global's OA Fee Waiver Initiative *encourages me to continue my research work without any hesitation*."

– Prof. Wenlong Liu, College of Economics and Management at Nanjing University of Aeronautics & Astronautics, China

For More Information, Scan the QR Code or Contact:
IGI Global's Digital Resources Team at eresources@igi-global.com.

Lightning Source UK Ltd.
Milton Keynes UK
UKHW051951020122
396528UK00005B/422